ADVANCE FORCE

PEARL HARBOR

Coming Soon!

CAPTURED 2-MAN JAP SUB

SEE YOUR NEWS-PAPERS ★ LISTEN TO YOUR RADIO FOR LOCAL DETAILS ★

"NAVY OFFICIALS SAID THERE ARE INDICATIONS THESE SMALL SHIPS ARE EXTREMELY DARING AND WOULD RESORT TO SELF-SACRIFICE TO CARRY OUT THEIR OBJECTIVES."

Washington Star Democrat, December 16, 1941

ADVANCE FORCE

PEARL HARBOR

■ BURL ■ BURLINGAME

Naval Institute Press
Annapolis, Maryland

LONGWOOD PUBLIC LIBRARY

Naval Institute Press
291 Wood Road
Annapolis, MD 21402

© 1992 by Burl Burlingame
All rights reserved. No part of this book may be reproduced or utilized in any form or by any means,
electronic or mechanical, including photocopying and recording, or by any information storage and
retrieval system, without permission in writing from the publisher.

Originally published in 1992 by Pacific Monograph
First Naval Institute Press edition 2002
ISBN 1-55750-211-0

Printed in the United States of America on acid-free paper ♾
09 08 07 06 05 04 03 02   8 7 6 5 4 3 2 1

PHOTO AND ILLUSTRATION CREDITS

Arizona Memorial Visitor Center: 63, 91, 99, 114, 149, 151–52, 161, 168, 193, 198, 200, 211–12, 214–17, 219–27,
  230–32, 376–77, 379, 422, 443
James Blears: 403
Burl Burlingame AirChive: All other photographs, maps, and drawings
Stan Cohen: 207, 331, 351, 420–21, 460–61
James P. Delgado: 390–91
Hawaii State Archives: 15, 125, 234, 367
Hawaii Undersea Research Laboratory / Erickson Air-Crane Co.: 435
Imperial Japanese Navy: 6, 8, 10, 48–49, 51, 57–60, 62, 64–68, 70–74, 83, 134, 139, 141, 176–78, 204–5, 229,
  242–43, 265–66, 301, 316, 354–55, 365–66, 381–84, 404, 442–45
Imperial War Museum: 13, 77, 80–82, 84–86, 399, 406
Japan Midget Submarine Association: 132–33
Mike Locke / Douglas McMurtry: 333–36
Kimo Wilder McVay: 437
Museum of the Pacific War, Nimitz Center: 2, 305, 425
National Archives via Arizona Memorial Visitor Center: 274, 282, 284–86, 419, 432
National Archives via James P. Delgado: 275, 283, 286, 288–90, 385–87, 430–31
Nippong Golden Network: 250, 394
Office of War Information: 340–41
Edward Redford: 352
United States Army: 251, 304
United States Navy: 4, 12, 24, 28–30, 34–36, 38, 105, 111, 127, 147, 169, 175, 180–81, 201, 213, 259, 268, 324, 327,
  344, 413–14, 451

LONGWOOD PUBLIC LIBRARY

ADVANCE FORCE
PEARL HARBOR

PEARL HARBOR SHONE RED
IN THE SKY LIKE A THING AFIRE . . .
A LARGE FLAME HEAVING
HEAVENWARD—LIKE A SHIP
EXPLODING IN PEARL HARBOR.

The battle report of *I-69* skipper Katsuji Watanabe helped
convince the Imperial Japanese Navy
that a midget submarine had sunk battleship *Arizona*.

ANY WAR IS WRONG—A MISTAKE OF
POLITICIANS. BUT IT WAS BEYOND THE
REACH OF ANYONE TO STOP THE WAR,
SOMETHING HUMAN STRENGTH AND WILL
COULD NOT STOP. THERE WAS NO CHOICE
BUT TO FIGHT THE GOOD WAR,
HONORABLY AND HARD.

KAZUO SAKAMAKI

The sleeve patch of a master
torpedoman in the Imperial
Japanese Navy features red
torpedoes and chrysanthemum on
a blue shield. This insignia was
phased out in 1942.

CONTENTS

PREFACE AND ACKNOWLEDGMENTS

When I moved to Hawaii in 1965, an eleven-year-old Tenderfoot scout in a military family, I had only two goals—to complete my advancement to Eagle Scout and to see Pearl Harbor. I had read about this famous battlefield in *Day of Infamy,* Walter Lord's wonderful, absorbing account of the December 7 attack. The real Pearl Harbor was oddly disappointing. I guess I expected to see the spirits of samurai barreling through the azure. It was a hot, gritty, stinking port, gearing up once again to feed American soldiers into the maw of Indochina. I eventually won the Eagle medal, and I read every book about the attack on Pearl Harbor I could find. The events of December 7, 1941, have all the elements of classical mythology; they are fundamentally mysterious and convey a genuine sense of history unfolding.

Advance Force Pearl Harbor began simply, as an attempt to tell the story of the little guys—the submarines, the destroyers, the yard craft—whose story has been passed over in favor of the more glamorous air attack. Conventional wisdom has it that because the submarines did not accomplish their mission, their role in the battle was incidental. But the historian's role is to distrust convention. The submarines were failures—why? Is it possible that American forces were not as unprepared as previously thought? Does the submarine failure indicate that the Japanese misdirected their resources or that the Americans directed theirs more shrewdly? In *Advance Force* I propose answers to these questions and try to explain why things happened the way they did at Pearl Harbor. If you're convinced, I have succeeded. If not, there will be another Pearl Harbor book along at any moment.

Most histories of the Pearl Harbor attack are concerned with the large view of cause and effect—who knew what when, and what could have been done and wasn't—but because historians have scant interest in the nitty-gritty of battle, little has been written about the technical details of the assault. Historian Gordon Prange's otherwise monumental battle accounts in *At Dawn We Slept, Dec. 7 1941,* and *The Verdict of History,* for example, contain multiple technical errors. This criticism is not an indictment of his methodology; Prange simply wasn't interested in counting rivets.

The confused, roiling smoke of battle militates against coherent history; public reality and personal mythology often fuse. Accordingly, in this book I tried to reconstructed some semblance of the real events from facts and bits of information gathered from hundreds of sources. Primary sources are listed in the bibliography. Dialogue and thoughts included in the book were either reported elsewhere or are reasonable interpretations of what was said. If a ship's log says, "The skipper ordered Full Steam Ahead," it was a short jump to "'Full steam ahead,' ordered the skipper." But I dared not jump further.

When the book was first published in 1992, a great deal of historical material was unfortunately still classified. For example, military interment records for Japanese corpses recovered after the attack were sealed. I was told I would have to prove that these people are dead before the records of their deaths could be opened, an Orwellian requirement. To date, only one record has been released, that of aviator Fusata Iida, and that one piece of paper required a year's worth of pressure from a congressman.

Despite President Clinton's blanket declassification of most World War II files in the late 1990s, these death records are still secret. Opening them, however, could solve some long-standing mysteries. For example, what really happened at dawn on December 8, as submariners Kazuo Sakamaki and Kiyoshi Inagaki said their farewells? A soldier who examined Inagaki's body told me that he appeared to have been shot in the back of the head. This is striking information, but it cannot be proven. This clue, along with others, such as the fact that Sakamaki's sword was recovered but not his pistol, plus his mental blocking of that period, plus a Japanese officer's traditional duty to his men, plus evidence from Sydney harbor that midget submariners helped each other commit *jibaku,* puts a grimly different spin on the pair's last moments on the deck of *I-24tou.* Did Sakamaki execute his own crewman? This is speculation, not history; readers are invited to draw their own conclusions. When no physical proof is available, the historian must rely on the fragile tissue of memory, in this case, Sakamaki's, but he passed away in 1999, still close-mouthed at age 81.

Since this book was first published, the Internet has become a powerful source of information. Much fascinating—albeit peripheral—material was forwarded to me after the book was published. This is available online at the book's web page at www.pacifichistory.net.

Computers have also helped to reveal new evidence in photos of the attack. The sidebar on pages 198–99 contains an aerial photograph of the attack that seems to show a *Ko-hyoteki* in the harbor. In late 1990, as I was finishing the initial stages of research, I was looking at damage photographs of the *West Virginia.* One of the torpedo holes in her hull was substantially larger than the others. Was it possible, since the midget-submarine torpedoes were larger than the aerial torpedoes, that the battleship had been hit by an Imperial Navy submarine? While looking for photographs that might give further evidence, I mentioned this possibility to the Dan Martinez, who works for the National Park Service as historian at the USS *Arizona* Memorial Visitors Center. Immediately interested, he showed me the well known photograph taken by a Japanese torpedo bomber. "I've always wondered what's going on here," he said, pointing to the turmoil in the middle of the harbor. I had noticed the tiny dark square before but had assumed it was a photographic imperfection. Closer examination, however, showed that its grain pattern was consistent with the rest of the image. Dan found me the highest-quality print they had on hand at the memorial, and computer guru Bob Goodman provided me with a beta copy of a then-new program he was testing for Adobe called Photoshop. Several passes with contrasting, equalization, and sharpening filters revealed something in the photo that looked like a submarine. I presented the images for the first time to naval historians at the "Gathering Storm" symposium in Austin in early 1991. Though the audience seemed impressed, little note was made of the image, and I decided to use it in the book as a speculative sidebar.

The images' lukewarm reception aside, a submarine in the harbor would mean that the history of the Pearl Harbor attack is incomplete, and that Kimmel's defensive strategy was essentially correct. After the book was published, the Park Service began to get inquiries about the image, and—by a stroke of luck—another clue was discovered, a stereoscopic mapping photo of the same part of the harbor taken on November 26, 1941. This earlier image would enable photographic experts to conduct a more rigorous study of the later one. Autometric, Inc., a Virginia-based photogrammetry firm with Defense Department experience, used higher quality image-processing software to study the wakes emanating from the object and used the mapping photo to determine precise sizing and location details in the original photograph. Though Autometric and I disagreed on the cause of the plume of mist arising from the area, we agreed that such a plume occurs when a midget-submarine broaches. The result of Autometric's professional analysis: the object is a "certain sub," matching in all respects the *Ko-hyoteki* class. The information was made public in a joint press conference on December 6, 1994, but the Associated Press managed to garble the details in its report.

Reaction to the discovery has been mixed. Using the Autometric report and materials taken directly from *Advance Force Pearl Harbor, Naval History* magazine turned our discovery into a cover story in 1999 for one of their best-selling issues. Even so, the revelation produced instant skeptics, such as Carl Boyd of the National Security Agency archives and John DeVirgilio, an independent historian, but they have yet to disprove the science. In 2000, deep-sea explorer Robert Ballard used this book in a National Geographic television special as he searched for the *Ward*'s sunken submarine. Ballard, however, neglected to contact experts on the subject and the hunt proved fruitless.

Quite a bit of the material in this book was obtained through the Freedom of Information Act, a wonderfully democratic institution currently threatened by a chilling wave across the land; the urge to reshape history to the tune of current public relations isn't limited to the Japanese.

To say that tons of material remained classified at the time of writing is not an exaggeration. I went through all of the 14th Naval District's intelligence records, which are stored in the National Archives branch facility in San Bruno, near San Francisco. Not only was the month of December, 1941, conspicuous by its absence, but data wranglers at the facility assured me that about 10 percent of these records were still classified. No federal worker at San Bruno at the time had a security clearance high enough to look at the documents they had in storage. At the U.S. Navy Storage Depot in Crane, Indiana, some fourteen thousand microfilm reels dealing with intelligence issues of the period were still classified, awaiting review. Considering that in early 1991, historian John Martini and I appealed to the Department of Defense to declassify photographs from the Civil War, the wait could be a long one.

The records that are available are disorganized and haphazardly boxed. The 14th Naval District records contained items like an officer's glove, sticks of fifty-year-old chewing gum, piles of rusting paper clips, and worn-down pencils, all indicating that the files were simply dumped and locked up.

Research was also hampered because many Japanese records were simply unavailable. In the two-week period between August 14, 1945, when Hirohito decided to knuckle under to the Potsdam Declaration, and August 28, when Allied troops arrived in Japan, the Imperial Navy's archives branch went into a frenzy of self-destruction. They burned and shredded massive warehouses full of documents, both governmental and private. They had already gathered sensitive papers just for this purpose. Photographs have survived only because an Imperial Navy worker loaded up a truck with as many photos as it could hold, drove them home, and hid the images until the late 1960s. For this reason, Japanese submarine movements were plotted by external sightings.

Also missing in action are all records of Sakamaki's POW years—in fact, those of all Japanese POWs. Those records have simply vanished. A high-level search by the National Archives of both the United States and Japan indicated that the records were supposedly shipped to Japan in 1959, as were the POW records for both Germany and Italy. The European Axis powers received theirs; Japan did not. The disappearance of what the shipping orders described as "7,000 documents" remains a mystery. In 1990 the Japanese consul general in Honolulu became interested in the case, and orders to retrieve the documents reportedly came from as high as the prime minister's office. Some Japanese archivists are convinced that the documents are stored in the FBI office in Honolulu, a notion that caused workers in that tiny room to burst out laughing.

The spellings of Japanese midget-submarine crewmen's names have created another obstacle to research because they vary widely across accounts. For this book, I used the spellings in *Special Attack Flotilla*, a Japanese propaganda booklet published in 1942, which is somewhat closer to the source than most Western accounts. References for the spelling of Japanese names are consistently inconsistent; I apologize in advance for variations. Japanese names here also do not follow the Asian tradition of using the surname first. This is an American book and follows English custom in this regard.

Despite the difficulties, material for this book wasn't hard to find. I used many of the standard sources but took a different point of departure. The forty-volume government publication of the congressional hearings on Pearl Harbor, for example, contained a wealth of previously unused information, including the ordeal of Katsuji Watanabe and *I-69.* The published hearings tell his story in full in the exhibits, and they include his own report, which was captured after the attack, but Watanabe's action rarely rates more than a footnote in most comprehensive Pearl Harbor histories.

Ship action reports were also useful, although it took some divining to see past the efforts of ship's officers to cover their butts. Most of the action reports are carefully worded statements by ship's officers who have been trained in the art of nonspeak. A notable exception is the log of yard craft *YT-153,* one of the most honest and clear accounts of the attack to survive, and one not written by an officer. Whenever possible, the actions of the Imperial Japanese Navy were carefully segregated from those of the Japanese people. They are two separate entities, and the deprecations of one should not reflect on the characteristics or capabilities of the other.

Even though the book was essentially complete in 1991, the fiftieth anniversary of the Pearl Harbor attack, I decided not to publish the book then because I wanted to include the rich materials and memories that the anniversary would likely bring to light.

Other books provided inspiration, though they didn't contribute to the data pile: Paul Fussell's *Wartime,* John W. Dower's *War Without Mercy,* and Edward Tabor Linenthal's *Sacred Ground.*

Dozens of people helped, among them: David Aiken, Buzz Belknap, DeSoto Brown, Bob Chenoweth, Bob Cressman, Stan Cohen, James Delgado, Bob Goodman, Harvey Gray, David Hackworth, Kevin Hand, Tom Harrison, Tom Kellie, Eiko Lynch, Arlene Lum, Alex Malahof, Danny Martinez, Johnny Martini, Kimo McVay, Mom and Dad, Jim Nikkel, James Clair Nolan, Kathleen O'Connor, Dean Sensui, Ed Sheehan, Mike Slackman, The SubCommittee, Lois Taylor and Mike Tsukamoto. The text was written to the music of Beethoven, Pink Floyd, and Kate Bush. Thanks to them too!

The key player on the home front was my wife, Mary Poole, who proofread and edited chapters despite a grueling work schedule at our newspaper, who bravely declared the work "interesting" even when it clearly was not, and who manages to keep World War II in its proper perspective, somewhere behind keeping the utility bills paid. Daughters Amelia and Katie now know the design features of the *Ko-hyoteki* better than their classmates; I'm sure this will prove invaluable later.

As the book neared completion, I was struck by how similar the fates were of Adm. Husband Kimmel and Ens. Kazuo Sakamaki. These were two men who gave their best to their countries, and then, because of a vagary of fate, were reviled and abandoned by the commanders to whom they had pledged allegiance. They deserved better.

This book began life during a chat about Pearl Harbor with Bill Cox, the late managing editor of the *Honolulu Star-Bulletin*. Bill was a good friend and a professional inspiration; he taught me that journalism is simply current history, that history need not be dull to be good, and that simple decisions can have far-reaching consequences. He challenged me to explore an aspect of Pearl Harbor that reverberates today, to focus on a single act or tactical decision and examine both its roots and its fallout. A tall order.

Bill did not live to see *Advance Force* completed. Editors who look beyond the daily avalanche of trivia and petty office politics are rare; Cox was passionately curious about the societal tremors caused by twists of fate, and this book is dedicated to his memory.

ADVANCE FORCE
PEARL HARBOR

SPECIAL FITTINGS

SPECIAL FITTINGS

1

A Rush to Join the Attack Force

Captain Hanku Sasaki, commander of the 1st Submarine Division of the Imperial Navy, was puzzled and angry. It was the middle of October, 1941, and something important was in the air. He could smell it. His new submarines should be at sea, undergoing training, shaking out the construction bugs, doing the thousand and one things a warship needs to be ready.

They weren't ready, and Sasaki knew it. In the previous 20 months, three Japanese submarines had been lost, due to crew error and possibly — but not admitted publicly — to design flaws. And now five submarines under his command had been ordered to Kure Naval Arsenal for "special fittings."

What did that mean? Mystified, Sasaki had been suddenly ordered to take newly built *I-22* from Saeki Bay, Kyushu, to Kure. As they pulled up to the dock a dozen technicians leaped on board and began making sketches. Sasaki asked what they were doing and they muttered "special work" and ignored the officer.

He stepped around the rattle and clang of workmen bustling on the decks of *I-16, I-18, I-20, I-22* and *I-24,* Sasaki's five fleet submarines, all of the same class. Some of the "emergency modifications" made sense — air-purifying equipment, protection against anti-sub nets, internal telephone lines.

Others did not, such as the weird structures on the subs' afterdecks. Huge half-moon-shaped clamps, looking like bent railroad ties, were being welded to the hull. Ports for electrical and phone lines were being opened nearby, leading into the sub's interior.

Sasaki discovered that Commander Kiyotake Ageta, the new skipper of *I-22*, was just as mystified as his superior officer and had gone to 6th fleet headquarters to find out what was happening.

"What are these?" Sasaki asked a workman.

The worker flipped up his face mask, said he didn't know. He only knew everything had to be in place by Nov. 10. There was a deadline.

Sasaki spotted Commander Midori Matsumura inspecting the

At first, Admiral Isoroku Yamamoto objected to including submarines of the Advance Force in the planned assault on Pearl Harbor.

work and hurried over to him. Matsumura had 15 years in submarines and was a staff officer. He should know what was happening. Sasaki asked.

"This equipment is to enable you to haul midget submarines close enough to Pearl Harbor to attack the U.S. Pacific fleet," said Matsumura, absentmindedly. "These are the Special Attack Unit."

Special Attack Unit? The news rocked Sasaki. Waiting until the last minute to give him the word seemed wildly irresponsible. *Would the hulls take the special equipment and the weight of the midgets?* The secret midget submarines were designed to be launched, like ducklings, off the backs of converted seaplane tenders like *Chiyoda*, not lashed to the deck of another submarine.

Sasaki knew that the massive Imperial Navy war games held in September had led to certain plans of attack against America and Britain. The games were held at the Army War college auditorium, as the navy auditorium was too small to seat all the interested officers. He may also have known that the brunt of the attack on Pearl Harbor would be borne by carrier aircraft.

Admiral Isoroku Yamamoto, backer of the air-attack plan designed by Imperial Navy aviators Minoru Genda and Mitsuo Fuchida, merely planned to have submarines of Admiral Mitsumi Shimizu's 6th Fleet engage in conventional, long-range undersea warfare. During the war game maneuvers, a large circle was drawn in a 600-mile radius from Pearl Harbor. This was the outside limit American search planes could fly from Oahu. This was the "danger zone" — all submarines in this area would operate with extreme caution, passively submerged by day and running quietly at night. Although every detail of the aerial operation was known when the war game maps were rolled up, the maneuvers ended with little decided about submarines. Not even the number of participants were estimated, nor details of their operation.

On X-Day, as the opening of war was called, Japanese submarines were to "observe and attack the American fleet in the Hawaii Area; make a surprise attack on the channel leading into Pearl Harbor and attempt to close it; if the enemy moves out to fight he will be pursued and attacked."

The five midgets' vague mission was to attack the fleet inside the harbor and prevent American warships from escaping. The five midget-carrying submarines and other I-boats would move inde-

SPECIAL FITTINGS

pendently and forward of the main striking fleet; they were the "Advance Force." Initial plans for the advance force included six vessels for a supply train, a concept soon abandoned as risky.

The Imperial Navy had 48 of the new I-class fleet submarines and 15 of the older, slower RO-class submarines. The ROs were considered a back-up force, obsolete and useful only for training and nosing around Japan's coasts. There were 18 submarines under construction for 1942 delivery, another 11 scheduled for 1943, and an additional 38 had been approved for rush construction in 1942. These figures don't include the 20 or so Japanese midget submarines, an unproven weapon sniffed at by the battleship admirals.[1]

Lieutenant Naoji Iwasa, a master of midget-sub tactics, worked hard to convince the practical Yamamoto that midgets could sneak undetected into Pearl Harbor. He and understudy Lieutenant Saburo Akieda had been the test pilots for the midget program and had faith in their capabilities. They considered the tiny submarines one of Japan's mysterious technological aces, like the Zero fighter.

The midget weapons were developed in line with Imperial Navy objectives, which since 1909 had been primarily concerned with using inferior strength against an enemy of superior strength, in other words, the U.S. Fleet. Every aspect of strategy, tactics, preparations, education and training was geared toward achieving a quick, decisive victory over American ships, without being dragged into a long-term, ship-eating conflict.

From the beginning, emphasis had been placed on submarines and their long-range torpedoes as a way of drawing out the American fleet. But the valuable submarines were still considered too slow, and the torpedoes too limited, to be useful.

The speedy, stealthy midget utilized the advantages of both torpedoes and submarines to overcome their defects. Instead of an elegant, skirmishing sword, it was a dagger meant for bloody, close-in work.

Yamamoto objected — it would be difficult to get the midgets close enough to Pearl without tipping off the Americans.

Iwasa suggested carrying them on "mother" submarines that could hide beneath the waves.

The wild notion had its romantic side, and Yamamoto gave the midgets a go-ahead during the maneuvers, depending on whether technical problems could be ironed out. He insisted that the midget crews be rescued after the attack.

From that moment, the plan could not be stopped; the midgets were an integral part of the assault. Iwasa was put in charge, and in October the ship fitters began scrambling in Kure.

And now Sasaki, who would have to command these jury rigged weapons into battle, found out — by accident — what he was in for.

Like many submariners, Sasaki was an orderly person. He was deeply troubled by what he perceived as scattershot planning.

[1] In December 1941, the Americans had 111 submarines in service and another 73 in the shipyards. Fifty-one of these were in the Pacific; 22 at Pearl Harbor and 29 at Cavite in the Philippines. In addition, there were 12 Dutch submarines in the Pacific. British submarines were all busily employed in the North Atlantic or the Mediterranean.

No photographs are known to exist of the midget submarine tie-down apparatus on the backs of the Advance Force mother submarines. The cable and wood block fittings on this C-class midget craft, pictured later in the war on a surface vessel, are probably a close match for the Pearl Harbor fittings.

"There was too much hurry, hurry, hurry," he recalled distastefully. Too many desktop pipe dreams, with too little experience to back them up. The "tubes," as they were jokingly called by the I-boat crews, were to be carried into battle on ships barely out of the shipyard, untested weapons upon untested warships, into the struggle that could determine the fate of the Japanese Empire.

I-24 was so new that she shook and rattled her way from the shipyards at Sasebo to the secret naval base at Kure. It was her maiden voyage. Torpedo Officer Mochitsura Hashimoto was alarmed to see bubbles rising from the forward starboard dive plane. At Kure, a diver discovered the heavy steel blade was attached to the hull with temporary wooden bolts — the shearing stress of an open-ocean voyage would have torn off the plane, leaving the submarine unable to dive or surface. Whatever the Imperial Japanese Navy needed submarine *I-24* for, thought Hashimoto, it was daunting enough to risk the lives of her crew.

At Kure, another load of workmen swarmed over the submarine's after deck, attaching a strange cradle-like apparatus. When Hashimoto asked what it was for, the workmen looked at him blankly. They were following the blueprints. Unknown to Hashimoto, the commander of the submarine fleet was nearby, wondering the same thing.

Eventually, a lance-like midget submarine was craned onto the cradle, lashed down, and a test run made at sea in the middle of the night. The main ballast tank crumpled on the midget and it took the rest of the night to repair.

SPECIAL FITTINGS

A COLLISION IN MID-OCEAN

2

The United States and Japan Square Off

The eventual collision was obvious. A Japanese-American struggle to dominate the Pacific had been predicted by everyone from Vladimir Lenin to H.G. Wells.

Japan shifted into colonialism at about the same time the Western nations were considering getting out. Long isolated, to outside influence and to internal change, the Imperial island nation rapidly caught up to the rest in terms of military capabilities. The crushing defeat of the Russian fleet during the Russo-Japanese War of 1905 served notice that Japan had arrived in the balance of powers.

The emergence of a strong, local power in the Far East was a worry to Western powers, whose reins were tightly stretched across the planet. Japan, figuring to move into the power vacuum created as the West moved out, rattled sabers so ominously that the United States — which considered the Pacific an American lake — was forced to divert military resources from traditional bastions on the East Coast.

Hawaii's sleepy frontier garrisons were considered vulnerable, particularly when Japan began to support Pancho Villa's Mexican revolution in 1913. Could such a revolt find root in Hawaii, itself seized by the United States only two decades before? The American government took no chances, and began constructing a massive series of fortifications on the island of Oahu, soon dubbed "The Gibraltar of the Pacific." These included a major naval base at Pearl Harbor, dozens of gigantic coastal cannon, airfields, fueling depots and regiments of infantry and armor. The United States had no global commitments at the time, so the fortifications were built with a single, potential enemy in mind — Japan.

The outbreak of World War I gave Japan an opportunity to capitalize on shifting alliances. declaring war on Germany and Austria, Japan marched on the German garrison at Tsingtao and laid siege, capturing it after a furious battle that also saw the introduction of war planes in the Pacific. Tahiti and Bora Bora were attacked by German raiders *Scharnhorst* and *Gneisenau*, under the command of

Admiral Graf Spee. Papeete in particular was heavily raked by shellfire, causing an unknown number of deaths.[1]

[1] Until the 1960s, the Yacht Club in Papeete bore a shell hole caused by an unexploded round, which drilled through the restaurant before exploding in a palm tree outside.

Japan sent few combat troops but many observers to the trenches in Europe. Flying general Billy Mitchell noted in his diary that Japanese seemed to be everywhere, taking notes.

Using the opportunity to occupy islands colonized by Germany, Japan was awarded title to them by League of Nations mandate at war's end. These scattered islands, popularly called the Mandates, lay north of the equator; Australia received title to those islands in the southern hemisphere. The carving up of the former German, Austrian and Ottoman empires was controlled by the League of Nations, and everybody got a piece or two. Britain grabbed Palestine and Iraq, France got Syria, New Zealand got Western Samoa. The League expected the conquering nations to improve living conditions for citizens of the mandated territories, and to prepare them for eventual democracy and, some day, a measure of independence.

Instead, the doled-out territories became the last gasp of European empire, and Japan, stung by a post-war Washington treaty that limited the size of her fleet, turned the Mandate Islands into top-secret Imperial Navy garrisons. U.S. Marine Corps intelligence officer Earl "Pete" Ellis may have been caught and executed there during 1923; Ellis also had a severe drinking problem, probably the real reason for his death. Had he lived, he could have brought the startling news that the formerly quiet Pacific island had been transformed into a mighty naval anchorage. Ellis also devised a plan for an amphibious war against Japan, anticipating the one-step-at-a-time "island-hopping" campaigns of World War II by nearly two decades.

America, in a burst of racially motivated legislation in the 1920s, shut the door on Japanese immigration and turned those Japanese already residing in the United States into second-class citizens. Japan, itself no stranger to racist motivations, regarded this as another slap; Imperial policy dictated that those of Japanese blood anywhere on the planet, regardless of successful assimilation into foreign cultures, were Imperial subjects at heart. This attitude would cast much suspicion on Japanese-American loyalty

Marine Corps intelligence officer Earl Ellis.

a few years later. Japanese political ambitions took practical form in the "New Order in East Asia" scheme, and its successor, the "Greater East Asia Co-Prosperity Sphere." The official line of the Imperial Foreign Office preached partnership and liberation from white colonialism. Retired admirals from the Imperial Navy were turned into instant diplomats and scattered across the capitals of Western countries; their British-based training allowed them to voice these goals with conviction. Many believed it.

The Japanese Imperial Army had other ideas. "The credo of

A COLLISION IN MID-OCEAN

Japan's dominance in Asia and the superiority of the Japanese over other Asiatics were sacrosanct," pointed out a French historian. "In the minds of the military elite, all of Tokyo's notions of equality had to fall before it."

More than notions fell. Military schemers were behind the assassinations of Prime Minister Takashi Hara in 1921, Yuko Hamaguchi in 1931 and Tsuyoki Inukai in 1932, and of other politicians and business leaders wedded to the Western notions of democracy and capitalism. Inukai's murder, in particular, was the final blow to a gradual democratization that had begun to flower during the Meiji Restoration of 1868. By the 1930s, in fact if not in policy, Japan was ruled by the military.

The Imperial Army began to set its own foreign policy, independent of the Japanese government. On Sept. 18, 1931, troops of the Kwangtung Army assaulted Mukden and went on to conquer all of Manchuria. The excuse given was to provide "living space" on the Asian continent. In Europe, Hitler used the same language before conquering Czechoslovakia.

The League nations protested Japan's move, and the Japanese delegation responded by walking out. The United States, in the midst of a great depression and nearly disarmed after The War to End All Wars, responded weakly by firing a flurry of diplomatic notes. It was "diplomacy by incantation," scoffed diplomat John Paton Davies. This feeble reaction heartened Japanese resolve.

What could Japan not do? The Shinto credo of *hakko-ichiu*

In 1921, Hirohito, then Crown Prince of Japan, made his only pre-war visit outside his empire. He went to England, and did not leave Japan again until 1971.

dictated Japan's holy mission was to rule the world, or to die gloriously trying. On July 7, 1937, at the Marco Polo bridge near Peking, the Imperial Army began a grab for all of China. Once again, the civilian government in Tokyo was powerless to prevent it, and governments in Europe and the Americas unwilling to stop it. In short order, Peking fell, then North China, then Inner Mongolia. By the end of the year, Shanghai was in Japanese hands, and by 1938, so were Canton and Hankow. China's rich coastline became an unwilling part of the Prosperity Sphere, and China's government withdrew into the barren interior. Western responses were once again limited to sputtering diplomatic cables and occasional protests when Japanese bombs fell too close to their warships.

The Sphere rolled south, taking advantage of colonial confusion caused by the outbreak of war in Europe. Japanese troops occupied French Indochina in September 1940, and strong-armed Thailand into proving a corridor to shuttle Imperial troops into Burma and Malaya. Thailand subsequently became the only other Asian member of the nine-country Axis powers of World War II.

In Japan as well, troops moved in and took up positions. On Oct. 16, 1941, General Hideki Tojo became Prime Minister as well as Minister of War. A canny fanatic, Tojo imposed a virtual dictatorship. Within a few weeks, on Nov. 4, an Imperial conference gave the go-ahead to war with the United States and Britain. Yamamoto's plan to neutralize Pearl Harbor was given the highest priority.

Hawaii, the string of islands that sheltered Pearl Harbor, had ties to both sides of the Pacific.

In less than half a century, the Meiji period of 1868 to 1912, Japan had become a world power, a modern state with a Prussian-inspired constitution, an American-inspired and motivated bureaucracy, and a British-inspired military that had triumphed over powerful Russia. The Japanese fast became the most literate nation on the planet, and the island empire became industrialized without incurring inflation or unemployment.

These achievements reflected on Japanese living abroad, the largest colony of which had settled in Hawaii, barely 1,200 miles from Japanese possessions in the Marianas, Caroline and Marshall islands. The Japanese empire was far closer to Hawaii than the territory was to the United States. A number of Hawaii-Japanese had served in the Imperial Army against Russia.

King David Kalakaua of Hawaii in the late 1800s urged Japan to lead a federation of Asian nations, of which Hawaii would be a key member, and even offered a niece in marriage to a Japanese prince as a royal seal on the pact. Japan politely turned down Kalakaua, concerned that creating such a coalition might offend British and American interests in the Far East. Besides, the idea was just a bit too democratic. The Sphere pursued in the '30s would have Japan as conqueror, not leader.

Flooding the islands with Japanese immigrants would eventu-

A Collision in Mid-Ocean

ally lead to a Japanization of Hawaii, in any case. Overseas Japanese, called *doho*, were regarded as emissaries of the Imperial empire. Their status, or lack of status, in host countries created sympathetic vibrations all the way back to Tokyo. For the first two decades of the Meiji period, Japanese workers were barred by their country from emigrating to Hawaii, for fear that they would be treated like lowly Chinese immigrants. This position reversed itself when a flood of Japanese immigrants began to overwhelm the islands — restrictions on Japanese immigration was considered a slap at Japanese national honor.

As Japanese poured into the islands during the late 1800s, mostly to work in the sugar fields, they were perceived as a potent political threat should they get organized. The propertied, largely white, ruling class of Hawaii began talking annexation with the United States as a way to counter the tide of immigration, an idea that found support in Washington. Alfred Thayer Mahan, the leading naval strategist of the era, had his own rather direct strategy for the islands. In 1897, he wrote Assistant Secretary of the Navy Theodore Roosevelt and suggested that America "take the islands first and solve the (Japanese) problem afterwards."

In the spring, the newly founded Hawaii Republic refused permission for three boatloads of Japanese immigrants to land. The Japanese foreign minister protested, backed up by the warship *Naniwa*.

The June 1897, treaty of annexation between Hawaii and the United States threw cold water on hopes of Hawaii remaining an independent country that could be peaceably made dependent on Japan. The Japanese nation was startled and dismayed at the development. Tokyo drafted and sent a stern protest just about the time President McKinley submitted the treaty to the American Senate.

Minister Toru Hoshi, Japan's man in Washington, sent a telegram to Foreign Minister Shigenobu Okuma urging "the only

In the late 1880s, Japanese workers coming to Hawaii poured across the "immigration bridge" on Sand Island, near Honolulu.

possible means of frustrating (the) scheme of Hawaiian annexation, that is, is our occupation of that Island by dispatching, without any delay some powerful ships under the name of reprisal, taking advantage of present relation(s) between Japan and Hawaii."

Two days later, Tokyo's official protest arrived in Washington, and was delivered to Secretary of State John Sherman by Hoshi. To Sherman, Hoshi claimed that Japan "did not have and never did have" schemes for seizing Hawaii.

Clearly, Hoshi was talking out of both sides of his mouth. He knew *Naniwa* was still in Hawaii, and could have initiated a seizure of government facilities, just as American marines had done a few years before.

In any case, Japan did nothing more. *Naniwa* eventually steamed home, carrying Japanese diplomats outraged at their country's feeble response to a prime opportunity. One, Masanosuke Akiyama, attempted ritual suicide on the voyage.

By 1941, Hawaii had 160,000 residents of Japanese ancestry, the third-largest number of overseas *doho* in the world — China and Brazil had more, though widely dispersed — and they comprised the single largest ethnic group in the islands, some 40 percent. No wonder a Tokyo book, published in 1932, called Hawaii "a second Japan."

Approximately 75 percent of these Japanese were *nisei*, born in the islands, and rapidly Westernized. By virtue of birthplace, all were American citizens. Those born before 1924, however, were also Japanese citizens, and these comprised a majority of *nisei*. Until that year, Tokyo had regarded all children born of Japanese men, anywhere in the world, as Japanese citizens.[2] Under these terms, dual-citizen *nisei* were subject to the laws of both countries, liable for military service or other draftings.

Before the age of 17, the *nisei* could apply for expatriation, casting off Japanese citizenship. In the 20-year period between age 17 and 37, the *nisei* could be drafted into the Imperial Army or Navy. A number of Hawaii-born *nisei* served in Japan this way. It was the same throughout the China adventure up until 1945.

Jiro Nakahara of Hilo, a Hawaii *nisei,* served throughout the war as a radio monitor on Japanese submarines. He was aboard one in 1944 when 180 male and female survivors of two sinking transports were massacred by Japanese sailors. He later testified to the incident at the war crimes trials.

In 1924, the Japanese government let slip the blood ties between overseas Japanese and the mother country. The parents of a new-born *nisei* had two weeks to register their baby at a Japanese consulate, or the child became a permanent citizen of the new country.

Between 1924 and World War II, only eight percent of Hawaii *nisei* had formally renounced Japanese citizenship. At the same time, 40 percent of newborn *nisei* were registered at the Japanese

[2] *The fruit of Japanese women married to foreigners were not recognized as "Japanese."*

A COLLISION IN MID-OCEAN

consulate in Honolulu, a task made easier by a network of consular agents throughout the territory. These *toritsuginin*, whose business it was to maintain links between Hawaii-Japanese and Japan, were suspect as espionage agents.

Other suspects included *kibei*, Hawaii-born *nisei* who had returned to Japan to be educated and, it was presumed, indoctrinated. The practice of returning to Japan for schooling tapered off quickly after October 1940, when Congress passed the Nationality Act, part of which stated that American citizens of foreign parents would lose their citizenship if they lingered in their parent's homeland for more than six months.

The remaining number of Japanese in Hawaii, about 40,000, were *issei*, Japanese immigrants. They were complete subjects of the Emperor by law, if not by fact. This group spoke little English and many followed proudly their country's conquests in Asia. The Tripartite Alliance was treated as a glorious step into the rank of nations. Hawaii newspapers catering to this group generally carried both English and Japanese versions of the same story, the tone of the English version usually being relatively detached, the Japanese version verging on jingoistic apoplexy. The English version would refer to "Japanese planes," for example; the Japanese version called them "our angry eagles."

Japan was perceived by Hawaii *issei* as saving China from her own decadence, while simultaneously challenging the Western power structure on its own terms. It was a "holy war" of great national import, so psychologically seismic in its spirit of self-sacrifice that tremors were felt in patriotic Japanese communities around the globe.

The jolts permeated American military intelligence services and the FBI. *Issei* were regarded with suspicion by the U.S. government. Particularly bothersome were visits to Hawaii by Japanese naval ships, which turned the patriotism crank a little

Consul General Toyokichi Fukuma and local toritsuginin *greet Imperial Navy tanker* Hayatomo *at pierside in Honolulu, 1937. Arthur Carroll, the U.S. Navy intelligence operative who took this snapshot, was subsequently harassed by consul Fukuma, wearing the white hat at center.*

Japanese Consul General Suyeyuki Akamatsu escorts Admiral Kichisaburo Nomura and staff during a courtesy call at Fort Shafter, 1929. In 1941, Nomura himself would become a diplomat.

tighter each time. Such visitations occurred 41 times between 1876 and 1939. Officially, such visits provided Imperial Navy officers a chance to regard their opposite numbers on a one-to-one basis, as well as provide diplomatic courtesy, one nation to another. It was also a way of showing the flag. The local Japanese press seized on the notion that Japanese naval officers who had visited Honolulu retained a psychic link to the islands, and their combat exploits in China were followed breathlessly.

Many sailors with the Imperial Navy had relatives in Hawaii, and warm family reunions were in full swing whenever warships ported. At least one Hawaii-born *nisei* girl fell in love with a visiting Imperial Navy cadet; their own war with governmental bureaucracy on both sides lasted for 10 years as they tried to marry. By the time they were actually wed, in 1941, he was a Japanese naval fighter pilot — an "angry eagle" — and she had renounced her American citizenship.

Despite these displays of racial affection, Hawaii *nisei* were often looked down upon in Japan. In mid-summer 1941, at the height of international name-calling between the two powers, a Tokyo newspaper demanded that *nisei* then in Japan be shipped back to the United States, as they were "too Americanized" to understand the delicate strengths of being a proper Japanese.

In the Imperial Navy intelligence offices in Tokyo, a lieutenant commander was detailed to pick up sacks of mail from patriotic Hawaii *doho*. Often, money was enclosed to help conquer the

A COLLISION IN MID-OCEAN

decadent Chinese. It was widely rumored among Hawaii-Japanese that the mail contained patriotic litmus tests by *toritsuginin*. Speak ill of the Emperor, and you might run into trouble on your next visit to the mother country.

The mail included *imonbukuro*, comfort bags, for the troops in China. Prized among the Japanese soldiers, these bundles typically contained Camel and Lucky Strike cigarettes, Sunkist oranges, Sun-Maid raisins, chocolate candy and a Hawaii staple, Dole canned pineapple. Some contained thousand-stitch belts, a patriotic totem that required nearly religious sacrifice from the makers, as each stitch was begged from a stranger.

Delegations of Hawaii-Japanese periodically visited the China front to cheer up the troops. By 1938, troupes of Hawaii "comfort visitors" were continuously touring behind the lines. A large Hawaii contingent also attended the Empire's 2,600th birthday in 1940, as part of a "Grand Congress of Overseas Compatriots." The head of the Hawaii group was Dr. Iga Mori.

The Hawaii *doho* were treated to a tour of Yokosuka Naval Base, and were greeted by base commander Admiral Koichi Shiozawa, who said, "An unseverable relationship binds overseas compatriots and the (Imperial) Navy. We are thankful for your warm hospitality whenever our training squadrons enter your ports."

Shiozawa was thanked by Hawaii delegate Takashi Isobe, a Shinto priest who called Hawaii's Japanese "emigrant warriors." As an inelegant footnote to the celebration, some of the papers presented by Hawaii-Japanese at the congress referred to non-Japanese residents of Hawaii as *gaijin*, foreigners.

Fictional accounts of Japanese conquests of Hawaii began to circulate as early as 1909, when "The Conflict of Nations" by Ernest Hugh Fitzpatrick and "The Valor of Ignorance" by Homer Lea were published. Each imagined hordes of blood-thirsty veterans of the Imperial Army slipping into Hawaii disguised as immigrant workers, and suddenly wiping out the American garrison. Lea, an 88-pound hunchback from Cripple Creek, Colorado, who liked to wear Chinese generals' uniforms, became much admired for his skill in describing the fictional campaign. "The Valor of Ignorance" became required reading among Kaiser Wilhelm's commanders, and Adolf Hitler quoted passages from it in "Mein Kampf."

Homer Lea, in one of his many ersatz Chinese military costumes.

Hector Bywater's "The Great Pacific War," published in 1925, focused on Japanese-American naval engagements. Bywater's book also imagined a carefully planned, spontaneous uprising among Hawaii Japanese, but left the rebels to fend for themselves — the Imperial Navy was busy elsewhere in the Pacific. In the book, internecine fighting leaves Honolulu in ruins and the Empire plans to pick up the scraps at a convenient date.

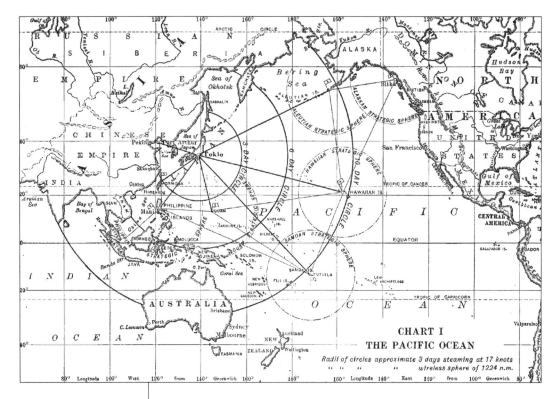

Radii of circles approximate 3 days steaming at 17 knots
"   "   "   "   wireless sphere of 1224 n.m.

CHART I
THE PACIFIC OCEAN

Homer Lea's turn-of-the-century campaign map for "The Valor of Ignorance" foreshadowed the Greater East Asia Co-Prosperity Sphere.

[3] *The book was gang-written by a group calling itself the National Military Affairs Organization.*

During the Great War, Bywater had been a British secret agent in Germany. He later became a leading authority on the world's navies, writing for newspapers and magazines on both sides of the Atlantic. He was present at the humbling naval disarmament conferences in London and Washington following World War I. He was aided in the novel by a source in Tokyo, English journalist Melville Cox.

"The Great Pacific War" profoundly influenced Admiral Isoroku Yamamoto, who read the novel in 1926 as Japanese naval attache in Washington. When he returned to Japan, Yamamoto lectured on Pacific war strategy, using concepts paralleling Bywater's. The admiral later spent an evening with Bywater at the 1934 London naval conference, where they debated seagoing strategy while finishing off a bottle of Scotch.

Bywater's novel was translated into Japanese and was furiously passed around by Japanese navy officers. It also inspired Japanese imitations that switched endings and had the Japanese winning the war. These novels, including earlier daydreams such as 1913's "*Nichi-Bei kaisan yume monogatari*," or "Fantasy on the Outbreak of a Japanese-American War,"[3] codified two prevailing Japanese perceptions about the Hawaiian Islands — they were a natural part of Japan, and Americans wouldn't mind handing them over if suitably humbled in a decisive engagement.

Yamamoto later followed Bywater "so assiduously in both overall strategy and specific tactics at Pearl Harbor, Guam, the Philippines and even the Battle of Midway that it is no exaggeration to call Hector Bywater the man who invented the Pacific War," said William H. Honan, author of a book about Bywater, "Visions of Infamy."

According to Honan, the U.S. Navy also capitalized on Bywater's concepts. The first two chapters of "The Great Pacific War" exposed weaknesses of the U.S. war plan, in which the Navy would recklessly rush reinforcements across a hostile ocean to relieve the Philippines.

Bywater had the U.S. fleet getting intercepted, severely mauled and humbled, prompting the United States to redesign its strategy. It became a step-by-step advance to Manila across a bridge of islands in the Marshall and Caroline chains. It was the first time a naval expert had publicly spelled out a campaign of amphibious landings.[4]

Later Japanese novels about a theoretical war between Japan and America assumed that Hawaii *doho* would spring to the aid of Imperial forces. One novel claimed the U.S. Pacific fleet would be lured to Midway and destroyed in an enormous, sea-going battle, the Jutland of all time. Demoralized white Americans would be set upon by minority groups, led by Jamaican nationalist Marcus Garvey, and Texas would once again be attacked by Mexico. The novel ends with a surprise Sunday-morning attack on New York, with Japanese commandos sweeping into the city on dirigibles.

In Lieutenant Commander Kyosuke Fukunaga's "An Account of the Future War Between Japan and the United States," war begins accidentally, when an impetuous destroyer skipper torpedoes *U.S.S. Houston* near China. One thing leads to another, and the Japanese wind up occupying Hawaii. A statue of the destroyer skipper is erected in Waikiki as the novel closes. When copies of "Future War" arrived in Hawaii, part of the cargo aboard the *President Taft*, they were seized by a territory customs official. The tale "was not so good for local Japanese to read," he decided.

The date in 1933 that the books were seized was Dec. 7. They were forwarded to the U.S. War Department for study.

In another book, a Japanese submarine commander eyes the silhouette of Diamond Head through his periscope and shouts, "Let's hurry up and take this island! I'm dying to eat some of those bananas!"

In 1932, Commander Hironori Mizuno, superintendent of the naval archives, published a sobering account of a Pacific conflict that flatly declared Hawaii to be the "Waterloo, the Verdun which will determine victory or defeat in a Japanese-American war… because America occupies Hawaii, America can attack Japan. But if Japan were to seize Hawaii, it could attack America."

Admiral Kanji Kato, commenting on another fanciful scenario for attacking the islands, said that as long as Hawaii remained American it would be "a cancer in the Pacific."

Conflict between the two nations was presented as an elaborate

[4] Both Bywater and his Toyko source Cox died in mid-1940 under mysterious circumstances. An autopsy, hampered by German air raids during the Battle of Britain, reasoned that Bywater died of a simultaneous heart attack and alcohol imbalance. Cox died in an unwitnessed fall from a window at Tokyo police headquarters. London Daily Telegraph reporter E.A. Harwood theorized in 1987 that Yamamoto ordered Japanese agents to liquidate Bywater and Cox, to keep the Englishmen from alerting the United States to his war plan.

game in these Japanese novels, an exciting sport that belonged best between the covers of pulp thrillers. And yet they were often written by Japanese naval officers, with ponderous forwards penned by Imperial Navy admirals. The novel with the hungry submariner was deemed "an important book for laymen and professional officers alike," by Vice Admiral Nobumasa Suetsugu, commander-in-chief of the Combined Fleet. "It would be simply splendid if the war turned out as (the author) imagines."

It was all a tease. "Books like these, in which descriptions of Japanese naval glories are substituted for meaningful analysis of strategy or tactics, were obviously less intended to inform the Japanese public of the strategic or material requirements for victory than to provide them with satisfying visions of Japanese expansive power and military ardor," Japan scholar Mark Peattie has pointed out.

In the cold light of analysis, a Japanese attack on Hawaii was discounted by American tacticians. Strategically, it didn't make sense. To the Japanese, however, it made a gut-level, unanalyzed kind of sense, fueled by emotion.

In any case, the average Japanese believed that Americans considered Hawaii to be a vassal state, a colony of non-whites whose loss would be little mourned. But the Japanese did not attack Hawaii; they targeted the American fleet anchored there.

Hector Bywater and Melville Cox.

THE FLEET PROBLEM

MILITARY MANEUVERS AND POLITICAL PLOYS

3

For the Americans, the direct road to Pearl Harbor began when Admiral Claude C. Bloch, Commander in Chief, U.S. Fleet in the Pacific — called CINCUS in the naval habit of acronymology — received this order on Sept. 22, 1939, from Naval Operations:

> FROM: OPNAV
> 1: CINCUS
> IN ORDER FACILITATE TRAINING OF THE FLEET, DEPARTMENT DESIRES FOLLOWING UNITS WITH AP-PROPRIATE TASK GROUP COMMANDER BE TEMPO-RARILY TRANSFERRED HAWAIIAN AREA BASING PEARL HARBOR; TWO HEAVY CRUISER DIVISIONS ONE FLOTILLA FLAGSHIP CARRYING FLOTILLA COM-MANDER TWO DESTROYER SQUADRONS ONE DE-STROYER TENDER ONE AIRCRAFT CARRIER OF CARDIV TWO AND SUCH BASE FORCE UNITS NECES-SARY FOR SERVICING ABOVE TASK GROUP X …

Bloch, known throughout the Navy as an officer both likable and capable, passed responsibility for this deployment to Vice Admiral Adolphus Andrews, commander of the Pacific Fleet Scouting Force, berthed aboard heavy cruiser *Indianapolis*. He set sail with this large force on Oct. 5. Andrews, wearing the additional cap of Commander Hawaiian Detachment, may have had doubts about this order, but did not question it. Moving so many ships to Pearl Harbor, at the time just a protected anchorage, would certainly not facilitate training, but it did move the fleet provocatively closer to Japan. It also split the fleet, which to the minds of some command-ers, weakened its war-making potential.

At the time, Pearl Harbor was a permanent base only for submarines. For ships of the U.S. Fleet, it was a pit stop on transpacific crossings, or a temporary berth during war games. Bloch himself soon moved to Hawaii as Commander of the 14th Naval District. He was relieved as CINCUS on Jan. 7, 1940, one day

[1] The majority of
American naval
ships were stationed
in the Pacific at this
time. Officially called
the "U.S. Fleet," its
commander was
known as CINCUS
— pronounced "sink
us." In 1942, the title
was changed to
CINCPAC.

after the Navy issued a major revision of its operating plan for the fiscal year.[1] The state of "limited emergency" declared by Roosevelt in September, as war rolled across Europe, pumped juice into the strained naval budget. Manpower was to be increased by a third, the number of ships by a quarter. The number of combat-worthy aircraft was to increase by only seven aircraft, but the number of training planes nearly doubled.

Even by reactivating reserve ships, the Navy lagged behind its program. A shortage of trained crews, faced with Buck Rogers technologies like degaussing gears, radars and voice radio — and their attendant problems — and the task of modernizing antique anti-submarine gear slowed things up. The problems accumulated.

They rolled down on the new commander of the U.S. Fleet, Admiral James O. Richardson, a tall, prickly perfectionist who was nonetheless much admired by his men.

At the time, Richardson viewed the command as another one of the intermediate steps on the flag ladder, and welcomed the chance for sea duty. He was a "small boat" admiral, and preferred the lean, racing destroyers to the waddling battleships.

He immediately began to beef up training and streamline logistics. "The cruising dispositions of the Fleet had to be vastly improved in antiaircraft and antisubmarine defense if the Fleet was going to be able to make a transpacific crossing in the early days of an 'Orange War,'" he memoed. He also lobbied for additional personnel and more Pacific island air bases.

The admiral was particularly worried about the latter. Navy air-search capabilities had improved tremendously since the first war, and "the planes were excellent, and the officers and men who manned them were superb in their skill," he wrote. But, in order to detect Japanese forces moving eastward across the Pacific to Hawaii, the West Coast or the Panama Canal, the United States lacked sufficient service facilities to keep the planes in the air. There also weren't nearly enough aircraft to go around.

Vice Admiral Claude
Bloch went from
Commander in Chief
of the U.S. Fleet to
command of the 14th
Naval District at
Pearl Harbor.

The Navy was well aware of the problem and made the most of its limited budget. After three years of congressional arm-twisting, work began in 1939, in piecemeal fashion, on aviation bases at Kaneohe and Pearl Harbor in Hawaii, on the Pacific islands of Midway, Johnston, Palmyra, Kodiak and Sitka, Alaska; also Tongue Point, Oregon; at Pensacola and Jacksonville, Florida; and at San Juan, Puerto Rico.

In 1939 the U.S. Navy had 194 ships assigned to the Shore Establishment. These included small combat craft like 75-foot patrol boats or submarine chasers, and tugs and barges. The patrol boats and subchasers were used by district commanders for general training of Naval Reserve forces, and specifically for training these reservists for in-shore anti-submarine operations. When war broke

THE FLEET PROBLEM

out in Europe, most of these boats had skeleton crews or were classified as "out of commission, in service." No use to anybody. The 553 aircraft assigned to the Shore Establishment were tabbed for training duties as well, or served as hacks so that brownshoes on shore duty could rack up flying hours.

Money for capital ships was tight, and the Navy was forced to air out its Reserve Fleet, dozens of ships mothballed during the 1920s. Many were swift "flush-deck" destroyers that made good submarine sniffers. "Some of them had been in the Reserve Fleet for a goodly number of years and, consequently, their anti-submarine gear was either obsolescent or obsolete," observed Richardson. "But, these destroyers, properly modernized and improved in operating condition, were essential if there was to be any anti-submarine protection of our coastal merchant shipping and if overseas movements of our Orange War Plan were to be practicable." Orange was the code word for Japan, and had been since the First World War.

Admiral James O. Richardson, although placed in command of one of the most powerful fleets of battleships in the world, still preferred the swift, deadly destroyers.

Though war plans were a relatively new military science, one of the first drafted was a "War Plan for War With Japan," drawn up in early 1914 and signed by Admiral George Dewey. Dewey had been incensed for years by the lack of prepared U.S. strategy at the outbreak of the Spanish-American War, and once the war was over, initiated a series of war-plan studies. These were generally treated as educational dissertations rather than serious documents. When the U.S. entered the war against Germany and Austria, no plan existed for executing strategy in that direction.

The 1914 plan for war with Japan was complete with separate expositions on "The Strategy of the Pacific," "Estimate of the Situation," and breakout documents on the problems of administration and logistics. The plan was completed despite the lack of an official office within the Navy Department to handle war planning. The emergencies of the Great War led to the creation of the Chief of Naval Operations title — despite the bitter opposition of Secretary of the Navy Josephus Daniels and President Woodrow Wilson — and a planning wing was created in the shadow of the CNO slot.

The study for war with Japan, tweaked over the years, became known as the Orange Plan because it never referred directly to the Empire of Japan, instead calling it "Orange" and the American

THOSE 'OLD' DESTROYERS

In most histories of World War II, the flush-deck destroyers brought back into service during the war emergency are often referred to as "antique" or "decrepit" or otherwise wanting. This is inaccurate. The four-stack, Wickes-class destroyers were the zenith of fast-ocean technology when they were built, and when recalled to service, none were more than 25 years old.

There are few ships in today's Navy younger than that. Most "four-stackers" had been comfortably mothballed and had sound frames, and were overhauled before being brought back into the line. They were swift, superb anti-submarine craft, but were second-stringed because of cramped quarters and topsides — they simply did not have enough room for the brace of weapons required of a fleet-class destroyer.

forces "Blue." By 1923, the Army was in on the planning under the auspices of Joint War Plans. Three separate plans for war with Japan had been created. Richardson studied the latest in Washington before leaving for the Pacific, and was aghast. Despite its heft of 800 pages, it had, he felt, no foothold in reality. Should the Pacific Fleet have to carry it out, the results would be disastrous.

Of all possible war plans developed, the war with Orange was considered the most likely, and the hardest to win. All but nine of 130 strategic war games played at the Naval War College before World War II focused on war with Japan. The weakest point developed was the supply convoys called Fleet Trains. Carrying the war to the enemy "will require the Blue fleet to advance westward with an enormous train, in order to be prepared to seize and establish bases en route," wrote Lieutenant Chester Nimitz in a 1923 thesis. He had been sent to the war college after establishing the submarine base at Pearl Harbor.

During the '20s and '30s, training on supply ships took second stage to combat exercises. The resulting softness of the supply problem was apparent to both Richardson and the Imperial Navy. The 1934 edition of the plan assumed that Blue ships would have to arrive in the Philippines before Orange forces achieved a toehold there, a logistical impossibility.

The 1934 Orange Plan called for a rapid advance into the Mandates as soon as 20 days after the start of hostilities, "regardless of enemy movements." Admiral J.M. Reeves studied the plan and some months later wrote the Chief of Naval Operations, Admiral W.H. Standley, that "Orange control over the Mandate Islands has given her potential bases which can be used as strong flank positions for operations of submarines and aircraft against Blue passage to the Western Area…" He also pointed out that "rapid strides" in the development of air-carried torpedoes had "enhanced the strength of Orange in the Western Pacific."

War planners continued to tinker with "0-2-Orange," as it was known. Standley himself inserted an interesting paragraph: "That in the event of war between Orange and Blue, hostilities will be initiated by Orange in the Far East without warning."

By 1935, the Army was sufficiently involved with war planning to be included in the process, and the U.S. Fleet and the U.S. Asiatic Fleet were merged into a single task force. This was a paper measure — the long stretch of the Pacific dictated operational independence between the two.

The war plans could be tested during war games. The Fleet Problem was the Navy's annual big event, and generally bounced

back and forth between the Atlantic and Pacific on alternate years. In the 1935 maneuvers, the fleet formed up off Hawaii and steamed west to Midway, in an imaginary advance on Japanese ships. Though this was precisely the move assumed by Imperial Navy planners, it was unsettling to witness American ships bluffing their way past the mid-Pacific.

The 1938 games were more interesting. In it, "enemy" waves of aircraft from carriers *Langley, Lexington* and *Saratoga* succeeded in sweeping down on Hawaiian airfields and moored ships, causing much pretend damage. Klaus Mehnert, a professor at the University of Hawaii, wrote an article dissecting these maneuvers, adding his own thoughts on Hawaii's vulnerabilities. In short order, the article appeared in a Berlin-based political magazine, where it spurred speculation among Japanese naval officers stationed there.

Fleet Problem 21 was scheduled for the Hawaii area during April and May of 1940. During the planning, Richardson was cautioned by the naval attache in Tokyo that "according to information I have, the Japanese Navy is making plans which are unusually elaborate to cover our fleet problem. In the operating areas, they will have tankers in addition to destroyers and submarines."

This threw radio security out the window. It meant that the thousands of radio messages sent during the maneuvers would need strictly husbanded cryptanalysis, for one error could provide Japanese intelligence with a key for cracking top-secret American codes. A trained ear also could learn much about American tactics

During the years prior to Fleet Problem 21, Pearl Harbor was an out-of-the-way stopover in the Pacific, home only to submarine squadrons and oil tanks. This picture was taken in 1925.

The U.S. Fleet comes to Lahaina Roads in 1940, protected by Maui mountains but anchored in deep water. Note that the ships have not deployed anti-torpedo nets, although they are in a "wartime" exercise.

and weaknesses from listening to "plain-language" radio traffic.

When the fleet arrived in Lahaina Roads for Fleet Problem 21, Richardson immediately established aerial skirmish lines, dawn and dusk patrols that extended about 30 miles from the anchorage. Anti-submarine destroyers were set up at the wide entrances to Lahaina, Maui's old whaling port. Long-range air patrol became common, ranging up to 180 miles out to sea.

At the time, these token patrols seemed to be prudent exercises. There were never enough ships or aircraft to develop an airtight screen. As the fleet settled into Hawaii, Richardson continued the scouts. "I feared that there was, at any time, a possibility that some fanatical, ill-advised officer in command of a submarine or a ship might attack," explained Richardson.

Lahaina Roads, Richardson pointed out at the time, was "2,000 miles nearer enemy submarine bases than our normal Pacific Coast bases."

THE FLEET PROBLEM

The Fleet Problem for 1940 had two phases, each scenario developed out of a possible war with Japan. The fleet was split in two parts, each taking turns at playing the enemy. Particular emphasis was given to realistic submarine and air attacks, with the Orange forces duplicating, as near as was known, the capabilities of the Imperial Navy.

A specific directive assumed "that submarines, air, and/or surface vessels, including small craft and surface vessels, of a determined and resourceful foreign power, may execute an attack on ships of the United States Fleet while in anchorages outside Pearl Harbor and off Honolulu." This increased list of suspects called for additional aerial patrols of the operating areas. At the time, it was assumed, 12 aircraft were all that was needed to maintain all-week, dawn-to-dusk patrols.

An exercise on April 9 assumed an all-out dawn raid on Pearl Harbor by bombers and submarines. The airplanes were picked up in short order by alerted crews. The submarines, however, were able to close in on the fleet and get clean shots. "We had a heavy swell with white caps so that it was difficult to see the submarines," reported Richardson. The problem of spotting submarines in rough water persisted, particularly in winter.

Planning for air operations took another twist when British carrier *Courageous* was torpedoed by a U-boat while steaming on a steady course to recover aircraft. Contingencies to launch and recover aircraft in submarine-infested waters were developed, often centering around a protective herd of destroyers.

U.S. Fleet destroyers Hull (DD350), MacDonough (DD351) and others form an anti-submarine skirmish line during pre-war maneuvers.

Joint operations of submarines and patrol planes also were developed as the fleet war gamed furiously around the Hawaiian Islands. This called for better identification of the notoriously hard-to-identify submarines, a problem eventually addressed by keeping American submarines in strict localities and cruising schedules. The tactics paid unexpected benefits later in the war during air-sea rescue operations.

The airplanes and crews of Patrol Wing Two, long based in Hawaii, became expert at being refueled at sea by submarines.

During Fleet Problem 21, the usual peacetime restrictions on maneuvering were lifted in the interests of realism. This included torpedo-dodging; expensive torpedoes were fired and surface craft danced around them, and then destroyers would chase after the runaway fish, recovering them to fire another day. These were still

artificial conditions, which limited the use of screening smoke, set up minimum distances, and called for attacking submarines to signal torpedo firings on the radio. Even so, conditions during this exercise were more realistic than past maneuvers.

Destroyers, aircraft and submarines all launched torpedoes. Aircraft had the best results, with 50 percent of their torpedoes striking home; destroyers the worst, with a quarter hitting the target. Submarine torpedoes were a third successful, and despite heavy anti-submarine patrols, a periscope was sighted only once, during a launching, and all completely submerged submarines were passed over. This was a sobering statistic, as the destroyers and aircraft were plainly visible on their runs and therefore vulnerable. The success of the submarines in wartime scenarios spooked the planners.

Admiral Harold Stark, Chief of Naval Operations.

The U.S. Fleet continued Fleet Problem 21 exercises in the Hawaii area, confident they'd soon return to the havens of San Diego after May 17, when the maneuvers ended. Richardson received a terse telegram in late April from Stark, warning that with "the possibility of Italy becoming an active belligerent in May, you may receive instructions to remain in Hawaiian waters…"

The new CINCUS was angry at the thinly veiled order. On May 1, Richardson wrote a letter to Stark, addressing him by the familiar "Betty," demanding the fleet return to the West Coast, and that he be sent to Washington "in order that I may talk to you, and the President if you approve, about the present war situation … and our present war plans. I feel that it is highly inadvisable for me to attempt to write what I feel it is my duty to say."

Richardson also stated firmly that it would be in the American interest to steer well clear of conflicts elsewhere in the world.

Three days later, the CNO again waffled in a dispatch. "It looks probable but not final that the fleet will remain in Hawaiian waters for short time after May 9." On May 7, Richardson got a handwritten dispatch from Stark, ordering Richardson to publicly announce that he had requested permission to remain in Hawaii "to accomplish some things I wanted to do."

Richardson was horrified. Not only was he being forced to take a public position completely opposite of his own — "something, on its very face, every tyro ensign would recognize as phony" — but the fleet was to remain in Hawaii while the tugs, target ships, repair ships and other yard craft remained on the West Coast. Training could not continue without the support ships, and CINCUS didn't know whether to send for them or let them wait for the fleet. The Navy in 1940 had only two ammunition ships, neither of which was assigned to the U.S. Fleet. Shells reached critically low reserves during training, and replenishment didn't arrive until August.

THE FLEET PROBLEM

Stark let Richardson know that it was Roosevelt who wanted the fleet "concentrated" in Hawaii. Further instructions from Washington contained wandering discourses on how the British felt about the Italian situation, or rumors concerning the Japanese "status quo" with the French Foreign Office. Richardson was given no definite orders concerning disposition of the fleet, so that he was unable to set up a base of operations, or given a reason to continue treading water in Hawaii, so that training could be set up accordingly. Pearl Harbor's facilities were stretched to the breaking point.

After repeated entreaties from Richardson, the normally circumspect Stark was unusually blunt in a personal letter dated May 27: "You are there because of the deterrent effect which it is thought your presence may have on the Japs going into the East Indies… with Italy in, it is thought that the Japs might feel just that much freer to take independent action. We believe both the Germans and the Italians have told the Japs that so far as they are concerned she, Japan, has a free hand in the East Indies… I wish I could help you."

Roosevelt's June address at University of Virginia, in which he warned off the Axis powers, startled Richardson when it was rebroadcast in Hawaii. "It's as near as making a personal declaration of war" as could be, he noted in his diary, and he asked again to come to Washington. The President then established a "defensive sea area" in Pearl Harbor and in the nine-square-mile area in front of the channel on June 14. The order gave specific boundaries, and specified that the area was out of bounds for all except the U.S. Navy. The borders were defined by lighthouse positions. Specific penalties were not established for violating the zones, but the Navy was empowered to prevent movement within them with whatever resources it could muster.

The 14th Naval District was directed to establish an in-shore patrol "consisting of a destroyer patrol at the entrance of Pearl Harbor, a boom patrol, a harbor patrol, and daily mine sweeping operations."

Richardson was instructed to catch the June 18 Pan Am clipper out of Pearl, and was about to board the plane when the orders were canceled. The reason given was the fall of France.

Later that day, Richardson was last in line to find out that the Army on Oahu had been placed on alert, ready to receive the brunt of a "trans Pacific raid." Army Lieutenant General Charles Herron, out of inter-service courtesy, had shared the warning with his opposite number at Pearl Harbor, Rear Admiral Claude C. Bloch. Bloch himself had received no such warning, but decided to launch aerial patrols of the paths to Pearl Harbor. Vice Admiral Adolphus Andrews, as the senior officer afloat in Pearl Harbor, had approved, and wanted to ask Richardson if additional patrols were necessary. He took the leisurely step of addressing this in a letter, delivered to Richardson back at Lahaina Roads. Richardson knew nothing about the alert until the letter arrived.

The admiral immediately got on the horn to Bloch, asking him if the alert was an Army exercise, or prompted by the War Department. Bloch responded by saying the alert was a directive from Washington. The U.S. Fleet waited for three days before receiving word from Washington about the alert, and even then it was hidden in official musings about possible sabotage on the Panama Canal.

Back in Pearl Harbor on June 21, Richardson asked Herron if the alert was genuine or bogus. Herron said he didn't know himself, but assumed it was real. Richardson assumed it was artificial. "It did not seem possible that the Navy Department and the War Department could be so far out of step with each other, or out of touch with each other…," he wrote.

Unable to stand the suspense, Richardson fired off a dispatch the next day to the Navy Department requesting clarification, 20 hours later, a return dispatch urged the Navy to "continue to cooperate" with the Army. "Reason is for a measure of precaution." In other words, it was a drill, unless it turned out to be real.

On June 24, Herron wrote a chatty letter to Army chief General George C. Marshall that indicates he knew the drill was false:

"This is to report that the Hawaiian portion of your domain is quiet this morning. I have just come in from seeing the dawn patrols take the air, and the anti-aircraft men roll out of the blankets at the first gray light at the sound of the Klaxon and stand at their guns. The Infantry at (businessman) Walter Dillingham's bathing beach on the North Shore were standing by their guns and looking out to sea.

"I have been highly gratified with the promptness and precision with which the planes get off the ground every morning promptly at 4:30. It is further encouraging to see the discipline and quiet efficiency among the ground crews. It is my belief that the Air Corps here comes on well.

"A week ago today I gave the command for a surprise alert, which went off smoothly and efficiently. In view of the disturbing state of the world I thought that the command might as well get accustomed to having live ammunition, but did not realize how much this would excite the post war portion of the Army. However, they are all quieted down now, as is the city, which buzzed for a couple of days. Some of the young people thought M day had come and two or three young couples that had intended to get married this month hustled around and did it at once just as in 1918!

"We really worked the young men for the first few days but have now eased up so that not more than 25 percent of any command is on actual reconnaissance or observation at any one time…"

On a brief trip to Washington in July, Richardson lunched with General Marshall, who said Herron had not been told the alert was a drill in order that "things were not simulated in Hawaii."

The alert had also highlighted a shortfall in craft to guard against submarines. Bloch pointed this out in a memorandum: "The local defense forces have no destroyers attached and it is my opinion

THE FLEET PROBLEM

that there should be destroyers on hand for district patrol purposes to be used in case of actual or approaching hostilities... there appears to be no answer to the fact that Army planes composing the in-shore patrol are untrained in submarine detection, submarine bombing and the identification of naval vessels."

Vice Admiral William Smith, in command of cruiser *Brooklyn*, held gunnery training off Oahu one summer evening and approached Pearl Harbor. He received orders to stand by and to black out the ship — a submarine had been detected lying in ambush off the channel entrance. *Brooklyn* paced the ocean until word came hours later to proceed normally. The contact seemed to be false, probably a "large fish."

Spooked by the softness of the harbor approach, Richardson began searching for destroyers to attach to the in-shore

patrol. His war plans noted that the 1939 "Jane's Fighting Ships" showed "over 40 submarines... easily capable of projection in this area. An Orange surface raiding force would be far removed from their base and would almost certainly be inferior in gun power to our surface forces..." Stealthy submarines, with their talent for vanishing into the cloak of ocean, were far more dangerous, and likely.

Richardson considered the alert a fiasco, and told Stark so in no uncertain terms. He urged that future alerts to both services be simultaneously transmitted.

By Dec. 7, 1941, this "sound principle" still had not been put into practice. Only the Army was alerted that day, and this message faltered before arriving at its destination.

In late June 1940, though, Stark was still only hinting that the fleet might be permanently stationed in Hawaii. By that point, the fleet had already settled in, to the extent of ruining Hawaiian fish catches and angering Army gunners, who complained that Navy aircraft wandering aimlessly around the islands had fouled up coastal battery ranges. The routine was broken only by a dummy "cruise" to Panama in June, in which a task force sailed off in the direction of the canal and milled about just over the horizon, sending and receiving lots of artificial radio traffic. This was during the Army alert, and the ships were gone just six days, hardly enough time to make a round trip to Panama. The Japanese consulate in Honolulu dutifully reported that the fleet had gone to Panama, however, and after their return the Navy Department was pleased with the deception. Richardson received official congratulations by

On July 1, 1940, during the Fleet Problem, Isaac C. Kidd became a rear admiral while serving as chief of staff to Commander Battleships, Battle Force, U.S. Fleet. Kidd subsequently became commander of Battleship Division 1, with battleship Arizona as his flagship. He was killed aboard the battleship on Dec. 7, 1941.

telegram: "This message consists of only two words X Well done X And therefore takes considerable padding."

By mid-August, approval was granted for small detachments of ships to "visit" the West Coast, so that married crewmen could be reunited with families that expected them home four months earlier. Stark had to lobby the president for this concession.

Richardson had lunched also with Roosevelt during the July visit to Washington during which the admiral had traveled under the assumed name of Mandley — and the President had told him, under the present circumstance, the fleet would not be sent to the Far East. Richardson lobbied hard on three points; that the Navy could not fight so far from bases, that war with Japan would be long and expensive, and that the Navy needed more men. That night, Richardson dined with the Starks and the Nimitzs. With Nimitz listening sympathetically, Stark assured Richardson that he also was working to secure more personnel.

On July 9, Richardson visited Secretary of State Cordell Hull and Under Secretary Sumner Welles, telling each that the Orange war plan as it stood was worthless. The admiral got the distinct impression that Washington was inclined to posture toughly with Japan, and that holding the fleet in check at Hawaii was part of the bluff.

Secretary of State Cordell Hull.

Unmollified, Richardson continued to complain, and Stark's replies were sympathetic, so much so that Richardson assumed the CNO agreed with him. The disadvantages to staying in Hawaii were many, including the lack of adequate maintenance facilities and a scarcity of naval target systems — gunnery scores for the Pacific Fleet actually fell during this period. Re-enlistment also dropped as sailors were separated from their families.

"I am sure it will come as something as a shock to the Honolulu Chamber of Commerce, but in 1940, the Commander Destroyers, Battle Force stated, "Enlisted men, on the whole, do not desire duty in the Hawaiian area," remembered Richardson. With no families to console them, no athletic or educational facilities to occupy them, and no supplies to keep them in training, sailors found little to do in Honolulu. Even Hawaii prostitutes refused to service them, and Honolulu whorehouses were forced to import talent from the coast.

"I was not looking for a secure place to hide the Fleet. I wanted the Fleet to be positioned where it would have the highest state of readiness for its war missions," said Richardson, who stated after the war that the Japanese could just as easily have attacked the Fleet at Puget Sound as at Pearl Harbor. "Certainly, the Navy wasn't determining where the Fleet would be prepared for war."

President Roosevelt had been advised by his Far East expert Stanley Hornbeck that stationing the fleet closer to Japan would bluff the island empire. Richardson, aware that Japan had the edge in warships and training, assumed that the Army-led government

would make a decision to attack purely on the basis of military expediency. Moving the fleet away from the protective shoulders of the West Coast and placing it in harm's way, like a ripe tomato, might actually incite Japan to act.

After mulling over the dead ends of his trip to Washington, Richardson called together all of the available commanders of the U.S. Fleet. Speaking to them on Aug. 3 at the Submarine Base Theater in Pearl Harbor, he gave an off-the-record pep talk, answering their own questions about the long deployment. *Why were they there?* Naval policy. *For how long?* Indefinitely. *What about additional men and promotions*? Until further notice, all were frozen in their billets.

He ordered the officers to be cheerful in their work, because the attitude reflected down to the men, and to be stricter disciplinarians. "We are in a profession where many people are going to be killed," said Richardson. "You cannot have discipline until you do your part to maintain it.

"I am not crying 'war' because I do not know anything about it, but I do know this, that if we don't get ready we may be sorry. If we do get ready and we have no war we will not have wasted one stroke of work. We will only have performed our simplest duties."

Upon getting transcripts of the talk, Stark and Nimitz were miffed. "We have been working together like two brothers" on procuring more men, Stark complained.

And so things continued. Knox visited the fleet in August and suggested to Richardson that he make another trip east, and when Richardson broached the idea to Stark, the CNO decided the admiral was better off in Hawaii. Stark had an abrupt change of mind a few days later, when Knox rushed into his office and insisted Richardson come to Washington. Stark wrote Richardson on Oct.

CINCUS Richardson visits Washington. From left, admirals Harry Yarnell and Harold Stark, Secretary of the Navy Frank Knox and Richardson.

1, telling him to "come East at your convenience," and courteously concluding, "Personally, I am looking forward as always to seeing you. I will keep the decks clear and will arrange our evenings according to your desires."

The details were unknown to Richardson, but the administration was considering a flotilla to the Far East. Stark and Knox wanted Richardson's support in shooting down this scheme, and were therefore suddenly solicitous.

CINCUS arrived in Washington, on the morning of Oct. 7, after a rapid cross-country trip on American Air Lines. He met immediately with Stark, Knox and Nimitz, and then rushed over to the White House for lunch. There he met Admiral William Leahy, a friend, formerly Chief of Naval Operations, now retired and serving as governor of Puerto Rico. Both dined with Roosevelt, and while Puerto Rican affairs were discussed, Richardson dozed upright in his chair, exhausted.

Ignoring Richardson, Roosevelt then asked Leahy's opinion of sending more ships to the Asiatic Fleet. Richardson's opinion on this was already a matter of record. Leahy's diplomatic response was to send none, but if ships had to be sent, to send the least valuable. Richardson decided this was an opportune moment to bring up the fleet's return to the West Coast.

In August, 1940, Navy Secretary Frank Knox visited the fleet in Hawaii and was shown new construction by naval district commander Vice Admiral Claude Bloch. It was at this time Knox strongly suggested that Admiral James O. Richardson return to Washington to face Roosevelt.

"The Fleet is being retained in Hawaii to restrain the actions of Japan," said Roosevelt.

"In my opinion, having the fleet in Hawaii might restrain a civilian, political government," countered Richardson. "But Japan has a military government. They know that our fleet is undermanned, unprepared for war and has no (supply) train, no auxiliary ships so that we could undertake active operations.

"We'd let the Japs know we meant business if the fleet were to return to the Pacific Coast and be fully complemented, fueled up, supplied with ammunition, and stripped for war operations."

The president eyed the commander-in-chief and dug in. "Despite what you believe, Joe, I believe the presence of the Fleet in the Hawaiian area had — and is now having — a restraining influence on the actions of Japan."

"Mr. President!" protested Richardson. "I still do not believe it, and I know that our Fleet is at a disadvantage in preparing for war operations."

In the heat of it, both were leaning forward, the military man considering a formula for disaster, the politician weighing public

THE FLEET PROBLEM

attitude. "I could be convinced of the desirability of returning the battleships to the West Coast if — if! — I could be given a good statement which would convince the American people and the Japanese government that we're not stepping backward," said Roosevelt.

"Are we going to enter the war?" asked Richardson.

"Not if the Japanese attack Thailand, or the Dutch East Indies, or even if they attack the Philippines," said Roosevelt. "But if they do, and expand their area of operations, sooner or later they'll make a mistake, and pull us into it."

Richardson, as he had done in July, protested that there weren't enough trained personnel to man a war. Roosevelt, also as he had done in July, maintained that men in civilian trades could be mustered into the Navy and become "adequate sailormen."

"Seasick garage mechanics are of little use at sea," retorted Richardson, and continued to press his reservations about pushing the fleet without support. Roosevelt remained intransigent — he had taken a preelection public profile of avoiding a military buildup — and Richardson grew hot.

"Mr. President, I feel that I must tell you that the senior officers of the Navy do not have the trust and confidence in the civilian leadership of this country that is essential for the successful prosecution of a war in the Pacific," he said.

"Joe, you just don't understand that this is an election year and there are certain things that can't be done, no matter what, until the election is over and won," said Roosevelt. The president, who considered himself a naval expert, was "shocked and crushed" at this outburst from Richardson.

And there the matter stood. Richardson knew he was putting his neck on the block to avoid what he considered probable disaster. And he had deeply embarrassed Roosevelt in front of Leahy, an old friend of the President.

The next evening, Stark held a dinner party at which most of the Navy command made an appearance. Talk turned to the war plans, and Knox wondered if there was a current plan for dealing with Orange. Richardson laughed, and said, "We had better have a plan, or ideas for one, or some cockeyed plan would be forced on us from above!" He met with Hornbeck the day after, who surprised Richardson by refusing to take credit — or responsibility — for basing the fleet in Hawaii. The next day, Richardson continued to make the rounds, meeting with Congressman Carl Vinson, chairman of the House Naval Affairs Committee, who plotted with Richardson to bring Leahy out of Puerto Rico and back to naval society in Washington, where he could lean on Roosevelt. The admiral then tried to head toward the airport.

Late that day, Oct. 10, as official Washington shut down, Knox sent for Richardson and Stark, canceling Richardson's return plane reservations. Knox announced that he had just came from the

President, that Roosevelt was concerned about the recently concluded Tripartite Pact and, in particular, Japan's reaction to Britain reopening the Burma Road. If the Japanese reacted strongly, the President wanted to do the same. He wanted to shut off trade with Japan, and place picket lines of small ships in the Pacific.

The admirals were silent for a moment before one asked if the picket line would be empowered to stop Japanese ships. "Wouldn't this be an act of war?" was the response.

"Is the President considering a declaration of war?" asked Richardson.

Secretary of the Navy Frank Knox.

"That's all I was told," said Knox. Richardson followed up by saying that the fleet was not only unprepared to carry out the embargo, but that it would be disastrous in practice. War planning had led to that conclusion, and no other.

Knox, annoyed at the general lack of enthusiasm in the room, barked, "I am not a strategist; if you don't like the President's plan, draw up one of your own to accomplish the purpose!"

Richardson, who rather liked Knox, was surprised by the secretary's peevishness on the matter. He and his war plans officer Murphy stayed up all night drafting a list of assumptions if the picket line idea were carried out, and they left the next day for Pearl Harbor. Richardson told his staff that they would soon be at war.

They weren't, and nothing more was heard of the President's plan to draw a line across the Pacific.

On Oct. 28, the *Kiplinger Letter* reported that Richardson would be relieved of command because of his opposition to war with Japan. In the months that followed the report, the admiral heard nothing from Washington, not even a single personal letter from Stark, so he hoped the matter had blown over.

There were plenty of operational matters that needed his attention. Exercises had not really slacked off since the Fleet Problem, and surprising holes kept appearing in defenses. The plan against Orange was modified on nearly a daily basis. By this time, the threat of submarines was obvious to all from the war games, and antisubmarine training was stepped up.

To January of 1941, the fleet often operated out of Lahaina's anchorage, still waters nestled in the crook of Maui's lee side. Security measures were carried out, guarding against surprise attacks by aircraft, submarines and surface craft, and in water shallower than 20 fathoms, mines. Prior to the installation of radar, the cover of night markedly increased the danger from assault. Evenings saw a doubling of watertight integrity, additional watches at torpedo defense stations and increased watches. Ships at anchor were often busier at night than during the day.

The anchorage at Lahaina Roads was considered to be in some

THE FLEET PROBLEM

danger from air attack, but greater danger from submarine attack. The only advantage was that ships could quickly get under way and disperse. The U.S. Fleet deployed to protect itself against the expected submarines, and crowded into Pearl Harbor. Plans for submarine attack were referenced only for operating areas outside the harbor — the harbor itself was considered vulnerable only to air attack, considered much less likely than a submarine assault.

At the throat of the harbor was an anti-torpedo net, made of surplus World War I material. An anti-submarine net was considered unnecessary in the constricted entrance; no known submarine could get by the net without causing a commotion.

By the end of the year, American warships in Hawaii sailed at night with lights secured, a standard precaution against submarine attack. Often they sailed under Condition 3 readiness, in which the guns were continuously manned in case of submarines. Carrier groups had a continuous daytime screen of aircraft fanning ahead of the groups, looking specifically for submarines.

The Atlantic blockade wicked away men and ships. The Orange plan depended entirely on the U.S. Fleet being up to full strength, which it was not, and as the situation in Europe deteriorated, the fleet was drained. Richardson resisted siphoning away his forces, often against direct pressure from the White House. The admiral argued that, if war came, the Pacific would be an offensive war, and the Atlantic a defensive conflict.

He also opposed moving forces to the Asiatic Fleet; these ships, he felt, "would be lost in the early days of the war."

The West Coast admirals also had to contend with the distance to Washington. Atlantic admirals were able to drop in at the capital with ease, and lobby for their commands.

American submarines were schooled in carrying the attack to the enemy. Despite this, in December 1940, 63 of the Navy's 93 submarines were based in the Atlantic, where there were few enemy surface ships to stalk and fewer enemy bases to spy upon. The 30 American submarines assigned to the Pacific Fleet were insufficient even to man patrol stations under the Orange plan.

Richardson's sailors did the best they could under the circumstances, and concentrated on anti-aircraft tactics. In the U-boat-rich Atlantic, the Americans received excellent on-the-job training in anti-submarine warfare. Richardson insisted on a "rapid interchange of information in these two areas of readiness," resulting in the Atlantic serving as a test site for Pacific anti-submarine training.

Ships since World War I had been equipped with paravanes for minesweeping. Trailing behind a sweeper, these tethered "brooms" flew through the water and cut moored mines. The new war in Europe, however, revealed a new menace. Magnetic mines, often sown by submarines, would lie on the ocean floor awaiting a steel hull to cause fluctuations in the earth's magnetic field. The mine sensed by this that a ship was overhead, and exploded.

Magnetic mines were neutralized by "degaussing" a ship, passing the entire craft through electromagnetic coils and aligning the magnetic fields in a consistent direction. Before degaussing, all compasses and similarly sensitive gear were removed. By the summer of 1940, degaussing piers were constructed at all major naval stations. At Pearl Harbor, the degaussing facilities were in West Loch, as far away from the Navy yard as possible, yet still within the harbor.

The continued presence of the fleet had spurred construction of air fields in Hawaii. Ford Island's air field was widened and lengthened to handle larger patrol planes, and maintenance facilities were erected. One million dollars was spent on seaplane parking and ramps, some of it on landfill created for the project. A major base at Barbers Point was well under way, designed to eventually replace the neighboring strip at Ewa. Seaplane facilities at Kaneohe were in operation, and a runway there was being laid. Smaller, satellite fields were built on the islands of Maui and Molokai.

The scope of the building was enormous, even though the Navy was having trouble manning the ships and aircraft it already had. Slightly more than one-fifth of $400 million, the entire Navy budget for 1940, was spent on Hawaii construction. The flood of money brought a boom in the local economy, and a subsequent influx of workers from the United States. Navy intelligence officers noted soon afterward that racial conflicts in the islands had increased, and credited them to white construction workers unschooled in island ways.

General Marshall noted in an *aide memoire* that "the island of Oahu, due to its fortification, its garrison, and its physical characteristics, is believed to be the strongest fortress in the world."

By the close of 1940, the Navy was rushing into construction 17 battleships, 12 aircraft carriers, three battle cruisers, 48 cruisers and 168 destroyers. To service these new warships, only two repair ships and six destroyer tenders were allocated. This lack of maintenance planning gave Richardson one more thing to complain about — Pearl Harbor's repair facilities were already in overdrive trying to keep a peacetime Navy afloat. What would happen if these ships had battle damage?

Under the existing Orange plan, argued Richardson, the problem of supply could still cripple the fleet, which would have had to scurry back to the West Coast, strip the ships for combat, and then assemble a huge transport train of supplies. By December 1940, Richardson had cleaned his ships of peace-time inflammables and

Army Chief of Staff General George C. Marshall.

THE FLEET PROBLEM

run the hulls through the new degaussing coils in West Loch, but the problems of thin supply remained.

Intelligence officer Lieutenant Commander Edwin Layton joined Richardson's staff in late 1940. As the year drew to a close, destroyer *McDougal* made a mysterious contact off the mouth of Pearl. The *McDougal's* skipper claimed, after tracking the echo for 14 hours, that it was definitely a submarine. Others in the screening group held onto the target for 44 hours. A temperature gradient began to interfere with the search; and when it dissipated, the contact was gone.

Subsequent to that contact, Layton began to receive dozens of similar reports from Hawaii and the West Coast. Destroyer skippers were convinced something was under there.

These contacts were reflected in updated war plans. Captain Charles McMorris, war plans officer for the Pacific Fleet, submitted Pacific Fleet Operating Plan for Rainbow Five, the Army's plan for war with Japan, to Admiral Stark with one primary reservation. The U.S. Fleet, he pointed out, had far too few destroyers and other anti-submarine vessels to successfully carry it off its part of the scenario.

"I estimated that there were likely to be heavy submarine concentrations in the Hawaiian area and the approaches thereto," testified McMorris later. "I believed that submarine attacks would be directed primarily at our task forces operating at sea and that there was likelihood of attempts being made to sink a ship in the Pearl Harbor Channel. It seemed not unlikely that the war might be initiated by an attempt to torpedo a valuable ship making ingress or egress to Pearl Harbor Channel."

McMorris also predicted similar tactics would bottle up West Coast ports.

The plans addressed submarine danger to ships in operating areas and entering or leaving the harbor, but no anti-submarine planning was applied to ships inside the harbor. Pearl Harbor was considered submarine-proof. "We found we were unduly complacent," McMorris said in retrospect.

Consideration was giving to lining the approach with defensive mines. Swift currents and the narrow shelf mitigated against it, however, studies showed that mines stayed put only a few weeks or so before tearing loose and drifting away. As for the underwater contacts, Richardson was not convinced — perhaps he didn't quite believe in the arcane technology of sonar — but ordered depth charges to be dropped on such echoes anyway. He later rescinded the order, influenced by a suggestion from Stark that destroyers should simply follow the contacts around instead of bombing them.

Another problem surfaced in January 1941. The U.S. Fleet was directed to escort naval transport *Chaumont* from Honolulu to Guam, where the Asiatic Fleet would take over and run interference for the transport on the leg to Manila. Richardson was curious about this change in policy — transports had sailed on their own and

Nomura visiting Richardson, 1941.

2 Of course neither suspected, at the time, that the other was being kept out of the decision-making loops of their respective governments.

unmolested to this point — and sent a dispatch to Stark asking why. The reply he got back essentially told him to mind his own business.

Later, in Washington, he again asked why, and was given a blindside by the CNO: There were rumors of German raiders in the North Pacific. It wasn't until after the war that Richardson discovered that *Chaumont* was carrying "Magic," a cryptographic decoding device capable of translating Japanese radio messages. At the time, Richardson was not even aware that the U.S. had this capability. The U.S. Fleet, once again, was out of the information and intelligence circuit. Only Washington analysts and Gen. Douglas MacArthur seemed to have access.

While *Chaumont* sailed to Manila protected by a phalanx of warships, Richardson received an old acquaintance, Admiral Kichisaburo Nomura of the Imperial Navy, on his way to Washington as Japan's new ambassador. The two had met when Nomura was Japan's naval attache in Washington, and became friendly. Richardson had high regard for Nomura's intelligence and friendliness, and he entertained the ambassador at a variety of functions in Honolulu. There's an irony in this last moment of friendliness between Japanese and American naval officers.[2]

Richardson felt that Army-Navy cooperation during his tenure in Hawaii was excellent. The problems that arose were with communications channels established by Washington, and with unfamiliarity of the other service's mission. No matter how many exercises and training sessions were held, for example, Army aviators had serious difficulty identifying ships at sea as friendly or hostile. Submarines were impossible to recognize.

The primary bomber used during this period was the B-18 Bolo, a ponderous aircraft that resembled an obese Douglas DC-2, with which it shared the same wing design and engines. The aircraft had poor downward visibility, a short range and a skimpy bomb load. It was expected to shoulder most of the patrols around the islands.

Combined exercises highlighted the futility of using these aircraft as anti-submarine warriors. An exercise in January 1941, that allowed hostile submarines to close on friendly forces prompted Herron to write, "I believe this exercise was of considerable value in bringing out some of the problems that will arise whenever Army aircraft are called upon to establish an anti-submarine patrol."

THE FLEET PROBLEM

Vice Admiral Bloch, his opposite number at the 14th Naval District, responded, "The communications between Army aircraft and naval vessels functioned well throughout the exercise. No issue is taken with the conclusion of the commanding general, Hawaiian Air Force, that the B-18 type airplane is unsuitable for submarine search."

Other aircraft were tried out, notably the whale-like 0-47, before the Army settled on the B-17 for overwater patrols, primarily for its range and bomb load. Until the time of the Pearl Harbor attack, however, the Bolo was the Army's primary anti-submarine patrol plane in Hawaii waters, a job at which it was a notable failure. Japanese submarines were never spotted by B-18s.

Army fliers had trouble throughout the war properly identifying surface vessels, and precision bombing at sea by B-17s proved to be a daydream. Ironically, once it was fitted with a MAD — Magnetic Anomaly Detector — boom in its tail, the B-18 finally came into its own as an anti-submarine weapon. By that time, however, it was employed only against U-boats in the Caribbean.

The need for aircraft was critical. In the fiscal year between July 1, 1940 and June 30, 1941, the number of patrol planes in the Navy inventory was scheduled to increase from 198 to 324 aircraft. Only 12 of these additional planes were assigned to Hawaii, however, and these were the last planes assigned, a situation Richardson later attributed to "direct Presidential pressure." The others were concentrated in the Atlantic and Caribbean, where Hitler's U-boats hun-

Construction workers arrive en masse at Pearl Harbor. Roosevelt's decision to throw the fleet forward into the Pacific created a massive building program at the once-quiet harbor.

grily circled convoys bound for England. Those 12 planes were it, Richardson was told. Additional patrol planes could not be expected before June 1943.

Captain Patrick N.L. Bellinger took over Patrol Wing Two, based at Pearl Harbor, on the first day of November 1940. His initial impression wasn't favorable. "I arrived here on Oct. 30, 1940, with the point of view that the international situation was critical, especially in the Pacific, and I was impressed with the need of being ready today rather than tomorrow for any eventuality that might arise."

Bellinger found a handful of PBYs being flown long hours on inadequate patrols, exhausted pilots and burned-out engines, and distressing equanimity from the Navy Department over the situation. He estimated PatWing Two needed to be tripled in strength, and even that was a conservative number compared to the Army's request for hundreds of B-17s.

"I was surprised to find that here in the Hawaiian Islands, an important advance naval outpost, we were operating on a shoestring and the more I looked, the thinner the shoestring seemed to be," he wrote. There were periods when the wing was unable to provide even the six planes needed for minimum patrols of shore areas.

Richardson's requests for complete patrols strained the wing. By December 1940, Richardson and Stark were again locking horns over the need for patrol planes. By Christmas, Stark ordered that there was "an advantage in making occasional sweeps by aircraft and surface craft, but it is not yet necessary to make these continuous." Richardson's mind wasn't changed, but he was forced to comply. PatWing Two eased back on the patrol schedule.

At the same time, Richardson ghost-wrote a letter by Bloch to Stark that detailed inadequacies in Hawaii defenses. At Bloch's request, Richardson then endorsed the letter he had composed. In January 1941, Secretary of the Navy Frank Knox lifted portions of this composition to appeal to the Secretary of War, indicating that an air attack on Pearl Harbor was probable. Although he pretended to have nothing to do with this wide-ranging communication, other than adding his seal of approval, Richardson was the principal instigator.

While these desktop maneuvers were raging, Richardson received orders relieving him of command at the end of January. He was shocked and disappointed — "My God, they can't do that to me," he blurted out when the message was delivered to him on a Hawaii golf course — but worked at readying the fleet for the war he felt was inevitable.

The War Department subsequently announced that 180 B-17s were being allocated to the Hawaiian Department, and a hundred PBYs were to be added to Bloch's command in the 14th Naval District. This was lip service, however. Of the promised aircraft, only 12 PBYs and 12 B-17s were delivered by Dec. 7, 1941.

THE FLEET PROBLEM

President Roosevelt ceremonially carves the Thanksgiving turkey, 1941.

Responding to a query from Richardson on Jan. 28, one of the last by the admiral, Bellinger said that the planes of Patrol Wing Two could not make sudden, long-range searches unless "radically reducing present training work and keeping a definite number of planes in ready Standby Status." He added that this also assumed the planes were not armed with anti-submarine weapons like depth charges, except for bomb or machine guns, and that a one-to-three hour lead time was available.

Richardson filed the response, making it available to his successor. The PBYs had been reduced to making occasional sorties by order of the CNO. Richardson later wished he had gone against Washington's wishes, and continued long-range reconnaissance flights fanning out from Hawaii. Even without enough airplanes to sweep the clock, it might have spotted the Japanese fleet on the way in, and certainly tracked them on the way out.

The matter was out of his hands. Richardson packed his sea bag on Jan. 31, 1941, and handed over the reins of the U.S. Fleet to Admiral Husband E. Kimmel. The thorn in the side of White House was gone, replaced by a man no less concerned, but very much a team player. Kimmel generally kept his opinions to himself.

4 KIDO BUTAI

A Sudden Sword Thrust to Protect the Flank

Admiral Isoroku Yamamoto's inherited response to the American war plan was, in many ways, complementary to it. The Americans had an edge in ship numbers, but worried about stretching them across the vast Pacific. War Plan Pac-46 called for a concentration in the central Pacific, to seize the Mandates and disrupt Japanese trade routes, while assuming Indochina would fall.

Basic Japanese strategy was predicated on a replay of the battle of Tsushima, when Admiral Togo bushwhacked a top-heavy Russian fleet that had sailed halfway around the world. The plan to control the Pacific called for the American Fleet to be lured beyond easy replenishment and then nibble away at them, piranha-like, with submarines. When the U.S. Fleet was whittled down to parity with the Imperial Navy, the Japanese intended to strike headlong in a mid-ocean Gotterdammerung, where superior — it was assumed — Japanese training and motivation would carry the day. The great battle to come was called *Kantai Kessen*.

Japanese war plans were drawn up every year by 10 staff officers of the First Section (Planning) of the First Division (Operations), refined with Army strategists and then submitted to the Emperor for his stamp. The plans looked 12 months ahead, and were in effect for a modified fiscal year, between April 1 and March 31.

Over the years, the plans changed little. Drawing on the impact that U-boats had on Britain in the World War I, Vice Admiral Nobumasu Suetsugu in the early '20s added submarines. As the American fleet advanced across the Pacific to its rendezvous with destiny, the I-boats would harry the U.S. ships, reducing their numbers by as much as 30 percent. This strategy, called *Yogeki sakusen*, a plan for forced attrition, became Imperial orthodoxy.

The only other change in Japanese war planning before 1941 added Britain as a potential adversary.

The American fleet's move to Pearl Harbor in 1940, and the expected beefing up of the Asiatic Fleet, exacerbated the Japanese dilemma. Yamamoto had to modify the original war plan. Japan's eastern flank had to be protected, while simultaneously allowing a swift grab of Indochina.

Zenshiro Hoshina, secretary general of the Imperial Navy and Hirohito's naval adviser, often argued against the coming war. He was accused of being an American naval officer in disguise by the Army, including General Hideki Tojo. Hoshina, still alive 50 years after the Pearl Harbor attack, came to believe that Yamamoto, who also opposed war with America, staged the brilliant strike at Pearl Harbor not only to cripple the U.S. Fleet, but to give the Imperial Navy political parity with the Japanese Army.

Yamamoto's solution was aggressive: smash the U.S. Fleet before it had a chance to sortie from Pearl, and use the second-string forces to hit at Dutch, British, Australian and American units in the Far East. America, it was hoped, would roll over and concede the Pacific. Both the plan and attacking fleet were titled *Kido Butai*.

The only drawback to this scheme was that it left the home islands largely unprotected. A short distance to the north was the Soviet Union, which the Imperial Army had scrapped with indecisively in China a few years before. The German attack on Soviet Union, however, shattered the delicate balance of power halfway across the globe. The Japanese military was free to strike without fearing the bear.

With the original grand-battle strategy for the Imperial submarines out with the bath water, Yamamoto decided to include them in Kido Butai, a combat role for which they had not trained. Yamamoto guessed — and subsequent war games proved him

Prewar planning called for a massive slugging match between battleships, with aircraft and submarines playing supporting roles. Here, battleships Hyuga *and* Ise *patrol the Japanese coast.*

47

correct — that the air wing would have a difficult time at Pearl Harbor. Buttressing the primary aerial forces with auxiliary undersea forces seemed like a good idea at the time.

The year 1941 was a period of feverish activity for the Imperial Navy's submarine crews. Long-established tactics were abandoned, shipyard schedules stepped up and new technologies were developed.

Foreign Minister Yosuke Matsuoka met with Hitler in Berlin on April 4, 1941. In addition to talk of diplomatic maneuvering, Matsuoka point-blank asked the Fuehrer to instruct the *Kriegsmarine* to open facilities to Japanese naval investigators. In particular, said Matsuoka, Japan needed to closely study German U-boat tactics and technologies. In return, Japan would do its best to avoid war with the United States, unless the Americans decided to enter the war after Singapore was attacked. In that case, Japan would limit the Pacific war to guerrilla actions in the south.

Hitler thought this sounded fine, and promised to place German naval authorities at the disposal of the Imperial Navy. Matsuoka then pleaded with the German leader to keep the conversation a secret, perhaps not trusting the current Imperial government, and once more pressed for submarine technology, specifically asking for periscope optics.

There was little the Nazis could give Japan in the way of torpedo development. During the opening moves of the Pacific War, the Japanese Type 95 oxygen-propelled torpedo had longer range, higher speed, a larger warhead and far more reliability than any comparable Allied or Axis weapon. In June, each submarine of the 6th Fleet had been allowed to fire one torpedo each against the rocky, steep shoreline of Oshima, just south of Tokyo Bay, which were the final operational tests of the Type 95. The Japanese also gave the Nazis 70 aerial torpedoes of the type used at Pearl Harbor.

Imperial Navy staff officers plan the assault on Pearl Harbor in this reenactment, made in mid-1942 for propaganda purposes.

Kido Butai

On Oct. 2, primarily due to intensive training, Lieutenant Commander Takashi Hirokawa's *I-61* was accidentally hit by a gunboat in home waters, sinking with the captain and most of her crew. It was the third training disaster in 20 months.

The most secret program in the Imperial Navy was the midget submarine, the stealth fighter of its day. The leading exponent was Lieutenant Naoji Iwasa, who headed the training program for midget submarine pilots. Except for Iwasa and his protege Lieutenant Saburo Akieda, no one in the midget program was a volunteer, though all were chosen for their enthusiasm and devotion to duty. It was considered quite an honor.

The weapon had been designed for open-ocean warfare. Iwasa's experience with the agile sub convinced him that it could do anything, even penetrate a foreign anchorage. His excitement over the machine's potential infected Lieutenant Keiu Matsuo, an aide to submarine expert Commander Toshihide Maejima, and the two spent many evenings plotting midget tactics.

The stealthy attributes of the craft could logically be used during a surprise attack during the outbreak of war. The flaw was that the midget crews were placed in greater danger.

Iwasa pitched the idea to Captain Kaku Harada, skipper of *Chiyoda*, and Harada was so impressed that he had Iwasa present the concept to Lieutenant Commander Ryunosuke Ariizume, a submarine expert on the Naval General Staff.

Upon meeting Ariizume, Iwasa blurted out, "Sir! Our weapon can do so much more damage to an enemy on his doorstep than in the middle of the ocean!" Ariizume laughed and was impressed with the young officer's enthusiasm. And he agreed with Iwasa's arguments: Enemy ships hit in port would not be able to inflict damage on Japanese warships. Enemy ships at anchorage are stationary targets and easier to hit.

Captain Kaku Harada, skipper of Chiyoda.

Ariizume carried the concept to Yamamoto, and before long the two lieutenants were called before the admiral to explain their scheme. Yamamoto didn't like the midget submarine's limited range. He felt it was a suicidal flaw, and rejected the plan. Midget submarine carrier *Chiyoda* simply couldn't loiter in Hawaiian waters to recover returning midget submarines while the rest of the Imperial task force raced to safety.

Iwasa and Matsuo were determined to iron out this problem, and solved it, at least in theory, by transporting the midget submarines on the backs of "mother" submarines, fleet-class warships that could hide beneath the water while waiting for the midget submarine crews to return from the attack.

Yamamoto accepted their plan, reluctantly. His abrupt consent left little time to reconfigure fleet subs to motherhood. The reason

the usually phlegmatic Yamamoto would consent to such a wild notion is a mystery. Perhaps he wanted merely to placate the submariners, who were demanding a piece of the action in Kido Butai; maybe he was struck by the two lieutenants' romantic military enthusiasm; perhaps the admiral wished a back-up in case the air wing's still unproven shallow-running torpedo got stuck in Pearl Harbor's mud; or maybe he made the harsh realization that the results might be worth the lives of the midget submariners.

On July 29 Yamamoto consulted with Vice Admiral Mitsumi Shimizu, and decided to commit a large pack of I-boats to the operation.

Shimizu's plan called for 25 fleet craft and five midget subs, but it didn't ease the worries of the Navy General Staff. Captain Kameto Kuroshima, a staff officer with the Combined Fleet, visited Captain Sadatoshi Tomioka of the General Staff in August and complained that the submarine plan was risky, bizarre and threw resources too far out of home waters. It was the same apprehension that greeted the air plan.

To ease their doubts, and perhaps assuage their own, the Combined Fleet staff devoted a portion of the fall map exercises at the Naval Staff College to war gaming the Pearl Harbor assault.

Security during these Pearl Harbor war games was woefully inadequate, according to a Japanese yeoman involved, who was later captured and interrogated. Classes at the Naval War College continued as usual, and "any man with a half-official air could easily have walked in."

The first round cost the Japanese 50 percent casualties. The second, which incorporated a stealthy, northern approach, played out better, but was still costly. And the games, as the proponents of Kido Butai pointed out, were mathematical exercises that ignored the factors of luck and divine guidance.

Those opposed to the plan felt their position was strengthened. Vice Admiral Shigeru Fukudome told the rest of the Navy General Staff that Kido Butai would result in disaster, and admirals Osami Nagano and Seiichi Ito agreed. Traditional naval orthodoxies were closing ranks on Yamamoto.

In October, Yamamoto threatened to resign if his plan wasn't carried out. The bluff worked; opposition to the plan dissolved, and Nagano gave the go-ahead sometime in late October or early November.

Kido Butai by this point could only be derailed by an outbreak of peace talks. Yamamoto's Combined Fleet Secret OpOrder #1, detailing the Pacific-wide assault on the Allies, contained a single paragraph concerning Imperial Navy submarine operations in Hawaii:

"The Commander of the Surprise Attack Force (Submarine Force), having the 6th Fleet (Submarine Fleet) as its main element, will have most of the submarines leave the western part of the Inland

KIDO BUTAI

Sea on X-20 Day to attack Pearl Harbor. Its entire strength will be so disposed so as to command the harbor mouth. It will attack any enemy warship which may have escaped from the harbor. It will also carry out reconnaissance before the attack, and if the opportunity presents itself, will carry out surprise attacks on enemy warships with midget submarines. The time for such attacks will be after the flights of planes have attacked Oahu. Every possible means for recovery of midget submarines should be considered."[1]

Kido Butai orders also indicated that any ship encountered within six hundred miles of the objective would be promptly sunk, no questions asked. The plan called for the hapless ship to be seized by a destroyer crew before a radio transmission could be sent. A more realistic plan — and the probable reason three I-boats were subsequently detailed to precede the fleet — would be to blast the ship with torpedoes, without warning, from beneath the sea. There would be no chance to get off an SOS implicating the Imperial Navy.

Submarine experts Maejima and Matsuo were chosen by the Naval staff to develop a more detailed plan for the midgets. One decision concerned a safe area in the islands where the midgets could be recovered. On the basis of Japanese intelligence, they settled on Niihau, an isolated, remote island southwest of Kauai where the sheltered residents spoke only Hawaiian. Independently, the air strike force also picked Niihau for the same purpose.

Sheer luck and chance were necessary, they admitted, for no one could predict American patrols at the entrance of the harbor. They also wanted a closer look at Pearl Harbor.

When the Japanese liner *Taiyo Maru* set sail from Honolulu's Pier 8 on Nov. 5, Matsuo and Maejima were aboard, disguised as doctors. Also on board was Lieutenant Commander Suguru Suzuki, an aviation expert. He had been one of the intelligence drones in the General Staff who had pored over mail from adoring Hawaii *doho*. On arrival, the liner swung near the entrance of Pearl Harbor, shadowed by a suspicious Coast Guard cutter. The two submarine men watched carefully from the rail, hoping to gather the latest observations of American ship moorings and sub nets.

The liner remained at the pier for the first week in November, closely guarded by American Marines who were under orders to keep all Japanese nationals sequestered aboard ship. Neither officer got ashore, though information from the Japanese consulate was smuggled aboard. They were visited by Consul General Nagao

[1] *Nowhere in these orders is there a command for the midget submarines to enter the harbor. On the other hand, the orders give plenty of latitude; Yamamoto realized that submarines can best operate independently and in the dark.*

Matsuo and Maejima set off on Taiyo Maru.

NYK liner Taiyo Maru, *the last Japanese ship to call on Honolulu before the December attack.*

Kita, whom they handed a wish list of 97 questions they wanted answered. Kita gave the list to the consulate's resident spy, Takeo Yoshikawa, who answered the list and threw in a couple of hand-drawn maps. The list was smuggled on board in newspaper bundles.

No information was available about American activities off Lahaina, but on the voyage back to Japan, Suzuki befriended some Maui *doho* who were being repatriated. Over drinks, he learned that the U.S. Fleet had, by and large, abandoned Lahaina Roads.

Suzuki presented his report on Nov. 17 to Rear Admiral Matome Ugaki, Yamamoto's chief of staff. Suzuki suggested that an invasion of Oahu could be aided by Hawaii Japanese. Ugaki was intrigued, but tossed back the idea; how would an invasion force be resupplied? The idea was dropped for the time being.

For Maejima and Matsuo, Pearl Harbor was as they expected. No one outside the harbor could see within. In daytime, the narrow entrance could be recognized from a distance of several miles only if the midget skipper climbed atop the bridge when the sub was surfaced. Using only the periscope, they'd have to be within a couple of miles. Recognizing the entrance at night would require a navigational fix on landmarks, in an area of Oahu remarkable for its paucity of landmarks.

Back in Japan, submariner Lieutenant Commander Tatsuwaka Shibuya was posted to the 1st Air Fleet on Nov. 5. It was unusual to have a submarine officer assigned to the air-attack fleet of carriers, but fleet commander Admiral Chuichi Nagumo needed him for such a closely coordinated operation. On Nov. 9, aboard *Akagi*, Shibuya briefed Nagumo and other staff officers.

The plan was to have Shimizu, as commander of the submarine 6th Fleet, direct the overall attack by his I-boats. However, for the three days immediately after the aerial attack, command would be shifted to the carrier group. It was imagined the two forces would be operating in the same area, fighting for their lives against angry American warships, and would need on-the-spot coordination.

The next day, Shimizu's staff presented the just-completed

52

operational plan to the submarine commanders. Twenty submarines of the 1st, 2nd and 3rd Submarine Squadrons were to take part, plus the five mother subs of the "Special Attack Unit" of Sasaki's 1st Submarine Division, a force of nearly 3,000 men. Before the attack, other submarines were to reconnoiter Lahaina Roads, the Aleutians an outposts in the South Pacific. During the attack, while the midget submarines were in Pearl Harbor, larger submarines were to ring Oahu, nailing any ships that got under way. Others were to snipe at American shipping between Hawaii and the West Coast.

Since the submarines would be in Hawaiian waters far ahead of the attack fleet, they were designated the Advance Force. They were the tip of the spear aimed at the U.S. Pacific Fleet.

The simple plan was quickly approved, highlighting the political advantage Shimizu's submarines had over Nagumo's carriers at this point in history. After the German undersea successes in World War I, the Imperial Navy brass needed no convincing that submarines were prized weapons. Whatever Shimizu asked for, he got — supplies or men or bulldozing through red tape. The airmen and their expensive, delicate carriers had never proven themselves in the forge of battle.

Shimizu had the 25 submarines and five midgets placed under his command, most of Japan's underwater fleet. During the Nov. 10 briefing, aboard *Katori* in Saeki Bay, the submarine commanders and division and squadron leaders heard from Matsumura for the first time — except for Sasaki — that their target was Pearl Harbor.

In the briefing, the air-attack portion was minimized, perhaps because the admiral remembered the 50 percent casualties of the September board games. They were also told war wasn't a sure thing, so it was a good idea to maintain radio discipline at all times, in case an all-clear was sounded. Enemy ships were to be tagged, but no torpedoes fired until after the air raid.

There was every expectation that the submarine attacks would be highly successful. The subs had a range of more than 10,000 miles without refueling, the crews were highly trained, and a submarine blockade could take place over weeks, while the air attack would be over in a couple of hours.

Admiral Ugaki also gave an informal talk to his commanders, hoping to smooth out the ambiguities in the secret order. "Our Navy, in engaging a worthy enemy, is about to realize an ambition which dates back to the foundation of the Imperial Navy many years ago.

"The alliance with Germany was not desired by the Navy, but was a project favored by the Army, which thought it would hold the Soviet Union in check.

"All of the planes of the carrier divisions will be concentrating on Oahu," If any ships escape, it was up to the submarines to pick them off. "Almost the entire submarine strength of the 6th Fleet will be in command of the harbor mouth and will concentrate torpedo attacks on them."

Commander Mitsuo Fuchida, leader of the Kido Butai air attack, was outraged when he learned of Advance Force involvement.

As for the rumored secret weapons, Ugaki shrugged. The midget submarine unit has been studying and training at the Kure Navy Yard with the *Chiyoda* for a year and a half, but it is still too much to hope that it has reached a state of perfection. In any case, the crew members are supremely confident. The 6th Fleet will attempt to use them in attacks within the harbor."

About the same time, during an idle chat with Eta Jima naval academy classmate Shibuya, Commander Mitsuo Fuchida, leader of the planned air attack, found out for the first time about the midget mission. "What possible good could the subs do?" cried Fuchida, furious. "If the air attack succeeds, they'd be useless." It was an additional risk in a risky venture.

Fuchida was also disappointed in Yamamoto. Was he risking the entire plan to give the conventional surface forces a taste of glory? His airmen faced certain slaughter if the plan went awry and the submarines were discovered lurking outside the enemy naval base.

Fuchida didn't doubt the midget submariners' bravery, but he was upset about their participation and railed against them throughout the Navy. The aviator knew nothing of the midgets' characteristics, operational objectives, organization or even of their reason for participating in the attack, and proudly maintained this facade of ignorance up until the attack.

Even so, he had reason to worry. The entire mood of the submarine attack had been sacrificial from the beginning. The airman were prepared to die, but only if the results justified it. The submariners were prepared to die for a grand gesture.

PATRIOT SONS　5

One Last Snapshot Before They Go

At the end of October 1941, Captain Kaku Harada of *Chiyoda*, home ship to the midgets, told the midget submarine skippers their presence was required by Yamamoto, after which they'd be given a 10-day leave. Yamamoto entertained them aboard his flagship *Nagato*, moored at Hashirajima. He said their work was highly important and meant much to the Navy.

"Dangerous operations such as you are about to embark upon could have far-greater success than conventional surface actions," toasted the admiral, who privately had doubts about the mission. "You could outshine the older officers. Be diligent, courageous and dutiful."

The midget officers fanned out over Japan on leave. Before they left, they were advised a "long maneuver" was coming up, and it would be a good idea to say goodbye to their parents.

Ensign Kazuo Sakamaki, one of the midget skippers, felt the prickling of fear as he rode a train home. This time it may be the real thing, he thought.

Being with relatives wasn't easy, even for someone trained, as he was, in suppressing emotion. Whenever a relative or friend clapped him on the back and said how proud they were of him, Sakamaki looked away and mumbled a reply. It was a relief to get back to the emotional discipline of the attack plan.

Born a week after the end of World War I, in a small village on the islet of Skikoku, Sakamaki was named Kazuo — "peace boy" — to commemorate the war's close. For nearly two decades, he grew up among fondly remembered hills and gentle rivers, a quiet place where Japanese mythological legends seemed to breathe the same air.

Sakamaki was disappointed when he discovered the legends were fables. He wanted to believe them just as they were taught.

This was the atmosphere in which Sakamaki lived as Japan went to war with China. Soldiers marched away to the glory of battle as Sakamaki and other school kids cheered them on with *banzai* cries and the national anthem.

As he grew, Sakamaki — and the rest of Japan — became convinced that there was indeed a national emergency, that Japan's very existence was threatened by the massed economic forces of the West. Instead of becoming a schoolteacher like his father, he was determined to enter the military.

One day, while still in high school, he came home and gravely announced to his parents, "Father and mother, everyone at school is going to join the Army or Navy. I wish to enter the Naval Academy. May I?"

They were astonished. "The Naval Academy?"

"Yes, that's where the country's best boys go."

"But, son — it's a difficult place to enter…"

Sakamaki's parents were apprehensive for good reason. The Naval Academy at Eta Jima was perhaps the most exclusive fraternity in Japan, with 95 percent of applicants rejected on the basis of intellectual and physical requirements. The remaining few were hammered into sharp blades, the cream of an elitist society, and many broke in the forge.[1]

Sakamaki's parents weren't sure he could take it. None of his ancestors, all schoolteachers and village leaders, had entered the military. The whole Sakamaki family was drawn into the debate, and Kazuo's teachers were quizzed. Would this country boy disgrace the family by failing, or would he bring honor on them by succeeding?

It was decided to let him try. Sakamaki was elated to discover he was one of 300 cadets — out of 6,000 applicants — to make the initial cut.

He entered the academy on April 1, 1937, just before the military fiasco on the Marco Polo Bridge that escalated into full-bore war with China.

Eta Jima is another small island in Japan's sheltered inland sea, templed with evergreen trees and surrounded by blue water all year. The cadets wore white uniforms with seven brass buttons and ornamental daggers. The training was so rigorous that Sakamaki barely had time to enjoy his surroundings. The day began at 5:30 a.m. and ended at 9 p.m., seven days a week. There were no relaxation periods.

Eta Jima's reputation for harsh discipline was well-deserved. Punishment for minor offenses consisted of blows to the face with a clenched fist while the victim stood at attention - there were rarely major offenses. After six months, beatings tapered off, as the cadets became psychologically unable to question authority, or became more adept at hiding it.

Classes were interspersed with drills and gymnastics. During summer, they swam for three hours a day and an annual camp out at Miyajima Island was capped off with a mass rough-water swim back to Eta Jima, a 10-mile course that took 13 hours. This swim alone would wash out 10 percent of the candidates.

[1] Adolf Hitler once said there were only two things Germany could learn from Japan — the Imperial Navy and the *Yamato Damashii, the martial spirit that linked soul and country.*

PATRIOT SONS

Imperial Navy cadets rowing at Eta Jima. The harsh discipline and rugged training took a physical toll on these young men, but the mental toughening also robbed many of initiative and imagination.

Cadets at Eta Jima sing the academy song in rank.

The cadets would row until blood ran from their fingers and soaked into their clothes. The boats would charge headlong into a wave-tossing storm, and they would not turn back, even if all the cadets were miserably seasick and stained the water around them with greasy vomit.

On land they wrestled, rising again and again from the floor, panting with exhaustion. The coach administered training with sudden blows to the face, hard enough to cuff the cadet to the floor.

But Sakamaki considered the physical training the easiest part of the cadets' life. Eta Jima also honed his mind, with a standard college curriculum — the equivalent today of 36 hours a week — as well as learning everything there is to know about military life. Cadets studied history, engineering, battle tactics and seamanship.

Young men sickened under the assault on their minds and bodies and dropped out. Some committed suicide. Those who were left, like Sakamaki, were proud of their fortitude and believed themselves to be disciplined masters of Japan's destiny, a fairly heady notion.

Their souls also went back into the shop for a spiritual tune-up. "We were taught, and we came to believe," wrote Sakamaki, "that the most important thing for us was to die manfully on the battlefield — as the petals of the cherry blossoms fall to the ground — and that in war there is only victory and no retreat. There was, however, technique in both…" And that was why they were in the academy.

As graduation loomed, the international situation darkened. Life for the cadets became even more grim, and they decided there was no room for individual thinking. "Absolute obedience to our superiors was the only behavior becoming a cadet," wrote Sakamaki. "This meant I had to rule out all thoughts of pleasures of life and concentrate on becoming an instrument for world peace, even if that should require fiercely fighting in war."

The great adversary was seen from the beginning as the United

PATRIOT SONS

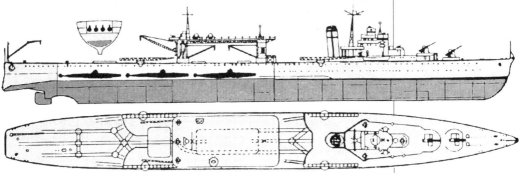

States Fleet. Sakamaki's officer-instructors drummed into them warnings about America's strength on the seas, about how rigorously trained Annapolis officers were — "more so, than you are."

Japan's only ace was the theory of "sudden attack," which supposed in advance a willingness to make a suicidal assault against superior forces. The Eta Jima cadets took this in stride, welcomed the concept for the edge it gave them over future opponents.

Sakamaki graduated in August 1940, and the new midshipman didn't get the customary world-wide cruise, because the world was deeply at war by then. He instead bounced from command to command, starting with maneuvers near the China coast, the Japan Sea and the Western Pacific.

He received a month of aviation training, then one month each as gunnery officer and deck officer on the torpedo cruiser *Abukuma* as it sortied to Taiwan and Saigon. Sakamaki was willing to become a career officer, but so far a specific specialty had eluded him.

The Imperial Navy decided what to do with Sakamaki on April 1, 1941, when he was promoted to ensign and posted to *Chiyoda*, the Navy's mystery ship. Officially she was a seaplane tender, though her maneuvers were always top secret, so much so that virtually no one in the Imperial Navy knew what she was about.

Sakamaki and 23 other puzzled young officers reported to duty aboard *Chiyoda*. They were all cast from the same tough mold — body strength and physical endurance, fighting spirit and intelligence. None were married. All came from large families with several sons.

Tender Chiyoda *was modified to hold a dozen midget submarines in her belly, and could deposit the craft out her stern in a few minutes. The roofed area amidships protected the ship's maintenance shops.*

Clockwise from the bottom, Lieutenants Furuno, Otosaka, Chuma, Ban and Yokoyama while training on Chiyoda. All would die in midget submarines during the first year of war.

[2] Harada remained a training officer through the war, and died in a Philippine detention camp.

None were volunteers. They had been ordered into this mystery without explanation, and no one objected; they were unquestioning, fatalistic. In fact, they felt honored.

They were gathered together and addressed by Captain Kaku Harada, *Chiyoda's* commander; "Fellows, you are going to receive a very special type of training from now on …"[2]

He let the words sink in for a moment. "You must pledge to keep it an absolute secret because you are going in a secret weapon — the midget submarine." They were then shown the weapons, drawn up black and glittering in the ship's sheltered belly.

They were then given leave. Sakamaki tried hard not to let his family know of his dangerous assignment, but they suspected something from his drawn-out goodbyes. He acted as if he would never see them again.

Back at *Chiyoda*, the new officers slept aboard the ship while it was completely converted at Kure to carry midget subs. During the day they clustered around the new weapons being built at the Kure naval torpedo factory. They learned the midget concept had been approved only the year before, and the first midget officers had completed their training only a month previous.

Sakamaki and the second group were themselves tutored by these freshly trained midget submariners, who had a single month of experience in the weapons.

By June, Sakamaki considered himself a seasoned skipper. He had his own midget submarine assigned to him, the 19th one built, as the craft were idiosyncratic. He practiced realistic exercises from an isolated fishing village called Mitsukuye, in the Inland Sea. They were closely guarded. Torpedo boats and patrol craft shadowed the maneuvers, keeping away curious spectators and preventing accidents between the swift but nearly blind midgets.

The town's harbor had been chosen for its similarity to Pearl

Patriot Sons

Harbor. The town, with a population of less that 4,000 farmers and fishers, was aware of the exercises, though not the details.

These peacetime exercises were not unusual for the Imperial Navy, which engaged in far more realistic and dangerous maneuvers than Allied navies. Their crews went to war with a practical idea of how their weapons would behave in the heat of battle.

Both midget tenders *Chitose* and *Chiyoda* could hold as many as 12 midgets. Launching from *Chitose* meant grabbing the midget with a crane and swinging it into the water. *Chiyoda*, by contrast, had been modified with two doors in her tail, and she could lay a smooth trail of midget submarines in the water, like eggs from a fish, all 12 of them in 17 minutes.

By September, the midget skippers were confident they could handle any emergency. They could sneak up to almost any ship in mid-ocean without being detected, and despite frequent midget-to-midget scrapes and shallow-water grounding, no one had been injured. They had implicit faith in their exotic weapon and in themselves.

They were an elite within an elite. Compared to the rest of Japan's military, the Imperial Navy's ocean-going warriors ate and smoked better quality provisions. Officers and men generally ate the same portions, and their dally caloric intake was about 3,300 calories, easily double that of a citizen in wartime Japan.

For submariners, this included a diet of pickled vegetables, dried seaweed, eggs, beef, pork, fish and miso soup, buoyed with a sticky platform of boiled white rice. Tea was available in quantity, but little coffee. Beer and sake were rationed during shore leave; at sea the skipper would issue alcohol only for special circumstances.

With little or no refrigeration space, fresh meat and vegetables usually disappeared during the first week of patrol. Rats were common. The narrow, humid gangways were piled up with cumbersome canned foods and rice sacks that were always underfoot. Often boards for walking on were placed atop the food. They were gradually cleared away as the crews digested them, and the length of the patrols were limited only by the amount of food on board.[3]

Later-model submarines had limited cooling systems, devoted to maintaining the food supply. The boats were usually swelteringly humid, and the perspiring crews dressed only in *fundoshi*, or loin-cloth. Showers and clothes washing were allowed once or twice a week, and in the dank submarine environment, uniforms were rarely dry.

Crews looked forward to shore leaves at forward bases, where they could take hot, soapy showers on the submarine tenders, eat fresh fruit, take advantage of the Imperial Navy's prostitute corps, see movies, go swimming or fishing, or watch the officers play tennis.

By October, Sakamaki noticed something important was brewing. There was an abrupt change in tactics. Harada called them in

[3] *This is common even on modern nuclear submarines.*

and pointed to harbor maps on the wall: Hong Kong, Singapore, Sydney, San Francisco, Pearl Harbor.

"Learn the peculiarities of these harbors," he said. "Commit them to your memory."

Sakamaki figured that, if war came, the midget crews would be split up to make solitary assaults against all these harbors. The midgets and their crews were hurriedly transferred to the north coast of Shikoku for a week or so of practice at entering a narrow inlet at night. Not enough, perhaps, to switch tactics so suddenly. Then came a surprise meeting with Yamamoto in early November, and a train ride home on an unexpected furlough. Saying goodbye as a soldier, with *banzais* ringing out, wasn't the glory Sakamaki expected. It was an hour of agony.

The oldest midget submariner in his group was 29. There were 10 in all, five pilots and five crewmen. The midget submarines had individual idiosyncrasies, and were assigned permanent pilots. They called them "tubes," although the craft had serial numbers. Sakamaki's midget submarine was *Ha-19*, the 19th craft built in the Ha-series of light submarines. Fleet submarines were designated by the prefix "*I*," the first letter of the *kanji* alphabet. Second-string, older submarines were prefixed by "*Ro*," the second letter, and "*Ha*," the third letter, denoted midget or various "coastal" craft. It is possible, although unconfirmed, that the "tube" term was deliberately used to mislead, much as Winston Churchill had dubbed the new land battleships "tanks" in the first World War. Sakamaki's midget submarine was assigned to be carried aboard fleet-class submarine *I-24*. Among themselves, the midget submariners called the craft *I-24tou*, or *I-24's* boat, for example, or *Sakamaki-tei*, Sakamaki's boat.

Snapshots of midget submariners at play — at top, Ensign Yanaki shows off fish caught during maneuvers. The other submariners are, from left, Otosaka, Furuno, Akieda and Kanda. Below, a last picture of submarine crewmen Shigenori Yokoyama, Naokichi Sasaki and Sadamu Uyeda.

PATRIOT SONS

Sakamaki's crewman aboard *I-24tou* was Kiyoshi Inagaki, who had none of the blazing drive to excel that characterized his fellow midget submariners. The stolid child of a religious family, his classmates could remember little about him. His most noticeable attribute was an attention to detail. He labored long to polish his work, leaving no job half-done.

While in sixth-grade at Kawai, in Miye, Inagaki heard about submarine commander Lieutenant Tsutomo Sakuma, who died in an underwater accident in the Inland Sea. For some reason, the incident had a profound effect on the boy, who for the rest of his life carried a newspaper clipping detailing the dead lieutenant's career.

The Inagaki family came upon hard times while Kiyoshi was in grade school, and he had to drop out for four years. This was another reason his classmates did not remember him. As soon as he was old enough, Inagaki enlisted in the Navy, where his compulsion to fine-tune made him an excellent torpedo man.

Above, Sakamaki and Kanda visit friends at a "hotel" near Kure; below, Uyeda plays for an Eta Jima baseball team.

Masaji Yokoyama, pilot of *I-16tou*, "was the most handsome of the midget submariners," recalled Captain Takayasu Arima, Yamamoto's liaison officer with the midget squad. "When he smiled, he looked like an innocent child. But he was a hard worker and had a lot of raw courage." Yokoyama had a gentle nature that belied a crushing sense of responsibility; his father, a member of the Imperial Guards Cavalry, served in the Russo-Japanese war and died in China when Yokoyama was six. The family, eight brothers and five sisters, was left in Kagoshima to be raised by mother Taka Yokoyama. These circumstances left Masaji both independent and sympathetic. He liked being around people, and doing things for them. Possibly because he didn't want to further strain his mother, he became a stoic, enduring pain without crying. Once, when he was in grade-school, he dislocated his shoulder in a fall and insisted on visiting the doctor alone.

THE CREW
OF *I-24TOU*

A DREAMER NAMED FOR PEACE WHO LUSTED FOR WAR, AND A STOLID, UNIMAGINATIVE STICKLER FOR DETAIL.

SKIPPER: **KAZUO SAKAMAKI**   CREW: **KIYOSHI INAGAKI**

As a boy, Yokoyama listened avidly to tales of great military heroes, as he considered his father to be; those who, by stint of bravery and faith, rose above the masses, or at least above the mass of brothers and sisters. At the Naval Academy, Yokoyama developed a fixation on Admiral Heihachiro Togo, hero of the Russo-Japanese conflict, who was also from Kagoshima. Whenever Yokoyama visited home thereafter, he'd spend long hours at Togo's grave, meditating.

In his academy notebook, Yokoyama distilled the four vital attributes of a heroic officer — vigor, spirit, patience and honesty. These words were written on the cover, so that he would see them every time he opened the notebook.

During his last visit home, Yokoyama seemed unusually animated about something, but told the family nothing.

Yokoyama's crewman, Warrant Officer Sadamu Uyeda, was born high in the mountain fastness of Kawaseko, a hamlet that commanded spectacular views and little industry. The family was poor, and Uyeda had to beg his parents to allow him to enter middle school, the equivalent of high school. This was a difficult step, as the boy was so quiet that his teachers were unsure of his scholastic abilities. Further schooling also added to financial hardship and his father had to work at another job to make up the shortfall.

Acutely aware of the strain on his family, Uyeda noticed that other middle-school graduates were joining the Navy. This he decided to do as well. After entering as a seaman, Uyeda was posted to torpedo school, and then to submarine school. He was assigned to a submarine in the summer of 1940, and from there was drafted into the midget program.

PATRIOT SONS

SKIPPER: **MASAJI YOKOYAMA**   CREW: **SADAMU UYEDA**

THE CREW OF *I-16TOU*

A DASHING OFFICER WITH AN AFFINITY FOR PAIN, AND A QUIET MOUNTAIN BOY WHO PREFERRED BASEBALL TO BOOKS.

On his last day ashore, Uyeda gathered up everything he owned, and packed his possessions into one trunk and one suitcase. He left them in the care of a Kure flower shop.

I-18tou was commanded by Lieutenant Commander Shigemi Furuno, whose family and neighbors expected much from him. His grandfather had been such a pillar of the little community of Onga, in Fukuoka, that villagers erected a monument to the man. Furuno's earliest memories included annual gatherings of the family before the shrine, where the "great deeds" of ancestors were endlessly replayed.

His mother Maki, an orphan, did her best to indoctrinate her children in the Furuno family legend. Her punishments were at times harsh. Neglecting homework earned her children several hours in front of the family altar, meditating on their sins. Her bedtime stories were about famous patriots who died for Japan.

Once, when Furuno was in primary school, his mother accused him of misbehaving, and threw him out of the house. The boy, then eight, refused to apologize, and stood outside in the cold through the night, shivering defiantly.

Shigemi Furuno's stubbornness and anger came out on occasion, even when he was very young. At the age of six, he went berry picking with friends on a faraway mountain. His companions suddenly cried out; they had seen a fox. Furuno picked up stones and pelted the animal until it ran away howling. On another occasion, he accepted a dare from his older brother to swim across a lake. The boy barely knew how to tread water, but kept at it until he emerged sputtering at the other side. He enjoyed testing himself in these ways, and when he entered middle school, Furuno loved

The Crew of *I-18tou*

An unhappy man haunted by family demons and a stubborn veteran who slept during maneuvers.

SKIPPER: **Shigemi Furuno**

CREW: **Shigenori Yokoyama**

the push-and-tumble of sumo. Furuno entered Eta Jima on the advice of a classmate. Even there, the hold of family discipline remained strong; he wrote his father once and asked permission to begin smoking. When the family pressured him to get married, he resisted, claiming he had to be able to die at any moment.

Furuno seemed enchanted by the prospect of early death. Without much prodding, he could be cajoled into a loud serenade of his favorite song, which contained the line "I'll come back surely in a small casket."

When Furuno visited home for the last time, he wore his civilian clothes. His father was greatly angered, and thundered at the young lieutenant to wear his naval uniform at all times, or he wouldn't be allowed to enter the house. "Don't worry," said Furuno. "The next time I come home, I shall be wearing a wooden casket." The comment, expressed as a joke to defuse his father's anger, was taken as such.

Furuno's stolid crewman aboard *I-18tou*, Sub-Lieutenant Shigenori Yokoyama, had a nickname in primary school; *Gambariya no Shige-chan,* or Never-Give-In-Shige, for his refusal to surrender while playing with toy soldiers, no matter how badly the sandbox battle was going. He saw little of his farmer parents, who were generally working in the fields. When he failed the entrance exam to naval flight school — a notoriously difficult course — "Never-Give-In" studied deep into the night and entered the Navy as a volunteer seaman.

Yokoyama's first duty station was aboard battleship *Fuso*, where, once again, he spent his spare time studying. In 1936, he entered torpedo school and became so expert at the tin fish that he

Patriot Sons

SKIPPER: **AKIRA HIRO-O**

CREW: **YOSHIO KATAYAMA**

THE CREW
OF *I-20TOU*

A SHORT, BOYISH
OFFICER WITH
SOMETHING TO
PROVE AND A
FARMER'S SON
WHO WILLED HIS
MILITARY PAY TO
HIS SCHOOL.

graduated at the top of his class. He was given a silver watch by the principal of the torpedo school.

He went on to submarine school. Word of Yokoyama's skill at torpedo warfare had spread, and he was courted by officers aboard torpedo craft. But the sub-lieutenant refused to drop out of submarine school, saying he felt that submarines were important to the future of the Imperial Navy. He graduated again with high honors, and shipped out in time to see action during the Manchuria Incident and in China. He was the only veteran among the midget submariners, and sometimes he slept during training.

In command of *I-20tou*, Lieutenant Akira Hiro-o — at 22 the youngest of the midget submariners during the Pearl Harbor raid - was born late in life to two schoolteachers in Asahi-mura, in Saga. He had perfect attendance in school his entire life.

Even among Japanese, Hiro-o was regarded as short. An average student, he overcompensated by constant drill. He could never be as tall as his schoolmates, but he could out-test them.

His attitude was reflected in his last letter to his parents. "The true value of a man is revealed when he proceeds toward a righteous goal on a righteous path. Consequently, his brilliance or dullness is of secondary importance for all phenomena within the sphere of possibility can be accomplished through human efforts. If one fails to accomplish his goal, the failure is ascribable to a lack of efforts."

His final year at middle school, when he was told he might not get into the Naval Academy, he studied so much that he often fell asleep sitting on the *tatami* mat by the worktable. Hiro-o may have inherited this strong will from his mother, who did not miss her classes even when about to give birth, and refused the allow the

THE CREW OF *I-22TOU*

A FIERCE MASTER OF MIDGET SUBMARINE WARFARE AND A *KENDO* SWORDSMAN WHO LOVED TO READ.

SKIPPER: **NAOJI IWASA**

CREW: **NAOKICHI SASAKI**

babies to come to school for feeding. She also taught her children that poor conduct in school shamed not only them, but the entire family.

She raised Akira from the beginning to be a military man, which may explain his fever to get into Eta Jima; failure to do so would shame both his mother and family. This attitude was rarely revealed to his crew mates. Hiro-o was boyishly ebullient at everything he did, and pitched in as if the raid were a great adventure.

Though Hiro-o's torpedoman Yoshio Katayama was from a poor family of farmers, in the village of Gojo in Okayama, the Katayamas had managed to improve their fortunes over the years. Katayama's mother Cho had enough hard-earned leisure time that she asked to go to school along with her children, so that she too could learn things denied her as child. Her husband refused, saying education was unnecessary for farmers. She was touched when Katayama's military will specified that his unclaimed pay be sent to his school.

In the summer of 1940, Katayama pulled an elaborate deception on his parents. He wrote and asked them to find him a bride. They felt he was too young, however, and pretended to not have received the letter. A year later, on his visit home, his parents finally brought it up, but the warrant officer just smiled and ducked his head.

The next day, he confided in a cousin. "You know very well what is going to happen to me in case of an emergency," said Katayama. "I really didn't want to get married; but since I knew then, as I know now, that I might never return alive, I wanted, even for a short while, to put my parents minds at ease by pretending to be thinking of settling down."

Katayama then visited his nine-year-old niece Fumiko Ogawa, and took her to dinner at an expensive restaurant, where he urged her to order anything she wanted. He kept staring at her.

Afterwards he took the child shopping and bought her toys. On the way home, she saw his eyes in the streetlights, and they were wet with tears. Fumiko was frightened, and began to cry herself. Katayama put his Navy cap on the child's head, and the two solemnly saluted each other in the dark. "Goodbye, Fumiko," he said.

The remaining midget submarine, *I-22tou*, was piloted by Lieutenant Naoji Iwasa, the program expert. He wasn't about to miss his weapon's initiation into battle.

Iwasa's crewman was Naokichi Sasaki. His mother had died in childbirth, and the infant was given to an aunt and uncle. Sasaki's real father, beset by failing business, died when the boy was six. His foster parents were farmers and bean curd makers. The boy was a voracious reader at his Kokufu village school, a trait unusual in a "country boy," as one of his teachers called him. His only other hobby was *kendo*, fierce fencing with bamboo swords.

Upon graduation from primary school, Sasaki left home and took a job in a hardware store in Osaka, and then in a lumber yard. He then returned to home to study to enter the Navy. He failed the first time, due to an undiagnosed case of beriberi, but by the second round of tests, the illness was gone. His foster mother believed he had simply willed it out of his body.

During the entrance examinations, Sasaki also learned for the first time that he was adopted. He made an effort to reassure his foster parents that the revelation did not matter, and went out of his way to help his mother make bean curd whenever he visited.

Iwasa, the leader, was the oldest of the midget submariners. Born May 6, 1915, near the picturesque Tone river, in a region historically famous for its patriot-sons, Iwasa was the son of a hard-tempered farmer and his hard-working wife. The boy determined early that he wanted to join the Navy, announcing to schoolmates, "No strange death shall I die. When I die, it shall be in the middle of the Pacific — a glorious death!"

Statements like this were later attributed to inchoate patriotic fervor, but it is likely in Iwasa's case they were the bluster of an undersized youngster persecuted by rough classmates. The boy got no sympathy from his father, who chastised him for weakness, and pressed his son to excel in his studies as a way to get even. Iwasa rapidly became a splendid student, spending long hours in book work while the other boys played. Whenever Iwasa wanted to engage in extracurricular activities, such as swimming lessons, his father agreed only if the boy promised to become the best in the class, and in return, perform extra chores around the farm.

By the time Iwasa entered middle school, in 1928, he was wound up like clockwork, silent and unusually willing to accept

Captain Kaku Harada, center in the front row, and his staff pose for one last picture aboard Chiyoda with the ten midget submariners chosen to attack Pearl Harbor. Iwasa sits to Harada's left; Sakamaki stands behind him.

extra duties. He was fond of the abstract theorems of algebra and geometry. He applied for the Naval Academy, the only upper-level schooling the family could afford, and one far away from his home. When he was accepted, he had a souvenir photograph of himself taken, and wrote across the back, "Behold the visage of one whose dream has materialized."

The rigors and humiliations of the academy were, for Iwasa, easy to take. He did well. He became a compulsively correct officer, one not easy to approach, but not afraid to take initiative. He was perfect for the lone-wolf command of midget submarines. Perhaps, blanketed beneath the mail of ocean, he felt at peace.

At one time, Iwasa applied to the Navy Ministry for permission to be married. Though this was granted, Iwasa broke off the engagement. His parting words to his former fiancee were that he didn't want any ties to interfere with his duties.

In the spring of 1941, Iwasa returned to his middle school at Maebashi for a class reunion. Asked to give an address, Iwasa afterward then answered questions. A classmate asked, "What would you do if a superior officer were to ask you for your life?"

Iwasa stared the man down, in the now-silent reunion hall. "Just die," he replied and walked away.

PATRIOT SONS

SEDUCED BY TECHNOLOGY

6

A BLADE, ONCE DRAWN, MUST BE BLOODED

The weapons in which the 10 midget submariners were about to set off were the latest model of a design process that began in the early 1930s.

Inspired by "A Sure Hit With Human Piloted Torpedoes," a 1933 article by Captain Noriyoshi Yokoo, a hero of the Russo-Japanese war, the concept was adopted enthusiastically by Captain Kaneharu Kishimoto. "If we would launch big torpedoes with men on board them, and if those torpedoes went deep into enemy areas and launched smaller torpedoes, there would be practically no chance of a miss!" he said. Prince Hiroyasu Fushimi, Admiral of the Fleet, allowed two prototypes to be built under the stipulation they not be *tokko* — suicide — weapons.

Kishimoto's second prototype.

Japan's first two midgets were built in 1934 under the direction of Kishimoto at Kure. They were experimental, torpedo-shaped craft with no conning tower, designed as auxiliary weapons carried by fast surface vessels.

The pair, coded *A-Kanemono* — Metal Fitting, Type A — were built in secrecy and tested as *Ko-Hyoteki* — Target A — achieving the astounding underwater speed of 25 knots. The ruse was so successful that many in the Imperial Navy thought late into the war that the tube-shaped objects were only gunnery targets.

After testing, conning towers were added and two more midgets were built in 1936.[1] The following year, the small craft were launched off seaplane tender *Chitose* and test pilots Naoji Iwasa and Saburo Akieda realized that the midgets could be used as stealthy attack-craft, provided they were unloaded close to the target.

Mass production got under way in Kure, and they were given code prefixes of *HA*, used on small and midget submarines. Of the type used in the Pearl Harbor attack, *HA-1* and *HA-2* were the prototypes, *HA-3* through *HA-44* were designed to be carried by

[1] It is possible that one of the first four Ko-Hyoteki prototypes was captured after the war and is in storage. Further research is needed.

Another view of the second prototype.

submarines and surface ships, and *HA-46* to *HA-61* were built for coastal defense.

To ensure total secrecy, the hulls and frames were made in pieces in a private yard, then taken to a small island outside Kure to be constructed and fitted out. No one was allowed on the island who did not know what the submarines were.

Training was at Ourazaki, another isolated island 12 miles south of Kure, and known by the code phrase "Base P." Before the midgets would sally forth for a training session, the waters around the island would be swept of fishing boats and commercial steamers.

This was strict discipline, even at Yokosuka, at the time perhaps the most secure naval base in the world. The only approach to the peninsula by land was through nine tunnels, and the waters were always patroled by sentry boats. No one was allowed to live near the base — or near the tunnels — unless they worked on base. No one was allowed to own a camera.

Only 20 of the tiny submarines had been built by the time the Special Attack Unit sailed.

Captain Kaneharu Kishimoto.

Each A-type midget submarine displaced a mere 46 tons, measured approximately 78 by 6 feet and carried two 18-inch torpedoes fired by compressed air. The crew numbered two; a junior officer who steered, and a petty officer who operated the various ballast and trim valves.

Maximum speed submerged was 19 knots at full throttle, but the 600-horse engine could only run that way for 50 minutes. At 2 knots submerged, patrol radius was 100 miles on battery power. The batteries could only be changed or charged by a shipyard or a tender.

With these harsh technological limitations, midget submariners had to be astute judges of speed, distance and navigation. The first class of midget submariners, housed aboard the seaplane tender *Chiyoda*, graduated only a few months before the Pearl Harbor attack.

As the assault on Pearl Harbor drew near, midget tactics were still in the formative stage. It was supposed that the tiny craft would be used in three ways:

* When an enemy fleet was contacted on the high seas, the midgets would dart in for a surprise attack on the enemy's largest ships.

* To secretly enter enemy harbors and assault ships at anchor.

* And as a "trump card" should the occasion arise, whatever that meant.

The midget experts were trying to integrate themselves into the opening moves of the upcoming war. The probable scenario envisioned by Naoji Iwasa supposed that the first battle would begin with a struggle for control of the air, with the usual dogfighting and

SEDUCED BY TECHNOLOGY

The first five Holland-designed submarines in the Imperial Navy, here at Kure after the Russo-Japanese War.

torpedo attacks. During the confusion, the midgets would be launched from 30 miles away, well over the horizon, and strike the enemy battlewagons using a stealthy combination of great speed and low visibility.

This was the great battle the midget skippers trained for during the summer and fall of 1941. The midget submarine skippers were confident in the superiority of their weapon — seduced by technology, perhaps, but rightfully so. Well thought out and soundly engineered, no other country had a comparable weapon.

The A-type of midget submarine was refined as the war ground on. Mass production of Type D *Ko-Hyotekis*, better known as *Koryu* — Scaly Dragon — were under way at a Kure shipyard at war's end. Some 540 were ordered in June 1944, a production rate estimated at an unrealistic 180 a month. Only 115 were completed by the end of the war.

The Japanese experimented with other types of small submarines, notably the *kaiten* — Heaven Shaker — a manned torpedo which supposedly allowed the operator to bail out of the craft before it struck the target. Most never got to that point, and those who did elected to take the last ride all the way in.

Kairyu, or Sea Dragon, was the only midget submarine designed from the outset as a suicide craft. None were used in combat, though a three-man version was built and used as a training vessel.

Japanese interest in submarines dates before the turn of the century, when Japanese officers had repeatedly visited the *Holland VI* while it was under construction in Elizabethport, New Jersey, during 1897. The creation of submarine genius John P. Holland, *Holland VI* was accepted by the U.S. Navy as *SS-1* in 1900, the first official American submarine, but not before Imperial Navy lieutenants Takashi Sasaki and Kenji Ide of the Imperial Navy had taken it out for test dives.

Japanese submarine number 1, laid down in Massachusetts in 1904 and scrapped at Yokusuka in 1922.

Japan was among the first nations to deploy a submarine in wartime. During the Russo-Japanese War, five Holland-designed boats were acquired by the Imperial Navy, but the war was over before the transported boat components could be reassembled and training had been completed. Japan then constructed two Holland boats of an improved design, and the director of the Kawasaki shipyard became a habitue of Holland's building ways.

Russia had also acquired submarines from Simon Lake, Holland's American competitor, and from Germany, but was equally unable to deploy them in combat. Japan also captured a small Russian submersible that had been scuttled at Port Arthur.

During the next decade, the Imperial Navy imported a wide variety of designs from other countries, and built several British, French and Italian designs. Japanese submarines saw no combat in World War I, although the Imperial Navy did field an anti-submarine squadron in the Mediterranean. The Imperial Navy received seven U-boats at war's end, but only on the promise that they not be used for military purposes.

The design of these German boats profoundly influenced I-boat design during the '20s, as the Japanese shipyards began producing submarine "cruisers," capable of long-range patrol and carrying heavy torpedo and gun batteries. At a time when most navies considered submarines only capable of coastal defense, the Imperial Navy was clearly thinking in terms of carrying the fight to the enemy shore. Naval analyst Hector Bywater, who had originally considered war between Japan and the United States impossible because of the vast stretches of the Pacific, changed his mind upon learning of this added capability. He began to speculate in newspaper columns on a future war between the two countries, with long-range submarines performing a vital duty. An in-print debate soon

SEDUCED BY TECHNOLOGY

broke out, between Bywater and former assistant secretary of the navy Franklin Delano Roosevelt, who maintained that such a conflict was impossible. "The whole trend of the times is against wars," Roosevelt wrote.

By 1941, Roosevelt had changed his mind, and Bywater had died mysteriously. At the outbreak of war, the Imperial Navy had 48 I-boats in service and 15 RO-boats, many of which were consigned to the Advance Force.

By orders of Admiral Mitsumi Shimizu, the hulls of all subs were painted black and numbers on the conning tower "sail" white. At war's outset, however, most of the fleet submarines were painted the same gray shade as other Imperial Navy craft. The first letter of the Japanese phonetic alphabet is "*I*" — pronounced "A" — and looks somewhat like the Greek character lambda. This was appended to the titles of all fleet-class submarines, followed by the hull number. *I-15*, for example, was a first-line submarine. Older, obsolete fleet-class boats were preceded by "*Ro*," the second letter of the alphabet, and some miscellaneous classes, including midget submarines, were prefixed by "*Ha*," the third letter in the alphabet.

Having the most highly developed midget submarine did not assure Japan of leadership in the field. Other countries had their own programs, just as secret and esoteric.

The midget concept goes back to the beginning of submersible warfare, the first used in combat being David Bushnell's egg-shaped *Turtle*. The craft featured a snorkel-like breathing system, a depth gauge and a detachable explosive, refinements that wouldn't be again seen for several decades. During the American Revolution, Sargeant Ezra Lee made a number of attempts in *Turtle* to attach a 150-pound explosive, complete with watchwork timer, to the hulls of British warships anchored near New York. The plan called for Lee to sneak up beneath the ships, augur a hole in the hull, leave the explosive and drift away. The missions ended in failure, reportedly caused by the tough copper hulls of British man-of-wars. As Lee made his escape, he was pursued by a British guard boat, which he distracted by cutting loose the explosive. When the charge went off, the British fleet scattered. In a letter to Thomas Jefferson, George Washington called Bushnell's craft "an effort of genius."

Following designs were all small in concept, their operational use planned for harbor defense and attack. The Davids of the American Civil War that attacked the Union "Goliaths" were midgetary in size, though they contained a dozen or so men, who cranked the craft through the water. The craft never really submerged completely, instead hunkering down in the water with the conning tower showing as the submersible pushed a charge on the

John Holland's very first submarine design, created so his native Ireland could fight the mighty British fleet on something like equal terms, predated midget submarine designs by several decades.

end of a 30-foot spar. The *Hunley* became the first submersible to sink another ship, the *Houstonic*, though it destroyed itself in the process.

Russia and Italy designed small submersibles specifically for harbor defense. The submarines designed by Irish-born John Holland were also small, and the streamlined design was adopted as a standard by many of the world's navies. Russia had three Holland-shaped midget craft, known simply as *No.l*, *No.2* and *No.3*, ordered by the Army to defend the Black Sea. They had provision for two bow-mounted 18-inch torpedoes and four crew. *No.3* left the Black Sea for the Danube, hoping to see action against the feared Austrian Danube Flotilla. Instead, she was captured.

The British-Swedish partnership of Garrett and Nordenfelt built a number of small submarines, sold to Greece and Turkey. Josiah Tuck of New York built a 30-footer in 1884 that solved a critical propulsion problem; he stored power in electric batteries. In short order, British shipbuilder J.F. Waddington designed a 37-foot "electric" boat, which also had hull planes and two long-distance Whitehead torpedoes for armament.

In 1896, France held a submarine-design contest, the winner of which, Maxime Laubeuf, had drawn in two separate propulsion systems — accumulator batteries for running submerged, and traditional steam power for surface running, at which time the batteries were recharged. Laubeuf also designed a double hull, in which fuel and water ballast were stored. This design was the link between the Hollands and large, sea-going submarines, the most notable of which were the terrifying German U-boats of WWI.

John Holland, meanwhile, had emigrated to the United States from Ireland. He had for years tried to interest the U.S. Navy in submarine design, forming the Holland Torpedo Boat Company. Holland followed Navy dictates with *Plunger* in 1897, which was a failure, and of his own muse with *Holland VI* in 1898, the design from which all modern submarines have descended, and the craft which so interested the Japanese. *Holland VI* was midget-sized — 53 feet 10 inches long, with a diameter of 10 feet 3 inches, displacing 74 tons and powered by 50 horsepower gasoline and electric engines.

A few days after *Holland VI's* sea trials, the United States declared war on Spain. Holland offered to take his craft to Havana and decimate the Spanish fleet, but the Navy passed, preferring more traditional methods. Building the submarine had stretched Holland's company to the fiscal breaking point, and the company that supplied the batteries initiated a hostile takeover. The Holland Torpedo Boat Company became the Electric Boat Company, the name which it holds today.

The Navy accepted *Holland VI* in 1900, and the company built a larger craft, *Fulton*, the next year, which the Navy declined. It was sold to Russia. The next five Holland boats were the ones sold to

Japan, a country eager for military technological innovations. By the time of the Russo-Japanese War of 1904, Japan had the largest submarine fleet in the world.

A manned torpedo was suggested by Commander Godfrey Herbert of the Royal Navy in 1909, and turned down as being too dangerous.

The first true midget submarine was the Italian *Alpha*, built at Venice in 1913. It was the design craft for the later A and B classes of small midgets, used for harbor defense in the Venetian lagoon during World War I. Any potential for sneaking into the other fellow's harbor was apparently not realized.

In the predawn of Nov. 1, 1918, two Italian officers, Lieutenant Commander Raffaele Rossetti, an engineer, and Lieutenant Raffaele Paolucci, a surgeon, quietly swam into the enemy Austrian harbor of Pola. They shepherded a torpedo-shaped craft called *Mignatta* — The Leech — an antique bronze 14-inch Mk.B57 torpedo fitted with two 170 kg charges. The Italians sat astride the weapon, changing course by jumping off and pushing it.

The Italians eventually removed one of the mines from *Mignatta* and attached it to the hull of Austrian flagship *Viribus Unitis*, a monster that sported twelve 12-inch guns. They noticed that there seemed to be a celebration happening on deck. On their way out of the harbor, Rossetti and Paolucci were promptly taken prisoner, and they abandoned *Mignatta*. They were brought back to the flagship, where the Italians discovered that their captors were friendly Yugoslavians who were cheering the dissolution of the Austro-Hungarian empire. They told the Yugoslavian captain about the bombs under the hull, and the ship was ordered abandoned. The Italians jumped overboard and began swimming away from the flagship, but were overtaken by angry Yugoslav sailors convinced that the bomb story was a hoax.

While being interrogated again aboard *Viribus Unitis*, the charge went off at 6:20 a.m. with a "dull roar." Rossetti and Paolucci gained the main deck in the confusion, where they again met the ship's captain, who shook their hands and wished them luck. The Italians jumped overboard for the second time and from a safe distance watched the huge battleship roll over and sink within 20 minutes.

In the meantime, *Mignatta* wandered aimlessly about the harbor, eventually striking the liner *Wien*, being used as a depot ship. The spare charge went off, and *Wien* sank as quickly as the battleship.

This first successful midget submarine attack had no influence on the war's outcome, as Austria had already sued for truce. But the

Viribus Unitis begins to roll over in Austria's Pola Harbor in 1918, the victim of the first successful midget submarine attack.

feat became legendary among Italian sailors, and among submariners on the far side of the world, in Imperial Japan.

The overwhelming success of the larger U-boats in the Great War spurred other nations into developing submarines as fleet warships — the *Mignatta* episode seemed a fluke in retrospect. By the Armistice, anti-submarine warfare had become a highly skilled discipline against this proliferating weapon. By 1931, 245 submarines served in some 20 navies.

Another invention that was crucial to the success of steered torpedoes — underwater breathing apparatus, the ancestor of the aqualung. Here, an Italian Maiale *pilot tests his gear.*

World War II saw the first operational use of midget submarines as a tactical weapon, and only Japan had a successful vessel at the outset. The others, designed in desparation as stop-gap weapons, were man-guided torpedoes, often ridden into battle as if astride a horse, or submerged "chariots," built to deliver underwater demolitions teams.

Three types of midget submarine were developed during World War II:

* Human-ridden torpedoes, like the Italian *Maiale* ("Pig") and the British Chariot.

* Semi-submersible assault craft, like the Japanese *Kaiten*, German *Biber* and the British Welman.

* True midget submarines, like the Japanese *Ko-Hyoteki*, British X-craft, Italian *CA/CB* and the German *Seehund*.

Only the United States, France and the Soviet Union did not employ midget submarines in battle. American naval doctrine favored full-sized, capital submarines as free-roving strategic weapons; the French were knocked out early in the conflict; the centralized Soviet command structure frowned upon the piratical nature of midget operations.

The first midget submarine attack of the war was a misfire. At Gibraltar in 1940, a dual assault by the Italian-designed *Maiale* went awry when one was sunk in the harbor and the other eventually washed up in Spain. A year later, the Italian submarine *Scire* hosted three Maiale off Gibraltar. On Sept. 20, 1941, they sank storage ship *Fiona Shell* and seriously damaged merchant *Durham* and Royal Fleet auxiliary *Denbydale*.

The Italians, with the tacit compliance of supposedly neutral Spain, then converted interned tanker *Olterra* in nearby Algeciras harbor into a secret base for *Maiale*. The forward hold of the tanker was converted into a workshop, and an underwater exit hatch

SEDUCED BY TECHNOLOGY

created, large enough for the Italian craft to slip in and out of the tanker undetected. Raids launched from the tankers through 1943 resulted in the loss of six ships in Gibraltar.

The main targets were on the other end of the Mediterranean, where the British controlled the Suez Canal. On the night of Dec. 18, 1941, off Alexandria, Maiale crews knocked British warships *Queen Elizabeth* and *Valiant* out of action, and badly damaged tanker *Sagona* and destroyer *Jervis*. The Pig boats were led by Captain di Corvetta de la Penne, and launched, once again, from *Scire*.

The next morning, Admiral Sir Andrew Cunningham held ceremonies aboard *Queen Elizabeth*, his flagship, hoping that the pomp would fool onlookers into believing that the battleship was intact. In fact, the balance of power in the Mediterranean had been knocked askew overnight. In his memoirs, Cunningham wrote, "One cannot but admire the cold-blooded bravery of the Italians ..."

The Italians had plans of grandeur, including one that got to the operational testing stage — transporting midget submarine *CA.2* on the deck of submarine *Leonardo Da Vinci* to assault shipping in New York Harbor. *Regina d'Italia* folded before the plan could be tested in reality.

The four CA boats built were originally designed to haul two torpedoes, but were wildly modified midway through development, replacing the torpedoes with eight underwater charges and adding a third crew number, a diver, to place the charges. None of the CA are known to have been used in combat. A follow-on design, the CB, followed the same silhouette and was larger. Twenty-two are known to have been constructed, out of a contracted 72. The first six CBs were posted to the Black Sea to aid the Germans against Russia. *CB.5* was quickly sunk by Soviet aircraft at Yalta on June 13, 1942. The remaining five proved successful — *CB.3*, nicknamed *Sorrentino*, sank Soviet submarine *S-32* on June 15, 1942; *CB.2* (*Russo*) sank submarine *Shch-306* three days later; and *CB.4* (*Sibelle*) sank submarine *Sc207* on Aug. 26, 1943.

The surviving Black Sea CBs were transferred to Rumania in September 1943 after the Italian armistice. They were scuttled in 1944 to prevent capture by advancing Soviet forces.

The other 16 CB craft had equally lively careers, some being captured by the Germans and used for parts, others serving with the Italian Allied forces until 1948, and the rest holing up with

Italians ride a "Pig" in the Mediterranean. While moving slowly or at rest, the craft caused barely a ripple.

Italian mother submarine Scire, *with pressurized pigpens on the deck.*

The substantial wake of an Italian Maiale *while under way ...*

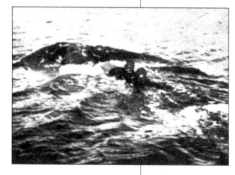

... and that of a British-designed "chariot," which was essentially a copy of the Italian design.

Mussolini's Italian Social Republic in northern Italy. Only three of these survived the war — *CB.16*, *CB.19* and *CB.22*.

The Royal Navy program began from scratch after the war was well under way, when Winston Churchill insisted that German battleship *Tirpitz* be dealt with in same way. The Admiralty's response was to copy the Italian Maiale underwater taxi, calling them "Chariots," and developing the futile Welman craft and the larger, successful X-craft. British midgets saw action in all three theaters of war, and the X-craft eventually crippled *Tirpitz* in September 1943.

The exploits of British midget submarines have been covered in excruciating detail by the English press, and have been the subject of a 1960s feature film starring James Caan.

The Chariots' first success was at Palermo, Jan. 3, 1943, when Lieutenant R.T.G. Greenland and Leading Signalman A. Ferrier on *Chariot XXII* and Sub-Lieutenant R.G. Dove and Leading Seaman J. Freel on *Chariot XVI*, slipped quietly into the Italian

SEDUCED BY TECHNOLOGY

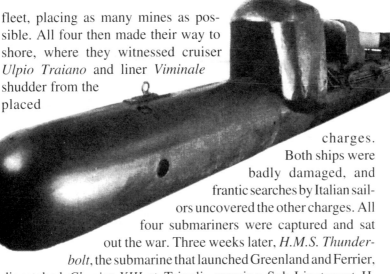

fleet, placing as many mines as possible. All four then made their way to shore, where they witnessed cruiser *Ulpio Traiano* and liner *Viminale* shudder from the placed charges. Both ships were badly damaged, and frantic searches by Italian sailors uncovered the other charges. All four submariners were captured and sat out the war. Three weeks later, *H.M.S. Thunderbolt*, the submarine that launched Greenland and Ferrier, dispatched *Chariot XIII* at Tripoli, carrying Sub-Lieutenant H. Stevens and Chief ERA S. Buxton. Their mission was to prevent the Germans from scuttling ships at the harbor entrance, but they arrived just as the ships settled in at the harbor mouth. Stevens pressed on and sank Italian warship *Guilio*, the secondary target. These two midget operators also were captured, but managed to escape and hide out in Vatican City until liberated by the American Fifth Army.

The Italian Maiale *and the British* Chariot *followed a similar design, being essentially a torpedo with guidance controls that could be ridden like a horse.*

The Italian cruiser *Bolzano* was sunk at La Spezia on June 22, 1944, by a combined team of Italian and British crews. Fearing that the abandoned ship would be sunk by the Germans to block the harbor, British Chariots were piggy-backed on Italian torpedo boats.

The "Terry" variation of the Chariot, in which the operators sat back-to-back, were used in a raid on Phuket, Thailand, on Oct. 27, 1944. Operating from submarine *H.M.S. Trenchant*, the Terrys sank merchants *Volpi* and *Sumatra*. This was the only operation carried out by Chariots in the Far East, as it was feared that the design could fall into Japanese hands, with predictable results.

A variation of the Chariot was the Motorized Submersible Canoe, called the "Sleeping Beauty." Crewed by a single underwater demolitions expert and capable of diving to 40 feet, the craft was used operationally just once. Leading a raiding force of 24 Sleeping Beauties into Singapore, Colonel Ivan Lyon's men were discovered before the attack could be pressed home. Fourteen of the raiders were killed on the spot, those remaining were imprisoned at Singapore, where one died in captivity. The nine left were beheaded after an impromptu court-martial, one week before the Japanese surrender in August 1945.

The British X-craft was the best-known midget submarine used in World War II. It carried a crew of four and a variety of limpet mines. The Operation "Source" assault on *Tirpitz* used six X-craft. *X8* and *X9* were lost while being towed across the North Sea. *X10*

A British X-craft
underway. In many
ways, these were
among the most
successful midget
submarines of World
War II, due primarily
to the thoroughness
of British training
rather than the
weapon's design
qualities.

bowed out due to mechanical difficulties. *X5*, *X6* and *X7* went on into the narrow, rocky neck of Kaafiord, where *Tirpitz* was believed to be safe from both bombardment and sea attack.

X5, piloted by Lieutenant H. Henty-Creer, disappeared. Lieutenant Donald Cameron of *X6* pressed on to *Tirpitz*, where he was spotted by Kriegsmarine sailors who thought they were looking at a porpoise. When *X6* was broached again a few minutes later, in the shadow of the battleship, the Germans began peppering the small craft with ineffective small-arms fire. Cameron planted both of his charges in the mud beneath *Tirpitz* before abandoning *X6*.

In *X7*, Lieuteant Geoffrey Place was briefly entangled in the anti-torpedo nets around the battleship before approaching it full-tilt and bashing into the hull beneath B turret. Place dropped a mine beneath the turret and worked his way down the hull before dropping the other. The Germans frantically tried to get steam up, hoping to move the battleship before the charges went off.

Place was on his way out of the harbor when the mine explosions crushed *X7*, causing him and his crew to abandon the vessel. Place and Cameron were both awarded Victoria Crosses for the action, and spent the rest of the war as POWs. *Tirpitz*' days as an ocean-going terror were over, and she was never completely repaired before the war ended.

British X-craft made other raids on occupied harbors, and were placed as navigation beacons off Sword and Juno Beaches during the invasion of Normandy. XE-craft were designed slightly longer and fitted with air-conditioning for conditions in the Far East. Six XEs formed the 14th Submarine Flotilla at Subic Bay in early 1945, where they were reportedly regarded with suspicion by American sailors.

The XEs were used to great success on July 31, 1945, when two craft penetrated Singapore harbor in Operation "Struggle." *XE1*, piloted by Lieutenant J.E. Smart, placed mines beneath Japanese

SEDUCED BY TECHNOLOGY

cruiser *Takao* before scooting back out to sea to rejoin her tow, submarine *Spark*. *XE3*, piloted by Lieutenant I.E. Fraser and crewed by a Leading Seaman Magennis, had a variety of misadventures trying to accomplish the same task. Magennis had serious difficulty placing the magnetic mines on *Takeo's* growth-encrusted hull, and when he finally returned to *XE3*, the midget was jammed beneath the cruiser's bilge keel, stuck fast by a rapidly falling tide.

Fraser wriggled the craft loose, but it became difficult to control and popped to the surface, under the nose of a Japanese liberty boat. Fraser rapidly submerged, only to find that one of the harbor-bottom mines had not released. Magennis, already exhausted, went back out into the inky water and pried the explosive loose with a crowbar.

Takao sank at her moorings a few hours later, her bottom blown out. Fraser and Magennis were both awarded the Victoria Cross for their efforts.

The 14th Submarine Flotilla's other accomplishment in the Far East, also on July 31, was cutting the underwater Saigon-Singapore-Hong Kong telephone cables.

All of the XE-craft were torched apart for scrap in Australia after the war, and in England, only *X24* escaped the acetylene. She is now on display at the Royal Navy Submarine Museum at Gosport.

Well-satisified with the success of the new generation of U-boats in the Atlantic campaign, Germany gambled on midget submarines only when invasion of the continent seemed imminent. Like many of their other desperation gambits, Kriegsmarine scientists came up with a confusing variety of clever prototypes. Only the well-designed Seehund was as deadly to the enemy as it was to its own crew.

"In many ways the German position was similar to that of Japan," wrote historian Paul J. Kemp. "The German decision to adopt midgets (as leading weapons) was an admission that their naval strategy had failed."

Head of the *Kleinkampfmittelverband* (Small Battle Weapon Force) was Vice Admiral Helmuth Heye, who almost single-handedly created Germany's midget submarine force. First off the drawing board was *Neger* (Nigger), essentially a G7e electric torpedo with the warhead removed to make room for a pilot, whose head stuck out a Plexiglas dome on top. *Neger* had another torpedo slung awkwardly beneath, and ran awash toward the target, while the pilot sucked on a rebreather and checked course by a wrist compass. When the target loomed ahead, the pilot pulled a lever

A continuing hazard for midget submarine crews were anti-torpedo nets. Here, a Japanese midget design tests out a sail-mounted net cutter.

which hopefully released the bottom torpedo; on occasion both were dragged toward the target. By most standards, *Neger* were the crudest of World War II midget craft. Even optimistic estimates figured the odds of survival at dead even. Many were lost because the pilots suffocated on the way to the target. Approximately 200 were built, as well as some 300 of an improved version called *Marder* (Pine). Between 60 to 80 percent of these submersibles were lost in combat, the largest number of midget craft used operationally during the

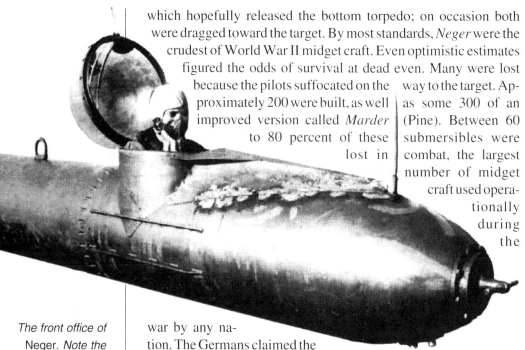

The front office of Neger. Note the crude welding on the fairwater in front of the observation blister. In practice, the pilot was nearly blind.

war by any nation. The Germans claimed the tiny craft were wildly successful, but it is thought that they sank only three minesweepers, two destroyers, and an LCF and a balloon ship, and damaged a cruiser and a destroyer.

The following design was *Molch* (Salamander), a more sophisticated craft that could drag two torpedoes, one on each side. Some 393 were built, and many had fierce-looking shark mouths painted on their snouts. The complicated craft confused the hastily trained crews, and *Molch* scored no successes whatsoever.

Even more complicated, though better designed, *Biber* (Beaver) was powered by a 32-horsepower gasoline engine for surface operations and a 13hp electric engine for submerged operations. It is believed that 324 were built. Biber had large grooves in either side of the hull, designed to cradle G7e electric wakeless torpedoes. *Biber* first operated off Normandy in the late summer of 1944, unsuccessfully, and many were destroyed in a ground engagement while being moved to another base.

A typical end for a German guided torpedo — the pilot was killed by engine fumes and the craft washed up.

SEDUCED BY TECHNOLOGY

Rebased in the Netherlands by December 1944, *Biber* attempted to terrorize the English Channel, accounting for a net-layer, an LST and a merchant ship. The *Biber* design was retired after a couple of months, during which 50 or so were lost in combat. It also had its share of bad luck; 32 men were killed in accidents in which *Biber* fired torpedoes while resting at their moorings.

Biber were more successful as mine layers, accounting for as many as seven Allied ships. *Biber* were also used in canals, including a fruitless attack against a bridge at Nijmegen in January 1945. Many pilots were killed by fumes from their gasoline engines, and some *Biber* were captured while drifting with asphyxiated corpses at the helm.[2]

The Germans salvaged and dissected the British X-craft scuttled during the *Tirpitz* attack, and put the knowledge to use in the *Seehund* (Seal) series of midget submarines, which also benefited from the light U-boat XXVII design. The *Seehund* also carried two externally mounted G7e torpedoes, but had considerable range and endurance, as well as a sophisticated steering mechanism. *Seehund* deliveries numbered 285, and 35 are known to have been lost in

combat. They scored no victories, arriving too late in the war to be properly deployed. Many never left their berths before being discovered and destroyed by the Allies. Four *Seehund* were conscripted by French, who used them until 1953.

Like other navies, the Kriegsmarine was attracted to midgets for

Another wrecked German minisub on the beach. This one is a Biber. *Note the shark's head insignia and the concave sides for torpedo storage.*

[2] *A captured* Biber *is on display at the Imperial War Museum in London.*

A Biber *with a "bird nest" of debris to camouflage the craft's telltale periscope wake.*

Too little, too late. The Nazi Seehund could have been one of the deadliest midget submarine designs of the war had it been deployed properly and manufactured more quickly. Here, a captured example is being examined by British troops.

what seemed to be compelling reasons in the heat of battle. The midgets could be built away from shipyards which were under constant Allied bombardment. By virtue of their stealthiness, midgets had — and still have — the capacity to deliver warheads precisely and devastatingly on target. They are inexpensive, can be built by unskilled labor and are easy to camouflage. And throughout the war, harbor defenses never stopped a determined attack by midget submarines.

The variable factors, however, were training and personnel. To successfully press home an assault, the midget crews needed a combination of highly individual personal initiative and rigorous training under realistic conditions. Underwater warriors of this caliber and training were scarce by war's end, and Germany and Japan dispatched hastily trained young men to ineffectual fates.

The British and Italians, by contrast, carefully winnowed their crews into an elite cadre of motivated volunteers, hardening them with realistic drill, similar to the training received by the Advance Force of Yamamoto's Kido Butai. The only notable midget submarine successes of World War II were a result of such skills.

SEDUCED BY TECHNOLOGY

SOUND CONTACTS

7

THERE'S SOMEBODY OUT THERE

Admiral Husband Kimmel's first few days as Commander in Chief of the U.S. Fleet contained an unwelcome surprise. A submarine contact off Diamond Head, eight miles from the Pearl entrance buoys, kept destroyer *Dale* on the scent for just over 24 hours, from 6 a.m. Feb. 3 to the next morning.

Scout planes from cruiser *Detroit* also canvassed the area, and reported only porpoises near the destroyer. *Aylwin,* another destroyer, was in company with *Dale*, but left after a few hours and was replaced by *Hull*, also a destroyer. When *Detroit* finished her exercises nearby, she caught up with the two destroyers and queried them. Both were in agreement — something large was definitely lurking below.

The noon turned, and still the contact beat brightly in the ears of the sonar men. Destroyer Division Nine was scrambled and split apart, with *Lamson* and *Mahan* joining the sonar corral and *Drayton* and *Flusser* attaching themselves to Battleship Division Three as an anti-submarine screen.

The contact kept circling. The ships sometimes approached within 500 yards of it, and once the contact teasingly sprinted through their patrol line.

During the evening, *Dale* was asked if the contact might be a whale. Their response was that other ships were maintaining the same contact, and besides, *this* contact was making realistic propeller noises.

At 6 a.m., Kimmel ordered Rear Admiral Milo Draemel, (Commander, Destroyers, Battle Force) to "bomb this thing, depth charge it!" Before the order went out, Kimmel canceled it.

At daylight on the 4th, PBY Catalina aircraft showed up to lend extra eyes. But the contact vanished at 7:25. The waters were clear; the sonar beat went whistling off into the depths. The destroyers milled about, and after a couple of hours *Dale* and *Hull* were ordered into the harbor for debriefing, with *Lamson* and *Mahan* continuing the search for the rest of the day. The only other excitement was a group of sampans showing up in the area. *Dale*, on her way back to

Admiral Husband Kimmel, the new CINCUS, arrives in Honolulu on Feb.1, 1941, and is greeted by newsmen Eugene Burns at left and Bill Ewing at right.

[1] It's an indication of how seriously the U.S. Navy suspected fishing sampans that the boats' serial numbers were noted during submarine hunts around Hawaii. By 1941, sampans and Imperial Japanese Navy submarines were intractably linked.

Pearl, charged the sampans, passing close enough to one to read her name; *Kasura Maru*, number FJ82.[1] The Catalinas began to fan out, covering a pattern 100 miles out from Oahu.

Kimmel's waffling on the sinking order may indicate he was second-guessing himself. Sinking another country's submarine in what were still considered international waters could have had reverberating consequences. Besides, the sonar contacts were so positive that the destroyer skippers seemed confident they could track the submarine, as if tethered to it by a sonic leash. They were ordered to attack only if the contact turned on them.

After the submarine — if that's what it was — disappeared, Kimmel decided that *Dale's* crew had vivid imaginations. "What motive would a foreign submarine have to operate submerged off Honolulu?" thought Kimmel, and said so in his report. The propeller noises could have been the destroyer's own machinery, looping back somehow into the operators' earphones. Lieutenant Commander John P. Womble, *Dale's* skipper, had two years experience tailing American submarines, and he disagreed. Womble had also heard propellers.

SOUND CONTACTS

This February contact spurred Navy officers to visit Honolulu's Bishop Museum to learn whatever they could about the waters around Hawaii. Their conclusion was that the sonar was bouncing off a layer of cooler water below the surface.

This thermocline, as it became known, was little understood. Sonar beams were deflected by it, like a flaw in window glass. Submariners later learned quickly to hide beneath it. Kimmel's staff decided that this reflective layer had fooled the sonar operators.

Kimmel reported to naval operations chief Admiral Harold Stark that he'd be "delighted" to take offensive action against solid sonic contacts, if the Navy Department wished him to do so. But he had no authority to issue such an order. Rather than giving the go-ahead, Stark waffled himself — Washington's response allowed Kimmel to bomb only within the three-mile limit.

Kimmel later considered allowing "depth charge practice" at sea on mysterious echoes.

Strictly speaking, anti-submarine warfare wasn't practiced by the fleet. Training was geared toward defense against submarines, and much trust was put in each ship's sound officer. The sound officer was responsible for the ship's sonar — Sound Navigation And Ranging — equipment, which, in active mode, would send out bursts of sound which would bounce off objects in the water, from whales to reefs to submarines. In the passive mode, the sound system could be used for listening, but only if the destroyer was moving slowly.

Once contact was made, the destroyer would veer toward it, hoping to overrun the signal. The depth and position of the contact could be roughly estimated by the distance at which the destroyer lost contact. Depth charges were set to explode below the target.

Lookouts were stationed to watch for periscopes; gun crews were also at the ready in case the target decided to surface and slug it out.

Battleships didn't venture into the open ocean without a destroyer screen, which preceded the battlewagons by several thousand yards, weaving at a slightly greater speed. If a contact was established, the destroyers would pounce while the battleship turned away. All sorties and entrances to Pearl Harbor were made in this fashion.

This essentially passive mode of defense had several weaknesses. Ocean sound conditions varied daily, making it difficult to predict a submarine's position before it was in attacking range. The minutes of sonar silence as a destroyer closed on the target, losing it under the bow, and the time it took the depth charges to reach their preset firing depth, often gave the target time to crash-dive, sprint or otherwise elude the onslaught from above.

Using recently installed sonars, American destroyers around Pearl had noted an escalating number of "suspicious" contacts in 1940 and early 1941. During the summer of 1940, while the Pacific

Fleet was away from Pearl Harbor on a highly publicized "run" to Panama, war plans officer Captain Charles McMorris was left in charge of the off-shore patrol. A destroyer reported a contact with a submerged submarine near Pearl Harbor and asked for instructions. McMorris, as the senior officer present afloat, responded that if the sub was in the restricted area, and not identified as American, by all means kill it.

The destroyer didn't get close enough. When Admiral James O. Richardson, the fleet commander, returned from the propaganda cruise, he canceled McMorris' order, grumbling that he was passing on the wishes of higher authority.

Believing these contacts to be Japanese submarines, Richardson's worries about the Imperial Navy were magnified, and he took his case directly to Roosevelt; take the fleet back to the safe waters of San Diego.

Roosevelt's response, indirectly, was to sack Richardson and install hard-nosed Kimmel in the commander's chair. Kimmel had the same fears, but kept them within his staff. After the scare of Feb. 3, Kimmel asked Lieutenant Commander Layton for his opinion.

Was it a Japanese submarine? The intelligence officer told Kimmel that he thought it was. "We've had several unconfirmed reports from unreliable observers that submarines are reconnoitering the approaches to Pearl," said Layton. "And the naval attache in Tokyo tells us that an Imperial submarine recently returned from a reconnaissance cruise of Hawaii and the West Coast. They're just repeating a rumor, of course."

As the contacts continued — there was a similar incident in mid-March — Kimmel declared that "anything other than a surprise submarine attack was most improbable." His commanders and planners agreed with him, at least in abstract. In various lists, the spectre of submarine attack was always near the top.

The current version of confidential letter 2CL-41 speculated that the Japanese could attack by both air and sea. The plan also said one could happen without the other.

Kimmel felt a mass submarine attack was well within the capability of the Japanese Imperial Navy. "At no time did I consider that a mass submarine attack had to be accompanied by an air attack.

90

SOUND CONTACTS

We were only talking possibilities and you could have one without the other ..."

Richardson's tough training regimen had pointed out deficiencies. Admiral Claude C. Bloch, commandant of the 14th Naval District, wrote Stark in December 1940, saying that the only "ideal defense against submarines" was to use a one-two punch of patrol vessels and aircraft. This notion of anti-submarine warfare teamwork has persisted from World War I to the present. At the time, however, Bloch had no aircraft and three newly arrived destroyers from a mothball fleet that still leaked around the newly installed sonar domes.

Just as pressing was a lack of minecraft. The Navy Yard had attached anti-magnetic coils to a barge and was in the process of converting three tugs when Bloch complained to Stark. No defense against moored mines was available in Hawaii, and Bloch warned that without these craft, Hawaii's harbors could be rendered unsafe.

Keeping the capabilities of submarines in mind, Kimmel quickly made a survey of Hawaii harbors after taking command.

"Four-stack" destroyers Bainbridge *(DD-246) and* Childs *(DD-241) in Pearl Harbor during the 1920s.*

Kimmel agreed with Richardson's assertion that Lahaina Roads was not safe from submarine attack, and continued standing orders not to moor there. The only way to make Lahaina unhealthy for submarines was to mine it thoroughly. Swift currents offshore there made it likely that mines would be torn off their cables and be dashed against American ships, and planning estimates figured the Navy would eventually sink more of its own ships from runaway mines than in combat with the enemy. The plan was abandoned, and the vast, deep fleet anchorage of Lahaina Roads stood empty.

The only other place outside of Pearl Harbor that could host warships was Hilo Harbor, which could barely squeeze in a couple of battleships and a few destroyers. Destroyers could also slip into Kahului, on Maui, and often did so on fleet maneuvers. As the situation tensed, these harbors were abandoned because they were too open to submarine attack. In particular, the docks of Hilo, protected only by a partial breakwater, were naked to the open sea. Torpedoes fired from the ocean could hit ships wharfside.

By the time Kimmel took the reins, only Pearl Harbor was considered safe for the larger ships. Only the speedy destroyers and the submarines, which could dive out of trouble on the spot, were allowed to visit the "neighbor islands." The Navy money tap that opened on Oahu was shut off for the other Hawaiian islands, a situation that continues to this day, and helped Oahu eclipse the others in economic health.

At Pearl Harbor, the narrow channel dictated that capital ships move in and out in single file. The fleet was drilled in rapid-exit. Even so, to sortie the entire fleet from Pearl took more than three hours. Ships were carefully moored to face the harbor entrance to simplify deployment maneuvers. Speed was limited to 12 knots — otherwise the waves generated wrecked light craft moored on either side of the channel. The big fear was that a ship would be sunk leaving the channel, victim to a lucky shot from an offshore marauder. The approaches to Pearl were heavily guarded.

A calm, shallow anchorage accessed by a narrow gauntlet, Pearl Harbor was considered the only place in Hawaii safe from

SOUND CONTACTS

submarine attack. No known submarine could get into harbor without showing its periscope.

"We thought that the danger from submarine attack in Pearl Harbor was nil — nothing," said Kimmel later. The alarm whistle for air attack inside Pearl Harbor was one long blast of 25 seconds, followed by a five-second whistle. No similar alarm was developed for submarine attack.

The channel into Pearl Harbor, straight as a spear, was blasted out of coral. This entrance corridor is less than 375 yards wide and 3,500 yards long. It is generally veiled by silt disgorging from the harbor, making ships rely on buoys and landmarks when approaching. The channels in Pearl Harbor average 40 feet in depth.

Where the throat narrowed to 400 yards from shore to shore, and 50 feet deep, two anti-torpedo nets were strung up in 1941, one backing the other. Each net hung down 35 feet, certainly deep enough, it was thought, to discourage torpedo shots up the throat of the harbor, and it was far too shallow for a conventional submarine to pass without being detected.

The nets, made of interlocking rings, were anchored on the shore side with heavy buoys and kept afloat with large buoys called baulks, actually wooden rafts. The rafts' topsides were studded with a wicked row of steel spikes pointed seaward, in case a small, fast surface vessel decided to leap the net at full speed. The gate end was handled by a ship containing generators and winches to haul the net open and closed. The anti-torpedo net was backed up on the harbor's shallow shoulders by underwater obstacles.

The net was not to prevent submarines from entering the harbor, but to deter a submarine from firing a torpedo down the throat. It was closed sunset to sunrise, opened only under orders of senior officers. During daylight hours the net was kept open, on the assumption that shore patrols would spot something so large as a submarine.

The torpedo nets installed at Pearl Harbor were left over from World War I. "1918 net!" sniffed Bloch, but he had been personally assured by the Bureau of Ordnance that a double-hung net would stop 90 percent of torpedoes fired through it.

Though the interior of the harbor was considered safe, operations around the islands were something else. Kimmel wanted security handled by someone permanently on shore. Bloch was it. "I felt I had enough to do already, but I was willing to take it," Bloch said, and used the new position to streamline the chain of command.

Taking advantage of his additional authority, Bloch wrote to Stark on May 7, 1941, titling his letter "Local Defense Measures of Urgency."

In it he pointed out that the only way submarines "can be kept out of an area or destroyed" was by small, fast ships fitted with listening gear, depth charges and guns; by aircraft or by mines; and preferably by a combination of the above.

"In any Pacific war, it appears very obvious that the principal

A crew of aviation ordnancemen at the newly built Navy base at Kaneohe move a bomb to a PBY patrol bomber.

[2] Kenneth Taylor, then an Army flight lieutenant and later credited with shooting down Japanese aircraft during the attack, said he remembers no ship-identification training of any sort.

effort of our enemy will be to concentrate its submarine activity in the area outside and near Honolulu, Pearl Harbor, the Island Bases and the other ports of the Islands. The protection supplied by existing arrangements for this area, exclusive of the Fleet, is very weak and unsatisfactory…"

Bloch went on to complain about the "four old destroyers" being overworked by the Navy and under-helped by the Army Air Force. "Complete reliance has to be placed (exclusive of the Fleet) on Army planes. This necessarily requires much indoctrination of the pilots and much training to qualify them for the recognition of various types of vessels and other matters pertaining to the sea before they become proficient in spotting and attacking submarines."[2]

Bloch's letter also pointed out the danger of cargo ships lying unprotected outside the reef fringes of Pacific atolls such as Wake. "This would appear to the undersigned as being a submarine picnic," he concluded.

When this letter was brought into evidence some years later, the penciled notation "All too true" was written across it.

Using aircraft as anti-submarine scouts was a continuing headache, not helped by an unreliable information flow. Ignorant of many of the destroyer submarine contacts near Pearl Harbor was Rear Admiral Patrick Bellinger, commander of Patrol Wing 2, the PBY wing tasked with perimeter security around Oahu. Considering that a primary concern of the patrol planes was to look for submarines, it's interesting that Bellinger later claimed he was left out of the loop. The Catalinas that aided the February search were

SOUND CONTACTS

from PatWing 24, stationed on Ford Island with the fleet. Although Bloch was charged with the ultimate responsibility for PatWing 2, he had no control over it. He also had, on paper, 108 patrol planes to guard Oahu. None were in Hawaii; most had not even been constructed yet.

Some confusion also reigned over the responsibility for long-range patrols. The Navy held Army strictly responsible for the defense of Oahu, and by mutual consent Army air patrols rarely ranged more than 100 miles from the island, and fighter patrols were limited to 15 miles. The Navy protected the fleet. PBYs were charged with the longer-range patrols, but many of these would have left with the ships had the fleet sortied to another base. This dilemma encouraged the Army to establish its own long-range patrols of B-17s, if it could get them.

The only target these reconnaissance planes were looking for were submarines. All PBYs in Hawaii were primarily armed with fused depth bombs. The 12 B-17s assigned to Hickam were highly thought of — Air Corps planners thought they could sweep the skies of enemy attacks — but they were too few in number. At any one time, due to a lack of trained personnel and spare parts, six planes or fewer were ready for long-range sweeps.

The long-range searches covered the coastal frontier of Hawaii, which extended 500 miles out from the islands, and included Johnston, Palmyra islands and Kingman's Reef. The only Army reconnaissance flights in the inshore area were flown by the widely disliked B-18. Brigadier General James Mollison, chief of staff for the Hawaiian Air Force, said the ungainly, underarmed B-18s were purposely kept within 20 miles of Oahu, not sent on any missions where they might contact enemy fighters, such as the Imperial

B-18s from Hickam Field patrol the inshore areas of Oahu. In Hawaii, this type of aircraft proved unsuitable for anti-submarine patrol, although it gave a good accounting of Nazi U-boats in the Caribbean.

Navy's lethal new fighter, which later was discovered to be the Zero. "That (would be) suicide," said Mollison. "It's just (got) no defense against most any reasonable fighter plane."

As 1941 wore on, Oahu's commanders did the best with what they had, assigning their few patrol planes only to sectors in which submarines were suspected. The only Navy long-distance reconnaissance was in the fleet training area to the south, an area approximately 30 miles on a side, while Army planes skirted the islands. Their single target was enemy submarines, which, to be effective in attacking the U.S. Fleet, needed to be massed south of Oahu. That is where the air searches proliferated. The fleet's own planes, primarily scouts on cruisers and battleships and the air wings on board carriers, provided on-the-spot anti-submarine patrols. Task forces did not move in the Pacific without a protective screen of aircraft looking for submarines.

On Oahu, drills were held once a week in which planes would fly over the harbor by day or night so gunners could track the targets.

Submarine training, now that the fleet was in town, became unusually realistic. "For the first time in all my experience in submarines, we had plenty of other ships to operate with," said Rear Admiral Thomas Withers, commander of submarines in the Pacific. The submarines were generally assigned to the opposing force to "prevent artificiality."

The realistic training extended to other areas. One plan recommended that whenever ships entered or sortied from Pearl Harbor, destroyers would salute them by setting off depth charges in the harbor entrance. Crews would get used to the concussive effects, argued the scheme, and any Japanese crews hiding below would get thoroughly rattled.

In the ongoing fleet exercises, destroyers attacked Withers' submarines, submarines attacked destroyers, submarines shadowed the fleet as it wheeled through the ocean, dogged the splinter forces, airplanes tried in vain to bomb submarines with realistic-

A B-17D on patrol from the 50th Reconnaissance Squadron, Hickam Field, during the summer of 1941.

SOUND CONTACTS

sounding charges. In one thrilling exercise, submarines stalked the great battleships and fired dummy torpedoes.

The destroyers became skilled at detecting submarines, knew what they sounded like at all attitudes and depths, became familiar with the tricky currents and fickle thermoclines surrounding the islands. Every time fleet forces put to sea, a submarine attack drill was staged at least once, becoming more frequent the closer the ships got to the harbor entrance.

To prevent misidentification, American submarines were required to enter the harbor on the surface and in the company of a fleet destroyer. To this day, American submarines approaching Pearl Harbor do so on the surface.

As tension with Japan increased, American submarines were assigned to picket duty, two each off Wake and Midway. All were armed. Withers warned submarine skippers before each sortie that war might be under way before they could return to the haven of Pearl Harbor.

An acute shortage of trained personnel and spare parts nibbled away at Withers' little fleet. In early November, 12 submarines were transferred from Pearl Harbor to Manila, leaving the submarine base pretty well deserted. Withers had to scrape to get the "long-legged" boats ready for duty off Wake and Midway.

During the first week of December 1941, there were only four American submarines in Pearl Harbor, with five more in the area.

This realistic training highlighted shortcomings in the American war plans. In March 1941, Bellinger and Major General Frederick Martin, commander of the Hawaiian Air Force, focused on the submarine threat while revising the war plan, now called Rainbow Five. They recommended that a strong part of the fleet always be at sea to deal with marauding submarines. "It appears possible that Orange submarines and/or an Orange fast raiding force might arrive in Hawaiian waters with no prior warning from our intelligence service ..." they predicted, and concluded that a declaration of war would be preceded by "a surprise submarine attack on ships in the operating area."

Their joint summary concluded that the air wings should hold "pursuit and fighter aircraft in condition of immediate readiness to counter a possible air raid until search proves that none is imminent. Dispatch armed shore-based fleet aircraft to relieve planes in the air over the attack area. Establish a station patrol by patrol planes two hundred twenty miles radius from scene of attack at one hour before daylight of next succeeding daylight period."

They also concluded that "the most likely and dangerous form of attack on Oahu would be an air attack ... launched from one or more carriers."

Without patrol planes to search for the carriers, however sporadically, defensive preparations concentrated on the submarine threat.

A memo co-written by Bellinger and Martin later that month quoted from the 1939 edition of *Jane's Fighting Ships,* which showed "over 40 submarines which are easily capable of projection in this area."

The two continued to list, in order of probability, Japan's possible actions preceding a formally declared war. First on the list was "a surprise submarine attack on ships in the operating area," followed by "a surprise (air) attack on Oahu including... Pearl Harbor," or "a combination of these two."

"Any single submarine attack might indicate the presence of considerable undiscovered surface force probably composed of fast ships accompanied by a carrier."

In this context, Rainbow Five's reading of "possible enemy attacks against the Oahu area in the order of probability are: **(A)** Submarine — torpedo and mine. **(B)** Sabotage. **(C)** Disguised merchant ship attack by blocking channels, by mines, or by air or surface craft. **(D)** Air raids carrier based. **(E)** Surface ship raids. **(F)** Major combined attack in the absence of the U.S. Fleet."

Rainbow Five addressed also "Possible and Probable War Situations," pointing out that "sea lanes from continental United States to Hawaii are open and that the garrison of Hawaii will be reinforced from continental United States..." This was of particular concern since the 11 oilers assigned to the Pacific Fleet were required to operate continuously between the West Coast and Hawaii to feed the thirsty warships. If the Japanese had a healthy strategic plan, these oilers would be prime targets.

"The Naval Operating Areas in Hawaiian Waters are considered submarine waters," bluntly stated Rainbow Five. Under the conditions under which American ships could operate at sea, eight of the 13 conditions were devoted to submarines.

Only submarines could anchor in unprotected anchorages. The destroyers' main mission wherever they were was as an anti-submarine screen. Steaming at night was carried out in blackout condition, in a defensive array. U.S. submarines were banned from operating submerged around other American ships, unless prearranged plans were available to all. Even so, American submarines were limited to specific operating areas. Task force commanders were provided with detailed itineraries for American submarines.

Capital ships coming from Pearl were required to have a destroyer attack unit preceding them, to "locate and attack hostile submarines." These screens had numbers of destroyers attached according to priority — top priority was given to battleships, followed by carriers and cruisers.

Should a submarine actually attack in the operating area, Rainbow Five was specific: "Originate a plain language dispatch, urgent precedence, containing essential details and addressed to all ships present in Hawaiian Waters." To ensure rapid distribution, the skipper of the "attacked ship" was supposed to transmit directly to

the Task Force commander, to all ships in Pearl on the harbor circuit, and to Radio Honolulu on an open channel.

In April 1941, Army and Navy commands in Hawaii sat down together and hammered out a "Joint Coastal Frontier Defense Plan." Areas threatened by submarines were singled out for special consideration. The coastal frontier itself consisted of Oahu and those areas considered essential for the defense of Oahu, which included most of the scattered bays and coves of the Hawaiian chain, any place that could shelter a submarine.

The same sites, as well as the oceans 20 miles from shore, were declared "Defensive Sea Areas." Pearl Harbor itself was a DSA, as it was called, with the harbor zone extending three miles out to sea from the channel entrance.

Liaison between the Army coast artillery and the Navy was maintained by two soldiers, an officer and an enlisted man, who were stationed in the Navy Harbor Patrol Station. The soldiers were there to help identify possible targets. Coastal artillery spotters were instructed not to fire upon submarines, unless directed to, which conflicted with another order to shoot if a submarine could not be positively identified as American.

To clear the way, all American submarines were shepherded by a destroyer. All unescorted submarines presumably belonged to the enemy.

The plans were next revised in October, calling for continuous patrols on the inshore area, the boom patrols and harbor patrols. Intermittent patrols included the offshore destroyer patrol, which prowled waters in an arc 10 miles from the Pearl entrance, a sweep

Destroyers Chew *(DD-106) and* Ward *(DD-139) pay a rare visit to Hilo on July 22, 1941. The pier they are moored to is open to the sea, and therefore to a torpedo-solution shot. The ships are also wearing the new Measure 11 camouflage, a dark bluish-gray on all vertical surfaces — compare to the light gray four-stackers on pages 90 and 91.*

by no less than three destroyers for 12 hours prior to sortie or entry of the fleet or any task force with heavy ships, and a "ready duty" destroyer standing by at all times to run interference for heavy ships coming and going. This last destroyer had to be ready to roll within an hour, which required continuously fired boilers and a larger-than-usual crew complement. This unpopular duty was rotated.

The local fishing fleet at this time was usually mentioned in the same breath as enemy submarines. The largely Japanese-American-owned fleet of fishing sampans in the Territory of Hawaii was highly suspect for its ability to disappear at sea and later return to bustling piers — too many to thoroughly check. The sampans clearly had the ability to rendezvous with submarines and smuggle spies ashore. There is no record that this was ever done, although there are a number of cases of illegal aliens jumping Japanese freighters and entering the territory in this manner. As a Navy Intelligence report from early 1942 noted: "If this was not an accomplished fact, it is only because the agents of the Japanese Government did not care to adopt this method and there is no question but that the opportunity existed and Japanese Naval Officers knew of the possibilities…"

It's also quite a leap from helping a "wetback" ashore to aiding spies of a foreign government. Besides, it was simpler for the Imperial Japanese Navy to book passage on any NYK liner.

General Sherman Miles, an intelligence officer in the War Department, testified before Congress in the summer of 1941, advocating a bill that would limit the number of Japanese-born fishermen. Asked if "Jap fishermen … were fishing right in Pearl Harbor itself," Miles answered that the trouble with them was "that they were American citizens, very largely; couldn't get them."

It was also known that the Japanese early warning line, on their approaches to the Imperial Islands, was achieved by equipping their fishing boat fleet with radio transmitters. Thousands of such boats dotted the waters as far as 800 miles from Japan.[3]

It did not help that local fishermen tended to be secretive about their movements. They were engaging in a competitive business, in which the location of prime fishing grounds were highly prized; yet their close-mouthed habits seemed highly suspicious.

From the beginning, Hawaii's fishing industry had been accelerated by incoming Japanese, who demanded seafood in their diets. Hawaiian fishermen fished for themselves and neighbors; the inadequate supply prompted Japanese to go into business. By the turn of the century, the sampan had been established in Hawaii waters and fishermen of Japanese descent in Hawaii monopolized deep-sea fishing. These fisherman were well-established before immigration limits were set in 1924, and hundreds of sampans plied island waters in the years before the war.

In March 1940, a customs law was passed that required sampans of five tons or greater to be registered by their owners, making

[3] *Before being blown out of the water by an American destroyer, such a fishing vessel radioed that aircraft carrier* Hornet, *bearing James Doolittle's B-25s, was bearing close to Japan.*

SOUND CONTACTS

it unlawful for aliens to own the wide-ranging fishing boats.

Even so, the business continued to flourish until 1941. On Feb. 28 that year, a federal grand jury indicted 70 people and three fishing companies for conspiracy, the particular charge being the false licensing of sampans. To get around the licensing law of the previous year, many alien owners had drawn up false bills of sale in the names of friends or relatives who were Hawaii citizens. Some of the defendants were in Japan when the indictments were delivered, a situation that prompted talk of espionage.

The fishing industry was dealt a serious blow. Nineteen sampans were seized by the government, and in late March another 42 charges of conspiracy were filed. Thousands of dollars were lost by Hawaii fishermen while the boats sat idle, and in an ironic twist, four boats were impressed into the Navy as inshore patrol vessels.

Harsh restrictions were laid down on the sampans, carried out

by local Coast Guard but inspired by initiatives from district intelligence officer Captain Irving Mayfield. Japanese aliens were barred from working on the boats; all boats were registered; the fishermen were limited to certain fishing areas and times, and barred from others; all radio equipment was removed.

To facilitate sampan inspection and beef up anti-submarine patrols, command of the local Coast Guard was transferred to Bloch's 14th Naval District. Three Coast Guard ships, cutters *Taney*, *Reliance* and *Tiger*, were outfitted with anti-submarine listening gear.

Stark wrote Admiral "Tommie" Hart in the summer of '41, revealing that there had been a long struggle with Treasury Secretary Henry Morgenthau to release the Coast Guard to Navy control. Morgenthau, at that point, had relented only in Hawaii. Hart, head of the Asiatic Fleet, was just as concerned in his own way about not receiving enough anti-submarine materiel.

In the same letter, Stark said he occasionally chatted with Japanese Ambassador Kichisaburo Nomura in Washington. "We have had very plain talk. I like him and, as you know, he has many

Coast Guard cutter Roger B. Taney — later known simply as Taney *— arrives in Honolulu, 1936. The threat from submarines was considered so great by late 1941 that Coast Guard craft were fitted with submarine detection gear.*

Tiger *during her days as a rum-chaser.*

friends in our Navy... In both the Far East and the Atlantic, there is plenty of potential dynamite."

Ralph "Doc" Nash was one of the Coast Guardsmen caught in the refitting switch. He was assigned to cutter *Taney* with his identical twin brother, which caused no end of confusion. Finally, the skipper called both of them into his cabin and flipped a coin to determine which one would be transferred off ship. Ralph Nash's new berth was in *Tiger*, a 125-foot "buck and a quarter" craft built as a Prohibition enforcer.

In August, *Tiger* skipper William Mazzoni called the crew together. "Men," he announced, "as of this date we're no longer Coast Guard. We're U.S. Navy, under the command of the 14th Naval District." The ship spent its patrols checking sampans by day and trolling for submarines by night.

Nash was impressed by the seriousness with which the Navy regarded the sampans, and was surprised when some humble fishing boats were found to contain excellent shoreline maps and high-caliber sonar and other electronic equipment.

The procedure called for the Coast Guardsmen to look the boat over while the sampan's papers were checked. The fishermen's hands also were inspected for callouses; a smooth hand was viewed with suspicion. More than once, the fishermen would pretend not to understand English when this inspection was requested, and Mazzoni would say to Nash, "Tell 'em to open their hands — or kick them in the nuts until they do it." Suddenly, hands were unfolded without further ado.

In October and November, the emphasis shifted to anti-submarine defense. *Tiger* spent most of her time listening to the water.

Kimmel and Bloch tried to enlist other small craft in the hunt for submarines. Local harbor defense was negligible. In late August, Bloch complained that his command had received no additional forces except for net guards. "I pointed out the very serious

condition, as I visualized heavy submarine attacks here, and I had to have patrol vessels …"

He suggested unmothballing some of the fleet laid up since the Great War. It was a matter of frustration. "The entire history of the World War indicates there have never been enough small craft," Bloch later explained. "The British trawlers, British sweepers and British destroyers during the World War operated 28 days out of 30 at sea. This fact has been known to us for years, as far back as 1933."

Another letter from the same time period, from Stark to Kimmel, reveals that the problem was known in Washington:

"Project is now under way to send twelve PTs to the 14th Naval District as soon as the boats can be prepared and transportation provided …" A handwritten note added, "Wish I had more. They will be coming. I know Xmas is too, but we are doing the best we can — and I am kicking all the time."

He urged all light craft in the Pacific be fitted with depth charges and listening gear. "This is *important.*" The new light-weight listening equipment JK-9 only weighed about 1,300 pounds, needed a small space and 115 volts to operate. The Navy received 10 a week of these in August 1941, hurriedly fitting out small craft.

Stark quoted Fleet Maintenance, explaining that destroyer/minelayers and destroyer/minesweepers had such gear authorized, some were already installed and the new model QC apparatus was being rushed into service, perhaps by September, 1941. *Too slow I know,* Admiral Stark penciled in the note's margin, *But I have been doing my d'-st.*

On the other hand, the unstable AVDs, converted destroyers, were having a hard time with the top-weight. An ever newer model of echo-ranging and listening gear, the "WEA," was on the way, with "deliveries commencing in October 1941." Stark listed the features of the WEA as if it were a Detroit special. One of the key features was that it could be installed on "most converted yachts."

Kimmel, with several sampans already under his control, lost no time installing these new weapons.

The 12 new motor torpedo boats sent to Kimmel were almost useless. Kimmel tested them by sending them on an October day trip from Oahu to Molokai. Against heavy fall swells in the Kaiwi Channel, the light craft could barely make 10 knots. Several turned back, and all reported injuries due to sailors being "thrown about." Kimmels wanted more substantial ships for anti-submarine operations, and requested more destroyers be broken out of mothballs.

On Oct. 17, Bloch pleaded for his own small, fast patrol craft with listening gear and depth charges, as well as more patrol planes. The only patrol ship the 14th had been given during the past year, other than net vessels, had been the old *Sacramento*, a waddling gunboat with inadequate weapons. Kimmel added comments of his own to Bloch's request, pointing out that borrowing fleet weapons systems for local defense wasn't efficient. The fleet, at any moment,

had to be able to sprint across the Pacific, which would leave Pearl Harbor defenseless.

The situation in the Atlantic, as Admiral Richardson had feared the year before, continued to bleed the Pacific Fleet. Stark ordered Kimmel, on Aug. 28, to deploy two light cruisers to the southeast Pacific. The perceived threat was from German and Italian raiders that might strike both sides of the Panama Canal. The two ships, and the forces of the Panama Naval Coastal Frontier, were told in no uncertain terms to sink such raiders, should they appear. These orders did not apply to Japanese warships.

On Oct. 8, under the outlines of Rainbow 5, the commanders of Atlantic fleet warships were given permission to fire upon German submarines and surface ships. War, de facto or not, existed in the Atlantic, at least on the American side of the 26th meridian.

The Navy Hemisphere Defense Plan No. 2 — known in the Navy as WPL-49 — had been in effect since April, when the convoy situation became critical. The updated version, WPL-51, went into effect on July 11. The order to shoot had been an amendment to the plan, as was Stark's deployment of the cruisers Kimmel could ill-afforded to lose.

On Oct. 16, Kimmel was formally advised of the possibility Japan would attack the United States and Great Britain, or perhaps Russia. At the same time, merchant traffic was ordered to new routes in the Central Pacific, away from northern routes that might contain Imperial Navy I-boats. A warning from Stark to his forward commanders — which didn't include Kimmel — pointed out possible Japanese intentions toward weakly held portions of the Pacific, and said Japanese "raiding and observation forces (were) widely distributed in the Pacific, and submarines in the Hawaiian area." Hawaii was left out of the planning stage, not being considered far enough forward for danger.

Kimmel was an action-oriented man, and despite his fears about hostile submarines operating under his nose, considered the main duty of the fleet was to dash across the Pacific and attack the Imperial Navy, should war erupt. In a Sept. 12 letter to Stark, Kimmel wondered about the situation in the Pacific. The options for direct action in the Atlantic seemed clear-cut; in the Central Pacific, his orders seemed hazy. "Of course I know the possibility of German or Italian submarines in that area is slight and Japanese improbable, but the question arises as to just how much we can discount the threat of Japanese action …" he wondered, and then he asked Stark point-blank what to do about "submarine contacts off Pearl Harbor and vicinity … As you know, our present orders are to trail but not to bomb unless they are in the defensive areas. Should we now bomb contacts without waiting to be attacked?"

At letter's end, Kimmel made it a point to "presume (he) will get official orders" concerning offensive action against "raiders in the Pacific and submarines off Hawaii."

A pair of paravanes aboard minesweeper Aroostook, *1923,* a sister ship to Oglala. These torpedo-shaped devices would "fly" through the water attached to a line, clipping off moored mines. Minesweeping was essential to defend Pearl Harbor.

Stark wrote back nearly a fortnight later, saying that the existing orders were "appropriate. If conclusive — and I mean conclusive — evidence is obtained that Japanese submarines are actually in or near United States territory, then a strong warning and threat of hostile action against such submarines would appear to be our next step."

The letter continued, "the longer we can keep the situation in the Pacific in status quo, the better for all concerned." In a show of mock patience, Stark then read Kimmel naval regulations; "Article 723 … reads as follows: The use of force against a foreign and friendly state or against anyone within the territories thereof, is illegal. The right of self-preservation, however, is a right which belongs to States as well as to individuals … (Force) can never be exercised with a view to inflicting punishment for acts already committed."[4]

By late October, the usually politic Bloch was still harping on his "four old destroyers" guarding the gate at Pearl and lack of aircraft dedicated to anti-submarine patrols. The oldest, destroyer *Allen,* was a real veteran, a four-stack, 1,000-tonner from World War I. "Nearly all of the failures of the British have been caused by what may be expressed in the cliche *Too little and too late.* It is hoped that we may profit from their errors," he signed off.

The destroyers of the Pacific Fleet continued to train hard, concentrating on anti-submarine sweeps. On Nov. 3, 1941, a PBY spotted an oil slick 50 miles southeast of Oahu, uncomfortably close to the fleet operating area. The Catalina scoured the ocean, and then called in destroyers *Worden* and *Dale* to beat the depths with sonar. Nothing turned up — or was long gone.

On Nov. 6, Kimmel forwarded to Stark his staffs' own intelligence estimate of Japanese strength in the Mandates, which ran "considerably" counter to the official word from Washington. "I think there can be no doubt that the Japanese have expended very large sums and much effort in their attempt to strengthen the Mandates and provide numerous operating bases for submarines and aircraft."

[4] Kimmel said later that "conclusive evidence" arrived on Dec. 7, 1941.

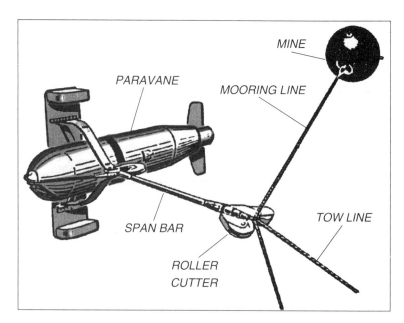

MINE

PARAVANE

MOORING LINE

SPAN BAR

ROLLER
CUTTER

TOW LINE

Details of the Type "D" paravane in action.

Submarine packs seemed to be thickening over the horizon. These estimates further fueled Kimmel's continuing desire for additional listening gear. "We have in this area 29 ships which can be fitted with sound gear and which are not so fitted. This is a very large number of potentially useful submarine hunters."

Kimmel also decided that the number of "flight deck merchant ships" should be increased ten-fold for each coast.[5] In addition to training purposes, these "mercantile aircraft carriers" would be most useful for sending out anti-submarine patrols.

The next day, Stark wrote to Kimmel, mentioning that "things seem to be moving steadily toward a crisis in the Pacific. Just when it will break, no one can tell."

[5] *Only one then existed — Long Island (AVG-1), built on the hull of M.S. Mormacmail.*

OVERLOOKED
LEAKS

8

IDLE RUMORS, BLIND ALLEYS AND HOT TIPS

While Admiral Kimmel was composing his thoughts on the submarine scare during his first few days as CINCUS, Admiral Stark was composing a most interesting letter to him. It dealt vaguely with war plans for a few paragraphs, then sprang an imaginative scenario:

"The Chief of Naval Operations believes it possible that Japan for some time maintained a vessel 500 miles north of Oahu. Indications are that some similar vessel is now stationed 1,000 miles southwest of Oahu. In connection with reports of unidentified submarines near Oahu, Panama, the Mexican coast, and in the open sea, it may be surmised that the vessel mentioned above is a submarine tender, and that Japan may plan storing war submarines on tenders in the open sea. It is considered most inadvisable that we not indicate too much curiosity in this respect for the time being. It would be well, however, to keep track of such vessels, and to take immediate steps to sink them on the outbreak of war."

Was Stark referring to *Chiyoda's* midget operations, or had his intelligence people simply made an informed guess? The last part of the paragraph certainly afforded Kimmel no clear direction, as Stark simultaneously suggested his commander both ignore and stalk the mystery ships.

Shortly before Kimmel took over the U.S. Fleet, cruiser *Augusta* was directed to pass through a position 600 miles north of Oahu as the ship returned from Asiatic Station. A Japanese naval tanker was suspected to be in the area at the time, and the cruiser was to surprise the tanker in the act of refueling submarines. PBYs were sent to the area also. This very secret operation wasn't even known by Lieutenant Commander Layton, Kimmel's intelligence chief, until long after it was completed. No tanker was found.

This situation was typical of intelligence scenarios of the period. Although the midget submarine was one of the best-kept secrets of the Imperial Navy, tantalizing hints of such a craft and other Japanese submarine mysteries were circulating in American intelligence circles long before the Pearl Harbor attack. Often, there

U.S. Representative
Melvin J. Maas goes
over plans for a
proposed two-man
midget submarine.

was a German connection — it was difficult, even at this late date, for American intelligence analysts to believe the Japanese could come up with schemes as sophisticated as these.

The November 1938 issue of the Japanese publication *Navy Club Magazine Picture News*, published by Kaigun-Kenkyusha (Naval Institute), contained a photograph of Colonel Melvin J. Maas, a Marine Corps reserve officer and a member of the U.S. House of Representatives from Minnesota. Maas was examining a blueprint of a Buck Rogers-like vehicle, which the magazine reported was a midget submarine.

Headlined "Suicide Squad of the Bottom of the Sea — The Appearance of the Two-Man Submarines," the article stated that "the American Navy reportedly is constructing super two man submarines … when an enemy ship is spotted, these submarines, traveling under water in a group, will be directed to approach the enemy ship to within a distance of about 250 yards and carry out a torpedo attack. At the same time, a method for the escape of the two men on board has been devised.

"According to one of the plans, the length of the submarine is 51 feet, the width is 10 feet, and the depth 7 feet. Its whole shape is like that of a fish and it is charged with a torpedo at its bow. The crew of two sits side by side, and the plan is for the submarine to return to its base or tender after releasing the torpedo, upon approaching within the range guaranteeing certain hits. The cost of construction of one reportedly is about $12,000."

Japanese military magazines of the period were virtually house organs. It's unlikely that an article such as this, which skates so closely to the truth of the midget project on the Japanese side, could be anything other than an attempt at disinformation. It would be

interesting to know what happened to the unfortunate writer if the story truly was a scoop.

An Oct. 11, 1939, dispatch by the United Press syndicate speculated that Germany was creating similar submersibles. The *Honolulu Advertiser* ran the story the next day, headlined "Midget Sub Developed By Berlin/Germany Has Fleet Of Pocket U-Boats, Built To Be Launched From Big Merchant Vessels."

Germany reportedly had perfected a fleet of "pocket submarines," according to John Tazwell Jones, a "former college friend" of President Roosevelt. Jones, who represented American business interests in Sao Paulo, Brazil, blurted this out after leaving a White House meeting. He had heard this from another friend, a German naval officer. The small submarines were supposedly capable of displacing 100 tons, were operated by a crew of 12 and could be carried on the decks of merchantmen and launched by crane.

As proof, Jones said he had personally seen a German merchant vessel in Brazil with a crane on deck.

In April 1940, a "personal friend" of Coast Guard Chief Boatswain L. Churchill was having a drink in a Eureka, Calif. bar when he noticed that the fellow next to him was not only drunk, he was German as well. The friend bought several rounds for the thirsty foreigner. The German revealed that he had been in the United States for a year, and bragged about a plan to sabotage the Panama Canal. A small vessel, said the German, would be outfitted with enormous mines attached to the bottom of the hull. The ship would detach the mines while transversing the canal, setting off a timing mechanism. Ballast tanks in the mother ship would draw in water as the mines were released to prevent an obvious change in the vessel's water line.

Churchill was so startled by this revelation from his friend that he repeated it to a Coast Guard officer inspecting the boatswain's duty station at Humboldt Bay. This report was soon distributed to the FBI, who searched in vain for the drunken, talkative German.

While visiting Shanghai in 1940, Nicolas Koumiotis of San Pedro, Calif., became friendly with a Japanese customs officer. One night the customs officer confided to Koumiotis that Japan "would soon declare war on the United States and England; that Jap submarines would attack (the) United States Pacific Coast; that Jap fishermen had already sunk drums of oil and drums of food in prearranged places; that even if all the Japanese fishermen were arrested, the stores had already been sunk, as arranged, and that these stores could not be found except by Japanese submarines."

Koumiotis repeated the above to Navy Intelligence as soon as he returned home, who in turn, filed the report.

Lieutenant Commander Henri H. Smith-Hutton, the U.S. Naval attache in Tokyo, reported in June 1940, that Japanese submarines were making observations of Hawaii and were replenished at sea by Imperial Navy tankers. Intelligence plotted the tanker tracks across

the Pacific and found that most passed through a point just to the north of Hawaii, a region that seemed to slow down the tankers by almost a day — as if they came to a full stop in mid-ocean.

PBY patrol plane crews were told to watch the waterlines of intercepted Japanese marus — tankers were reportedly sailing east riding low in the water and back west riding high. The explanation was that the ships were probably refueling submarines during the voyage.

Vague reports of Japanese submarines came in off the American West Coast, off Central America and as far south at the Galapagos Islands. The Japanese also had merchant ships stationed every 1,200 miles on a straight line from New Zealand to lower California, and all made periodic reports to Tokyo on the same radio band, 8400 kilocycles.

Rumors reached British intelligence that by the summer of 1940, German sailors were crewing Japanese submarines in the Pacific, hunting British ships. No hard evidence existed, though at least three German surface raiders were actually at large in the Pacific during the early part of the war, and were routinely replenished in Japan between sorties. One German raider carried a Type 95 Japanese seaplane painted in bogus British markings.

German raider *Kormoran*, disguised as a Dutch freighter, apparently ambushed Australian cruiser *Sydney* on Nov. 19, 1941, near the coast of western Australia. Both ships went down immediately without getting off details of the encounter.[1] Australian citizens were stunned that the ship could be lost so close to home after surviving the dangers of the Mediterranean war.

Participation in these actions, benign or otherwise, was routinely denied by the Japanese government. Japanese diplomats in Europe deliberately misled their Fascist partners, and the German ambassador in Tokyo had been reassured in late October 1941, that Japan had no plans afoot concerning their democratic enemies. Despite this, Germany pressured Japan to attack either the British in Singapore or the Russians at Vladivostok.

The Nazi naval attache in Tokyo was Admiral Paul W. Wenneker, for whom close relations with the Imperial Navy were essential, as he was required to monitor German submarines and raiders slipping through Osaka and Kobe. In late 1941, he sent a coded telegram warning of imminent war, hinted at by his colleague "Commander Shiba," that before "Christmas … He cannot, possibly, tell me a precise date in consideration of the need for surprise." Wenneker did not tell German ambassador Eugen Ott about the cable, though he did pass on Shiba's news.

There was good reason to worry about German moves in the Pacific. Nazi U-boats were tearing up the Atlantic, strangling the Lend-Lease lifeline to Britain. "Neutral" Americans flew active anti-submarine sweeps in the North Atlantic, occasionally spotting a U-boat. This breach of high-seas law infuriated U-boat Admiral

[1] It was a most mysterious battle. Despite being outgunned by the Mediterranean veteran, some 318 of the Kormoran's crew of 380 survived, while none of Sydney's 645 crew lived. A single lifeboat was discovered drifting, shot to pieces. On Nov. 24, 1941, the Australian Naval Board concluded that the cruiser was sunk by a Japanese submarine. A 1992 expedition to find Sydney's hulk may resolve this mystery.

Overlooked Leaks

Karl Donitz; it was "completely contrary to every tenet of international law (and) was of the utmost military, materiel and moral benefit to Britain!"

Roosevelt's politic response was that "when you see a rattlesnake poised, you don't wait until it has struck before you crush it."

The same anti-Nazi rumor mill produced the tale of German submarines being transported across Russia in pieces and being reassembled at Vladivostok, and that U-boat officers were putting to sea with Russian crews and performing Japanese missions.

Soon after the February submarine contact, Kimmel met with Captain Ellis M. Zacharias, skipper of cruiser *Salt Lake City* and a self-proclaimed Japanese intelligence expert. What was exchanged at this meeting was later the subject of bitter debate. Zacharias claimed to have warned Kimmel about the attack months in advance, and of having counseled everyone who would listen about what to do and when — not if — the Imperial Navy hit the harbor. He even claimed to have dictated the exact phrasing of the radio station KGU's war alert on the morning of Dec. 7, during a dinner engagement the week before with station owner Lorrin Thurston. Zacharias' influence with Thurston was such that, the day after the dinner, Thurston ran the headline "Japanese May Strike Over Weekend" in his newspaper, the *Honolulu Advertiser*. The story accompanying the headline indicated the target was southeast Asia, but the headline rattled nerves in Honolulu.

Zacharias supposedly told Kimmel in February that sightings of submarines off Pearl Harbor were "positive indications of intent to attack." During the hours prior to the Pearl Harbor attack, Zacharias was on his way to Wake Island, spending his time sequestered in his cabin on *Salt Lake City*, cruising the radio waves for Japanese chatter. What he heard seemed "intense."

Admiral Ellis Zacharias, who claimed to have warned Kimmel about the impending attack.

"Something was imminent," he said later. He apparently said nothing at the time.

Another intelligence report in June 1941, caused a bigger stir. In Mexico City, a Senor Villasenor, who was president of the Bank of Mexico, received some interesting information from one of his "agents." Villasenor passed it on to the commercial attache at the American Embassy, a Mr. Lockett, who in turn passed it to the embassy military attache, Army Colonel Gordon H. McCoy. Villasenor, when contacted, refused to reveal the name of his agent or the circumstances under which the information was received. "The agent is believed sincere and he reports what he gathers from subversive individuals," McCoy appended to the routing slip attached to the report. "These individuals may or may not be telling the truth. Their purpose may be propaganda or a form of a war of nerves, or it may contain an element of fact … on account of the

serious nature of the information, it is submitted without other comment."

The report did contain a germ of fact, which at the time, seemed wildly improbable. Drawing on information supplied by German navy agent Wagner Schioferle of Nicaragua, the report was about "a new type of light draft short radius submarine that is now being built in quantities at the Japanese Navy shipyards in Japan."

The midget submarine is described as carrying four torpedoes and a crew of 10, displacing only 350 tons. The engine supposedly was manufactured by N.A.M. of Germany and shipped overland across Siberia.

The mission described was even wilder. The midgets were to be sunk offshore at a strategic spot and fitted with lead-covered electrical cables which led ashore. Closing the contact allowed the submarine to automatically blow ballast and rise to the surface, ready for action. Light-weight anchors fore and aft prevented the craft from drifting; average depth for sinking the craft was 40 feet. If air pressure has bled off, an air hose attached to a wooden float crowned with kelp could be charged by air hoses on board a sampan.

By the summer of 1941, at least three and as many as 12 of these craft were rumored already in place, spotted around the island of Molokai, a short sea channel away from Pearl Harbor, and conveniently camouflaged near the "large Leper Colony" at Kalaupapa, Molokai. The crews were alleged to be hiding out among "large colonies of Japanese working in the sugar fields and pine apple (sic) plantations."

The report went into great detail over the technical details, noting for example, that it took exactly 35 minutes to recharge the submerged air tanks from a surface sampan. The new air also purged corrosive, foul air from the electrical storage batteries.

The midget submarines were towed to position. "The Japanese tanker called *Kenwo Maru* conducted an experiment recently on her way to Los Angeles, California, by taking one of these small subs from the Marshall Islands to where a base has been established in the vicinity of the Hawaiian Islands. At this point those submarines were again taken back to the Marshall Islands in tow by another Japanese tanker for the object of giving members of the sub crew experience in the deep sea towing of these vessels ... practically all navigation is done under water to prevent detection by other vessels ..."

The agent in Mexico added pencil sketches of the device, since lost. "If and when war comes between Germany and the U.S., or Japan and the U.S., the plan is to at once use this small' fleet of submarines on the U.S. Navy fleet anchored in Pearl Harbor!" the report stated, somewhat breathlessly. "A surprise attack of this kind would cause the loss of all United States Airplane Carriers, which is the principal objective of the Japanese High Command."

Not explained was why Molokai was chosen as the location.

112

OVERLOOKED LEAKS

From that island, however, the small submarines could just as easily reach the anchorage at Lahaina Roads. "If it can be used in Hawaii, it can be used in Santiago, Panama, and other Naval bases," McCoy in Mexico City warned.

By the time the report reached Hawaii, via Washington, newly assigned Army G-2 Lieutenant Colonel Kendall H. Fielder had written in the margin, "This is like a Rube Goldberg cartoon, hence, is of interest to read. No particular significance. Believe informer got tip on pygmy submarine and let his imagination run wild. Navy does not attach importance to theory."

Even so, Rear Admiral Bloch was directed to search the coasts of Molokai and other islands. Bloch derisively called the rumored craft "baby submarines." In October and November the neighbor island shores were scoured by Navy crews on land and in the water, and PatWing 2's PBYs shadowed the coastline at all times of day, hoping the changing light conditions would reveal the sleeping midgets.

Nothing was discovered.

And there was this top billing in a prewar intelligence bulletin: "In collaboration with German advisors, the construction of 75 submarines is projected in Japan. Shipyards in Osaka have allotted 20 of these jobs, of which the Osaka Iron Works are to build 4 …"

Then, a paragraph later, a curious statement labeled "hearsay information, given with utmost reserve." The Japanese were supposedly hiding construction of a new type of warship, using other ships to transport the new craft; "Same old hulks have been emptied of machinery and equipment, and 'pocket destroyers' are being constructed *within* them. As a further aid to secrecy, the position of these hulks are changed by towing from one place to another. This may be an exaggerated account of Japanese tendencies to secrecy, but there may be something in it, and the report is passed on for what it is worth …"

Change "pocket destroyers" to midget submarines, and "old hulk" to revamped auxiliary ship *Chiyoda*, and the report is worth something after all.

Books in prewar Japan, supposedly written under the auspices of the military government, often speculated on the probability of success of war with the United States. Many were hopeful; "When Japan Fights," by a civilian, code-named Hirata, spoke glowingly of the Imperial Navy as "a fast-stepping force that would be truly matchless and invincible."

The book rightly wondered if American commanders would be occupied by the threat of "Japanese submarines that hover near to the islands to attack or harass the Fleet … an attack off Hawaii would be the first battle of the Pacific War, and if in the very first

Col. Kendall H. Fielder, head of Army intelligence in the Territory of Hawaii.

engagement one can wrest the courage away from the enemy by one's own daring, it would put him in a funk or give him the jitters."

"When Japan Fights" made the rounds of Japanese-speaking American intelligence officers, and an English version was translated in Hawaii in 1940. An abridged version with Hawaiian highlights was in the possession of the war plans officer McMorris by October 1941.

There was enough real intelligence activity in Hawaii to keep a score of spies occupied. The FBI suspected that visiting Japanese tankers were routinely leaving personnel behind in Honolulu, who would then gather intelligence and return to Japan on the next tanker. Bloch complained to the Navy Department, which in turn leaned on the State Department to disallow such visits. The last Japanese oiler docked in Honolulu in 1940.

The Honolulu consulate of the government of Japan, above, just before it was replaced in the 1950s. At right is consulate spy Takeo Yoshikawa.

The Japanese Consulate in Honolulu had its own house spy, Ensign Takeo Yoshikawa, using the name Tadashi Morimura. Yoshikawa was not well-liked by the consulate staff, most of whom had no idea of his real function. They knew only that he arrived to work late, often took trips around the island, flirted with *geisha* and consorted with unsavory characters.

Yoshikawa was fascinated with Kailua and Waimanalo beaches on the eastern shore of Oahu, and often visited, walking up and down the sand and staring out to sea. The consulate staff also picnicked occasionally on the beach at the Lanikai home of Sam Woods. Woods wasn't home during these occasions or even aware of them; the consulate staff was invited on to the property by Woods' Japanese yardman.

Yoshikawa was ordered in late September to cut up Pearl

OVERLOOKED LEAKS

Harbor, cake-like, and keep track of which ships anchored in each slice. These zones, in the rigorous morning-after quarterbacking that followed the attack, clearly divided the harbor into zones that corresponded to particular weapons. It was a plot easy to follow if navigating around the harbor, either at sea level or just under. The significance of this "bomb plot" message, which was intercepted by American intelligence, was not appreciated until after the attack.

In mid-November, Yoshikawa was ordered to keep tabs on ships that frequented the harbor. "As relations between Japan and the United States are most critical, make your 'ships in harbor report' irregular, but at the rate of twice a week. Although you already are no doubt aware, please take extra effort to maintain secrecy," the message read.

As November slipped into December, Yoshikawa was also noting whether any barrage balloons were above the target, or planned in the near future, whether any anti-torpedo nets were strung out around the ships, or even which ships remained idle for extended periods.

Tokyo's interest in American destroyer operations grew as X-day approached. By the end of November, the consul in Honolulu was being peppered with specific requests. *Is the U.S. Navy laying mines off Pearl? How many destroyers patrol the entrance? Are there anti-mine nets?* And an urgent demand even as Kido Butai neared the jumping-off point: *What ships have moved in and out of the harbor since Dec. 4?*

This movement of ships in and out of the harbor was of particular interest. Their route charted the safe route past the choke point of the harbor entrance. In hindsight, admitted Navy intelligence officers, the Japanese were charting courses for their midget submarines. All of this was intercepted through Navy wiretaps and routed to Washington for perusal. None of it came back to Kimmel or other local commanders. At the time the consular requests were intercepted and decoded, the route charts were thought simply to be of general naval interest.

This area at the mouth of Pearl Harbor, with its assorted boat booms and harbor craft, was highly secret, and forbidden to photographers. A snapshot made by an Army sergeant of the boat boom in 1940 caused consternation all the way up to Admiral Bloch and Lieutenant General Charles Herron, who fired off memos to each other on the subject. "For your information I am enclosing a copy of our Departmental Regulations on the subject," needled Herron. "I had hoped the regulations would not be violated. Appropriate action in this case will be taken."

The hapless sergeant, resident of the post camera club, had his negative and prints of the boat boom confiscated. They were classified "Secret" until 1989.

The German connection to Honolulu spying activities was carried out over long distance. In late March 1941, a cab accidentally struck

SECRET

SECRET

The formerly secret picture of the harbor entrance boat boom, taken by an amateur photographer. The I-beams sticking up were meant to discourage fast boat attacks.

[2] *A suspicion has lingered ever since that the spy's death was engineered by the British.*

a man crossing Times Square in New York City. Another car then swerved and bounced over the body. The man never regained consciousness and died the next day. Police searched his pockets and found a passport in the name of Julio Lopez; the FBI was called in, and they grabbed the dead man's luggage from a room at the Taft Hotel. The bags revealed the dead man's name was actually Ulrich von der Osten, a Nazi Abwehr agent planted in the United States. Linked to Osten was a postcard sent from Hawaii to a mail drop in Shanghai, in Osten's writing though it was signed "Konrad," showing Diamond Head and a map of Oahu.

With the help of British Security Coordination — the BSC was Britain's overseas intelligence service — the FBI tracked down von der Osten's spy ring, certainly the largest then operating in the United States.[2] British operatives revealed that they had earlier intercepted a rather thorough defense report on Pearl Harbor, including photographs and maps, from a "Konrad" in the United States, also mailed to Shanghai. The Axis were beginning to work together; Asian faces like Yoshikawa's were denied access to Pearl Harbor, but a European would be able to walk right in.

Attempting to rebuild its U.S. spy network after Osten's death, the Nazi Abwehr assigned Yugoslavian playboy Dusko Popov to the job — his German code name was "Ivan." His code name from MI-6, the British counterintelligence corps, was "Tricycle," as he was a double agent. Popov was outfitted in the latest Abwehr

OVERLOOKED LEAKS

technology, including the microdot, which reduced a page of text to the size of a printed period. He was given two missions; rebuild von der Osten's spy ring, and, more importantly, carry out a "highest priority" mission for the Japanese.

The Japanese had prepared for Popov a detailed questionnaire about Pearl Harbor defenses, including pointed queries on "naval ammunition and mine depot on the Isle of Kushua (Ford Island). If possible, sketch ... Where is the station for mine search formations? How far has the dredger work progressed at the entrance and in the east and southeast loch? Depths of water? Exact details and sketch about the state wharf, of the pier installations, workshops, petrol installations, situation of dry dock number 1 and of the new dock which is being built."

Answers to these and other questions would greatly aid the crews of both the midget submarines and the torpedo bombers.

On his way to the United States, Popov thoughtfully left copies of the microdots with J.C. Masterman, chief of the British XX (Double Cross) Committee, and the contents were circulated by Aug. 16, 1941. Masterman's conclusion; "It is therefore surely a fair deduction that the questionnaire indicated very clearly that in the event of the United States being at war, Pearl Harbor would be the first point to be attacked, and that plans for this attack had reached an advanced state by August ... "

Another double agent, a friend of Popov's, had accompanied Japanese naval officers to Taranto, Italy, along with the German air attache assigned to Tokyo. Their goal was to examine exactly how British torpedo planes, in a swift, sneak attack, had swept into a protected harbor and decimated the Italian fleet.

Popov passed along this information to the FBI when he arrived in New York — his contact there was Special Agent Percy Foxworth, his British case worker for the BSC was a Commander Ian Fleming. Popov then waited for FBI permission to set up a phony spy system, in the meantime resuming a long-standing affair with French actress Simone Simon. When Simon left for Hollywood, the highly sexed Popov became "partial to twins, but, lacking a matched pair, often made do with a couple other accommodating ladies," recalled an FBI agent. Popov maintained the catting was good for undercover work.

Popov eventually met with FBI director J. Edgar Hoover, at the Stork Club, which they both frequented. Hoover was incensed to discover that Popov's lavish tips and enchanting female companions had made the playboy a club favorite.

Hoover told Popov that the FBI didn't need any help catching German spies. The director also seized the Abwehr funds Popov had been given to set up the spy network and threatened him with the Mann Act, as the Yugoslavian had taken an unmarried female companion on an interstate jaunt.

The British pulled Tricycle back. Popov believed that the FBI

had missed an opportunity to completely infiltrate German intelligence. The one useful result of his trip, he felt, was that the U.S. was duly warned about Japanese interest in Pearl Harbor.

Unknown to Popov, when Hoover prepared a precis of the German spy's microdot information for Roosevelt, the director withheld all references to Japanese intentions or to Pearl Harbor. The Japanese questionnaire was not made public until the mid-'70s, after Hoover's death, and even then the FBI tried to convince publishers that Popov's mission was insincere.

Looking appropriately James Bondish, Popov and his wife promote his memoir "Spy-Counterspy" in the 1970s.

The only person to gain from the incident was Commander Fleming, who later modeled his fictional spy, British Agent 007 - James Bond - on Popov's real-life adventures.

Without the needed information on Pearl Harbor coming from Popov, the Japanese turned to other Nazi sources. Working independently, but under Yoshikawa's direction, was a German "sleeper" agent named Julius "Otto" Kuehn. American intelligence had tagged Kuehn within a few years of emigrating to Hawaii. His function was to lie doggo and begin spying only after war had erupted, when, it was assumed, the consulate staff would be arrested or deported.

A sailor in the Kaiser's fleet when World War I broke out, Kuehn was captured by the British within six months. He remained in a British camp until 1918. He returned to the Kriegsmarine, married, and in 1920 inherited enough money to purchase a small sailing freighter, which he named *Antares* — a ship name that will later figure in the midget submarine assault on Pearl Harbor. He cracked up the boat and went to work for various manufacturing concerns. Hearing Adolf Hitler speak at a meeting in Kiel in 1930, Kuehn enthusiastically joined the Nazi party the same night, also enlisting his teenage son.

Soon Kuehn was running errands for the party, including making secret reports on the "immoral" activities of local police who were unsympathetic to the Nazi line. He was interviewed for a party job by Heinrich Himmler, who found Kuehn personally distasteful. Kuehn eventually went back to business in Berlin, where he had the apparent misfortune of speaking in public to Jews. Kuehn spent some weeks in a work camp, but was released because his son — by then a stormtrooper — and his wife were working for a Nazi welfare agency.

OVERLOOKED LEAKS

Rather abruptly, Kuehn announced that he was moving to Japan to study the language. He and wife Friedel traveled to the Empire, pausing briefly in Honolulu, and then moved on to Shanghai. From there Friedel went back to Germany and Kuehn returned to Honolulu, which, he later claimed, was the ideal location to study Japanese. Shanghai had a large German community.[3]

While living in Honolulu's Brooklands Hotel, Kuehn became chummy with several American submarine officers, including two lieutenants named M.G. Kennedy and W.A. New and a lieutenant commander named Edward R. Durgin. They were vying for a naval attache position in Berlin, and pressed Kuehn to teach them German. Durgin eventually got the job.

Friedel, two other sons and a daughter joined Kuehn in Hawaii in 1936, and no sooner had he settled them into a Lanikai home than he rushed back to Japan for more "language studies," staying less than two months. His Japanese studies in Hawaii were privately tutored by a Mr. Ikeno of the language school in Kailua.

The only labors performed by Kuehn in Hawaii prior to the war were at a furniture company that he owned for eight months — during which he lost $15,000 — and a six-week stint as a freight checker for Honolulu Iron Works, which he quit because the work was too hard. Friedel opened a Kailua beauty shop in 1940, and openly cultivated the wives of naval officers. The shop brought in only about $80 a month. Despite this meager income, Kuehn managed to lease several acres of land and purchase — in cash — three houses. Friedel also managed to send her son 50 marks a month through the Bishop National Bank of Honolulu. By then the young stormtropper was working for Nazi propaganda minister Josef Goebbels.

Large packages of cash arrived for Kuehn occasionally, routed through Japan. On Oct. 25, 1941, Yoshikawa personally called on Kuehn at home, handing over a cardboard box that had arrived on board *Tatuta Maru*. It contained $14,000 in $100-dollar bills, to help buy a house near the beach at Kailua where he could signal submarines.[4]

Kuehn told investigators he had first contacted the Japanese consulate in order to send money to his son in Germany, as money exchanges between Germany and America at that point were frozen. He claimed that the consul general refused unless Kuehn agreed to spy for them.

The German devised a Byzantine system for relaying information, using lights on the beach at Lanikai, just south of Kailua, sails on beached boats or arrangements of laundry on a line, all of which were supposedly visible from just offshore. His house at Lanikai had been rented to a pair of servicemen and their wives, who later stated that Kuehn had not visited prior to the attack, so it is not known if Kuehn was serious about using this site.

Kuehn also suggested using a series of short-wave radio sig-

[3] It was at this point that British overseas intelligence — MI-6 — got wind of Kuehn and alerted the FBI. Kuehn's Japanese code name was "Jimmy." The FBI's file on Kuehn stands at 683 pages and is still heavily censored, primarily to remove these early British warnings. The FBI did not begin to investigate the Kuehns until 1939, when the Germans were well established on Oahu. The Nazi connection in Hawaii is directly linked to the submarine, rather than the aerial operation.

[4] The house, with dormer windows looking toward the ocean, still stands in the Coconut Grove neighborhood of Kailua, although the ocean view has become crowded.

nals, though he didn't own such a radio. Kuehn's original system of signals was far too complicated, and Consul General Nagao Kita insisted he devise something simpler. Kuehn did this, and on Dec. 2 visited the consulate once more, carrying two envelopes; one contained an outline of the now-streamlined signals and the other contained American money for his stormtrooper son.

The simplified signals included placing broadcast want ads at 9:45 a.m. every day on radio station KGMB, a civilian radio station with enough power to be received at sea; as well as the complex series of night lights and daytime sail adjustment on a boat on the Lanikai beach. On KGMB, a Chinese rug advertised for sale, for example, meant the American battle fleet had vacated the harbor.

Should the Lanikai boat signal or the hanging laundry signal or the short-wave signal or the radio want-ad signal not pan out, Kuehn suggested a back-up. A German friend, Carl Basler of Maui, had once described vacant lots on that island that overlooked the sea. Kuehn's scheme was that a bonfire lit near Kula Sanitarium on Maui, visible from the flotilla rendezvous during certain hours, also would be effective.

Kuehn later insisted that Basler had no knowledge of these plans, and that he had not contacted anyone on Maui.

In any case, the waters off Lanikai for most of November and early December were too rough for sailing, and small boats were grounded. Kuehn would not have been able to use the sail message system without attracting the notice of neighbors.

The consulate sent out Kuehn's code to Tokyo so that it could be picked up by the I-boats. The coded radiogram was recognized as out of the ordinary by Dorothy Edgers, a research analyst in the Office of Naval Intelligence. Edgars, a 38-year-old former schoolteacher, had spent much of her life in Japan. The signal frightened her, and when Lieutenant Commander Alwin D. Kramer returned to the Cryptographic Section at 3 p.m. she rushed over and pressed it on him before he could sit down.

Edgars was surprised when Kramer seemed irritated with her for working overtime. He was trapped in the nuances of the message's writing style, and missed the evidence of heightened interest in Pearl Harbor defenses.

"This needs a lot of work, Mrs. Edgars," he said after examining the translation. "Why don't you run along now? We'll finish the editing sometime next week."

"But Commander — don't you think this intercept ought to be distributed right away?"

"You just go home, Mrs. Edgars," said Kramer. "We'll get back to this piece on Monday." The signal seemed too routine to Kramer, and over Edgar's protests, it was basketed. Unknown to Edgars, Kramer was distracted by the ominous and famous 14-part diplomatic message then rolling in.

Japanese naval intelligence also made use of alien Japanese

120

residing in Honolulu, sometimes without their knowing it. Japanese-Americans were not approached, Yoshikawa figured, correctly, that they were too Westernized. Military intelligence operatives and the newly organized Honolulu Police Department Espionage Squad began working in tandem, investigating, for example, reports made by suspicious neighbors that a Japanese family renting a Kailua house was raising pigeons.

Louis Kahanamoku of the sheriff's office of Honolulu, brother of well-known Olympic athlete Duke Kahanamoku, and a champion canoeist in his own right, reported his own encounter. In mid-1940, Kahanamoku had rented a house in Honolulu from a Dr. Tokue Takahashi, whose own home at 1385 Alewa Drive, alongside Kamehameha Schools, commanded a sideways view of Pearl Harbor and a splendid panorama of Honolulu Harbor.[5]

Takahashi approached Kahanamoku in October 1940, and asked the sheriff to take a group of Japanese naval officers out on a canoe ride among the American carriers anchored off Waikiki. The sailors were visiting from Japanese training ships *Iwate* and *Yakumo*, then in the harbor. Takahashi's houseguests on the heights included Vice Admiral Yorio Sawamoto, an old friend of Takahashi's brother, Admiral Ibo Takahashi of the Imperial Navy.[6]

American carriers often parked off Waikiki, and a destroyer was detailed to watchdog them. The anchored carriers were great tourist attractions on the beach. It was not known on shore that the big ships were bristling with manned machine guns, to defend against sabotage from sampans or other small boats.

Dr. Takahashi, a cancer specialist, was well-known in the small medical community of Honolulu prior to the war. He was president of the Japanese Medical Society. He organized a Red Cross unit and was an enthusiastic teacher of emergency first aid for Civil Defense. He often entertained visiting Japanese dignitaries in his Alewa Heights home.

Kahanamoku didn't reveal whether he performed this favor for his landlord. Takahashi, he said, was very interested in sailing and claimed to own his own yacht. A subsequent check of the berthing facilities at nearby Ala Wai harbor showed that Takahashi did indeed own a 38-foot boat, but that he was such a poor sailor "a couple of Japanese boys (had) to help him operate the boat whenever he went out."

The FBI already had an eye on Takahashi. During the 1930s, the doctor had traveled widely — and without apparent restraint — in the top-secret Mandate islands.

The interaction between Japanese NYK liners and the local community of Japanese aliens was also of interest. In 1940, the Japanese consul general and a group of apparent civilians posed pierside for a picture from an NYK liner. Their picture was also taken by a Marine photographer, an action that was noticed by the

Continued on page 124.

[5] *The house still stands, and still has a spectacular view.*

[6] *Two other Takahashi brothers also served in the Japanese military.*

THE VIEW FROM THE DOCTOR'S YARD

"As I take my pen and write, I distinctly recall in my mind all the memories of the palm trees in your yard near the beach; the native dance which I saw from the window that moonlight night …"

Also visible from the yard, across a few hundred feet of calm water, was most of the American Pacific Fleet. Imperial Navy Lieutenant Fukujiro Oshima, of cruiser Natori, wrote the words above to express his appeciation to a Japanese-American doctor who had hosted the officer at his Pearl City home.

Navy intelligence had their finger on Dr. Yokichi Uyehara for some time. A graduate of Tokyo University Medical School in 1916, he emigrated the following year, in time becoming a prosperous physician in Hawaii.

Uyehara was prominent in the Japanese plantation community of Waipahu, which rims Pearl Harbor to the west. He was known as a behind-the-scenes man, organizing, among other things, fund-raisers for politicians in Japan and festivities for Prince Takamatsu when the consort's naval squadron visited Hawaii in 1928. Uyehara's intelligence dossier rather stuffily notes how he grew rich performing illegal abortions and that he had numerous affairs with nurses in the small hospital he owned in Waipahu. None of this gossip could compare to Uyehara's choice of real estate.

In 1930, he purchased a waterfront home on Pearl City peninsula, looking directly out onto Pearl Harbor's Middle Loch and Ford Island. Uyehara's home became a regular haunt for visiting Imperial Navy officers, who would toast the emperor in the shadow of the American fleet. In addition, Uyehara's brother Shinko was a lieutenant and surgeon in the Imperial Navy, coincidentally stationed at the Naval Torpedo School in Yokosuka, home base of the midget submariners.

During the attack, the Uyeharas had a front-row seat to the furious midget sortie up the back of Ford Island, the rollover of target auxiliary Utah, and the shattering explosion when a Japanese aircraft ploughed into tender Curtiss.

When the skies were clear, Uyehara and adopted daughter Nancy Yukie Uyehara fled to the basement of his Waipahu hospital, staying there until picked up by FBI agents on Feb. 25, 1942.

They were looking for Uyehara because the doctor's name was found on Ensign Sakamaki's attack map of Pearl Harbor, penciled in at the approximate location of his home. Underneath was scrawled a phrase translated by the FBI to mean either "Enjoy the Mountains" or "Pleasant Retreat."

Sakamaki was briefed prior to launch by the gunnery officer of I-24, who had visited the doctor's house in 1939. He had suggested Uyehara's home as a place where a beached sailor might hole up.

When shown his name on the captured map, Uyehara professed surprise and "extreme nervousness," noted FBI agent Robert Shivers. It must be, the doctor said, because his house was "so famous" in the Imperial Navy.

While Shivers intimidated Uyehara, the doctor's waterfront home was scoured by the FBI. Found were calling cards from Japanese naval officers, as well that of Masao Takata, chief officer of Asama Maru, an NYK liner that routinely landed Japanese intelligence agents along its ports of call.

Also found were bundled letters from other Japanese officers reminding Uyehara of duties to his "mother country." Mixed in were a flood of notes from his mother, requesting money in

increasingly larger sums over the years. It's not known if the escalating matriarchal requests for funds were code for something else. During his initial interrogation, Uyehara didn't know where his mother lived, or if she was still alive. The doctor also revealed that he had another brother, Kashin, with whom he had lost contact. Kashin Uyehara, in fact, was a taxi driver in nearby Honolulu.

Little else seemed suspicious about Dr. Uyehara. He didn't belong to any Japanese organizations; he enjoyed a degree of professional respect from other Hawaii doctors, and he sent his daughter Nancy to a largely white private school called Punahou — instead of the suspect Japanese language academies. Still, Uyehara was interned for the duration.

The conclusions of District Intelligence officer Captain I.H. Mayfield noted that Uyehara was to be considered "dangerous to the internal security of the United States."

In the FBI-solicited opinion of Hans L'Orange, manager of Oahu Sugar Company and a Waipahu resident who had known Uyehara for two decades, the "subject is queer and not a person to be trusted in this emergency."

In the photograph above, Dr. Yokichi Uyehara, in ceremonial kimono, welcomes four unidentified Imperial Navy officers to the waterfront of his Pearl City home, October 1939. Also enjoying the view of the American fleet is Reverend Chiro Yosemori, priest of the Jikoyen Buddhist temple in Honolulu, and Shigeki Narahara, a clerk at Iida's, a well-known Japanese-goods shop in Honolulu. Yosemori later led two tour groups to Japan in 1941, and Narahara was discovered hiding a Roman candle under his bed after the Pearl Harbor attack.

Japanese. A scuffle ensued as the Japanese tried to grab the American's film. Even when the group was moved to the Honolulu police station, the consul general demanded the film, which was not handed over.[7]

[7] See picture on page 17.

The movie "Hell Below" was re-released at this time in response to growing war tensions. Filmed in 1933 on location in Hawaii, the Robert Montgomery action film focused on a fleet of American submarines based in Taranto Harbor during World War I. The film-makers decided that the closest double for the Italian port was Pearl Harbor, and the conclusion of the film featured a "suicide sub" attack against an enemy harbor with a narrow throat. Although the film played in Honolulu, no one in the military drew any comparisons between Pearl Harbor and Taranto.

By the fall of 1941, the Honolulu waterfront was a place of great tension. On Sept. 22, Army Air Corps Lieutenant Martin R. Connolly, on his way home from duty in the Philippines, got into an argument with customs guard John K. Yeung over a packet of photographs. Yeung settled the dispute by drawing his pistol and shooting Connolly to death. Customs collector Warde C. Hibberly later declared the incident "occurred in the line of duty."

A surreptitiously taken snapshot of liner Taiyo Maru *docked in Honolulu, Nov. 5, 1941.*

Mail going onto NYK ships for Japan was inspected, and the Japanese consulate was concerned. Only first-class mail was being examined, however, and soon the volume of parcel-post mail from the consulate increased.

The behavior of NYK liners, always of interest to American Intelligence officers, grew more bizarre during the summer of 1941. *Asama Maru,* for example, steaming for Honolulu in late July, allowed her passengers to receive radiograms, but not to send them. The entire ship was under strict radio discipline; no passengers were allowed to listen to radios in the lounges. On July 23, the ship turned tail and headed west; the next day she steamed north until reaching a fog bank along the 180th meridian; there *Asama Maru* hove to and huddled in the fog until the evening of July 26, at which time the liner's funnels were painted overall black and Japanese flags on the hull and deck were painted over.

Now incognito, *Asama Maru* headed toward Honolulu for 12 hours, then a notice was posted stating the ship was ordered back to Yokohama. Once again the liner headed west, but during the night of July 27, the ship reversed course and the notice disappeared. *Asama Maru* arrived in Honolulu on July 31 and discharged her befuddled passengers.

The last NYK liner to dock in Honolulu was *Taiyo Maru,* which contained the Imperial Navy submarine experts Maejima and Matsuo. Passengers arriving in *Taiyo Maru* were debriefed in a circumspect manner by Army Intelligence operatives. The majority of passengers getting off the ship in Honolulu that first week of

OVERLOOKED LEAKS

November were "local people" returning from Japan, read an Army report, and "every single one of the returning people was very glad to come back here and they were all determined to live here permanently." Hawaii-born Japanese were particularly angry over NYK regulations that prevented them from sailing with more than 10 yen in spending money. Residents of Japan were allowed as much yen as they could carry.

Those boarding the ship were inspected, and interestingly, nearly every one of the 350 families sailing for Japan was packing one or two brand-new Singer sewing machines. The only other luggage of note was that of Buddhist priest Katsuto Takumyo, whose bags bulged with a massive collection of "obscene pictures." It is not known if they were confiscated.

Movements of ships in general in the Pacific were largely a mystery during this time of increasing tension. In response, a group of Navy Intelligence officers, commanded by Commander Joseph Rochefort, set up shop in an air-conditioned basement at Pearl Harbor and devoted themselves to sniffing out the Japanese war machine. Using codes, radio signals, shipping schedules and first-hand intelligence, they made themselves invaluable.

They called themselves the Combat Intelligence Unit as a cover name, to dissuade questions. "It was a case of the tail wagging the dog, but it worked," wrote then-Lieutenant Wilfred J. Holmes, an analyst with the outfit, and an ex-submariner. "It met the need for an overt name that gave no clue to the real activity."

One of their tasks was to keep track of warships, and until this point, the Combat Intelligence Unit had managed to keep a handle on the Japanese submarines. They tailed Vice Admiral Mitsumi

Americans of Japanese descent began to quickly return from visits to Japan in the fall of 1941. Here, passengers from Tatuta Maru fill out papers as they disembark in Honolulu on Oct. 23.

Shimizu to the Marshalls, and reported a general eastward movement of the submarines. "We had located them in a negative sense," Rochefort explained later. "We had lost them. We did not know where they were." They only knew where they weren't.

This was set aside while intelligence operatives scrambled to find six missing Japanese carriers and their support ships, a peculiar mystery that had Admiral Kimmel concerned. "It became apparent to us that something was afoot," said Rochefort, in characteristic understatement.

The Japanese signal code was changed at the beginning of November and again at the beginning of December, a too-rapid shift that looked suspicious to Kimmel's intelligence head Lieutenant Commander Layton, who wrote in the daily summary to the admiral that the change was one of many "progressive steps in preparing for active operations on a large scale." The admiral circled the sentence, asked Layton to prepare a map showing locations of each Japanese ship.

When Layton showed up the next day with the map, Kimmel pointed out that the carriers were missing. Layton said they were probably in home waters. Maybe. "What? Do you mean they could be rounding Diamond Head and you wouldn't know it?" joked Kimmel.

Another American intelligence officer, University of Hawaii engineering professor Wilfred "Jasper" Holmes, wrote a variety of what-if military stories under the pseudonym Alec Hudson. The jacket of this prewar book accurately depicts an anti-submarine attack against a vaguely Japanese-appearing I-boat.

But no additional action was taken. When the carriers had disappeared before, it usually indicated they were inactive.

Some actions had been taken in the past based on signals intelligence. In September 1941, Bloch suggested that PBYs be sent as far west as possible, on a line running "betwixt Oahu and Jaluit," in an attempt to flush out I-boats operating in the area. He'd been tipped off by intelligence analysis of radio traffic that something might be brewing in the area. That far at sea, he reasoned, away from port, the two bristling powers would simply eye each other, and circle warily. The flights, however, discovered nothing, and were discontinued to concentrate on the Hawaii frontier.

Only one operation based on intelligence information took place north of Oahu during November. It was very intrusive, at night in blackout conditions. A destroyer was sent to stealthily prowl the north shore of Oahu, specifically trying to surprise Japanese submarines lurking there, perhaps even catching one in the act of signaling ashore.

By Dec. 1, the daily summary to Kimmel stated that a "large number of submarines believed to be east of Yokosuka-Chichijima and Saipan ..." The progress of the commander of the Imperial

126 **OVERLOOKED LEAKS**

submarine force from Japan to Chichijima to Saipan was tracked, as was his close radio association with Jaluit. A "large unit" of submarines also had seemed to arrive in the Marshalls; the Hawaii-based radio decipherers concluded that Imperial submarines were nesting in the area, a position contrary to Cam-16, the West Coast traffic analysis branch; "Every evidence points to a concentration, not only the small Fourth Fleet submarines there, but also a good proportion of the Fleet submarines of the Submarine Force." Kimmel and McMorris initialed this summary.

U.S. Fleet intelligence officer Lieutenant Commander Edwin Layton.

Other Imperial submarines were spotted on the move. A patrol plane saw nine heading south in the China Sea between Vietnam and the Philippines, and three others near Saigon.

In the meantime, destroyer crews were continuing to hear underwater echoes of a suspicious nature. A month before Dec. 7, the destroyer security patrol was ordered to have all guns loaded; shortly afterward the guns were ordered unloaded but the ammunition stowed nearby.

Sometime in the middle of November, at an engagement party for a fellow officer at Pearl Harbor, U.S. Navy intelligence expert Lieutenant (j.g) Forrest R. Biard was approached by an officer he didn't know, a scholarly looking man with steel-rimmed glasses.

"Hi," the fellow said, offering his hand. "Bill Outerbridge. I hear you're an expert on the Japanese Navy."

Biard sipped his drink. He had left the language school in Japan just a month previously, and regarded Outerbridge coolly.

"I just want an opinion," said Outerbridge, a little flustered at this breach of protocol. "I'm due to take command of a destroyer in a couple of weeks. We're going to be patrolling the entrance of Pearl. If we spot a Jap sub, what do think we ought to do?"

"Well, if he's in that close, he's up to no good," said Biard. "I don't care if he's a Jap or not — I'd sink the son of a bitch."

"Thanks," said Outerbridge. "That would have been my first reaction too."

9 | ACROSS THE PACIFIC

The Wolves Scent the Prey

Despite hints provided by intelligence sources, the overwhelming nature of the Advance Force's planned assault on the Pacific Fleet was not suspected by the Americans. More than 30 of the Imperial Navy's most advanced submarines, including the five midget craft, were thrown into Yamamoto's gamble. It was a sizable portion of the fleet, including many submarines not known to be on active duty. Four of the submarines were completed only days before they sailed into battle.

Within 24 hours of Vice Admiral Mitsumi Shimizu's briefing of his submarine squadron commanders on board *Natori*, the 3rd Submarine Squadron under Rear Admiral Shigeyoshi Miwa slipped out of Saeki into the Pacific. These nine submarines were older models and would have to refuel in the Marshalls. The time was 11:11, on the 11th day of the 11th month in the year 1 in the Japanese calendar.

Miwa was considered capable, but also very careful of political ramifications. He was the natural choice to lead the first wave of Japanese warships toward Pearl Harbor.

Sailing from Kwajalein, between Johnston and Palmyra atolls, Miwa headed for Oahu. *I-72* and *I-73* were to spy on Lahaina Roads, keeping tabs on the sheltered anchorage as well as the west coast of Maui and the east coast of Lanai. All intelligence was to be held until the day before the attack, giving Nagumo time to switch attack plans.

I-74 was to cruise off Niihau looking for downed airmen.

The others were to ring Oahu.

In Tokyo that day, the rest of the Combined Fleet began to gear up for the attack, the first major use of Japanese sea power since the Russo-Japanese War. Yamamoto, who had two fingers blown off in that conflict, presented himself to subordinates as pleasantly composed. But he feared the upcoming conflict would destroy Japan. During a quiet moment in the early morning, he wrote his friend Rear Admiral Teikichi Hori: "What a strange position I find myself in — having to pursue with full determination a course of action

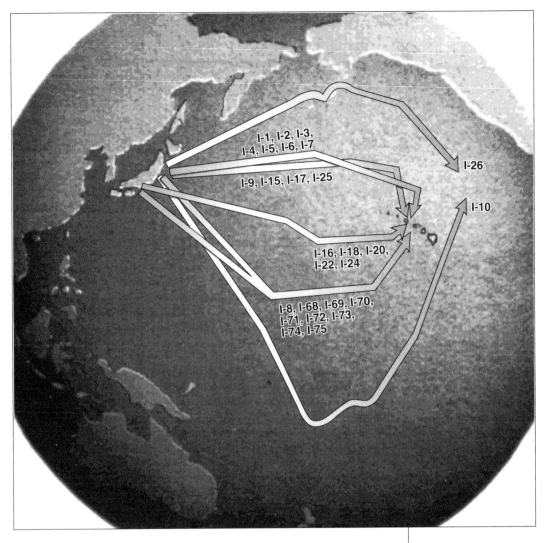

which is diametrically opposed to my best judgment and firmest conviction. That, too, perhaps, is fate ..."

He left by train later that morning for a series of briefings at the top-secret naval base at Yokosuka, where the submarines were converging.

At the base the next day, Nov. 12, Yamamoto was packing up to head for his flagship when Shimizu showed up to discuss in private the submarine portion of the attack. Yamamoto still was not convinced the midget submarine crews could be rescued from Pearl.

"You must feel free to cancel your portion of the operation," he said to Shimizu. "It may be suicidal."

"I haven't decided," said Shimizu. "I shall have to discuss this with the crewmen."

On Nov. 14, Captain Takayasu Arima hustled down from Tokyo, bearing second thoughts from Yamamoto. Arima, the torpedo staff officer at Combined Fleet Headquarters, wanted it

Including the five midget submarines, 35 I-boats comprised the Advance Force. I-10 and I-26 reconnoitered the north and south Pacific and were stationed northeast of Hawaii, and I-19, I-21 and I-23 were assigned to the Kido Butai task force.

positively understood that no midgets were to force their way into Pearl Harbor. Unless they could slip in quietly, they were ordered to abandoned the penetration and return to the pick-up point. "We don't want to lose the element of surprise," insisted Arima. And there was one more order from Yamamoto; no effort was to be spared in rescuing the midgetmen after the attack.

That day, Shimizu saw the "tubes" for the first time at Kure. Early the next morning, he ordered the crews to the private rooms of Naval Command.

They stood at attention and Ensign Kazuo Sakamaki wondered why the room was so cold. Shimizu appeared and stood before them, taking in their faces. He had a sheaf of papers in his hand.

"These are the orders from the headquarters of the General Staff of the Imperial Navy," he barked suddenly. "You are herewith directed to take positions of readiness for war with the United States of America."

Sakamaki was astonished, the words washing over him "like a sudden magic blow." The chill in the room evaporated, replaced by something raw and grim.

Shimizu handed each officer a copy of the orders. This was considered a great honor, and the midget officers beamed with fierce joy.

Shimizu then explained the plan as the officers stood at attention. Edging as close as possible to the mouth of Pearl, the midgets would be cut loose from the mother ships on the eve of "X-Day." They would enter the harbor by night, well before the air attack, fix their location and settle into Pearl Harbor's mucky bottom. They were not to rise and fire until sunset, long after the attack. The idea was to give them a chance to escape, however slim.

Lieutenant Naoji Iwasa, leader of the midgets, rose to his feet and objected. "I request permission to attack immediately after the air attack," he said. "To remain underwater for so long might be more dangerous. We might also get more effective results while the enemy is confused."

Shimizu refused. Daytime was too dangerous, particularly since the Americans would be both enraged and trigger-happy.

Iwasa persisted, and the other midget submariners stood behind him. "Maximum damage to the enemy is what counts, not our survival," they chorused.

Shimizu's heart pounded at this display of fighting spirit. "I agree," he said. He stared at their young, shining faces. He felt the attack would be a success. *The admiral would be proud.*

Still, he cautioned. "One mistake on the part of any one of you may be fatal to us all — the Sixth Fleet, the navy itself, and the whole country," Shimizu said. "I trust in your loyalty and ability. Best of luck to you! And now — will you meet me in the club for lunch?"

At the officers' club called Suikosha, many loud toasts were exchanged, to a smashing victory of an unspecific nature.

The 2nd Submarine Squadron (of 6th Fleet) left Yokosuka on Nov. 16, commanded by Rear Admiral Shigeki Yamasaki, a submariner since 1917. His obsolete subs dated to the '20s and Yokosuka had barely managed to make them operational in time. They were to sail northwest, above Midway, scouting for the enemy, and then approach Pearl from the north.

In the target zone, the 2nd would string a picket line between Kauai and Molokai, with Oahu plugging the middle.

Later that day, *I-10* left Yokosuka alone, commanded by Yasuchika Kayahara. He was to cruise to the Fiji islands, peep at Suva Harbor, note what was afoot there and then proceed to Samoa, Christmas Island and past the Hawaiian Islands to a point 900 nautical miles southwest of San Francisco. If he saw a ship in that area, he was to shadow it until X-Day before sinking it. If he spotted any crippled ships steaming for the repair shops at San Diego, he was to administer a *coup de grace* with torpedoes.

In Fiji, Kayahara sighted U.S. heavy cruiser *Astoria*. Since the American ship appeared to be making a solitary patrol, the submarine noted her position and gave her a wide berth.

As soon as *Taiyo Maru* returned from Honolulu, submarine experts Commander Toshihide Maejima and Lieutenant Keiu Matsuo left the ship to report on what they had seen in the enemy port. At intelligence briefings in Tokyo on Nov. 16, Maejima objected to the many problems the midget submarines would cause. It was far too risky to launch them close to the mouth of Pearl Harbor, he declared. Anti-submarine nets could close the harbor in moments, and there was the risk of detection. The midgets would have to use extreme care, otherwise the entire attack could be jeopardized. Matsuo, trained in midget submarine tactics, disagreed, but not strongly.

Operations chief Captain Sadatoshi Tomioka thanked Maejima and speculated that the Pearl Harbor plan "remained at best a gambler's move."

Afterward, on Nov. 17, Maejima went to Yokosuka to talk to the submariners. Then, with Matsuo in tow, he hurried to Kure to lecture the Special Attack Unit midgets on how to find Pearl Harbor's mouth (difficult), the transparency of the water (not very), and American anti-submarine tactics (skilled).

Matsuo wanted to participate as a midget skipper, and was disappointed at being left out. The force was to leave the next day and there was no time for training. Shimizu, recognizing Matsuo's recent intelligence prowess concerning Oahu, told Sasaki to take him in *I-22*, the squadron flagship. At the Kure Naval Club, the officers of the 1st Submarine Squadron were briefed on their destination.

Pearl Harbor. They had also never heard of or seen midget subs before this moment. Deployment was the next day.

The modified mother subs left Kure that day for Kamekakubi, where the midget submarines were loaded aboard in the early

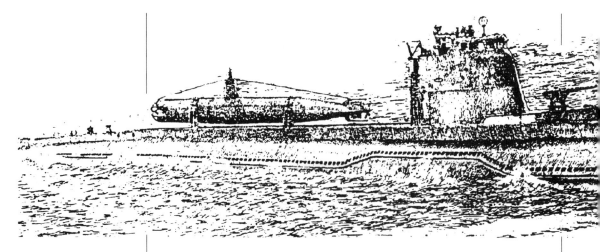

morning. The midgets rested directly abaft of the conning tower, strapped on papoose-style with steel belts. A telephone line from the midget's conning tower connected the two boats.

All five of the mother submarines were of the Cl class, recently completed and with new crews. *I-24,* the submarine to which Sakamaki's midget was strapped, had been completed only on Oct. 31, and her first war patrol was also her shakedown cruise.

Midget submarine officer Sakamaki and midget crewman Kiyoshi Inagaki were posted to the crew of *I-24* just before departure, as well as two midget technicians. None of the petty officers on the midgets knew the plan before departure. Mochitsura Hashimoto remembered them as being very confident. The torpedo officer was one of the few in *I-24* who had seen actual warfare, and had witnessed the accidental bombing of American gunboat *Panay* a few years before. Hashimoto was more worried than the midget submariners. He noted in his diary, "I saw the craft for the first time at Kure and had no chance of learning anything about its construction." He had been curious ever since seeing the cradle attached to *I-24's* aft deck.

For an hour, while Hashimoto watched, Sakamaki charged batteries on the midget while in harbor. It contained 192 trays of two cells each, with a total weight 33,600 pounds. The electrolyte was a solution of sulfuric acid.

In the cooling evening that day, Sakamaki strolled arm-in-arm through the shops near Kure with old friend and fellow midget skipper Akira Hiro-o. "This is our last night in Japan, Ensign," remarked Sakamaki.

"You are right," said Hiro-o, sobered. "When we go, we cannot expect to return."

They stopped at a novelty shop, where each bought a bottle of perfume to douse themselves with before going into battle. It was a samurai tradition to die gloriously while clean and scented, "like cherry blossoms falling to the ground."

Midget submariner Sadamu Uyeda, before leaving, stashed his

ACROSS THE PACIFIC

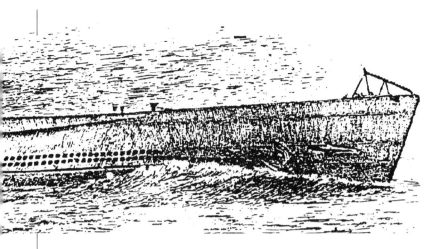

A sketch from a scrapbook of the Japanese Midget Submariners Association shows how the midget craft were attached to the mother submarines.

possessions at Kenji Yamane's flower shop in Kure; one trunk and one suitcase.

About this time Captain Kijiro Imaizumi was told verbally by Commander Ryunosuke Ariizumi of the Naval General Staff to speed the three submarines under his command to Hitokappu Bay, there to receive secret orders. Puzzled at this breach of naval etiquette and the odd order, Imaizumi left. *I-19, I-21* and *I-23* were considered a special group, so Imaizumi had not attended the Nov. 10 briefing of the 6th Fleet sub commanders.

These three submarines were assigned to the carrier battle group, forming a skirmish line 50 miles ahead of the main body as it stole quietly through the North Pacific. Their mission, in addition to scenting American forces in the path of the strike force, was to aid in rescuing downed pilots and to defend the fragile carriers from U.S. counterattacks.

During the day of Nov. 18, Sakamaki completed charging the midget's batteries. It was his birthday. He wrote a note to his parents. "I am now leaving," he lettered formally. "I owe you, my parents, a debt I shall never be able to repay. Whatever may happen to me, it is in the service of our country that I go. Words cannot express my gratitude for the privilege of fighting for the cause of peace and justice."

As he posted the letter, Sakamaki felt his ties to the world of the living break away. I am already buried, he thought, and the idea settled comfortably in his soul.

That moonless night, the Special Attack Unit submarines took off one by one, gliding into the dark waters like humpbacked wraiths. There were no cheering crowds to see the submariners off to war. Only the crews of training craft doffed their caps as the submarines slipped away.

The five submarines bearing midgets left Kure for the Pacific Ocean, passing single-file through Bungo Strait. Sakamaki stood on the deck of *I-24,* hating the feeling of salt in his eyes. "Goodbye, Japan," he whispered.

A submarine of the I-76 class sets off on a mission during wartime. The I-76 and the I-16 mother submarines were both variations of the KD6 design and were virtually identical. Note the flat, open area aft of the sail, where the midget submarines were tethered. The I-76s were primarily used for cargo runs.

I-22 was the last to leave, at midnight. In the early morning it passed the hulking shadows of the Combined Fleet.

Rear Admiral Matome Ugaki, chief of staff of the fleet, saw something odd in the water as he leaned against battleship *Nagato's* rail. "On our way out of Saeki Bay, we saw a queerly shaped submarine with no marks, heading south," he wrote in his diary. "It proved to be *I-22*, flagship of the 3rd Submarine Division, which had a midget submarine aboard ..."

Nagato challenged the odd shape, and *I-22* blinked back a reply.

Yamamoto's flagship then signaled, *Congratulations in advance on your success.*

Sasaki blinked, *I swear to be successful!*

Ugaki was impressed. He recorded:

"A surprise attack on X-day will be an entirely unexpected storm. How much damage they will be able to inflict is not the point. The firm determination not to return alive on the part of these young lieutenants and ensigns who smilingly embarked on their ships cannot be praised too much. The spirit of *kesshitai* (self-sacrifice) has not changed at all. We can fully rely on them."

The lights of a merchant ship paralleled them for awhile; the submarines sprinted ahead with the decks awash, hiding their cargo. In the morning, the ship was revealed to be a carrier. The submarines came to the surface, where they could make better speed, and began the dash to Hawaii, taking a dangerously direct route between Johnston and Howland islands. The other ships had already left.

The crew was new in *I-24*, and the skipper, Captain Hiroshi Hanabusa, drilled them relentlessly. Soon, diving stations were manned quickly. Lookouts were instructed to watch for "enemy detection devices," though further elaboration wasn't provided. Radar was still science-fiction technology.

The five I-boats spread out 20 miles apart, traveling on the surface until they reached the American patrol zones around Wake Island. They were under strict radio silence, but lined up so they could close up for blinker signals.

From that point on, they sailed submerged by day. The long periods underwater prepared the freshman crew for submarine life. The air grew foul and hot, making the crewmen sleepy and irritable. On the surface at night, the midget crews climbed all over the small subs, checking every detail. Sakamaki was washed overboard twice as he enthusiastically ran on *I-24's* deck. He was hauled back on board, smiling on his safety line.

On Nov. 19, *I-26* left Yokosuka, under Commander Minoru Yokota, to scout Kiska and Adak in the Aleutians, keeping any naval forces he ran across under observation. If nothing turned up, he was to proceed to Hawaiian shipping lanes and lie in wait.

I-26 was brand new, having been hastily completed on Nov. 6. Though Yokota had leagues of undersea service, he needed all his training and experience, because he didn't learn of the attack until a few days before setting sail in an unfamiliar and totally untested boat. *I-26* had a hangar for a fold-up reconnaissance aircraft, though she used the space to stock up on extra fuel and food.

Yokota had qualified to command submarines five years before, after returning from a trip to the West Coast of the United States as navigator on a Japanese tanker. He had fond memories of a stopover in Hawaii, watching Hilo schoolchildren walking to class with their shoes slung over their shoulders.

I-25 of the same class did have her aircraft aboard, a fold-up seaplane built by the secret naval factory at Yokosuka and numbered E14Yl, later dubbed "Glenn" by the Allies. *I-25's* mission was to provide overflights with the aircraft from a station about 100 miles northeast of Oahu. On the voyage there, Flying Officer Nobuo Fujita and crewman Petty Officer Shoji Okuda heard thumping noises coming from hangar deck as the sub ploughed through rough seas. When the sub surfaced at night to charge its batteries, Fujita checked the hangar and was furious to discover the plane damaged beyond repair.

On Nov. 20, Imaizumi's three reconnaissance submarines set sail from Hitokappu Bay, heralding the exodus of Yamamoto's strike force. Already far from the home islands, the special unit with the midget submarines was enjoying clear weather. Sakamaki convinced *I-24's* skipper to allow him to give the batteries another squirt for an hour, just before dawn. By this point, Sakamaki's midget was already known as *I-24tou*.

On board *I-15*, stilled moored in Yokosuka, Commander Nobuo Ishikawa sought out Executive Officer Zenji Orita on the morning of Nov. 21. "We will sail this evening," said Ishikawa. "Get her ready for sea."

"Where are we going, Skipper?" Orita asked.

Ishikawa scowled and said he'd reveal that when they were away. "I will tell all hands once we are clear of land," he said, tensely. Ishikawa then went to a final briefing on board *Katori*.

As a drizzling afternoon rain turned the naval base pine trees into silent sentinels, Rear Admiral Tsutomu Sato left Yokosuka with the last four submarines; *I-9, I-15, I-17* and *I-25*. Last-minute, vital repairs had kept his subs high and dry, and the 1st Submarine Squadron had to hustle to catch up with the 2nd Submarine Division, headed for the open sea between Midway and the Aleutian chain of islands.

Last in, first out. Shimizu's submarines, included in the attack plan at the last moment, were already on their way to battle while the important carriers loafed in Hitokappu.

As Sato disappeared into the misting rains, Shimizu returned to flagship *Katori*. The ship headed for Truk in the Carolines, where it was to lay low until Dec. 2, when it would head to Kwajalein.

In the fold of twilight, as *I-15* moved away from Oshima island, the trailing plume of Mount Mihara was lost in the glimmering distance. Orita gathered all hands on deck, aft of the conning tower, and was himself as curious as the rest of the crew.

"*I-15* is now beginning her first war mission," Ishikawa announced. "Our station has been established at a point 40 miles north of Pearl Harbor in the Hawaiian Islands. We will arrive there on December 7 (Tokyo time). Unless there is a drastic change in the international situation, Japan will go to war the following day against the Americans, British and Dutch. A great attack will be made on Pearl Harbor. I hope that you will, under my command, do your best, and show the skills you have trained so hard to acquire these last months and years. I hope that what you will achieve a glorious name for *I-15!*"

There was a brief cheer, and the men filed quietly off the deck and below. *I-15* had provisions for 90 days, gathered during three days of quick activity. The entire deck space except for the diesel engine room was covered knee-deep with containers of food.

"It looked like our crewmen were living in a tubular food warehouse," Orita wrote later. "Especially crammed was the torpedo room, near the bow, with a full wartime load of 20 Mk. 95 torpedoes, fantastic weapons that could make nearly 50 knots en route to target. Men in that compartment not only had a two-foot-thick floor of food, but had to squeeze between it and the 'steel fish' in order to get needed rest …"

Already far ahead, the Special Attack Unit of the 1st Division spent its time fine-tuning the midgets. On Nov. 22, after a couple

of days of clean-up aboard the mother submarine, Sakamaki climbed into *I-24tou* and was distressed to find seawater sloshing about the deck. He bailed it out and unsuccessfully hunted for leak. He re-oiled the propeller shaft. The next day, more water was found.

Away from Japan, Sato's squadron sailed right into a storm that completely covered their movements; they were able to proceed on the surface by day. *I-15* struggled through the mountainous troughs, and Orita looked up in fear at the thrashing crests high above the bridge. The waves thundered down on the black craft. Spuming water scoured the open bridge, and Orita clung to the compass to prevent being washed overboard.

At night, with black-out conditions in effect, the submariners fought against fear of the unknown as well as cold and fatigue. "All hands fell into a state of near-exhaustion, both mental and physical," wrote Orita. "With the massive load we carried, *I-15* had only slightly positive buoyancy. This would prove advantageous should we need to submerge quickly, but it made for sluggish movement along the ocean's surface …"

The men below suffered as well. When the giant waves smashed across the submarines, a large induction valve set on the conning tower would slam shut. As this was the only air supply to the straining diesel engines, the engines would get their air from somewhere else — the submarine's interior. With these rapid fluctuations in internal air pressure, the crews' eardrums vibrated like tympanis and gave them searing ear pains, so bad many dropped to the deck gasping.

The waves also forced exhaust gases back into the engine compartment, filling it with reeking fumes and rattling, popping noises. "It's a wonder (the engineers) could go about their duties," noted Orita.

On Nov. 26, all submarines received word that negotiations with the U.S. were considered hopeless, and the latest intelligence estimates on the ships in Pearl: two battleships. The crews were disappointed.

The weather improved as Sato's squadron headed east. The other I-boats, far ahead, were in considerably rougher seas. Iwasa was nearly lost overboard. Running out on deck without a lifeline one night, he was swept yowling down the deck by a foaming comber. The midget submarine leader grabbed one of the mounting racks, "by pure luck," and hung on. Captain Sasaki forebade him to show his face on deck again until the launch point had been reached.

Torpedo tests were carried out, one of which involved sliding the fish in and out of their slippery tubes while the I-boat crash-dived. Working with the heavy torpedoes as the slippery deck canted was dangerous. On *I-24*, Hashimoto took his customary position next to the watch officer in the control room, and ordered the maneuver. *I-24* took on water and began plunging into the ocean. The submarine didn't stop when cruising depth was reached.

"Blow the forward trimming tanks!" shouted the navigator. This was done, and the tank pumps cranked up, but still the submarine sank into the sea. The navigator tried a burst of speed, hoping to use the dive planes to "fly" up into shallow water. It was too late. Hashimoto raced forward in the submarine and discovered that the trimming tank blow valve was jammed. It was a J-shaped pipe with a wheel attached. Hashimoto tugged at the wheel, failed to move it, attacked it with a huge wrench.

At last it unfroze, and the submarine leveled off just under 300 feet down, just about at the ship's maximum design depth. Air flowed into the trim tanks, and *I-24* ascended. She broke the surface, and the submarine's trim was accurately adjusted.

It had been a near thing. A block of wood, left behind by a careless ship-fitter, was discovered jammed inside the valve. Hashimoto reflected that their mission must be important — the Imperial Navy was simply hoping for the best by sending out an untested ship.

Built for shallow running, one of midget submarine *I-24tou's* torpedo tubes was damaged by the sudden descent. The torpedo was crushed and jammed in the tube. At sunset, Hashimoto mustered a crew topside, drawing the damaged torpedo out of the tube and tossing it over the side.

That was the easy part. Another torpedo was brought up from below, pulled through the narrow torpedo hatch on the forward deck of *I-24*, an operation normally carried out in the still waters of a harbor. In the heaving seas, wrestling a high-explosive torpedo that weighed more than a ton across a narrow, slippery deck was a frightening proposition. Hashimoto took it slowly, walking the fish down to *I-24's* stern, where it was inserted into the midget. It was dawn before they were finished, and the sailors tumbled into their racks exhausted, lulled by the fetid air in the submarine.

On Nov. 30, the first submarine-launched reconnaissance flight of the war was over Suva Bay. Taking off from *I-10*, the plane did not return.

On Dec. 2, Yamamoto radioed the ships a code message: *Climb Mount Niitaka.*

Translated, it meant simply that the attack day was to be the same as the declaration-of-war day, Dec. 7, Hawaii time. Orita surveyed the message and knew there was more to it than that. Mount Niitaka, in Taiwan, was the highest point in the Japanese empire, higher even than Mt. Fuji. Yamamoto was urging all of his fighting men to strive toward heaven.

There was no turning back.

The arrow is loosed from the bow, thought Orita. *The arrow is loosed from the bow!*

Word was received later that day that the number of battleships had grown to eight, and the the I-boat crews were jubilant. It was nearly every battleship in the U.S. Pacific Fleet. The day's messages

138

ACROSS THE PACIFIC

also fixed the time of the attack at 8 a.m. The midgets would have to be launched the night before to avoid tipping off the Americans.

Sakamaki fiddled with I-*24tou* for the first few days of December. Every night it seemed that something new needed to be tested or fixed. He tested the periscope, noting that the electric motor noise was loud, and it took nine to 10 seconds to raise and lower the small periscope, quite slow compared to larger submarines. He got the radio ready, loaded on a small battery and examined the torpedo charging control. The flasks for the torpedoes needed to be charged, as did the oxygen bottles.

On Dec. 5, Sakamaki and Inagaki loaded on goods and adjusted the radio. A couple of holding bands were disassembled, leaving *I-24tou* with just a pair fore and aft attaching it to the mother submarine. The Special Attack Unit was within 100 nautical miles of Pearl Harbor. The midgets were given a final check that evening and the mother submarines redeployed themselves in a fan-shaped formation, the same arc that they traveled in across the Pacific. They began to creep toward Pearl, getting within 10 nautical miles of the harbor by daybreak. They settled in to wait.

Lights from the new Hickam airfield were plainly visible, and music drifted across the water from Waikiki hotels. The submarine gunnery officer, who had reconnoitered Pearl Harbor from a Japanese-American doctor's house on Pearl City peninsula the year before, briefed Sakamaki and Inagaki on naval yard landmarks. The pair seemed charged, almost buoyant, noticed Hashimoto. Too confident. They barely listened to the gunnery officer.

Sakamaki turned on the submarine radio, and American jazz music spilled out.

Inside an I-76 class *I-boat. Not enough detail is visible, though the two crewmen appear to be trimming the boat. The exposed ribs overhead are coated with sound-proof paint.*

"This must be from Honolulu," he said to Inagaki.

"Yes sir."

"This means we are in enemy water now."

"Yes sir."

The music was happy, not what Sakamaki expected of the enemy. It gave him a queer feeling. Inagaki seemed unconcerned.

As the submarines moved into position, the midget submariners began to talk and joke almost constantly. They tried to give every sign that the mission was no more complicated than a simple training outing. One midget commander kept fondling his pistol, telling his mates that after his submarine had fired her torpedoes, he intended to dock in Pearl Harbor, leap out and let fly with the pistol. Another put on clean underwear and his regulation uniform, and wistfully remarked that he wished he could go in his working clothes instead. It was just too hot for uniforms.

Advised by shipmates to keep an eye out for American depth charges, one midget crewman laughed and retorted, "We'll tear a big hole in the side of an enemy ship before we are attacked!" He then began to compose poetry on the spot; *"Roosevelt whined when he heard the news. And I heard his lamentations in the court of Hades,"* which set off the submariners in fits of laughter.

Hiro-o said to others staying behind, "The ice cream in Honolulu is especially fine. I will bring you some when I come back."

They laughed. "No, really," said Hiro-o. "I'm looking forward to landing on Oahu. I promise the Americans some hot action with my sword!" He whirled about, demonstrating, like a child at play.

After the Friday evening passed beyond midnight, the mother submarines came quietly to the surface. The midget crews and technicians dropped onto deck to finish preparing the torpedo tubes. The crews got into the midget submarines and sealed the hatch, the mother submarines then submerging slightly so that the midgets could test their steering mechanisms.

Back on the surface, the crews set the torpedo tubes' gyros and depth-setting spindles, with simultaneous settings by linkage to the control rooms. The torpedoes were set for five meters of depth; zero degrees gyro angles. The net dodgers, a cable running from bow and stern to the conning tower, were rigged and tightened. Battery power was checked at eight locations within the midget. As Sakamaki moved back aboard *I-24*, towering waves began to bracket the submarine, and the boat submerged into serene depths.

Sakamaki then prepared the supplies to be taken aboard the midget. A stop watch. A pistol. A sword. Two mirrors, for signaling. Cigarettes and matches. A bag of tools. Two electric lights. A duffel bag containing wool blankets. Life preservers. There were no uniforms — *We will go naked* he noted in the log. Soda lime "absorption cake" for two men to last 17 hours. Charts of ship types, firing angles, torpedo distances. Rations of pure water, fruit, alcohol, dry bread and chocolate.

ACROSS THE PACIFIC

Everything was carefully weighed and the kilograms noted in the log. Sakamaki drew tiny pictures of sun and moons rising and setting in flat horizons, and noted the times next to them — at least the time in Tokyo. He also figured that, for two men, the carbon dioxide in the enclosed midget would be at dangerous levels within three hours, and that the oxygen supply was only good for four and a half hours.

That finished, during the morning of Dec. 6, he wrote in the log; *I have many recollections from my childhood. Today, I will shoulder one important mission and, diving into Pearl Harbor, will sink the enemy's warships. I was born a man in our country and the present daring enterprise is really the peak of joy. Disregarding the hardships and bitter dangers of the past year, I have trained and the time has come when I will test my ability here.*

These tubes are the pick of our navy. Moreover, they are the result of the wisdom and skill of several tens of thousands of Japanese. In the present operation the strength of the crew is even more prepared than the torpedoes and certainly we are all completely affected by a feeling of self-sacrifice …

As for *I-24tou,* Sakamaki made a check list of troubles, winding up with 25 complaints. The depth gauge was frozen. Most of the valves were sticky. The oil pump leaked, as did water from the valve that adjusted air pressure. Air was bubbling out of the midget's horizontal rudder connection, and water was spilling into the sub from somewhere.

None of this concerned him as much as the discovery that the midget turned normally to starboard, but when he steered to port the submarine banked sharply and wallowed in the water.

A rather romantic propaganda photograph records another flotilla of Imperial Navy submarines departing Kwajalein during the war.

10 WAR WARNING

Clouds on a Darkening Horizon

As the I-boats of the Advance Force swarmed quietly across the Pacific in late November, Stark wrote a highly stilted letter to Kimmel and Bloch on the 25th, telling them that their frantic requests for aircraft and ships to be committed solely to ASW was being given "full consideration." One of the hold-ups was that the current version of Rainbow Five had not yet reached his desk.

"The joint plan should indicate what assistance to anti-submarine or other patrols will be rendered by the Army Air Forces," Stark wrote, in effect saying that the Navy commanders in Hawaii couldn't have their planes until they could prove the Army wasn't going to take over anti-submarine duties.

As 1941 wound down, Navy officials in Washington concluded that action by the Japanese was "expected, not in the Hawaiian area, except by submarines, but rather against Guam, the Philippines, and British and Dutch possessions in the Far East."

American submarines *Thresher* and *Tautog* left Pearl Harbor on Oct. 21, 1941, to patrol the picket line off Midway. The two submarines operated under wartime conditions, and for the first time in the Pacific since World War I, had armed torpedoes ready in the tubes.

The submarines maintained total radio silence, remaining submerged during the days and running on the surface at night. Any sign of Japanese shipping would prompt an urgent plain-language report. Any suspected offensive moves from the Japanese would elicit torpedoes from the submarines, without a go-ahead from Pearl Harbor. The submariners were surprised and concerned at this directive. Things were getting serious.

The routine grew quickly tedious, as fresh provisions lapsed into canned foods and fresh water was rationed.

In late November, exacerbated by poor translations of Japanese counterproposals, the diplomatic roundelay broke down between the United States and Japan. Admiral Stark and General Marshall each sent warnings to commands in the Atlantic and Pacific.

"This dispatch is to be considered a war warning," Kimmel read

142

on Nov. 27. "Negotiations with Japan looking toward stabilization of conditions in the Pacific have ceased and an aggressive move by Japan is expected within the next few days …" Stark went on to predict Imperial forces would strike in the Philippines, Thailand or Borneo, and commanded Kimmel to "execute an appropriate defensive deployment preparatory to carrying out the tasks assigned in WPL-46."

This missive later became known as the "War Warning" message. Kimmel instructed intelligence officer Lieutenant Commander Edwin Layton to paraphrase it for General Short, and inspected the message before it went to his opposite number. It could not match the original message, but had to parallel it so closely that no misinterpretation was possible. Layton typed up several versions and took them to Kimmel's cabin for approval.

Captain John B. Earle, Bloch's chief of staff, arrived at this moment, bearing a message from Short. The admiral read it and said, "This is almost like ours."

Kimmel then selected one of Layton's drafts and said, "All right — get this to General Short."

As Layton and Earle left Kimmel's office, they ran into a Lieutenant Burr, who had delivered Short's war warning to the Navy. Earle returned Short's message to Burr, and then gave him Kimmel's version, making sure the lieutenant read it first in case the general had any questions. It was about 5:30 p.m. when Burr left, and Short received the Navy message in the early evening.

Both commanders were then well aware of the war warning, having spoon-fed it to the other. Short's reaction to the message was to put his Army "on the march." By that evening, Army patrols had secured public utilities, rail heads and bridges — targets of sabotage. Short remembered the "Black Tom" German sabotage attack of 1916, when munitions-loaded trains on a New Jersey siding exploded mysteriously.

The War Warning ordered Kimmel to effect a "defensive deployment," a nebulous term that the admiral discussed at length with his staff. *What did it mean?* "It has always been our practice to use very precise terminology with definite known meanings," mused Bloch. "So far as I know, I have never encountered that terminology before."

In the absence of precise orders, Kimmel invented his own. He used this lever to immediately order the fleet to "exercise extreme vigilance against submarines and to depth bomb all submarine contacts suspected to be hostile in Oahu operating areas." A variation of this order extended the range to "fleet operating areas."

At this first scent of war, unable to go on the offensive, Kimmel's first reaction was to kill submarines. Like predecessor Admiral Richardson, Kimmel had chafed at Washington restrictions against attacking the undersea shadows that dogged his

Lieutenant General Walter C. Short, commander of the Hawaiian Department, U.S. Army. The "war warning" of Nov. 27 prodded Short to do both everything and nothing to get Hawaii ready for war. He chose to guard against sabotage.

warships. He belatedly informed Stark of this decision, in a P.S. added on to a letter dated Dec. 2.

In this action, Kimmel was exceeding, if not violating, his orders from Stark. In the Navy Court of Inquiry after the attack, Stark's staff officer Rear Admiral Richmond Kelly Turner, Director of War Plans, noted that Kimmel "ran the risk of committing an overt act against Japan, but did so feeling that it is best to follow the rule 'shoot first and explain afterwards.'"

Under questioning by Congress afterward, Turner equivocated mightily and said Kimmel "was never ordered, so far as I know, not to commit an overt act." He compared Kimmel's action to Richardson's during the war scare in the summer of 1940. "We were taking the precautions — with the purpose of taking precautions — against some irresponsible Japanese in a submarine around our areas," he said.

Kimmel's order was a go-ahead to depth-bomb every submerged contact within the operating area, which ranged several hundred miles from Pearl Harbor. "If a Japanese submarine had appeared on the surface, that would have been another story," he said later.

To explain this change of operations, Kimmel called a meeting of his flag officers on Nov. 28. Pacific Fleet submarine commander Tom Withers, upon whom this order had the most direct impact, was in Honolulu and the last to get word of the meeting. When he arrived at Pearl Harbor, he was mildly embarrassed to find he was the last officer into the conference room.

Kimmel handed him the war warning dispatch. Withers scanned through it, and Kimmel asked, "What do you think that means, Tom?" Withers stunned, muttered, "I think it means war."

Bloch snorted. "What are you going to do?" he said. "Sail out of here and sink ships?"

"If they come within 500 miles of here, and they don't turn back — yes, I will."

One of Kimmel's staff officers, Captain Arthur C. Davis, knocked and entered. "Have you seen Short?" demanded Kimmel.

"Yes sir, I have," said Davis.

"What did he say?" said Kimmel.

"He said, 'Somebody is drawing a long bow.'"

"Ah," said Kimmel.

After the flag meeting, Bloch had the commanding officer of Destroyer Division 80, the inshore patrol, call the skippers of the four ships — of which only *Ward* had listening gear installed — and give them a pep talk. "Be on your toes," they were advised, Kimmel had finally issued orders to depth-charge suspicious contacts. The most likely precursor to war would be an underwater assault on fleet ships in the operating area, they were told, and Japanese submarines "might make an effort to get into the harbor."

Kimmel also put out a bombing order for the PBYs of Patrol

Coast Guardsmen get caught up on war news aboard cutter Tiger, 1945.

Wing 2. Bloch felt the situation justified an additional inshore patrol at Honolulu Harbor, and directed the Coast Guard to run vessels back and forth across the harbor entrance, listening for submarines. Military transports and cargo ships put in at Fort Armstrong in Honolulu, not Pearl Harbor.

Commander Gordon T. Finlay, district Coast Guard officer, and the first port commander of Honolulu, passed on the order to cutters *Taney, Tiger* and *Reliance*. Finlay's guardsmen were already trained to seize "belligerent" vessels in territorial waters.

No other fleet action in Hawaii was taken in consequence of the war warning, other than to shepherd ships within the safety of Pearl Harbor. Only two days before, the approaching submarines of the Advance Force had been disappointed at the paltry number of battleships within the harbor. To Kimmel's mind, the legitimate Japanese threat, the submarines, was countered. Even while Kimmel was drawing his sword on Nov. 28, a sonar operator on cruiser *Helena* with no knowledge of the new orders became convinced that a submarine was within a restricted area and, on his own, issued an alert. Three destroyers searched fruitlessly.

Reports of suspected submarines became commonplace in the week that followed, and a number of depth-chargings occurred. The destroyers were keen on the prey.

On the same day that Kimmel's aggressive anti-submarine orders went into effect, the State Department, relaying a policy announcement from the White House, made it clear that American merchant ships traveling peaceful waters — essentially, everywhere in the world except the North Atlantic — would go unprotected. "American merchant vessels sailing on routes in the Pacific Ocean will not be armed under existing circumstances," the announcement added.

The captains of the Matson line, whose ships crisscrossed the Pacific, were given sealed orders in case of war. On receipt of war

Captain Hans O. Matthiesen, skipper of Matson freighter Lahaina. *Of German background, Matthiesen took reports of enemy submarines quite seriously.*

news, the ships were to sail 30 miles to the west of their usual track and to paint gray all surfaces visible from the air or sea.

On Dec. 2, 1941, Matson freighter *Lahaina* laboriously warped in toward the Ahukini wharf on Kauai, seesawing in the ocean until the ship's side tapped the pier. "Don't even open the hatches," the crew was told. "You're leaving tomorrow, back to San Francisco."

This was a curious development. The old ship normally followed the "Matson groove" worn in the North Pacific between Hawaii and the West Coast — San Francisco to Hilo, to Kahului, to Ahukini and back again. The cargoes were general. Sometimes a deck load of used cars. Maybe lumber out of the Columbia River. But the ship never traveled empty.

So, with 745 tons of molasses and 300 tons of scrap iron instead of the usual heavy load of sugar and pineapple, *Lahaina* cast off from Ahukini and headed into the North Pacific. Some of the crew had a standing bet over whether war would break out before they got back to San Francisco, or after. No one took odds that war would not happen. The journey normally took a week and a half, the freighter plowing through the ocean at roughly 9 knots, the speed of a man in full trot.

The skipper was Captain Hans O. Matthiesen, young, but a Matson professional who had jumped off a German freighter in 1922 and had family back in the Fatherland. He still had a German accent, and when excited, spoke in melodramatic flourishes.

Third Mate Douglas McMurtry had been with the freighter less than a year. After graduating from the California Maritime Academy in June 1939, he'd promptly married "Peggy" Mitchell, an island girl whose father was General Ralph Mitchell, operations officer at Fort Shafter.

They had met at a dance at the Waialae Country Club, during an earthquake. While the other dancers fled to the putting greens,

McMurtry bumped into Peggy under the drink table.

"Grab all the drinks you can," advised McMurtry, and Miss Mitchell found that charming.

The day after the wedding, McMurtry shipped out on *President Coolidge* for the Orient run. Later, as a deck officer on board *Lahaina*, he stood the 8 to 12 a.m. watch on the bridge.

While the deck officers steered the course, the engineering officers kept the ship running. Third Engineer Michael Locke, also an academy graduate, had reported aboard with even less ceremony. After an introductory chat with Chief Engineer Frank Laumeister, Locke was told to "get below and start 'er up."

Below, Locke became friendly with an oiler named Concezio del Tinto, an older man, an Italian, who had family somewhere. Locke never figured out if the family was in Hawaii or San Francisco.

The crew consisted of 34 men. The stewards were evenly mixed between mainland blacks and Hawaiians, and the deck crew was a "hodgepodge," including one Japanese-Hawaiian named Richard Takeo Hirashima. "Take," (Tah-kay) as he was called, was one of the most popular crew members. They functioned well together, any racism stowed away or hidden, like an embarrassing item in a duffel bag. Even potentially volatile union problems rarely erupted.

It was a typical merchant marine crew, with members of each section keeping pretty much to themselves, not even mixing much at mealtimes. Locke was friendly with McMurtry, who was similar in age and background, and their wives lived together while the men were at sea. Locke's relationship with Del Tinto was pleasant, but the fine line between command and service prevented them from becoming friends. That was the way things went in the stratified universe of the shipping business.

As *Lahaina* steamed away from Kauai, a sonar sweep by destroyer/minelayer *Gamble* that night produced a meaty, metallic echo in deep water 50 miles southwest of Oahu. Other destroyers rushed to the area, but found nothing to report.

Commander Arthur H. McCollum, the Far East expert in the Office of Navy Intelligence.

Little more arrived from Washington intelligence sources after the war warning, despite the efforts of Brigadier General Leonard Gerow and Rear Admiral Turner's staff to amplify the warning. The two war-plans officers had decided the Nov. 28 message was warning enough and could not be deflected from their course. Commander Arthur McCollum, Turner's Far East expert, approached the admiral on Dec. 5 with a message for Kimmel advising the fleet be further alerted, and Turner pulled out the war-warning messages of the week before. McCollum refused to be deflected, and Turner worried the text of the message reported little that was new or ominous. In the end, McCollum's warning was not sent.

This first week in December had been a busy one for American

Pre-war bombardment practice near Diamond Head. Shrapnel kicks up the water, a warning to any nearby submarines.

sailors. Lieutenant (jg) Victor Dybdal, the new gunnery officer on board destroyer *Helm*, was bitterly disappointed when the submarine scare sent the battleships scurrying for the harbor, calling off live-fire exercises. The destroyers were detailed to screen the big ships into Pearl. Dybdal had had only one such exercise, and felt the crew needed more practice. The emphasis had been on anti-submarine training at the expense of gun training.

On Dec. 4, the submarines on picket duty in the western Pacific were relieved, and all ran for the haven at Pearl Harbor. *Thresher* fought against the rising seas that camouflaged the Japanese fleet and lagged behind, plowing stubbornly through rough water. On the surface, the once-graceful undersea boat wallowed against the waves, and green water dashed against the conning tower, foaming as high as the periscope shears.

A lookout, Seaman William Dell Grover, was tossed from his post on the shears and thrown headlong to the aft portion of the conning tower, a small platform known as the cigarette deck. In pain from a shattered leg, Grover was carried below and placed in the skipper's bunk. The boat's pharmacist's mate stayed at Grover's side as the boy's condition worsened and he began to rave. During lucid moments, he spoke longingly of home and shore leave, and once, turned to the mate and predicted he would not live out the patrol. Grover's shipmates laughed and said the lookout was exaggerating.

Grover's skull had been fractured, however, and his bruised brain began to swell. Morphine eased the pain.

As carrier *Enterprise's* task group sailed away from Wake after delivering a load of Wildcat fighter planes, the company of ships commenced a new tactic, zig-zagging. There were 20 different patterns of zig-zag, all of which had to be executed in choreographic precision by the group. Escalating reports of mysterious

WAR WARNING

submarines nettled task group commander Vice Admiral William Halsey; he was taking no chances.

The maneuvers that eluded Helm's crew ended on Friday, Dec. 5. The ships sifted back to the harbor throughout that evening and into the dawn of the 6th. As destroyer *Ralph Talbot* steamed past Hickam Field, chief fire controlman Cleveland Davis looked up while checking buoys. His mind was on the maneuvers. "I think Pearl is very vulnerable," he said. "A sneak attack could be devastating." Standing nearby, Lieutenant R.A. Newton was surprised, but he thought about it and agreed. David went back to buoy-counting.

Lieutenant Commander William W. Outerbridge, who had wondered in mid-November about the intentions of Japanese submarines, that weekend took command of inshore patrol ship Ward. The patrol consisted of *Ward* (DD-139), *Schley* (DD-103), *Chew* (DD-106) and *Allen* (DD-66). *Ward* was a "four-stacker" destroyer, a type built in great numbers nearly two decades earlier. Though it was considered obsolete by some, Outerbridge was proud of his

Inshore patrol destroyer Ward *(DD-139) during World War I, painted in a "dazzle" camouflage scheme intended to mislead attacking submarines.*

ship. Dec. 6 was the first day of his first patrol of his first command. Born in Hong Kong of a British merchant captain and an Ohio girl, he graduated from the U.S. Naval Academy in 1927 and spent 14 years plugging away in the Navy's peacetime promotion platform, observing the war in China from cruiser *Augusta*. Now he was the only Academy man of a shipload of reservists.

Outerbridge a few days before had been executive officer on destroyer *Cummings*, where all officers were academy men except for one reservist, for whom he had felt sorry. Now the tables were turned. Lieutenant (jg) Oscar Goepner, recalled later that everyone in *Ward* felt sympathy for Outerbridge, alone among heathens.

Richard Phill, sight setter on *Ward's* No. 2 gun, joined the naval reserve at age 17 and cruised for two weeks on the Great Lakes, aboard training gunboat *Paducah*. Back on shore, he learned that the reserves had been called up in a national emergency; he and several other Great Lakes cadets were directed to proceed to San Diego's "Red Lead Row," there to de-mothball *Ward*.

This was all pretty exciting to Phill, a "Midwestern boy who'd never even been to boot camp." He noticed, however, that the older hands grumbled about it.

In the week since the war warning, Phill had been ordered to keep a keen eye out for anything submerged or partially submerged, and to shout it out if anything was sighted, even floating coconuts. *Ward* got underway at 7:21 Saturday morning to relieve destroyer *Chew* in the Defensive Sea Area.

At the same time, the ships of the Pacific Fleet began to nest in Pearl Harbor, safe from submarines. The destroyers, the first line of defense against submarines after the continuing disappointment of aerial observation, readied themselves for a quick exit should the balloon go up.

Helm spent the day removing electronic gear in preparation for deperming[1] Sunday morning. The gear was passed to destroyer *Blue* alongside at berth X-7. Like other ships in the tropical harbor, *Helm* had canvas awnings rigged over the deck to help keep heat out of the mess hall and living quarters. Since the deperming cruise was short and in harbor, these were left in place.

Blue also had returned Friday from a week of sea duty, and was scheduled for routine upkeep. She expected to be at sea again within a week. Eighty percent of the crew members were on board, about 135 men. Liberty was scheduled to expire for all except the chiefs at 1 a.m. Sunday morning.

Except for a six-week stint, *Blue* had been based in Pearl Harbor since 1939. The prolonged stay away from the destroyer's homeport in San Diego was a hardship for the crew. Though Chief Torpedoman's Mate Charles M. Shaw's wife was in San Diego, he had tried to sample Honolulu's nightlife, but lately begun to shun it. "Most of the fairly decent places are so crowded you can hardly get into any of them," he complained. Even the YMCA was swamped with sailors trying to sleep anywhere but their racks. Shaw's men behaved better in San Diego; he figured that they, like he, were happier in the port they considered home. The chief had spent the last six weeks sleeping on the destroyer.

Destroyer *Monaghan* returned from Maui Range and moored inside Pearl Harbor on the starboard side of a line of destroyers of Destroyer Division two, including *Dale*, *Aylwin* and *Farragut*. It was *Monaghan's* turn to lie in wait as the ready-duty destroyer. At

[1] "Deperming" altered a ship's magnetic field so that its mass wouldn't set off magnetic mines.

8:30 a.m., *Monaghan* signaled "assumed Ready Duty in readiness to get under way on one hour's notice." This duty would keep skipper Lieutenant Commander William Burford aboard for the next 24 hours. His wife, whom he called "Soldier," was to pick him up Sunday morning at 8 a.m.

Lieutenant Commander Herald F. Stout kept his crew on destroyer-minelayer *Breese* busy all morning with emergency combat drills — 20 percent of his crew were newly recruited and didn't know one end of the ship from another. *Breese* lay moored at berth D-3. Watch officer Ensign R.L. Carlson and Carpenter's Mate C.D. Willard received aboard four and a half gallons of ice cream and were busy sampling it.

In the early afternoon, skipper of cruiser *St. Louis* Captain George A. Rood welcomed aboard Rear Admiral H. Fairfax Leary, Commander, Battle Force, Cruisers. They sat in Rood's cabin and critiqued the maneuvers. Rood felt they had gone well, and that Pearl Harbor's cruisers were "in a good state of readiness."

St. Louis was moored to a dock in the southeast loch. Radar

"Four-stacker" destroyers converted to minelayers, at anchor in Hawaii, 1939. From left, they are Sicard *(DM-21, ex DD-341);* Tracy *(DM-19, ex DD-214);* Preble *(DM-20, ex DD-345) and* Pruitt *(DM-22, ex DD-347).*

Destroyer Ralph Talbot *(DD-390) near the Boston Navy Yard, 1938. Note the light gray pre-war paint scheme.*

was being installed and the decks were littered with scaffolding and cable reels. Three of her four five-inch guns were dismantled.

Throughout the afternoon, maneuver-weary sailors swarmed ashore, ready to tear up Honolulu. Rood decided to stay aboard; his wife and children were on the Mainland. He believed "if war came, Hawaii was no place for a family."

Sergeant June Dickens, U.S. Army, was sergeant of the guard at Camp Malakole, an antiaircraft battery on shore near the entrance to Pearl Harbor. His men had "sabotage trucks" rigged with machine guns, with one parked on the beach. On that Saturday afternoon, his men observed a sampan offshore. Dickens was called down from the guardhouse and told something strange was going on. The boat was within 50 yards of the camp, and two men were trying to swim ashore. Dickens pulled out his .45 and walked down to the surf line and waved the pistol.

"Come any closer," he shouted above the waves, "and I will shoot to kill."

The men treaded water and stared at Dickens, who stared back. They went back to the boat, and it moved away. Dickens ordered the sabotage truck on the beach to keep its machine guns loaded, and stationed an additional two men on BARs, telling the soldiers to open fire if the sampan came back within range. For the rest of the afternoon, the sampan slowly crisscrossed the area — waiting for something, it seemed to the soldiers on shore.

Finally, it disappeared into the dusk.

WAR WARNING

NIGHT MOVES 11

ENEMIES AT THE GATE

On the evening of Dec. 6, 1941, Gunichi Takahashi and Kimie Sera of Haleiwa were married, and threw a big luau for their fishermen friends. Sampans from around the island converged on Haleiwa, their skippers determined to make the most of the Takahashi wedding.

On any other night the nearly 200 sampans registered on Oahu would have been at sea, their crews fishing all night and returning to port in the morning. For the first time in many months, sampans were seen settling for the evening in the calm bays of the Hawaiian Islands. It contributed to a sense of false security.

At 7:03 that evening, off the protected cove of Lahaina Roads, submarine *I-72* radioed the attack fleet, reporting, *The enemy is not in Lahaina anchorage.* It was a disappointing message for attack strategist Minoru Genda; American ships sunk in the deep water off Maui would have been gone forever, unsalvageable. He scheduled a reconnaissance flight next morning, just in case, and turned his attention to Pearl Harbor, where the midget submarines would soon begin their clandestine approach. *The account of this most risking (sic) enterprise of the midget subs gave an enormous impression to the crews of the planes, encouraging them to the fullest extent,* he later wrote.

By this time, the remainder of Rear Admiral Shigeyoshi Miwa's nine blockading submarines of the Third Submarine Squadron had slipped into place, sealing off Oahu. Three submarine squadrons were spread out around Oahu, and a fair amount of radio traffic played between the islands and Admiral Mitsumi Shimizu's command center aboard *Katori*, safe on Kwajalein.

Halfway between Honolulu and San Francisco, *I-26* reached her pre-attack position and paused on the surface in the evening, awaiting word from Tokyo. A lookout, using binoculars, spotted a mast on the horizon. Commander Minoru Yokota was brought up on deck, where he could clearly see the navigation lights of 2,140-ton *Cynthia Olson*. Yokota ran *I-26* on the surface and drew slightly ahead of the freighter before submerging.

Cynthia Olson, a tough little steam schooner of a type peculiar to the West Coast lumber trade, was under contract to the Army,

delivering building lumber to Hawaii military bases. She was named after the grand-daughter of her owner, Oliver J. Olson. Her skipper was Captain Berthel Carlsen, and she carried a crew of 31, all under the aegis of the Army Transport Service. Two of the crew were regular Army, Private Ernest J. Davenport, the medical technician, and Private Samuel J. Zisking, the radio operator.

Third Mate James W. Mills — who had stashed a canoe on board in anticipation of lazy afternoons in Waikiki — had telephoned his sister before departing Seattle. During their conversation, he mentioned that on the previous voyage back from Hawaii, a submarine had surfaced right next to the ship as they neared the Washington coast.

Mills called for Captain Carlsen and they signaled the submarine. The sub, which had no markings, ignored the signals and promptly submerged. Mills assumed the submarine was American.

I-26 was one of Japan's newest submarines, completed less than a month before, and she carried excess fuel in the hangar space meant for her aircraft. She could have quickly finished off the small wooden cargo ship. Yokota held his fire, however, mindful of Yamamoto's desire not to have the fireworks go off prematurely.

Chief Gunner Saburo Hayashi wondered if the ammunition would even work. While loading *I-26*'s torpedoes in Japan, he discovered that the other submarines had depleted the stock of new torpedoes. Even though *I-26* could carry 17 torpedoes, all Hayashi could scrounge were 10 that had been warehoused for a decade.

Yokota shadowed his prey through the night, watching her through the periscope. The crewmen tried to relax by reading, playing bridge or listening to phonographs. On the morning of Dec. 7, they were 1,000 miles northeast of Hawaii.

The Navy tanker *Neosho* arrived at Pearl Harbor at 8 p.m. Dec. 6, carrying aviation gas and fuel oil. Under the new approach regulations, the ship came in darkened. As the heavily loaded tanker aimed for the gate, it hit something under water, twice.

"God almighty — we've hit something!" Machinists Mate Leon Bennett exclaimed to another crewman. "Somebody up there can't drive, or something."

But the ship was not aground, and she headed for Aiea Landing to discharge her fuel oil. Later that evening, *Neosho* wound up moored at Battleship Row.

Around 10 p.m., Kazuo Sakamaki looked through *I-24*'s periscope at the red and green landing lights of Hickam Field, next to Pearl Harbor. The moon had risen at 10:05 p.m. He turned to Lieutenant Commander Hiroshi Hanabusa, the mother submarine's skipper, who said, "What are you going to do?" They were so close to the target that music from the shore could be heard.

In reply, Sakamaki went to study recognition drawings.

Hanabusa was anxious. Sakamaki's gyrocompass had broken en route, and there were no spares. *I-24*'s gyro expert and midget crewman Kiyoshi Inagaki had struggled with the balky instrument for

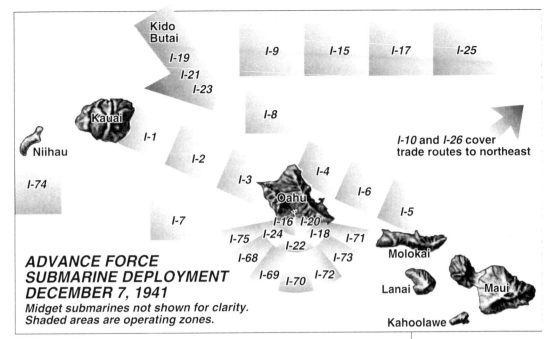

Kido Butai

I-19
I-21
I-23

I-9 I-15 I-17 I-25

Kauai

I-1

I-8

I-10 and I-26 cover
trade routes to northeast

Niihau

I-2

I-74

I-3

I-4

Oahu

I-6

I-7

I-16 I-20

I-5

I-75 I-24 I-18 I-71

I-22

Molokai

I-68 I-73

ADVANCE FORCE
SUBMARINE DEPLOYMENT
DECEMBER 7, 1941
Midget submarines not shown for clarity.
Shaded areas are operating zones.

I-69 I-70 I-72

Lanai

Maui

Kahoolawe

hours. Sakamaki would have to rely on the midget's tiny periscope, dipping through the waves, to navigate the fierce reefs and anti-submarine nets around the harbor.

His orders were to hit a battleship or a carrier, and he coveted *Pennsylvania*, unaware the battleship lay high and dry-docked.

The midgets were now scheduled to strike between the first and second aircraft waves, another change of plans. They were also to circle Ford Island counterclockwise and Sakamaki penciled in the course on his chart, marking it off in colored crayon. He added ship positions as last reported from intelligence operatives at the Japanese Embassy in Honolulu. The map dated from 1937, but the names of moored ships were accurate three weeks before. He then catnapped.

Sakamaki awoke at half-past midnight and went up to the conning tower for a last look at Oahu. He then went below and checked on Inagaki and the gyrocompass. The instrument was still stubborn, but the crewman was full of pep.

Worried but determined, Sakamaki packed his personal gear, including a farewell note to his family that contained a lock of hair and a fingernail. He washed and changed to his combat uniform, hooded overalls[1] and *fundoshi* — a sort of white loincloth. He wrapped matches carefully in waterproof oil paper. He dabbed on the perfume he'd bought in Kure and carefully tied on a *hachimaki*, the Japanese warrior's traditional headband.

He wandered through the mother sub and embraced the crew, one by one. Imperial Navy sailors setting off on a mission generally say, "*Itte mairimasu*" as they leave their officers: literally, "I am going, and will be back." The midget submariners, as they took their leave, said simply, "We will go."

I-22 surfaced 50 miles south of Pearl, the most distant of the

The submarines of the Advance Force were positioned to isolate Pearl Harbor from outside aid, and to snare ships leaving the protected anchorage.

[1] Reported in other accounts as a "leather jacket." The overalls were probably a flying suit.

Special Attack Unit mother ships, and probed forward gently in the night. Captain Hanku Sasaki stood rigidly on the wet bridge, eyes straining into the void. Gradually the lights and mass of Oahu became visible, with occasional half-hearted searchlight sweeps coning through the sky.

In the reflected light, Sasaki also could see *I-20* silently treading water nearby. He felt confident the attack would be a success. *See how careless the Americans are!*

I-20 left the company of *I-22* and moved forward, bracketing the mouth of the enemy anchorage.

Aboard *I-22*, Sub-Lieutenant Keiu Matsuo listened to Lieutenant Naoji Iwasa and Ensign Naokichi Sasaki discuss the mission. The talk rarely turned toward rescue — instead they chatted about how to make a final stand on Oahu and how best to mow down Americans with their swords and pistols.

Matsuo, who had visited Oahu the previous month aboard *Taiyo Maru*, was moved. "Please let me go with you," he pleaded.

"There's no room," said Iwasa, surprised. "And there's no air. We would have to run on the surface."

Captain Sasaki came up behind them and told Matsuo that he'd be more valuable remaining behind. "The Navy cannot spare you," he lectured. "You are here to learn all you can about the midget submarines. There is a possibility the midget submariners might not return. If that's the case, it's up to you to carry on the program, alone."

Iwasa called in the maintenance crew, bowed and thanked them for their diligence. "Now I am going to leave the ship with everything in good condition. I think the war will last a long time and in its course midget subs will be used more and more. I expect you to do your best in future operations."

Picking up brush and rice paper, Iwasa wrote *shi sei* — utmost loyalty — and tacked it to a bulkhead as a memento.

At approximately 1 a.m., Dec. 7 Hawaii time, seven miles off the channel entrance to Pearl Harbor, *I-16* released the midget craft containing Masaji Yokoyama and Sadamu Uyeda. Both had said their goodbyes, and written letters. Uyeda's was the most personal of the midget submariner's letters:

Forgive this negligent son for not writing these long months. I hope you are both in excellent health. As for me, I am in the highest of spirits, and striving to discharge my duties to the best of my ability. Please rest assured, for everything is well with me.

Though harvest time has come and gone, you must be more than pressed with work at this time of year. With the present lack of hands on the farm, you must find the work much too strenuous for you. I earnestly beg of you not to overstrain yourselves, for to do so is to injure your health. Please finish your work at your leisure, and above all things, I entreat you to guard your health.

You are aware that our country is now facing a grave situation — a period of great emergency. Consequently we are undergoing inten-

Night Moves

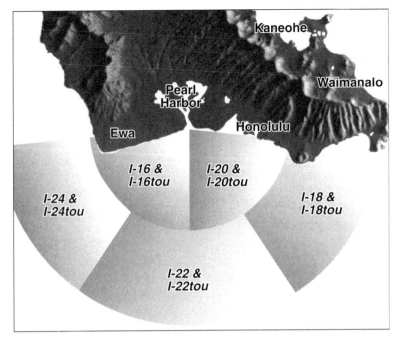

Each mother submarine was given a wide sector to drop off her charges. The midget submarines approached Pearl Harbor from five different directions, increasing their chances of being detected, but also increasing their chances of slipping into the enemy base.

sive training day and night. In this connection, too, we are soon to be dispatched to regions unknown. I should like to meet you again before I go, for there is much I should like to discuss with you, but my observance of military secrecy compels me to part thus with you.

Should anything happen to me, do not grieve or mourn, for I have dedicated my life in service to His Imperial Majesty. In performance of my duty in the service of the Imperial Navy, I am determined to sacrifice my life.

Of disobedience and disloyalty, I shall never be guilty. Of this, rest assured, for I shall do nought which will humiliate you or cast a slur upon your name.

Lest you worry at the gravity of my letter, let me assure you that there is no need for anxiety. What I have written thus far is but the expression of my resolution — to serve my country to the utmost of my ability in these troubled times. Only this I ask — should I join the rank of those who fail to return, I ask that you forget me. Instead, live a happy life, a peaceful life for the remaining years ...

Let me here emphasize the fact that you must not reveal, under any circumstance, the contents of this letter. I ask that you observe the utmost secrecy and seal your lips regarding the context.

Please do not write to me until you hear from me again. Should I fail to write, do not be alarmed, for in my silence lies the confirmation that I am well and discharging my duties faithfully.

With the approach of winter, the weather is turning colder; so look after your health, and refrain from doing too much strenuous work.

Good-bye. Sadamu.

In comparison, during his last moments on board *I-22*, Iwasa lettered an unusually formal farewell to his parents. *Forgive me that I was unable to fulfill my duty as a son*, he wrote. *Should I die after*

157

achieving my objective, I hope you will commend me. Should I die without accomplishing my task, I hope you will permit my spirit to depart to that land to which it needs must go …

In the margin, he added a poem:

As the cherry blossoms fall
At the height of their glory,
So, too, must I fall
That men may call me
A flower of Yamato,
Though my bones lie scattered
In the bleak wilderness
Of strange and distant lands.

That errand completed, Iwasa again turned to his checklist. He dressed in his uniform and stuck a ceremonial short sword through his belt. "Are you sure you can get inside with that thing sticking from your waist?" teased Sasaki, his crew mate. Iwasa tied a white *hachimaki* around his head — it signified his great resolve — laughed stiffly and clapped Sasaki on the back.

Petty Officer Sasaki climbed aboard *I-22tou* and Iwasa met with Captain Sasaki on the dim bridge to once more go over the attack plan. Sasaki gave Iwasa their exact position — Pearl Harbor lay dead ahead, 10 miles away. Visibility was good with an almost-full moon, the Americans were obviously not on the defensive.

They decided chances were excellent the midget submariners could navigate into the target area. Departure would be no problem; they figured the anti-submarine net would be open with all the American ships running for safety to the open sea. Then Iwasa entered *I-22tou* and dogged down the hatch.

They chatted over the telephone line while waiting to be cast off.

Captain Sasaki said to Iwasa, "Congratulations in advance on your success. I hope you will do your job well. Good luck!"

"Thanks a lot for taking me so close to the harbor. I will attack without fail," said Iwasa. His voice, distant and metallic, sounded excited.

"You are a good officer, Iwasa. Your deed will gladden the heart of the Emperor," said Sasaki.

"Thank you," said the faraway voice. There was a pause, Sasaki sensed Iwasa was coming to grips with the deadly nature of the situation. "I wish you to look after my private affairs," blurted Iwasa.

Before Sasaki could reply, navigator Lieutenant Tetsuaki Suga-masa tapped him on the shoulder and took the phone away, "The time has come," he said to Iwasa. It was 1:16 a.m., and by now Pearl Harbor lay only nine miles away.

"Goodbye! Take care of my belongings," said the leader of the midgets. "I've left them all bundled up." The connection broke, and the midget was cast loose.

On the other side of the Pacific, Japanese warships were already in action. Japanese minelayer *Tatsumiya Maru* began

depositing 456 mines in British-controlled waters near Singapore, then turned north along with *Chosa Maru*. They were picked up by British reconnaissance planes and *Chosa Maru* reversed course to split up their aerial shadow. This was the first overt act of war with Europe.[2]

Japanese submarines in the area included *I-56,* eying weather conditions off the coast of Kota Bharu, Malaya, in preparation for a seaborne invasion, and *I-121* and *I-122,* detailed to lay mines in Singapore approach routes. The mission was scrubbed for fear of tipping off the now-curious British.

Japanese troopships near Singapore were then discovered by a British PBY Catalina. Before it could get off a warning, the aircraft was shot down by a Lieutenant Ogata, flying a Type Zero float plane. At its Singapore airfield the Catalina was listed overdue, possibly due to stormy weather. It was actually the victim of the first shots fired between Japan and Britain.

As Japanese invasion forces closed in on Kota Bharu, lead destroyer *Uranami* surprised a Norwegian freighter. Taking no chances, *Uranami's* boarding party scuttled the freighter, though not before it squeezed out a distress signal.

In Hawaii, at 2 a.m., minesweepers *Condor, Crossbill* and *Reedbird* waddled out of Pearl Harbor. Part of the new war-footing routine was a late-night sweep for drifting mines. Nearly two miles south of the entrance buoys, *Crossbill* and *Condor* spread their paravane brooms and trundled back and forth. *Reedbird* went west.

The offensive end of offshore patrol was handled by destroyers *Ward, Chew, Schley* and *Allen.* They took turns, a week at a time, guarding an area two miles square at the mouth of the harbor. It was marked on maps as the Prohibited Area and the destroyers were quite serious about guarding it.

It was their duty to identify every ship running in and out of busy Pearl Harbor. That included lots of submarines, each of which was chaperoned by a destroyer, just in case.

There was a waning moon peeping through scattered clouds. It was a routine evening; ships marching on watch, like guards at a gate, traffic moving in and out of Pearl like a lazy river, signalmen gossiping by signal lantern. Quiet.

In the shallow, growling waters just off the glittering ribbon of Waikiki, *I-18* released the third midget submarine, containing Shigemi Furuno and Shigenori Yokoyama, at 2:15 a.m. They were more than 12 miles from Pearl Harbor. Unflappable Yokoyama spent the day of Dec. 6 sleeping soundly. He said goodbye to a single friend aboard the mother submarine, reaching into his pocket and pulling out a handful of beans as a gift. To the west, midget submariners Akira Hiro-o and Yoshio Katayama scrambled on the slippery deck of *I-20,* packages of wine and food in their left hands, shaking hands with their right. "We must look like high school boys happily going on a picnic," said Hiro-o, the class joker. They sealed themselves into the midget and were set loose at 2:57 a.m.

[2] *The only victims of Tatsumiya Maru's mines were Dutch submarines O-16 and K-17, a week after war broke out.*

In a last letter to his parents, Katayama spoke of his own death. Mid-way through the correspondence he suddenly changed wording to the third person, as if to distance himself from his own emotions.

Night-time, he wrote, *My dear parents.*

I take up my pen with a heart full of gratitude for all that you have bestowed upon me — love, kindness, tenderness.

We leave on the day after tomorrow, and even the bright autumn sky seems to be rejoicing at our impending departure.

Yoshio is in high spirits, determined to surrender his life for his country. Every man must die once, and Yoshio is profoundly grateful at the opportunity thus offered him — to die a glorious death. From the depth of his heart he offers you his thanks for the upbringing and care you gave him until he became fitted for this destiny.

When you receive the official report of his death, rejoice, and commend him for the only filial act of his life. What is one man's life when the great objective of this nation lies at stake?

From the grave I shall ever be praying for your happiness and long life.

Goodbye. Yoshio."

Katayama also wrote a last letter to his older brother, considerably chattier and less formal than the stiff goodbyes the others addressed to their parents. Perhaps they sensed that the letters to the parents might become public. Katayama urged his sibling to protect their parents from the demands of interviewers and well-meaning strangers with condolences. He also suggested that their younger brother Yoshito apply to the naval academy, and that brother Akio be given a watch in his name upon graduation.

At 3:42 a.m., a ghostly plume appeared 50 yards off the port bow of *Condor*. A stick-like periscope was silhouetted against the waning moon, moving at cross-purposes with the other waves.[3]

[3] In 1991, physics professor Donald W. Olson calculated the moon angles during the night of Dec. 7, 1941, and discovered to his surprise that the moon was in a direct line between Condor and the periscope.

Ensign Russell G. McCloy, officer of the deck, called to Quartermaster 2nd Class R.C. Uttrick, asked him what he thought. Uttrick looked through binoculars at the strange white wave in the darkness. "That's a periscope, sir, and there aren't supposed to be any subs in this area."

Helmsman R.B. Chavez could only see the glimmering wake, not the periscope. It was headed right at them. Chavez turned *Condor* to starboard, and at the same moment the sub turned to port, heading for the harbor. This was suspicious enough behavior, believed *Condor* skipper Ensign Monroe Harmon Hubbell. Identification wasn't positive enough, however, to report it to other than the Senior Officer Present Afloat — Lieutenant William Outerbridge in *Ward*. At 3:57 a.m. *Condor* used her yardarm blinker to report *Sighted submerged submarine on westerly course. Speed nine knots.*

At the other end of the signal was Lieutenant (jg) Oscar W. Goepner, who had just taken the watch on board *Ward*. The destroyer was cruising at 15 knots, sweeping the two-square-mile area off Pearl.

Ward radioed back: *One moment, please stand by.*

NIGHT MOVES

Minesweeper Condor (AMC-14) in the light gray colors of early 1941. Note the four-color minesweeping insignia next to the bow number.

A reserve officer from Northwestern University, Goepner had been doing inshore patrol for more than a year, and this was the first time he had received a message like this one. He told Ensign Louis F. Platt to wake up *Ward's* new skipper. Outerbridge was bunked in the chart house, next to the loudly pinging sonar apparatus. Though the sonar operators did their best to keep quiet, Outerbridge had learned to sleep through the electronic racket during a previous assignment as executive officer in destroyer *Cummings*.

Relations between Japan and the U.S. were at critical mass, and Outerbridge considered it highly likely *Condor* had seen exactly what she had reported. Besides, reasoned Outerbridge, the signal was an opportunity for late-night drill.

He joined Lieutenant Hartwell T. Doughty on the bridge. "Sound General Quarters," said Outerbridge. It was 4:08 a.m.

Come in, radioed *Condor*.

Ward edged as close as she dared to *Condor's* trailing brooms, then drifted away to the west at slow speed, lashing the sea with sonar. Nothing bounced back, and after half an hour a frustrated Outerbridge radioed, *What is the distance of the submarine?*

He paused and repeated, *What was the approximate distance and course of the submarine you sighted?*

The course was about what we were steering at the time, 020 magnetic, and about 1,000 yards from the entrance, apparently headed for the entrance, sent back *Condor*.

By this time, *Ward* was near Barbers Point, quite a distance from the entrance. *Do you you have any additional information on the sub?* he asked as *Ward* headed back toward Pearl Harbor.

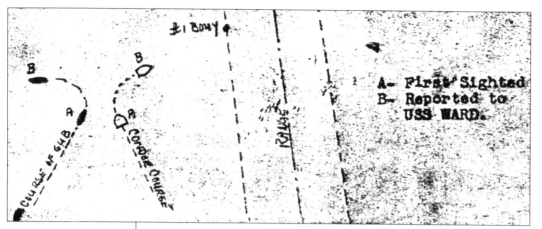

A- First Sighted
B- Reported to USS WARD.

This sketch, from minesweeper Condor's *after-action report*, shows how they and the periscope they had spotted in the darkness went in opposite directions.

No additional information, said *Condor*.

When was the last time approximately that you saw the submarine? Outerbridge persisted.

Approximate time 0350, and he was apparently headed for the entrance.

Please? queried *Ward's* radio operator.

"Thank them for their information," snapped Outerbridge to the radio operator. *They probably saw a buoy*, he thought. "Notify us if you have any more information."

Nobody at this time realized there had been a mix-up — the original message gave the course when the sub was last seen, moving away from the minesweeper. This latest update gave the course when first seen.

Outerbridge fretted he'd been searching the wrong area and then mistakenly went east, where the midgets were not.

Condor, Ward and a nearby radio station that picked up the signals didn't report the contact to higher-ups. Mistaken sightings were common. Communication watch officer at the shoreside radio station was Ensign Oliver H. Underkoffer, being aided by Ensign Gordon F. Kennedy, who was in the coding vault, and could not hear the radio. Their shift was 8 a.m. Saturday morning to the same time Sunday, and both were dog-tired. This "loudspeaker watch" required the officer to listen in on minesweeper radio traffic. Paperwork was taken care of while ears were set for the call sign. For ComFourteen, the radio station, it was DW2X. "You listen to it subconsciously," said Underkoffer, explaining after the war why he didn't seem to hear anything unusual that night. *Condor*, using DZ5Y, and *Ward*, using DN3L, only conversed between themselves.

Not that it mattered. Underkoffer had fallen asleep at 2:30 a.m., trusting that his "subconscious" would filter his call sign through the wall of sleep. Sometime between 4:35 and 4:58 a.m., *Ward* secured from General Quarters. Outerbridge and most of the crew padded sleepily back to bed. The regular watch was told to keep an eye out. Whatever had been nosing around the harbor entrance was long gone.

Ward announced, *We are finished* to *Condor*. For the next couple

of hours, the only radio traffic consisted of routine checks to see if the circuits were open.

While things seemed quiet, at 4:30 a.m. Hawaii time the Japanese liner *Tatuta Maru*, came to a stop in mid-ocean. The ship was on a well-publicized voyage around the Pacific, picking up Japanese nationals in Honolulu, Mexico, Panama and San Francisco, a trip that implied an officially sanctioned peace, at least for the duration of the voyage. When she sailed from Yokohoma on Dec. 2, 37 American and other evacuees from Japan were on board.

As instructed, at the stroke of midnight, Tokyo time, the ship's master opened a sealed box given to him by the Imperial Navy. Inside were orders to reverse course and speed back to Yokohoma under radio silence. Also in the box were 20 pistols in case the passengers rioted.

At two minutes before 5 a.m., the anti-submarine net guarding Pearl Harbor was swung open by gate vessel *YNG-17*, to receive minesweeper *Crossbill*, followed closely by *Condor*. The gate crewman wrote *Gate open — white lights* in the gate log at that time. *Crossbill* passed through at 5:08, *Condor* at 5:32. As *Condor* stood in to Pearl, visibility was very good, noted skipper Hubbell. Sunrise was due at 6:27 a.m., with twilight scheduled at 5:35 a.m., becoming quite bright by 6 a.m.

The gate remained open. Tug *Keosanqua* was due out at 6:15 a.m., so the gate crew decided to skip closing the nets. *Keosanqua*'s task was to lead in stores ship *Antares*; transport *Argonne* provided extra hands for handling *Antares*' lines.

It was at this point, a quiet moment in a routine night, that things began to go wildly wrong for the Americans. The gate didn't actually close again until 8:40 a.m., well after the attack was under way. The submarine reported by *Condor* could easily have entered the harbor at any time, perhaps snuggled between *Condor* and *Crossbill*.

Lieutenant Commander William W. Outerbridge, a post-war photograph.

The nets probably didn't matter. The anti-torpedo nets were made to deter standard-sized submarine weapons and, accordingly, went down only 45 feet. The deepest part of the channel entrance was 72 feet. The Type #A midget submarine could have crabbed under the net with 10 feet or so of leeway.

Inside the harbor, the heavy warships of the fleet were nested safely. The exceptions were carriers *Enterprise*, then 200 miles west of Oahu, returning from Wake Island with an escort of three heavy cruisers and five destroyers; and carrier *Lexington*, also with three heavy cruisers and five destroyers, en route to Midway with a load of Marine scout-bombers.

Four submarines were stationed off Wake and Midway atolls, a pair at each; and stores ship *William Ward Burroughs* was near Wake.

Riding Piggyback Into Battle

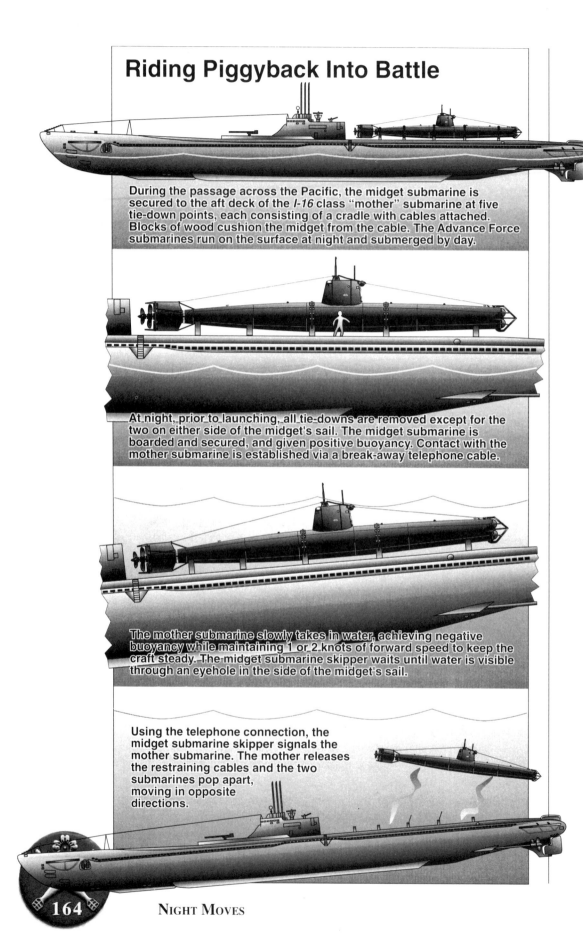

During the passage across the Pacific, the midget submarine is secured to the aft deck of the *I-16* class "mother" submarine at five tie-down points, each consisting of a cradle with cables attached. Blocks of wood cushion the midget from the cable. The Advance Force submarines run on the surface at night and submerged by day.

At night, prior to launching, all tie-downs are removed except for the two on either side of the midget's sail. The midget submarine is boarded and secured, and given positive buoyancy. Contact with the mother submarine is established via a break-away telephone cable.

The mother submarine slowly takes in water, achieving negative buoyancy while maintaining 1 or 2 knots of forward speed to keep the craft steady. The midget submarine skipper waits until water is visible through an eyehole in the side of the midget's sail.

Using the telephone connection, the midget submarine skipper signals the mother submarine. The mother releases the restraining cables and the two submarines pop apart, moving in opposite directions.

At Johnston Island, testing of the new Higgins landing craft was under way, requiring heavy cruiser *Indianapolis* and five destroyer-minesweepers.[4] In the fleet training grounds 25 miles south of Oahu, a heavy cruiser and four high speed-minesweepers were conducting exercises. Another destroyer kept a submarine company as it approached Pearl from the southwest — this was standard procedure for approaching friendly submarines.

Heavy cruiser *Pensacola* was escorting an eight-ship convoy near Samoa. Heavy cruiser *Louisville*, with a two-ship convoy, was in the Solomons. Two tankers were halfway between Hawaii and California, four auxiliaries were anchored at Lahaina Roads, and seaplane tender *Wright* was 300 miles to the northwest, by herself. *Wright's* log for the night of Dec. 6 indicated sighting a "vessel bearing one point abaft port beam running without lights ... distance four miles." Later, the vessel was judged to be a submarine.

About 25 civilian-owned, government-chartered troop and cargo carriers were scattered between Hawaii and North America.

Three PBYs were scheduled to search for submarines 120 miles south of Oahu. Each plane had 1,000 gallons of fuel, two depth charges and armed machine guns, limiting its range to about 800 miles. Four more Catalina patrol planes near Lahaina Roads — *24-P-1, 24-P-2, 24-P-4* and *24-P-5* — were exercising with submarines; they had armed machine guns but no depth charges.

North of Oahu, in the comparative safety of the open sea, *I-15* lolled on the surface. Nearby, the carriers of Kido Butai raced toward Oahu, hidden behind a wintertime bad-weather belt boiling on the fringe of the trade winds, a wall of rain 300 miles north of Oahu. It is an area of near-constant low ceilings, poor visibility, squall and rain, a predictable meteorological phenomenon noted by Japanese oilers.

Executive Officer Zenji Orita tried to sleep on board *I-15*, but kept imagining American warships sniffing out their oil spoor. Finally, at dawn, he gave up and went to the bridge. It was the first day of the war, and he didn't want to miss it.

I-15 sank beneath the waves as dawn lightened the sky. Only the periscope and radio antennae poked above the water.

By the time Sakamaki had made all his farewells on board *I-24*, it was nearly dawn. Time to go. Lieutenant Commander Hanabusa showed him a message just received from Yamamoto.

The moment has arrived, it read. *The rise and fall of our empire is at stake. Everybody do his duty.*

Hanabusa was still worried. "Ensign Sakamaki, we've arrived at our destination, but your gyrocompass isn't working. What are you going to do?"

Sakamaki remembered the lights of Hickam, dancing across the waves. *The target is right in front of me*, he thought. *How can I miss?*

Sakamaki glanced at Inagaki, discovered him flushed with excitement. "Captain, I am going ahead," said Sakamaki, flatly.

Moved by the young officer's pluck, Hanabusa seized Sakamaki's

[4] *Indianapolis had just unloaded one boat from shore when word came of the attack. The ship notified the commander on Johnston that they were leaving. The big cruiser, sitting motionless off the atoll, was "in quite an exposed position, exposed submarine waters, and I was immediately conscious that they might have submarines at sea or at each of the islands," Vice Admiral Wilson Brown of the scouting force explained.*

shoulders. They stared into each other's eyes as the mother submarine yawed in the dark waves.

"On to Pearl Harbor!" they shouted.

Sakamaki's and Inagaki's few possessions were already bundled and addressed, Torpedo Officer Mochitsura Hashimoto saw, as if they did not expect to return. Even stolid Inagaki had written a poem:

For the sake of His Majesty the Emperor, nothing do I grudge to sacrifice. Young as I am, I'll lay down my life gladly in his Imperial Majesty's service. On my war mission I now go forth, defying the network of barriers and mine fields. Ready am I to perish, once I have crippled the enemy. Oh, how serene this morning's sky looks, as my heart turns up to it full of joy at the thought of joining my dead comrades at the Yasukuni Shrine.

Unseen in the darkness, destroyer *Ward* was nearby, moving away in the opposite direction, back toward the restricted area. Sakamaki paused in the tiny conning tower of the midget submarine, just southwest of Barbers Point Naval Air Station. There wasn't much room. The small sail held the periscope, a bulky, rubber-clad radio antenna, battery exhausts and covered lights.

His body was wedged into a tube that led into the midget's control room, and shears for net-cutting arose like wings on both sides of the hatch. The hatch could be opened only from the inside, and if he sucked in his breath and looked dawn, past his chest, Sakamaki could see the luminous dial of the directional gyroscope. It appeared to be working perfectly, unlike the balky gyrocompass squatting next to it.

The last to be fitted out with the midget-carrying apparatus, *I-24* did not have a telephone link to the small submarine, as did the other mother submarines.

Sakamaki wriggled down into the midget and spun the hatch dogs. They were running late, perhaps by as much as two hours, and Pearl Harbor was more than 10 miles away.

I-24, moving steadily and slowly forward at two or three knots, delicately filled her tanks, inching down into the water. The midget, facing aft, was attached to the cradle just behind *I-24's* conning tower, now held in place by a pair of steel cables. *I-24* sank until *I-24tou's* own tower was awash, and then cut free the cables, which were designed to separate along the midget's spine. The slightly buoyant midget submarine popped to the surface, away from *I-24*, and the two submarines departed one another.

I-24 dropped out from underneath Sakamaki's midget. The crewmen could feel the quiet purr of their electric motors and the rushing momentum of the mother sub.

The steel cables of the releasing gear slid away with a metallic whang, but instead of squirting forward smoothly, the midget nose-dived. Sakamaki and Inagaki tumbled forward as their little steel world turned on end.

NIGHT MOVES

FIRST SHOTS 12

"This Is a Lot of Activity For a Sunday Morning ..."

The scuttlebutt below decks as *Antares* returned from the resupply run to Canton Island was that a mysterious submarine had been dogging their trail. Not that the trip had been uneventful. The day the ship arrived at Canton, a fire broke out in an island warehouse, and from the ship the crew was entertained by the sight of beer bottles exploding in the flames.

On the return trip, a radioman, a friend of Fireman Apprentice Bill Ellis, told him that *Antares'* skipper Commander Lawrence C. Grannis had attempted to contact the apparition by radio, and got no response. The fire room gang was somewhat reassured when they were told a destroyer — an "older vessel, a four-stacker" — would provide cover on the last leg back to Hawaii, as *Antares* had no armament of her own other than a three-inch cannon, with no ammunition.

Fleet auxiliary *Antares* was a lumbering, slab-sided ocean truck, and she was towing an empty 500-ton H.D.S.2 supply lighter as well. *Antares* passed Barbers Point, on the ship's port side, at about 5:45 a.m., moving through the same waters as Sakamaki and *I-24tou.*

Ward saw her lights as they appeared over the horizon, and noted her arrival. Inside the harbor, American ships gradually became visible, silent against the lightening sky. As Chief Engineer William Blackmore was dropped off at Berth #9 by his wife, she observed, "This is the quietest place I've ever seen."

"You'd be surprised what goes on around here," winked Blackmore. He went on board *Keosanqua,* underway at 6:10 a.m.

Grannis had been on *Antares'* bridge since the sweeping signal from Diamond Head lighthouse was spotted. He was tired from the grueling replenishment trip from Palmyra and Canton atolls and eager to be taken into the harbor. All that remained was an early-morning rendezvous with *Keosanqua,* taking on board a harbor pilot.

As dawn rouged the sky, Grannis paced the deck and chatted with a sailor who was peeling potatoes.

At 6:20 a.m., *Antares* began drawing in the tow line that connected her to the lighter. They expected to transfer the barge to tug *Keosanqua* and then enter Pearl Harbor.

Antares (AKS-3)
during World War II.

Ten minutes later, the tug wasn't in sight yet, so *Antares* turned slightly east to burn off some time. The sunrise was spectacular and Grannis was distractedly marveling at the heavens when someone noticed a bizarre object about 1,500 yards away on starboard quarter.

It looked like a broaching conning tower, and it was shadowing the supply ship. *She's obviously having depth-control trouble and ... trying to go down,* thought Grannis, signalling *Ward* for a closer look. *Keosanqua* passed through the submarine net and was loafing in the channel entrance, about two miles away.

Fireman Ellis was on the 4 to 8 a.m. watch in the fire room, and halfway through his shift, the room lost airflow. The rods that normally controlled the intake of air from below were broken and bent, so Ellis was ordered to go topside and trim the vents by hand, angling them into the breeze.

Ellis was in the midst of doing so when he noticed officers scrambling for the bridge. The signalman was out on the wing, throwing messages at destroyer *Ward* and a PBY seaplane nearby. In the water astern of *Antares*, Ellis spotted a black conning tower, pointing directly at the ship. He assumed that the submarine and the four-stacker were the same ships talked about during the return voyage.

Goepner was still in charge on *Ward's* deck. At the helm, H.E. Raenbig saw the object first, and said, "Put a glass on that thing, Harry," to Quartermaster H.F. Gearin.

Tug Keosanqua *in
her post-war guise
as merchant tug* SS
Edward J. Coyle,
*near Seattle in the
1950s.*

FIRST SHOTS

Gearin showed the object to Goepner. "Looks like a buoy to me," shrugged Goepner. "Keep an eye on it."

Gearin did. "Sir, it looks like a small conning tower," he decided. "And I've never seen a buoy move at five knots through the water."

As the two men agreed "they had never seen anything like it," a PBY of Patrol Wing 2 from Kaneohe began circling over the object. The plane's pilot, Ensign William Tanner, thought the object was an American submarine in distress. His co-pilot on *14-P-l* was Ensign R.B. Clark.

That was convincing enough for Goepner. "Captain, please come on to the bridge!" he called.

From his bunk in the navigation chart room, Outerbridge pulled a robe over his pajamas and hot footed it to the bridge. The robe was a blue-and-white patterned kimono the lieutenant had picked up in China.

She's going to follow the Antares *in, whatever it is,* Outerbridge thought. It can't be anything else but a sub. *Whose?*

Ward's executive officer, Lieutenant H.T. Doughty, arrived on the bridge.

"What's up, Captain?" he asked. Doughty was shown the object, conning tower awash.

"He probably thinks he's submerged," said Outerbridge.

"Oh," said Doughty, "What are you going to do?"

"I'm going to shoot at it as soon as we're ready," said Outerbridge. "General Quarters, please."

At 6:40 a.m., General Quarters sounded again on *Ward*. Sailors fell out of the sack for the second time in three hours, some so sleepy they didn't bother to button their uniforms. Seaman Ambrose Domagall, a loader at No. 3 gun, was doing double duty as a bridge messenger. When the rest of the gun crew assembled, they found him waiting with a shell in his arms. Richard Phill, the sight-setter on No. 2 gun, which shared the galley platform with the No. 3 gun, stumbled into position, figuring this was another drill.

Once again, ammunition was hauled up and guns loaded. *Ward* stoked her boilers and lit off after the sub, the engines humming through the hull.

P. Allen Dionisopoulos' duty station was fire control talker, on the flying bridge above the navigation bridge. From Dionisopoulos' vantage point, it looked as if the sub was trying to ram *Antares*.

"Come left!" Outerbridge ordered Raenbig, and the narrow hull heeled hard in the water. They aimed for the gap between the barge and the conning tower, now closing quickly at 400 yards.

Gunner's Mate Louis Gerner dogged down the hatch to the anchor engine and then ran aft on the bow deck. Outerbridge leaned over the bridge rail and frantically shouted for him to watch out — the big deck gun was swinging toward the target and Gerner's head was in the way.

Tanner dropped some smoke floats from the PBY.

Ward dashed to 100 yards abeam the object, accelerating from 5

Ensign Goepner

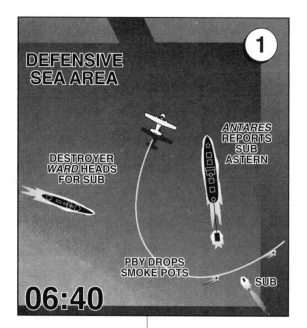

DEFENSIVE SEA AREA

①

DESTROYER *WARD* HEADS FOR SUB

ANTARES REPORTS SUB ASTERN

PBY DROPS SMOKE POTS

SUB

06:40

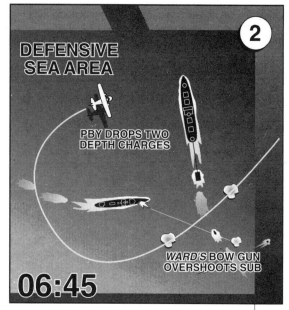

DEFENSIVE SEA AREA

②

PBY DROPS TWO DEPTH CHARGES

WARD'S BOW GUN OVERSHOOTS SUB

06:45

to 25 knots. About two feet of conning tower could be seen slicing through the water. Fascinated gunners on the destroyer caught glimpses of the slim dark shape, close enough to make out rust and moss.

It continued to dog *Antares*.

"Commence firing," ordered Outerbridge. Goepner passed the word to Dionisopoulos, who told Gun No. 1 on the destroyer's bow to fire, followed by Gun No. 3 on the starboard side of deck house.

They were too close to use the gun's sights, so Boatswain's Mate A. Art aimed the forward four-incher "like a squirrel rifle."

At 6:45 a.m., the first shot of the Pacific war missed, "passing directly over the conning tower" and splashing in the water beyond.

"Keep firing! Keep firing!" Outerbridge shouted at Gun No. 1, but in the confusion they thought the order was "Cease firing."

With the conning tower now only 50 yards away, at No. 3 gun behind the bridge, Gun Captain Russell Knapp's round hit the midget "at the waterline … the junction of the hull and the conning tower." It was a "square positive hit." Outerbridge noted the projectile did not pass through the submarine and explode outside. Instead, the sail shuddered over to starboard — but continued toward Pearl.

Tanner's PBY dropped a brace of depth charges, missing the midget but exploding close enough to the destroyer to lather the ship with spray.

Looking over their shoulders, Phill saw the black rectangle knifing through the water. *The PBY came awfully close*, he thought. *This is awfully weird. Is this enemy action?*

Gerner excitedly gripped the rail as *Ward* closed on the submarine. The object was slimy with black-green moss. It was sucked into the destroyer's bow wave and hung bobbing alongside for an eternal moment, long enough for Gerner to stare into the dark, wet eye of the periscope.

FIRST SHOTS

Then it bounced away, shaking and bucking in *Ward's* wake.

At the sound of a whistle, Chief Torpedoman W.C. Maskzawilz rolled four depth charges off the stern. It was a killing pattern with the pistols set for 100 feet, and the submarine disappeared in the stems of thundering geysers. *She*

seemed to wade right into that first one, Maskzawilz thought, with some satisfaction.

My God, Goepner shuddered on the bridge, *I hope she wasn't an American sub. I hope this wasn't a mistake.*

On *Antares,* Ellis was startled and excited to see *Ward* open fire on the black shape, and was concerned that the hurtling destroyer would accidentally ram *Antares.* The other ship heeled about as the depth charges erupted. Ellis saw the small submarine racked up in the air, a view not reported by *Ward's* crew.

Ward roared by, and Ellis gaped. The whole thing had taken just moments. The fireman tossed himself down the ladders into the boiler room, sliding with hands on the rails and ignoring the rungs; he was on fire to tell his fellow stokers the details. They chattered below, excitedly, and decided the submarine was probably Japanese. Ellis claimed that craft was full-sized; *no, it was huge!*

In the patrol bomber above, Tanner was horrified. He decided *Ward* knew what she was doing and made another pass. He tersely

An image once thought to show Ward *dropping depth charges on the midget submarine, analysis shows the four-stacker is actually* USS Stewart, *probably near Shanghai in the early 1920s.*

reported the attack to Kaneohe and glumly resumed his patrol, convinced a courts-martial awaited him.

On board tug *Keosanqua*, now a mile away, the crew watched all the crashing and splashing with amused interest. Another drill. That attitude was shared by many still below deck in *Ward*.

Just as the Japanese airmen had feared, a blundering midget had triggered a shooting match. The first blood shed at Pearl Harbor was Japanese, the first ship sunk belonged to the Imperial Navy.

"He never saw us," mused Outerbridge. "We ran on him for five minutes, but he was bent on following the *Antares* into port." There was a large scum of oil on the surface. *Ward* tried to locate the submarine with her sonar, and detected nothing. She must have gone to the bottom.

In contrast to the bewildered mood on the deck, Outerbridge decided to radiate confidence. He ordered the ship to chase a sampan only 500 yards away. It was in the Prohibited Area, a violation. The sampan, number 248 clearly visible on her stern lit out to the west, toward Barbers Point. A sampan with a similar number had been reported on November 6, making a run across the area at about the same time every morning. They'd been warned away once; it was time to do it again.

Inside the harbor at this time, about 6:50 a.m., the action at the gate was far away. Yard tug *YT-153* chugged away from the main landing about this time, Boatswain's Mate Ralph L. Holzhaus at the wheel. She was ferrying harbor pilot Captain Oscar L. Otterson out to *Antares*.

Destroyer *Helm* prepared for a day of passing through the deperming buoys in Pearl Harbor's West Loch, which degaussed the ship's hull and made it unattractive to magnetic mines. Accordingly, magnetic compasses and chronometers were already deposited on destroyer *Blue* at the next buoy; deperming would throw them out of whack. The boilers were lit, and the watch mustered the crew on deck. Two were missing, probably not too bad after a Saturday night.

While noses were being counted on board *Helm*, Outerbridge rang up the 14th Naval District watch officer at 6:51 a.m. *We have dropped depth charges on sub operating in defensive sea area*, he messaged.

That didn't sound tough enough. "Stand by for more messages …" *Ward's* radio operator said to shore.

Your last priority? wondered the shore.

Outerbridge wanted them to know he was shooting at something, and not getting trigger-happy. He recomposed the message and resent it two minutes later; *We have attacked, fired upon, depth-bombed and*

KICK-OFF TIME

For the Japanese, war with the West actually began on Nov. 21, when the assembled ships of Kido Butai were messaged to begin the second phase of operations. The British Far East Combined Bureau in Singapore, FECB, had already divined this; Captain W.W. Mortimer there had been busy the month of November tracking the movements of Japanese commercial shipping, and noticed that the ships were on their way back to the Empire. At the outbreak of war in Europe, German merchant ships were caught flatfooted in Allied ports. The Japanese learned from this. None of their ships would be in foreign ports by the end of the month.

When this information was transmitted to London, British intelligence analysts predicted war would break out any time after Dec. 5.

When the dust had settled from the attack on Pearl Harbor, the Navy lined up the crew of No.3 gun on destroyer Ward *for publicity pictures.*

sunk submarine operating in defensive sea area. Underkofler, transcribing *Ward's* message at the Bishop's Point radio station, excitedly wrote that the destroyer had "dripped depth charges."

That should let headquarters know something was growling at Pearl Harbor's doorstep. The message was logged in on Ford Island at 6:53 a.m., while Fuchida's airplanes were still an hour away. *Ward* continued chasing the sampan. *Did you get last message? ... Stand by for further messages,* radioed *Ward,* following up.

Behind them, *Antares* had finally skidded to a stop in the channel entrance and was waiting for *Keosanqua,* only a few minutes away.

Hidden around the corner of Oahu, Coast Guard cutter *Tiger* loafed near Waianae, heading south. Since Dec. 3, she had spent her days patrolling the area between Kaena and Barbers Points, boarding sampans at random and demanding to see registration Form 2686, which would confirm the fishing boat's identity. Coxswain "Doc" Nash, the helmsman with the twin brother on cutter *Taney,* was at the wheel. Nash and the executive officer, a chief named Wells, chatted about the daily topic, which was whether or not war was imminent. Wells remarked that his landlord, a Japanese-American woman, was convinced that the Japanese would strike sometime in December.

Silva, the radioman, appeared and announced that he had overheard *Ward* engaged in enemy action to the south. Skipper Mazzoni was called to the bridge, and *Tiger* went down the coast to render assistance. Silva, who doubled as sonar operator, immediately started listening to the water beneath her. *Tiger* headed for the defensive sea area, hoping to be of some help.

A few minutes after 7 a.m., hot on the trail of the sampan, *Ward's* sonar bounced off something vaguely submarine-like. The destroyer steamed over the sound trace and dropped more depth charges.

Black oil bubbled to the surface behind *Ward.*

A Boat Dogged By Bad Luck

The picture above, taken in 1940 at Honolulu's Kewalo Basin, shows Hawaii's fishing fleet with American flags flying. The sampan in the foreground is *Ebesu Maru No. 2*, which blundered into the first American battle of World War II. The boat, built in 1931, had a history of similar hard luck. The year it was completed, Ichimatsu Kimura and fisherman Yukitoshi Nakashima were severely burned in a gasoline fire at Kewalo Basin. The boat was gutted and had to be rebuilt.

Two years later, another gasoline explosion injured four men, and slightly damaged the sampan. The Coast Guard towed it back to Kewalo Basin in 1939 when the engine failed off Black Point. *Ebesu Maru No. 2* was seized by the government during World War II, and the last record of it is in 1949, when it became part of a fraud judgment against an "ex-bootlegger" involved in a "fake diamond enterprise." The sampan was liquidated to defray court expenses.

"This is a lot of activity for a Sunday morning," said Outerbridge, to no one in particular.

Outerbridge ordered the sampan to halt through a bullhorn, and when she did not, a gunner's mate cracked rifle shots across her bow.

"But stand by ... but stand by for message at any time," *Ward* radioed ashore.

Phill saw officers shouting at the sampan, trying to make them understand they were in a restricted area. His impression was that the sampan crew had trouble with English. After the rifle fire, the sampan halted quickly. The captain appeared on deck frantically waving a white flag — understandable under the circumstances, but Outerbridge laughed at the man's discomfort.

The sampan, *Ebesu Maru No. 2*, serial #248 32A453, was a 34-foot "akule boat," owned by 88-year-old Ichimatsu Kimura of Hawaii Suisan Kaisha Fishing Co. Hawaii Suisan was one of three fishing outfits charged with illegally registering U.S. citizens as owners of the boats to get around a mandate requiring the fleet to be American-owned. The usual crew consisted of two alien Japanese and one citizen.

On the morning of Dec. 7, however, *Ward* simply ordered the sampan to return to Honolulu and decided to escort her until Coast Guard cutter *Reliance* could relieve them of shepherd duty. *We have*

FIRST SHOTS

Matson liner Lurline *steams through the Golden Gate.*

intercepted a sampan into Honolulu, signaled *Ward. Please have Coast Guard send cutter to relieve us of sampan.*

Underkoffer at Bishop's Point asked the destroyer to repeat the message. *Ward* did.

The sun was well up and the seas were quiet.

Just as *Ebesu Maru No. 2* returned to port, *I-26* rose out of the sea ahead of *Cynthia Olson*, a thousand miles to the north.

Commander Minoro Yokota was tired of shadowing the little wooden freighter and he knew the precise time of the attack, which was drawing close. Although he had heard nothing about the attack on the wireless, he had implicit faith in the Imperial airmen's ability to deliver a war on schedule. It was his turn.

At 2,000 meters, he ordered a shot across her bow. The freighter, possibly confused, kept coming. *I-26* fired another round. *Cynthia Olson* got the message, and stopped to lower her two lifeboats.

The Matson liner *Lurline*, two days out of Pearl Harbor, and 320 miles due south of *Cynthia Olson*, picked up Private Samuel Zisking's distress call — *SOS* — *Am under torpedo attack by surfaced submarine.* The message was also picked up by *I-26*, and Yokota noted the error in attack methods.

On *Lurline*, chief officer Edward Collins was chatting with another officer, "Tiny" Nelson, who was on watch in the liner's radio shack, when the signal came in. They were both stunned by use of "torpedo," and Nelson directed radio operator Rudy Asplund to query *Cynthia Olson* about the attack. Zisking signaled that the attack was actually by gunfire, and then contact was broken.

Collins hustled the information to the chart room, where First Officer John van Orden plotted *Cynthia Olson's* location; uncomfortably close. The skipper, Commodore Charles A. Berndtson, was apprised of the situation.

ADVANCE FORCE — PEARL HARBOR

I-26 at sea. The heavy cables abaft the sail are radio antennae.

[1] *Asplund and Grogan had heard mysterious Japanese naval signals on the trip to Honolulu, and when* Lurline *moored there on Dec. 3, their transcripts were confiscated by Navy Intelligence.*

[2] *In 1966, F. Kent Loomis, acting director of the Office of Naval History, with the help of Dr. William Markowitz of the Time Service Division of the Naval Observatory, calculated the attack actually occurred at 7:30 a.m. Pearl Harbor time.*

Asplund and asistant radio operator Leslie Grogan, in the meantime, attempted to relay the message to Navy stations in California and Hawaii, and failing that, tried Coast Guard frequencies.[1] Asplund eventually raised the Globe Wireless station at KTK in San Francisco. Globe operator Ray Farrill called the Navy radio station at Mare Island immediately, and got no reply.

Farrill ran to a telephone and called the Office of Naval Communications in the San Francisco federal building.

A few minutes later, the Globe operators received more bad news over the wireless. An attack was under way at Pearl Harbor.

This information was also picked up by *Lurline*, 55 minutes after she received the SOS from *Cynthia Olson*. Due to the then-complicated nature of world-wide time zones — which wasn't straightened out until 1947 — there still exists some confusion about the exact time *Cynthia Olson* was attacked. Many believe she sent out her distress signal a full hour before the Pearl Harbor attack.

Like the rest of the Advance Force, Yokota and *I-26* were living on Tokyo time. They knew, perhaps, a few minutes one way or another wouldn't help either the freighter or Pearl Harbor. He claimed after the war that the first shot had been fired at 3:35 a.m. Tokyo time, which translated to 8:05 a.m. Pearl Harbor time.[2]

Yokota waited until the lifeboats were away from the ship before attacking again. *I-26* played with the freighter, prowling around her while submerging and surfacing, and Yokota drilled his men as they ran to their guns. Each time, they fired a couple of shots at the freighter, as if she were a target ship. Yokota kept *I-26* in constant crash-dive readiness, as he expected counterattacks by American bombers.

The freighter kept floating, and Yokota was losing patience. *I-26* switched to torpedo attack, but drifted too close to the now-blazing ship and had to shift into full reverse. When they were safely away from *Cynthia Olson*, 400 meters or so, Chief Torpedoman Takaji Kamaba fired the submarine's first wartime torpedo.

The old torpedo went berserk traveling to the target, spinning in the water, and barely missed the freighter before sputtering out.

Dismayed, the Japanese submarine dived again. When she re-emerged, the freighter was listing heavily, and the deck gun was once again used to slam shells into her. After a half-dozen shells were fired, the electric ammunition elevator froze, and another dozen shells were hand-carried topsides. Chief Gunner Hayashi got permission to take a snapshot of *Cynthia Olson* broken and burning in the water.

FIRST SHOTS

After seven hours of hammering the stubborn freighter with shells, *I-26* left her there and proceeded to the planned patrol area halfway between Hawaii and California. From there, *I-26* went on to the seas outside Seattle, hoping to intercept aircraft carrier *Enterprise.*

Yokota did not actually see *Cynthia Olson* sink, but there was no doubt in his mind. He claimed the first open-seas victory of the new war, even if it did involve the Imperial Navy's newest submarine and an unarmed, 22-year-old wooden ship.

Over the airwaves, nothing more was heard from the freighter. On Berndtson's orders, *Lurline* went off the air and charged away at full speed for San Francisco. Collins spent the rest of Dec. 7, breaking open the paint locker, using dark blue trim paint to black out hundreds of portholes. Berndtson also closed the ship's bars and secured the liquor. Mystified passengers weren't notified of the war until 5 p.m., where Berndtson gathered them together in the First Class Lounge. They were ordered to surrender all radios and electrical apparatus — in case Japanese submarines were able to get a fix on them — to eat meals as quickly as possible and to carry life jackets at all times. Berndtson also

SS Cynthia Olson *in Seattle, above, and her last moments afloat, a snapshot taken by* I-26's *chief gunner.*

said he had no idea where the ship would eventually dock.

Blackout completed, Collins was disconcerted to discover how bright the moon was that evening. "The moon reflecting on the water was a ribbon of silver from horizon to horizon, and with the white hull of the *Lurline* illuminated by the moonlight, we felt as though the periscope of every Japanese submarine was watching us," Collins recalled.

The next day, *I-19* passed through the area and spotted *Cynthia Olson's* lifeboats. The submarine pulled alongside and her medical officer scrutinized the hapless Americans. *I-19* then passed food to the lifeboats and vacated the area.

The crew of *Cynthia Olson* were then swallowed up by the vast Pacific. When interviewed in 1966, Yokota claimed to be startled to hear this. He had assumed American ships and planes would swarm the area, a factor that also contributed to *I-26's* hasty departure.

Radioman Grogan was upset by the radio intercepts being taken from him in Honolulu and he wrote a nine-page, single-spaced memorandum detailing the voyage to and from Hawaii. As *Lurline* approached the Matson dock in San Francisco in the early morning of Dec. 10, an air raid siren went off and the piers were plunged into darkness. Berndtson's crew barely managed to keep the liner from hurtling into the pier.

No mention of the loss of *Cynthia Olson* appeared in public print until more than a year after the war. A Navy Intelligence officer immediately boarded *Lurline* in San Francisco and seized the radio logs as well as those of Globe Wireless. He also demanded Grogan's memorandum, but the radio operator refused, giving it instead to Berndtson. Under orders, the commodore surrendered that document as well.

These records, which could settle the question of attack time, have since vanished. The Navy claims it has no record of the incident.

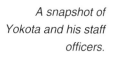

A snapshot of Yokota and his staff officers.

INVISIBLE MOMENTUM

13

THE DELICATE SOUND OF THUNDER

Ensign Oliver H. Underkofler, the communication watch officer who had been sleeping at Bishop's Point radio station, was "broken out of his bunk" when destroyer *Ward* called the first submarine-sinking flash at 6:53 a.m. The message startled him. By the time the second arrived, the ensign was alert and immediately dispatched it to duty officer Lieutenant (jg) Albert E. Kilhefner.

The chain of command responsibility began to clink into place. A few minutes later, Underkofler was directed by Kilhefner, at 14th Naval District Chief of Staff Captain John Earle's order, to request verification from *Ward*.

"Should we encode it?" he asked, and was told to make it so. The verification query was translated into a strip-code cipher, which took several minutes, requiring alphabets on pieces of paper to be misaligned in groups of five letters. The substituted message was then spoken over voice radio, a letter at a time, and delivered in phonetic equivalents, such as "Affirm, Baker, Charlie," and so on.

The system was very slow, but the only one in use on *Ward*.

On board Coast Guard cutter *Tiger*, at that moment rounding Barbers Point, Silva the radioman was operating the sonar as well. He picked up a definite echo. The executive officer, named Wells, suggested that it was a whale; the equipment was picking up the signal inshore of the boat and paralleling their course.

"If it's a whale, it's an awfully small one, because it's in very shallow water," said Silva. Odd, though, because the creature was making motor noises. Wells instructed coxswain "Doc" Nash to shadow the echo, and *Tiger* began to feel her way down the coast toward Pearl Harbor.

The cutter was almost certainly following Ensign Kazuo Sakamaki's *I-24tou*. The midget submarine, freed of the mother ship an hour before, continued to tumble through the water. Somehow, on the rough voyage from Japan, the small craft's trim had become unbalanced.

The ensign and crewman Inagaki frantically worked at trimming the submarine, wiggling one at a time through the tiny tunnel that ran

the length of the midget, wrestling lead ballast and shifting water from tank to tank.

They finally massaged the craft upright and aimed it at Pearl, trusting a magnetic compass instead of the faulty gyrocompass. Sakamaki and Inagaki rested for a moment in the sweating, tiny control room, chewing on rice balls and trading cups of grape wine. They held hands and vowed a successful mission. Minutes later, Sakamaki rose to the surface, risking a peek through the periscope.

They were running away from Pearl. The magnetic compass was defective as well, and had swung the midget 90 degrees off course. The craft skewed around in floundering circles.

Sakamaki was shocked. He tried slowing to minimum speed and using the periscope to put the submarine on course, worried he wouldn't get into harbor before the air attack. But the stubborn ship insisted on setting her own course.

Inagaki was worried, and Sakamaki reached down and clapped him on the shoulder. "Have no fear," he said, "now that we have come this far, it is our duty to complete our task. We will somehow break through that guard line and pierce into the enemy harbor.

"Once inside it, we will dare to make a surface run at full speed. We'll let our torpedoes go at an enemy battleship. If necessary, let's dash into a battleship ourselves.

"That's our mission. In a few hours, our fate will be decided. So cheer up!"

Sakamaki's little speech emboldened the ensign as well, and he raised the midget near the surface and popped up the periscope.

A ship raced by so closely Sakamaki could see the white uniforms of the crew. "Just a couple of destroyers!" he jeered, and Inagaki laughed.

The ship was *Ward*, and at 7:03 a.m., the destroyer got a blind sonar contact and rolled five depth charges near Sakamaki, thoroughly rattling the sub. The ensign passed out, and awakened some time later to find the sub misty with white smoke and acrid fumes from the straining batteries. *I-24tou* had drifted west, a victim of invisible momentum and unseen currents.

Lieutenant Clarence E. "Dick" Dickinson drew an anti-submarine patrol preceding carrier Enterprise as she returned to Pearl Harbor.

Hugging the shore, Sakamaki headed back east, unaware that they were being followed by *Tiger*.

Other watches were being kept for submarine activity. The *Enterprise* task force, returning from the delivery of 12 VMF-211 Wildcats to Wake Island, was 250 miles west of Oahu on the morning of Dec. 7. At 6:15 a.m., the carrier nosed into the wind and launched the morning scouting force, nine flights of two planes apiece. Each pair of SBD dive bombers was given an arc of of 10 degrees radiating out from the task force. All planes were in the air by 6:30.

180

Lieutenant Clarence E. "Dick" Dickinson, flight officer of VS-6, took off with Radioman First Class William C. Miller in the rear seat. Dickinson used Miller, a confident "country boy … with a good ol' farm boy gait," as his radioman every chance he got. Miller's home-grown sense of direction was more accurate than Dickinson's book-learned navigation skills, or so the pilot believed. As they buckled in, Dickinson noticed that Miller was uneasy. Miller explained his dis-comfort by joking that out of the 21 men in his radio class he was the only one without an ocean crash. "Hope you won't get me wet today, sir," he said.

Dickinson knew Miller was going on leave soon to get married. "This will probably be our last mission together," he pointed out. "That's all we've got to get by — this morning's flight."

The mission that morning was to sweep the oceans ahead of the ships, looking for anything suspicious. The task force was a day late returning to Pearl Harbor, having been slowed by the same rough seas that battered the Advance Force. Accordingly, the planes were in-structed to land at Ford Island when the sweep was completed.

The morning flight of Dec. 7 was to have been Radioman First Class William C. Miller's last — his enlistment was nearly up and he was engaged to be married.

There wasn't much to see. The Japa-nese submarine net was arranged to catch vessels entering Pearl Harbor, or to inter-cept those coming from the northwest; the planes were flying into the only hole in the net. In the west, only *I-74* lurked in the waters near Niihau. The only ships spotted by the SBDs were Richfield tanker *Pat Doheny*, 50 miles south of Niihau, and submarine *Thresher* and destroyer *Litchfield*, which had rendezvoused to transfer Seaman William Grover, the criti-cally injured sailor on the submarine.

Three SBD Dauntless dive bombers of VS-6, in November 1941. The middle aircraft is 6-S-4, flown by Dickinson and Miller on Dec. 7.

At 7:12 a.m., Lieutenant Commander Harold Kaminski, the officer in charge of net and boom defenses, was passed *Ward's* signal about the submarine action a half-hour earlier. Kaminski's men had been on alert since Nov. 12, when he decided that he "did not like the way things were going … no sir, I did not like the looks of things."

Despite being tired — he had been on duty since the previous morning — the signal seemed ominous to Kaminski. His orders in such situations were to ring up the district chief of staff and the commandant's aide. The aide didn't answer his phone, so Kaminski moved down the list and tried the fleet duty officer. That that day it was Commander Vincent R. Murphy.

Coast Guard 125-footer Tiger *pierside in Honolulu.*

He got the duty officer's assistant, Lieutenant R.B. Black, and read *Ward's* attack signal to him. Black thanked Kaminski and went off to tell Murphy.

Black found the duty officer dressing in his quarters. "Did Kaminski say what he was doing about it?" wondered Murphy. "Did he say whether Admiral Bloch knew about it or not?"

"No," said Black.

"I've gotta finish dressing," said Murphy, holding his pants in his hands. "Call Kaminski back and see what he's doing about it. See whether or not he's contacted Bloch."

Black was still holding the telephone. "I've dialed and dialed, but Kaminski's line is still busy," he complained to Murphy.

Murphy considered. "All right, you go to the office and start breaking out the charts. Check the positions of the ships involved. I'll dial Kaminski one more time and then I'll be over to the office."

Kaminski's line was still busy and Murphy called the base operator. "Tell Kaminski to call me immediately, and break in on any conversation I might be having, unless it's of supreme importance." He then hustled over to the duty office.

On his own initiative, Kaminski had used the phone to order destroyer *Mahan* out to sea, which he thought was the ready-duty destroyer. *Mahan* was with the *Lexington* task force near Midway.

"Get underway immediately and contact *USS Ward* in defensive sea area," he ordered, and instructed the communications office to send a copy of the order to *Ward*. By this point Kaminski was positive that "we were in it."

The message was sent visually to where *Mahan* was supposedly moored, and intercepted by destroyer *Monaghan*. Kaminski then rang up Captain Earle.

"I want to speak to Captain Earle!" he shouted when Mrs. Earle

INVISIBLE MOMENTUM

answered. As she handed the phone to her husband, she remarked that the fellow on the other end seemed "quite excited."

Earle listened to Kaminski, and said, "Oh, it's probably just another false report. Our boys are seeing submarines everywhere."

Kaminski explained that shots had been fired, and Earle was astounded. This seemed serious, more so than the message passed on to him earlier by Underkofler. For some reason, Earle had the impression that the submarine had fired upon *Ward*.

"Why, I can't believe it!" he sputtered. "Call the district operations officer — Commander C.B. Momsen. Tell him what you told me. I'll call (Admiral) Bloch."

Bloch listened to Earle's account, and then asked if he felt it was a false report. Earle read Bloch the substance of the *Ward* encounter.

"I can't understand from the nature of this dispatch. Is it a real submarine or a report of a submarine, is it bona fide, or a sound contact, or a sight contact, was *Ward* fired upon, or had *Ward* fired?" wondered Bloch. Earle admitted he didn't know.

"Get it cleared up immediately, John," said Bloch.

"The enemy's a little more active with their sub campaign, or *Ward* made a mistake," said Earle.

Their first reaction was that it was probably a mistake. If it wasn't, they decided, then *Ward* could certainly "take care of the situation and the relief destroyer could lend a hand." They were only vaguely alarmed, and could see no specific threat except that posed by a snooping submarine. The bugaboo of an air attack was something promoted by aviation officers, said Earle, later.

In the end, the admiral instructed Earle to "find out about it" and hung up to await further developments. By this point, Bloch figured, Kimmel surely knew about it.

Earle dashed into the bathroom to shave and dress, shouting at his wife to fix breakfast. The phone rang again; it was Kaminski with the news about the fugitive sampan. Earle was somewhat relieved. *If the situation was so dangerous out there at the harbor mouth, why would* Ward *leave her post to chase a frightened fishing boat back to Honolulu?* Besides, with *Monaghan* routed out, there was nothing more they could do anyway. It was in Kimmel's hands. Earle returned to the bathroom, intending to shower before shaving.

While Earle was pondering events in the shower, Kaminski was being deluged with calls, all of which he had to handle himself. Kaminski often complained about the men on telephone watch. They were locals, whose pidgin English was indecipherable to Kaminski. Besides, they had not been trained in the teletype. Kaminski often had to operate the machine himself, which made him furious.

He briefed Momsen, who was the officer in charge of turning on the air raid siren, and called another officer, an Ensign Harold E. Logan. Both promised to hustle down to the office. Kaminski then tried calling his own people, and could not get through. He made contact with a switchboard operator, whom he knew only as Miss Jones, and

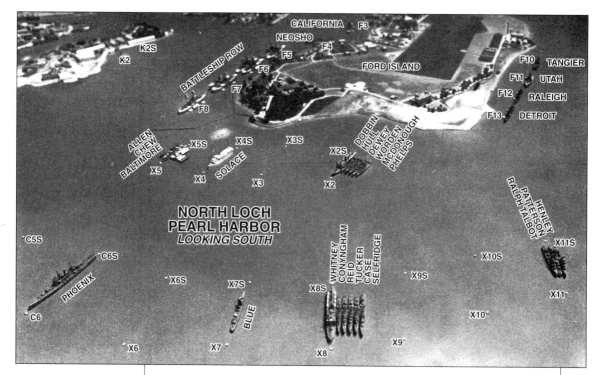

NORTH LOCH
PEARL HARBOR
LOOKING SOUTH

she promised to stay at her board and forward his calls. Jones was at her switchboard the rest of the day, a performance Kaminski later termed "wonderful. I don't know what I could have done without her."[1]

While the command structure at Pearl Harbor was trading telephone calls, business went on around the shipyard. At 7:15 a.m., *Keosanqua* finally eased alongside *Antares'* towed lighter. With all the excitement, they were running late. The supply ship also required a customs check upon arrival. Customs inspectors Andrew Buta and John Williams, notified that *Antares* would arrive about 7:30, showed up at the Yard Duty Office at 7:20. They were told the ship was running about an hour late, so they cooled their heels.

At 7:26 a.m., destroyer *Helm* moved away from the nest next to *Blue*, and leisurely proceeded up the channel for deperming, the only warship underway inside the harbor. They were followed by the ship's two boats, containing seven men. Gunnery officer Lieutenant (jg) Victor Dybdal was at his station on the fantail, supervising the stowing of the mooring lines. Half the crew was immediately sent below for chow, so they'd be ready to deperm right after mooring.

At Buoy X-11 nearby, destroyers *Henley*, *Patterson* and *Ralph Talbot* were nested together and sailors were gradually waking up. Except, on *Henley* — a green hand had sounded General Quarters instead of Quarters for Muster. The sleepy, cursing crew, like that earlier on *Ward*, took their stations. At the time, it seemed like a monumental screw-up.

At sea, *Tiger* was still tailing a mysterious object in the water. The Coast Guard cutter went in circles trying to locate the object, and finally cut her engines to reduce interference with the listening apparatus.

[1] Verva N. Jones received a civilian commendation ribbon on July 10, 1951, for her steadfast courage on Dec. 7. The award was recommended by Bloch.

184

Nothing—the echoes faded away. *Tiger* resumed steaming toward the defensive sea area and kept a sharp lookout. The signal returned and *Tiger* fell in behind it. It was headed directly for Pearl Harbor.

All that was visible, notes *Tiger's* log, were "friendly destroyer" *Ward* and a "naval auxiliary ship with barge and tug laying to off the Pearl Harbor entrance"; *Antares*, her tow and *Keosanqua*. Apparently not visible was submarine *Plunger*, at that moment rounding Diamond Head and heading for the barn after a cruise to the West Coast.[2]

By 7:39 a.m., *Keosanqua* had hooked up to the lighter in record time. From the bridge of *Antares*, Commander Lawrence Grannis watched in satisfaction.

Ward was still some distance away, and the crews of *Antares* and *Keosanqua* were concentrating on the task at hand. So only a few soldiers at the coast artillery batteries at Fort Kamehameha saw an odd object nosing around the harbor passage. It looked like a black stick, and made a small plume in the water as it moved past the shore battery.

Monaghan, the harbor's ready-duty destroyer, lay at berth X-14, snuggled up with *Aylwin*, *Dale* and *Farragut* of Division Two.

It was nine minutes to 8 a.m., at which time *Monaghan* would be relieved as the ready-duty destroyer. Lieutenant Commander William Burford, the skipper, was at the deck rail, watching the liberty gig tie up alongside. In nine minutes he could go ashore and see his family.

Burford was handed the message from Kaminski — *Proceed immediately and contact* Ward *in defensive sea area.*[3]

It takes a while for ships to get up enough steam to sail — an hour for a destroyer, two for a larger ship. The *Monaghan* skipper would not be seeing his family any time soon. Burford went below to reflect on his ruined Sunday morning.

Commander Murphy arrived at Kimmel's CINCUS office in the Submarine Base building in time to hear his phone ringing. It was Commander Logan Ramsey, operations officer of Patrol Wing 2. He was calling from his home on Ford Island to tell Murphy about Ensign William Tanner's PBY attack.

"That's funny," pondered Murphy. "We got the same sort of message from one of the DDs on the inshore patrol." Any doubt about the authenticity of this report was beginning to evaporate from Murphy's mind.

Ramsey pulled on slacks and an aloha shirt and drove the short distance to the operations building on Ford Island. He began to draw up a search plan for his three airborne PBYs, to the northeast, considered the most likely attack corridor.

Murphy replaced the receiver and it rang again. It was Kaminski, who told him that Bloch had been notified, the ready-duty destroyer had been ordered out and the standby destroyer advised to fire up her boilers. Also, the Coast Guard had received the same signals from *Ward* and was standing by for orders.

"Oh," said Murphy. *Things seemed to be slipping out of their hands.* "Do you have any more details? I'll have to call Kimmel."

[2] This is according to Plunger's *action report that day. It seems unlikely they would head unescorted toward the harbor.*

[3] Unfortunately, Burford's thoughts at this moment are not recorded.

"The message came out of a clear sky," admitted Kaminski. "There's no word of a preliminary chase or search of any kind."

"Thanks," said Murphy. It seemed as if most members of the Navy brass in Pearl Harbor were calling each other up and chatting about the *Ward* attack. [4]

[4] Nobody thought to notify the other services, however, and Army Air Force pilots lounged sleepily at the air fields.

Murphy joggled the phone cradle to clear the line and called Kimmel. The admiral was preparing for a ritual golf date with Army commander General Walter Short, and was preparing to shave and shower. Despite that, he listened carefully to Murphy and promised he'd be right down.

Murphy set the phone down; it rang again. It was Ramsey, calling from operations, wanting further instructions. "I dunno," said Murphy. "It might be wise to make your planes available in case the admiral wants them."

He set the phone down.

It rang.

It was Kaminski with the news about the sampan. "Give me details," said Murphy, who then called Kimmel back and told him about the sampan.

Murphy set the phone down. It didn't ring. Outside, he heard the growing thunder of airplane engines.

At the radio station at Bishop's Point, Radioman Richard Humphery arrived at 7:50 a.m. Humphery, checking the log, noticed that the conversation between *Ward* and *Condor* in the middle of the night had been picked up, but had not been directed toward his station. Because it only seemed to be a conversation between the two ships, nothing more was done to alert the inshore patrol. Besides, the later messages, about the sinking near *Antares*, had been passed on. There was nothing more to be done.

At this moment, *Ward* was once again nearing the harbor mouth, having passed the sampan on to *Reliance*. At 7:54 a.m., the watch noted several airplanes flying over Barbers Point, heading in the direction of Pearl Harbor. On the bridge, the destroyer's reply to Earle's request for verification was still being decoded.

Closer to Pearl Harbor, *Tiger* had followed the echo right up to the entrance of Pearl Harbor, and lost it in the reef on the west side of the channel. By now, they were convinced it was a submarine. *Tiger* entered Pearl Harbor in the hopes of once again picking up the echo. The gates were open, and *Tiger* was well into the mouth at 7:54 a.m.

The little Coast Guard ship was surprised by what appeared to be shell hits striking the channel water. *Were they from a ship over the horizon?* Airplanes, the same ones spotted by *Ward*, suddenly swept past her. A couple dropped small bombs, which missed; several fired machine gun bursts at the cutter. Rounds laced the water, framing the cutter. The airplanes sped away into the sleeping shipyard.

Tiger appears to be the first American ship fired on during the attack on Pearl Harbor.

INVISIBLE MOMENTUM

THE HARD PLACE

14

GOING AGAINST INSTINCT

The hurricane of destruction that visited the U.S. Fleet at Pearl Harbor that Sunday morning in December 1941, remains one of the hinges of history, a salient point upon which the modern world began. It is also a major embarrassment for the U.S. Navy, whose personnel losses in the attack were three times that of the Spanish-American War and World War I combined.

Fairly or unfairly, Admiral Husband Kimmel's grasp of the tactical situation prior to the attack is often called into question by historians. Both Kimmel and his opposite number in the U.S. Army, General Walter Short, were publicly humiliated by the disaster, primarily because official Washington at the time decided to make them scapegoats.

The reasons Americans were caught asleep at the switch have been hotly debated ever since. Many clues to the impending attack were available that seem obvious in retrospect, from the radar traces picked up north of Oahu that morning, to the decrypted radio intercepts, to *Ward's* sinking of the midget submarine more than an hour before the bombs began to fall.

On the other hand, the Imperial Navy did its best to ensure a secret operation, and it remained so. Japanese intelligence goals also were specific rather than scatter shot. They began with a fair idea of American fleet disposition at Pearl Harbor; Kimmel's men, by contrast, had absolutely no idea on which side of the Pacific the Imperial warships steamed.

"Japan evidently brought to bear upon this attack the best brains, the best equipment, and the finest intelligence, with the most expert planning, which it had," admitted Army intelligence head Major General Sherman Miles. "It was a bold and considered venture."

The airplanes of Kido Butai slashed across Oahu, leaving broken warships and shattered airplanes behind. The awful destructive power of the aircraft carrier was as much of a surprise as the attack itself. The air attack has received the lion's share of historical analysis since; the long view of Pearl Harbor has always been from the air. But until the first bomb fell, the practicality of aerial attack was still just a theory.

Kimmel and his commanders were concentrating on the proven threat, submarines which prowled the depths outside the harbor.

In World War I, and in the two and half years of war prior to the Pearl Harbor attack, the most potent strategic weapon in modern warfare was the submarine. Hitler's wolf packs were starving out England, the U-boats appeared suddenly out of the depths, delivering crushing blows with torpedoes — a weapon that, pound for pound of high explosive, had no equal in destructive potential — and the submarine then retreated into the stealthy deep. Even the residual threat of submarine attack was also of strategic significance, tying up men, weapons and materiel that could have been used elsewhere. [1]

Submarines were expected, uninvited guests around American naval bases. The many underwater alerts in the months prior to the attack convinced the admiral and his staff that they were already at the gate. Kimmel discounted estimates by war planners that fixed an air attack as the number-one danger. "It's (just) not in the order of probability," he said. "I'd think that what they're going to do in the case of war in the Pacific, is have a mass submarine attack in the operating areas around Pearl Harbor."

And that is what he prepared for. Taking his cue from his predecessor Admiral Richardson, who was also concerned about submarine stalkers, Kimmel's destroyers trained constantly in anti-submarine tactics. Mysterious echoes were dealt with quickly and hounded out of existence. With the largest concentration of destroyers in the U.S. Navy, the anti-submarine crews of the Pacific Fleet became experts. Kimmel, who had displayed a positive genius for gunnery as an ensign, didn't neglect gunnery exercises either.

No Washington warning delivered to Hawaii indicated to Kimmel that an air attack was imminent. "We *did* expect a surprise submarine attack upon our ships at sea," he testified later. "This readiness to meet the submarine menace is evidenced by the fact that when a submarine was discovered near the entrance to Pearl Harbor on 7 December, it was promptly attacked by the nearest destroyer."

No matter where the Japanese attacked, and it seemed that they might hit anywhere, Imperial Navy submarines were expected off Pearl Harbor. So, when one was reported, it simply seemed to confirm the vague war warning of November; the Japanese were on the move *somewhere*.

"I am very happy to report that at 6:57 on the morning of December 7, one of these destroyers commanded by one of those men who had been put on the alert, sighted a submarine, and he opened fire on it, and he sank it," testified Admiral Claude Bloch, 14th Naval District commandant.

"So he was on the job, and that part of the alert was satisfactory, and I wish it had been with everything else, sir," Bloch wistfully concluded.

Rear Admiral William W. Smith, Kimmel's chief of staff, agreed. "We were very submarine-conscious and one reason for that was that

[1] *The unseen dagger remains a threat today. During the Falklands War, even with sophisticated anti-submarine gear, the mere rumor of Argentine submarine activity paralyzed the British striking force, as frightened Royal Navy sailors pounded the waters with depth charges.*

we had several sound contacts — perhaps all of them were false," he said, explaining why the destroyer men were on their toes. "I think every one in the Fleet expected if an attack came, it would be by submarines rather than (by) aircraft … people of the Fleet felt little danger of an air attack on Pearl Harbor."

"It should be recalled that we were not in a state of war," said Battle Force commander Vice Admiral William S. Pye. "The (offshore) patrol was primarily to determine the possible presence of submarines."

The danger focused on the unknown, explained Pye, and his comments are illustrative of the kind of mild paranoia engendered by invisible assailants. "An attack by a submarine, if fired when the submarine is submerged and the submarine is not definitely sighted, cannot be proven. If attacks had been made by submarines, and the submarine not sighted or sunk or captured, there would have been no way for us to prove definitely that it was not an internal explosion in the ship rather than a torpedo.

"In addition to that there was always the possibility that German crews might man Japanese submarines or might, in the last analysis, even bring their submarines to Hawaii to try to force us into war. It was therefore considered that the possibility of submarine attack was greater than any other form of attack of which the nature could not be uncertain."

"We did expect that there would be Japanese submarines off

Operations Officer Captain W.S. Delaney, CINCUS Admiral Husband E. Kimmel and Chief of Staff Captain William W. Smith worry about the world situation in the fall of 1941. The map is the 1940 National Geographic *edition of the Atlantic Ocean.*

Hawaii, that there would be Japanese submarines off our Pacific Coast, that they would be a line of communications between Pearl Harbor and our Pacific Coast, that there might be an attack on our outlying possessions, such as there were on Midway and Guam," then-Rear Admiral Royal Ingersoll of Naval Operations testified at later hearings that attempted to fix blame for the surprise. "I am sure Admiral (Harold) Stark did not anticipate an attack which the Japanese made at Pearl Harbor, although it was always a possibility; but he did not anticipate it as a probability."

Battle Force commander Vice Admiral William Pye was well aware of the psychological aspects of submarine assault.

The inescapable fact that the fleet was at Pearl Harbor virtually guaranteed an underwater assault. After all, if the tables were turned, that's how the Americans intended to deploy their submarines against the enemy.

Rear Admiral Richmond Kelly Turner, the Navy's war plans officer, expressed his worries about berthing the fleet at a forward post like Pearl Harbor. "Operating for a considerable period here, habitually, would make it certain that the Japanese could concentrate a considerable number of submarines in one relatively small area. If they were boldly and skillfully used, they would (find) numerous opportunities to inflict serious damage," he warned.

Despite the four American shoot-to-kill picket submarines arrayed near Midway, the U.S. Fleet deliberately played passive.

"We didn't want to send any submarines out near the Japanese islands. It was an attempt to retain the peace as long as possible, and to make sure that when the war came, that it would be initiated by Japan and not by the United States," said Turner. The American submarine killers operated in island waters, waiting for the inevitable attack. There were too few of them to range afar, anyway.

[2] Destroyer Reuben James *(DD-245) was sunk; destroyer* Kearny *(DD-432) and oiler* Salinas *(AO-19) were attacked.*

Stark, Chief of Naval Operations, explained the overall situation to a Navy board later. "The Atlantic was in a turmoil … Along late in October and early November, as I recall, we had three ships sunk.[2] We were at our wits end for escort vessels in the Atlantic. I was being pressed to bring escort vessels from the Pacific into the Atlantic …"

If Stark couldn't transfer ships, he moved apparatus. For example, the sonar gear earmarked for the four-stack destroyer/minelayers in Pearl Harbor was suddenly rerouted to the Atlantic

190

in the fall of 1941, a matter that angered Kimmel. He had lost extra sets of underwater ears, ones that couldn't be replaced until a new construction contract was approved. The admiral had counted on these ships being outfitted with the gear by the first week of December.

Kimmel is usually criticized for not doing enough after the "war warning" of Nov. 27, or even of taking it seriously. [3]

The war warning, however, gave Kimmel a convenient excuse to use deadly force against submarines. In doing so, he was exceeding his orders, jumping into a sticky political arena even Richardson didn't dare tread. The situation by the end of 1941 was far more dangerous than it had been the year before.

"Who started the war?" a startled Bloch was quizzed later. The line of questioning by one congressional committee led down the path of American willingness to shoot too quickly, because of Kimmel's go-ahead. Had Outerbridge and his destroyer started the war by sinking the midget, which had not directly provoked them?

"Well, the President issued a proclamation prohibiting submarines from running submerged within the territorial waters and the area three miles south of the entrance to Pearl Harbor, three miles square, and that vicinity is the area in which all ships are prohibited from entering without the consent of the authority in command," said Bloch, testily. "The legal grounds are sound."

Historian Gordon Prange blames "Roosevelt's don't-rock-the-boat policy" for Kimmel's previous hesitancy to act against suspected submarine contacts. The President, a master politician, believed he held the upper hand, the initiative, in diplomatic dealings with Japan. Given enough time, perhaps he could have finessed the Japanese into behaving.

Meanwhile, Roosevelt wasn't allowing Kimmel any operational slack that might provoke the Japanese. Kimmel, well-aware that he had jumped ahead of dozens of other admirals to command the Pacific Fleet, let the President have headway, and complained mostly for show.

The "war warning" message, as interpreted by Pacific Fleet war plans officer Captain Charles McMorris, was to keep the fleet on a steady course. Months of training and alert led him to feel "that the situation was already well in hand … (it) would, in effect, be a message to keep doing what you are doing now."

The only clear signal from above, said McMorris, was "an injunction to be particularly alert for possible enemy submarines."

That was enough for Kimmel. After 10 months on the job, any threat from aircraft carriers seemed distant and abstract to Kimmel, the province of gaming boards. Submarines had been sniffing the admiral's ankles for months, or so he imagined. "Kimmel took measures against the danger which seemed real to him, submarines," wrote Prange.

An enemy I-boat force moving up from "the Marshalls was accepted as almost A-l, and submarine activity was anticipated," said Lieutenant Commander Layton, Kimmel's intelligence officer.

[3] *Rear Admiral Walter Anderson recalled that the war warning was "received with all the solemnity and intense interest at the time that its context manifestly entitled it to — there was nothing light-hearted about the way it was received!"*

Kimmel's decision to treat all submarines in Hawaii waters as enemy was largely based on Layton's analysis, as well as the gut feeling that when the balloon went up, the deep water off Pearl would swarm with undersea raiders. The admiral also was worried about the safety of destroyer crews in these close encounters near the harbor.

"The Pearl Harbor operating area was some 2,000 miles from the nearest Japanese possession. I knew that if we sent any submarines into a Japanese operating area they wouldn't hesitate a moment to bomb them. (So) I felt that any submarine operating submerged in the Pearl Harbor operating area should be bombed. I had felt it for a long time, and I decided on 27 November to bomb them anyhow."

In later testimony, Stark waffled mightily on giving Kimmel firm direction regarding submarine contacts. "I would have left it to his judgment," was a favorite response.

Closer to Pearl Harbor, there were no gray areas. Said Rear Admiral Bill Calhoun, commander of the base force, "there wasn't any question about the fact that if they had encountered a Japanese submarine out there that they were to destroy it; not in my mind."

Coolly and professionally, destroyer *Ward* was acting under Kimmel's shoot-to-kill order of Nov. 28 when it blew away the midget submarine trailing *Antares*. The gunnery was superb, but Kimmel would have not expected less. Other than being in the wrong place at the wrong time, the shape in the water had made no hostile moves. As reported, no one ashore knew whether the encounter was real or imagined, whether the sub had attacked *Ward*, or whether *Ward's* new skipper had imagined the whole thing and depth-charged a whale. Many of the crew on *Ward* assumed the thing in the water was a new type of practice target; it was too small to be a real submarine. Outerbridge's follow-on signal about a trespassing sampan confused things as well.

Under the circumstances, and in the war plans already drafted, little action was called for. Kimmel was offense-minded, and the snug, warm harbor at Pearl tended to take the edge off. Training for the Great Sea Battle was the first priority. "A protracted state of complete readiness to meet a surprise air attack on Pearl Harbor would have completely disrupted training, upkeep and maintenance," Kimmel protested to a skeptical Navy board.

So he and his officers awaited verification of *Ward's* encounter.

In any case, the Pacific Fleet was more protected in Pearl Harbor than out of it. The snaking entrance to the harbor was the only effective shield against an ocean-based underwater assault, and the reason the Pacific Fleet had been banned from other Hawaiian harbors some months previous. If hostile submarines were really massed outside Pearl Harbor, only the destroyers could deal with them. The valuable battleships were safer anchored behind the shoulders of dry land.

The fleet's war doctrine implied no action, except to scramble the ready-duty destroyer. An alert would have made no difference in this situation.

THE HARD PLACE

"But you can be sure that, at that time and upon the facts then at hand, no one reasonably would have or should have been expected to sound an air raid alarm," said Kimmel to a Navy board. "The effort to obtain confirmation of the reported submarine attack off Pearl Harbor was a proper preliminary to more drastic action in view of the number of contacts which had not been verified in the past."

Even if the American fleet were to leave port and been relocated at sea, Kido Butai was prepared for an open-ocean assault. The midget submarines were already trained for that eventuality, in fact, desired it. The ideal situation would be to catch the battleships coming out of the narrow channel, and sink them in the harbor's throat, choking the naval base.

Prange wonders in the ominously titled "Verdict of History" why "the Navy authorities did not realize that the mini-sub heralded a larger force ... such a tiny craft could not have come all the way from Japan except by mother ship."

All that had been reported ashore before the aerial attack was a white wake in the night and a bit of conning tower, which had been promptly holed by the destroyer. Moreover, Outerbridge's message had not indicated the submarine was undersized.

General Short claimed afterward that the *Condor* sighting four hours before the attack was significant. "That would, under the conditions, have indicated to me that there was danger. The Navy did not visualize (the incident) as anything but a submarine attack." The

Lacking complete air protection, the Pacific Fleet turned to its destroyers to provide safety from the submarine threat. Here at San Diego in the 1930s are Aylwin *(DD-355),* Dale *(DD-353),* Farragut *(DD-348) and* Monaghan *(DD-354).*

Army commander also never received word of the submarine incidents, as the Navy considered it a purely naval problem.

Prange also criticized the supposedly slow reaction of naval commanders that morning, blaming it on an American tendency to evaluate rather than act. This was the style from the President on down.

Once put into motion, deficiencies in the war plan were revealed too late to do any good for those ashore. The plan called, for example, for hostile contacts outside the harbor to be reported in "clear," on radio wavelengths broad enough to be picked up all over the fleet.

The initial report by *Ward* was in clear, but Outerbridge's confirmation and later follow-up were translated and sent in code, a laborious process. The destroyer's reply to the verification request was still being decoded when bombs started to fall.

Outerbridge's error was in not continuing to broadcast the encounter in clear language, on enough frequencies so that everyone tuned in would know something odd had happened at the doorway to Pearl. So far as is known, he was not questioned about it, though Kimmel certainly blamed him later.

Outerbridge was following his orders to the letter — he was supposed to broadcast in clear if he *were under attack.* But his destroyer had sunk a submarine that was simply trespassing.

Captain Grannis, who witnessed the encounter on board *Antares*, regretted not putting out the warning himself in plain language, "telling everybody that it had actually been a submarine and it had actually been sunk."

The patrol bombers of both the Army and Navy were not being utilized to their fullest. This also can be blamed on the submarine threat.

Commander Harold M. "Beauty" Martin, commander of Kaneohe Naval Air Station. His PBY patrol planes were stretched to the limit.

Rear Admiral Bellinger, responsible for the island's fleet of PBYs, felt he did not have enough planes to maintain daily patrols in all directions from Oahu. The planes and their crews were being run ragged by around-the-clock training. So PatWing 2's aircraft concentrated on fleet areas where submarines could be expected to attack. Fleet planes, after all, protected the fleet, not Pearl Harbor.

Air searches by the PBYs only covered areas in which the fleet was going to operate that day. On Dec. 7, these areas extended 200 miles to the south, and that's where the planes were concentrated in the early morning. The Japanese attack fleet was to the north, a route chosen precisely because it would not cross American training zones.

Bellinger didn't find out about his own PBY's participation in the *Ward* incident until the attack was underway. When the first bombs fell, his staff had just completed a search plan for his approval.

The responsibility for general long-range reconnaissance fell

194

through the cracks, the victim of inadequate inter-service communication. General Short assumed the Navy, with the long legs of its PBY bombers, was making the reconnaissance, but the Navy was actually conducting flights only incidental to the maneuvers of the fleet, looking for Japanese submarines that might interfere with training. The Navy, he said later with some bitterness, was "submarine- and training-minded."

Rear Admiral Bloch was thus forced to rely on Air Corps bombers, but never asked for them. Navy aircraft temporarily posted to Ford Island could be utilized, but not counted on; they sailed with the fleet.

Major General Frederick L. Martin, commander of the Army's Hawaiian Air Force, considered his overwater patrols "very alert" in regards to enemy submarines, though admittedly his planes could only look for submarines lurking close to shore. The Air Corps was largely constrained to coastal flights only, as deep blue water was considered Navy property. [4]

Until mid-1941, these training flights were the only distance flights attempted by the Army in Hawaii. The new, long-legged B-17 Flying Fortress changed these tactics. Whatever the airframe, the aircrews were instructed to keep an eye out for "suspicious-looking objects under the water," according to Martin, who later testified that these over-water navigation field trips were primarily anti-submarine patrols.

By Dec. 7, there were only a dozen B-17s in the islands, half of which were down for routine maintenance. Other Army planes, primarily B-18s, had already demonstrated numbing ineptitude in identifying seagoing targets. In any case, *Ward's* encounter with the midget submarine in the restricted area didn't result in a call for Army Air Corps help in hunting submarines.

In postwar Pearl Harbor hearings, Kimmel reacted explosively to suggestions that long-range reconnaissance was wanting. He told Senator Scott Lucas of Illinois that "on Monday, Tuesday, Wednesday and Thursday of the week preceding the attack we did, in fact, send

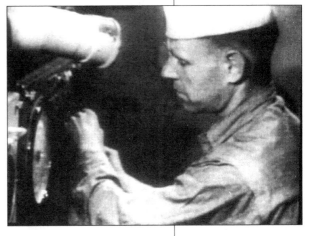

out patrol planes in the northwestern sector about to a distance of about 400 miles." The admiral offered this up as proof that patrols were underway, while at the same time claiming there weren't enough planes or men to patrol fully.

These mid-week excursions, offered as evidence by Kimmel, weren't idle patrols. They were, once again, following the fleet, covering the routes of the Halsey and Newton task forces to Wake and Midway. They were looking solely for submarines. Running across Kido Butai would have been a surprise bonus. But with no American

[4] In the late '30s, a Wheeler-based lieutenant named Curtis LeMay argued successfully to allow navigation-training flights to other Hawaiian islands, "Otherwise, our only choice when flying was whether to go around the island clockwise or counter-clockwise," he said. Soon, Army planes were making flights of hundreds of miles on a regular basis.

A Navy sonarman calibrates his equipment. These men were the ears of the anti-submarine force.

The debacle at Pearl Harbor led directly to a shakeup in the Navy chain of command, with these two profiting directly from Admiral Kimmel's fall from grace. Admiral Ernest King became Chief of Naval Operations while Admiral Chester Nimitz became commander in chief of the Pacific Fleet.

capital ships north of Oahu on Sunday morning, there was no *perceived* need for a patrol in that direction.

By Dec. 6, the only American aerial patrols were sniffing the path ahead of Halsey's ships. On the morning of Dec. 7, the only aerial patrol was south of Oahu, where American ships were maneuvering, and where a submarine was flushed out right where it was expected, in the guarded area around the harbor mouth. Until Imperial planes hit Pearl Harbor, Kimmel's long-range policy was sound, and got results.

Prange and other historians have suggested that Kimmel was negligent in this use of his few patrol planes. "What he should have done — and what he had planes and crews to have done — was cover the critical northern sector," wrote Prange, and this often-repeated accusation haunted Kimmel to his grave.

Doing so, however, would have left his fleet units at sea naked to submarine attack.

It was the literal rock and a hard place for Kimmel; send planes blindly north to search for a then-improbable threat, or protect his ships to the south from certain attack. At the time he made it, the choice seemed clear.

THE HARD PLACE

READY DUTY DESTROYERS

15

"A GREAT SUCCESS — ENEMY SHIPS ARE BURNING!"

Colors were normally raised on ships berthed in Pearl Harbor at 8 a.m. At 7:55 every morning color guards would assemble and raise the Blue Peter, or "Prep" flag, from the signal bridge, as a signal to prepare. Across Pearl Harbor, from the biggest battleship to the smallest destroyer, flag crews were in place at 7:55, just as Japanese aircraft appeared. The exact time of the initial attack was thus fixed in everyone's mind as they stood on deck in their dress whites, preparing to raise the jack and ensign.

Chugging placidly out the harbor channel, tug *YT-153*, taking the harbor pilot to *Antares*, was 500 yards past Buoy No. 4 when aircraft swept past. "Aren't those funny-looking airplanes?" the tug engineer remarked casually. "I believe they are Japanese planes. There's a big red ball on every one of them."

Boatswain's Mate R. L. Holzhaus, at the wheel, was startled at this revelation and looked aft, just in time to see an explosion among the hangars at Hickam Field. It didn't seem real. The tug crew milled about on deck, watching airplanes swarm over the harbor. Holzhaus was transfixed as he watched a small yellow training plane flutter down in flames over John Rodgers Field, next to Hickam. The tug plowed forward.

"Come about!" shouted Captain Otterson, the harbor pilot. "Get back to the yardcraft area!" Holzhaus spun the boat around and headed back into Pearl, now mushrooming with fire and smoke. He felt sick, certain the tug alone in the harbor channel would attract the attention of fighters. Some Zeros flashed by and shot up the water around them, so Otterson ordered the tug closer to the shelter of the shore. Holzhaus obliged while the crew put on life jackets and cut loose the life raft. Ford Island loomed ahead, and *YT-153* aimed straight for it while Holzhaus and the crew "all had a good session of swearing."

They passed destroyer *Helm*, which had begun turning into West Loch to head for deperming buoys to degauss the ship. As planes passed low near *Helm*, directly up the channel, a pilot cheerfully waved at Quartermaster Frank Handler, who waved back. "Look at that," he said. "I didn't know we had planes with fixed landing gear."

A Classic Image Reveals an Intruder

An excited crew member reported to Lieutenant Commander William P. Burford's cabin on board destroyer *Monaghan* that Japanese planes were in Pearl Harbor. *Monaghan*, that day's ready-duty destroyer, was in the midst of preparing to cast off to help *Ward* chase submarines.

Burford, already angry over having his Sunday interrupted, stepped outside and verified the report. He saw black clouds over Schofield Barracks and a torpedo plane making a run on battleship *Utah*.

"Hell, I didn't even know they were sore at us," another crewman complained to Boatswain's Mate Thomas Donahue. Sporadic shooting snapped back at the darting planes. CTM(AA) Gilbert S. "Al" Hardon realized it was no drill and sent men scurrying for .50 ammunition. TM2c Andrew F. Parker heard the alarm and went to his station at the ship's amidships torpedo tube.

He wasn't there long. Hardon sent the torpedoman's mate for additional ammunition; Parker hauled some up on deck, and then was sent by Hardon back to stand by the depth charge tracks and prepare the charges for dropping. In the midst of this, Parker was ordered by *Monaghan's* executive officer to carry projectiles for Gun #5, then to take in lines trailing in the water aft of the destroyer.

READY DUTY DESTROYERS

The first few minutes of the Japanese assault on Pearl Harbor were devoted to the slashing attacks of dive and torpedo bombers. As Lieutenant Hirata Matsumura's B5N "Kate" bomber pulled up after a torpedo run on Battleship Row, his rear-seater captured this classic image of the attack. In the foreground, battleships Nevada *and* Arizona *await their turn while shock rings spread out from* West Virginia *and* Oklahoma. *In the harbor, torpedoes kick up spray as they're dropped. All eyes were on the sky at this moment. Under computer enhancement, however, the action in the harbor's center shows what may be a midget submarine firing at* Oklahoma. *The splashes are uncomfortably near an American whaleboat, while just behind the boat the sail and upper hull of what may be a* Ko-Hyoteki *can be seen broaching in the water, a common problem when midgets fired torpedoes. The whaleboat gives the scale, confirming that the object is the right size and shape. More research is needed — no original prints or negatives of this famous photo are known to exist, and the testimony of the whaleboat sailors would be most interesting.*

On board destroyer/minesweeper *Breese*, skipper Herald F. Stout had left standing orders never to sound General Quarters before 8 a.m. on a Sunday. The day before, he'd kept his sailors jumping with emergency battle drills — a fifth of them were green hands. When it sounded, he shot up from his breakfast to go chew out the watch. He never finished his meal. Looking around, he saw a plane drop a bomb on Ford Island and thought, "I always knew one of those screwy aviators would pull a stunt like that."

Stout reached the starboard deck rail in time to see a plane angle out from behind Ford Island, ripping across the surface of the harbor. It headed for *Breese*, and the destroyer's machine guns chattered loudly behind Stout. "Stop!" screamed Stout. Aren't these American planes? Suddenly the deck jumped as Japanese slugs chewed up across *Breese*, and bits of wood, steel and paint blasted over Stout. The plane bellowed overhead. Stout saw a flash of red insignia, and said out loud, feeling perhaps a little stupid, "Why ... he's a Jap!"

Lieutenant H.G. "Steve" Corey, executive officer of destroyer *Henley*, woke up to the sound of gunfire and looked out the window in time to see flames sheeting Pearl Harbor. He flipped on the bedside radio; it said, "All military personnel are under orders to return to their

stations immediately," and then returned to a Sunday morning musical interlude. Corey hurriedly dressed and ran outside, where he was picked up by *Henley's* skipper, Lieutenant Commander Robert Hall Smith. Smith gunned his car and they reached Aiea Landing in a few minutes, where they had stashed the destroyer's whaleboat. They preferred this smaller dock to the larger Fleet Landing, figuring correctly in case of an emergency the fleet dock would be a madhouse. They ran for the whaleboat, but a large Hawaiian woman jumped in front, waving an appropriated rifle and screaming "Halt!" She was the hot-dog vendor and it took a few minutes to convince her of their identities. Corey and Smith could see men swarming over their ship in the distance and they were in a fever to get aboard her.

Destroyer *Blue* was tied up at the north end of the harbor, at berth X-7. She had been moored next to *Helm* the night before and had the other destroyer's compasses and instruments which would have been affected by deperming.

Craven-class destroyer Blue.

CTM Charles H. Shaw had been fretting about one of his torpedomen, who had just came in after a night on the town; he had missed liberty curfew. Some men were still hung over, although the range finder operator would say later that he had never sobered up so quickly his life. The ship's alarm went off during breakfast, confusing the sailors — the alarm was generally tested every morning except Sunday. The chief quartermaster went up on deck and returned quickly; *Japanese planes!*

The four officers on board *Blue*, all ensigns, had rushed for the wardroom to rendezvous when the attack started, and there they heard cries from topside about *Utah*. The four ensigns — Nathan F. Asher, M.I. Moldafsky, J.P. Wolfe and R.S. Scott — each broke away in opposite directions to duty stations, Asher in charge for the time being. At the bridge he paused, stunned at the sight of Japanese aircraft swarming over the harbor.

Asher called the engine room and instructed the crew to light off No. 2 boiler. No. 1 was already lit, simmering along for auxiliary purposes. At the sound of machine gun fire breaking out from the other ships, Asher told the gun control officer to release the men to fire at will.

Blue's .50 machine guns were already primed with 960 rounds belted at each gun. The 5-inch guns, however, were unarmed, with

READY DUTY DESTROYERS

rounds locked in the magazine. It took 12 long minutes before the guns began to fire.

A muffled, distant rumbling rattled the windows of the Earles' cottage. Mrs. Earle looked out the kitchen window and saw the windows of a hangar on Ford Island blow out in smoke and flame. She screamed. Captain John Earle, chief of staff of the naval district, ran out of the bathroom, lather on half of his face. Planes thundered low over their home, bombs and torpedoes visible on their bellies. "It's an attack!" reasoned Earle, and he hastily dressed. It was a couple of days before he finished his shave.

The executive officer of light cruiser *St. Louis*, Commander Carl K. Fink, burst into Captain George Rood's cabin. "Skipper, there's some sort of air raid on!" he shouted. Startled, Rood levitated out of his bunk, noticing noises like "the loud twanging of guitar strings" up on deck. He pulled his uniform on over his pajamas, slapped on a cap and slipped on slippers and dashed for the bridge.

There he saw Japanese planes strafing overhead, as well as his own gunners firing back. There had been no order to commence firing — many combat drills had put the men on autopilot. Rood watched his men with satisfaction, and felt a swelling of pride.

Cruiser *Honolulu*, moored next to *St. Louis*, blocked Rood's field of fire. A large warehouse nearby didn't help either. The planes would suddenly appear and disappear before *St. Louis*' gunners could aim accurately. A dock chief solved the problem by positioning himself on the cruiser's exposed fantail. When a Japanese plane headed their way, he'd wave his arms frantically and hit the deck.

It worked. Rood's gunner's set up a cross-fire and a torpedo bomber flew right into it. "When they hit him, it sounded like thick pancake batter smacking against the wall," Rood described. "The barrage cut the head of the torpedo right off. The plane crashed into water, and when he did, the torpedo also shook loose and landed in the harbor."

Everyone who wasn't firing into the air prepared the cruiser for sortie. The four-foot access hole in her side was welded shut in jig time, and scaffolding was simply pushed over. Big beams and metal railings rained down on the decks and dock.

Outside the harbor, *Antares* continued to wait for relief for her towed barge, essentially cruising in circles.

Eventually the next watch drifted in, and fireman Bill Ellis filled them in on the morning's excitement. A few minutes before 8 a.m., the firemen left their post to take showers and eat breakfast. Ellis and his shipmates were about to turn on the showers when bullets chewed through the wooden hatches overhead, loudly thrashing through the compartment.

The sailors turned and began to rush topside, but the first ones out turned and dove back in. The skies were full of Japanese planes, they said. Something was going on in Pearl Harbor.

Explosions in the harbor were echoing across the water. As the

Captain George Rood, skipper of light cruiser St. Louis.

crew was mustered to stations, Commander Lawrence Grannis heard the bullets "zing and whine" as they chattered through the ship's decks. A morosely serious paymaster, "worried as all hell, " scooped all the pay receipts, government funds and accounts into a sealed bag, just the way combat regulations insisted they be secured. The paymaster then charged onto the bridge and shouted, "Sir! Permission to scuttle ship's accounts." He feared the ship would be sunk outside the harbor.

"No, hang onto the bag," snapped Grannis. "We aren't sinking yet." The paymaster disappeared below, clutching the valuable bag.

Japanese planes wheeling out of the harbor continued to strafe *Antares*. The ship was unarmed except for two water-cooled machine guns that could not be elevated high enough. As one Japanese plane circled around to attack, Grannis saw the pilot clearly. The Japanese "grinned one of those typically arrogant Japanese grins of the time" as he looked over *Antares*. Grannis was furious, and spotted the potato peeling mess man standing nearby. "Throw a spud at him!" shouted Grannis. "Sorry, skipper," said the rating. "But I threw 'em all already."

Submarine *Plunger*, off Waikiki, was also strafed. It dove and headed south, submerged, through the lurking I-boats.

Caught in mid-turn, destroyer *Helm* hit her engines on full reverse and backed into the main channel. *Helm's* two whaleboats, following the destroyer, were just passing Waipio Point when they were strafed by planes — one boat had 15 holes right at waterline. The crews bailed out and beached the boats, taking shelter in a wooden shack and later in a cave. They were stuck there until noon.

Now, occupied with the antiaircraft batteries, Lieutenant Commander C. E. Carroll turned to Handler and said "Take her out. I'll direct the battery. " Speed limit in the channel was normally 14 knots, but that was in peacetime. Handler ordered 400 rpm from the engine room — they questioned the command — and *Helm* leaped forward at 27 knots.

A Zero flying over was shot at by GM2c W. C . Ruff on the after machine gun; it crashed at Fort Kamehameha. Many ships claimed the quick kill.

Gunnery officer Lieutenant (jg) Victor Dybdal ran forward from the stern, toward the ladder going up to the gun director, above the navigation bridge. Men streamed out of the mess hall, asking, "Where's the fire?" Dybdal shouted at them to man general quarters stations.

At the director, Dybdal discovered the number one crew somewhere astern in the whaleboat, and they shifted to the second-string team. But the 5-inch gun was not ready to fire. The gunner's mate had the firing locks squirreled away in the ship's workshop and had to break them out. The ammunition also was locked away, and the locks were broken. The awning prevented the forward gun from traversing, so Dybdal's men began to slash away at the stubborn canvas.

The initial, muffled explosions from the harbor rattled destroyer *Ward*. "Pretty noisy ashore," said Lieutenant H. T. Doughty.

READY DUTY DESTROYERS

"There's a new road being built between Pearl and Honolulu," said Lieutenant Outerbridge. "They're probably blasting."

"Look at those planes. They're diving straight down," said Doughty, uneasily.

"Probably Halsey's boys, putting on a show. *Enterprise* is due in today."

The *Ward's* crew was astonished to see a plane drop bombs near a sampan. "That's Japanese!" Outerbridge shouted, and whirled on the helmsman. "Turn, turn! Give me 30 knots!" *Ward* sped forward and churned up the Prohibited Area in a series of figure-8s.

An oil pool was spotted, but there was no time to concentrate on sub hunting with airplanes buzzing overhead. *Ward* couldn't elevate her main guns above 15 degrees, and the 3-inch antiaircraft gun on the stern was primarily used for firing star shells. The first few shells were defective, and the cursing gunners who manned the 3-incher flung them overboard. Machine guns also jammed; salt had plugged the water cooling lines. A pair of bombs fell nearby, not causing damage. They were observed from *Antares*, who believed the bursts to be depth charges.

On the north side of Ford Island, gunnery training ship *Utah* had her belly ripped out by torpedoes, and began to turn over. Moored at a spot usually reserved for carriers, she was the victim of excited bomber pilots. Nearby, seaplane tender *Curtiss*' boilers were ordered lit off; underway emergency! On board *Breese*, Commander Stout heard someone yell, "They've got the *Utah*!" He turned and watched, thinking, *That old ship isn't much account, but she's got our boys on board.*

As the initial impact of the assault evaporated, Navy crews scrambled to shoot back. Tug *Keosanqua*, outside the harbor to take on *Antares*' barge, broke out her few machine guns and futilely sprayed at far-off planes. Newly arrived torpedo bombers began to shoot at *Helm*, now moving forward in the main channel. The destroyer was unable to fire back immediately because her guns were coated with preservative grease.

A gunner's mate burst in on Carroll, yelling, "Sir, may I have permission to get the keys to open the magazine locks?"

Carroll couldn't believe his ears. "Forget the keys!" he roared. "Cut the locks!"

On *Monaghan*, the locks were being sawed off. Donahue spent the first minutes at No. 4 gun, his old duty station, flinging monkey wrenches at low-flying planes, apparently without result.

Someone called up from below. "What do you need?"

"Powder! I can't keep throwing things at them," said Donahue, and they took him literally. He received a package of drill powder for his trouble, no shells. He threw it at the planes as well.

When *Blue* opened fire, Asher was amazed the crew got the guns loaded so quickly, swifter than their fastest drill time. *Blue* blazed away continuously until the #4 ammunition hoist stopped. The gun captain

ADVANCE FORCE — PEARL HARBOR

203

from No. 1 gun raced into the ammunition handling run to get it going again, but it stubbornly froze.

He threw himself to the deck and cried "Oh Lord, Oh Lord! Make this ammo hoist work — just this once!" Tears burst from his eyes.

A tall black sailor paused while carrying away ammunition and said, "Why sir, you got the oil turned off."

The gun captain leaped up, grasped his hands once more and prayed loudly, "It's all right, Lord. I've got it covered."

In the channel, opposite the coaling docks where the minesweepers nested, mud and bubbles boiled to surface. Minesweeper *Bobolink* fired three shots at the disturbance, thinking perhaps a submarine had brushed the opposite shore. The sweeper observed, *Suspicious sign of Japanese submarine* and signaled such to destroyers. The signal was apparently ignored.

Ten miles south of Barbers Point, Catalina *24-P-4* spotted a submarine on the surface near American ships. The submarine made a crash dive and the PBY marked the spot with float lights.

To the east, another PBY was in the midst of submarine-to-plane tactics, practicing visual communications. First Class Petty Officer Maurey Meister coordinated the maneuver, and the American submarine was spotted five miles off Molokai. Aboard the PBY the First Radioman was on the signal gun while the Second Radioman operated the radio. The man on the radio suddenly threw off his headset and showed Meister a message.

The periscope wake of a Type #A midget submarine, from an Imperial Navy propaganda film.

"Are we using some special code for radio today?" he sputtered. "I just received this message and I can't decode it!"

To Meister, the letters on the paper strip "looked at least six feet tall." It read *WAR WITH JAPAN COMMENCED WITH AIR RAID ON PEARL.* Meister showed it to the man on the signal gun, who transmitted it to the submarine. There was no reply; the submarine crash-dived.

As Meister re-examined his relationship with his Deity — "Praying to a God I did not know" — the Second Radioman canvassed other units for confirmation. None responded, and he raised Pearl Harbor, asking "Is this a drill?"

"No! No! And get the hell off the air!" he was told.

"Here we are, about a thousand feet above the Pacific Ocean, about 50 miles from our base at Ford Island," observed Meister. "Our country is at war with Japan and we have nowhere to go."

The PBY circled the area, vainly waiting for a submarine — friend or foe — to reveal itself.

Closer to Pearl Harbor, through *I-24tou's* periscope, Sakamaki spotted roiling, black clouds of smoke belching from inside the harbor. It was obvious the air attack had started.

"Look! Look!" cheered Sakamaki, hauling Inagaki to the submarine periscope.

READY DUTY DESTROYERS

"Just look at that smoke!" said Inagaki. "A great success — enemy ships are burning!"

"We'll do the same!" vowed Sakamaki. They grasped the other's shoulders, swore on it and resumed trying to thread Pearl's needle.

They prepared *I-24tou* in case any American ships came their way. Sakamaki ordered Inagaki to spin the screw sleeve on the torpedo safety mechanism — unless a small valve bonnet closed the air line leading to the stop cylinder, the impulse blast of air that fired the torpedo would not charge. It worked like the safety latch on an enormous air pistol.

Sweat burned in Sakamaki's eyes. The midget had an air-cooling system in which air was pumped in channels next to the submarine's thin steel hull. The air's warmth was whisked away by the cool

A reenactment of a midget submarine crew invading Pearl Harbor, from the propaganda film "Hawaii Sakusen."

water surrounding the midget, and the re-cooled air discharged in the aft battery room. Even so, normal operating temperatures were between 110 and 130 degrees in a buttoned-up midget.

Sakamaki worried about foundering on the reefs surrounding the harbor. *I-24tou* sat too low in the water to see the rocks, and the submarine could easily run into them while submerged. He despaired. On the controls, his hands grew slick with sweat and he cursed the prowling destroyer.

The sub suddenly ground into the coral, lifting it partly out of the water, within sight of shore.

About this time, *YT-153* was passing Hospital Point in the harbor mouth, the wide-eyed crew watching "the Navy Yard and Ford Island both catching hell." With most of their attention directed at the aerial display, Holzhaus ordered Ludwig to watch the harbor itself. Ludwig grabbed a pair of binoculars and stood next to Holzhaus.

He immediately spotted something strange in the water, a tiny periscope gingerly wheeling around Buoy #19, headed for the channel north of Ford Island. Straight ahead floated the slurry pipe running from dredge *Turbine*, effectively closing off the south channel route toward Battleship Row. From water level, the floating pipe looked enormous, like an anti-submarine net. Ludwig handed the glasses to Holzhaus, who confirmed the little periscope.

"What do we do?" asked Ludwig.

"All I can think of … is run him down, I guess," said Holzhaus. He swung the tug sharply toward the tiny target and headed after it.

The tug bore steadily down on the periscope swishing through the dirty water. About 150 yards away, the glass eye atop the periscope swiveled back toward the tug, and the slim black rod abruptly disappeared.

Holzhaus and Ludwig cursed, wishing the water were less murky.

There was no sign of the submarine. The tug sledded over the spot where the periscope had been, and Holzhaus reversed course and ran over the area again. Nothing. The shallow draft of the tug couldn't probe deeply enough into the harbor.

They began to cruise around slowly, watching the water southwest of Ford Island, in case the intruder reappeared.

Pharmacist's Mate 3c Edwin Soreside, on shore and detailed to watch things waterside at Hospital Point, saw something cutting through the water. It looked like a periscope — probably the same midget that had escaped *YT-153* a few minutes before. Soreside called the signal tower about the sighting. Soreside neglected to leave his name, but the watch log noted he was "excited" and that he hung up before any details could be obtained. A sailor in the tower was ordered to watch the harbor channel carefully, but he saw nothing.

Caught in the bottleneck of the Pearl Harbor channel when she lost the spoor of *I-24tou*, the little Coast Guard cutter *Tiger* was nearly rammed by *Helm*, which rushed by to port. "Hard left rudder!" sang out Chief Wells, and "Doc" Nash complied. The craft made a U-turn in the narrowest part of the channel and dashed out to open sea. A stricken Zero fighter passed only a few dozen feet overhead and smashed onto the beach at Hickam.[1]

Tiger left the rattling maelstrom of Pearl Harbor as quickly as possible, taking up patrol off Waikiki.

Outside the harbor during the first minutes of the attack, from the bridge of the *Antares*, skipper Grannis surveyed the "confusion, blackness and disaster" of the aerial assault. He was angry. Suddenly, a destroyer darted through the boiling black shroud of smoke, bow waves arching and glistening in the morning light, making a run for the harbor entrance. To Grannis, it was one of the most stirring and beautiful sights he'd ever seen. It was *Helm*. She "came out like a bulldog ready to fight and every part of her spoke defiance."

"Go!" he shouted. "Go!"

The paymaster chose this moment to bother Grannis. "Don't you think I should throw the bag overboard now, Captain?" he pleaded.

"Go away and don't bother me again!" seethed Grannis.

Quartermaster Handler at the helm, the destroyer roared out of Pearl Harbor at 8:17 a.m. It was the first time he'd ever held the wheel by himself.

As *Helm* popped through the chokeway, lookouts saw Saka-maki's midget struggling on the reef, on the starboard side of entrance channel. It was nearly on the shore skirting the town of Ewa Beach. To Dybdal, "it looked like a garbage can with a periscope."

It disappeared as they were looking at it, then reappeared, then disappeared.

Helm passed the entrance buoys and cranked starboard, toward the submarine, which surfaced once again.

With the 5-inch guns now primed, *Helm* opened fire. Once again, the submarine disappeared. It was so close to shore that the morning

READY DUTY DESTROYERS

swell was lapping over it. *Helm* began to circle, two or three times, giving all her batteries a chance to pop off at the target. As *Helm* held speed to 25 knots, her guns began blazing away at Sakamaki. Shots rained down around the black intruder, rocking it back and forth. A lone rifleman on shore started to shoot at the midget also.

The explosions walked around the target, seemingly having no effect. The guns were loaded with anti-aircraft rounds, with the fuses set on safe, which meant the shell exploded only on impact. Dybdal was in the middle of resetting the fuses to scatter shrapnel over the area when the midget slipped away.

Simultaneously, *Helm's* controls froze. During a circuit, water had shipped over the fantail and down an open hatch, shorting out the steering gear switchboard, a main contact relay on the power panel. *Helm* shifted to hand steering and maneuvering by engine. The ship wobbled, out of control for a moment. Luckily, it was headed away from the reef. Main circuit breakers were opened and the ship lost all power for a full minute.

While frantically changing to hand steering, men on *Helm's* stern observed a torpedo pass close underneath the fantail and disappear to the northwest. No one thought to notify the bridge.

The shot didn't come from Sakamaki. Inside *I-24tou*, Sakamaki simply couldn't decide whether to fire one of his torpedoes at the destroyer; he wanted a bigger, more glorious target. The decision was made for him when a close shot rang him against a bulkhead like a clapper in a bell. He passed out. One of Sakamaki's torpedo tubes was dented, trapping the torpedo inside.

Inagaki excitedly shifted ballast. The submarine wiggled off the reef and vanished.

As she sped away, looking for other intruders, *Helm* signaled *Ward — Small Jap sub trying to penetrate channel.*

Ward signaled back that they were well aware of submarines in the vicinity. *Helm* headed for patrol off Waikiki, the predetermined post for the first destroyer sortie in wartime.

Pearl Harbor explodes. A portion of a motion picture frame from a Japanese bomber circling over Ewa Field shows the first strikes on Battleship Row and Ford Island, as destroyer Helm *continues to steam into West Loch in the right foreground.*

16

STAND BY TO RAM!

SWORDS OF THE EMPEROR

Far away, on board battleship *Nagato* at Kure, Admiral Isoroku Yamamoto awaited results of the attack. Minutes crawled away, and Yamamoto quietly smoked two cigarettes — he only smoked when there was a battle. The radio suddenly crackled with messages. As the surprise victory at Pearl became clear, the room hummed with excitement, as if they were listening to a football game.

One intercepted American message warned of ships operating in the harbor.

"Good!" cheered Rear Admiral Matome Ugaki. "That means our midget submarines are getting through!"

Yamamoto stared at the radio, and lit another cigarette.

He wrote a poem:
What does the world think?
I do not care
Nor for my life;
For I am the sword
Of my Emperor.

In the flame and blood of Pearl Harbor, battleship *California* hoisted a signal directing Task Forces One and Two to "get underway." The harbor signal tower relayed this information to the gate vessel, warning that an emergency sortie could be expected any moment. The gate vessel messaged back that everything was under control, and the harbor entrance was clear, except for *Antares*' imminent entrance. The tower officer, a Commander Hayes, arrived breathlessly while these dispatches were being transmitted, and he ordered *Antares* — by searchlight — *Under no circumstances enter!*

Antares was busy at the moment, having spotted another submarine off the port beam. Skipper Grannis' riggers were unprotected, engaged on the heaving lighter deck casting off *Antares*' tow bridle. Grannis was ordered to stay clear of Pearl — his slow ship was too tempting a target in the harbor channel. He headed his ship for Honolulu Harbor, dodging and jinking inshore of the combat ships. As soon as the ship got there, at 10:54 a.m., Bill Ellis and the other stokers were ordered below to secure the fires and boilers. It

was a long wait before the jittery harbor master allowed the ship to enter the harbor. *Antares* didn't moor until 11:46. Grannis bolted from the ship to tell his wife the ship was safe, then instructed her to call all the other *Antares*' officers' wives and repeat the message.

With the lighter in tow, tug *Keosanqua* followed *Antares* toward Honolulu. The little tug blazed away at planes, which maddeningly stayed just out of range. Several "bombs" fell nearby.[1] The tug's skipper ordered the lighter pulled in tight for easier maneuvering.

[1] Almost certainly misfused antiaircraft shells.

Keosanqua reached Honolulu Harbor about the same time as *Antares*, and within 15 minutes was moored at Pier #5. More shells fell nearby, around the Honolulu Iron Works complex, and *Keosanqua* moved to the better shelter of Pier #6.

Coast Guard craft *Tiger* noted an oil slick four miles away from the entrance buoy and then proceeded to her designated combat zone off Honolulu Harbor, watching all the while for submarines. Her log estimated 16 close calls from bombs or unidentified shells.

Customs agents Andrew Buta and John Williams were left behind in Pearl Harbor. Hearing explosions, the agents rushed to the window and saw Japanese aircraft peeling down from Aiea Heights. With nothing better to do, and unwilling to go outside, the two stayed in the administration building until 10:15. Buta then pointed out to the yard captain that "no customs duties could be performed under the circumstances." Released, the agents dashed downtown to the federal building. By that time, *Antares* was already in Honolulu Harbor. It's unknown if the ship ever formally checked in with Customs.

During the initial attack, communications with *YNg-17* and Section base went out. Lieutenant Commander Kaminski detailed Ensign John H. Hoefer to visit the area and report back. Hoefer did that, and subsequently delivered extra weapons, ammunition, gas masks and helmets to the net and boom crews.

The submarine scouting flight from *Enterprise* fell in to the attack. Lieutenant Clarence Dickinson and Radioman First Class William C. Miller, in formation with another *Enterprise* SBD dive bomber, had scouted the waters far south of Oahu, where no Japanese submarines were. They then turned north and arrived over the Ewa plain around 8:25 a.m. Dickinson noticed the water below sprinkled with shell splashes and assumed an Army battery was engaging in some Sunday morning target practice. The three ships off the harbor mouth didn't seem to be doing anything.

The splashes were antiaircraft shells dropping into the water, mixed in with *Helm's* frantic firing at Sakamaki's submarine near the Ewa beach. Misreading the situation at a glance, Dickinson predicted to Miller that Army heads would roll for disturbing a quiet morning.

Looking ahead, Dickinson noticed the ragged black puffs of antiaircraft shelling over the harbor, as well as the furious column of greasy smoke roiling up from Battleship Row. *Something was definitely amiss here.* Motioning the other SBD into a tighter formation, the two planes climbed to 4,000 feet above Barbers Point.

Two flights of Zero fighters bounced the American planes, forcing them down to the deck in a screaming dive. Dickinson's wingman, Ensign John R. McCarthy, was hit, his plane flaming and flopping through the air. McCarthy bailed out; his parachute blossomed just above the ground. The pilot landed in a tree and broke his leg climbing down. Radioman Mitchell Cohn, McCarthy's rearseater, was still in the SBD when it impacted south of the Ewa runway, near the beach.

The Zeroes, now numbering five, concentrated on Dickinson and Miller. As the pilot danced the Dauntless around, Miller unlimbered the single .30 Browning machine gun in the rear cockpit. Dickinson heard the gun chatter. Miller said he had been wounded, then said he'd scored strikes on a Zero.[2] Bullets drummed against the SBD, and Miller reported that he'd been hit again.

Dickinson then heard Miller scream, and, startled, sideslipped the aircraft. A Zero overshot the stricken dive bomber, and Dickinson fired a few futile rounds after it. The Dauntless, however, wasn't coming out of its spin, and the left wing was ablaze. The pilot shouted at the radioman, got no answer, and decided to depart the aircraft at 1,000 feet. The wind blast pulled the goggles from his head.

Once on the ground, Dickinson commandeered the first car that would stop for him and made for Ford Island. There he found only three Dauntlesses of the 18 that had taken off from *Enterprise* a few hours before. That afternoon, Dickinson and other *Enterprise* pilots were organized into a sortie north of Oahu in fresh airplanes. They didn't see anything.[3]

As the first wave of attackers began to dissipate that morning over Pearl Harbor, around 8:30 a.m., the fleet's destroyers tried to get underway. On board destroyer *Breese*, skipper Stout was frustrated as his ship built up boiler pressure. She was ready to "haul tail," but was stuck with destroyer/minelayer *Ramsey* tied up alongside. *Ramsey's* engines were still cold, and if *Breese* disengaged her mooring lines, *Ramsey* would drift in the harbor.

Officers Smith and Corey of destroyer *Henley* finally reached their whaleboat, and found *Henley's* engineer and whaleboat coxswain awaiting them. They shoved off and putted briskly toward the destroyer, noting in despair that she was moving away from her buoy. Lieutenant Francis E. Fleck Jr. had assumed command and gotten her screws turning by 8:30.

Henley was following ready-duty destroyer *Monaghan*, already underway and steering southwesterly between Pearl City and Ford Island, Lieutenant Commander William Burford in command. They were ordered out by Destroyer Division Two commander Ralph S. Riggs, via flag system from cruiser *Detroit*. It was their second set of orders that morning — the destroyer had been firing up to support offshore destroyer *Ward* when the airplanes struck, and Burford wanted "to get out of that damn harbor as fast as possible." They poured on the coal.

As *Monaghan* maneuvered to sortie from Pearl via the north

[2] Probably that of SEA1c Isao Doikawa, from carrier Soryu.

[3] When the smoke cleared, it was determined that five SBDs had been shot down by the Japanese, one by over-eager American ground gunners, and the rest were widely scattered and damaged.

STAND BY TO RAM!

Destroyer Henley (DD-391).

channel, a third set of orders was received by voice over TBS, for DesDiv 2 to establish offshore patrol.

At 8:30 a.m., destroyer/minesweeper *Zane*, on the other side of *Breese*, noted "Sighted enemy submarine 200 yards astern *U.S.S. Medusa* at berth X-23." *Zane* appears to have been the first major ship to notice an intruder in the harbor. It was spotted next by *Breese*, moored in a nest of other aging destroyers turned out to shallow-water

Destroyer/ minesweeper Zane DMS-14 (ex DD-337) in 1943.

pasture, near the Pan American landing ramp on Pearl City Peninsula.

Within minutes, the submarine was well into the north channel, its conning tower visible to observers far away in the harbor signal tower. Kimmel's headquarters messaged "Japanese submarine in harbor" and heads began looking down as well as up. *Breese* signaled that two submarines were involved; the ships couldn't fire because other destroyers were in the way.

Tenders *Medusa* and *Curtiss*, busy testing their main engines, flagged a "sub in harbor" message at 8:35. The submarine was spotted 200 to 300 yards away on *Curtiss*' starboard quarter at Berth X-22. *Curtiss* began to shoot at the tiny target with guns No. 3 (one round over, two just under the periscope) and No. 2, and machine guns No. 3, 9 and 11. Ensign G.K. Nicodemus was battery officer.

At 8:39 a.m., a signalman pointed out *Curtiss*' submarine warning to Burford on *Monaghan*, then fast approaching the scene.

"Well, *Curtiss* must be crazy," snapped Burford.

"That may be, Captain — but what's that down there?" said the crewman.

Burford looked 1,200 yards off the starboard bow and saw "an over-and-under shotgun barrel looking up" at him. The tubes were pointed directly at *Monaghan.*

"I don't know what the hell it is, but it shouldn't be there!" Burford shouted for flank speed and right full rudder. He intended to ram the intruder. The destroyer swung too far to starboard, and then it steadied on a collision course.

Gunfire from *Medusa* joined that of *Curtiss*, shredding the water around the object into dirty foam. Vigorous cross-fire came from *Tangier*, moored at the northwest end of Ford Island.

Monaghan moved abreast of Buoy 7, followed closely by *Henley*. By now the periscope and part of the conning tower were visible. To Gunnery Officer Lieutenant (jg) Hart Kait, the object seemed to bob and zigzag near Ford Island's west bank, perhaps as the submarine glanced off the channel bed. D.E. Williamson, at the helm, was directed to head for the sub as soon as he could see it.

Chief Torpedoman's Mate "Al" Hardon found another torpedoman's mate, named Varnado, to help charge the two torpedoes *Monaghan* had ready on deck. Torpedoman's Mate Andrew F. Parker was sent aft to the depth charge racks. When Parker heard there was a submarine ahead, he cut the safety lines and let the charges into the trap, setting one of the pistols at 30 feet.

On second thought, Parker wondered if the depth setting was wrong, so he asked executive officer E.J. Verhoye the depth of the harbor. The lieutenant said, "30 feet," so Parker set the rest at that depth. The torpedoes were armed by this point, and Hardon ran back to the depth charge racks, leaving Varnado. Parker had completed setting the pistols, so Hardon stood by the release mechanism.

It was a long moment — the destroyer sprinting down on the mysterious object through a gauntlet of blazing ships and wild gunfire, Japanese planes screaming overhead, the rattle of anti-

aircraft fire and the sizzling rain of shrapnel "God … a lot was going on in just a few minutes of time," said Burford.

Cornered, the midget submarine loosed a torpedo at *Curtiss*. The lightened midget popped to the surface and was slammed with 5-inch and .50 caliber rounds from the seaplane tender. The torpedo porpoised out of the water and hit a Pearl City dock near a pile driver.

A large round lanced through the conning tower into the harbor, taking the submarine skipper's head with it. Another round clipped his coat button. His body was "blown into a mass of crumpled steel."

Torpedo officer Ensign P.W. Gill dashed aft on board *Monaghan*, saw Hardon ready at the depth charges and decided the chief could handle them alone. Fearing serious damage if the destroyer hit the submarine squarely, Gill ran forward, sweeping up loose men into a repair party.

When the submarine came within range, *Monaghan* bore down on the midget, firing her own guns. Gun No. 1 had a hang fire; the first round from the No. 2 gun skipped across the water and exploded in a derrick attached to shore, setting it ablaze. Another round severed a cable on the derrick, dumping hanging gear nearly atop a civilian yardworker. The civilian, as witnessed by Carpenter's Mate 3c Glenn J. Bennett, dashed off the barge into shallow water, tossing aside his hardhat and nearly walking on water. Once ashore, he threw himself into a car, discovered it didn't have keys, and slid out the opposite door and disappeared into the canefields.

Within 75 yards, the submarine turned sharply and fired its other

One of the first illustrations of the Pearl Harbor attack released to the public was this Navy sketch showing a midget submarine about to be rammed by a Navy destroyer, with a ship resembling Curtiss *blazing away in the background. The details of the submarine are surprisingly accurate, although the artist mistakenly depicted Japanese aircraft as biplanes.*

torpedo directly at *Monaghan*. The missile porpoised twice, passing on the starboard side within 20 yards. Bennett hit the deck, convinced the fish would leap out of the water and strike the destroyer's propeller guards. The torpedo ran on, barely missing *Dale*, following in *Monaghan's* wake.

Communications officer J.W. Gilpin clearly saw the yawning bow tubes aimed at his ship. It seemed very small. Gilpin was more afraid that *Curtiss* wouldn't stop firing, but as *Monaghan* drew close, the other ships held both fire and breath.

To Lieutenant Kait, the submarine looked like a whale blowing.

The order was passed: *Stand by to ram!* The shock was expected forward; the submarine had disappeared from bridge view and collision seemed imminent. Gill's repair party crouched breathlessly at Gun No. 1. "Stand by the depth charges!" Verhoye yelled.

Once again Hardon verified Parker's charges. The starboard pistols were locked at 30 feet, but Parker, unwilling to leave his post, had not set the port charges. Hardon raced over to reset the charges, in case they were needed. He saw the submarine for the first time and wondered at the oddness of it. He couldn't tell if he was looking at the bow or stern. Hardon also wondered if the charges would explode—they were exercise charges filled with low-grade TNT and had been in the racks since leaving Mare Island in 1939.

Behind *Monaghan*, the torpedo hit the bank of Ford Island, vomiting up a 200-foot geyser of mud and water.

The destroyer sledded into the midget, mashing her under the water and spinning her against the hull as the destroyer railroaded overhead. There was a momentary, hideous screeching of metal as the ships tore at each other, and then the water pressure from *Monaghan's* surging hull pushed the small submarine away. The ship listed slightly to port.

Monaghan's ramming of the midget submarine inspired this scene in the 1943 film "Navy."

The shock was so slight that Gilpin thought *Monaghan* had completely missed the submarine. Two men sent below by Gill to check damage found none. *Monaghan* had succeeded in doing what *YT-153* had tried just half an hour before.

The noise was such that Hardon released the first depth charge on his own initiative when he saw the submarine pass under *Monaghan's* stern, then dropped the second when he heard Kait's order. The explosions jackknifed the speeding destroyer's stern clear out of the water. Braced against a forward impact rather that a jolt to the rear, nearly everyone on deck tumbled off their feet.

The second explosion violently threw the midget to the surface — in the signal tower, the first plume showed white; the second, black. Kait claimed he saw the submarine's bow and superstructure blown above the water.

STAND BY TO RAM!

The depth charges "tore hell" out of the midget, twisting off the bow like a cigarette butt being ground away. Though he had been signaled to roll his charge, Parker decided against wasting it when he saw Hardon's results.

Men on board *Curtiss* and the line of following destroyers of Division Two were heard to cheer as the plumes of water misted toward them. *Monaghan*, out of control from the moment her rudders were lifted out of the harbor, skewed through the water toward the derrick barge she had set afire moments before.

"All engines back — emergency full speed!" ordered Burford. It was insufficient to slow the ship. Gill ordered his repair party and the crew of the forward gun to stand by the anchor; Gill himself leaped onto the forecastle to drop the anchor, hoping to slow the ship. Burford waved him back. Kait, in the rear of the destroyer and unable to see the onrushing shore, ordered another brace of depth charges released, just in case.

Monaghan bashed into the dredge derrick moored at Beckoning Point, a glancing blow on the starboard bow, mushing the destroyer deep into the mud bank. The burning dredge wound up wedged against the ship's starboard side, near the bridge. The anchor that Gill had wanted to drop was tangled in the wreckage. It was a sudden stop; *Henley* swerved to avoid rear-ending *Monaghan*, and raced into the main channel, the third ship to sortie from Pearl Harbor.

The other classic Japanese aerial view of the Pearl Harbor attack looks north from West Loch — torpedo bursts are raising spray on Oklahoma. The midget submarine proceeded up the channel in the foreground. At left, near the bottom, the dredge derrick accidentally shelled and rammed by Monaghan *hugs the shore.*

This pre-war photograph of Monaghan *on joint maneuvers — aircraft in the background are spreading smoke screens — gives an idea of the tremendous speed generated by Farragut-class destroyers.*

Feeling the impact, and once again on his own initiative, Hardon decided not to drop a third depth charge when he heard the ship was fouled in the derrick. The explosion certainly would have damaged his own ship.

While sailors played a fire hose on the blazing bow, others yanked the anchor free of derrick debris. There was an oxy-acetylene tank on fire on the derrick, and *Monaghan's* crew played water on it to keep it from exploding. The destroyer drunkenly lurched astern, pushed by the harbor's outgoing current. The ship seemed to be moving clear of the burning dredge when the derrick moved sharply toward the bow; the destroyer was snarled in the platform's anchor cables.

Carpenter's Mate Bennett prepared to chop it free, throwing an ax onto the derrick and getting ready to jump over. Burford tried gunning the destroyer's screws, surging the ship back and forth off the mud.

It worked. *Monaghan* popped free of the derrick debris, but in very shallow water. The ship moved cautiously away, an easy target from the air. Men not on guns were told to lie down and take cover. Bumping her bottom again slightly, *Monaghan* swung into the harbor astern of *Dale*, who had paused while they were aground. *Dale* had already witnessed a close call; while backing out of her berth, an aerial torpedo aimed at cruiser *Raleigh* passed under *Dale's* bow and exploded on Ford Island.

"We were bombed while in the channel, but they all missed us, we were going too fast," remembered Richard Geiger, who served on destroyer *Dale*. "Over 30 knots, and zigzagging to boot, but our quartermaster knew the channel as well as the fish, so nothing but mud soiled the ship."

STAND BY TO RAM!

Destroyer Dale (DD-353).

Damage appeared light on *Monaghan*, and Burford headed for the open sea as ships cheered nearby. Gilpin looked back as they dashed into the channel, seeing for the first time the horrifying damage on Battleship Row.

Another brief submarine scare turned out to be a black cage buoy, and Gun No. 2 fired a round at it for good measure.

The harbor signal tower sent out a message to all ships. *Witnessed* Monaghan *sink enemy sub by ramming and depth charges,* it said. *Excellent piece of work!*

Holzhaus, on board tug *YT-153*, saw the shooting and heard the cheers, and figured that's where the submarine had gone. At the moment though, the tug was busy dodging loose timbers and other floating debris from *Utah* that was fouling the harbor. With the submarine dispatched, Holzhaus promptly forgot about it and headed for the yardcraft pier to deposit pilot Otterson. The tug then helped battleship *Nevada* beach herself opposite Hospital Point.[4]

Nevada's determined run for the harbor entrance had attracted the attention of Japanese dive bombers. She was hit several times, and Battle Force Vice Admiral William Pye, wary of other submarines possibly lying in wait in the channel, ordered the battleship to stand fast. A battleship sunk in the narrow harbor channel would cork the bottleneck.

As *Nevada* lurched ashore, a few hundred feet from blocking the channel, Kimmel ordered that no other capital ships would sortie from Pearl Harbor.

In the shipyard, the message about enemy submarines in the harbor was received with a grain of salt. On board cruiser *St. Louis*, crews continued to frantically clear away rigging. The gangway was burned away with an acetylene torch, held by a shipfitter dangling on the ship's flanks.

The water hose, a foot thick, was chopped free with fire axes, and a plate welded over the hole in 10 minutes. Some sailors paused to watch a disliked petty officer chop away scaffolding, not realizing he was standing on it.

At a few minutes past 9 a.m., a dive bomber dropped a bomb

[4] *Aiding in this effort was* YT-146 Hoga, *which recently retired as a fireboat in Oakland.*

between the bow and the dock next to cruiser *Honolulu*, making *St. Louis* alongside buck on the tumescent swell.

Light cruiser *Phoenix* was already underway, skirting the blazing disaster on the east side of Ford Island by going through the north channel, the path of choice for most of the destroyers. For some reason *Phoenix* signaled the tower "Japanese submarine in harbor submerged," and on the strength of this warning the tower issued a blanket "emerg sail" signal, only to withdraw it a few minutes later.

Phoenix, curiously, was told not to sortie — submarines were in the harbor, that the submarine nets were being closed, and that they should return to berth. Frustrated, her crew got her there just in time for the second wave of Japanese bombers.[5]

Though destroyers continued to speed for the exit, the harbor was being shut up tight. The submarine scare had badly rattled the admirals, but the harbor was still the safest place to shelter the fleet from the horde of I-boats that surely stalked outside.

Lieutenant Commander Kaminski finally got through to the harbor anti-torpedo nets and ordered the officer in charge, Ensign Richard Eastman, to shut the gates. The noise from outside increased dramatically as the second attack got underway. At this point, Captain Earle arrived quite breathlessly.

Kaminski then turned his attention to the Honolulu gates, and could not get through. He called the home of the officer in charge, Lieutenant James H. Ottley, and was told Ottley had departed for his station some time before, which Kaminski still could not contact.

Around noon, Kaminski raised Ottley and ordered Honolulu Harbor sealed. Ottley told him that the mess hall on Sand Island, near Honolulu, had been bombed and one of his men was injured. And that Ottley was no longer in charge — Captain Finlay, the senior Coast Guard officer, had arrived.

The only ships allowed out of Pearl Harbor in the wake of the *Monaghan* incident were destroyers and minesweepers, and they were tasked to hunt submarines. For the first time that morning, the harbor's submarine nets were being closed much too late.

At 9 a.m. sweeper *Cockatoo* got underway to drag the channel, followed ten minutes later by *Condor* and *Reedbird*. *Reedbird* also was ordered to sweep the entrance waters.

Other destroyers were joining *Monaghan's* sprint to the sea, broken water running to avoid bombers. Destroyer *Blue* was speeding through the harbor, with Ensign Nathan F. Asher in command; he would remain there for 30 hours. While waiting for the boilers to steam, the crew had blasted away wildly at Japanese aircraft. One plane wobbled and slammed into the water near the Pan American ramp; *Blue's* crew stopped shooting and danced on the deck in ecstasy.

Asher, without a gun, had thrown his field glasses at a plane. "I guess I just was kind of mad," he later explained. Seeing the signal to sortie, Asher unshackled the berthing chain and chopped through the connecting wires.

[5] Phoenix *was later sold to Argentina, renamed* General Belgrano *and sunk by a British Royal Navy submarine during the Falklands War.*

STAND BY TO RAM!

Blue's route took her away from the devastation of Battleship Row. Machinist Mate Charles Etter tossed lines to men struggling in the blazing water. Some were hauled aboard. Others slipped off and fell behind, and Etter watched their bobbing heads recede in the smoke and fire. *Blue* passed around the north side of Ford Island, and as the destroyer came abreast the overturned gunnery training ship *Utah*, they stopped engines and drifted because of heavy timber deck planking carpeting the surface.

Asher's orders were to sortie eastward, and patrol a sector off Waikiki. Asher wondered if they'd get out of the harbor; at least four aircraft attacked the ship as it entered the channel, and bomb explosions around *Blue* were so fierce that Asher thought the ammunition dump was going up.

Behind *Blue*, destroyer *Farragut* cleared her nest and headed for sea, followed six minutes later by *Aylwin*. In her haste, *Aylwin* snapped her anchor chains and stern lines at the buoys.

Like many other ships underway, *Aylwin* left her skipper on shore. She was handled by Ensign Stanley Caplan, in civilian life a chemistry major at the University of Michigan. The four ensigns on board had between them slightly more than a year of sea experience, and were convinced they couldn't get the destroyer out of the harbor in the hail of explosives.

Aylwin skipper Lieutenant Commander R.H. Rodgers chased the destroyer out to sea in a commandeered launch, but shore command wouldn't allow the fleeting destroyers to slow down in possibly dangerous waters. Half of all the destroyer officers were on shore when the attack started, and Rodgers and other marooned *Aylwin* officers cooled their heels on destroyer *Chew* until the following day.

Burdick H. Brittin, one of the four ensigns in charge aboard *Aylwin*, later explained they were afraid to slow the ship because of possible submarines; "As destroyer after destroyer gained the sea, more and more contacts were reported, depth charges were exploded with marked frequency.

"Whether there were many submarines present, I still do not know; however we considered it foolhardy to stop despite the fact that the captain's small boat tried to close us numerous times. The opportunity is rare indeed for an ensign to refuse his captain's request to come aboard, and to sail off with his ship. We did just that!"

There wasn't much time to think about it. Brittin had clapped on a steel helmet and commanded a repair party that stripped the ship for action as she got steam up. Everything not essential or tied down was tossed overboard — even the accommodation ladder.

Minesweepers Cockatoo (AMc-8), above, and Reed Bird (AMc-30), below were trawlers purchased by the Navy in 1940. Although in the same same class, there are many differences between the individual AMc boats.

Henley cleared the channel at 9 a.m.. Corey and Smith, frustrated at chasing their destroyer, steered toward *Selfridge*, which was standing pat. They discovered *Selfridge's* boilers were still cold, so they chugged after *Trever*, then coming to life, the better to transfer to *Henley* later. The air was thick with greasy smoke and misting water from bomb blasts, and the two officers held seat cushions over their heads to protect from raining shrapnel, which fell hissing all around the boat. Even with the cushions, they felt silly and somehow naked.

Out alone with destroyer *Helm* for nearly 40 long minutes, the crew of *Ward* saw the fleet standing swiftly out of Pearl Harbor, like cavalry coming to the rescue. First *Tiger*, then destroyer *Henley*, followed by *Dale, Monaghan, Blue, Patterson*. More followed. But no battleships, noted Dybdal in *Helm*. He wondered why.

Farragut-class destroyer Aylwin (DD-355).

When a call went out for additional men to crew the short-handed destroyers, 200 wet and angry sailors from the capsized *Utah* volunteered. The 55 chosen didn't wait for a launch, they jumped overboard from auxiliary *Argonne* and swam to the ships.

Like the other destroyers, *Blue* entered international waters at a speed averaging 25 knots. Dodging the minesweepers lumbering slowly in front, *Blue* still managed to nip off a sweeper's starboard paravane cable. The minesweeper crew cheered *Blue* as she thundered past.

Soon as *Blue* cleared the channel, No. 3 and No. 4 boilers were lit off. At such a speed, with the ship reacting violently to every wave impact, it was nearly impossible to load the depth charge tracks, but the men did it. After the ammunition-shortage problem of the previous hour, Asher had the skipper's stateroom and the communications officers' room packed with shells.

Blue was followed by destroyer *Patterson*, in turn chased by a small boat containing *Patterson's* captain. He pulled up alongside as the destroyer slowed down and leaped onto the Jacob's ladder at 9:30 a.m., two miles south of harbor entrance.

While *Patterson's* skipper gained the deck, destroyer *Ralph Talbot* was out at sea by 9:35 a.m.

The hemorrhage of destroyers from Pearl Harbor slowed, and

STAND BY TO RAM!

Crossbill streamed out Oropesa gear on her starboard side and waddled out into the channel, screening the area astern of the destroyers.

Ashore, Lieutenant Commander Harold F. Pullen of destroyer *Reid* and his gunnery officer pulled into a parking space near the officers' landing. They ran down to the water front, where the impact of the scene set Pullen reeling. "My God, it looks like a movie set," was the best he could come up with.

They were surprised when *Reid's* 24-foot gig pulled up, with *Reid's* cook at the controls. "Everybody else had a gun, so I thought I'd look for officers," the cook said.

The destroyer had undergone complete overhaul just a week before and Pullen was afraid she'd be stuck in the dangerous harbor with mechanical difficulties. He was a proud man when he stepped on board and an officer greeted him with "Skipper, everything's under control."

The chief engineer chimed in, "Captain, we can get going in half an hour." Pullen could not believe what he was hearing.

Nested next to tender *Dobbin* on a "cold iron" watch, *Phelps* took until now to light boilers and push off, leaving behind the rest of Destroyer Division One: *MacDonough*, *Worden*, *Dewey* and *Hull*. *Hull*, ironically, had been the first destroyer to start firing back at Japanese aircraft — the gangway watch blazed away with his .45.

Outside the harbor, "when things started to pop," as Lieutenant Outerbridge put it, good metallic contacts began crowding the sonar. So many that destroyers began to run out of depth charges.

Unusual explosions burst out mysteriously along the reef. Outerbridge thought they were torpedoes being fired into the reef. *Can't be bombs,* he thought, *they can't be missing by that far!* He didn't consider antiaircraft shells falling back into the sea.

On patrol south of the harbor, *Dale* came across fishing sampans, flying white flags and frantically making for Kewalo Basin harbor. *Dale* skipper Lieutenant Commander Anthony Rorschach noted that "difficulty was had in restraining several members of the crew" from firing on the fishing boats.

Up in the gun director on board *Helm*, gunnery officer Dybdal heard the after machine guns rattle and turned just in time to see a dive bomber crank out of a low dive, barely a hundred feet above the ship.

Note the design differences between '30s destroyer Aylwin *and destroyer/ minesweeper* Trever *(DMS-16, ex DD-339), which was built during World War I. The later model has a raised forecastle, trunked stacks and heavier weaponry.*

⁶ The ship's action
report assumes
these bombs came
from the same
aircraft, however,
none of the D3A dive
bombers were fitted
out with more than
one weapon for the
Pearl Harbor raid.

Bombs bracketed the bow, 20 yards to starboard, 50 yards to port.[6] The ship shook violently as those forward were deluged with water. The plane disappeared in the distance.

For the first time that morning, sudden quiet surrounded the ship. The bombs had waffled the forward peak tanks, springing leaks and short-circuiting equipment, including the just-fixed steering gear. *Helm* continued her patrol despite having no boats, no power steering and waterlogged radio equipment and sonar gear.

A later examination revealed *Helm's* back had been broken by the bracketing bombs, though she is not one of the ships listed as damaged in the Pearl Harbor attack. She was not completely repaired until she put into Australia, several months later.

An hour and a half after the Imperial Navy first hit Pearl Harbor, the only American ships on station outside the port were

Craven-class destroyer Helm *(DD-388).*

the destroyers. Their strategy, in light of the harrowing submarine attack on Ford Island's northern backside, was codified by a radio dispatch from Admiral Pye, commander of Task Force One:

Battleships remain in port until further orders. Send all destroyers to sea and destroy enemy submarines. Follow them by cruiser to join Halsey.

One minute later, the Navy radio in San Francisco had an additional message; *USAT* Cynthia Olsen *sent distress reports — enemy submarine.*

First blood.

STAND BY TO RAM!

SHADOWS IN THE SEA

17

DESTROYER COUNTERATTACK

"Out from the silver-surfaced mouth of the harbor, a flotilla of destroyers streamed to battle, smoke pouring from their stacks," marveled the *Honolulu Star-Bulletin,* on its famous and hurriedly prepared first edition that day. The newspaper hit the streets before 10 a.m. The main headline said "WAR! OAHU BOMBED BY JAPANESE PLANES." The submarine threat was little known, and little understood, and so little reported.

By some atmospheric trick, Commander Mitsuo Fuchida's signal to begin the attack — translated as *Tora Tora Tora* — carried all the way to Hashirajima, in Hiroshima Bay, where Yamamoto's wireless operator on board battleship *Nagato* picked it up.

Closer to Oahu, on the picket line north of the island, *I-15* heard the message, which signified the attack was underway, the surprise successful. "This is good! This is good!" chortled skipper Nobuo Ishikawa. "Orita! Pass the word throughout the boat!"

Zenji Orita dashed down the narrow passageways, shouting that the attack was starting, and going well. As he ran, cries of *Banzai!* rang out behind him; sailors threw their arms around each other and sobbed happily. Orita reflected on the Japanese national passion for sudden, spontaneous displays of emotion, weeping openly at times of peak emotion. He wept himself. *We are the arrow of Empire,* he thought.

As soon as the cheering died down, the radiomen in *I-15* listened carefully to the American circuits. Out there in the dawning Pacific, *I-15* could easily have been thousands of miles away from the battle. The American radio traffic was confused and frantic. Obviously, something profound was going on at Pearl Harbor.

For the first time, Orita wished he were on one of the midget submarines. If things were going right, they had front-row seats.

America's first ally to go into action was Dutch freighter *Jagersfontein,* strafed as she stood into Honolulu Harbor. The ship quickly shot back, as the Dutch had already been at war for more than a year and were prepared.

Japanese aircraft began to thin out. In Middle Loch, at 9:30 a.m., a plane flopped into the harbor 500 yards off destroyer/minelayer

Montgomery's port beam. The crew saw the pilot climb out of the sinking aircraft and sent a boat over to capture him, but he created a such a fuss that one of the sailors shot him. The body was taken back to *Montgomery*.

At 9:32, *Aylwin* cleared the harbor, followed by *Breese* at 9:42 and *Phelps* at 9:50, the last of the first outrush of destroyers. Amid the floating, burning debris in the harbor, others got up steam and began to move out more cautiously, picking up speed only when hurtling out of the channel. *Bagley* was underway from berth B-22 at 9:40 and stood seaward, pausing only to pick up officers trying to catch *Blue*.

Porter-class destroyer USS Phelps *(DD-360).*

Bagley was the last destroyer to sortie while the attack was under way, with Lieutenant Philip Cann as senior officer aboard. Moored at the Navy Yard near *St. Louis* and *Honolulu*, undergoing repairs on a dented bilge keel, *Bagley* had to hurriedly relubricate an engine before she could fire up. She sortied north of Ford Island to avoid becoming entangled with the beached *Nevada*.

At 10 a.m., *Selfridge* pulled out of nest at berth X-9 and stood for sea, followed by *Case*, *Tucker* and *Reid*. *Conyngham* was left behind.

Fuchida's airplanes were scrambling pell-mell back to Nagumo's carriers, the last leaving Oahu around 10 a.m. The crews aboard the northern submarines grew tense. This was their moment. If the American carriers counterattacked, it would be through their line.

In his bones, Kimmel felt the Japanese carriers lay to the north. At 10:18 a.m., he radioed his sea forces, *... some indication enemy force northwest Oahu ...* and directed ships to that area. A Japanese submarine picketing Oahu picked up this message and and relayed it to the Imperial task force.

Though the Japanese were alerted, American ships apparently ignored this instruction. *I-15* waited throughout the day and surfaced after sunset, watching the seas south toward Oahu. No ships appeared.

The action was to the south of Oahu, as reports of submarine contacts escalated throughout the morning. The immediate job was to flush out the I-boats, and the destroyers that escaped Pearl Harbor concentrated on the port approaches. Unless the undersea threat was neutralized at the naval base's doorstep, any northern maneuver was academic.

SHADOWS IN THE SEA

Cruiser *St. Louis*, under Captain George A. Rood, also scrambled to get out of the harbor. The warship was the largest to leave that morning, and it wasn't simple; she needed a large hole in her flank welded shut first. She backed out of berth B-17 at 9:31 a.m.

Rood felt thirsty as the ship began to move and called down for water. As Japanese planes strafed the backing ship, Pharmacist's Mate Howard Myers took the captain a pitcher of iced water and a glass. "Nothing was too good for Captain Rood," he later explained.

Doing 22 knots in an 8-knot zone, *St. Louis* charged out of the harbor. Rood, an ex-submariner and well-liked by the cruiser's crew, figured correctly that if any Japanese submarines were present, they'd be lying in ambush right outside the entrance to Pearl, hoping to bottle up the channel with a fat target like *St. Louis*. Rood ordered full power, hoping to shorten the subs' moments of opportunity.

Rood aimed the cruiser at the open sea, ignoring a steel cable stretched from Dry Dock No. 1 to *Turbine*, the dredge that had deterred the midget submarine from Battleship Row. *St. Louis* "hit the cable a smashing blow and snapped it like a violin string," sang historian Gordon Prange.

Boatswain's Mate Howard C. French, busy on Ford Island, stopped to admire *St. Louis* sweeping past. "It was a great thrill," he

Battleship California *burns in the foreground, the hull of* Oklahoma *lies at center and cruiser* St. Louis *picks up speed at right — within a few moments the ship veered hard to port, scraping against the quays and nearly slamming into Ford Island.*

recalled. "That ship was moving beyond all knots I had ever seen in the channel."

Booms laden with boats and a gangway were scraped off the ship's side as she grazed Ford Island's piers. "I wondered what kept her from hitting bottom," marveled French. "Everyone on that ship seemed to be at their battle stations and no one seemed to give a damn as that cruiser dashed out to sea … That skipper was really moving and it looked as though no one but God himself was going to stop him!"

The channel was crowded with minesweepers *Condor* and *Crossbill* and their apparatus and the cruiser charged straight ahead. At 10:04 a.m., Rood saw what appeared to be two torpedoes, one following the other, flashing toward his starboard bow.

ADVANCE FORCE — PEARL HARBOR

"We're going to get smacked good and proper," thought Rood, and he called out to Commander Carl K. Fink, "If you want to see a ship torpedoed, come take a look!" Fink took one look and agreed with the skipper — in the narrow channel there wasn't much they could do. In the foremast structure, with a great view of the on-coming weapons from 1,000 to 2,000 yards, Lieutenant Charles A. Curtze tensed as he watched the torpedoes arrow toward the ship.

Rood ordered *St. Louis*, already sprinting at 22 knots, to Emergency Full. At 25 knots, he tried a tentative zig zag, cranking the ship sharply in the narrow, coral-rimmed channel. The first torpedo was aimed directly at the starboard side of turret No. 3, but struck a coral spit near Buoy No. 1, on the west side of dredged channel, and exploded 200 yards from ship, sending geysers skyward in an explosive blossom of water and coral.

It drenched the ship with water. "That Jap got over-anxious," observed Rood.

The second torpedo was "running hot" on a diverging track, about 10 degrees off of the first, and was apparently caught up in the explosion. The track disappeared.

St. Louis burst out of the coral throat too quickly to avoid the two minesweepers, so the cruiser flashed between them, slicing the thin broom cable and, Rood thought, probably scaring the hell out of the two minesweeper skippers.

A small, dark shape broke the surface nearby, on the starboard quarter. It didn't resemble anything anyone on *St. Louis* had seen before, so the cruiser opened fire with 5-inch guns; the gunners believed they hit the "top of the periscope fairwater." The shape plunged underwater within 30 seconds, and destroyers came over to investigate.

Condor witnessed *St. Louis*' dash, and noted in its log that the cruiser mistook *Crossbill's* Oropesa minesweeping float for a midget

SHADOWS IN THE SEA

Cruiser St. Louis during the summer of 1941, showing off her newly applied Measure 1 camouflage, with a complex Measure 5 false bow wave added to fool submarines into thinking the ship was making greater speed than it was. By Dec. 7, 1941, the wave had been overpainted.

submarine, swerving away from the object and shooting at it. Doing so, she cut across *Condor's* cable approximately 100 yards from the outboard end.

Condor switched to "O" type Oropesa sweep as her severed paravane floated away in the direction of Barbers Point, trailing the clipped cable into the depths. *Cockatoo's* starboard gear was also cut by *St. Louis*, though it was recovered. She continued to sweep with the port gear.

Rood later saw a captured "baby sub" at the submarine base and was convinced his target was the same object.

Whatever it was, this incident was the last major naval action of the attack. *St. Louis* continued her mad sortie to the sea.

From on high, Curtze watched in admiration as Rood, with "uncanny prescience and shiphandling," twisted *St. Louis* past Waikiki on the edge of the five-fathom curve, keeping the ship shielded by shallow water. Her mission was to join up with carrier *Enterprise's* task force and search for the enemy fleet. The cruiser began to zigzag at 25 knots, and Rood ordered destroyers *Blue, Phelps* and *Monaghan* to screen him.

Just as *St. Louis* turned past Diamond Head, another torpedo rushed toward the cruiser. Rood pulled the ship parallel to the track and the fish sped by. This attack was not entered in the cruiser's battle log, though destroyer *Blue* got a firm sound contact on the submarine headed for *St. Louis*. Contacts were all made at 1,400 yards and the destroyer signaled the emergency, dropping two depth charges while tracking the submarine's course. A scum of oil was observed bursting to the surface. There were no bubbles, and *Blue* did not credit the attack.

The incident was *Blue's* third depth charging within an hour. After

This sketch from Condor's *action report shows how* St. Louis *cut* Condor's *paravane free and shelled* Crossbill's *paravane.*

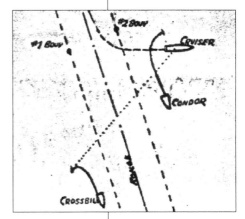

leaving the harbor, the destroyer had slowed to 10 knots and began methodically using her echo ranger. Within 20 minutes, a good sound contact was reported by CRM(PA) W.J. Matthews, who was manning both sonar and radio equipment. *Blue* pushed over the contact and dropped four depth charges on it, then circled, running through the foaming water where the target had been.

By 9:48 a.m., *Blue* had regained the sound contact, dropping two more depth charges. Once again, she investigated the location, this time spotting a large oil slick and air bubbles appear over a 200-foot length. Because the air bubbles might indicate a surfacing submarine, all guns were run out to starboard, ready to open fire when it appeared. Other sailors crowded the deck to watch the show, but the I-boat didn't oblige them. [1]

The destroyer, like others, stripped for action as she continued patrol. Flammables were cut away and tossed overboard; weapons were locked and loaded. *Blue's* four torpedo mounts could hold up to 16 torpedoes, though only nine were on board. Chief Torpedoman's Mate Charles M. Shaw went to his position as soon as the depth charging stopped and started bringing up the six torpedoes that were stored below. Two weapons were already on deck, and one was disassembled in the torpedo shack, the after body lashed to the deck. He charged the water compartments and fuel cells, getting eight ready to go, and then worked at getting the other one put back together. It was noon when he finished.

They put the last weapon in the tube and locked down the tripping latch. All the torpedoes were ready except for the impulse charges that, when ignited, blew the missile out of the tube. The fore and aft racks of tubes were facing one another. Shaw and another sailor closed the impulse charge chamber and were in the midst of placing another impulse charge in it when the torpedo fired, rocketing forward out of the tube and striking another torpedo in the fore racks. The guide stud atop the torpedo sheared off against the air flask, and the missile twisted, the warhead wrenching off and bouncing onto the deck.

The torpedo body strained and horsed as it hung halfway out of the tube, pushed by compressed air but blocked by the sheared guide stud. Shaw crawled under the rack and shut off the air, and did the same to the forward rack. He was afraid they would bolt their tubes as well. Ensign Asher slowed the destroyer to five knots to smooth out the bumps.

The hissing warhead was ordered overboard. The ship leaned into a turn, and Shaw used the shifting inertia to manhandle the weight to the starboard side and over. He braced for an explosion, though none came. He figured the arming bail inside the torpedo's nose had been damaged when it struck the fore rack.

The little task force of *St. Louis*, *Blue*, *Phelps* and *Monaghan*

[1] Blue *felt the submarine was "definitely sunk," and noted the coordinates — 21*-11'-30"N and 157*-49'-45"W.*

A scene from an American training film shows a depth charge "rack" on the fantail of a destroyer, with an exploding charge ripping up the water behind.

were sent to investigate reports of enemy transports off Barbers Point. They dashed there, prepared for combat, found nothing. More reports came in. They were hunting for themselves. They banged away at an "enemy aircraft" nonetheless, and when Rood saw a ship pop up over the horizon due straight for Barbers Point, he said "There are the Japanese! And this time we're ready and itching to knock hell out of them." The oncoming ship turned out to be cruiser *Minneapolis*.

During the late morning, submarine *Thresher* began a wide swing to approach Pearl Harbor through the approved sea corridors for friendly submarines. The boat's injured seaman, William Dell Grover, was beginning to rave from his head injury, and the submarine's medic was anxious to get him ashore. *Tautog* and the other two sentry submarines were already in Pearl.

Thresher met up with destroyer *Litchfield*, their escort to the harbor. Word of the attack convinced *Thresher*'s skipper, Lieutenant Commander William Anderson, to release the escort so that the destroyer could dash west and join *Enterprise*'s task force. *Litchfield* faded over the horizon, and *Thresher* began to submerge. A radio message came in, warning American submarines not to lose their escorts. *Thresher* signaled *Litchfield* for another rendezvous.

I-69, the flagship of Japan's 12th Submarine Squadron, had been running her batteries hard, dashing about close to Oahu. As the attack started, the sound detectors picked up the sound of bomb and torpedoes crashing through the water, as well as the rumble of depth charges. Judging by this, skipper Katsuji Watanabe declared that the Advance Force "was engaged in heavy fighting."

Soon orders were received directing *I-69* within eight and half miles of Pearl Harbor, there to survey the battle action and to "annihilate" remaining American forces.

The midget-submarine carriers were also in the area. At dawn, a few miles southwest of Barbers Point, *I-24* dove to 90 feet. The seas were so rough that even at that depth the submarine rolled in place. The swells tended to suck the craft toward the surface, and the crew compensated by continually flooding and blowing tanks. The new tanks were balky, and once, by accident, the submarine burst to the surface in the light of day. Skipper Hiroshi Hanabusa ordered the trim tanks crash-flooded, pulling instantly in 20 tons of water, but *I-24* continued to loll on the surface. Two airplanes were sighted, closing in on the

I-69, flagship of the 12th Submarine Squadron. The tall radio antennae indicate her importance as a message sending and receiving center.

USS Wasmuth (DMS-15, ex DD-338), a flush-deck destroyer converted into a fast minesweeper.

submarine. The error was found, in the main ballast pump, and the I-boat sank once again to 90 feet. The trim tanks were damaged, and the submarine adapted an awkward bow-down stance.

Distant thunder rolled through the thin steel bulkheads, the pulse of faraway depth-chargings, carried through the thick ocean like the pounding of veins in the skull. The crew of *I-24* tried to imagine the furious battle, and could not.

Another American warship commanded by a junior officer, Lieutenant Bernhart A. Fuetsch, destroyer/minesweeper *Trever* cleared the harbor a few minutes behind *St. Louis*. Lieutenant Robert Smith and Lieutenant Steve Corey, skipper and XO of *Henley*, had hitched a ride aboard *Trever*, hoping to flag down their destroyer. More than an hour later, though they'd spotted their destroyer, Fuetsch refused to loan them *Trever's* whaleboat, figuring he'd need it to get his own skipper aboard. Lieutenant Commander D.M. Agnew, *Trever's* commander, was cooling his heels on board *Wasmuth*. He finally made it aboard his own ship at 4:34 that afternoon.

Smith and Corey decided to swim for *Henley* and cut their trousers off at the knee. They paddled furiously, but *Henley* drifted faster than they could swim. Smith and Corey climbed back aboard *Trever* to catch their breath.

Inside the harbor, *Jarvis* made for the sea at 10:15 a.m., from Berth No. 6. At 10:40, *Worden* unmoored from *Dobbin* to do the same thing. At the same moment, *Cummings* cleared the harbor from Berth B-15 and joined the anti-submarine patrol, tossing off some depth charges for good measure.

She wasn't alone in this promiscuous use of weapons. Between the last aerial action around 10 a.m. and noon, the waters bracketing Pearl Harbor shuddered continuously with high explosive.

Destroyer *Ward*, the first to shoot that day, attacked another contact at 10:20 a.m., dropping three depth charges. Running across an oil slick at 10:31, she rolled two more charges, and the concussion jammed her steering gear hard left. The destroyer floundered around in circles for three minutes before it could be hammered out.

At 11:27 a.m., *Ward* heard another contact on her sound gear, dropped four depth charges, and got an oil slick in response. At 11:50, *Ward* made an additional, though futile, depth-charge attack; none of the weapons exploded.

Destroyer/minesweeper *Wasmuth* dropped an "ashcan" with no result on a suspected submarine at 10:23 a.m.; 13 minutes later she dropped another and was rewarded by an oil slick 3.4 miles off the harbor entrance.

Chew got a "supersonic" contact 1,000 yards west of the channel buoys at 10:30 a.m, and dumped a depth charge that didn't explode. The destroyer got three more contacts before noon, none close enough to attack. By the end of the day, *Chew* had dropped 28 depth charges on an estimated eight different submerged contacts, all in the area southwest of the entrance buoys. "Evidence indicated that two submarines were sunk," claimed an after-action report.

Just after 11 a.m., PBY *11-P-23* reported two submarines of "unknown nationality" that dived when the airplane approached.

USS Worden (*DD-352*), a Farragut-class destroyer.

The excited crew of a motor torpedo boat led destroyer/minelayer *Breese* to a spot where a periscope had been sighted, near the channel entrance. At 11:15 a.m., *Breese* dropped two depth charges. There was no result, and *Breese* continued the search to the west. Within a few minutes, she began to track a submarine off the port bow.

Breese charged over the target, scattering two charges by sonar. A "great deal" of debris and oil boiled to the surface in the wake of the second explosion. No sound contact reappeared after that, but on the second pass a positive ping was heard off the sea bottom. Four more deep-set depth charges were fired with no apparent result.

At the same time, about 11:40 a.m., the sound operator in

USS Gamble (*DM-15, ex DD-123*), *like* Breese, *was converted into a light minelayer in the early '30s.*

Virtually no photographs survive that show destroyers during the attack on Pearl Harbor — attention was centered on the battleships and many destroyers cleared the harbor before photographers dropped their rifles. This image, apparently taken from a moving car about 9:26 a.m., shows tender Dobbin *with destroyers* Hull, Dewey, Worden *and* MacDonough *alongside. In the background,* Phelps *gets underway.*

Cummings picked up "propeller noises … close aboard." Two depth charges were tossed over, with the usual reward of an oil slick. A radio signal over the naval district net reported *Submarine due south Aloha Tower 4 miles has been bombed. Surface covered with oil slick.*

Reid's engineer's promise of half an hour to get underway had proved optimistic, but she pulled away from from the buoy by 10:40 a.m. As the destroyer steamed past, the turtled *Utah* was "quite a shock," remembered Lieutenant Commander Harold F. Pullen.

Reid cleared the channel at 11:40 a.m. at high speed, 30 knots. *Boy, I'll bet I catch hell for this,* Pullen thought. He felt a curious relief at gaining blue water. *Reid,* the last ship to clear Pearl Harbor before noon, joined a task force and didn't return for three days.

By this time, the eminently frustrated Smith and Corey had figured out a way to transfer from *Trever* to *Henley* without stopping the ships. *Henley* let out a life raft pulled along on manila lines, and the officers leaped on it as the two ships raced through the water.

Finally aboard his ship, all Smith wanted to do was rest on his favorite stool on the bridge and catch his breath. When the skipper got there, the stool was missing. "I threw it over the side," a seaman said proudly.

"Now why in hell would you do that?" Smith wondered.

"Because it was made of wood, and wood's inflammable," explained the sailor patiently. It was a rule picked up from the experiences of the Royal Navy. Smith sat on the deck, simply glad to be back aboard his own ship.

SHADOWS IN THE SEA

SLIPPING INTO DARKNESS

18

THINGS THAT ECHO IN THE NIGHT

The afternoon of Dec. 7 settled into a routine for the hungry destroyers, vigorously running down contacts and hammering them with high explosive. The weather turned cloudy and brisk, and the sea chopped at their hulls. After the sunny casualness of most Hawaiian days, the afternoon seemed grim and gray, a routine run by the numbers.

Destroyer *Mugford*, stuck without fuel at Berth 6, didn't get underway until noon. She was preceded by *Chew*, which had been detailed to relieve *Ward*. *Chew* picked up a sonar contact on the way out, a few minutes past noon, and tossed two depth charges, one of which exploded. *Chew* didn't make another contact until 3:15 p.m., just west of the entrance buoys, this time rolling four depth charges, two of which exploded.

Chew took *Ward's* post at 12:45. Lieutenant Outerbridge's ship dashed back into Pearl Harbor, dog-legging all the way. For the first time, the crew saw the damage in the harbor; it was a grim experience. All the crew began to tie on life jackets, not taking them off while they were on board.

Ward tied up to the ammunition dock in West Loch with engines simmering at 1:40 p.m. Ten minutes later, 300-pound depth charges began to be wrestled on board, 47 of them. Like most Americans, Outerbridge was fearful the Japanese would attempt a landing that night, and he wanted to be well-armed.

Rearmed, *Ward* cast off from the ammunition dock and bolted out of Pearl at 4 p.m., slowing only to pull up alongside destroyer *Allen* to take on 14 extra sailors to relieve *Ward's* tired crew.

By 5:45 p.m., *Ward* was back on the inshore patrol circuit. The antiaircraft gang slept next to their gun that evening, not waking even when depth charges thundered around the ship. Over the next three days, *Ward* dropped another 172 depth charges.

Another veteran of the first shots fired that morning, tug *Keosanqua* shed *Antares'* lighter in Honolulu Harbor and hauled a floating crane into Pearl Harbor for salvage operations. She spent the rest of the night pushing target rafts around the smoldering harbor.

The only known photograph of a Pearl Harbor destroyer in action on Dec. 7. This is USS Chandler *(DMS-9, ex DD-206), caught at sea with the* Minneapolis *task force 25 miles south of Oahu in the Fleet Operating Area. Taken in the afternoon, this image shows* Chandler *searching for the Advance Force; the waves have turned brisk, choppy and cold. The original print shows three other destroyers on the horizon.*

SLIPPING INTO DARKNESS

At 12:35 p.m., destroyer *MacDonough* poked out of Pearl and joined *Worden* and *Phelps* screening light cruiser *Detroit*. At 3 p.m., *Dewey*, the last of Destroyer Division 1 and *MacDonough's* nest mate, cast off from tender *Dobbin* and went to sea. *Dobbin*, left by itself off the northeast shore of Ford Island, then had her own excitement. Pacific Fleet Radio Unit reported that afternoon that the destroyer *had Japanese prisoners aboard. Men approached* Dobbin *by boat. Prisoner believed off submarine.* The signal wasn't verified.

As for *Detroit's* little group, steaming to rendezvous with Admiral Halsey's task force, destroyer *Aylwin* was already on station, dogging the light cruiser's starboard flank, about 600 yards out. The destroyer crew witnessed two torpedo wakes rip through the water toward the cruiser, but they passed astern and headed out to sea. A few minutes later, there were two explosions on the horizon, which the sailors assumed were the torpedoes' end-of-run self-destruction.

While this was going on, the two ships were ordered to veer toward Nanakuli Beach on the west side of Oahu, where Japanese troops were reportedly swarming ashore. Finding nothing there, they wheeled west and hastened to catch up with the task force.

Far to the south, off Johnston Island, heavy cruiser *Indianapolis* also reported torpedo tracks, just before 3 p.m.

There were submarine scares within the harbor as well. *Curtiss* reported another submarine at 3:08 p.m.; destroyer *Case*, on her way out of the harbor, depth-charged what she believed was a sunken submarine at 5:15.

At 6:40 p.m., with night glimmering wetly and punctuated only by the dull bellow of oil fires, destroyer/seaplane tender *Hulbert* sighted a periscope near Battleship Row. *Hulbert* swerved toward the area, intending to ram, and went over the location twice. A few minutes later, battleship *Maryland* saw a submarine periscope at the south end of Ford Island.

Americans continued to depth-charge the harbor throughout the night of Dec. 7, in case any stray midgets still lurked.

American submarines were in danger of friendly fire. *Pollack* and *Pompano*, enroute to Pearl Harbor, stayed well away until Dec. 9 and then entered under escort — they received battle stars for the raid anyway. *Plunger*, in the same group but ahead of the other two submarines, came in at the same time. Her log indicates she had been off Waikiki when the attack started.

Thresher had a pressing need to enter the harbor. Seaman William Grover, injured in a fall a few days before, was slipping into delirium as the lesion on his skull went untreated. *Thresher's* morning rendezvous with escort destroyer *Litchfield* had been interrupted by the attack, and the two ships were scheduled to meet up once again.

In an hour, the destroyer signaled *Thresher* that the rendezvous had been reached. The submarine reached the agreed-upon location and used a sonar recognition signal. At periscope depth, a smoke flare was released so the destroyer's gunners could correlate the sonar

signal and take bearings on the flare. *Thresher* surfaced, comfortably near a destroyer's silhouette.

Destroyer/minelayer *Gamble*, seeing a surfacing submarine, opened fire with her No. 1 gun. Bullets bounced off the water and rattled against the submarine's conning tower, denting the thin metal without penetrating. The first 5-inch round splashed short, and as the submarine hurriedly submerged, a second round jammed in the breech. The submarine quickly sent up an emergency signal: she was *U.S.S. Thresher!*

Sensing an enemy submarine contact, *Litchfield* had darted away without warning *Thresher*.

The reef shallows at Fort Kamehameha, at the entrance to Pearl Harbor. Sakamaki and Inagaki's I-24tou had trouble navigating this area, and the black midget submarines would have been highly visible from the air.

Thresher headed for deep water and stayed submerged through the night. As the crew watched helplessly, Grover died without again setting foot on land, as he had predicted.

Thresher ventured near Pearl Harbor the next morning to be driven down again by excited Army aircraft. The submarine was finally escorted into the harbor by destroyer/seaplane tender *Thornton*.

When Maurey Meister's PBY returned to Ford Island, he saw the cold-weather flying gear accidentally shipped in from California getting a workout. Handling crews were wearing it to keep off the thick oil scum as they waded into the water from the seaplane ramp.

Meister was told to stand by while his plane was refueled. He managed to cadge some food, and had just sat down to eat when General Quarters sounded. He rushed to his post past the hangers, and there he peered down the long channel to the sea. Meister saw destroyers hounding something at the entrance, and from the great distance, believed he saw a "miniature sub" lifted out of the water, within the corona of a depth-charge plume.

The devastating impact of the raid was just beginning to hit home in Washington. President Roosevelt, going over the incoming reports with ten invited congressmen as well as his cabinet, wondered about the proper response. Someone asked if there were casualties on the Japanese side.

"It's a little difficult," said Roosevelt. "We think we got some of their submarines, but we don't know …"

"There's a story coming over the radio that we got one of their airplane carriers," some one hoped.

"I don't know. Don't believe it. It was reported about eight o'clock. I didn't believe it. A Japanese carrier has been discovered off the Panama Canal and sunk by our forces," mused Roosevelt. "I wish it were true. But about the same time, the commanding officer in Canal Zone said they were on the alert, but very quiet."

Roosevelt continued to speculate that some of the Japanese aircraft shot down "had swastikas on them."

Senator Tom Connally of Texas, chairman of the Foreign Relations Committee, rose from his seat in agony. "I am amazed at the attack by Japan, but I am still more astounded at what happened to our Navy," he cried out. " They were all asleep. Where were our patrols? They knew these negotiations were going on!"

Roosevelt knew about *Cynthia Olson*, calling her "an armed transport supposed to be carrying a load of lumber. Is that right, Harry?"

"Yes sir," confirmed aide Harry Hopkins.

"And the other one is — that was 1,500 miles off San Francisco — the other report which might release the same — that an American merchant ship had been sunk 700 miles (off). But they are just flabby ..." and the President snarled something inaudible.

"If that report is true," said another cabinet member. "It is pretty close to California, is that right, Harry?"

Connally turned on Navy Secretary Frank Knox, berating him for the strategy of sequestering the fleet from the submarine menace. "Didn't you say last month we could lick the Japs in two weeks? Didn't you say that our Navy was so well-prepared and located that the Japanese couldn't hope to hurt us at all?" Connally raged. "Why did you have all the ships at Pearl Harbor crowded the way you did? And why did you have a long chain across the mouth of the entrance, so that our ships couldn't get out?"

Knox explained that the expected threat had been submarines, not aircraft.

"Well, they were *supposed* to be on the alert," insisted Connally.

Later, Roosevelt began to look back, trying to put the day in perspective. The tenor of the conversation, however, became a blueprint for strategic use of submarines. "Back in 1922-1923, I wrote an article for the *Asiatic* [1] magazine, and I pointed out at that time from what I had seen of the Navy Department, war between the United States and Japan would be won by us; but it would be won primarily by the starvation and exhaustion of Japan — starvation or exhaustion.

"And always remember that they have no naval bases. They have nothing ... And the Japanese know perfectly well that the answer to her attack is proper strangulation of Japan. Strangulation altogether ...

"Remember that out there it is nearly just about dawn. They are doing things, and saying things during the daytime out there, while we are all in bed."

"We are in bed too much," muttered a cabinet member.

As the politicians filed out of the White House, they gave no comment to reporters. Upton Close, an isolationist, was interviewed on Washington radio and insisted the Hawaii attacks "might well be German submarines trying to provoke us into war, and that the Japanese government would probably disavow the attack even if it's own navy were responsible."

[1] *Actually, Asia magazine.*

That night, Rear Admiral Bloch described the damage to Admiral Stark in a telephone call.

"The fires in the Navy Yard are very well under control," he said. "We have had reports of parachute troops landing, but I have not been able to verify those. We have sunk some submarines. One has been sunk in the harbor here. I don't know whose it was, but it was fired on by the ships in the harbor and sunk."

Stark was incredulous. "A submarine sunk in our harbor?"

"Yes, one was sunk in our harbor, and we believe there have been three sunk outside near here. One by airplane, and two by destroyers," said Bloch, who then went on to describe papers recovered from the Zero shot down at Fort Kamehameha.

Stark was still dwelling on the submarine, and blurted out in the midst of Bloch's account, "The submarine sunk in the harbor, is it German?"

"We don't know what it is yet," said Bloch, who paused before going on with his report. Stark listened this time.

As night fell over Hawaii, Oahu lay smothered by blackout. Sutematsu Kida, skipper of sampan *Kiho Maru*, aided by son Kiichi and crewmen Kiho Uehara and Seiki Arakaki, was fishing west of Barbers Point. *Myojin Maru* loomed out of the darkness and hailed Kida. "Turn off your lights!" Sannosuke Onishi shouted from the other sampan. "There's a blackout!"

Kida was dumbfounded. Onishi, whose sampan had a radio, explained that Japan had attacked Pearl Harbor. He had formed up with sampans *Sumiyoishi Maru* and *Shin-ei Maru* in the darkness, and they were going to make a run for Honolulu in the morning light. Probably figuring there was safety in numbers, Kida agreed to abandon his fishing trip and join the other three boats.

The crew of the sampan had seen smoke rising from Oahu during

A colorful sampan crew enjoys a meal in this staged picture for the Hawaii tourist industry.

SLIPPING INTO DARKNESS

the day, and had wondered what was going on.

Kiho Maru doused her lights. Kida and his crew ate rice and corned beef in the darkness. "I'm a Japanese alien, though I've lived here most of my life," mused Kida. "I was told that — as an alien — if there's a war with Japan, I won't be able to fish offshore any more. If I can't fish, how can I support my family?"

Kiichi Kida, who was nisei, pointed out that he was an American citizen. He would be free to fish. His father complained that the boy was too young, only 21. On the other hand, Uehara had more experience …

The four men spent the black evening trying to figure out the future.

Destroyer/minelayer *Breese* slipped through the ebon waters nearby. The only light came from phosphorescent splashes as porpoises played tag with the ship. Lieutenant Commander Stout, leaning on the starboard bridge rail, watched the mammals and thought the night "was as black as the inside of a hat. We were running on dead reckoning. We would look ashore and not see a damn thing except the waves washing in." Nearby, Stout saw a porpoise head for the ship, glimmering in the inky waves. It was joined by another. He stared. The two were arrowing directly for the ship's flanks.

Sutematsu Kida and son Kiichi Kida

They were fish, all right, "but not the type of fish I thought it was," said Stout. He shouted for *Breese* to increase speed and swerve seaward, and the torpedoes raced away in the darkness.

There was no sign of the submarine that had launched them, and *Breese* continued her patrol. "There was no use dropping depth charges just for the hell of it, because people were jittery enough as it was," explained Stout.

A shrouded launch pulled up behind cruiser *Honolulu* and deposited figures on the dock. Seaman Clair E. Boggs leaned over the side of the cruiser and challenged them; if they didn't identify themselves, he'd open fire. The men below said something indecipherable. Boggs warned them again, and a voice from below yelled, "Go ahead and shoot!"

Boggs let them go. "A Jap would be more polite about it," he explained. The next morning, he saw the sailors return to the launch and asked why they'd called his bluff. They hadn't, said one; in fact they had been scared into calling out the name of their destroyer — "*U.S.S. Chew!*"

That night the seas were rough. Ensign Burdick H. Brittin, stumbling in exhaustion about destroyer *Aylwin* in filthy dress whites, recorded 47-degree rolls. *Aylwin* and other destroyers had formed a

scouting line that afternoon and had sped off to the southwest at 30 knots, hoping to run across the Japanese battle force. Instead, rushing through a "tumultuous void" without running lights or radar, they almost ran into each other.

Lieutenant Dybdal, unwilling to leave *Helm's* gun director — some of the sailors were catnapping on deck — noted with curiosity that the heavy director pitched in different directions than the destroyer. When *Helm's* bow splashed dawn, the six men in the director would reel backward.

Using a shielded flashlight, Dybdal inspected the base of the director. Three of four welds securing it to the deck had snapped in the dive-bomb attack when *Helm* left Pearl Harbor in the morning. Dybdal reported the potentially dangerous situation to the bridge, and was told to shore it up as best he could.

The destroyers were directed to swing to the northeast and rendezvous with *Enterprise*, but *Aylwin* didn't decode the order promptly. The other destroyers switched back while *Aylwin* continued blindly. As they pitched on through the swells, a black shadow humped out of the darkness and rushed at the destroyer, which promptly leveled guns and swung torpedo tubes at the intruder. Luckily, the stranger blinked for identification. *Aylwin* learned the shape was sister ship *Farragut*, bearing a change in orders.

Reported landings at Ewa on the night of Dec. 7 were an effort by Japanese fifth columnists to lure U.S. ships "into a submarine trap," or so the initial report on the attack read. Destroyer commander Rear Admiral Milo Draemel supposedly wised up just before reaching the spot, and wheeled his forces away as Japanese torpedoes reached out for them.[2]

Intelligence analyst Edwin Layton was riled about the radio chatter of Dec. 7, calling it, "The greatest collection of erroneous, foolish fantastic reports that was ever passed on a radio circuit, and until these were observed to be so fantastic, so exaggerated and so imaginary … they were passed in plain language on to the fleet."

At least one rumor caused a cruiser and some destroyers to head for Barbers Point to investigate. The expected Japanese landing force didn't materialize, though once there, a torpedo was fired at them. Which in turn led to another rumor — the wild radio reports themselves were a Japanese trap.

Hounded by eager destroyers, the Japanese were having enough trouble just trying to stay in one place. Commander Katsuji Watanabe was the youngest skipper of a standard submarine in the Hawaiian Operation and considered the "most brave." He spent the day dodging destroyers, on occasion pumping out oil and Japanese sandals to fool the hunters. His *I-69* lurked 17 miles southwest of Pearl, until sunset, when he was ordered to close to within 8 miles of the harbor. It was an area overrun with prowling destroyers.

At 8 p.m., Watanabe was spotted by four ships, who attacked him with depth charges but did no damage.

[2] In fact, the area off Ewa did swarm with I-boats, and American forces passing through were clean targets. The astonishing thing is how few shots were actually taken while the submarines had the advantage of numbers and weather.

SLIPPING INTO DARKNESS

Kiho Maru, *the Kida family sampan, at the Ala Wai boat basin near Honolulu Harbor. Diamond Head is in the background.*

After sunset, *I-69* broke the surface and began cruising at battle speed, recharging her batteries. The bridge crew kept an eye out for potential targets.

They soon sighted patrol ships and reversed course. When a destroyer charged toward her, the I-boat was obliged to submerge with the batteries only partially charged. Back on the surface, waves racked the submarine and decks were continually awash, playing havoc with depth control. The battery power was being depleted faster than it was being replenished.

Watanabe was fascinated with the hard red glare hanging over the harbor. "Pearl Harbor shone red in the sky, like a thing afire," he remembered. "It was (as if it were) already dawn …"

At a minute past 9 p.m., Watanabe saw "a large flame heaving heavenward — a flame like a ship exploding in Pearl Harbor. After this very heavy anti-aircraft followed."

Ashore, anti-aircraft guns were firing at shadows, the shells lighting up the skies. When a flight of F4F-3 aircraft arrived from the carrier *Enterprise*, four Wildcats were shot out of the air by nervous gunners. The exploding aircraft made it appear to Watanabe that a ship had blown up.

The fiery light also silhouetted the submarine against the island's dark mass, and once again an American destroyer bore down on *I-69*, firing green Very shells to signal other submarine hunters.

Rattled, Watanabe took the submarine far to the southwest, away from the destroyers. At 5:36 a.m., Watanabe felt obliged to take his submarine down again, despite the bad news that charging was only 73 percent completed. He nosed carefully toward the harbor channel, even though destroyers scented his sonic spoor and rolled depth charges randomly near the craft.

The mother submarines of the Advance Force stole away from the apron of south Oahu and headed southeast, to the rendezvous point seven miles west of Lanai. Air was forced into the ballast tanks, and instead of rising gracefully, *I-24* pitched to starboard, flinging the crew off their feet. Once again, a piece of rubbish from the shipyard was discovered jammed in a valve. It was quickly cleaned out. *I-24* and the other midget mother ships rendezvoused in the calm lee

waters southwest of Lanai island, and waited for the midgets to return. The scheduled meeting was for 3:30 a.m. Dec. 8. The original rendezvous near the island of Niihau, in the opposite direction from Oahu, had been canceled. *I-74* was detailed to rescue the aviators.

Sakamaki's belongings and farewell letters were discovered carefully bundled on his bunk. There was a note explaining what to do with them, and some yen for postage. Most of the midget submariners left writings behind, thanking their superior officers. *For the sake of his Majesty the Emperor, nothing do I grudge to sacrifice,* began one. *Young as I am, I'll lay down my life gladly in his Imperial Majesty's service. On my war mission I now go forth, defying the network of carriers and mine fields.*

Ready am I to perish, once I have crippled the enemy. Oh, how serene this morning's sky looks, as my heart turns up to it full of joy at the thought of joining my dead comrades at the Yasukuni Shrine …

Since no word had been received from any of the midget submarines all day, the mother I-boats did not know if their wait at the rendezvous would be in vain.

Into the cusp of Dec. 8, at 41 minutes past midnight, the crew of *I-16* was surprised when they received a signal from Ensign Masaji Yokoyama, her midget skipper and the first attacker launched. *Successful surprise attack,* signaled Yokoyama.

This was the only radio message passed on from any of the midgets, although *I-16* said communication with Yokoyama abruptly ceased at 1:11 a.m. It's possible Yokoyama was shooting at *Breese,* which was in her general area at the time.

Based on the juxtaposition of Watanabe's sighting and Yokoyama's brief message, the Imperial Navy later decided at least three midgets had penetrated the anchorage and had inflicted serious damage, perhaps even sinking *Arizona.*

On Dec. 12, after Watanabe's report of the night explosions had been digested, the commander of the submarine division radioed Tokyo's approved version of the incident to the Advance Force: *Regarding the Naval Section, Imperial headquarters SMS No. 487 (message) the conditions actually observed were as follows:*

At (two minutes after moonrise) there occurred one great explosion in Pearl. Apparently an explosion occurred in the magazine. It was accompanied by a conflagration and the scattering about of red hot articles. The firing into the air of the AA guns and machine guns went to extremes in violence and was very rapid, but in several minutes the fire disappeared rapidly. It was confirmed that an enemy capital ship was sunk by the raid of a midget submarine. There was great rejoicing.

Images of great resolve — Japanese actors in "Hawaii Sakusen" portray determined I-boat crews pressing home the assault on the American fleet.

SLIPPING INTO DARKNESS

Yokoyama's call-in confirmed that at least one midget was stalking American prey that Sunday night, into the midnight hour. While Pearl Harbor burned, Sakamaki and Inagaki were adrift in their damaged *I-24tou*, nearly unconscious. They had spent the day trying to run the coral gauntlet in their uncontrollable submarine, each time bashing into the rocks. The second torpedo-firing mechanism was damaged about this time, and the two exhausted, battered crewmen collapsed into a stupor.

"What are we going to do, sir?" said Inagaki.

Sakamaki comforted his crewman in the darkness, wondered if Inagaki felt as sick at heart as he did. "We're going to plunge into an enemy battleship, preferably the *Pennsylvania*," said Sakamaki. "We're going to crash against the ship — and if we're still alive, we're going to kill as many as we can."

"Full speed ahead!" cried Inagaki, to Sakamaki's surprise.

They labored through the afternoon as the air grew foul and the batteries sputtered white smoke. Electrolyte spilled on the metal deck

plates gave them vicious electric shocks as they wrestled 11-pound lead-ballast "pigs" in the hold, trying to trim the ship.

Sakamaki heard someone sobbing in the dark, and discovered it was himself. He wiped crusting tears off his face. He looked through the periscope and saw Diamond Head racing by to port. They were beaten.

Sakamaki set a course for the Lanai rendezvous, opened the hatch and fell into bitter unconsciousness. On the surface, the midget drifted to the east. The two Japanese were past caring if they were spotted.

Off Waimanalo Beach, on the southeast coast of Oahu, a nervous soldier saw something dark and ominous in the water, heading for the shore. He phoned a report to Bellows Field to the north, and Air Corps men grabbed light weapons and piled into trucks. It looked for a moment like the Japanese planned to invade. But when the excited soldiers arrived at the beach, the mysterious shape had vanished into the night. The soldier who had sent the warning was chastised.

It's possible he saw Sakamaki's midget submarine.

At midnight, Sakamaki awakened. He still had a fierce grip on the periscope handles. Climbing stiffly into the conning tower, he noted with some surprise the hatch had been open for hours, dangerously close to the waves.

Sakamaki filled his lungs with fresh air. The night was quiet, the sub gently rocking on the surface. Starlight was the only illumination playing on the sea; the night before had blazed with light from shore. Oahu was thoroughly blacked out, appearing only as a dark patch torn from the bowl of stars.

Inagaki stirred below, and passed out again. Sakamaki rested his chin on the edge of the sail, a wave occasionally licking his cheek.

The batteries gradually wore down, and at dawn *I-24tou's* propellers stopped. In the pinking light, Sakamaki saw a humped mass he assumed was Lanai. They were near the rendezvous point!

He tried the motor. *Nothing.* He waited for a few minutes and tried again. The small submarine bolted forward and crunched into another reef. Sparks and smoke showered from the batteries and Sakamaki thought they would explode.

This was the end. Using the matches he had wrapped in oil paper, Sakamaki and Inagaki lit a fuse to scuttle the submarine, watching it blaze for a few seconds. The flaring glare limned their exhausted, haggard features.

They climbed out on the slippery, curved deck of the trapped midget. Waves thundered around them, and 200 yards away was the dim crescent of a beach. The moon was setting, and overhead they could hear enemy aircraft beginning search patterns.

"I should stay with my ship," Sakamaki thought aloud. "That is the way of a naval officer."

Inagaki said nothing.

"Why not try to live?" Sakamaki wondered. "Why not? I am not a weapon. I am a human being." Inagaki nodded, and they shed their leather coveralls and shivered in the salt spray. They were wearing only *fundoshi* and military watches loyally set on Tokyo time.

"We're leaving now," Sakamaki said to *I-24tou*, as if it were a war horse. "Explode gloriously!" He dived overboard. His watch stopped. It was 6:40 a.m., Hawaii time.

Sakamaki's actual location was near the new Bellows airfield on the east coast of Oahu. The island he had sighted was Manana, one of the Mokulua islets fringing Lanikai.

The young officer was suffering from breathing poisoned air and nearly two days of unimaginable nervous exhaustion. The water, pumping over the reef toward shore, was colder and rougher than he thought it would be. It was another shock, and he struggled.

"Inagaki!" he called.

Inagaki's head bobbed nearby. Sakamaki heard him gasp, "Sir, I'm over here."

The waves began to roar, and hump up between them. His crew mate vanished.

Sakamaki listened for the submarine's scuttling charge to explode. There was only the rush of surf. He felt sickened; he had failed even to destroy his own submarine. It no longer mattered what happened to him, and as a breaker seized and flung him into the dawn, he let it carry him along, welcoming the headlong rush into oblivion.

Nearby, in the roaring darkness, Inagaki still struggled, fighting, fighting, even against the water.

Slipping Into Darkness

PRISONERS OF WAR

19

Strangers on the Beach

The bloom of dawn revealed the four fishing sampans huddled together near Maili Bay, on the leeward coast of Oahu. Sutematsu Kida and his crew in *Kiho Maru* ate breakfast, changed into clean clothes and put on raincoats to protect the fresh clothes from salt spray. They were going ashore to face who-knows-what. From a distance, they were all dressed alike.

"Shall we leave now?" suggested Sannosuke Onishi on *Myojin Maru*. The four boats formed a line and headed southeast, toward the fishing harbor at Kewalo Basin. Kida's sampan lagged behind, cursed with puny horsepower. Skipper Kenji Takumi on *Sumiyoshi Maru* kept the sampan close to the shore as he rounded Barbers Point. Small splashes around the boat puzzled him; they looked like raindrops. Then the sampan was solidly thumped, and Takumi looked toward shore. Marines on the beach were shooting at him. Takumi steered out of range, followed by Onishi, who had witnessed the shooting.

From the jostling air, to an excited imagination, the four boats advancing around Barbers Point may have looked like the tip of an invasion force. On a return flight to carrier *Enterprise*, a Navy SBD Dauntless dive bomber plummeted out of the sky and swept toward the sampans from behind. Kida was in the stern of *Kiho Maru*, handling the steering rod, looking ahead and fretting as the other sampans pulled away from his boat. Kiichi Kida and Kiho Uehara also were looking toward the bow. Something crunched on deck. Seiki Arakaki looked back, and his eyes widened.

Kida never knew what hit him. The skipper's body jerked backward, ripped open by .30 machine gun slugs from the SBD's nose guns. Then he slumped over the steering rod. The bullets marched forward, hitting the younger Kida and Uehara in the back and throwing them to the deck. Arakaki dived for the engine compartment; a bullet punched through his left leg just below the knee.

The plane roared over, paused on one wing tip, and attacked again from the port side. Arakaki could hear Kiichi Kida moaning wetly. The fusillade had torn away his jaw. Arakaki could see the exposed muscles on his face, moving.

Bullets raked the boat again, throwing up splinters and blood. The Dauntless swung around for a third time, approached from the bow, and once again worked over the craft. By this time, Kida's linseed oil-soaked raincoat had been set on fire by tracer rounds, and the man lay burning, hanging on the rudder pole. His son was quiet.

The SBD flew in the direction of the other sampans.

Arakaki dragged himself out on the now-silent deck. Strange, he thought, his leg didn't hurt. *Kiho Maru* was going in tight circles, the rudder jammed by Kida's smoldering body. Arakaki beat out the flames and disentangled Kida from the steering rod. He could hear the bomber shooting at the other sampans.

On *Myojin Maru*, skipper Onishi watched the Dauntless approach. He was familiar with the bluff lines of the aircraft, recognized it as U.S. from the red-white-and-blue insignia. He was surprised when the plane opened fire. One round sliced through the fuel line; another bounced and blew a gobbet out of his arm.

The spilling fuel ignited. Onishi tried to put out the fire, but his arm was slippery with blood and wouldn't function properly. He saw the aircraft begin to turn.

"Hide!" he shouted. "Some damn fool pilot thinks we're Japan boats!" The SBD augured in toward the tiny craft, and the crew leaped overboard, on the side away from the dive bomber. Protected by the sampan's stout side, the crew ducked their heads anyway as slugs shredded the deck. The Dauntless flew on toward *Shin-ei Maru*.

Between 9:15 and 9:30 a.m., Coast Guard tender *Kukui* passed by and radioed for help, proceeding directly to *Kiho Maru*. Another Coast Guard craft arrived and dropped a ladder for Onishi's crew. Despite his arm wound, Onishi climbed up the ladder, but one of his crewmen wouldn't move from the safety of *Myojin Maru's* freeboard. He was frozen by shock.

Coast Guard lighthouse tender Kukui *in Honolulu, 1924.* Kukui *served in Hawaiian waters for 36 years.*

PRISIONERS OF WAR

"Don't worry — we'll use a smaller boat to pick him up. Tell him to hang on!" an officer yelled. Onishi complied, and then he began to shiver as shock began to overtake him. The Coast Guardsmen provided blankets, hot coffee and crackers.

Onishi was asked why his boat hadn't been flying a large American flag. The sampan skipper was puzzled. He had fished off Oahu for 15 years without having to hoist colors. The Coast Guard officer explained that the military expected an amphibious landing on Oahu, and that unidentified craft were going to be attacked.

Onishi was asked more questions as he watched *Myojin Maru* being towed away. Had he smuggled in any Japanese nationals? Had he taken any food, oil or messages to foreign submarines? Onishi could see additional fires flaring up on his shattered boat as it disappeared. He never saw it again.

Skipper Takumi on *Sumiyoshi Maru* was creased by a bullet, but crewmen Kichimatsu Urakami and Eiji Goto were untouched. A Coast Guard cutter pulled alongside the sampan and presented the crew with a large American flag, and then escorted the fishing boat safely into Kewalo Basin. The three fishermen were treated, then placed in the city prison in Iwilei.

Three men aboard *Shin-ei Maru* also were killed; skipper Shinichi Yokoyama and crewmen Kaichi Okada and Ryozo Okogi, who also used the name Maeda. The lone survivor was crewman Tetsujiro Yamamoto. As *Kiho Maru* was being towed into Kewalo Basin by *Kukui*, Arakaki saw the bodies being placed in bags. Arakaki's wounds were treated at The Queen's Hospital, and then he was arrested by military police, along with Onishi and the surviving crewman from *Shin-ei Maru*.

They were kept for a couple of weeks, then released. Dead and wounded sampan fishermen were listed on Civil Defense records as "war prisoners" rather than as civilian casualties. The sampan crews were told that the bullets found embedded aboard their boats were Japanese.

The sampans had been attacked because they were suspected of meeting submarines at sea, as if Hawaii's fishing fleet were the stealthily placed weapons of a foreign power. Suspicion boiled over into unthinking action after the attack on Pearl Harbor. The distinctive lines of the boats were easily identifiable from the air, and the Imperial Navy used landing craft of similar design.

After Dec. 7, all sampans began to fly large American flags, and the boats were required to be painted white. Previously they had been bright blue, a Japanese fishing tradition going back more than 300 years.

Despite these protective measures, several sampans were strafed on Dec. 12 by American planes off Kailua and Kahala. On Dec. 19, ships were warned that fishing vessels may be "rendering aid to enemy forces," and that American warships were now empowered to "examine, seize or sink" suspicious fishing boats.

When this picture was taken on Dec. 20, 1941, American flags were flying over most of the sampans at the Ala Wai boat basin.

Virtually everything that floated or swam in Hawaiian waters was suspect. The overriding priority for American aviators after the Sunday attack was to get back into the air and search the islands for signs of the enemy; the hard lesson had been drummed in at great cost.

At Bellows Field on the morning of Dec. 8, damage from the attack was surprisingly light. The Japanese had meticulously hammered only the P-40 fighters on the ground, sparing all but one of several whale-like 0-47 observation planes of the 86th Observation Group.

Lieutenant Phillip Willis, a pilot without an airplane, was issued a pistol and told to patrol the beach.

At dawn, all the 0-47s were in the air, flying search missions around the islands. As they pulled out over Waimanalo, an 0-47 piloted by Captain J.T. Lewis spotted something slim and black in the surf. Lewis and his observer, Captain Jean Lambert, decided it looked suspicious. Perhaps it was a downed aircraft. They radioed for air support.

Staff Sergeant Quiniro F. Olegario of Oahu's Home Guard was high in the Waimanalo hills, alone and cold in an isolated lookout post. Sometime after 7 a.m., he watched detachedly as a Navy plane dropped out of the clouds. Planes had been in the air all morning. None of them were Japanese, despite several scares.

This plane began circling the water off Bellows. Olegario leaned forward.

It dropped a bomb, which sent a geyser of water into the air. Olegario excitedly grabbed a phone as the explosion's dull echo rattled through the hillside.

In the surf and misting bomb spray, Olegario couldn't see what

PRISIONERS OF WAR

was under attack, and he couldn't leave his post. So he told the guy at the other end of the line to send people to the beach, pronto. *The Japanese were back!*

Corporal David M. Akui of Company B, 298th Infantry, was digging out a machine-gun emplacement on the northeast shore of Bellows when Lieutenant Paul G. Plybon trotted by.

"Get a couple of men!" said Plybon as he went past, buckling his helmet. "Something's going on down the beach."

Akui collected a couple of soldiers as Plybon backed out a jeep. They piled on and raced through Bellows' weepy iron-wood trees and sand dunes, jerking to a stop behind the cover of a grassy dune. Plybon and Akui cautiously reconnoitered the quiet beach while the others stayed in the jeep.

Nothing. And this was the exact area designated by Olegario. Three Navy utility planes began circling and dropping 50-pound bombs in pairs. Bracketed between bomb geysers, the two soldiers saw a tiny submarine rocking on the reef. They counted 12 bombs, of which maybe six exploded within 50 feet of the midget.

An Army O-47 at Bellows Field in the fall of 1941.

They walked down onto the beach slope, now joined by Willis, a short distance away. Akui spotted something small and dark bobbing in the ocean, near the shore. It looked like a turtle. A large wave suddenly lifted it up, and Akui clearly saw the head and arms of a man floating in the agate water, lit from behind.

"There's somebody out there," he pointed out to Plybon.

"Just one man?" wondered Plybon. "What's he doing?"

"I doubt any local boys would be swimming here. Not now. This is a military beach, sir."

"Right," said Plybon. "Fire a warning shot."

Akui borrowed a rifle from one of the men in the jeep and aimed carefully. The round splashed near the man's head, but he appeared not to notice.

"Don't do that!" shouted Willis. "What do you see?"

"It's a Jap, sure as hell," explained Akui.

"Well, my God, we need a prisoner," said Willis.

"He's still coming in," said Plybon. "Cover me." The lieutenant drew his .45 pistol and waded out into the shore break. Akui angled off to the side, keeping a clear field of fire between Plybon and the man, just then reaching shore on his hands and knees.

The bombing had stopped, and the beach was quiet and deserted except for the four men.

A wave threw the stranger past Plybon onto the foaming shore

and he collapsed, his face in the streaming sand. He was a slight Japanese, just 127 pounds and bedraggled-looking. He was wearing only a military undershirt and what looked to Plybon like a G-string. A watch hung on a lanyard around his neck.

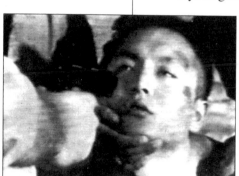

A dramatization of Sakamaki's capture from the Nippon-TV special "P.W.1."

Plybon grabbed the man by a wet arm and roughly hauled him to his feet. He stuck his big pistol in the man's face. "You're under arrest!" he said loudly, over the surf noise. Akui approached and also aimed his weapon at the man.

The Japanese man's face was blank and miserable. He stood numbly as the Americans searched him for weapons, finding only a prayer belt into which was sewed 15 cents in Japanese money, which Plybon appropriated.

They had just captured Prisoner of War Number One, Ensign Kazuo Sakamaki. It was 7:07 a.m. They had no idea who he was. The man just stood there, quivering with fatigue.

"Well," said Plybon, finally. "Let's take him to the guardhouse."

Startled, Sakamaki stared at Akui, a hawk-faced Hawaiian in an Army uniform. *Where had he come from?*

They were standing on a beach, with another American, a burly man with a pistol. *How had he gotten here?*

Sakamaki remembered a day in school when he was playing ball and had been knocked into unconsciousness. He'd suddenly stood up. He'd run around wildly, body in overdrive, mind in neutral.

On the beach, as his memory clicked slowly into place, he felt as numb and as spent as that time in school.

At about 8 a.m., the phone was ringing at headquarters when Captain James W. Lovell, staff officer of the 298th Infantry, returned from the beach at Bellows. The caller was from a field artillery unit. The Navy planes had all missed the submarine target, and the gunners wanted a crack at it.

Lovell had just seen the submarine wallowing about 200 yards offshore — the bombings had dislodged it, and everyone was dashing down to the beach to gape at it.

Lovell cradled the phone in his shoulder while he tried to figure out the coordinates. As he figured, another phone rang.

It was Navy Combat Intelligence. *Under no circumstances*, Lovell was informed, *should the submarine be harmed.* It was a prize of war, and potentially a valuable intelligence item. They were sending a Lieutenant R.L. Rutter out to inspect it.

Lovell told the artillerymen to stand down. They were disappointed. They wanted to shoot at something.

Nearby, 2nd Lieutenant Steve Weiner had been handed a .45 pistol and a shovel and told to dig foxholes. Hand-to-hand combat, he was assured, could happen at any moment. A communications and crypt-analysis officer, this was the first gun Weiner had ever been issued. He

250

also had never before dug a foxhole.

He shrugged and began tearing at the sandy soil that fringed Bellows air field.

The Army rules were explicitly laid out for prisoners of war. They were to be searched at once, grilled by unit S-2s, and then sent to a 24th Division Prisoner of War enclosure in the Post Stockade at Schofield Barracks. There they would once again be questioned, this time by high-ranking G-2s; one was on duty at all times from the Provost Marshall's office.

Prisoners would be restrained from destroying documents. Any papers found on them or their craft would be couriered hastily to the G-2 officer at the division command post. Documents identifying organizations, or the use of chemical weapons, would get the highest priority.

Injured prisoners would not get special treatment, unless they were badly wounded. If they were so badly injured that they could not be moved, the division G-2 would come to the prisoner and interrogate him on the spot.

When Weiner looked up from his freshly scrabbled hole in the ground and saw Sakamaki approaching, guarded by Akui and Willis, he knew something important was afoot, or at least more interesting than foxhole digging. To Weiner, the Japanese man looked as though he had been in the water for a long time. Sakamaki's skin was "crinkled … he looked like a prune."

"Where in the hell did you get him?" asked Weiner.

"He walked right out of the water," said Akui.

Curiously, Weiner vividly remembers this incident as happening about 11 p.m. on the night of Dec. 7. Most histories of Sakamaki's capture rely on the man's own account in "I Attacked Pearl Harbor," but if Sakamaki were actually captured earlier it would account for the speed with which American officers interrogated him. One thing is certain — at this point, Sakamaki was in no shape physically or mentally to be precise about details.

Weiner took Sakamaki to the Operations shack and then tried to find the commanding officer or a staff member. He came up only with another lieutenant.

The four of them, the three officers and Akui, took turns questioning Sakamaki. They also took turns holding a heavy .45 pistol to Sakamaki's temple.

He only stared at his interrogators, glum and defiant, pretending not to understand. He couldn't help shivering, and the Americans gave him a blanket.

All the cadets at Eta Jima were taught English, though Sakamaki's instructor had been dismissed before the essentials had sunk in. He

David M. Akui went on to serve with Merrill's Marauders in Burma and continued with the Hawaii Guard. Here he examines Viet Cong booby traps during the 1960s.

still understood enough to know they were quizzing him about fleet movements. So he keep quiet — it might be a point in his favor if he ever returned to Japan.

The American officers were more nervous than their Japanese prisoner. Weiner pressed the .45 hard against Sakamaki's head,

hoping the cold threat would loosen his tongue. It didn't. To Weiner, Sakamaki's dead stare seemed to be saying, "Go ahead, *shoot* me."

The little bastard, thought Weiner. *He's defying us. He wants us to kill him. We're all shaking and embarrassed and he's not scared at all.*

The frustrated Americans finally gave Sakamaki a hard-boiled egg and a shot of booze and sent out for an interpreter. Sakamaki made a formal bow after receiving the food and drink, which annoyed Willis. A local Japanese-American was brought in and the lieutenants told him which questions to ask Sakamaki. He and the prisoner chatted for a moment and the Japanese-American said he couldn't understand Sakamaki's dialect.

The flying suit worn by Sakamaki over his fundoshi, *here being shown off by Americans. It has since disappeared.*

The soldiers didn't believe him and pushed the local man into a corner, calling him a traitor and waving the pistol. The lieutenants ordered Akui to go find a Japanese-speaking kid who wouldn't try to outsmart them, and he came back with a 12-year-old boy. The boy couldn't understand Sakamaki either.

Sakamaki sat quietly watching this. He then said, "Give me pencil, paper" in English. Weiner grabbed a manila envelope off a desk and Sakamaki wrote: *I am Japanese Naval officer. My name Ensign Sakamaki. My serial number (this is lost). My ship catch on coral. I jump into water. Swim to this airplane land. No tell about ships. Kill me an honorable way.*

The Americans kept Sakamaki at Bellows until a truck arrived. Willis placed Sakamaki in a large laundry bag and pulled the drawstrings tight around his neck, a kind of straitjacket. As the truck hauled Sakamaki to Fort Shafter, overlooking Pearl Harbor, the prisoner was in no mood to fight his way out. He slept the whole way.

Later, in a small, windowless room on the sixth floor of the Alexander Young Hotel in Honolulu, an interpreter questioned Sakamaki in Japanese. The prisoner insisted on being shot.

"We don't shoot prisoners," said the surprised interpreter.

"I saw the *Arizona* explode!" screamed Sakamaki. "I came here to sink it! It is not honorable for an officer like myself to be captured. I am an enemy to you. Why don't you take me before the sinking *Arizona* and kill me properly?"

He stood there, quaking. He had a fever brought on by his exposure to the cold surf, and his throat was raw.

Lieutenant Colonel Kendall J. Fielder, G-2 of the Army Hawaiian department, was called in to put his intelligence skills to work on the recalcitrant Sakamaki. He found the young Japanese officer hunched

252

on a stool, wrapped in an Army blanket, shivering and miserable. The Japanese stubbornly refused to answer questions, and he was moved to a quickly built internment facility on Sand Island, near Honolulu.

The American guards called a doctor down from Fort Shafter to treat him, though they told Sakamaki that the doctor was actually going to execute him.

Oddly, the news calmed the prisoner. In a foul, self-recriminating mood, Sakamaki believed he had been the only midget to draw the destroyers' attentions outside Pearl Harbor and the other four midgets had gotten inside, achieving spectacular success. He wanted to die.

When Captain Herman L. Metzler, the doctor, arrived, the prisoner leaped to attention and cried something in Japanese.

"He said, 'I am ready to die for my country. Please do it quickly,'" said the interpreter. The guards laughed, and Metzler discovered their trick. He was not amused.

The doctor chastised the guards, treated Sakamaki, and left. He did not return, and Sakamaki was surprised at the man's unexpected kindness. [1]

Sakamaki also was not above disinformation, claiming the midget had traveled "more than a hundred miles" to reach Pearl Harbor and that he was closing in on an American warship when he grounded off Bellows. He revealed the midget had a mother ship, but not the mother's type, tonnage or whether the midget was diesel or electric powered. He said the midget was a variation of a one-man torpedo. He worried aloud that the Americans might examine the midget submarine. At the time, his questioners thought the craft had been bombed into oblivion by Navy aircraft.

He carefully drew the insignia of the Imperial Navy petty officer, Naval Pilot, and explained the details to intelligence officers Edwin Layton and Fielder. He also made a sketch of the midget submarine on the back of a mother submarine.

Morosely, Sakamaki then stared at Fielder and said quietly, "My greatest mistake was being captured. This is the first time I have failed. Please do not advise Japan about this.

"Please," Sakamaki pleaded. "Kill me."

The sketch of the mother submarine-midget submarine combination made by Sakamaki upon capture. No one in the U.S. Navy had a clue where the midgets had come from until the prisoner volunteered this information. Note that the midget correctly faces aft behind the mother submarine's sail.

[1] In 1979, through Navy veteran Charles Jackson, Metzler wrote Sakamaki and wished him continued good health. Sakamaki did not reply.

20 | THE CARRIER CHASE

The Scent of Blood in the Water

After the attack on Pearl Harbor — plus the surprising appearance of a Japanese submarine within the harbor and a pack of I-boats massed at the gate — defensive plans changed quickly. No ship was kept in the harbor longer than absolutely necessary, certainly no longer than 48 hours. The stately parade of big ships passing by the Hickam officer's club changed overnight into a furtive scrambling. Battleships and carriers generally slipped out at night; the workhorse destroyers and sweepers dashed continuously in and out.

Prior to the attack, the Navy had trouble securing enough liaison officers to deal with the Army. Afterward, the Army was swamped with jobless naval officers whose ships were on the bottom of Pearl Harbor.

Eventually, Admiral Bloch had 13 more destroyers assigned to the 14th Naval District, enough to begin offshore patrols, 10 to 15 miles out, to act as tripwires for approaching submarines.

More nets were hung to protect the caissons of the dry docks and the length of 1010 Dock. Target rafts had an additional 5 feet of steel plate added below their waterline, and they were trooped in front of the moorings as anti-torpedo buffers.

The devastation littering the harbor was more than enough warning for the fleet. Destroyer *Helm* returned the night of Dec. 8, witnessing the carnage for the first time. The crew had heard wild rumors on the radio, and wondered what they'd find. The magnitude of the destruction was sobering.

As cruiser *Salt Lake City* pulled into Pearl Harbor that day, communications officer Church A. Chappell was warned about dangers still stalking the harbor, including "drifting mines (and) one-man subs which come to the surface and throw hand grenades (and) spies swimming in the harbor." Chappell passed the word.

Destroyer *Blue's* Ensign Asher remained on the bridge until the ship returned to port Monday night. During the day, he had ordered Ensign Robert S. Scott, a newcomer, to circulate through the ship, bolstering morale, "giving them the glad hand," and feeding the men. Three regular messes were served, and then Asher ordered the men

below to sleep. Nothing doing. They insisted on sleeping by their guns, with at least one man standing watch at all times.

At Johnston Island, cruiser *Indianapolis* quickly recovered her planes from anti-submarine patrol and departed the atoll at high speed with Vice Admiral Wilson Brown on board. She was to rendezvous with other fleet ships 500 miles to the north. On the way, Kimmel changed her orders. The destroyer/minesweepers were to continue to Pearl while *Indianapolis* backtracked toward Johnston. If the Imperial task force was retreating southwest toward Jaluit, the cruiser would be alone in their path.

Nothing happened. The cruiser rejoined the fleet on Dec. 9.

At midday on the 8th, near Honolulu, cruiser *Detroit* lurched suddenly to avoid a torpedo. In the galley, food went flying. Coast Guard cutter *Taney*, which had spent the previous day moored in Honolulu Harbor enthusiastically shooting at any and all airplanes in the sky, went to sea early on the 8th and patrolled the city harbor entrance. By noon, she had a sound lock on an "unknown" and dropped depth charges.

During the next week, she made several more contacts and dropped a couple of dozen depth charges, never bringing up more than an oil slick on Dec. 10. In the twilight that day, a few miles south of Aloha Tower, the cutter noted tracer bullets from the harbor entrance hosing down something invisible in the water. Investigating, *Taney* got a strong hydrophone echo and rolled off three depth charges. The slick that resulted, smelling strongly of fuel oil, persisted in the location for several days.

The sound contacts were not what the crew expected from previous prewar maneuvers. *Taney* skipper L.B. Olson noted in the log that all "contacts were made at short range, 800 yards or less, indicating that the target was considerably smaller than submarines on which practice had been conducted when contacts of 1,500-2,000 yards had been made. With this type of contact the probability of false contacts with wake knuckles and large fish is increased. One very large manta badly injured was observed at one time and a slightly smaller one floating dead was observed later … it is possible they were actually targets for some attacks, not necessarily by this vessel."

These contacts persisted. Through Dec. 31, a total of 52 depth-charge attacks on submarine contacts took place in Hawaiian waters. Destroyer *Ward* alone dropped 107 depth charges in the 10 days following the attack. "Killed a lot of fish," joked skipper Outerbridge.

The enemy was closer than even *Ward's* inshore patrol suspected. About 9 a.m. on Dec. 8, as *I-69* carefully nosed back toward Pearl Harbor, skipper Katsuji Watanabe retired to his cabin to get a few moments of sleep. As he shut his eyes, an unusual vibration seized the submarine. The navigator commanding the bridge ordered all four engines stopped. Watanabe popped into the conning tower and the officers decided *I-69* was caught in an anti-submarine net. Watanabe ordered full reverse. Though the submarine strained, it did not move.

The officer decided that the "pit log tube" may have been broken by the net, making it impossible to determine underwater movement. He ordered the submarine to the surface.

I-69 was seized again by tremors. Watanabe stopped headway. Again, he tried reverse, but the ship stubbornly refused to move. The helmsman reported that trim wasn't responding normally, and that the submarine was beginning to sink.

"Blow main tank!" shouted Watanabe, now alarmed. "We must regain negative buoyancy!"

I-69 shot to the surface, in daylight, within a few miles of a thoroughly alerted Pearl Harbor. The submarine's commanding officer quickly examined the forward end of the submarine through the periscope. Nothing seemed amiss, and *I-69* crash-dived. Control problems persisted. *I-69* twice more surfaced, and the CO spotted two American destroyers dead ahead. Their position, he reckoned, was four miles southeast of Barbers Point.

"We cannot continue either submerged or on the surface," Watanabe said. "We will lie submerged and wait until sunset."

The electric motors were stopped, but the submarine continued to be dragged down. "Blow main tank!" shouted Watanabe. The depth gauge passed the extreme limit of 85 meters, plunging past 100 meters. Hoping they were free of the net, Watanabe commanded "Ahead standard!" and the submarine began to shudder violently and slew through the water.

"Stop," said Watanabe.

I-69 sank deeper, the hull groaning in protest. It reached 125 meters.

"Blow main tanks," breathed Watanabe.

I-69 rose again, twisting in the grip of the undersea obstruction.

At 87 meters, with what was hoped to be slight forward speed, the I-boat smashed blindly into something solid. Despite the crew's best efforts, the submarine was in the grip of the reef. They settled in to wait.

That evening, *I-74* spotted carrier *Enterprise* south of Niihau. The prize target was accompanied by a screen of destroyers, and *I-74* was content to stay put and radio the sighting.

By and large, the submarines of the Advance Force were quiet on Dec. 8. The exceptions were the mother submarines, which surfaced at the rendezvous point near Lanai, waiting one more night for the midgets to return. It was a fruitless wait. Near dawn on the 9th, Captain Hanku Sasaki, commander of the Advance Force, signaled the five mother submarines under his command:

The subs have not yet taken aboard the midget sub personnel. Judging from the state of enemy scouting on the night of the 7th, we can well imagine — be certain — that the midget subs were able to enter the harbor and attack the enemy. However, the state of things after that and the battle results are not clear.

"*If they arrive by daybreak of the 9th, the I-20, I-18 and* I-24 (*submarines*) *will take them aboard and remove the equipment and*

take up work in the patrol sectors. After the I-22 *and* I-16 *(submarines keep) searching the neighboring coast until daybreak of the 10th, they will take up their duties in the scout area.*

Commander Kaoryu Yamada, skipper of *I-16*, signaled Sasaki back in response: *At 1811 on the 8th received communications from the midget submarine using 'To Ra'[1] and even though we had contact up to 1914 of the same day, after that the calls ceased.*

All five mother submarines were ordered by Tokyo to leave the area together. They sailed to the great Japanese naval and submarine base at Kwajalein atoll, arriving in time for New Year's, and they were treated to a display of dancing by the natives there. The new war seemed very far away.

I-16, however, went straight on to Harashijima, where Yamamoto wanted to debrief Yamada about the midget attacks. Shimizu, commander in chief of the 6th fleet, signaled a precis of the situation to the Naval General Staff on Dec. 11: *Report the success of a raid at 1811 on the 7th from the midget sub carried on the* I-16, *viewing the situation at this time even though we knew that each tube would be able to penetrate into the harbor and attack. Up to the present time we have not been able to rescue even one person.*

The American translator noted that the message seemed to mean that *I-16* was a midget sub carrier. This, coupled with Sakamaki's sketch, confirmed the Ha-boats' mode of transportation.

When told that the midget submarine crews had vanished, Yamamoto looked grave and said, "I would never have sent them if I'd known we'd achieve so much with air units alone."

The mother submarines left just in time. Admiral Kimmel, remembering the intelligence tip from Mexico City, believed midgets were serviced and recharged near Molokai, and ordered intensive air searches around the area. They revealed nothing. Some bombing was done anyway.

American submarine *Plunger* returned to Pearl Harbor on the morning of Dec. 9 and spent the next 24 hours replenishing supplies and fuel. Early the next day, just in case the Japanese struck again, she moved away from Sub Base and moored to a buoy north of Ford Island to load food.

A submarine at the next buoy reported a sound contact in the harbor. Earl D. Bronson, a machinist's mate on *Plunger*, watched as the sound crews of both submarines pinpointed a submerged object in the harbor. It wasn't moving.[2]

Bronson passed a grapnel and line to the 50-foot provisions boat and dragged the spot. The grapnel hooked something which could not be lifted or towed. Since it seemed dead, the submarine crews shrugged their shoulders and assumed it was uncharted wreckage. They returned to work and *Plunger* went to sea at daybreak, Dec. 11.

Plunger was unmolested by the Japanese, who considered enemy submarines small fish. The I-boats were hunting American carriers, spreading a wide rake around Hawaii and the West Coast, hoping to

[1] *Tora — tiger — was the abbreviated signal meaning "Surprise attack successful." There were a number of these brief signals, used by both the airmen and submarine crews, including* Kito, *meaning "Enemy Fleet is departing in large numbers"; and* Yunu, *or "Results unknown."*

[2] *The object may have been American submarine* F-4, *sunk in 1914, raised that year and used as a floating marker, and then scuttled in 1940 to make room for the U.S. Fleet. It is still at the bottom of Pearl Harbor.*

snag a carrier. The submarines patiently dodged destroyers and torpedoed an occasional merchant while waiting for big targets.

Kido Butai, the Imperial Navy task force, patrolled constantly in fear of American submarines on their way back to Japan, and several were claimed spotted. In fact, none were on the carriers' route.

The real action was to the east of Hawaii as an American carrier and Japanese submarines mixed it up in the trade lanes to the American mainland.

Despite his reliance on battleships, Yamamoto himself was carrier-fixated. He knew they were powerful offensive weapons and thus, logically, they were the targets of choice. The attitude percolated down. The admiral promised five dozen bottles of beer to the first torpedomen to sink a U.S. carrier.

I-70 spotted a carrier entering Pearl Harbor on the 8th, and signaled the Advance Force. The ship was *Enterprise*. Following the attack, the *Enterprise* task group had searched the oceans west and south of Hawaii without luck, and returned to Pearl Harbor at sunset for a fill-up and a change of orders. Looking at the damage, Halsey muttered, "Before we're through with 'em, the Japanese language will be spoken only in hell."

Combat Intelligence correctly divined that some of the submarines might be headed northeast to harass the West Coast, and *Enterprise* sallied forth in that direction herself at dawn, Dec. 9. She wore an enormous American flag, "the biggest I had ever seen on a ship," said one pilot. It was her battle flag, worn only in combat.

At 4 a.m., while standing sentry duty in Kauai channel, *I-6* spotted "two cruisers and Lexington-class aircraft carrier on the northeasterly course" go streaking past in the northern Kauai Channel, accompanied by a pack of destroyers. Skipper Tsuso Inaba reported the carrier to Shimizu on board flagship *Katori*, who then ordered the 1st Submarine Group to run the carrier down and kill it. She could conceivably close in on Nagumo's strike force, which was hampered by slow tankers in the convoy.

I-9, *I-15*, *I-17*, *I-19*, *I-21*, *I-23* and *I-25* broke position and headed toward the carrier, with orders to *I-10* and *I-26* to "stand by" between Hawaii and the West Coast.

After the inactivity north of Oahu, the men on *I-15* cheered the news, jubilant that the three days of strain were broken. If the war wasn't going to come to them, then they were going to the war.

Unaware there were enemy submarines in her wake, *Enterprise* raced to the northeast. It was a spirited chase. Admiral Halsey noted in his memoirs that lookouts "were spying periscope feathers in every whitecap and torpedoes in every porpoise." He signaled the task force, "If all the torpedo wakes reported are factual, Japanese submarines will soon have to return to base for a reload, and we will soon have nothing to fear. In addition, we are wasting too many depth charges on neutral fish." Not everyone got the joke.

A couple of hours after passing *I-6*, and about 200 miles north-

THE CARRIER CHASE

west of Oahu, Ensign Perry Teaff of Scouting Squadron Six spotted a Japanese submarine while flying patrol. He nosed over his Dauntless dive-bomber and believed he punched a bomb hole in the side of the submarine, but it did not sink. Two other submarines were sighted, but managed to get away.

The recent horror of what they had seen in Pearl Harbor motivated *Enterprise* pilots to viciously attack submarines, a tricky proposition as the bomb had to be released from an altitude of at least 1,000 feet or it would not arm itself before striking the ocean. Halsey liked to tell the story of one of his brownshoes who bombed a contact that other aviators had decided was a whale. Fed up by the ribbing he received after landing, he said, "Well, if it was a whale it was the first whale I have ever seen that exhausts through his tail!"

Another submarine sighting on Dec. 9 was attacked by destroyer *Balch*, and later a submarine was reported dead ahead, prompting maneuverings to evade it.

Sightings came thickly on the morning of the 10th. Scouts were launched at 6 a.m., and within 20 minutes Dauntless *6-B-17* reported a submarine, as did *6-B-2* a few minutes later. Lieutenant Clarence Dickinson, with RMlc Tom Merrit as his backseater in *6-B-17*, had methodically begun to search for enemy submarines using sighting on the 9th as his starting point. Flying along the line suggested by the sightings, Dickinson saw the submarine from 1,800 feet. It looked huge to him, compared to American submarines. He buzzed the ship and noticed men and debris floating alongside.

The submarine crew saw him and began potting at the airplane with machine guns. Dickinson pulled the SBD over the top at 5,000

Escorted by an I-boat screen of PT boats, Enterprise *leaves Pearl Harbor in the summer of 1942.*

feet, turned around and squarely planted a bomb next to the submarine, which broke up and sank "in a vertical manner" with all hands.

The death of Miller, Dickinson's backseater on the morning of Dec. 7, was avenged. The target was *I-70*, not part of the sub pack hunting *Enterprise*.

Once the planes were up, the *Enterprise* group zigzagged through the ocean. Hydrophone contacts by outlying destroyers teased throughout the day, with the usual spurts of speed and course changes reverberating through the task force. At 1:27 p.m. destroyer *Fanning* reported torpedo wakes heading toward *Enterprise* and rolled depth charges in their path. More elusive contacts were heard; nothing seen. Lookouts aft reported seeing a periscope just after 3 p.m.

Heavy cruiser *Salt Lake City* soon reported seeing a submarine as well and opened fire. The submarines disappeared, but another was reported dead ahead immediately after. The *Enterprise* aircraft began to return at 5 p.m. and the carrier went to general quarters while she steamed into the wind to collect them. All planes were stowed within half an hour. A submarine was sighted by *Balch* on the horizon. The carrier jumped to full steam ahead, cranking hard right. *McCall* fired depth charges, as the task group resumed zigzagging.

By the time other aircraft could be launched, the silhouette had vanished.

The submarine scares became so intense that even Halsey lost his sense of humor. One panicky junior officer became such a pest that Halsey threatened to heave him overboard.

Once again, the night was uneventful and the next morning charged with stress. In the battle group defensive screen on the 11th, destroyers continued to make depth-charge attacks, and cruiser *Salt Lake City* fired 5-inch shells at what she believed to be a submarine at 8:34 a.m.

Destroyer *Fanning* saw it too, and rolled depth charges. The submarine seemed to dart between them; at 9 a.m., *Enterprise* sailors were shaken to see a torpedo dance by astern, within 20 yards.

Nothing more was seen until noon, when a rash of hydrophone contacts sent the task force zigzagging all over the ocean. A periscope was simultaneously spotted starboard of *McCall* by both that destroyer and *Balch*. *McCall* swerved in that direction, and dropped depth charges.

That evening, Dickinson and some of the other pilots went up on deck to get a breath of fresh air. It was twilight, with just enough illumination to see the familiar shadow of the "plane guard" destroyer dogging the carrier. She was there to pick up airmen forced to ditch.

Suddenly, all of us were staring at a startling thing, Dickinson wrote in his diary, rather romantically. *Astern, no more than 150 yards, the bow of a submarine had broken out of the water. Her shape was told plainly because she was solid blackness, fringed and streaked with the merest whispers of light, ghost fire from phosphorescent animalculae of the sea ...*

THE CARRIER CHASE

The vision was real enough and the pilots whooped like cowboys. The destroyer sprinted ahead and cranked over to her right, hard, intending to ram. All the ships were speeding along at about 25 knots, but the destroyer didn't turn quickly enough and she swished past the submarine's bow, almost touching.

Six depth charges were rolled off, and water rose behind *Enterprise* "as if we were right over an active volcano,*"* remembered Dickinson. The submarine's bow was suspended between the blasts, and then she slid into the inky depths.

On the morning of Dec. 12, destroyer *Benham* reported a submarine to starboard, and an hour later, what appeared to be a torpedo wake. Hydrophones rang all morning; the ships zigzagged in response. Ahead of the task force, at 2:30 p.m. *6-B-2* saw a splash on the surface, reported a submerged submarine and attacked it. Other planes swarmed on the area, and other "submerged" submarines were spotted. *Benham* wheeled out of formation to join the fray as bombs rocked the ocean. In half an hour *6-B-2* rather sheepishly reported that the original submarine sighting was most likely a school of flying fish breaking water.

A few minutes later, destroyer *Gridley* reported a submarine to the now unprotected rear of the task force, dropped charges, and *Fanning* dashed out of formation to signal *Benham* to rejoin the group. While this was going on, another submarine was spotted astern of *Salt Lake City*. The cruiser's two SOC scout aircraft were launched and searched the area as the task force sprinted away, and saw nothing.

After this, the barrage of hydrophone warnings began to lessen. Suspected submarines were reported only a couple of times on Dec. 13, 14 and 15, none considered serious enough to warrant rolling depth charges. But the task force had spent a week charging back and forth over the ocean, burning up precious oil and not getting very far. The implied threat of submarines remained potent.

The battle group wheeled around and returned to Pearl Harbor on the 15th. The pilots were convinced they'd sunk "four and maybe five submarines," according to Dickinson, but *I-70* was the only victim. Along with two destroyers sunk at Wake Island later that day, she was the first Japanese fleet ship lost in the Pacific War. She was skippered by Commander Takashi Sano, who had survived the sinking of *I-63* three years before.

With *Enterprise* no longer a threat to the Japanese task force, Shimizu directed the 1st Submarine Group, as well as *I-10* and *I-26*, to leave Hawaiian waters and continue east. Off the West Coast, they were to attack shipping and shell coastal cities.

Back at Pearl Harbor, before daybreak on the 11th, *I-1* spotted a "10,000 ton cruiser" headed southeast, but there was no opportunity for an ambush. *It made a most vigorous enemy patrol in the sector before Pearl Harbor,* reported the submarine.

Carrier *Lexington* was about to enter the swept channel at Pearl on Dec. 13 when orders were transmitted to turn around and steam south

at full tilt. Two hours later, *Lexington* was given the all-clear to approach Pearl, and the big carrier rushed toward the harbor. Just outside the entrance, an I-boat was spotted within two miles of the carrier, to the east, and destroyers swarmed over it, dropping six depth charges. *Lexington* dashed into the channel at 25 knots, slowing abruptly after passing the anti-torpedo nets.

The enemy spotted was *I-1*, who reported *Lexington* as an auxiliary of some sort, perhaps to cover the shame of missing her. A half-hour after the carrier was moored and refueling under way, a surprise submarine alarm in the harbor "caused some disturbance."

On Dec. 14, ammunition ship *Pyro* was attacked but not damaged by a submarine 85 miles from Barbers Point.

The submarines were becoming more elusive, and not just because many of them had left the area to chase *Enterprise*. After a week of war, Rear Admiral Draemel reported that the Imperial Navy submarines were tricky to track: "Many destroyers have made good contacts with enemy submarines near Pearl entrance and destroyer captains have stated that as they make the approach, with almost perfect contact, and are within 150 yards of the submarine and are ready to attack, they lose contact very quickly on one bow or the other."

The Japanese submarines' tactic was to turn in on the American destroyers, presenting a smaller sonar cross-section. "The enemy submarines are very maneuverable, probably small, and are well-trained in eluding surface attacks," he concluded, and added that midget submarines "of the type recently captured" had to operate at shallow depths that made detection easier. Even if contact was lost at the last second, a normal-sized barrage of depth bombs would flush them out, he predicted.

On Dec. 15, frustrated at missing the carriers, Admiral Shimizu signaled *I-71* and the 11 submarines of the 1st and 2nd Squadrons that "all vessels which you discover should be attacked and sunk." The Advance Force was declaring total war.

In reply, *I-72* signaled back that one "large type merchant vessel" was anchored in Kahului Harbor at Maui, and it hadn't been attacked. No other ships were spotted in other ports. Also, "the calm sea surface in this place is satisfactory for flying operations." Later that day, *I-72* crept in past the breakwater boundary at Hilo Harbor on the island of Hawaii, to lie in wait until the evening of the 17th, planning to rise occasionally to spy on vessels in the harbor. On the 17th, *I-72* planned to burst to the surface and open fire on the ships, whose locations had been carefully mapped out.

Back on Oahu, *I-75*, patrolling in vain off Kailua for spy Otto

THE IMPLIED THREAT

Kimmel's daily summaries to Stark during the weeks following the attack concentrated almost exclusively on the submarine threat.

Typical was the report of Dec. 15:
"Only new development Hawaiian Area were submarine activities. In addition to sinking reported by Com-14, unsuccessful moonlight attack was made on Pyro *north of Oahu,* Chew *was attacked by a second submarine while she was attacking one west of the island. We are vigorously following up all contacts but no positive results can be claimed."*

THE CARRIER CHASE

Kuehn's signals, took advantage of *I-72's* report and began to occasionally venture over to target ships in Kahului Harbor.

The "calm sea" report inspired Shimizu to order an aerial reconnaissance. The next day, the 16th, he radioed Rear Admiral Shigeki Yamasaki, commander of the 2nd Submarine Squadron, *to inform us on the "sunk vessel" situation. In addition, among the 4 battleships stationed there, how many (can be identified by) the cage type mast?*

At dawn, *I-7* launched a Type 96 floatplane near Oahu. Eleven of the 25 submarines involved in the Pearl Harbor assault carried fold-up floatplanes, and the Imperial Navy put them to good use for intelligence purposes.[3]

I-7's plane stole over Pearl Harbor in the morning light and confirmed the claims of Fuchida's airmen. The crew then flew back and landed beside the submarine, now running scared on the surface in daylight. They leaped off the tiny plane and swam to the submarine. "Patrol of the enemy's action within 40 miles of Pearl Harbor was rigid," they reported. As soon as they were aboard, *I-7* dived, leaving the aircraft abandoned and drifting. Intelligence was more important, and the submarine raced back to Kwajalein for debriefing and photo developing.

The immense devastation at Pearl Harbor was accurately reported to Tokyo, creating a curious twist on the propaganda front. Official accounts from Tokyo of the damage at Pearl Harbor were more realistic than those coming from Washington at the same time.

Before the proof was in hand, the Imperial Naval staff broadcast the results of the Pearl Harbor attack on the 17th. Three battleships were estimated sunk, three or four more badly damaged, an aircraft carrier and three or four cruisers also badly damaged, two destroyers and three submarines sunk.

"America formerly underestimated the Japanese Imperial power and its navy, but at the beginning of the war very large losses were inflicted by surprise attack operations of the Imperial Navy, and as even the American agencies concerned admitted that the damage was greater than was imagined, the Army, people, and officials of America all received a violent shock," boasted Imperial Navy propagandists. "Within the American homeland all sorts of rumors of an invasion by the Japanese Army flew about. Even on the East Coast, it is said, they are having dimouts."

U.S. Navy ships reportedly had hightailed it to the West Coast, leaving Hawaii unprotected, the propaganda broadcast went on. "Much shipping is moving in and out" of the "Hawaii Area," but the only reinforcements expected were heavy bombers. Some ships were expected to sail from the Atlantic to bolster the West Coast.

"The American Navy, in the face of such a defeat as this, is endeavoring to restore the prestige of the Navy, raise morale, and restore damaged ships, etc. ... in order to completely restore the prestige of the Navy they are frequently attacking our homeland shipping when an occasion arises."

[3] According to Zenji Orita, these planes were launched toward the stern of the submarine, which had to run in reverse at full speed into the wind to launch. This bizarre notion is not supported by other sources.

While this Pacific-wide wash of wishful thinking was being aired, Admiral Kimmel was relieved as commander in chief of the U.S. Fleet. Normally gregarious and combative, he became quiet and moody. He was ordered to remain in Hawaii awaiting investigation, and he spent his evenings with Captain Earle and his wife, obsessively going over details of the attack.

The new CINCUS, Admiral Chester W. Nimitz, was angered when he first read of minesweeper *Condor's* night-time confrontation with the midget. This was "information not previously reported to the Commander-in-Chief, United States Pacific Fleet," he wrote on Dec. 30, in an otherwise benign endorsement of an analysis of the Dec. 7 bat-tle. "It is requested that the report be confirmed, if possible, and the Commander-in-Chief, United States Pacific Fleet, advised what action, if any, was taken to inform either the Commandant or the Com-mander-in-Chief, United States Pacific Fleet, in this case."

The use of his full title, three times in two sentences, indicates the gravity in which Nimitz viewed this oversight. Nimitz became known as a commander who haunted his own intelligence offices.

On Dec. 18, Admiral Nagumo broadcast his own version of the attack to the Imperial Fleet, the "Striking Force advancing to a posi-tion 200 miles north of Pearl Harbor at dawn on (7) December, with trust in divine assistance under the influence of the Emperor."

The aircraft, according to Nagumo, "braved dense clouds and … severe defensive fire" while sinking four battleships and damaging four others, and destroying a total of 450 American aircraft. He gave an inordinate share of credit to the midget submarine crews. "It is certain that, by the glorious and incomparable surprise attack by the Advance Expeditionary Force, Special Attack Units, very great suc-cesses were achieved, and thereby the main strength of the enemy's Pacific Ocean fighting units and also the enemy Army and Navy air strength in the Hawaiian area are considered to have been almost annihilated within one and half hours after the beginning of the war."

Three hours after Nagumo's broadcast, Yamasaki radioed the observations of his scout plane. The Imperial Navy's battleship fixation was obvious from the described details of the sunken war-ships: *The greater part of some was (sic) submerged and we have no details, but observations were, in general, as follows: Place of sink-ing — 600-700 meters north to south area, in succession, two objects appearing to be bridges (one of the basket type), and in two places there were ones thought to be parts of hulls. Although these are above surface in the harbor, their mutual relations are not clear.*

Of the remaining battleships, one is of the basket mast type, and the others are watchtower type, or, having badly damaged super-structure of unknown type.

The U.S. Fleet was confirmed as out of action, and the glorious targets of opportunity were not going to sail out of Pearl Harbor — they were in the mud at the harbor bottom. The eight remaining submarines of the 3rd Squadron were ordered back to Kwajalein soon after Yama-

264

THE CARRIER CHASE

saki's report. A later report from him indicated "no warships entering or leaving" the Hawaiian area after Dec. 18.

I-16 was being debriefed in Harashijima by this point. On Dec. 19, Rear Admiral Matome Ugaki, chief of staff of the Combined Fleet, incautiously signaled the other submarines of the 6th Fleet: *Of the Special Attack Unit, one ship has been assigned at present to combined maneuvers with the special model midget submarines in the Hiroshima Bay area, and so, when this unit returns to base, with the report of the attack on Hawaii and with future special model midget subs, we will improve our methods of attack. Then having made a digest of our observations, it is desired that the means of dispatching them in this area be prepared, in collaboration Lt. Matsuo and the personnel designated by Combined Fleet (message) #470, the orders to be issued on (their) return. Also, we wish to be informed of the names of the ships and at what time they will be able to depart.*

Ugaki's signal contained too much information about the secret weapon. Two days later, the Chief of the Bureau of Military Affairs cautioned the 6th Fleet submarines: *Regarding the present special submarine attacks on Pearl Harbor, although Naval Imperial HQ have published a dispatch concerning them, secrecy is still absolutely necessary, and it is strictly required that those persons designated for this work maintain absolute silence.*

In any case, there were only a half-dozen I-boats of the Second Submarine Squadron in Hawaii, all of the I-1 class, huge submarines that carried enough fuel for an extended tour. The prized American carriers were proving to be elusive. There was never more than one in port at any time, and they slipped in and out of Pearl Harbor in the dark of night. The carriers' phalanx of aggressive destroyers were dangerous as well, running down contacts at the least hint of underwater noise. They were also getting better at it; the slight oil sheen that resulted from prewar depth charges didn't fool them any more.

On Dec. 20, *I-1* spotted an auxiliary, but was unable to get into position. On Christmas Day, *I-1* was depth-bombed, with no apparent damage. On Dec. 31, *I-3* reached her deployment line, and then received a report of an American carrier in the area. She left her post to chase the report, found nothing. The carrier was *Saratoga*, newly arrived in the islands, and on her way to patrol Midway. On New Year's Day, *I-1* — which seemed to have bad luck on American holidays — was sighted and attacked by U.S. planes.

I-16 *at sea. Note the broad, flat after deck behind the sail — ideal for strapping on a midget submarine.*

On Jan. 2, 1942, *I-3* was back in position. The submarines were discovered by destroyer *Ward*, still successful at sniffing them out. In a division-wide attack on a good contact, *Ward* skated over the signal and rolled over depth charges. The starboard explosion threw something big and black to the surface, witnessed by destroyer *Allen*, trailing astern of *Ward*. No one on board *Ward* saw it.

To help out the older submarines, *I-24* left Kwajalein for Hawaii on Jan. 3, her buoyancy tank valve freshly repaired. On Jan. 6, *I-1* made another unsuccessful attack on an American destroyer, while *I-3* sighted and attacked some auxiliaries to no avail. An SBD of the *Saratoga* task force, then returning from the cruise off Midway, pounced on a surfaced I-boat running to the east that day, dropping a 500-pound bomb square on the submarine's deck. But the bomb was unarmed and the submarine crash-dived and disappeared.

The next day, the 7th, another *Saratoga* pilot spotted the same submarine ploughing through heavy waves 47 miles southeast of the task force. The plane attacked; again the bomb was unarmed and the target escaped.

I-18 *at sea.*

The stormy seas overwhelmed the fleet and all flying was canceled. Enormous waves shipped over the carrier's huge bow and flooded the elevator well. *Saratoga* gingerly continued southeast, back to Hawaii, planning to exchange planes with *Enterprise*.

Fuel low, and equally racked by the storm, *I-1* left Hawaii on Jan. 9. The same day, an American carrier was spotted at 6:30 a.m. by Commander Otani aboard *I-18*, which had returned from Kwajalein to help. *I-24* had joined up with the 2nd Squadron as well.

Once again, the carrier chase was on. Otani reported the "Lexington-class" carrier 300 miles northeast of Johnston Island, about a third of the way to Hawaii, and signaled the carrier's heading, speed and position to Shimizu in Kwajalein.

This was a solid lead, far from the covering aircraft of Oahu. Shimizu pulled several submarines off picket duty in Hawaii to run down the carrier. I-boats returning from the West Coast also were directed into the area.

Unaware she had been targeted, *Lexington* launched a routine anti-submarine sweep the morning of Jan. 10. Twelve SBD Dauntlesses cleared a path 300 miles ahead of the task force, while four F2A Buffalo fighters closely patrolled the flanks and stern. At 10:20 a.m.,

THE CARRIER CHASE

pilots Fred Simpson and Doyle C. Barnes surprised a submarine running 60 miles to the south. The I-boat dived before the Buffaloes got close, and Simpson firewalled the fighter back to the task force. At 10:57, he buzzed *Lexington's* deck and dropped a beanbag message giving the sub's position, now 100 miles west of Johnston Island.

The carrier trapped the morning search teams and launched another at 12:30, joined by four TBD Devastators carrying depth charges. The submarine was quickly picked up again by a Buffalo team flown by Lieutenant (jg) Clark Rinehart and RM1c Charles E. Brewer. Rinehart stealthily pulled the Buffaloes up in the sun and radioed the position of his patrol at 1:25 p.m. *Lexington* vectored two TBDs to the scene, flown by Ensign Norman A. Sterrie and AOM2c Harley E. Talkington.

Rinehart waited until the Devastators slipped into bombing position, and then he and Brewer dropped onto the submarine from out of the sun.

Sterrie salvoed his two depth charges from 2,000 feet when the submarine started to dive, but Talkington's charges clung to his TBD. The Buffaloes opened fire from the other side, holding their triggers open as they hurtled downward. "We could see our tracers bouncing off his deck as he went down, so I know bullets were going into him," reported Rinehart. "And don't let anyone tell you those .50-calibers won't tear a hole in anything they hit!"

They kept hosing the submarine until they were forced to pull out, Brewer flashing over the ocean within 100 feet. Talkington, meanwhile, shook his charges loose and they went into the sea about 50 yards ahead of the rapidly submerging I-boat. Brewer reported that these near misses "jerked sub abruptly to the right," probably inflicting damage. Within moments there was no sign of the ambush other than a small oil stain on the water. The four Americans searched for a hour, after which Rinehart wrote a description of the incident and returned to *Lexington*.

His delivery method gave a thrill to those on deck. He horsed the little Buffalo across the ship at bridge level, turning the plane sideways to avoid catching the stack with a wingtip. With the plane "hanging on his prop," Rinehart roared over the bridge — where everyone was taking cover — and flung out the message in a beanbag, which fell at the feet of Vice Admiral Wilson Brown.

Though Brown detached destroyers *Phelps* and *Monaghan* to finish off the possibly crippled submarine, no sign of it was found. The craft was possibly *I-19*, returning from the West Coast, although skipper Takaichi Kinashi did not report the attack. Whatever it was, the two Buffaloes fired 650 rounds at it.

After two days at 20 knots, high-tailing it for the presumed location of the carrier, *I-24's* valves stuck again, leaving the submarine foundering at sea. Repairs were made, enough so that *I-24* could crash-dive, though not much else.

Directly north, still slowly approaching a southeast rendezvous

Freshly repaired from the Advance Force's successful torpedo attack on Jan. 11, carrier Saratoga *stands into Pearl Harbor in June of 1942.*

with *Enterprise*, carrier *Saratoga's* planes remained grounded due to the stormy weather. On Jan. 11, 420 miles southwest of Pearl Harbor, the shuddering seas had smoothed a bit and *Saratoga's* planes prepared to take off for combat air patrol. The morning mission was canceled, however, and the pilots filed below for routine duties. The ship ground on at 15 knots. As darkness fell at 7:15 p.m., while the pilots enjoyed dinner in the wardroom, a "terrific explosion" knocked them away from the table.

I-6, under Commander M. Inaba, had stalked the carrier until a good torpedo solution was available. A single torpedo had crashed into *Saratoga* hard amidships, on the port side, bursting into three fire rooms and killing six firemen. Oil bunkers ruptured and sprayed aircraft on the flight deck, and metal fragments from the explosion littered the ship's deck. As the pilots ran for their ready room, the crippled carrier took a fierce list to port, taking on 1,100 tons of seawater. The water contaminated oil tanks and caused a loss of fuel suction, and *Saratoga* lost headway, drifting helplessly for a few moments before engineers could finesse the problem.

Inaba could see that the ship was badly damaged and had begun to heel over before he had to flee the destroyer patrol. Full of joy, he radioed that *I-6* had sunk a Lexington-class carrier.

The hit was to be the most successful Advance Force strike against an American warship. Morale soared throughout the 2nd Squadron.

First into the enemy camp and last out, the submarines were the only warriors of Kido Butai to hit the highly valued American carriers. Yamamoto paid off his beer-bottle bonus to Inaba's torpedo officer, who shared his booty with the crew of *I-6*.

The admiral was convinced *Saratoga* was sunk, and was quite surprised when she showed up in Hawaii in June, during the Battle of Midway.

THE CARRIER CHASE

MYSTERY SUBMARINE

21

THE UNINVITED GUEST PROVES FASCINATING

After the war, Senator Homer Ferguson of Michigan, leaned forward — astounded! — at a congressional hearing concerning American unpreparedness at Pearl Harbor. "You mean," he sputtered, "that our intelligence was such that we didn't even know that Japan had these small submarines?"

Harold Stark explained that intelligence on Japanese naval matters was notoriously hard to get, illustrating his point by saying that window curtains on trains were pulled down whenever the cars rolled past a naval base. Later, Admiral Husband Kimmel protested that the midget submarine was a "surprise type ... and a very ineffective one, in my opinion."

Ineffective or not, and despite prewar rumor, the type came as a complete surprise to Americans. Seizing Ensign Sakamaki's submarine was more difficult than capturing the man. It proved to be an intelligence bonanza.

Lieutenant Royal L. Rutter of Submarine Squadron Four, the promised Navy observer, showed up at Bellows Field on the morning of Dec. 8, 1941, in time to see three Navy planes hurl 25-pound bombs at the submarine, all of which missed. The impact craters of the bombs on the reef were clearly visible from the air.

While this was going on, an Army Air Force officer called General Short from Bellows and said the Navy was bombing the submarine. Short said that it shouldn't be destroyed, but if the Navy wanted it gone, a piece of field artillery could do the job more quickly and accurately. By the time a piece was trained on the target, the Navy had already loosened it from the reef with near misses.

Rutter quizzed Captain Lewis, the pilot who first saw the submarine. He confirmed it had a large oil slick near the stern and that despite the best efforts by American bombs, it was still in one piece.

Rutter cadged a ride on an Air Corps 0-47 and buzzed the midget submarine. As the plane passed with 100 feet of the craft, Rutter determined it was dull black with no distinguishing marks, and guessed it was 40 feet long, which was half-right. The submarine was jammed on the coral by its stern, and as waves winked over it, Rutter

could see a "basket-like projection" on the streaming black bow. This was the mangled torpedo guard, twisted out of shape on the reef outside Pearl Harbor.

The midget looked like an easy recovery job to Rutter, and he reported it so.

Later that morning, Navy crews showed up at Bellows armed with cables and bulldozers. A sailor swam out with a rope, which was then used to drag out cables. They were roughly attached to the battered submarine and the bulldozers pulled it to within 50 yards of shore, where it was tethered to palm trees.

Captain Lovell sent the submarine base repair officer, Lieutenant Commander Daniel T. Eddy, to examine it, and warned others to stay away. Eddy, a large man, couldn't get into the thing, nor could the electrician's mate with him. [1]

Another man swam to the craft at noon and, Kimmel's impression aside, easily entered it to briefly rummage through the control tower, bringing back a map and some papers, as well as empty rice cans, empty vegetable cans and empty fruit cans, two each.

Lovell figured rightly from this there had been two crew aboard and started a search for the other crewman. The map looked important — it was marked up with notes in colored pencil — and Lovell hustled it back to Pearl Harbor.

Eddy reported that the sub could be salvaged with assistance, and Intelligence Officer Edwin Layton directed him to do so. More cables were attached to the midget submarine, and the salvage crew stood down for the day. While all this was going on, 0-47s from Bellows circled overhead. Periscopes were continuously spotted in the water.

Later that afternoon, Yeoman Leonard Webb at 14th Naval District headquarters answered the phone at Captain Earle's office.

"This is Major (So-and-so) at Bellows Field. We have a submarine tied to a tree."

"Tied?"

"You goddamn sailors come over here and disarm these torpedoes!"

"What torpedoes, sir?"

"It's got torpedoes sticking out of the front end of it!"

Webb rolled his eyes. Earle caught the motion and said, "What do you have there, Webb?"

"I have an Army Air Corps major here, sir, that I think must have been shot in the head."

"Why?"

"He says he's got a Japanese submarine tied to a tree."

Earle considered. "He does sound like he's been hurt."

Webb brushed off the major by passing him on to the submarine base. He was embarrassed to discover a couple of days later that the major had not been exaggerating, much.

While the Americans were tying up *I-24tou*, the crew of *I-69* continued their efforts to escape from the ocean bottom, right at the

[1] *This incident led to bizarre, racist notions about the submarine's size. Said Admiral Kimmel later, "It is so small that a white man could not get into it. They had to cut the thing apart in order to get a white man to the seat where they drove it ..."*

MYSTERY SUBMARINE

gate of Pearl Harbor. Despite the danger, it seemed to skipper Wata-nabe and his crew as if a miracle had occurred while they were plunging into the deep with an "anti-torpedo" net tangled around their submarine. Though 17 meters below safe submerged depth, and in waters charted as being hundreds of feet deep, the submarine was resting snugly on the bottom.

The captain ordered unnecessary machinery switched off, and the crew heard an enemy destroyer steam directly over their heads. Other patrol vessels were heard in the distance, occasionally stopping to lash the water with active sonar. Watanabe decided the Americans were listening carefully, and directed rigid sound-control measures.

All pumps except the oil-pressure pump were switched off, all mechanical movements were suspended, such as electric fan, ventila-tors and gyrocompass. Watanabe decided to wait until sunset to surface, but the tempo of destroyer activity above convinced him to try and tough it out until the next night, if possible. "We are a few miles from the harbor entrance," he said. Surfacing in daytime, however briefly, "offered considerable chance of discovery, and consequent battle to the death."

The crew settled in to wait. The air grew acid and leaden, the chemicals used to purify the air unable to keep up with the demand on oxygen. On three occasions, the sound of destroyers grew faint enough to switch on electric blowers for a few moments. Soon, the crew complained of headaches. Walking a short distance caused

I-24tou is pulled ashore at Bellows Army Air Field, near Waimanalo. The dank overcast of Dec. 8 is apparent.

panting. Those not on duty were urged to sleep, which came quickly in the thick air.

Cold biscuits and canned fruit were served as meals. With the heads out of commission, the crew used empty oil cans to relieve their bowels, parking the stinking containers in passageways.

Once an hour, bilge water was measured. This far below the ship's design depth, seawater was forcing its way into the hull. The bilges rose, imperceptibly at first. The temperature rose as well — pressurized seawater could not be let in for cooling purposes without shattering the pipes. The engineer suggested circulating bilge water to cool the ship.

Watanabe knew the submarine would only have a few moments on the surface before it was detected by Americans. He wanted as much control of the I-boat as possible. The air reservoir needed charging. The high-pressure air compressor could not be used without broadcasting the submarine's position, so high-pressure air from the six reserve torpedoes was bled into the reservoir.

Dinner the evening of Dec. 8 was curiously formal. For the first time since leaving base, sake was served to all hands. Watanabe assumed the next day would be spent in furious battle, and wanted to treat his men.

Night passed slowly in the half-light of the submarine passageways, undetectable except by time piece. In the morning, Watanabe checked the air reservoir and was shocked to see that it had leaked during the night. He decided to risk the air compressor, and charged the reservoir once again.

Bilge water continued to rise. Waste material was stuffed into the propellor-shaft packing, and all valves to the outside were tightly dogged with hammers. Despite this, bilge water rose until it splashed beneath their *zorii*. *I-69* rested in a slight nose-up attitude, and bilge water collected deepest in the motor room. Concerned that the electric motors might become swamped, men spent the day hand-pumping the filthy water into the aft torpedo room, which began to fill.

Watanabe decided to surface just before midnight, the point between sunset and the waning moon, the darkest portion of night. Should they be able to easily free the ship and dodge the destroyers, he wanted to retreat at high speed to a place of comparative safety, to charge batteries and listen to the radio for orders.

More likely, there would be a battle. Watanabe had all weapons checked thoroughly, torpedoes set for two meter depth to knock out the expected destroyers. Small arms were issued to the deck crew, and the machine guns cleaned. Code books and other secret documents were cut to ribbons and pulped in containers of sea water.

A total of 19 men were assigned the task of spilling out on deck and slashing away at the submarine net that held them fast. They were instructed to ignore enemy gunfire. Other men were to throw waste material overboard, such as slippers, trash and oil, to give the impression a submarine had been sunk on the site.

Mystery Submarine

Watanabe considered his options should the submarine not be able to escape the net as American warships closed in. Ten cannon rounds were opened in the magazine, exposing powder charges, and arranged around two open cans of kerosene. If escape looked impossible, *I-69* would make a run for the harbor entrance, where the message "We are unable to communicate" would be broadcast in clear. As soon as the I-boat entered the harbor mouth, it would self-destruct gloriously, locking in the American fleet.

Watanabe made a mental note to install proper self-destruction materials in Imperial Navy craft, if he got through this ordeal. *It's unbearable,* he thought. *The crew is already suffering in this foul air — they shouldn't have to watch the kerosene flames try to ignite the ignition charge.*

They settled in for the long day.

That Tuesday morning, radioman Charles L. Jackson was on duty in the temporary transmitter room at Sub Base, Pearl Harbor, when Lieutenant Commander Donald C. Beard, radio officer on Admiral Kimmel's staff, stopped by.

Would Jackson consider volunteering to do a job for the admiral? Beard asked.

Jackson, surprised, said he'd be glad to do anything he could.

Beard sent the radioman to the Sub Base Repair Office, where two other specialists had gathered, a lieutenant commander who was a weapons expert and a chief petty officer. They learned — for the first time — that a Japanese midget submarine had been captured, and that they were the prize-of-war crew. It was their job to examine it, and if necessary, disarm it.

The midgets had been a complete surprise to Navy intelligence units at Pearl, and there was considerable curiosity about the metal creature bucking in the surf on the other side of the island. Even Lieutenant (jg) Forrest R. Biard of Navy Combat Intelligence, who had advised Lieutenant Outerbridge to take definitive action against mysterious submarines, confessed years later that the midgets seemed to have "appeared out of nowhere."

News of the midget's capture was withheld from the public for a week, and then only briefly mentioned in an official Washington dispatch.

Radioman Jackson's mission was to remove the Japanese radio transmitter and receiver from the midget and haul them back to the Sub Base transmitter room. There, they were to be hooked up to American equipment for testing.

The little salvage party boarded a truck and rode across the Pali in the Koolau Mountains to Bellows. There was a cold rain pouring down as they stood on the beach. The midget thrashed around in the surf, dark and menacing.

"Jackson, strip down and get yourself out there and take a look," said the salvage chief.

Jackson jumped shivering into the water and swam to the midget

The midget submarine is braced with timbers to keep her from rolling over in the surf. The lines used to haul the craft ashore are tangled up in the submarine's net-jumping cables, which later led to erroneous impressions about the complexity of the cable arrangement.

as quickly as he could. He started to haul himself up on the bow's twisted framework when he heard a shout from shore.

He turned around to hear better. "Get yourself away from there!" the chief yelled. "Those are torpedoes sticking out!"

Jackson hadn't noticed the shiny warheads nestled, one over the other, in the tangled net cutters, but now he saw them clearly, and they looked as deadly as sharks. He backpedaled furiously and then swam down the sub's flank.

He hauled himself onto the deck near the conning tower and rested for a moment. When he looked back toward shore, the chief was signaling for him to enter the ship.

Jackson opened the small hatch at the top of the conning tower and got a violent blast of rotten air. He gagged. It was the stench of vomit, battery fumes, perspiration and despair.

He waited a moment for the smell to vent away, and took a couple of deep breaths before climbing in.

There were navigation charts and instruments on the port side, communications gear on the starboard, including the radios. Underfoot in the control area were the remains of a meal, including an apple and sake bottles. There was also a filled toilet.

Jackson policed the area, dumping small items into a collapsible bucket and making a couple of trips to shore with the miserable booty. Convinced it was safe by the third trip, the officer and CPO joined him.

Jackson concentrated on the radio while the officer crept forward to inspect the torpedoes and the chief poked around in the aft portion of the hull, where the batteries and propulsion units were housed.

MYSTERY SUBMARINE

"Hey!" cried the chief. "Look what I found!"

Jackson and the officer scurried back and aimed their flashlights at the deck. An unburnt fuse rose out of a puddle of water and plunged into a mass nestled between two batteries. It was 300 pounds of explosive, Sakamaki's scuttling charge that had failed to detonate.

The chief poked at the explosive, and the officer, round-eyed, told him to be careful. They then told Jackson to get the radio gear off, because they wanted to leave.

The officer and CPO swam ashore, got dressed and waited for Jackson. He disconnected a small motor generator, ferried it to shore and swam back, towing an inflated Mae West life vest. The idea was to float the radio equipment in it, high and dry.

Jackson manhandled the radio equipment up the conning tower and held it up while he surveyed the control room one last time. He popped out of the tower, wrapped the life vest around the radio and, balancing it on his head, strolled to the bow and watched the waves pump past. Jackson figured he'd jump straight in and walk up on the beach with the package dry.

The mangled bow of I-24tou is pulled up onto the sand. Note the identification plate on the top torpedo cover. Like many small pieces of the midget submarine, this item vanished shortly after these photos were taken, almost certainly liberated as souvenirs.

He jumped in during a likely swell and was driven in far over his head. The waves pushed him forward and he stumbled in the swirl of salt water and sand particles. Jackson felt his lungs strain and he thought he'd have to drop the bundle and jump to the surface.

His face broke clear of the water and he gulped air before another wave pitched him forward. He stumbled up on the beach and dumped the radio, gasping.

"Get dressed," said the chief. "It's time to go. We're done here."

A Navy crew then dragged the sub up onto the beach, where it was photographed. Hauling the vessel in required a jury mast, a sled of 12-inch timbers and an army tractor. It was dismantled into three sections, which turned out to be surprisingly easy — they were just bolted together. Each section was then craned onto flatbed trucks commandeered from the Oahu Railroad Company.[2]

Sakamaki's midget finally made it into Pearl Harbor that afternoon, driven right through the front gate. A "small" enlisted man scoured the submarine for remaining items, finding documents, maps, recognition pictures, a small note book, sewing thread and needle, morphine syringes, a first-aid kit, rations and a toilet resembling a small cuspidor. All were badly smudged from lying in the oily bilges.

Only a few miles away, in *I-69*, as the moment drew close to fight to the surface, Watanabe gathered together his officers. They drank toasts to the Emperor with carefully hoarded beer, and prayed aloud for a "good battle."

[2] *General Short saw the midget submarine, and asked for the details of its capture. "Some fellow from Texas, probably, lassoed it," he commented.*

ADVANCE FORCE — PEARL HARBOR

The crew assumed battle stations. The throb of destroyer engines overhead grew faint, and a half-hour ahead of his timetable, Watanabe ordered the main tanks blown.

I-69 rumbled back to life, but did not move.

"We're not floating!" shouted an officer.

"Cut in the motors — port and starboard motors ahead standard," said Watanabe.

The submarine lurched free of the bottom, standing on its stern. It arrowed toward the surface as men tumbled backward and an estimated 50 tons of bilgewater and collected excrement coursed aft. Though Watanabe frantically ordered to stop blowing the forward tanks, the abrupt change of balance kept the submarine bow-high. Vents in the forward main tank were opened, and seawater rushing into the nose stabilized the angle of ascent.

The extreme angle caused the oil sump tank in the engine room to slop over and both engines seized. The submarine was without means to pump air or water.

In the already flooded stern of *I-69*, the tsunami of oily bilge water and human waste blasted crewmen away from their posts. Batteries broke open and acid steamed in the passageways. Electrical wires shorted out. Men choked in the fetid brew. As the submarine broke surface, high-pressure pumps immediately sucked clean air into the ship. *I-69* had been on the bottom for 38 hours.

A second miracle occurred — no enemy destroyers were within sight. The net-cutting crew burst out of the steel coffin, carrying army-supplied wire-cutters. They searched quickly and were unable to find any submarine netting, which greatly puzzled Watanabe. Only a single strand of cable was found, which was thrown over the side.

The port engine was restarted, but the starboard propeller refused to rotate. *Was that mysterious cable wound around the prop?* wondered Watanabe. He was about to order a diver overboard, to feel the shaft in the black water, when the propeller energetically burst back into life. *I-69* was whole again.

Their good luck was running out. The I-boat had drifted dangerously near the coast, and a curious destroyer was drawing near, challenging them with signal lights. Though air pressure was only partially replenished, and 25 tons of bilge water remained, the submarine began to submerge and run south.

Trim was unsteady and the submarine pitched up and down in rollercoaster fashion, exacerbated by the bilge water splashing down the corridor from one end of the submarine to the other. Pressure in the reservoir fell as the engines again lost their oil sump, and Watanabe resigned himself to returning to the surface.

The destroyer disappeared in the distance, and Watanabe ordered the submarine to run northwest, keeping the coast of Oahu to starboard to guide the helmsman. If more Americans were encountered, it would have to be a surface battle.

The passageways were slimy with bilge water flooding, and the

MYSTERY SUBMARINE

submarine reeked. Most of the damage was to electrical systems. Gradually, the engines were brought on line, and *I-69* picked up speed. By dawn, she was a hundred miles from Oahu, moving at flank speed. No Americans were seen.

It took the best part of the day to repair radio equipment enough to transmit a report and await orders.

What entangled the submarine outside Pearl Harbor has remained a mystery. No submarine nets were used in Hawaiian waters, and the submarine certainly never got close enough to the channel to run into the anti-torpedo nets. [3]

American intelligence experts had already begun to study Sakamaki's *I-24tou* and were intrigued by its capabilities. "Many times I had piloted a surfaced submarine through Pearl Harbor channel," wrote ex-submariner Lieutenant Wilfred J. Holmes of the Combat Intelligence Unit. "I knew that, even on the surface, a submarine had to navigate that long channel with caution, so I evaluated as ridiculous the report that a submerged Japanese submarine was in Pearl Harbor. It was, in fact, one of the few accurate sighting reports to reach us that day …"

On Thursday, Dec. 11, Lieutenant Commander Harold Kaminski examined the midget submarine, and later recommended that the anti-torpedo baffles around *YNg-17* be tightened. Kaminski had the nets inspected by a diver on Dec. 12. The diver reported that the "nets had not been penetrated or disturbed." [4]

On Dec. 16, Kaminski measured the midget and declared "it would be extremely precarious … for an underwater craft of this type to directly penetrate or even go under the Pearl Harbor (nets) when the gate was closed, without advertising its presence."

Lieutenant Outerbridge of destroyer *Ward* visited Sakamaki's submarine in Pearl Harbor. Inside was a torpedoman, trying to get the torpedoes out without exploding them. Outerbridge carefully inspected the craft and confirmed that it was the same type he had seen on the morning of Dec. 7.

The documents found aboard were fascinating, and promptly given to the FBI for translating, as they had the best language experts.

"All the necessary data to facilitate a submarine attack was in Japanese possession" and discovered aboard Sakamaki's midget, a Navy official testified after the war.

Found were two commercially available panorama photographs of Pearl Harbor, looking down from Aiea Heights. Other recovered documents showed sea-level views of Hawaii and the approaches to Pearl Harbor. [5]

Sakamaki's note "Tube released" caused some puzzlement when translated. American intelligence experts assumed it meant that torpedoes were fired at this point. It took a while before they realized "tube" was the midget submariners' slang for their weapon.

Inagaki's corpse was recovered from the water near Bellows on Dec. 11. From the condition of the body, there was speculation that

[3] *The likely explanation is that* I-69 *had the great bad luck to blunder into the cable hanging from* Crossbill's *drifting paravane, severed the day before by cruiser* St. Louis *as she sortied wildly from the harbor. On-shore currents go in that general direction, and the device would have floated toward Barbers Point, into the path of* I-69.

[4] *Kimmel later claimed there was a hole in the net.*

[5] *They suggest that reconnaissance was carried out prior to Dec. 3, 1941, which the Japanese government continues to deny.*

277

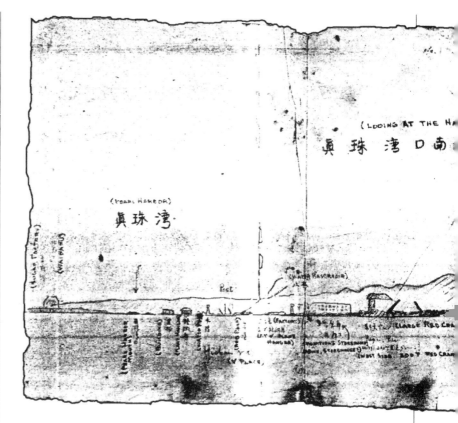

(LOOING AT THE HA
眞珠湾 口南

(PEARL HARBOR)
眞珠湾

The sea-level view of the attack route into Pearl Harbor, found aboard Sakamaki's midget submarine.

[6] *Inagaki's actual cause of death remains a mystery, as his forensic certificate is still classified by the U.S. government.*

he had either been attacked by sharks, had been too close to the bombs dropped near the submarine or that he had held a small explosive charge, like a hand grenade, to his stomach. [6]

Also found on Inagaki's body was a map, apparently charting an attack route through Pearl Harbor. It showed three separate tracks laid down for approaching the harbor, one for leaving. Some of Sakamaki's notes were in English. Sakamaki marked his intended approach in blue crayon, changing to red crayon as he entered the enemy waters in Pearl Harbor.

The map was an exact copy of a prewar U.S. Geodetic Survey map — "This Japanese map is an excellent example of subversive Japanese activities," the Navy testified during the congressional hearings — and the "route" goes counter-clockwise in straight-line segments around Ford Island, with what appears to be times and bearings noted.

The trapezoidal track around Ford Island reached Captain Rochefort a few days after the attack, with the Japanese writing already deciphered by FBI translators. The FBI was convinced that the midget had reconnoitered the harbor and sailed out again before the attack. Though the FBI declined to interview Sakamaki, Special Agent Robert Shivers was impressed by the careful tracking marked off on the maps, and deduced that Sakamaki had entered the harbor. This view was widely distributed and not refuted until the Hewitt investigation made a careful study of the maps and concluded "that

MYSTERY SUBMARINE

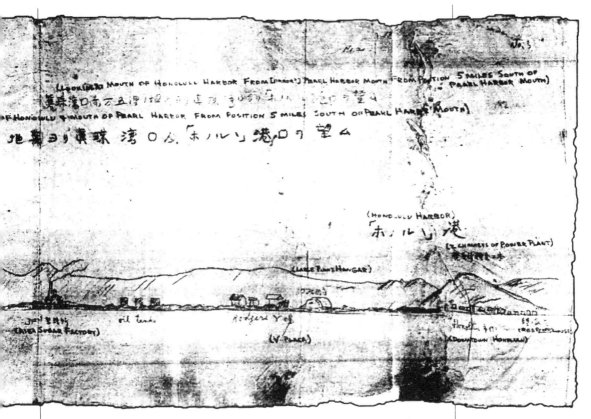

there was no evidence warranting the belief that any Japanese submarine entered Pearl Harbor prior to 7 December."

The Hewitt investigators presumed the midget attack plan was to lie in the channel, to sink ships attempting to escape and thus block the channel, and then, after the air attack was finished, proceed into the harbor and use the rest of their torpedoes. They cited captured Japanese sub orders, which stated, "Will make a surprise attack on the channel leading into Pearl Harbor and attempt to close it." There was nothing about making a circuit of the target.

Even the best translators in the FBI and Navy Intelligence were unable to determine if Sakamaki's track showed that he had already penetrated the harbor, or was laying out his course. "Jasper" Holmes of Combat Intelligence also interpreted the markings as check points for navigation, because he had seen navigators on American submarines go through the same routine before entering a harbor.

Taking the opposite view, Naval Intelligence's Layton decided that "it is too exact to be an exact track" and that "figures were written

Inagaki is prepared for a simple burial.

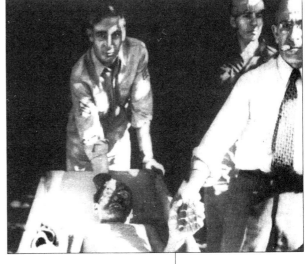

The map of Pearl Harbor supplied to attacking forces of the Imperial Navy.

too carefully to have been performed by the captain of the midget submarine while controlling the submarine." Sakamaki had to operate the periscope, the control trim and maneuver the craft by himself; Inagaki opened and closed switches, cut in and out of the CO_2 absorbent material and tended the engine. A man in the midst of skulking through a battle in an enemy harbor simply wouldn't be so neat about it.

The Army Pearl Harbor Board concluded that submarines "must" have been in the harbor a few days prior to attack, a rather unkind swipe at Navy security. They were "of the opinion that Japanese midget submarines operated freely inside of Pearl Harbor for several days prior to the 7th of December, for the purpose of gaining information."

A Navy report, not surprisingly, concluded the opposite. The positions of American ships "differed substantially from the actual berthing arrangements on Dec. 7," the Navy counterclaimed in its own defense. [7]

This, in turn, led the Army to retrench; the positions were charted prior to the attack. Nobody apparently thought to compare the chart with berthing positions in the weeks prior to the attack; a match would have pinpointed when the information was transmitted.

Admiral Kimmel rather defensively speculated on the possibility of Sakamaki's submarine touring Pearl Harbor. "There was no reason," he said. "It didn't make sense. They could see from the hills, so why risk a submarine going in there? ... I would strongly discount anything except the most positive evidence that the Japanese were stupid enough to send a submarine in there merely for the purposes of observing."

Clearly, the map was a political hot potato. The FBI made an internal investigation following the war and during the congressional Pearl Harbor hearings, making an attempt at damage control should the bureau be chided for misreading the captured maps. They concluded that one of the two charts actually came from the midget submarine rammed by *Monaghan*, and "thus Sakamaki's views on the failure of his mission do not obviate the possibility that the course actually is a logged track."

[7] On the other hand, the Navy at this time thought cruiser Raleigh *was hit by a torpedo fired from a midget submarine already in the harbor when the attack started.*

MYSTERY SUBMARINE

In other words, a definite maybe. Details of this internal ethics audit were not released until 1990.

Even if the submarine had entered the harbor to survey the ships, it would have done Kido Butai no good, as there was no way to transmit the information before the attack without tipping their hand.

Ships were plugged in according to information received from the consulate weeks before. Sakamaki wrote *Saratoga* at the berth where *Utah* was moored on Dec. 7, a move later interpreted by FBI translators to mean he had mistaken the old battleship for a carrier — which in turn helped fuel the rumor that all Japanese attackers had hallucinated a large carrier where an ex-battleship squatted. Though *Utah* was spectacularly knocked out almost immediately, within plain sight of attacking forces, none of the Japanese aviators claimed a carrier kill during debriefing.

Nevertheless, the rumor that a midget had cruised smoothly through Pearl Harbor days before the attack was given wide credence, and is still believed by many Pearl Harbor veterans.

Another recovered map also showed the track chart around Ford Island, fainter, but still there. This map, however, was recovered by Layton himself from the Zero that crashed at Fort Kamehameha early in the attack. Apparently the two maps were not compared, as there is no reason for an aircraft to make a similar circuit of the harbor. The most likely explanation is that the track was on the original Geodetic Survey map, and was faithfully copied by the Japanese. The track roughly corresponds to dredging paths in the harbor.

These questions could be resolved by a study of Sakamaki's original map, but it disappeared from FBI custody. Soon after it was photostated, it was "purloined by a souvenir hunter," an embarrassed admiral testified before Congress. [8]

Another chart taken from the Zero had the positions of task force screen submarines *I-19, I-21* and *I-23* marked. Sakamaki, when questioned, explained they were there to protect Kido Butai during the high-speed run to launch, and then covered the rear of Kido Butai as it retired.

Also made much of was Sakamaki's drawing of the midget submarine being carried on the deck of a mother submarine. [9] His drawing skills were such that it is difficult to tell fore from aft on the mother submarine, and Navy intelligence documents during the war often indicated that the midgets were carried in front of the mother's conning tower. As late as 1991, official information handouts from the National Park Service, using information from the Navy, showed the midget carried on the forward part of the I-boat.

The midget submarine rammed by *Monaghan* was not raised for at least three weeks, since salvage crews were too involved trying to rescue sailors trapped in sunken battleships. When it was pulled up, it was studied for two days, but a month of silt, brackish water, leaching acids and decaying corpses had wiped away virtually everything of value, even electrical leads and pipes had disintegrated.

[8] *The original photostats are held at the Army Intelligence School in Fort Huachuca, Arizona. The maps reproduced here are from those copies.*

[9] *See page 253.*

Layton claimed Japanese documents from the *Monaghan* midget were unusable, yet papers collected from Sakamaki's submarine *Ha-19* sometimes refer to *Ha-13*, which may have been the rammed submarine. It is possible that other papers were mixed up with Sakamaki's, before or after the attack.

Another rumor widely accepted at the time was that Sakamaki's submarine was loaded with Love's Bread, a brand made by an island bakery. Such gossip confirmed suspicions that the submarines were provisioned by sampan.

The first letter from Kimmel to Stark after the attack, on Dec. 12, was both subdued in tone and betrayed fascination with the submarine assault. The air raid, Kimmel explained, was considered " a very remote possibility." The "primary effort" of patrol aircraft in the air that morning "was directed against the submarine menace which everyone fully recognized ... the submarines were promptly, and I hope effectively, dealt with."

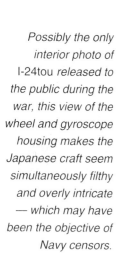

The crude flags carried aboard I-24tou.

Later, Kimmel notes that details and photographs of the midget submarine were being given express service back to Washington. He gives details: "This submarine, 74' by 5', bolted together in 3 sections and capable of 24 knots submerged, can pass under and around most nets.

"The Pearl Harbor anti-submarine net was down at the time the raid started. The submarine carried photographed silhouettes of Oahu from every angle of approach; and among other things in its locker, it had an American Ensign. I shall forward shortly, considerable detailed information of this vessel."

The American flag carried aboard *I-24tou* was crudely hand-

Possibly the only interior photo of I-24tou released to the public during the war, this view of the wheel and gyroscope housing makes the Japanese craft seem simultaneously filthy and overly intricate — which may have been the objective of Navy censors.

MYSTERY SUBMARINE

drawn on cloth, and has not been satisfactorily explained. Perhaps Sakamaki thought the midget submarine could pass for a buoy.

The initial report on midgets by Lieutenant Commander William R. Smedberg III stated they were 41 feet long. Actually, the Ko-Hyoteki was about 80 feet long. Confusion reigned throughout the war, with Navy intelligence reports carefully differentiating between the 41-foot "Pearl Harbor-type" midget and the 80-foot "Kohyotekis." Actually, they were one and the same, as anyone with a measuring tape discovered. Sakamaki's midget was examined and dissected in detail. Other than the Mitsubishi *Reisan* "Zero" fighter, also a surprise at Pearl Harbor, no Japanese weapon was given as thorough a going-over.

The 10-foot periscope, for example, was "of Japanese make but almost an exact copy of our Zeiss 30' periscope … made by Japan Optical Manufacturing Company, May 1941."

The gyrocompass was similar to the German "Anschutz" gyrocompass, dating back to 1926. Curiously, when set up at the submarine base, it worked perfectly after some poking and prodding.

The torpedoes, complete with warheads and exploders, went to the Naval Ammunition Depot at Lualualei on Oahu's leeward side; the radio to the CINCUS radio officer; the sound gear to the minecraft base; Sakamaki's personal articles to the intelligence officer; and the high-pressure air tanks to the diving and salvage unit at Pearl Harbor.

This picture of the aft battery compartment presents a clearer view of the submarine's sturdy craftsmanship. The technician is measuring rubber bumpers that protrude from the ribs, providing shock absorption for the battery racks. Note the monocoque construction, similar to that of an aircraft fuselage, and the white and red interior.

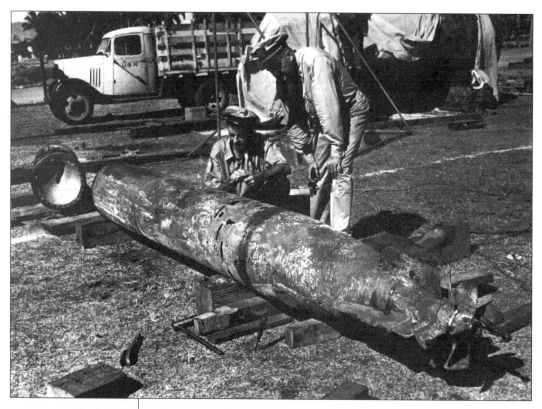

Navy technicians disassemble Sakamaki's supposedly balky gyrocompass and torpedoes.

The screw sleeve on the torpedo safety was found in the closed position, so the Navy assumed that was why *I-24tou's* torpedoes didn't fire. The explosives to scuttle the submarine were found to be several years old, some dating back to 1905.

"In general, the workmanship, construction and design of the battery is considered excellent for the purpose for which it was designed," concluded a portion of the technical analysis.

Midget submarines used at Pearl Harbor had a battery section removed to make additional room for compressed air and oxygen. Hydroplanes were controlled by compressed air. The periscope was raised electrically, the radio had a raiseable, rubber-covered mast, there was even a small chart table in the control room.

The U.S. Navy was impressed. A technician named Bernard Butler was afterward rushed to the West Coast with information about the Pearl Harbor attack, meeting with commandants

MYSTERY SUBMARINE

of 11th Naval district and the Navy Yard at Mare Island. The commanders were particularly impressed with details of the "two-men submarines which might provide a serious menace to the West Coast." The Mare Island commandant personally called the 12th and 13th Naval District commandants to brief them on this surprising submarine type.

The information gathered from on board *I-24tou* didn't help Rochefort's radio-traffic unit track submarines still in the Hawaiian

Continued on Page 290

I-24tou is taken apart at the Pearl Harbor submarine base.

ADVANCE FORCE — PEARL HARBOR

Mangled torpedo guards on the bow of I-24tou at Pearl Harbor; the plaque has already disappeared.

A battery vent on top of the forward fuselage. At right, close-ups of the top of the sail, showing the hatch and housings for the radio antenna and periscope. The Navy has added draft markings.

IMAGES
OF A
SECRET
WEAPON

Dozens of pictures of the midget submarine were taken by Navy Intelligence and remained classified during the war. Here, three sailors provide scale as they pretend to inspect damage on the sail caused by towing the submarine ashore. The hull and periscope have by this point already been scraped and primed with fresh paint.

MYSTERY SUBMARINE

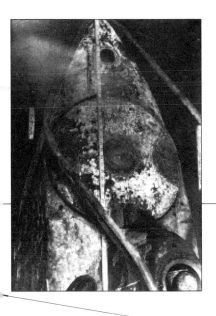

The light housing on the sail was blanked off.

An American officer shows off the small scale of the Ha-boat. On the original print, dozens of grafitti can be made out on the hull.

Sakamaki's damaged prop at Pearl Harbor. This was removed.

ADVANCE FORCE — PEARL HARBOR

The submarine's reduction gear and screws.
Behind them is the tail section in the process
of being repainted.

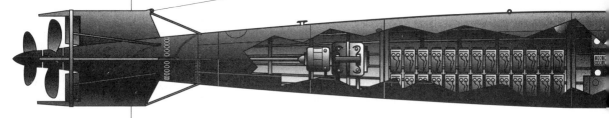

Looking forward into
the bow section of
I-24tou *reveals
torpedo tubes, air
flasks for charging
and various type of
plumbing. Note the
bolt holes in the rim
for mounting the
sections of midget
together — these
ribs were the
strongest structures
in the craft.*

MYSTERY SUBMARINE

A rack of batteries, removed from the submarine.

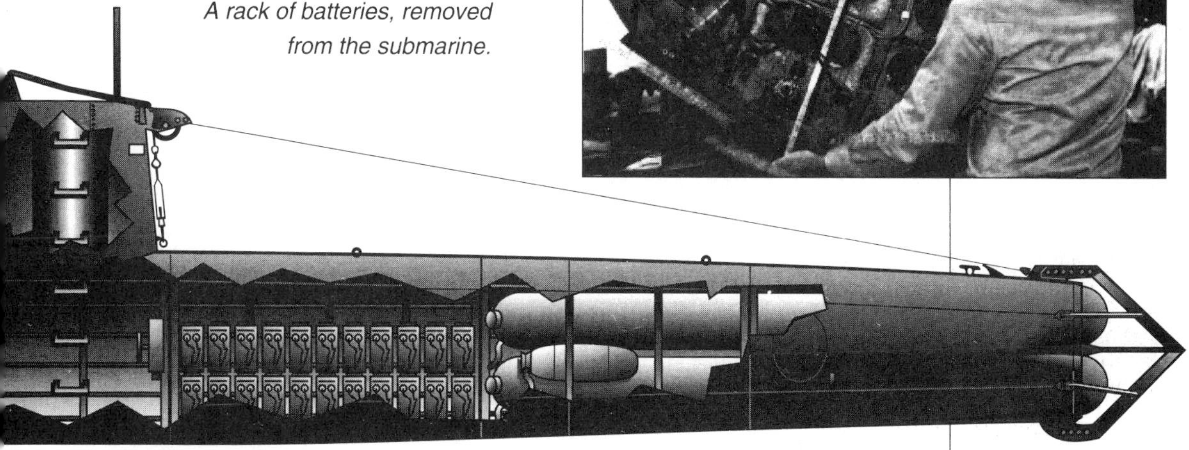

The aft end of the center section, above, shows how limited access was to the battery racks. Bolted to this section was the forward end of the tail section, left. The plywood bulkhead covers the engine and gearing compartment.

*Investigating the aft
battery compartment.
The plumbing at the
top houses the air
purification blowers.
The white and red
interior is obvious:
the white upper
works were intended
to provide additional
light from overhead
bulbs.*

frontier. He had solid information on the carriers and support ships of Kido Butai before the planes had fled back to their roosts. The large submarines did not show up in his radio plots until the evening of Dec. 7. Other than the sunken and captured midget submarines, there was no solid evidence that the Advance Force was even in Hawaii.

A Japanese radio broadcast on Dec. 12 admitted that five submarines were lost in the attack, but didn't say what type.

Rochefort's communications-intelligence summary for that day capitalized on the flurry of sightings around Hawaii — "It appears that practically all submarines are away from Empire waters, or that our estimates of Japanese submarine strength were lower than actual numbers." His outfit also picked up "four or five single bearings of submarines in the Oahu area."

Other bearings obtained from West Coast direction finders indicated Japanese submarines all over the North Pacific when triangulated with the Hawaii bearings. Tokyo broadcasts were powerful and all inclusive, not aimed in any direction, "an additional safeguard for widespread submarine units." The estimate from direction finders indicated that the number of submarines in the northwest Pacific, including Hawaii, was eight to 12.

Until the I-boats opened fire — and they were lying in wait for a carrier or a battleship — the Americans had no way of knowing if the Advance Force was still in Hawaii.

MYSTERY SUBMARINE

It didn't take much to rattle nerves. On Friday the 12th, the same day that Rochefort's analysis concluded that enemy submarines must still be around Pearl Harbor, and as the harbor settled into a routine of ship salvage and clean-up, Radioman First Class Aubrey E. Cox reported for duty. He was posted to the Magnetic Survey Group, one of the few sailors working at Fort Kamehameha, near the entrance of Pearl Harbor.

Cox's specialty was the Esterline-Angus Fluxmaster, which was, for its day, a wonder. It monitored slight variations in the Earth's magnetic field along a given track, like the entrance to Pearl Harbor through the anti-submarine nets. If a big ship went by, a needle made a big jump on a continuously feeding paper tape. The smaller the ship, the smaller the jiggle.

Cox was watching the tape just after 8 a.m. that day when a ship went by, and accordingly, marked its passage on the tape. Another ship followed, and did the same. But, halfway between the two tracings, was a smaller, but clearly identifiable, magnetic tracing.

He had seen nothing go by, at least on the surface. Cox called over a captain, who looked at the tape, and then looked out the window. He saw only two ships. He said not to worry about it, and walked away.

The same three sailors from page 286 pretend to inspect the repaired torpedo guards. The mangled guards and screws from I-24tou were replaced by undamaged parts from the midget submarine rammed by destroyer Monaghan — note the differences in texture. The most important part of I-24tou's career still lay in the future.

Cox, an expert at deciphering these tracings, was dumbfounded. He managed, through the enlisted men's grapevine, to get word to his commander, Lieutenant Commander Thales S. Boyd. Then, remembered Cox, "all hell broke loose!"

Cox and other Magnetic men were ordered to commandeer a whaleboat, making sure it was made out of wood. They wrapped coils of wire around it and attached a sensitive galvanometer to the center.

They dumped this jury-rigged floating magnetometer into the harbor and went midget hunting.

Despite several false signals from trash on the bottom, they found something large skulking near Pearl City. It scooted away and they gave chase.

At this point, other American ships suddenly went berserk, charging around the harbor and dropping depth charges. The target tried to hide several times, once under hospital ship *Solace*.

Solace moved out of the way, and that spot was bombed as well.

By 2 p.m. the target made a run for the open sea, where a Navy PBY dropped a killing brace of depth charges. Cox believed this last attack finished off the suspected midget, and they returned to duty.

Bloch ordered three of Pearl's PT boats loaded with depth charges and stationed behind the channel nets, specifically to watch for more midget sorties. They were moored at the old "Q" station at Fort Kamehameha, under the command of Boyd. The PT boats were empowered to attack any suspicious contact without reporting to shore first.

More sampans were commandeered, 25 in all, and fitted with machine guns and depth charges for inshore patrol — which now extended all the way around the island.

At 7:35 a.m. on Saturday, destroyer *Ward* reported a Japanese body floating two miles southwest of the channel entrance buoys, not far from where the PBY bombed the midget submarine contact the day before. Within a couple of hours, a PT boat had scooted out of the harbor and picked up the body. The next day, at almost the same time, another Japanese body was discovered in the same location.

This corpse, when pulled aboard *Ward*, was bloated after floating in the water. It was wearing tan overalls, green webbing and a leather helmet.

When flopped over on the deck, gun sight-setter Richard Phill saw that the face had been chewed off by scavengers. He was promptly sick.

"It was the only dead Japanese I saw the entire war," he said later.

The first official pictures released of the attack on Pearl Harbor were those of I-24tou on the beach at Bellows Field. The Los Angeles Herald Express featured it on the front page of the Dec. 16 edition, while the Los Angeles Examiner devoted a full page on the inside of the newspaper. Public interest was building.

LIFEBOAT

22

MEN AGAINST THE SEA

On Sunday morning, Dec. 7, the weather was heavy and Matson freighter *Lahaina* punched steadily through roiling swells. It was unpleasant. Third Mate Douglas McMurtry had just taken the watch.

With all the war talk going on, McMurtry halfway anticipated a course change en route. Still, he was startled when Captain Hans Matthiesen rushed onto the bridge.

McMurtry had never seen the skipper so excited. "Something terrible has happened!" blurted Matthiesen. "The Japs are attacking Pearl Harbor!"

"Pearl?" said McMurtry, stunned.

"Keep a good lookout. Look around," said Matthiesen. "We might be in the area where the Jap ships are."

"Never expected an attack on Hawaii. Submarines, though — we should watch for subs," said McMurtry. He peered through the bridge ports at the sea, gray and heaving. The wind was gusting, tearing swells into whitecaps, and the sky hung low, leaden and threatening. Anything could be out there.

Matthiesen returned a short time later. "Turn her around. We're going back to Hawaii," he said. "14th Naval says for all American ships to return to the nearest U.S. port. For us, that's Kauai."

"We're already five days out."

"Orders," said Matthiesen.

"Aye aye, sir."

As *Lahaina* doubled back, the ship's speed cranked up to 10 knots, Matthiesen got all hands not on watch busy repainting the ship. The freighter wore typical Matson colors; black hull, white topsides, beige stack with a blue Matson emblem. Third Assistant Engineer Mike Locke drew the duty of scraping up soot in the engine room, which was mixed with white paint to make a passable gray color. McMurtry, who wondered where the gray paint came from, reasoned it had been stored as part of a war plans contingency.

Matthiesen put a sack of raw potatoes in each lifeboat. The captain was nothing if not thorough, something the crew chalked up to his Teutonic background.

On the 9th of December, an airplane appeared. It looked like an amphibian, perhaps the kind carried on naval cruisers. It circled the ship, banked, then scooted by the stern, close enough to read the ship's name. It then flew off.

The aircraft that spotted *Lahaina* was not American, unless the pilot didn't report the sighting. It's possible that the aircraft was an ElYl "Glen" from a Japanese submarine.

To the east that day, the Advance Force zeroed in on its second civilian target after *Cynthia Olsen*. *I-10* under Yasuchika Kayahara intercepted and sank *Donerail*, a 4,473-ton freighter of Panamanian registry. [1] *Donerail's* crew of 43 escaped into boats, but were then machine gunned by *I-10*. Only 16 of the merchant seamen survived the fusillade. This bloody incident became the first of notorious atrocities by Japanese submarine crews.

On the 10th, *Lahaina* received an urgent radio message, broadcast in the clear: *Reverse course and proceed to continental U.S.* The message was not even in Matson's own code system, and some believed the message was faked. "We're only about 700 miles from Hawaii," the navigator pointed out.

Matthiesen wasn't sure the waters around Hawaii were any safer than those between them and the Mainland, so he decided to reverse course yet again and dash for the coast. Besides, it was a whole lot farther from Japan. Matthiesen was sure the airplane of the previous day had relayed their position and that the Navy had decided the safest course was east. He settled on San Francisco, their original destination.

That evening, somewhat indirectly, another civilian ship ran afoul of the Advance Force. Freighter *Mauna Ala*, bound Portland-to-Honolulu with a load of 60,000 Christmas trees, 10,000 turkeys, 3,000 chickens and crates of eggs, pears, apples and other Christmas cheer, had been ordered on Dec. 7 to return to Portland.

She reached the mouth of the Columbia River late on Dec. 10 and ran blindly into the blackout. The ship also had her radio direction finder turned off and the wireless disconnected for fear of giving a fix to Japanese submarines.

Attempting the bar crossing without lights, she ran aground at Clatsop Beach under the big gun batteries at Fort Stevens. The next day a Coast Guard cutter and two tugs tried mightily to pull the 6,256-ton *Mauna Ala* off the beach, but a growing ocean groundswell began to pound the ship, tearing away the rudder. Captain C. W. Saunders ordered the crew to escape as the ship tore herself open in the surf.

Beaches for miles were carpeted with Christmas trees and turkey carcasses. Soldiers poured onto the beach, pulling turkeys and chickens out of the water. "I've had chicken in the rough and chicken in the basket, but this is the first time I've ever had chicken in the surf," a soldier told the *Benton County Herald*.

The morale of the *Lahaina* crew seemed excellent. Matthiesen overheard a fair amount of bravado and reflected on the seasoned

[1] Some sources call this ship Donnyvale.

Matson freighter
SS Lahaina, *just*
prior to World War II.

stoicism of the professional seaman. "We'll just take whatever comes, Captain," said one.

The weather had been clearing, and by noon on the 11th, the seas were fairly calm and *Lahaina* was making good headway. McMurtry surrendered his watch to Second Mate Bernard Kuckens at noon and went below to sleep. Many of the other men began a leisurely lunch.

At 1 p.m., a black shape rose to the surface on *Lahaina's* starboard quarter, between them and the sun. The sunlight glared across the waves, hiding figures running onto the shape's deck, setting up a cannon.

"Submarine!" shouted *Lahaina's* lookout. "No markings — nationality unknown!"

The submarine was *I-9*, under Commander Akiyoshi Fujii. The submarine was one of four manning a picket line north of Hawaii, on the sidelines while the other Imperial Navy submarines prowled in the American waters south of Pearl. The Japanese captain couldn't believe his luck — a fat, slow freighter, far out of reach of help from Hawaii. *I-9* also carried one of the fold-up Glen reconnaissance aircraft, which might explain how Fujii located *Lahaina*. It's possible that the fly-by on Dec. 9 came from his submarine.

Fujii moved quickly to disable the target. *I-9* perfunctorily fired a shell across *Lahaina's* bow, then immediately fired a ranging shell that splashed the ship.

Matthiesen, assuming the submarine was acting under interna-

tional rules of war, ordered *Lahaina* stopped, and waited for orders from the submarine.

McMurtry, jarred awake, pulled on his uniform and raced for his emergency station, the No. 1 lifeboat on the starboard side. He threw his leg in and was hoisting himself up when a third shell exploded just below the wooden boat. He was tossed away; the boat splintered and buckled as shrapnel raked it. Engineer Locke, also near the boat, was blown back by the concussion, winding up on his back 15 feet away. He had been in his bunk reading when the attack started.

Matthiesen quickly pulled the freighter to port, shielding the other lifeboat. The next round blasted out the deckhouse and bridge, destroying the radio. *They know exactly what they're shooting at,* thought McMurtry, examining the lifeboat. It was a total loss. He scrambled to the other lifeboat. The hands were pulling on life preservers.

THE SUB QUICKLY OVERTOOK THE "LAHIANA".

WITH LITTLE EQUIPMENT TO COMBAT THE RAIDER, CAPTAIN MATHIESON MADE A SWIFT DECISION.

ALL HANDS STAND BY TO ABANDON SHIP 'I'M DESTROYING' OUR PAPERS!

The April, 1944, issue of True Comics *carried an illustrated version of* Lahaina's *ordeal. Despite some creative spelling, the account was reasonably accurate.*

"Take" Hirashima, *Lahaina's* lone Japanese-American sailor, stood on the deck, gaping at the submarine. "Get that boy out of sight!" bawled someone, and a couple of deckhands pulled Hirashima down, behind the railing. It seemed logical at the time.

Matthiesen found radio operator Leonard de Geus. "Did you get anything off?" he asked.

"Yes sir. S.O.S., our position, sub attack — repeated until the radio got hit," de Geus said.

"Have to do," said Matthiesen. The deck bounced beneath them as more rounds punched into *Lahaina's* hull. Smoke blanketed the men, fed by the blazing deckhouse. *Lahaina* was dead in the water.

"Abandon ship," said Matthiesen.

"Aye aye, sir," said McMurtry. Second Mate Kuckens ran up to the bridge and threw the chronometer and sextant into a waiting bulldog valise, zipped it up and tossed it to Matthiesen. Bag in hand, the captain trotted back into his quarters and grabbed a box of cigarettes.

LIFEBOAT

Men were already crowded into the remaining lifeboat and it dropped into the water. Matthiesen tossed the instrument bag and cigarettes down and shouted, "I'm going back to get the ship's papers!" As he straightened up, another shell ripped through his cabin, setting it afire.

Matthiesen shrugged, and climbed down into the lifeboat. The two seamen manning the falls jumped into the water, near the lifeboat, and were hauled aboard.

Lahaina's newly painted hull began to peel and bubble as she burned inside. The lifeboat pulled away from the stricken ship. A shell punched through the hull, demolishing the falls and landing about 50 yards from the lifeboat before exploding.

"Man alive!" exclaimed Matthiesen. "That could have been disaster if we'd been closer!"

The lifeboat stuck close to the shelter of the burning freighter. *I-9's* nose appeared around the edge of the ship, Japanese sailors on deck. "They're watching like hawks," remarked Matthiesen.

She's got a net cutter on her bow, thought McMurtry, numbly. *Never seen a U.S. sub with a net cutter.*

"Everybody down!" ordered Matthiesen. "Sit and be quiet. Don't make a move of any kind. The first guy who makes any kind of movement gets brained!" McMurtry and the other officers arranged themselves within braining distance of the huddled crew.

The submarine fired another shell, which geysered near the little boat. Another round burst against the ship's hull, ripping up the water around the lifeboat with shrapnel.

"They're after us, boys!" shouted Matthiesen. "Pull her around to the lee side!"

The crew rowed frantically, attempting to put *Lahaina's* burning bulk between them and the submarine. Another shell slammed into the freighter, near their heads. They could see the enemy sailors attempting to set up a machine gun, could hear shouting in Japanese.

"They want to kill us all," said one of the hands.

"Shut up and row," said another.

"They want to shoot us," seethed Matthiesen. "Dastards! It's the most cowardly thing I've ever witnessed in my life." Some of the men wondered what *dastard* meant.

The Americans could see the submarine had succeeded in hitting *Lahaina's* engine room, which was now rapidly filling with seawater.

After what seemed like hours, the lifeboat pulled into the pall of smoke on the other side of the freighter. Matthiesen told the men to watch out for the submarine, but nothing appeared. The only sounds were the groans of *Lahaina* as she burned.

SHIP IN DISTRESS?

Ever since the sinking of Lahaina, *some have believed that the ship's signals for help were ignored. Her S.O.S. was received at 1:10 p.m. by Coast Guard listeners in Honolulu and duly noted in the 14th Naval District watch log. At the moment, however, all attention in Honolulu was focused on a freighter that seemed to be sinking just south of Waikiki, which turned out to be a false alarm. The next day, Stark was notified by Kimmel of the attack on* Lahaina, *including the position report, in the daily summary of events. Nothing more, however, seems to have been done.*

"What's that? Listen," said Matthiesen. "They're yelling."

"What are they saying, Take?" said a sailor.

The Japanese-American cocked an ear. "They're cheering," he said, finally. The crew could hear faint shouts of *"Banzai, Banzai"* from the other side of the freighter.

They carefully pulled the boat forward, until she just peeked around *Lahaina's* bow. McMurtry could see the Japanese sailors going below, buttoning up the submarine. "The rats!" he exclaimed. "They're leaving, like a bunch of rats!"

The submarine disappeared to the northeast.

"They heard our distress call. They know we're alone out here!" McMurtry complained.

"Maybe they're worried that some of our Navy is in the area," said Matthiesen. "Maybe our boys heard the distress call too. In that case, we should hang around."

The encounter had taken only half an hour, and Matthiesen estimated 25 shells had been fired at *Lahaina.* He took stock of the situation. The 30-foot lifeboat was dangerously overcrowded, holding twice as many seamen as it was designed for. The boat's freeboard dipped low, close to the water — most of the men bailed continuously, just to keep her from swamping. The boat had only a case of hardtack and a single breaker, or small wooden keg, of water. Many of the men were wearing light clothing.

On the plus side, no one was injured and the boat's sailing rig was in good shape. Seas were smooth, with no wind.

They circled the burning freighter as she threw a column of dense black smoke straight up in the still afternoon. Anybody in the area would see it from miles away. As night came, the ship glowed and sputtered like burning coals, occasionally booming hollowly and sprouting bright flame, as high as 100 feet. It was a beacon in the black night. As if hypnotized, the men threw out a sea anchor, bailed and talked very little. At one point, something aboard *Lahaina* exploded. They assumed it was the fuel oil tanks.

The next morning, *Lahaina* still rode the surface and the smoke had died down. The engineer's house appeared unburnt and the ladder was intact. Matthiesen decided to take Chief Engineer Frank Laumeister — a hard-drinking type with a well-hidden distrust of school-educated officers — and radio operator de Geus to reboard her, to see if anything could be done. Laumeister refused, and First Assistant Engineer Ken Madison and Third Assistant Engineer Locke went instead.

They scrambled up the sooty sides and went below. Matthiesen and the engineers weren't surprised to find water standing 16 feet deep over the main engine. A shell hole three feet across was hemorrhaging water into the hold, and the main condenser was smashed.

There was no hope of pumping her. The ship's back was broken and she was flooding inexorably. A careful examination of the No. 1 lifeboat confirmed McMurtry's instant diagnosis of the previous day.

LIFEBOAT

The five-gallon breaker of water aboard the shattered lifeboat was intact, however.

The boarding party lined up at the water fountain near the officers' quarters and drank their fill.

Matthiesen scoured the ship looking for provisions. A case of eggs was carefully carried up the sloping deck, as were quarter-cases of lemons and apples, five loaves of bread, 25 pounds of carrots, a pound of butter and a case of biscuits. *Lahaina* had begun to settle in the water, leaning precariously to port, and the food was handed to the waiting lifeboat. The case of eggs proved unwieldy, but Matthiesen insisted that it be brought off.

The midship house exploded in ribbons of flame and chased them off the ship.

They rowed in place, reasoning the smoke still made a good beacon. Lunch was served, a half-cup of water and a choice of an apple or carrot. There were no complaints.

An hour later, *Lahaina* shifted in the water. A deep explosion bulged out the plates on her flanks. She suddenly rolled, hull glistening blackly in the sunlight as seawater coursed over the rough surface. The men unconsciously took off their caps as the ocean began to chew up the ship. Debris and trapped air boiled to the surface.

"Goodbye, old friend," said Matthiesen.

The men watched as the ship vanished beneath them. The ocean seemed very quiet.

"Where's the damn Navy?" Laumeister complained.

"Why did this happen to us?" said some others.

"They probably can't spare anybody," said Matthiesen. "We're not important enough."

"Hell, nobody asked me," said McMurtry, and some of the men laughed. He figured if they were complaining, they were doing all right. For sailors, complaining was like breathing. Only Hillard Moore, a cook, a big, brooding man, was quiet.

"With all the fuss on Oahu right now, we'd better go to Maui," said Matthiesen. "It's only about, oh, 700 miles. Lay to, boys."

The hands began to bail the low-riding lifeboat and rowing watches were set. The sail could not be rigged in the windless water. The men pulled away enthusiastically, glad the waiting was over. Imperceptibly, the lifeboat began moving south.

As the sun touched the horizon, a single raw egg and a half-cup of water was served to each hand. In the darkness, the men rowed silently, pulling for the south. At 10 p.m., the sound of an airplane passing over made them pause. Matthiesen fired a Very pistol, the flare arching futilely into the sky.

Breakfast the next morning was another raw egg, with a slice of bread and butter, and a half cup of tepid water. Soon, a soft breeze arose and the sail was raised. The men shipped oars and rubbed their aching fingers.

Lunch was skipped, and supper that evening was a biscuit and a

half cup of water. A light overcast had set in and the boat darted through the waves, light spray misting over the gunnels.

In the evening, Moore suddenly jumped to his feet. "Hear me, Lord!" he screamed.

McMurtry's head jerked around. *Oh no,* he thought.

"Save me!" shrieked Moore. He danced and waved his arms at the sky. "Take me from this evil man! Protect me, Lord!" The lifeboat rocked as Moore began to thrash wildly.

"He's out of his head," said Matthiesen. "Secure him — *now!*"

A seaman attempted to grab Moore, but the cook struck him down. Water splashed over the gunnels. "That evil man will kill us all!" he shouted, pointing at the captain.

"Take him down!" snapped Matthiesen.

Engineer Madison, who had been a Golden Gloves contender in his native Portland, gave Moore a vicious roundhouse punch. Moore blinked at him and pulled a small knife from his back pocket, with which he tried to stab Matthiesen. Madison picked up a broken piece of ash oar stock and slammed it hard into Moore's forehead, a skull-crushing blow that merely stunned the cook. Moore fell to his knees, and other sailors grabbed him.

"We've gotta do something for him, Captain," said a seaman.

"The evil man will take us all to hell with him," mumbled Moore.

Matthiesen detailed a couple of men to watch over Moore and tie him up, and as the lifeboat sailed through the night, the cook calmed down. By morning, Sunday, Dec. 14, Moore apologized and sat sullenly in his lashings. He seemed confused, although he accepted the breakfast of an egg, biscuit and water.

The weather was cloudy, with trade winds reversing their direction and pulling the boat to the northwest. Dinner that evening was four ounces of raw potato. The ocean began to swell and cold water splashed aboard through the night.

The next three days went by in a routine of constant sailing, bailing and rowing. Mates Kuckens and McMurtry took horizon sightings by standing on each others' shoulders and clinging to the mast, setting height of eye. They had a sextant, chronometer, compass and a book of charts. Depending on the vagaries of the trade winds and guesstimates of speed, the officers figured they'd make the islands in 10 days.

Kuckens revealed a bitter, hostile streak. Much of his venom was directed at Hirashima. To Kuckens, the Asian sailor began to look more Japanese and less American after several days at sea. At one point, Hirashima was attempting to get a compass reading as the boat pitched mercilessly, and Kuckens castigated him relentlessly.

Hirashima finally threw the compass at Kuckens. "Screw you, you asshole!" shouted Hirashima. "If you can do a better job, goddammit, then do it!"

Matthiesen had had enough. "If any of you guys gives Take a hard time 'cause he's Japanese, I'll blast you. Got that?"

Among some of the men, resentment shifted from Hirashima to Matthiesen. Tempers flared under the wet, miserable conditions. The skimpy meals didn't help. Fresh water was limited to two ounces a day per man.

Moore occasionally raved. He remained lashed in the bottom of the boat, where his thrashings would not upset the craft's delicate balance.

The seas grew steadily rougher, and the crew steadily more irritable. All hands were cold and wet, their joints aching from the constant strain of bracing themselves against the ship and against each other. Matthiesen cautioned them against too much talking, at one point ordering complete silence. If an airplane flew over, they'd want to hear it.

The sun beat down on them, and salt water softened their hands and feet, causing skin to slough off in red, peeling strips. The average temperature of the ocean was 60 degrees, and despite the fierce sun, the men shivered. McMurtry was glad he'd worn his officer's uniform. They learned to sleep with eyes open, backs braced against gunnels and feet wedged in the bilge.

Violent waves sometimes shocked them awake again, but that was better than lying down in the sloshing bilge. "You never know how heavy a man's head is until he tries to use you as a pillow," said Matthiesen.

An Imperial Navy propaganda painting celebrates the sinking of a merchant ship by I-boat gunfire. The accent is on the beauty of the sea and sky rather than the submarine hurtling death into the distance.

De Geus got the feeling that any time he couldn't stand it any more, he'd just go below and get a cup of coffee. *Yes, that's it.* He leaned against the rail and looked out over the ocean, watching skyscrapers, islands and bridges pass by. *Why aren't we stopping?* he cried out, and shakily realized he'd been dreaming or hallucinating — with his eyes open.

The quiet desperation that settled on the crew set Moore off again, and it required eight men to truss up the cook. Moore claimed the "evil captain" was hoarding beer in his pockets.

Thirst began to take a toll. Some of the men pulled off coat buttons to suck on, Locke selecting one about the size of a quarter. Fred Schuster, an oiler, and Cliff Lanigan, a fireman, began gulping seawater, and as the salt water burned in their throats, began to push the others away and scream. Lanigan waved around a pocket knife. Matthiesen ordered the other hands to tie them up. Gradually, Schuster and Lanigan were calmed, and they sat dully and stared at Moore, who wriggled at their feet.

"I'm going to catch a bus and go home," Moore informed them.

Dinner was a rubbery carrot and half a lemon. The lifeboat waddled south under steel-wool skies that made the gloomy weather fade darkly into night.

A large shark was spotted in their wake, shadowing the boat. Among the old salts, it was an ominous sign.

The seas grew heavy in the evening and the wind began to shriek. Moore screamed along with the wind. Night clamped down on the ocean and the little boat raced through the black waves, driven before the wind. Nothing could be seen. The men worked furiously, keeping the boat bailed, riding the edge of disaster. They used hands, hats, whatever they could find to throw out the ocean, grateful the boat had steel flotation tanks built in.

By morning, the storm began to dissipate. Light filtered across the sea, revealing haggard men. "We made a hell of a lot of speed last night," said McMurtry.

The dawn position sighting indicated they'd traveled 150 miles in the last 24 hours.

"My God," said someone.

"What's the matter?" said Matthiesen.

"It's Moore. He's dead."

The cook lay lifeless on the lifeboat's bottom, still tightly tied up. His face looked peaceful for the first time in days. Matthiesen dropped the rudder and scrambled forward, confirming for himself Moore's death.

"What happened? Did anyone see it happen?" he asked. "Did Moore drown? Did he have a seizure?"

"Skipper, we didn't see it," said a sailor miserably. "We couldn't see anything last night."

The men were gloom-struck, yet somewhat relieved. Moore had been a danger to them all.

LIFEBOAT

Matthiesen felt it best not to dwell on Moore's death. "We'll have to commit him to the deep," he said.

The men untied Moore, handling him gently. They looked for something to weight the body down — Matthiesen was afraid the body would float on the surface and haunt them. But there was nothing they could spare. The dead man's bindings were removed.

"Let's have a moment of silence," Matthiesen said. The sailors bowed their heads, each committed to his own thoughts. After a long moment, the captain nodded and two sailors lowered Moore over the side. McMurtry glanced at his watch. At precisely 7:30 a.m., Dec. 19, the cook slid into the water and vanished, swallowed up by the blue. McMurtry was shocked by how quickly it happened. *It was as if Moore never existed.*

"Come on, boys," said Matthiesen, quietly. "Let's get away from this place."

It was an unwritten rule of survival — no man on board was given more consideration than another. Moore could not have been ministered to. Still, his death sobered the crew.

Matthiesen decided to serve a large breakfast to the crew; an egg, a biscuit and a cup of water for each man. The two who had been tied up the day before were rational by this point and were released.

As the morning wore on, Herman Freedman, a sickly crewman, moaned and collapsed. He was dying, most of the crew realized. He had been ill on the ship, so much so that the other seaman wondered what he was doing at sea. He was continually taking medication.

The weather alternated between squalls and mountainous seas. Dinner was a biscuit and half a lemon — the last of the lemons — and a half cup of water. As on the previous evening, the skies blackened and the water churned. The boat skated before the wind, into the night, as if it were sliding downhill into a endless, velvet tunnel. Waves broke continually over the shuddering gunnels and the men bailed frantically.

McMurtry wondered if they'd make it through the night.

23

BOUND BY HONOR

A Cipher to His Captors

Intelligence Officer Edwin Layton's impression of prisoner of war Kazuo Sakamaki in the days following the Pearl Harbor attack wasn't favorable. The Japanese was delusional and self-abasing, to the point where he had to be watched almost constantly.

Sakamaki's explanation for his capture was that he was "sneaking up on a capital ship and opened the hatch in order to navigate — whereupon water came into the hatch and swamped the motor ..."

So far as Sakamaki knew, the "attack was a disappointment; they had expected (to deliver) a paralyzing blow" to the U.S. Fleet.

Layton noted that Sakamaki "appreciated the treatment afforded him by the Naval questioners to that of the Army." With precisely applied mental milking, said Layton, "further information *might* be derived from this officer."

The American guards continued to harass Sakamaki, turning bright lights on unexpectedly, tossing mess kits clattering to the floor while the prisoner slept, and purposefully keeping Japanese food for themselves. When he found out, Lieutenant Colonel Kendall H. Fielder brought a swift halt to this hazing. "He's an officer of the Imperial Japanese Navy and will be treated as an honorable prisoner of war," he lectured.

The prisoner was moved to Sand Island, on the ocean side of Honolulu Harbor. A former smallpox quarantine station, the Sand Island detention center held "enemy aliens," mostly Japanese. It was run by Captain Carl Eifler, an imposing man who had been a policeman in California and a customs inspector on the Mexican border. Considered tough but fair, Eifler originally feared he'd also be interned because of his German ancestry.

Captain Carl Eifler

Sakamaki was not allowed to speak to the Hawaii internees, and was housed separately, in a wire enclosure called "the bird cage" by other prisoners. They could see him walking around and around the small yard for exercise, his eyes focused on some inner horizon.

Security around the camp was the responsibility of 2nd Lieutenant Dave Dingeman, who until the Pearl Harbor attack had been enrolled at the University of Hawaii. "I was the 'outside man' at Sand

Island," he recalled. Pulled out of school, Dingeman immediately began to wrestle with interpreting the Geneva Convention's codes for prisoner-of-war housing. "That's why the prisoner rated his own building, separate from the internees," said Dingeman. "Considering how fast we put it up, Sakamaki's quarters were actually a pretty nice little hoochie."

The prisoner's main contact with the world was through Sergeant Launcelot Moran, the "inside man," a gangly fellow who towered over his charge. Moran had taken a shine to the "enemy alien" internees on Sand Island and often spent his own money to bring them small presents.

The lone POW was allowed one cigarette a day. Learning that his picture was to be taken soon, Sakamaki lit the cigarette and pressed the burning tip against his cheeks, just below his eyes, branding neat, charred triangles in his skin. In this way Sakamaki proclaimed to the world his disgrace.

When the picture was taken, the prisoner grinned wildly, triumphantly. He looked crazed.

The burn scars around his eyes were routinely noted in his physical description. The POW form was a lash-up from Immigration, with "Interned Enemy Alien" crossed out and "Prisoner of War" typed in. Because it wasn't legal, the form was tossed out and a new one filled in. [1]

When the internees saw the burned pits on Sakamaki's face, they were scandalized. They assumed Sakamaki had been tortured by his guards. Moran, offended, told them to look closely at the marks — the prisoner had inflicted them on himself.

Once again abiding by the Geneva Convention, Dingeman was obliged to set up an investigation into Sakamaki's self-mutilation. "It was a kind of forlorn hope that we'd understand why he did it," said Dingeman. "What we were really trying to decide was whether to allow him more cigarettes." They settled on allowing Sakamaki to smoke while under observation.

Dingeman had little contact after that with Sakamaki, and would

Sakamaki's improperly filled-out POW form. This is the only official record of his prisoner of war years.

[1] *The alien property officer, a civilian lawyer from Honolulu, fished the improper form out of the wastebasket, figuring it might have historical value. In the late 1970s, it was given away by the U.S. Army Museum in Hawaii and wound up at a Pacific War museum in Texas.*

see the prisoner exercising madly, trying to work something out of his system. "It was no good trying to talk to him. The only thing I remember him saying was that he was an officer, and expected to be served by an orderly," said Dingeman.

The days on Sand Island were a daze. Sakamaki recalls only attempting suicide and failing. "I cannot write anything intelligible about those days. My life was completely shattered. I was not myself," he wrote in a postwar memoir, "I Attacked Pearl Harbor."

Layton tried vainly to question the surly prisoner, and reported only that, "In accordance with the samurai code, the prisoner requested that he only be allowed to commit suicide."

Control of Sakamaki's destiny had passed into American hands, and they didn't realize the significance of their role. Suicide to a Japanese soldier was a ritual of atonement, not a simple self-killing. Psychologically, Sakamaki needed their permission to end his life.

When asked why he simply hadn't run away from his rescuers Akui and Plybon, forcing the solders to shoot him, Sakamaki muttered excuses about rejoining the Japanese Navy. In reality, getting shot in the back on a deserted beach wasn't the Japanese ensign's idea of a noble death. Killing himself, while his white American captors watched, was.

In the meantime, he was theirs to command. This psychological scenario repeated itself with dozens of Japanese prisoners in the war.

Eager to please Fielder, and anxious to put his own feelings in order, Sakamaki began writing a letter on Dec. 14 to the intelligence officer. It gives an insight into Sakamaki's disordered mind during this period:

"I thank you for your kindly visit of yesterday. Now I will write down your requests of yesterday in Japanese. Please pardon my poor writing and composition.

"1. BRIEF PERSONAL HISTORY

"In August 1940 I was graduated from the Naval Academy and became a midshipman. In April of this year I was commissioned at sub-lieutenant in the navy, my present rank.

"2. RECORD OF BATTLE

"Your honorable 'have' country instituted an economic blockade of Japan, a 'have-not' country, refusing to sell us oil, cotton and the like, until we had no choice but natural collapse. Because of this we began diplomatic negotiations with your country, but these ended in failure. Therefore, with a friend, I set out for Pearl Harbor with the purpose of sinking a battleship, but due to an accident, although we were able to reach the mouth of the harbor by creeping underneath your bombs falling like rain, since the accident was fatal to the submarine, we determined to proceed without hesitation to the surface of the water, and dashing into the harbor, and climbing the gangway ladder, hoped to leap onto the deck and die simultaneously with blowing up the enemy warship just as in olden times, during the Mongol Invasion, our Tsuyo Kawano lowered the mast and boarded

306

the enemy ship with it. However, because of our accident suffered at the harbor mouth, we struck a reef which given ten seconds we would have safely cleared. With the difference of ten seconds the fate was decided and one of the warships of your country was saved.

"Seeing the success of our sister submarines and the splendid achievements of our air force, I left the mouth of the harbor, compelled to do so due to my submarine being disabled. Later, finally being unable to do anything with the submarine, I swam through the ocean and reached an enemy airport. Due to my exhaustion, I was captured without having time to even fight. And thus my sad fate began.

"Due entirely to my inexpert navigation and strategy, my honor as a soldier has fallen to the ground. Thus I betrayed the expectations of our 100,000,000 (people) and became a sad prisoner of war disloyal to my country.

"3. The talk I had with an understanding naval officer in the home of an army man in 'Honolulu' was very pleasant. Because I thought about the trouble I would cause your country later on, and because I was unable to endure my shame, committing suicide or being shot to death became impossible, and thus began my sad life as a prisoner of war. Now that things have come to such a pass, I have started the life of a peaceful Japanese naval officer abiding by the rules of international law.

"In olden times, Hakui and Shukusei of China, refusing to eat millet of a foreign land, went into the mountains and ate grass until they starved, but I, since I began eating your country's bread, have thought what a cause for the shame and sorrow it is.

"Although I have caused you much annoyance, I have done things right along according to righteousness. However, such incidents as that which happened yesterday which is from the standpoint of your country a sad thing which has continued. My righteousness made scores of men of your country withdraw all day long, with their guns pointed at me and made them afraid, but as a result of this, I must face a death which to me is not too 'pleasing.'

"My willingness to die need not be mentioned; to be killed by one of your bullets of your country shall make me very happy. I pray for your country's lasting military success.

"An uprighteous pistol has been aimed at me. This is my end. Good-by.

"4. To the Japanese people, especially to officers like ourselves, becoming a prisoner of war is inexcusable. Of course, whether or not there is a record of the incident or not, I will commit suicide upon my return to my native land. Even though we are unarmed, to bite with teeth and fight to the last is the Japanese spirit.

"I pray that my death will forgive me for all my failures and I pray that my spirit will be enshrined at the Yasakuni (Shrine)."

Sakamaki then wrote an equally confused "Last Will and Testament," which he requested be forwarded to the Imperial Navy:

The internee and POW camp at Honouliuli near Pearl City, later in the war. Prisoners show their defiance by wearing underclothes rather than prison uniforms.

"Although I planned into the mouth of the harbor, and sit and struck terror into the hearts of the people of the (undecipherable), I arrived at a situation where I could do nothing. For this I have no excuse to state. I do not desire to grasp this opportunity to become a prisoner of war. I am about to die after fighting for righteousness until the very end as an officer of the Japanese Navy.

"Long live His Imperial Majesty!

"POEM COMPOSED AMONG THE ENEMY (ON THE UN-FORTUNATE DAY THAT I BECAME A PRISONER OF WAR)

When cherry blossoms fall,
Let them fall!
Wet are its branches and leaves
With the sorrow of today!

"5. I like best 'DOWN THE TORPEDO' and 'AMONG THE SHOTS THROUGH THE MARGARET.' I experienced all these things in this current battle which is the goal of all naval men's ambition, and I manifested the *Yamato Damashii* (Japanese spirit). Last night, again scores of bayonets and muzzles were pointed at me from the front door and from the window and from above my head. However, righteousness won. And although as a result of this regrettable situation has come about, I hope all will be forgiven with my death. On the eve of my 'fairly death' lamenting the many sacrifices of your country due to my 'call of righteousness,' I earnestly hope

BOUND BY HONOR

that this will be clearly understood, that supreme desire and joy in dying as a soldier by your country's bullets.

"I appreciate your many kindness shown me up to now, and I pray for your success in the war.

"Respectfully,

"Kazuo Sakamaki"

Fielder's reaction to this epistle is not recorded.

On Feb. 17, 1942, the internees were rousted out of bed, including Sakamaki. Of the group, 172 were told to collect their things and report to the barge that would take them to the Immigration Station on the other side of Honolulu Harbor.

The internees assumed that they were being released. Instead, they were photographed and fingerprinted, and given numbers. Sakamaki's was Number #1. The processing took most of the day.

The next morning, the stunned internees were told they were being sent to the Mainland.

On Feb. 20, the prisoners were driven to the embarkation pier in Army trucks, guarded by MPs with shotguns. Three armored cars with anti-aircraft guns bracketed the procession.

Sakamaki was placed on board *U.S. Grant*, part of an eight-ship convoy that included *Lurline* and two destroyer shepherds. Many of the internees were shipped on another transport that also held German spy Otto Kuehn.

As Sakamaki paused on the top of the gangway onto *U.S. Grant*, he tried to salute the quarterdeck. Guard George E. Fisher became outraged and knocked the prisoner sprawling onto the deck. Other guards grabbed Sakamaki's arms and dragged him into his cabin, and locked the door.

The convoy arrived in San Francisco on March 1, 1942. An FBI report noted that the ships contained *196 enemy alien internees (172 Japanese), 2 native citizen internees (Hawaiian-born Japanese), and prisoner of war Kazuo Sakamaki. Sakamaki was transported to San Francisco in an officer's stateroom and received excellent treatment, however, Sakamaki refused to answer any questions and would not submit to a medical examination. In contrast, the other internees were very cooperative in carrying out their orders. The internees and Sakamaki were temporarily held at Fort McDowell on Angel Island in the San Francisco Bay, and later sent by train to a concentration camp in the state of Wisconsin.*

To the internees, the camp on Angel Island seemed like heaven compared to the dank, dangerous passage. On March 6, Sakamaki and the others were sent to Camp McCoy, Wisconsin, deep in the heart of America.

24 SHOOTING AT ISLANDS

A DEADLY GAME OF HIT AND RUN

Immediately following the attack on Pearl Harbor — which tied up most of the Imperial Navy's newest I-boats — third-string submarines *RO-13*, *RO-64* and *RO-68* used their 8cm guns to shoot up "enemy flying-boat installations" on Howland and Baker islands near the equator, south of Hawaii.

What they actually shot at were shacks manned by Hawaiian teenagers, there because of a bizarre territorial dispute which had erupted six years before. The shellings instituted a new phase of the Advance Force's mission.

Pan American Airlines had plans to pioneer air travel across the Pacific, and in 1935 came to an understanding with the U.S. government. It would establish refueling bases on remote atolls for its short-legged flying boats with help from the U.S. Navy. The Navy agreed. It gave them an excuse to establish hegemony over far-flung areas of the Pacific, a concept essential for countering suspected Japanese buildups in the mandated islands.

Bill Miller, director of the Bureau of Air Commerce—a single desk within the Department of the Interior—came up with the idea of colonizing uninhabited atolls known as the Equatorial Line Islands, sun-blasted guano heaps called Jarvis, Baker and Howland. The islands had been claimed by the United States according to the Guano Act of 1856, and had been steadily mined of bird droppings for 20 years. The phosphates gleaned from the droppings were turned into explosives. Americans abandoned the islands in 1877, and the British briefly inhabited them before they, too, left them to the sea birds.

By the 1930s both countries were competing for air routes, and the Equatorials, almost halfway between America and Australia, were once again tempting. In Hawaii, Miller sprang the colonization idea on Albert Judd, a trustee of Bishop Estate, a vast land-holding trust in Hawaii. Judd suggested that boys from Kamehameha Schools would be ideal candidates for settlers. Kamehameha Schools, not coincidentally, is an institution for native Hawaiians managed by Bishop Estate.

The Hawaiian background of these boys made them excellent

pioneer material, according to Judd. He pointed out that they were used to hot weather and to living off the sea, and were disciplined by years at a private school in which ROTC was a requirement. Miller was sold, and the operation began in 1935.

England got wind of the developing plan and sent her own settlers to the islands, using New Zealand as a stand-in. Lieutenant Harold A. Meyer of the 19th Infantry, who advised Miller on military aspects of the settlement, made the extraordinary step of telephoning Washington directly from Schofield Barracks. In a two-hour call, Meyer begged for swift action.

Meyer was placed in charge. Within the day, March 20, 1935, the Coast Guard cutter *Itasca* was outfitted with supplies and Hawaiian settlers, and raced off for the Equatorials. Lieutenant Commander Frank Kenner, skipper of *Itasca*, later recalled that the little cutter never made better speed.

Coast Guard 250-foot cutter Itasca *during the 1930s. This ship became famous in 1937 as Amelia Earhart's last radio contact.*

The Hawaiians had no clue as to their destination, nor did the dozen or so soldiers who accompanied them. They had been told simply that it was a security matter. Despite a scare when the ship spotted another vessel, and a brief stop at Palmyra atoll to dig up some palm trees for transplanting, the Hawaiians and the soldiers managed to raise the American flag first on the contested atolls.

Every six months or so thereafter, depending on the availability of *Itasca*, four boys were deposited on each of the three islands. By the time of the Pearl Harbor attack, some 135 had participated in the settlement.

"When we were invited to participate, there was a rush of applicants," recalled Abraham Piianaia, one of the first recruited. "They only wanted graduates, and for boys right out of high school, at the height of the Depression, the $3 a day they paid was good money." It was more than the soldiers made, who were rotated off the islands after a few months, leaving the boys alone.

At first the Hawaiians lived in pup tents, eventually graduating to wooden shacks dubbed "Government Houses," which were open on

On the beach at Jarvis Island, a group of Hawaiian students wave goodbye to the supply ship. For the next six months or longer, the teenagers were on their own.

the sides to let the cool night breeze blow through. All fresh water had to be brought to the islands. The 50-gallon water drums were too heavy to boat to the shore, so each was dumped over the side of the supply ship and allowed to drift ashore. If the drums landed on the wrong side of the island, the boys walked across the island to get a drink. Whenever it rained, open containers on the island were set out.

Jarvis Island, nearly 1,000 miles east of Baker and Howland, had a ghost town still standing, testimony to American and British guano miners of the previous century. A 25-foot-high sign still read "The Pacific Phosphate Company of London and Melbourne." On the beach was the wreck of the barkentine *Amaranth*, which provided lumber for furniture, shacks and surfboards.

The settlers' main tasks were logging hourly weather reports, clearing land for a runway and servicing a small lighthouse. They also collected wildlife samples for the Bishop Museum of Honolulu. Otherwise, it was very much a Robinson Crusoe existence on the islands, which rose barely a dozen feet from the sea. Responsibility for the project was transferred to the Department of the Interior. Meyer's involvement was remembered in a billboard-sized sign, which declared Baker's few buildings to be the town of "Meyerton."

In the opening days of 1937, Howland Island was suddenly taken over by Navy engineers who put in a short airstrip. The runway was built in anticipation of Amelia Earhart's planned 'round-the-world flight. When Earhart cracked up her Lockheed on the runway at Luke Field in Pearl Harbor, while taking off for Howland, the flight was rescheduled for the summer.

Shooting At Islands

Earhart next tried to fly around the world in the opposite direction. On the leg between Lae and Howland, her aircraft disappeared, the last radio signals being picked up by *Itasca*, which had paused along her route to give bearings. Earhart and her aircraft vanished despite a massive Navy search. A shower and private bedroom the Hawaiians had built expressly for Earhart went unused. They grieved for her, and built a 20-foot sandstone monument which they called the Amelia Earhart Lighthouse.

Things were quiet for the next few years, marred only by the death of a colonist in 1938 of peritonitis brought on by appendicitis. Coast Guard cutter *Taney* traveled 1,310 miles at full speed to save the boy, but arrived too late.

Canton and Enderbury islands were added to the program the same year, and were the subject of an exchange of notes between the United States and Great Britain in 1939, the upshot being an agreement to joint administration for at least 50 years, after which the agreement could be extended indefinitely. Each government was to be represented by an official, and the islands were to be available for communications and airports for international aviation — but only of American or British-empire airlines.

Similar circumstances prevailed at Christmas Island, under administration of British High Commissioner of the Pacific, headquartered in Suva. America claimed a seaplane base there, as both countries claimed sovereignty based on occupancy. Britain, however, controlled the island from the end of World War I to 1941. Johnston Island, actually a string of islets that were technically part of the Hawaiian Sea Frontier, was under sole jurisdiction of the United States. All the islands were prized solely for their location.

The Kamehameha students serviced the islands' meager facilities, and spent the rest of their days fishing and working on their tans. "Lobster every day, which we ate raw," said Piianaia. "And the island had these big rats, which ate the pili grass. Vegetarians. We used to catch them and roast them for red meat. They were delicious!

Itasca *approaches Baker Island. The small size of the atoll is apparent.*

"We were paid our salary in a lump sum when we went back to Honolulu, and it was quite a bit of money. We let our hair and beards grow long, it made us feel like explorers. But as soon as we went home, we hit the barber shop."

At night, the bowl of universe blazed above the isolated atolls. Falling stars were so bright they'd cast a shadow. One night, the waters roiled with hundreds of porpoises, a pod that seemed to stretch to the horizon. Some evenings were reserved for ghost stories, punctuated by the sound of birds crying eerily in the night.

Given driftwood, a crab net and a softball, basketball could be played on Baker Island.

There was magic there. Piianaia went back for a second tour, and one morning smelled something in the wind.

"What is that?" he said, and the boys stood around sniffing. "Smells like teriyaki!" joked one, but to Piianaia it did smell like Japanese cooking. Soon they saw a gray warship pull up alongside the island — Piianaia describes it as looking like a cross between a destroyer and a freighter, probably a seaplane tender — with the flag of Japan on her stern. The ship put over a launch, which began pulling for shore. The boys decided that the ship couldn't see the Government House too well, so they ran up a pole with a large American flag on it. Immediately, the launch turned around and went back to the ship, and the Imperial Navy hastily departed the Equatorials.

The Japanese didn't forget about the strategic islands. In December 1941, the boys on Baker were Walter Burke, Blue Makua, James Coyle and James Pease. On Howland, the colonists were Richard Whaley, Joe Keliihahanui, Thomas Bederman and Elvin Matson. By then, too far out of flying routes, Jarvis was deserted.

On the morning of the 8th, Burke went outside to raise the American flag and saw the RO-boat just offshore, ungainly in the water. The submarine fired a round and ripped off the top of the Government House. Burke dashed inside and told the dazed colonists that they'd "better skeedaddle out of there." The four ran across the island in record time, and sought shelter by digging foxholes. Burke ordered the others to disperse across the island, so that a lucky shell wouldn't get them all. The RO-boat walked shells across the island, methodically demolishing the building and other facilities, including the Earhart light station.

That night, the boys went back to survey the wreckage. Pieces of tin were scattered from the Government House roof, which they used as sunshades the next day. At noon, a four-engined H6K "Mavis" flying boat passed over the island, and let go a salvo of bombs.

The boys piled brush atop their foxholes for camouflage. The bomber came back nearly every day from its base in the Marianas or Marshalls, gutting the atoll with high explosive. Not much of the food was saved, and rats got into the rest, but there was a little coffee, and

SHOOTING AT ISLANDS

palolo leaves to chew on, and the ocean provided fish and squid. The flag which never got raised on the morning of Dec. 8 was wrapped in a gunny sack and buried, marked by a cairn of stones.

The boys settled in to wait, cut off from the rest of the world. Christmas dinner was lobster under a full moon and carols into the dawn. They kept a low profile, going to ground whenever a Japanese submarine or destroyer came by. After weeks of bombing, they expected the Japanese to land any moment.

Closer to Pearl Harbor, at a few minutes before 7 p.m. on the night of Dec. 15, submarines surfaced near Kahului, Maui, and Johnston Island. The submarine near Kahului, probably *I-1*, fired 10 shells at the town before running for the sea. Two fell into the harbor, and three hit the cannery of the Maui Pineapple Company, racking up $700 in damage. Panicky residents grabbed their valuables and started to flee the town, but were eventually persuaded to return by Maui police and Boy Scouts.

At Johnston, the attackers were *I-16* and *I-22*, stopping off on their passage to Kwajalein. The two submarines approached the tiny, flat island in cloudy weather and were surprised when it appeared less than 1,000 yards away.

Using the deck gun of a submarine was a difficult proposition, and rarely done except in ideal circumstances. The couple of minutes it took to surface and prepare the gun leaves the submarine wallowing defenseless, and the rangefinders were portable and therefore not very accurate. The usual way of hitting a target was to bracket it with shells. The chances of successfully using a manually loaded deck gun during the moil of battle were slim. The gunnery officer on board tended to be the most junior.

Japanese submarines carried about 20 rounds of deck gun ammunition stored in waterproof lockers in the deck. If the submarine intended to fire more rounds than those, additional ammunition was hauled up from the magazine on a hoist. This arrangement was slow and awkward, and had the disadvantage of requiring a hatch to be opened on deck that could not be sealed from the inside. The combination of a crash dive and an improperly sealed ammunition hoist could result in water cascading into the I-boat.

The guns were virtually useless against attacking aircraft. Japanese submarines were not equipped with ranging radar, not even by war's end, and the only submarines that fired back at aircraft were those that couldn't dive out of harm's way.

In circumstances where the submarine could creep toward the target unseen and on the surface — or where no return fire was expected — the deck gun could be used to good result, as the 4.7-inch round packed a wallop. The targets of opportunity were seacoasts by night, or undefended shipping. Both tended to become scarce after the first few months of war.

Against shore targets, ranges were calculated by estimating the distance from the submarine's presumed location on a seacoast map.

Blazing away on the gun deck of an I-boat. Although this is a posed picture for propaganda purposes, the size of the large gun is noteworthy.

Where the first round landed was a matter of great curiosity to gun crewmen, who were literally taking a shot in the dark.

"It was quite useless to aim for a small target, and the usual practice was to plaster a particular area with the idea of frightening the populace," Torpedo Officer Mochitsura Hashimoto wrote later. He also explained that shore bombardments were unpopular with submarine skippers, who worried about counterattacks against their fragile craft.

I-16 got lost as she approached Johnston, leaving the attack to *I-22*. Both submarines were unaware Navy transport *William Ward Burrows* had arrived early that afternoon with barge *PAB-7* in tow. The transport had slowly steamed from the now-dangerous oceans near Wake Island, and while trying to enter the calm waters of the atoll, the tow bridle snagged a coral head. It was late afternoon before the transport unloaded the barge and 77 civilian contractors on Johnston. The rest of the cargo would have to wait until the next day.

The civilian workers were ordered to remain on Johnston until a runway, bombproof shelters, sewage and saltwater lines and a number of other amenities were completed.

Captain Ross A. Dierdorff anchored *William Ward Burrows* over the shallow coral shelf south of Johnston, reasoning the ship was safer there from submarine attack than cruising the blue water beyond the lagoon. The coral heads that caused problems earlier that

SHOOTING AT ISLANDS

day were well-known, and considered enough to scare off any submarines. Even so, a full submarine lookout was posted, the bridge fully manned and the engineering department told not to get too far from their engines. Satisfied, Dierdorff went down to dinner.

On the island, the newly emplaced American gun batteries observed flashes winking on the northern horizon, as did a radio striker strolling toward the radio shack. He ran into the shack and informed the supervisor of the mysterious flashes, and they both peered northward. Through a small squall obscuring the distance in that direction, the flashes were timed at 20 seconds apart. Behind them, the south was clear and *William Ward Burrows* stood out in relief, etched by the setting sun against the darkening sky.

At 6:10 p.m., dinner on the transport was interrupted by a General Quarters alarm — officer of the deck Ensign J.A. Paterson also saw the flashes, correctly deducing they were muzzle blasts. Moments later, shells began striking the atoll. As the officers rushed out on deck, they saw shell hits "laddering up and down the island." Overshoots and ricochets bounced into the water near them, one raising a geyser 30 yards from the stern.

One of the first salvos landed near the civilian contractors' power house, one shell making a small hole as it passed through the wood-frame building without exploding. Another burst on a telephone pole outside the building and showered the area with hot shrapnel, as well as abruptly cutting communication between Johnston and Sand Islet to the south. The splinters riddled both a 1,200 gallon oil tank, setting it afire, and a 50,000 gallon water tank, quickly emptying it.

Oil flames touched off the power house and the two civilian operators ran for their lives. Blazing oil spread quickly behind them as more shells landed nearby, apparently targeted on the prominent water tower. One civilian leaped into a manhole beside the road, not realizing the burning oil would follow him in. He climbed out quickly, his hands covered in flames.

The damage control party arrived and began to fight the fire with sand and salt water. Two shells shredded an additional power building, and another passed through the mess hall without exploding.

At the naval air station on Sand Islet, the damage on Johnston gave observers the impression the "island seemed doomed." The oil fire was upwind and threatened to sweep the entire island from one end to the other. A wall of flames blossomed more than 50-feet tall, throwing the remaining buildings and scurrying people into silhouette and throwing greasy coils of black smoke into the air.

Radio reports received in Pearl Harbor, arriving on top of accounts of shelling in Kahului, said "Johnston Island ablaze!" The 14th Naval District sent out a Hawaii-wide warning; *Contemplated Japanese uprising among Jap sympathizers tonight. Be especially alert.*

On the transport, Captain Dierdorff conferred hurriedly with Lieutenant Commander E.I. McQuiston, his executive officer, and

gunnery officer Lieutenant W.B. Colborn. The glare from the raging oil fire reflected across the lagoon surface, punctuated blackly by splashes of shrapnel. They decided that discretion was the better part of valor, particularly since they had 132 civilians still on board and their own guns couldn't reach the raiders. The ship ran for it.

The transport frantically surged forward at 6:30 p.m. and then shuddered to a stop. The port anchor was fouled in the coral and Dierdorff ordered the chain cut. The ship cleared the anchorage and headed out into deep water, where, several miles out, Dierdorff spun the ship around and cut the engines. Shrouded by rain squalls, she rode quietly for several hours, skirting the shoal.

The island's 3- and 5-inch guns fired several shells in the direction of the faraway muzzle flashes. Nothing could be made out in the misting rain and oil smoke, and the flashes stopped as soon as the island began firing back.

Perhaps because of the extravagant damage on Johnston, observers who did pick out "dim objects in their telescopes" were positive the attackers were capital ships, much larger than submarines. The battle report speculates that the attacking force was a light cruiser and a destroyer that turned tail at the first sign of resistance.

The fire burned wildly for nearly an hour and was finally brought under control by bulldozing the blazing power house. Without communications, a small boat was launched from the Navy base to determine damage and casualties at Johnston, and on the way back, skewered itself up on a coral head. The crew remained stuck there overnight.

At 11:30 p.m., with communications restored, Dierdorff asked Johnston if further help was needed. Johnston replied there were no serious casualties, and therefore, no pressing reason to return. *William Ward Burrows* got under way for Pearl Harbor shortly before 1 a.m., presumably still loaded with Johnston's cargo.

The next morning, another Pacific island held by Americans was giving the Japanese headaches. A spirited defense by American Marines on Wake was exacerbated when two Imperial submarines collided while on patrol. Part of the invasion screening force, *RO-66* accidentally rammed *RO-62*, commanded by Lieutenant Hideyuki Kurokawa. Most of the submarine crew were saved before *RO-62* foundered and sank.

"That island is almost bewitched," Rear Admiral Matome Ugaki recorded in his diary.

On Dec. 20, the chief of staff of the Japanese 6th Fleet signaled the 2nd Submarine Squadron that "in the event of shelling a Hawaiian strong point, the principal target must be shipping and military installations in order as far as possible to avoid harming our own nationals."

At the same time, frustrated at their lack of success in Hawaiian waters, the I-boats of 3rd Submarine Squadron were ordered home to Kwajalein, leaving behind the 2nd Squadron.

SHOOTING AT ISLANDS

Three of these 3rd group submarines paused on Dec. 22 to shell Johnston Island again, as well as Palmyra. Apparently, their aim was off, as there is no record of notable damage. *I-71's* shells ranged Johnston, but skipper T. Kawasaki reported inconclusive results "because visibility was bad."

Not mentioned was that *I-71* ceased firing as soon as the shore battery fired back. Third Squadron I-boats were given the reason for the shelling attacks on the 23rd: "Progress report part IV: (2) Concerning the atrocities of the American Army, mentioned above, which factors have a great relation to the fate of a majority of Japanese on future battlefields, first of all, these cruel killers of Japanese will be thoroughly investigated, and you will take note of the above mentioned and give orders for punishing quickly those involved, at a ratio of 50 to 1." The "atrocities" referred to the Wake defense by American Marines.

That night, *I-73* shelled Johnston's Sand Islet and destroyed the CAA homing tower. "Knocked down a large radio tower!" skipper Akira Isobe noted. The pair of five-inch guns on Johnston fired 20 rounds at *I-73*, estimated at 7,000 yards range.

I-75 also shelled Palmyra and "destroyed a structure which apparently (is) a radio transmission station." In the excitement, *I-75* ran aground but managed to get away. *I-68's* turn came on Christmas Eve, when the air station was shelled from 3,000 yards distance. Six rounds were fired, one of which hit U.S. Engineer Department Dredge *Sacramento*, causing minor damage. The Americans fired two star shells and 12 "navy common AP (armor-piercing) shells." No hits, and the submarine submerged.

On Christmas Day, the civilians were placed under the command of the island commandant "for necessary defense and protection measures in the present emergency." The next day, an order from

This charming domestic vignette — familiar to military families — was taken on Johnston Island in 1946 and meant to show off the pleasant living conditions there. Beyond the cottages is the aircraft ramp, and beyond that, the sea. There is not much more to Johnston.

Pearl negated the instant draft. The commandant of Johnston was ordered to retain as few civilian workers as possible to finish the runway. By the end of December, a third of the island's 307 civilians were evacuated to Honolulu.

I-74 spied on Howland Island between Dec. 23 and 25 and "recognized installations for ships."

On Dec. 27, the I-boats still in Hawaiian seas were ordered, *to carry out a reconnaissance attack on the important areas of the Hawaiian Islands according to the following table.*

Submarine I-2 *at Kahului Harbor. Submarine* I-3, *Nawiliwili Harbor (Kauai Island). Submarine* I-1 *at Hilo.*

The time is fixed at twilight and night on (30) December.

Targets for attack are ships, harbor and bay installations, and other military installations.

After completion of the attack, sub I-2 *and* I-1 *shall proceed to Alenuihaha Channel and* I-3 *to the sea area of Kauai Island and perform observation duty. After sunset on 2 January it shall return to patrol area.*

On the 29th, an addendum: *In the attack on strategic point of 31 December, if no enemy ships are anchored at said place, all ships will carry it out as quickly as possible after about 2100.*

I-1 and *I-2* also were given patrol sectors in the channel, *I-1* riding on the Kona side and *I-2* cruising near Kohala.

In the brilliant moonlight of Dec. 30, the towns of Hilo, Kahului and Nawiliwili were shelled within a three-hour period. Shells splashed short of the Kahului pier, and others passed completely over the town, in the direction of Puunene. Army guns wildly returned fire.

In the teachers' cottages bordering Kauai High School, which sat on a bluff overlooking the Nawiliwili Harbor, the whistle and explosion of shells awakened 10-year-old Ellie McCollom. *Bombs!* she thought, excited. *But I don't hear any airplanes.*

She ran onto the front porch of the blacked-out cottage, joined by her mother, grandmother and 9-year-old brother. Nothing was vis-

The harbor of Kahului, Maui, in 1938. Shells fired from the sea burst around these piers.

SHOOTING AT ISLANDS

ible, though the shells seemed to scream by directly overhead before detonating up the slope. Ellie's father had died some months before and her mother fretted in the darkness. Their neighbor in the cottage duplex, another teacher named Katashi Nose, reeled sleepily out his front door. "Woke me up," he complained.

Mrs. McCollom asked advice, and Nose suggested they head for a cave up the road. He herded the family there while the shells impacted. "My brother and I skipped along, excited," McCollom recalled. The little group crowded into the cave, and Nose went back to sleep, undisturbed by the explosions.

After a while, the shelling ceased, and the McColloms woke up their sleepy neighbor. The excitement was over for the night.

At least 15 shells crashed into Nawiliwili, although damage was limited to a canefield fire and $500 worth of shrapnel rips in a gasoline tank and a home. The next morning, Ellie McCollom saw a dud shell in the road next to her home. It sat there like a malignant animal while guardsmen routed traffic away. The shell was the first sign of the enemy the girl had seen, and she stared at it, fascinated, until she was chased away by a soldier.

Two shells fired at Hilo had better luck, one knocking a hole in a pier and the other starting a fire in some hala trees by the airport. *U.S.S. Hulbert* fired one round in response, and the 55th Coast Artillery shot back as well. Since *I-1's* target seemed to be some oil tanks, a long-delayed camouflage program was enthusiastically renewed at daybreak.

Also on the way to Kwajalein from the West Coast in late December, *I-25* picked up enemy radio transmissions on the I-boat's direction-finder apparatus. Curious, the boat followed the signal, which lead them midway between Johnston Island and the Marshalls.

The signal was presumed to come from an island, but upon approach during Jan. 8, was described by the skipper as an aircraft carrier. Peering through-the periscope, he detailed the flight deck, derricks and aircraft to the bridge crew. He smiled and ordered a spread of four torpedoes. The crew heard the explosions and happily claimed an aircraft carrier.

No other ships of any kind, Allied, Imperial or neutral, were in this area. Perhaps the crew of *I-25* successfully hit an atoll.

Also on her way to Kwajalein at this time, *I-9's* floatplane made a clandestine visit at Pearl Harbor.

On Jan. 19, while lying in wait for targets northeast of Hawaii, submerged at 90 feet, *I-24* heard the sound of successive explosions. The submarine crew believed they were the targets. After a time, the periscope was cautiously raised but nothing seen. Perhaps, they figured, a search aircraft had jettisoned its bomb load.

I-24 formed up with *I-18* to shell Midway Atoll. Arriving in the dark of night, they were forced to dive by a patrol vessel. *I-24* popped back up to fix position and target, down again at sunrise. In the morning, they sighted a merchant vessel through the periscope.

Officer Mochitsura Hashimoto recalled great excitement among the crew at the unexpected target, though when the I-boat moved closer, he discovered the merchant ship was well shielded inside the atoll lagoon.

There was an argument at the noon meal as to whether they should shoot at the Midway targets right at the appointed time, even if not in the proper position, or wait until only the right angle was achieved. Hashimoto was anxious to get it over with — as first lieutenant, he was in charge of trimming operations, and would be working below with no inkling of what was going on topside.

On Jan. 23, in company with *I-18*, *I-24* crept up on the atoll on a brilliantly star-lit night. *I-24* surfaced with five minutes to spare, and so was able to jockey into position. Hashimoto began to fill buoyancy tanks in preparation for a possible crash-dive.

The submarine started shooting at what skipper Hiroshi Hanabusa thought was an aircraft hangar. Seven rounds were readied. By the fifth round, lights were twinkling on shore. The gun crew congratulated themselves on what they thought were secondary explosions caused by their gunfire. Suddenly, *I-24's* bow was braced by shellfire. The lights on shore were muzzle flashes. Hanabusa ordered a crash dive, catching Hashimoto by surprise. The tanks weren't completely prepped, but *I-24* went down quickly anyway. The seventh round was left sitting on deck, unfired.

I-18 never got a shot off before being targeted by the shore batteries. Hashimoto considered the raid a complete failure, and complained that it would have been better to wait until the anchored merchant had left the safety of the lagoon. The two submarines then ran west for four hours, submerged in case Midway sent patrol aircraft after them. Surfacing, they found themselves "in the teeth of a rising sea."

The waves continued to grow restless. Near the Bonin Islands, the weather was very heavy, and waves slammed greenly against the windows of *I-24's* bridge. Standing watch, Hashimoto got soaked, and was happy to be relieved by the navigation officer. The torpedo officer lowered himself off the bridge, ready to go below and change into dry clothes.

The open hatch above Hashimoto suddenly exploded with sea water and broken glass; he was knocked off the ladder. Stunned, Hashimoto heard voices shouting in pain. He scrambled back up the ladder and found skipper Hanabusa, the navigation officer and rest of the bridge crew writhing on the deck, which was slippery with blood and sea water.

A wave had crashed through the thick glass bridge windows, shattering them into razor-edged shrapnel. Hashimoto applied what first aid he could and cried for help. When the deck was clear, Hashimoto took over the aborted watch and spent the next several hours alone and shivering on the damaged bridge.

At Baker Island, a warship showed up on Jan. 28. The teenage

SHOOTING AT ISLANDS

colonists hid in their foxholes and watched the gray destroyer put over a boat, which began pulling for shore. "Oh boy, we've had it now!" said Burke.

They saw a blonde head among the sailors and realized that the boat must be American. It was destroyer *Helm*, making the dash from Pearl Harbor to retrieve the colonists. "We found those guys living like Robinson Crusoe," remembered Victor Dybdal.

The boys threw off the brush cover and rushed to shore, where the boat halted just at reef's edge. In his haste, Burke badly cut his foot on a piece of jagged shrapnel buried in the sand. Blood poured out, and he was concerned the scent would attract sharks. The Navy officer in charge of the boat refused to row to the other side of the island, where the waters were quieter.

Makua swam back to shore and convinced Burke to swim for the boat. Even sharks were better than the daily bombings from the Japanese Navy.

Aboard *Helm*, the Hawaiians learned that Whaley and Keliihahanui had been killed by the shelling on Howland, and that they were buried there. Bederman and Matson were still in shock, their adventure turned tragic.

The "Government House" and weather hut on Baker Island. By the time help arrived from Honolulu, these had been blown away by the Advance Force.

Skipper Chester Carroll secured from General Quarters as the destroyer moved away from Baker, and he came down to quiz the survivors. Just as they told the lieutenant commander that a Japanese bomber came over every day promptly at noon, they heard the sound of feet running on deck, always the first sign of impending danger on a destroyer. Dybdal looked at his watch: noon. As he gained the deck, a pair of bombs bracketed the destroyer; Dybdal could see the "Mavis" flying boat circling around for another run.

The aircraft made three passes, missing each time. By the third run, the destroyer's anti-aircraft guns were hosing the sky around it. The plane fled. *Helm* turned around and raced back to Pearl.

By the beginning of 1942, radar was in operation on these isolated islands and Japanese submarines couldn't get close without tipping their hand. After this month of aggressive shellings, Japanese submarine attacks against islands thinned out. In March 1942, *I-4* attacked Cocos Island, which was attacked again by *I-166*[1] in January 1943, to cover while Guadalcanal was evacuated. *I-8*, along with cruiser *Nara* and a destroyer also fired on Canton Island to cover the Guadalcanal evacuation.

On Aug. 31, 1942, the flying-boat base in Graciosa Bay in the Solomons was shot at by *I-19* from outside the bay. There was little damage, so a week later *I-3* entered the bay and repeated the attack, actually hitting some targets.

[1] The number was changed from I-66 in 1942.

In mid-October 1942, *I-7* shelled the airfield on Espiritu Santo, and repeated the attack a few days later. Damage was claimed.

Despite the real, though minor, damage caused by submarine-based shellings, balanced against the imaginary successes of the midget submarines at Pearl Harbor, I-boats returning from Hawaii in the spring of 1942 were impressed into a new squadron, the 8th, comprised of *I-18, I-20, I-21, I-22, I-24, I-27, I-29* and *I-30*. Under the command of Rear Admiral Ishizaki, the 8th was to train for "special operations" — which included midget submarines. But no such "special operation" for the rest of the war would equal the wide-ranging scope of the Advance Force offensive.

Hawaiian teenagers Walter Burke, Blue Makua, James Coyle, James Pease, Thomas Bederman and Elvin Matson show their relief at arriving safely home in Honolulu. Classmates Richard Whaley and Joe Keliihahanui were killed during the Advance Force offensive.

TORPEDO JUNCTION

25

"One Insane, One Injured, And Proceeding Honolulu."

Peggy McMurtry began to haunt the Matson office in San Francisco when *Lahaina* became overdue. "Where's that ship?" she demanded. She was usually told that it must have been diverted to another port. One day, she asked about *Lahaina* and was startled to see the people behind the counter look knowingly at each other and shake their heads.

"What's going on? Where is my husband's ship?" she insisted.

"We're not sure, actually," said the clerk. "By the way, your husband — was he a good swimmer?"

Peggy McMurtry's husband had been sunk by submarine *I-9* on Dec. 11. The sinking had been a stroke of good fortune for the Japanese — freighter *Lahaina* had come to them. Japanese submarines had little luck when first hunting in Hawaiian waters. Although *I-9*, *I-10* and *I-26* each sank a merchant ship during the four days after the attack, none were within range of Hawaii-based air patrols. The blockading submarines were constantly harassed in the sea and from the air and rarely got an opportunity to get off a shot. The carrier chase of Dec. 9 to 15 provided some excitement, but was fruitless, and resulted in the loss of *I-70*.

The 2nd and 3rd submarine squadrons were ordered to patrol the Hawaiian sea frontier until late December, just in case something came up. The 1st squadron *I-9*, *I-15*, *I-17* and *I-25* — and the three screening submarines for Kido Butai *I-19*, *I-21* and *I-23* of the 2nd Submarine Division — were ordered to proceed to the West Coast, "charged with the duty of destroying communications and raiding ships." As the submarines went east they hoped to pursue ships going to the American mainland. They either saw none, or were outrun by their prey.

Added to the group were *I-10* and *I-26*, already halfway to the coast. *I-26* proceeded directly to the Seattle area, off Cape Flattery. The rest of the group arrived in the sea area 500 miles from Seattle on the 16th, with no enemy observed. The submarines then dispersed, taking up stations off West Coast shipping ports.

The risk of running supplies to the about-to-be-besieged Hawai-

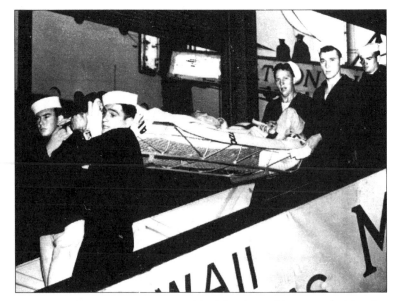

The first military casualties of the attack on Pearl Harbor arrive in San Francisco, carried by ship through the ineffective Advance Force blockade. The censor has marked out part of the gangway lettering, but enough remains to make out the details.

ian Islands began to seem acceptable. Merchant ships grew bolder. On Dec. 14, 29 miles from Makapuu Point on the northwest tip of Oahu, *I-4* under K. Nakagawa torpedoed *Hoegh Merchant*, a 4,858-ton Norwegian motorship. The ship's 35 survivors were picked up at sea by destroyer/minelayer *Trever* and deposited in Honolulu by 9 a.m. *Hoegh Merchant's* cargo of oil barrels drifted ashore at Kauai.

"With reference to the *Hoegh*," Kimmel reported to Stark, there were "no signs of submarines prior or later by explosions."

On the evening of Dec. 17, *I-15* surfaced off California's Farallon Islands and carefully moved toward San Francisco.

Through his binoculars, Executive Officer Zenji Orita could see the lights of the city gilding the Golden Gate. "They certainly don't act like there's a war going on, allowing such illumination to silhouette their shipping along the coast," Orita thought.[1]

1st Squadron commander Captain Tsutomo Sato joined them on the bridge and joked with skipper Nobuo Ishikawa. "I've never been to America," he said. "If we weren't at war, this would be an excellent opportunity to pass through the Golden Gate and visit that famous city of San Francisco."

Orita couldn't resist joining in.

"Sir, if you wish, we could launch our aircraft," he said. "That would give you an excellent chance to do some sight-seeing!" Their laughter carried over the water.

The next night, San Francisco was dark. American patrol boats sliced through the corrugation of cold, choppy water near the Farallons, chattering on their radios. These intercepts gave the Japanese submarine ample warning, but also drove her underwater. They spent a week dodging American patrol boats and missed any firing angles at American freighters.

Also on the 17th, the day after leaving Honolulu for a destination not revealed to her crew, *S.S. Manini* was torpedoed at 6:40 p.m. The

[1] *The Japanese were contemptuous of American attitudes toward the new war footing. Off Long Beach,* I-19 *reported Americans sunning themselves on the beach by day, and at night, the beams of car headlights were "so bright" the crew read newspapers on the bridge.*

3,253-ton freighter was 180 miles south of Hawaii. Many of the crew were in the ship's saloon, finishing the evening meal and listening to the Eddie Cantor program on the shortwave. Bosun Orrin Jewell had a blackjack game going on one table, and was 12 dollars ahead.

The freighter shuddered as a blast punched a massive hole in her port side. The topmast snapped from the concussion, taking with it the wireless antenna. Seaman James McVicker died in a nearby gangway when he was catapulted from the deck into the steel overhead.

Within six minutes, *Manini* had slid back into the ocean until her bow pointed upward. The ocean rocked the ship violently back and forth, rattling loose everything on deck.

Twenty men, dodging deck cargo as it tumbled around them, got into lifeboat No. 2. Second Mate George Jahn and eleven other men got into lifeboat No. 1. In the evening darkness, Jewell could just barely make out the silhouette of the submarine.

The sub was *I-75* under Sunao Tabata. She had reported shelling an "enemy merchant ship" two days earlier — an act unnoticed by the Americans — and was confirming the identity of her kill. The submarine turned on her white and green running lights and began to play a searchlight on the sinking freighter.

The crew of Manini Lifeboat #1. Jahn and Jewell are the first two on the left, front row.

"Hey! I'm stuck over here," a voice called out. In the searchlight's white glare, the men in the lifeboats could make out Seaman Michael Tompkins clinging to debris near *Manini's* hull. Around him, heavy timbers churned and snapped as they slid off the now-vertical deck.

"Hang on — we'll come and get you," Captain George Sidon shouted at the 19-year-old seaman.

Tompkins advised them to wait a moment, as the tons of thrashing lumber made the area unhealthy. The submarine flipped off her lights at that moment and Tompkins' screams were swallowed by darkness.

Over the horizon, the crew of freighter *Prusa* had spotted the light and reported "flares on horizon."

The crew of Manini Lifeboat #2. Captain Sidon wears the white shirt in front row center.

The *Manini* survivors rowed for several days in the heavy seas, and the boats became separated. Water often flooded the lifeboats up to their knees, and on the first day a sea anchor snapped, making the boats unmanageable.

Several American planes were spotted, which failed to respond to signal flares. Four days out, a bomber ran across the 12 men in Lifeboat No. 1 and dropped some food. The plane signaled "six

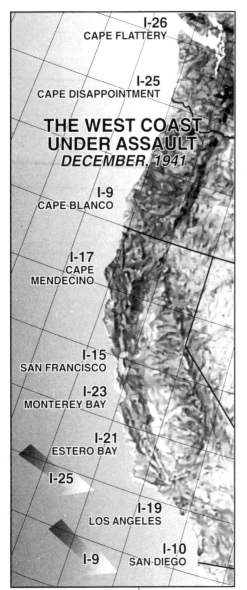

THE WEST COAST
UNDER ASSAULT
DECEMBER, 1941

I-26
CAPE FLATTERY

I-25
CAPE DISAPPOINTMENT

I-9
CAPE BLANCO

I-17
CAPE MENDECINO

I-15
SAN FRANCISCO

I-23
MONTEREY BAY

I-21
ESTERO BAY

I-25

I-19
LOS ANGELES

I-10
I-9   SAN DIEGO

marines sighted in a boat" at 8:30 a.m. The next day, another bomber dropped water. On Christmas Eve, a patrol plane dropped a note asking if they needed help. The reply, by flashlight, was, *We sure do!*

Jahn's boat spotted a Kauai mountain peak on Christmas Day. *It's obviously no cloud either,* he noted in the boat's log. But no help arrived. The next day, the sea anchor was carried away in rising seas, and the crew in frustration began to row toward the mountain peak.

Coast Guard cutter *Reliance* searched the area, unable to find the lifeboats. They were repeatedly spotted from the air, and promises of imminent help were dropped. Finally, on Dec. 27, a day when submarine sightings blossomed thickly around Kauai and Niihau, the stranded men were picked up by destroyer *Allen.*

With the survivors, *Allen* raced back to Oahu, radioing ahead, *One insane, one injured, and proceeding Honolulu.* Once ashore, a reporter asked Jewell how he was doing, and the bosun shrugged. "I left 12 dollars on the table, back on *Manini,*" he said. "But what the hell."

On the other lifeboat, 20 men including Captain Sidon were infrequently dropped inadequate supplies. One day, it was a can of tomatoes; another, a single biscuit and a quarter-cup of water. It was as if the aircrews were tossing out the remains of their lunches. Then the planes lost their location, possibly confusing the two boats.

Late in the afternoon of Christmas Eve, just as saloon keeper Bob Lashon was reading aloud from the Bible, a lone patrol plane was spotted. The captain took a chance and fired off the last flare. As the plane circled above, the ship's name was spelled out by flashlight, and the plane flew off. Sidon figured it was time for a celebration. It was Christmas Eve, after all. Each man was given a quarter-cup of water.

The flare was seen from Oahu, and reported as a "searchlight pointed at sky on and off twice." Action on the sighting was given to Army Intelligence, which decided the light was a Japanese signal. Throughout Christmas Day, no help appeared.

The next day, Messman Jules H. Simmons died of thirst and exposure. After a short service by Sidon, his body was consigned to the deep.

Three days after Christmas, on the evening of Sunday the 28th, the men were in the midst of a heartfelt religious service when Navy planes buzzed overhead. A dropped note said, "Help is coming!"

One big plane, a Navy "torpedo bomber," circled low enough for

the sailors to see the air crews stuck up their thumbs. Several of the 19 surviving sailors stuck up thumbs and middle fingers in reply.

Destroyer *Patterson* appeared on the horizon, dropping a launch as soon as it came close. The launch was well-stocked with fresh water, something the thirsty seamen appreciated most of all.

At 5:30 on the morning of Dec. 18, less than 10 hours after glimpsing *I-75's* searchlight playing on the stricken *Manini*, the Lykes Brothers' freighter *Prusa* was torpedoed near the Big Island. The 5,113-ton "Hog Islander" freighter, running with lights extinguished, was hit by *I-72*, under I. Togami. Navy intelligence had Togami's signal deciphered nearly as quickly as it reached Kure: *Have sunk one 5,000-ton freighter, at point (censored), about 120 miles southwest of Hawaii.*

Eight of the 34 men aboard *Prusa* were killed in their bunks when the torpedo slammed into the stern. The lookouts, one in the bridge and one in the forecastle head, plus the mate on the bridge, all saw the torpedo appear foaming out of the night, with no time to maneuver away. The explosion blew out the doors of the poop deck, the pressure bubble tearing the awnings away, which shredded and fluttered back down onto the deck.

An order to abandon ship was sent down immediately and radio operator Lawrence H. Gianella hurried into the radio shack to send out an SOS. The equipment was damaged; Gianella was in the midst of rigging an emergency set when an officer told him the boats were being lowered.

Gianella stalled. *It would only take a few minutes to get the set working.* The men in the boats waited for Gianella to escape, but he did not. The ship sank in nine minutes, with no chance to SOS. [2]

I-72 also played a searchlight on the ship and watched her go under. Engine wiper Alfred Dyer was thrown into an alleyway below decks. In the dark confusion, he found himself tumbled into a heap with Delores Martinez, another wiper, and fireman Sam Taylor.

The other two men were screaming, and Dyer felt something wet in the darkness. "Turn on the light! There's no light!" shouted one of the writhing shapes. The submarine's searchlight played suddenly through a hole in the bulkhead, and Dyer gasped when he saw himself covered with other mens' blood. Dyer could hear water rushing into the freighter, so he dived through the hole.

The submarine was only about 250 feet away, and to Dyer it looked enormous. He swam toward one of the lifeboats just then settling into the water.

Two lifeboats were provisioned and launched, Captain G.H. Boy in command of one and Chief Mate Levi Plesner in charge of the other. The two boats set course for the Marshall Islands. Two hours later, a plane flew over, too high to spot boats.

During the next six days the boats separated after drifting at least 500 miles from Hawaii. Plesner's boat, aided by favorable winds, beat back toward Hawaii for three days. Nearly 250 miles from Honolulu,

[2] *Gianella was posthumously awarded the Merchant Marine Distinguished Service Medal. Navy Secretary John Lehman named a T-5 tanker after Gianella in 1983.*

the whaleboat was located by scouting planes on Christmas Day, which dropped tomatoes, fruit juices and water. Coast Guard cutter *Tiger* was sent out to retrieve them. A morning flight on the 26th was planned to relocate the boat, and then remain in position to guide *Tiger* to the scene. The scheme worked, and *Tiger* recovered 13 men a bit past noon. They were deposited in Honolulu on the 28th.

The other lifeboat, commanded by Boy, disappeared until Jan. 19, when it landed on Nikuau Island in the Gilberts, 2,500 miles from Hawaii. One man died en route. The fourth officer, a fellow named Baker, set off for Beriun Island, where he contacted British authorities. Of the 34 men on board *Prusa*, 24 survived.

The I-boats off the West Coast began to find targets as soon as they arrived on station. At 1:30 a.m. on the 18th, as she crossed the mouth of the Columbia River, Union Oil tanker *L.P. St. Clair* drew ten rounds from *I-25*. John Ellison, skipper of *L.P. St. Clair,* ordered the tanker hard to port, into the river channel, as soon as the first flashes erupted in the darkness. All missed.

A few hours later, as dawn lightened the horizon, the 70-foot commercial fishing boat *Jacky-Joe* stood out of Catalina Island. Skipper Andy Mardesich, brother Mike Mardesich and engineer Tom Johnson were heading for Santa Cruz, shadowing the shoreline, when the skipper spied another boat moving into the Catalina Channel.

"Let's get in on his luck," decided Andy Mardesich, describing the other craft as a "strange, black-colored fishing boat." *Jacky-Joe* dogged the other ship, hoping it had stumbled onto a school of fish.

The strange boat abruptly disappeared. "My God — it's a sub!" shouted Andy Mardesich. "Let's get the hell out of here!" Mike Mardesich revved the engines, and *Jacky-Joe* flew toward the Palos Verdes Peninsula. An engine self-destructed under the load, and the fishing boat limped into San Pedro that evening. [3]

Also before dawn, at almost the same moment *Prusa* was going under near Hawaii, five gun rounds and one torpedo were fired at lumber steamer *Samoa*, near Santa Barbara. The ship was carrying lumber to San Diego, and had run into heavy seas on Dec. 15. The thrashing had damaged one of the ship's lifeboats and swept away the Lyle gun.

First Mate John Lehtonen spotted light leaking from the bridge of *I-17,* under Commander Kozo Nishino. "A submarine is attacking us!" cried Lehtonen. Below, Captain Nels A. Simmes bolted out of his bunk and shouted into crew's quarters to man lifeboat stations.

Nishino's torpedo exploded in the water, short of the target. The ocean geysered; fragments fell hissing onto the deck of *Samoa*. *I-17* began popping away at the radio shack, littering the ship with more shrapnel. The submarine abruptly stopped shooting and moved within 40 feet of the steamer. Someone on the I-boat shouted *"Hai-ya!"* and Simmes shouted, "Hi yourself!"

There was no reply. The submarine disappeared into darkness. The ship had a congenital list to port, caused by shifting water in the

[3] On Christmas Day, the Navy commandeered Jacky-Joe *for the duration.*

Tanker Emidio *drifts onto the shore of Crescent City, Calif. Pieces of the ship are still on display there.*

ballast tanks, and Simmes figured the Japanese captain believed his shot had struck home. *Samoa* stood quiet until daylight, and then proceeded under high steam to San Diego.

On Dec. 20, *I-17* used deck guns and torpedoes again against Sacony-Vacuum Oil tanker *Emidio*, 6,912 tons. Captain Clark A. Farrow was running the ship empty between Seattle and San Pedro, in an area the Navy had declared sub-free. A lookout spotted a submarine between the tanker and land, and Farrow took no chances — *Emidio* poured on the coal and lit out for Eureka, 25 miles north.

Nishino gave chase, and *I-17* steadily closed on the tanker. When he was within a quarter-mile, he fired a shell into *Emidio's* midships. Tanker radioman W.S. "Sparks" Foote sent out a quick SOS, appending, "Under attack by enemy sub!"

I-17's next six shots all hit home, one blowing away the radio mast, another killing three men[4] lowering a lifeboat. Two others died in the engine room. While Foote and a skeleton engine crew remained aboard, Farrow and crew took to lifeboats and watched the submarine continue to pour shells into *Emidio*. The submarine also fired shells at the retreating lifeboats, which was interrupted by a Navy bomber passing overhead, flying from San Francisco to Seattle. Two depth bombs bracketed the submarine. Though one was a dud; *I-17* disappeared below. After a few minutes, Nishino partially resurfaced and dispatched a single torpedo, which caused *Emidio* to settle stern first into the water. Foote, back on the air after rigging another antenna, added *Torpedoes in stern* to the SOS and leaped overboard.

Oiler B.F. Moler, fireman Kenneth Kimes and Third Engineer R.A. Winters were in the engine room when the torpedo struck. The missile burst through the bulkhead, knocking aside an astounded Moler, slithered across the engine room and detonated on top of Kimes and Winters. The engine shielded Moler from the blast, though he had three broken ribs and a punctured lung from being knocked down. The oiler swam his way up passageways to the deck as water flooded the ship, where he joined Foote, treading water.

Satisfied, Nishino declared the tanker sunk and rapidly departed, a move which may have been exacerbated by more Navy bombers arriving on the scene.

[4] *R.W. Pennington, Fred Potts and Stuart McGillivray.*

Emidio's crew rowed to the Blunts Reef light ship — about 18 miles away — where they arrived at 11 p.m. They were taken off the next day by Coast Guard cutter *Shawnee* and deposited in Crescent City. *Shawnee* had attempted a rescue the day before and had been foiled by foul weather. Five volunteer Coast Guardsmen set off in *Shawnee's* motor lifeboat, arriving on the scene long after *Emidio's* crew had rowed away.

Chief Boatswain L. Garner Churchill[5] then spotted another ship, "long, low, and without masts or stack." He signaled it; the other craft turned and began bearing down on the lifeboat. When it was within 50 yards, Churchill was shocked to see that it was a submarine, apparently bent on ramming the Coast Guard craft. The boatswain floored the engine and cranked the rudder, reversing the lifeboat's course, and the onrushing submarine hurtled by in the darkness.

Emidio drifted, her decks awash, eventually grounding at Steamboat Rock next to Battery Point lighthouse. She remained there for 18 years before being towed to Long Beach and smelted down. Pieces of her hulk, removed in 1950 and '51, are on exhibit in Beachfront Park in Crescent City.

On Dec. 20, *I-23* under Commander Genichi Shibata, used deck guns to damage tanker *Agwiwold*, 6,771 tons. At 2:15 p.m., an explosion shuddered through the tanker, bringing skipper Frederick Gonclaves full-tilt into the bridge. *I-23* was on the surface, 500 yards west. "Hard to port — head straight at it!" ordered Gonclaves, reducing the target size. Another round rattled the tanker, and while the Japanese were reloading, Gonclaves wheeled and presented his stern to the I-boat. *Agwiwold* scooted away at high speed, weaving, presenting the smallest possible target. *I-23* gave chase, but was unable to land any rounds on the tanker.

Golfers at seaside courses watched the tanker zig-zag madly, and remarked on the huge clouds of smoke billowing from her stack. None saw the submarine, although many of the eight shots fired landed close enough to pitch water on the tanker's deck.

Some miles to the north, garbage scow *Tahoe's* regular dumping run that day off the Farallon Islands was interrupted by an I-boat incident. The scow's crew claimed she had sighted, rammed and sunk a submarine in broad daylight. A later drydock inspection revealed that the 37-year-old former lumber ship had been bruised against a "steel object," which sliced the scow massively — a cut a foot wide and 80 feet long.

What was it? The U.S. Navy denied any knowledge. Japanese sources don't mention it. *I-23* was in the area — that morning she had blown a hole in *Agwiwold* off Santa Cruz, 40 miles away. *I-15* was also in the area, using the Farallons as cover while scouting the Golden Gate. Neither Japanese submarine reported any heavy-metal encounters with garbage scows. It's possible that the first strike from the West Coast against the I-boats had been inflicted by a garbage scow. A poem soon appeared in the *San Francisco Chronicle:*

[5] *The fellow who had reported sharing drinks with an inquisitive German in California during 1940.*

TORPEDO JUNCTION

The Tahoe's *back on the job today,*
She's ruined a sub, her crewmen say;
The Tahoe *rides the waves today,*
A queen for sure in her own sweet way.

General Joseph Stillwell, writing in his diary, was more succinct. The *Tahoe* incident was a "two-pound bundle of crap."

While the I-boats arrayed themselves by night off the West Coast, in *Lahaina's* overcrowded lifeboat near Hawaii, wet bodies slammed against Douglas McMurtry; hands scraped at his face. He tumbled back against the bulkhead, fighting off the shroud of sleep. He became aware of voices shouting.

Once again, seamen Fred Schuster and Cliff Lanigan had gulped seawater in the night and were berserk. In the weak predawn light, they fought against the others. McMurtry rubbed his salt-burnt eyes and made out black shapes struggling, etched against gray water, gray sky.

A comber racked under the boat's stern, catapulting men into the air. The boat slewed sideways, water bursting over the gunwales. Men seized ropes, oars, each other, to prevent being separated from the boat. Big waves thundered broadside over their heads, swamping the boat with foaming water.

Surprisingly, the seas smoothed out for a few moments, allowing the frantically bailing men enough time to fling out most of the water. The boat rose out of the sea.

By dawn — an unusually clear dawn, as if the skies had been scrubbed clean by storm — heads were counted and the boat squared away. No one had been washed away, although seaman Freedman looked near dead, pale and shivering even as the sun began to beat down.

Douglas McMurtry during World War II.

As daylight filtered across the horizon, clouds began to take on distinct shapes. One cloud, low in the sky off the port bow, began to harden. Captain Matthiesen took a look with the glass when the cloud refused to move.

"Boys," he announced. "That's Mauna Loa!"

It was Saturday, Dec. 20. The first mate was unsure if the mountain was actually the Hawaiian volcano because the angle didn't agree with his navigation. Matthiesen reset his course anyway, riding the sudden good cheer of the crew.

They were still far from safety. Matthiesen hoped to be spotted by Navy patrols. There was also a good chance Japanese warships could be lingering in the area. For all they knew, Hawaii might have been invaded.

Breakfast was a quarter cup of water, a biscuit, and for those who could stomach it, the last of the raw eggs, now turned explosive from the heat. The ocean was still mountainous, pushing the boat to the west on the breeze. It surfed down the crests, rocketing upward on the wave shoulders and dropping again. The men, pressed against each other so tightly that each jumbled contact chafed agonizingly, suf-

fered through each sickening fall. They continued to bail, and Mauna Loa disappeared as the day began to haze.

Freedman continued to sink into illness. He stood up, so suddenly that the other sailors were caught flat, and he grabbed a line from the mast, wrapped it around his neck and attempted to hang himself on the spot. He was discouraged by the others, and returned to the deck.

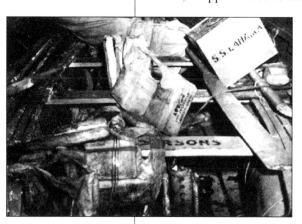

In the early afternoon, while the men began to doze under the sun, the boat swamped again. Matthiesen ordered sail to be shortened, hoping to trade speed for seaworthiness. Heavy squalls spat down.

By late afternoon, the seas moderated enough for dinner to be served. It seemed substantial; half a cup of water, half a raw potato and a single biscuit royally slathered with jam. Somehow, engineer Mike Locke missed out on the jam. As they ate, the men speculated on the whereabouts of the U.S. Navy. Not a single ship or plane had been spotted all day. "We could be the whole Jap navy!" someone cracked.

The battered interior of Lahaina's lifeboat. At right is the broken stock of the oar used to subdue Moore.

Full sail was hoisted after dinner, and just at sunset, Maui rose over the horizon, glimmering. McMurtry was sure he'd never seen anything so lovely.

The boat rode through the night, much as it had the previous eight nights, except that this time the men were sure it was the last. One way or another, by tomorrow, they'd be off the little craft.

Near 9 p.m., a voice called out, "Goodbye!"

"Who's that?" said Matthiesen.

"Now try and stop me!" said the voice. The boat rocked, and something heavy splashed into the water.

"Grab him!" shouted Matthiesen. "Douse the sail! Damn!"

The men stretched over the sides, grabbed at the inky sea. Nothing. The ocean was still rough, making it impossible to mark their position, or to work their way back.

Matthiesen called roll, discovered the missing man was AB Albert Lindquist, who had once served in the Swedish navy. Lindquist was one of those who had been drinking seawater, and Matthiesen suspected the man was 'round the bend.

Through the weak moonlight, Maui could be made out to starboard. The island looked huge, and water gleamed as it foamed over the reef. Matthiesen and McMurtry, who were familiar with Maui, decided they were near Spartan Reef, on the Kahului coast.

Matthiesen fired the Very pistol, trying to alert the shore defenses. The signals were spotted and interpreted as Japanese codes, and a detachment of the 299th Infantry hustled down to the beachfront, expecting an invasion and rattled by the previous week's shelling of Kahului, a few miles away. The soldiers waited all night, vexed by not

TORPEDO JUNCTION

having boats or heavy guns of their own. Frantic phone calls to Oahu, alerting them of the expected assault, were cut off by a security-minded operator.

At 1:30 a.m., Locke's friend, oiler Concezio del Tinto, leaped into the water and struck out for shore. "So long!" he shouted. "I'll be the first one ashore. I'll tell them you're out here."

The oiler apparently thought he could make it, despite the weakness and cramps of the voyage. Distraught, Locke tried to jump in after the older man and was restrained. Matthiesen ordered the boat about, but del Tinto disappeared into the darkness. The crew heard him screaming. The oiler was never seen again.

Under shortened sail, and sometimes with oars, the boat worked throughout the night to stay in place. As dawn lightened the sea, Freedman was discovered dead, still propped up between two sailors. Three men had died within a few hours of sighting land, and Matthiesen was determined not to lose any more. He ordered the men to wait until they could see the reef plainly.

But in the calm morning light, no suitable breaks were spotted in the combers. Matthiesen said, "Get the sail up! Let's get some speed and we'll go right through the breakers and land there."

"Are you crazy? D'ya want to kill us all?" complained a sailor.

"For crying out loud — you're so goddamn weak you can't even see me, and now you holler because you're afraid to get your feet wet," snapped Matthiesen. "Get that sail up. We're going in!"

A Navy airplane buzzed by overhead. Matthiesen shook his fist at the sky. "Where were you when we needed you?" he joked.

Lahaina's lifeboat on a Maui beach. The temporary gray paint has been battered off the boat's bottom, exposing the original white color.

The boat skated over the reef, riding the surf beautifully and finally grinding up on the beach. The seamen fell out and staggered onto their hands and knees, the surf foaming around them. The beach seemed to rock violently, and McMurtry realized it would be some time before he got his land legs back.

Thirty men had survived. They sprawled on the sand, waiting for the vertigo to pass. Locke spat out the coat button he'd kept in his mouth for a week, a placebo against thirst. It was in pretty sad shape.

Matthiesen rose unsteadily and looked around. There was a terrible pain in his stomach. He laughed.

"Damn!" he said. "That's Frank Baldwin's house!"

Covering Freedman's body, the crew began to crawl up the beach toward the Baldwin residence. Baldwin, a Matson executive, had often hosted parties for the officers at his Spreckelsville home.

"We missed Kahului by a mile and a half," remarked McMurtry.

Matthiesen laughed again, and pointed. Mrs. Baldwin had appeared at the door, hesitating, apparently at a loss to deal with the strange, ragged creatures advancing slowly on her home. A milk truck pulled up, directed by a soldier, and the sailors scrabbled at the sides, forcing it to stop.

"Hey! Slow down!" protested the milkman, as the crew opened the truck and began pouring cool milk down their throats.

"Sorry," said Matthiesen, milk on his peeling lips. "Wartime, you know. We're the crew of the *S.S. Lahaina*, sunk by the Japs nine days ago."

"Jeez, you're lucky you hit dry land," said the milkman.

"Luck?" laughed Matthiesen. "Luck had nothing to do with it. We're professional seamen, buddy."

Mrs. Baldwin had recognized them by this point and ran up breathlessly. "My God, we thought you boys were dead," she cried.

McMurtry self-consciously brushed at the salt encrusting his one gold stripe. "Please excuse my appearance," he said.

Lahaina survivors gather for a group portrait. In the front row, Hirashima is third from left, McMurtry is fifth. In the back row, Locke is first from left, Laumeister is 10th, Matthiesen is 11th, Kuckens is 13th.

A fleet of ambulances appeared, called in by the Maui Civilian Defense, who were slightly embarrassed at allowing an unknown craft to land undetected. Two blankets were clapped over each survivor, and hot coffee was brewed by a Japanese-American woman.

Arriving at the hospital, they were given hot showers, a hot breakfast and slid into heated beds, a technique recommended for shock victims. McMurtry drifted into sleep, and next remembered waking up at night, everything blurring in the darkness. In the morning, his newly cleaned uniform hung loosely on him, and he discovered he'd lost more than 30 pounds. The men regained their water weight by alternately drinking and passing full quarts of water.

Schuster and Lanigan were kept in the Spreckelsville hospital, while the other 28 were arranged for a group portrait.

For private reasons, Chief Engineer Laumeister insisted on being called "Frank Connelly" on the survivors' listings.

McMurtry sent a Mackay Radio message to Peggy, saying simply, *Safe. Well.* All the survivors were allowed to send the same two, unrevealing words.

On Dec. 21, the day the *Lahaina* crew reached Maui, an I-boat was seen surfaced a mile off Point Fermin, near Los Angeles Harbor breakwater. It was the same area where Japanese freighters had, with curious frequency, broken down due to mechanical malfunction and had to lie at anchor after leaving port.

The next day, 110 miles to the north, and visible from shore two miles off the treacherous hook of Point Arguello, *I-19* under Takaichi Kinashi used deck guns to damage Standard Oil tanker *H.M. Storey*, 10,763 tons. From the bluffs, where he was rabbit hunting along the railroad track, high school student Jack Sudden "heard a dull explosion and saw smoke arising from the sea."

He had no idea what it was. The smoke looked heavy and viscous, and settled on the water "like a smoke screen. To the northwest of the screen and about three miles from shore I could see the tanker speeding up the coast ... I later saw a long dark object leave the smoke screen, heading in the general direction of the ship."

I-19 had launched a torpedo at *H.M. Storey*. "It closed the gap between itself and the ship and at times came to the surface and kicked up a white spray," Sudden said. "The last I saw of the torpedo, it passed in front of the ship."

A woman walking on the beach, whose identity was withheld by the Navy, plainly saw the submarine that Sudden couldn't spot. "It was between the tanker and the shore when I saw it, less than two miles away. I saw what I thought were three torpedoes fired from the submarine at the ship, but they all went behind it."

The tanker escaped behind its own smoke screen and zig-zagged away. Patrol planes arrived and scattered bombs, frightening the woman on the beach. "They were so heavy that when they exploded they shook the ground where I was standing. The explosions raised great columns of water."

H.M. Storey darted for the little coastal town of Surf, where it was intercepted by a Navy PBY. Unwilling to wait to debrief the crew, Navy officers transferred from the plane to the tanker while still at sea.

I-10, which was near San Diego, was teamed with *I-19*, supposedly reconnoitering ships predicted to be passing through the Panama Canal and heading north to San Francisco. "Be prepared for enemy battleships," Vice Admiral Shimizu radioed, but none were encountered. After the 22nd they noted a sharp increase in patrols and a decrease in shipping. "We recognize that together with our causing considerable blows on the maritime transportation of the same sea area there is a great reaction which influences public opinion," added Shimizu.

ALL'S FAIR IN ...

A possibly apocryphal submarine was reported the same day off the twisted thorn of Palos Verdes peninsula. An anonymous tipster said, "My lady friend and I were in one of those romantic canyons of Palos Verdes admiring the scenery, when we saw this object in the water." He had never seen a submarine before, but it was confirmed by his companion. "My lady friend told me, and she ought to know ... because her husband is in the Navy."

Frank Knox, Secretary of the Navy, had a somewhat different opinion, bolstered by the poor score of the Imperial Navy in the first five assaults on the West Coast. "We have effectively dealt with several Japanese subs in the Pacific," he proclaimed.

Knox had "buck fever!" according to an anonymous Navy source in Washington. "The Japanese are far from their home waters, apparently too fearful of prowling United States destroyers to take time to aim carefully."

These opinions were quickly mooted by events. On Dec. 23, three ships were hit by the Advance Force. *I-17* used deck guns to lightly damage *Larry Doheny*, 7,038 tons, 80 miles southwest of Eureka; *I-21* torpedoed *Montebello*, 8,272 tons, near Santa Barbara; *I-21* later used deck guns to damage *Idaho*, 6,418 tons, in the same area.

Nishino, chasing *Larry Doheny*, was frustrated by the ship's harried zig-zags, and launched a torpedo. The Long Lance missed and detonated inside Estero Bay, awakening nearly everyone in the hamlet of Cayucas. "It nearly threw me to the floor!" exclaimed the wife of the town constable.

Union Oil tanker *Montebello*, carrying a full load of gasoline, had an abrupt change of command at midnight. The skipper, a fellow named Andreassen, had suddenly refused his commission and retired to his cabin, locking the door. First Mate Olaf Eckstrom assumed command, and at 5:30 a.m. lookout William Srez informed the skipper the tanker was being haunted by a dark shape astern. "Srez was right — it was the silhouette of a Jap submarine, a big fellow, possibly 300 feet long," reported Eckstrom. "I ordered the quartermaster at the wheel, John McIsaac, to zig-zag. For ten minutes we tried desperately to cheat the sub, but it was no use …"

Montebello's lifeboats reach the rocky shore of Santa Barbara.

A torpedo erupted square amidships. "There was a big blast and the ship shuddered and trembled and we knew she was done for," remembered Srez. "The skipper was cool as a snowdrift. He yelled an order to stand by the lifeboats and then an order to abandon ship, and there was something in the way he gave those orders that made us proud to be serving under him."

Montebello's crew scrambled safely away as Matsumura in *I-21* began hammering at the stricken vessel with gunfire. Eckstrom ordered the lifeboats to stay within sight of the tanker. "But 45 minutes later, just as the dawn was breaking, she went down," he said.

The sinking was visible from shore, where scores of awakened Californians were watching from the beach. "She upended like a giant telephone pole and slowly settled into the sea," reported M.L. Waltz, editor of a weekly newspaper. "But there was no fire or explosions about the ship that we could see."

TORPEDO JUNCTION

Rain obliterated the view from shore. Matsumura then opened fire on the lifeboats. "Shell splinters hit our boat and she began to leak like a sieve," said Srez. "We began rowing shoreward, with some of us leaning on our oars for all we were worth and the others bailing."

Luckily, no one was hit. The leaking lifeboat didn't reach shore until noon, when it tumbled over in the surf and Eckstrom nearly drowned. Srez was furious. "As soon as I dry out, I'm gonna look for another ship," he seethed. "Those Japs haven't scared me yet and they never will."

Idaho, tiny compared to the other merchant ships, had been shadowed by a submarine since Dec. 20, possibly *I-9*. She blundered into the area of *Montebello's* sinking and was harassed by gunfire from *I-21*. The tanker was damaged and put in to Long Beach in the afternoon.

At dawn the next day, Christmas Eve, *I-19* fired a torpedo at *Barbara Olson*, also off Long Beach. The torpedo detonated prematurely, only a hundred feet from the merchant's flank. By the time Navy subchaser *Amethyst* rushed to the scene, there were no subs to chase.

I-19 had moved near Point Fermin, in the Catalina Channel. Port Fermin resident William Anderson called the Coast Guard station at San Pedro at 10 a.m. to report an odd fishing boat; it seemed to ride "too smoothly for the heavy sea that was running."

The Coast Guardsman taking the call was amused that Anderson was claiming to see a "submarine camouflaged like a fishing boat." The civilian was instructed to "maintain watch and call back with a progress report."[6]

An Imperial Japanese Navy photograph of an I-boat leaving a sinking freighter in her wake. The casual nature of the image suggests it wasn't taken during the frenzied attacks off California — she may be a Dutch ship in the Indian Ocean.

[6] *A newsman, Anderson relayed his sighting to the* San Francisco Chronicle, *which headlined "Sub Uses Fishing Boat Camouflage."*

Absaroka founders within sight of the coast, kept afloat only by her cargo of lumber. The image below was taken from shore, and shows three lifeboats leaving the wallowing ship.

Opposite, starlet Jane Russell gives scale to the torpedo hole in Absaroka.

Fifteen minutes later, McCormick Steamship Company's *Absaroka*, 5,695 tons, passed across the point with a load of lumber for San Diego. Seaman Joseph Scott saw a whale to port. "At least I was going to say, look over yonder, a whale, when I changed my mind," he recalled.

"There's a goddamn Jap submarine!" Scott screamed. The 48-year-old sailor had had four ships torpedoed under him during World War I; he knew what he was looking at before anyone else could react.

"You know how a guy will lose control and cuss at a time like that, caught by surprise and all," he apologized later.

The first torpedo fired by *I-19* missed, followed in its wake by another. The second missile struck the vessel squarely amidships.

At a machine gun post below the old lighthouse at Point Fermin, Sergeant James Hedwood saw "a fountain of water spout 100 feet in the air at the stern." The force of the Long Lance strike whipped the freighter around the clock, pointing her in the opposite direction, her "stern to sea and her bow facing toward land."

The blast tossed deckhands in the water and vaulted tons of lumber into the sky "as if a man were throwing matchsticks around."

Harry Greenwald was one of the hands blown off the deck. As he fought his way back to the surface, Greenwald was astonished to see the ship's railing within reach. *Absaroka* had heeled so far over from the force of the blast that her deck had gone vertical. He grabbed the rail and was lifted out of the water as the ship righted herself.

TORPEDO JUNCTION

Another seaman thrown overboard, Herbert Stevens, had his leg shattered by the blast. He yelled for help. Deckhand Joe Ryan slid to the teetering rail and tossed a line to Stevens. Ryan began pulling Stevens back to the ship when what was left of the deck load of lumber shifted and fell on Ryan from behind, pulping his head and neck. His body fell into the sea, beside Stevens.

Bombers and subchaser *Amethyst* showed up and peppered the sea with charges. *Absaroka*, in fact, though awash, was buoyed by her lumber cargo and in no immediate danger of sinking. Skipper Hans B. Olson hitched the ship onto a Navy tug and soon she was beached on a sandspit near Fort MacArthur.

Wearing a suitably solemn expression, starlet Jane Russell was posed inside *Absaroka's* massive torpedo hole, holding up a sign warning "A slip of a lip may (have sunk this) ship."

Near Monterey Bay the same day, *I-23* used her deck gun on "an old gunboat" but failed to tag the enemy ship until its rudder was struck. Steamship *Dorothy Philips* floundered around in circles, watched by concerned citizens on shore. The steamer eventually ran aground, and *I-23* fired a few more rounds at her for good measure and beat it back into the open sea.

The underfunded and undertrained West Coast anti-submarine forces were making up for their shortfalls with energy and imagination. Any boat or airplane that could be spared was prowling for the Imperial Navy, and spoiling for a fight. It became dangerous even to poke up a periscope.

An order from Vice Admiral

Shimizu told the nine submarines to leave the West Coast area on Christmas Day and return to Kwajalein. But there was a "Christmas present" — all the deck shells they could fire at Mainland targets.

I-15 surfaced on Christmas Eve, near the Golden Gate, and the crew began running out 4.7-inch ammunition. A cease-fire order suddenly flashed from Tokyo — Admiral Osami Nagano was over-riding Shimizu's Christmas bonus. The disappointed crew packed away the shells and swung the submarine to the west. Although he asked, Orita never learned why the assault was canceled. [7]

If the I-boat wasn't near a city, the plan was to shell lighthouses on Christmas Eve, and there was great anticipation. On *I-25*, a lottery was held so non-gunners would have a chance to fire a round into the enemy camp, which was won by the I-boat's cook.

On the way to the West Coast, *I-25* had dodged four bombs dropped by *Enterprise* planes. Once, after surfacing, the I-boat got a wireless report about enemy transports, but couldn't track them down. The crew was restless and impatient to get into the shooting war. Aviator Nobuo Fujita, babysitting his busted airplane aboard *I-25*, got an idea and hashed it out with executive officer Tatsuo Tsukado. He wanted to arm the Glen, not only to scout for enemy ships, but to attack them as well. Their imaginations went wild, and they spun out probabilities; attacking the Panama Canal, aircraft factories, what-ever. Tsukado wrote it all down and promised to prod higher-ups. [8]

I-25's Christmas target was the Cape Disappointment lighthouse at the mouth of the Columbia River in Oregon, but the submarine was routed south by Shimizu's order of Dec. 22, to intercept Navy ships reputed to be swarming north out of the Panama Canal. By Christmas, *I-25* was near Monterey, where it reversed course. Once again, the war had eluded them.

On Christmas afternoon, a periscope was spotted near Redondo Beach, within yards of *Kohala*, a decommissioned barkentine schoo-ner used by the city as a fishing barge. Only a few miles from where *Absaroka* now lay beached, it was assumed that this was the same submarine, and an Army harbor defense unit quickly wheeled a 75mm howitzer onto Redondo Pier.

The soldiers began lobbing shells at *Kohala*. Word reached the nearby Los Alamitos Naval Auxiliary Air Station and the pilot trainees scrambled, led by a visiting Royal Air Force bomber pilot. The hard-working *Amethyst*, called to the scene, was advised that the planes would "mark position of disabled submarine." A few minutes later, she rounded Palos Verdes peninsula and witnessed a frenzy of bomb-dropping and water-strafing.

Amethyst charged the target, firing her three-inch gun. Her log then states, *Puzzled at the apparent lack of response from the enemy sub, despite the shelling, bombing and now depth charging ... at 1706 lowered boat to investigate target which proved to be a roof off a small fishing vessel with galley chimney attached. At 1808 picked up boat and took target in tow ...*

[7] This order coincides almost exactly with a similar don't-shoot order sent to the Japanese commander on Wake Island, who was preparing to execute several hundred captured Marines. Perhaps the Imperial Navy got rare cold feet concerning world opinion. A partial clarification sent out later stated that the Imperial Navy was concerned the shells might hit Japanese-Americans.

[8] Imperial Navy submarines built to bomb the Panama Canal were on their first operational cruise when the war ended.

TORPEDO JUNCTION

Kohala was split in two by the attack, and the drifting halves became menaces to navigation. Battery F of the 105th Field Artillery got a commendation for firing their 75mm off the Redondo Pier.

Advance Force submarines were grudgingly leaving the West Coast. A radio message on Dec. 26 from Rear Admiral Tsutomu Sato, commander of the First Submarine Squadron, directed his large blockade and raiding submarines — *I-15*, *I-17* and *I-19* — to rendezvous off Oahu. The next day, another message was sent to all Japanese submarine commanders in the Pacific, giving them the numbers and sizes of American ships currently in Pearl Harbor. Where this intelligence was obtained is not known, though it may have been divined from the Dec. 16 overflight by *I-7's* floatplane.

On Dec. 27, Sato reported to Shimizu as the submarines sailed west, noting that the Panama Canal watch hadn't worked out. *Submarine I-9 continued patrol since the 22nd south of San Francisco but could not ascertain enemy condition. Left Guadalupe island, bound for Kwajalein.*

And then, almost as an afterthought, *On 12 December, at grid point (censored), we sank an American freighter, the* Lahaina.

On Dec. 29, Sato ordered the three submarines to attack American ships around Oahu on New Year's Eve. The attacks were not carried out, for reasons unknown.

Another message, also intercepted by the Americans, complained about the cold and treacherous currents along the Pacific coast. Complaints also were registered about the 20-foot periscopes that rose from the I-boat conning towers, too short to peer above the waves and not reveal the submarine from the air. *Suggest new submarines be fitted with longer periscopes, to allow deeper running depth,* said one. Japanese submarines began releasing false periscopes during this period, a length of black-painted bamboo with a weight on one end. They bobbed vertically in the ocean, and caused no end of false sightings.

The only I-boat left off the coast by Dec. 27 was *I-25*, still futilely searching for targets. That night, in miserably dark and rainy conditions off the Columbia River, *I-25's* skipper Commander Meiji Tagami chased tanker *Connecticut*, 8,684 tons, right up the river. Hit with one torpedo, *Connecticut* stopped dead. Tagami was readying a second torpedo when the tanker suddenly began to heel over. Tagami watched the crew get away in boats, and later heard on radio they had reached shore. The Japanese skipper didn't know that *Connecticut* had stopped because she had run aground in the shallow river.

RACIAL FALLOUT

The West Coast remained in a siege mentality that would soon have tragic consequences for Americans of Japanese descent. Typical of the hysteria of the period was this J. Edgar Hoover communique to all Pacific Coast commands: There is a plan for an air and sea attack against San Diego, San Pedro and San Francisco, to take place about dawn either New Year's Day or the following Sunday. It is possible that the attack will be made against San Diego or San Pedro first. The attack will be by German airmen from across the border where planes are now under cover, taking off before dawn and coming over flying high. If air forces are alert, this can be broken up before they reach their objectives. Source and reliability of this information uncertain. Remember Pearl Harbor.

THE PACIFIC COAST "Q-SHIP"

Rumors of hidden Japanese bases deep in Mexico and on the Baja Peninsula reached a fever pitch at the end of 1941, resulting in several punitive expeditions into the area. They were delicate operations as Mexico had not yet declared war on Japan. An American colonel — referred to in Stillwell's diaries as "XYZ" to save face — was teamed up with seven Mexican generals and several Mexican divisions. The final, and largest sweep was called Expedition E-Easy; it lasted two months and established five search bases on Baja.

Teamed for this covert operation were a platoon of Mexican infantry and a dozen Spanish-speaking American officers from 115th Observation Squadron. The Americans wore civilian clothing, and their vehicles and aircraft had the white American star painted out; the word "Brown" was added atop the blue circle, in white letters.

In January, 1942, small seaplane tender Pelican (AVP-6) was hustled to San Francisco's Hunter's Point shipyard and hidden behind raised curtains at the end of a pier. She emerged as Normandie II, apparently an innocent fishing vessel. Well-hidden, however, were sonar and radar gear, a bristling complement of machine guns, light cannons and K-gun depth charge racks. In a "bait box" on the stern was an SOC scout plane that could be lifted into action by the "net winch." The concept was similar to the "Q-Ships" of the first World War, armed bait to attract enemy raiders. The crew, dressed in civilian clothes, remained at sea for a year, searching the waters off Southern California and Baja for Japanese submarines and an oiler supposedly refueling the I-boats. Normandie II's orders were to sink the oiler, capture her renegade crew and destroy her shore facilities. The decoy rarely put in to port because of her secret mission, which wasn't scrubbed until May, 1943. Once again Pelican, she served in the Atlantic as an AVP.

Above, Pelican disguised as Normandie II plies the Baja coast, hoping to entice Japanese submarines. The large crate on the stern contains a seaplane. Below, the crew poses in civilian fishing clothes. Note the screens in the background; they hide Pelican's reconstruction.

I-25 abandoned the coast, running to Kwajalein. On the voyage, Tagami ran across a ship near Johnston Island that he claimed looked like a seaplane tender, perhaps the *Langley*. He fired torpedoes at it, claiming a kill. Since *Langley* was actually sunk Feb. 27, south of Java by bombers, the ship *I-25* fired at has never been identified.

On Kwajalein, *I-25* rested and refitted, the crew enjoying fresh vegetables and repainting the battered I-boat. After the long month sailing under the noses of the Americans, an officer was killed in a tragic accident. The watertight door on the aircraft hangar was jammed shut; he pressed on it, releasing the internal pressure. It burst open, swatting him across the deck.

I-8 made a West Coast sortie, arriving off San Francisco in early February. She cruised up toward Seattle, but claimed seeing no targets. She returned to Japan in March, with torpedoes still in her tubes.

Submarines continued to strike in Hawaiian waters. On Jan. 23, oiler *Neches*, 7,383 tons, was blown out of the water a few hours after she left Pearl Harbor. Killed by *I-72*, *Neches* was the only oiler in the Central Pacific and was on her way to rendezvous with the task force that had attempted to relieve Wake Island. Without oil available, the task force returned to Pearl Harbor.

Five days later, Army transport *General Royal T. Frank*, loaded with Big Island inductees on their way home after completing basic training on Oahu, suddenly exploded in the channel between Hana on Maui and Kohala. The round-bottomed, 224-ton *Royal T. Frank* — an ex-minelayer called *"Rolling" T. Frank* by seasick servicemen — was accompanied on this trip by a four-stack destroyer and small freighter *Kalae*, which was towing a barge. The three ships had been tied up in Kahului harbor for 24 hours while a barge was hurriedly loaded with half a million dollars' worth of heavy earth-moving equipment, urgently needed to complete Army runways at General Albert Lyman airfield in Hilo.

PEAKING EARLY

The only "glorious target" to present itself during this period was aircraft carrier Saratoga, *the U.S. Navy's largest warship design. Torpedoed on Jan. 11 within 400 miles of Pearl Harbor, the carrier was knocked out of the war. After this event — the high point of the Advance Force assault on America — the remaining submarines ran out of fuel and time, and had to retire to Kwajalein. All subsequent attacks were simply follow-on sorties, carried out piecemeal and without the overwhelming numbers and planning that characterized Advance Force operations.*

I-71 tried the following night to torpedo *Kalae* and her barge of equipment, but the torpedo missed and slammed amidships into *Royal T. Frank*. A second torpedo also missed. A survivor reported "the ship did not seem to blow up or sink, she just disintegrated and disappeared in 30 or 40 seconds." The ship went down within 30 seconds. Twenty-four men were lost, the largest loss of life in a Hawaiian sinking. Seventeen draftees and 12 crew went down with *Royal T. Frank*. *Kalae* cut loose her tow and began pulling soldiers out of the water.

Ship radio operator Private Victor Rabinowitz was trapped by a mast cable which pinned his leg — the ship went under and the cable loosened, and he popped to surface. Chief Engineer Francis Wilson was also pinned by debris, which included an automobile.

Army transport
General Royal T.
Frank.

Kalae took 36 injured men to the isolated town of Hana, Maui, where they overwhelmed the small hospital. The 13 most seriously injured were treated by First Aid volunteers in the Kaeleku Sugar Company gymnasium.

The barge, meanwhile, drifted away in the fierce current. Colonel William Lyman, commander of Army engineers in Hawaii, placed a radio-telephone call to Oahu requesting a military aircraft from Maui be shaken loose and assigned to locating the barge. *Royal T. Frank* had sunk so quickly that this call was the first indication on Oahu that something was amiss.

The next day, *Kalae* was guided by military aircraft to the barge, which was again taken in tow and pulled to Hilo. Just as freighter and barge slipped into the city breakwater, another torpedo raced by.

I-71 never reported firing on *Royal T. Frank*, and it is possible that the old transport might have had an internal explosion, or struck a floating mine or expired torpedo. The blast was so all-consuming that the only piece of *Royal T. Frank* found floating was the ship's wooden pilot's wheel. [9]

On Feb. 1, Admiral Halsey's planes swept over Kwajalein. Using information supplied by submarine *Dolphin*, which had spied on the atoll on Jan. 27, the bombers suspected Kwajalein was filled with Japanese submarines, resting after harassing the West Coast.

As the aircraft blasted buildings on shore, the massed submarines pulled their plugs and sank to the bottom of the lagoon. By the time the planes turned their attention to the ships, none of the submarines were visible, and none were damaged. Shimizu was injured, however, and through blood and tears, ordered the aroused submarines to dash after the enemy carriers.

The American were too far away; the subs never caught up. *I-9* and *I-23* continued on to Hawaii, joining *I-24*, since they were already going in that direction. *I-17* went on to the West Coast. Shimizu was relieved of command and returned to Japan to convalesce.

[9] *The wheel wound up in the Army Transportation Museum at Fort Eustis, VA.*

I-17 sank merchant *William H. Berg* by torpedo off San Francisco on March 1. The I-boat surfaced to administer a coup de gras with her deck gun, but was herself fired on. Skipper Kozo Nishino submerged, surprised that the Americans had armed civilian ships so quickly. The rules were shifting. Future patrols off America were fleeting.

I-26, which had fired the first torpedo of the war at *Cynthia Olson*, didn't get a chance to shoot again until June 7, 1942. In her favorite hunting grounds off Seattle, Commander Minoro Yokota blew the belly off of 3,286-ton *Coast Trader*. The ship sank within 40 minutes. The submarine was close enough to shore to see the startled faces of Americans gawking at the action, and Yokota dived and raced out of the area. American planes failed to turn up any sign of the submarine, although they did spot *I-25*, nearly 500 miles away.

A Naval Board of Inquiry decided *Coast Trader* had suffered some kind of catastrophic internal malfunction, rather than submarine attack, a conclusion that *Coast Trader's* survivors disagreed with.

On June 20, *I-25* torpedoed steamship *Fort Camosun* on her maiden voyage, 70 miles southwest of Cape Flattery, but the steamer managed to limp into port with the aid of four tugs lashed alongside.

On July 14, *I-7* sank freighter *Arcata* in the North Pacific. The ship was demolished with gunfire, and the crew took to the lifeboats. They were rescued near Kodiak Island on July 22, and most needed medical attention.

Caught out in the open by American bombers while the crew was taking a smoke break in August, *I-25* barely submerged when the bombs hit, the shearing force snapping off the submarine's aerial and causing a leak.

Though she couldn't message, *I-25* continued to patrol. *Larry Doheny*, which had been targeted by *I-17* in December, was sunk by the ubiquitous *I-25* on Oct. 5, 1942, five miles south of Gold Beach, Oregon. After this sinking, no more American ships were lost along the West Coast. The final victim in every sortie east of Hawaii had been sunk by *I-25*.

With one torpedo left, *I-25* cruised west. On Oct. 11, about 800 miles out, Sonarman Kou Maki declared there were two other submarines just ahead. Commander Tagami decided they must be American, and when *I-25* was within 500 yards, he touched off his last torpedo. The missile struck the lead submarine, breaking its back in a terrific explosion. The explosion sprang rivets in *I-25's* hull. The target submarine sank within 20 seconds, her mate firing five futile rounds at *I-25* before racing away in a zig-zag pattern.

Tagami reported the sinking as an American submarine. It was later determined that he had sunk Russian submarine *L-16*. At the time, the Soviet Union was not at war with Japan, and claimed the "cruel and foul blow" was at least partly the responsibility of the United States.[10] Despite *I-25's* score of victories, bad judgment seemed to dog the I-boat.

[10] *Among those lost on L-16 was Sergei Andreevich Mihailoff, a naturalized American citizen who had volunteered to serve as interpreter aboard the Russian ship. He is not listed among America's war dead.*

26 STRIKING AT AMERICA

The West Coast Under Assault

At the end of December 1941, a progress report was signaled to those I-boats still east of Kwajalein, as well as Rear Admiral Matome Ugaki, Chief of Staff of the combined fleet.

On the basis of reports received from all ships, all phases of action were quickly completed. To judge from enemy radio reports we believe the psychological threat visited upon enemy peoples has been very great, said Rear Admiral Tsutomu Sato of the 1st Submarine Squadron, who also noted that the timetable and methods agreed upon in the attack plans weren't followed, for a variety of reasons.

It appears that patrol of enemy shores has become very strict, and control of the movement of vessels is being exercised. The execution of this operation in quick succession is becoming difficult and there is the feeling that chances of its effectiveness are decreasing ...

Sinking enemy shipping, in other words, was becoming a difficult proposition now that the Americans were fighting back. It looked to Sato as if the submarines were in for the long haul.

This didn't go down well with the Japanese submariners, trained not for the stealthy cat-and-mouse game of commerce raiding, but for briefly furious, glorious naval engagements with enemy capital ships.

To keep the submarines active, Sato suggested it would be *expeditious not to hold to any one area but to carry out surprise attacks in many places, appearing unexpectedly at irregular intervals.*

Even this had its problems in the stormy waters off the American coast. *It is almost impossible to use (dive) planes to cover the surface of the sea,* reported Sato. *And it is very difficult to maintain periscope depth, especially north of San Francisco Bay, where there are strong winds and waves are high. Torpedo warfare and gun warfare are both extremely difficult to effect.*

Accordingly, Sato suggested that new equipment and procedures were "urgently" needed: strengthening the buoyancy tanks, increasing the length of the periscopes, and practice in shooting torpedoes while "deeply submerged and in high waves."

Following these new tactics, *I-17* arrived off Santa Barbara on Feb. 21, 1942. Seaman Genji Hara, skipper Kozo Nishino's radio

operator, recorded the event in his diary: "*I-17* is once more off the coast of America, but this time we are alone. Our movements have been slow, and the sea ripples softly along the sides of our ship. The vast spread of the Pacific seems like a watery waste to me. Wireless reception from the 6th Fleet communications tower on Kwajalein was very good today, but I could not hear much of what *I-23* was sending. She is in the Hawaiian area, and must be having trouble with her transmission equipment …"

Around midnight, as he began to bunk in, Hara heard a lookout reporting a lighthouse to port. It turned out to be a small boat, and Nishino turned away from it and increased speed. It might only be a fishing boat, on the other hand, it could be a submarine chaser.

By coincidence perhaps, the small boat turned in the same direction as the submarine and sniffed at her wake. The loudspeaker brayed, "There may be an enemy patrol boat after us. All hands rig for depth-charge attack!"

I-17 slipped into the ocean's dark envelope and all unnecessary equipment was switched off. There were long breathless moments as the crew waited for the lashing of sonar, or the hammering of depth charges. After a safe interval, *I-17* surfaced and turned back toward the coast. Hara, now wide awake, went to the radio room and was surprised by a stack of recent messages from Tokyo Bay.

"They listed places we were to bombard, and others (like San Diego), we were to avoid," recorded Hara. "I felt a thrill, as though we would really carry out the task this time and not have it canceled, as it had been in December."

This was a reversal of policy. The December shellings were called off to dampen negative publicity, as well as to not endanger West Coast citizens of Japanese descent. These Japanese-Americans were being relocated to the interior by executive order — Roosevelt had speculated on creating "concentration camps" for Japanese-Americans as early as 1936 — and this racial hysteria was well publicized in Japan.[1]

I-17 boiled to the surface on the night of Feb. 24, and when systems were secured, Nishino spoke to the crew.

"We are now entering Santa Barbara Strait," Nishino announced. "We will lie submerged tomorrow, doing reconnaissance with our periscope. Then, tomorrow night, we will surface after dark and bombard the Elwood Oil Field, inside the strait."

Hara, a substitute gunner on the deck crew, was thrilled. *We are really going to do it this time!* he thought. Hara went out onto the pitching deck to check out the weapon. Thirty-knot winds rattled the waves into whitecaps. A dull moon shone down, a nimbus of haze blurring it.

Hara stood back as the regular gun crew poked at the weapon. He looked up into the sky, located the Big Dipper — the Japanese thought of it as the Great Bear — and following its lip, the North Star. He tried to estimate the direction in which Japan lay.

[1] *The relocation benefited only those who illegally seized Japanese-American property, and the Imperial Japanese Navy, which then resumed its assault on the American mainland.*

The vast distances yawned before him, an abyss of water and war. Hara felt woozily sentimental. He hoped that if he died, his family and neighbors would know that *I-17* had shot across thousands of miles of Pacific to strike a blow for Japan.

Throughout the next day, Hara hung out in the sound room with a friend, a seaman named Nagashima. Nagashima listened carefully for the chop-chop of American destroyers, and laughed suddenly when they were surrounded by bleating fish. They shared a lunch of sushi; vinegared rice papered in bean curd. An officer passing down from the conning tower told them land was within sight.

I-17 trundled slowly and blindly into the strait, not displaying even her periscope. Hara tried to read a book. *No use.* He had just decided to distract himself by eating again when, "All hands to battle stations" issued from the loudspeaker. It was about 5:30 p.m.

Ten minutes later, Nishino gave a "battle-surface" order. "Man the deck gun!" he snapped as *I-17* rose from the ocean. The three-man gun crew dashed onto the draining deck.

Jealous, Hara listened below. "Captain Nishino kept calling out, asking the distance to land and the submarine's depth, giving instructions about the targets," Hara wrote later that evening. "He ordered that shells be fired only at the oil tanks.

"The rest of us in our 'windowless barracks' could only imagine what it was like from the sounds and shocks that came through the hull. *One ... two ... three ...* we could imagine the gunners loading each of those rounds; the trainer and the pointer trying to sight on the target. We had counted up to 17 when the shooting suddenly stopped."

Hara flipped on the radio and listened for American reaction. *Nothing.* He spun the receiver dials. There was only the hiss of night static. No warnings or calls for help.

The gun crew dropped back into *I-17* and the craft began to pick up speed. Two of the gun crew, named Onodera and Nagata, stuck grinning faces into the radio room to tease Hara.

"What did we hit?" bubbled Hara.

"I don't know. I only saw flashes," said Onodera. "I had no time to confirm anything."

"It was beautiful!" crowed Nagata. "I could even see the headlights of automobiles."

I-17's navigator joined in. "We surfaced and started shelling right after sunset," he explained to those who had missed the excitement. "There was no reply from shore until we started to speed away. Some enemy planes tried to drop flares on us, but they were far away from our position."

As *I-17* beat a retreat, the chief gunner tossed phony bamboo periscopes into their wake.

Someone realized they were the first in the Imperial Navy to strike directly at the American heartland, and the sailors beamed. "Even if we didn't hit a thing, they know *I-17* has been here," noted Hara. "We all felt like heroes."

350

STRIKING AT AMERICA

Though the damage was minimal, it was the first foreign attack on the continental United States since 1814. Most of the shells had peppered the Goleta oil field, causing — at most — $500 damage to one oil pumping house. Captain Bernard Hagen, an artilleryman, was wounded while deactivating the fuse of a dud shell — it exploded, throwing shrapnel into his right thigh. Hagen received 50 days in Hoff General Hospital in Santa Barbara for his trouble, plus a Purple Heart. He's probably the only servicemen to be wounded within the United States by the direct result of enemy action during the war.

There is a widespread story that *I-17* skipper Nishino had been embarrassed by American laughter when he fell into brambles while touring the site before the war. This tale, certainly apocryphal, was repeated by the Associated Press as recently as the mid-'80s.

The Santa Barbara attack spun imaginations into high gear. On the night of Feb. 24 there was a terrific aerial battle over Los Angeles, with 1,440 anti-aircraft rounds bursting over the blacked-out city. By morning, it was apparent to military authorities that it was all a colossal case of the heebie-jeebies.[2]

Nishino sank *William H. Berg* on March 1 and then returned to Imperial Navy territory.

In April, *I-15*, *I-16*, *I-19* and *I-25* were resting cheek to jowl in a Yokosuka drydock when Jimmy Doolittle's B-25s attacked Japan. The submarine tender *Taigei* suffered a close-by bomb burst, which tore open a hole in the ship and thoroughly rattled the submariners in the area. Mochitsura Hashimoto, in *I-24*, claimed additional plans to attack the U.S. Mainland were in retaliation for the Doolittle raid.

I-26 got her chance to lob shells at a lighthouse on June 20, when she fired 17 rounds at Estevan Point lighthouse, on Vancouver Island, British Columbia. No shells hit the lighthouse, although the bracketing bursts caused consternation in the tiny farming community of Hesquiat just behind the tower. On the submarine's bridge, Com-

[2] The movie "1941" was based on the so-called "Battle of Los Angeles," which actually occurred in 1942.

A Japanese shell among the shore debris near Point Estevan lighthouse.

mander Minoro Yokota could hear pigs squealing in terror after each explosion.

The enemy shells were the first to land on Canada since the War of 1812. The enemy then had been America; some believe that the 1942 shells were American as well. Lighthouse keeper Robert Lally claimed the shells actually came from a cruiser, a notion that Canadian lighthouse historian Donald Graham has interpreted as a secret American attempt to goose Canadian attitudes toward the Pacific War. The shells, he figures, must have come from a U.S. Navy ship, because they all missed their target, and the Japanese writing on the unexploded shells could be easily washed off. The Americans were baiting the Canadians, trying to alert them to poor defensive measures along the coast.

Whoever fired the shells, it worked. The day before, an argument had begun in the Canadian parliament over conscription; after the shelling was announced, the pro-conscription forces carried the majority. Graham's feelings about Japanese submariners are clear in his book "Keepers of the Light." "There's no more despicable trade in warfare than commanding a submarine," he wrote. "It takes a man with a shriveled soul to peer through a periscope … and order torpedoes away."

One of the shells was found on June 8, 1973, and detonated by a Canadian EOD team. The resulting explosion splashed bright yellow-green picric acid around the area, which identified the shell as Japanese. Americans had stopped using picric acid as an explosive in the early '30s because it was so unstable.

After this adventure, whether Yokota was the shriveled soul or not, *I-26* returned to Yokosuka.

The next night, June 21, *I-25* used a fishing fleet as cover to enter the Columbia River, Commander Meiji Tagami correctly guessing the boats would know where the minefield lay. Once well into the mouth, Tagami swung the submarine around, pointing her nose at the open sea, and her stern gun at the lights on shore. He was near where *Mauna Ala* had spewed Christmas trees on the beach.

Tagami's intelligence estimates placed an American submarine base close by. He didn't know the base had never been build. He also didn't know the Columbia was rimmed with heavy firepower.

Chief Gunner Sensuke Izutu elevated the gun 30 to 40 degrees and began pumping shells toward the lights. In the gun batteries on shore, startled Americans jumped off their cots and rushed to their posts. One man raced into a dark parking lot and slammed his head into a parked truck. He wheeled back into his barracks, blood coursing down his face, and the other artillerymen figured there "must be Japs all over the place!"

One round impacted about 300 yards short of Battery Russell. The duty officer was Jack Wood, of The Dalles, Oregon, and he was playing cribbage with his executive officer when *I-25's* shells hit. He raced upstairs onto the battery observation platform, and clearly saw the submarine gun flashing, far beyond the range of his own guns. He elected to hold pat until the submarine either drifted into range or fled into the night. [3]

By then most of the Americans at nearby Battery Pratt could clearly see the submarine as well. They weren't given permission to fire and this rankled many. The official explanation was that the submarine appeared to be out of range which might be true — and that firing at it would only expose the shore batteries to counter-fire — which might be speculative. The Americans did not yet have radar on the coast batteries, although visual triangulation had been developed to a fine art .

Most of the 17 shells fired by *I-25* exploded harmlessly on the beach and among the skunk cabbage marshes. One smashed the backstop of the Battery Russell baseball diamond.

I-25's air officer Nobuo Fujita had a more radical plan. Arming his little "Glen" E14Y amphibian with fire bombs, he dropped the charges on Oregon forests in September. It was hoped that the entire northwest would burn down to the ocean's edge. Fujita was an expert in the tiny planes, having already flown reconnaissance missions over Sydney, Melbourne, Wellington, Auckland, Hobart in Tasmania and Suva in Fiji. The top speed of the airplane was only 150 miles per hour, and the submarine was helpless on the surface while recovering aircraft. But Fujita was never spotted.

During the year beginning with the attack on Pearl Harbor, 38 Glen flights were made, from Zanzibar to Oregon. A quarter of the planes were lost, primarily to landing and recovery accidents. *I-19's* plane was ruined on May 27, 1942, while it was being prepared for a night flight in the Aleutians. An American destroyer loomed up out of the darkness, and the I-boat crash-dived with the plane still on deck.

A Japanese intelligence document captured in 1944 listed all known E14Y flights during this time period, but records for actions in the Aleutians are fuzzy. A July 7, 1942, battle between a Japanese submarine and 125-foot USCG cutter *McLane* — paired with halibut-schooner-turned-patrol boat *YP-251* — near Cape Addington, Alaska, for example, officially ended in the sinking of *RO-32*. This claim is complicated by *RO-32* apparently surviving the war as a training hulk in Japan, and by the appearance of a seaplane the day after the encounter.

The aircraft, a "small unmarked floatplane," approached *YP-251* and signaled "Follow me" by light. The crew aboard the schooner followed obediently, supposing that the plane was leading them to another submarine. Skipper Captain Niels Thomsen had second thoughts, and ordered the lightly armed "yippie boat" back toward the safety of the coast; the plane could just as easily be setting them up for

[3] Although of smaller caliber, deck guns could elevate to 45 degrees for optimum range. Standard coast artillery guns could usually reach only 30 degrees.

ambush. Although the aircraft appeared twice more with the same message, *YP-251* refused to follow. A later investigation revealed no Allied aircraft in the area during that time period. During the years since, Native Americans have occasionally reported Japanese military artifacts found at remote lake encampments in the Aleutians. It is possible the aircraft was a Glen previously launched by the submarine sunk the day before. No I-boat is reported lost in the area, though several disappeared during 1942.

The plane could have been supplying a secret Japanese "coastwatcher" weather station, similar to those established by the Nazis on Greenland. Abandoned canning stations along the British Columbia coast are widely rumored to been used as Japanese provisioning stations, although any proof has not appeared.

With navigator PO2 Shoji Okuda in the back seat, on Sept. 9 Fujita dropped a pair of 170-pound incendiary bombs on a forest called Wheeler Ridge, near Brookings, Oregon. On Sept. 29, they repeated the mission, dropping two more bombs near Port Orford. The small blazes resulting from each mission were quickly found and put out.

Fujita spotted two merchant ships on the way back from Port Orford. After landing, Fujita's airplane was folded up and stuffed in the hangar envelope. He gave the navigators the ship coordinates and went below to take off his flight suit. *I-25* was just getting ready to submerge when an American dive bomber appeared out of the sun, straddling the submarine with small bombs.

They crash-dived. The last man down the water-tight hatch caught his clothing on the rim. He pulled and swore at the balky cloth while water poured in through the hatch. Finally, it pulled free and the hatch was tightly dogged.

At 25 meters down, an explosion rattled *I-25*. Another blast a few meters deeper burst pipes and lights. The switchboard room was flooded as water gushed from a shattered conduit tube.

Fujita was tossed about in his cabin, and then raced forward to find out what was going on. He heard Commander Tagami saying, "What a rascal! His action was close and speedy. Ha!"

Ordering silent running, Tagami kept the submarine at a depth of 60 to 70 meters. *I-25* drifted into the harbor of Port Orford, where it sloughed smoothly into the bottom silt. They remained there, quiet, until nightfall, and then slipped away. The ship's physician, a Dr. Hoshi, treated scraped heads.

Nobuo Fujita, the only Axis airman to bomb North America.

A Glen nuzzles up to her carrier sub. At left is the I-boat's bow with the plane catapult; in the foreground is the collapsible crane used to pull the plane from the water.

354

Another view of a Glen launching. The I-boat is headed into the wind, and the plane will be catapulted forward. The lifting crane is turned toward the camera. This image was probably taken in 1942; the Glen has been camouflaged with dark green paint and the pre-war dark gray of the submarine is beginning to be overpainted with black on the hangar forward of the sail.

The attack on *I-25* was made by Captain Jean H. Daugherty of the 42nd Bomb Group. Flying a Lockheed-built Hudson, he spotted the sub on the surface, circled into the sun and dove on it. He dropped his bombs just as the ship went under; seeing no slick, Daugherty figured he had missed.

Damage was actually extensive, causing some flooding inside the submarine, and broken pieces topside. It was the closest West Coast forces would come to hitting an I-boat during the war. It was after this incident that *I-25* sank the Russian submarine while on the way back to home port.

Air defense forces were caught by surprise by the initial thoroughness of the Japanese submarine assault. I-boats seemed to be everywhere during the weeks of December 1941. Every available aircraft was called to duty for anti-submarine patrols, including planes of the Army and the Civil Air Patrol.

B-25 bomber pilot Lieutenant "Brick" Holstrom claimed he sank a submarine off the Washington coast on Christmas Eve, 1941. Lieutenant Ted Lawson in another B-25 confirmed the slick on Christmas Day. [4]

Anti-submarine patrols off the West Coast had a life of their own, much different from the tense U-boat situation in the Atlantic. Soon after the attack on Pearl Harbor, newly drafted pilot trainee Wyman Spalding was sitting in a train station in Riverside, California waiting

[4] Holstrom and Lawson and their B-25s saw more action in the spring, flying with Doolittle off carrier Hornet. *Lawson wrote "Thirty Seconds Over Tokyo."*

for the coach to Thunderbird Field, Arizona. A tired-looking lieutenant colonel slumped down on the bench next to Spalding and idly asked where the recruit was headed.

Spalding told him. "Good, we need as many of you boys as we can get, out there," said the officer, indicating vaguely in the direction of Hawaii. He pulled a large chunk of shattered steel out of his trenchcoat pocket and showed it to Spalding. "This is what they were throwing at us," said the colonel.

"Sir, I've got some sad news to give you — I probably helped them get that stuff!" said Spalding, explaining that as a civilian he had helped load freighters with scrap metal and drums of chemicals destined for Japan.

"Crazy," said the officer, shaking his head.

"Bad, wasn't it?" said Spalding, referring to Pearl Harbor.

"Can't discuss it until I get to Washington," said the officer. "But yes — it was bad."

By summer of 1942, Spalding was training on the hot, new B-26 Marauder in Tampa, Florida. Some of the instructor pilots already boasted of sinking a U-Boat with the craft, and Spalding was itching to get in on the action overseas. In August, Spalding was given his assignment, and was disappointed to be sent back home to California, to the 41st Bomb Group, based at Hammer Field near Fresno. Pilots rated for twin engines were sorely needed for anti-submarine patrol.

Spalding made the transition from the supercharged B-26 to the relatively docile Hudson. The Army pilots were quartered at the Navy base at Alameda, the Navy being critically short of long-range patrol planes at the moment. Patrol blimps, which would eventually take over much of this duty, were still not off the ground.[5]

Spalding eventually logged 90 hours and 15 minutes of sub patrol off the California coast, the longest flight — a "butt-buster" — lasting seven and half hours. Most of the time was spent at about 2,000 feet droning lazily offshore, occasionally dropping down to the deck to buzz a ship. Spalding felt vaguely guilty as the Hudson roared by, himself warm and comfortable in the cockpit, as aircraft turbulence spun off and blasted sailors hanging on to the frigid freighter.

The idea was to check code flags strung up on the ships mast, the pattern of which seemed to change daily. Spalding was typical of the young pilots tapped for this important duty, eager beavers who found the long, dull flights an exercise in boredom. He heard others brag about shooting up whales, or rattling fishermen. And there was the possibility of running into an enemy submarine, like the Atlantic patrols were doing on a daily basis. A couple of missions flown out of the Navy field at Alameda in the fall of 1942, however, didn't fit the mold.

On Oct. 20, the Hudson was patrolling off Big Sur when radioman Charles Coffman shouted that enemy troops were landing at Santa Cruz. "Just got the word from Navy Intelligence!" he confirmed.

"Hot damn!" said Spalding.

He reversed the aircraft and pulled back on the throttles. The

[5] The L-8, a Goodyear-type blimp drafted by the Navy, caused a minor sensation in August when it drifted in from the ocean minus its crewmen. The airship had been seen some hours earlier, performing some traditional anti-submarine spotting operations at sea. It crashed in Daly City, south of San Francisco, and a Navy inquiry concluded the crew had fallen out while trying to observe something closely.

Hudson went howling over Point Lobos at 800 feet and the crew spotted hundreds of khaki-clad figures jumping off landing craft and swarming ashore.

Spalding charged the .30s in the plane's nose, instructed Coffman to drop bombs as soon as the first landing craft passed underneath. Gunner Anthony Franciosa[6] would open up with his .50 as the Hudson pulled away. Then they'd do it all over again.

[6] Not the actor.

The soldiers were square in Spalding's sights when Coffman yelled, "Hold it! The Navy says it's a mistake! They're our guys."

The landing craft were part of an exercise from Fort Ord. During the excitement, the Hudson crew neglected to notice that there were no bigger ships in the area that could have carried the landing craft.

Two days later, fog smothered the Golden Gate. Only Alameda was open, and at 4 a.m. Spalding was informed by Navy Intelligence that 17 Japanese submarines had been picked up near Pigeon Point. Once again crewed with Coffman and Franciosa, as well as new navigator John Rife, Spalding climbed above San Francisco Bay by dead reckoning and went 50 miles west, over the presumed location of the submarine flotilla. The sun, when it came up, revealed a carpet of cloud to the horizon, a flat, fluffy shroud that began at 2,000 feet and seemed impenetrable.

Spalding speculated that a little flying room might exist between the fog bank and the ocean. He asked the crew if they were game to try diving in; they were. The Hudson carefully began to let down into the void, a hurtling gray blankness that enveloped the craft.

The fog hung low, and Spalding had to warn himself to loosen up. Still, at 100 feet, nothing. At 75 feet, "Hey!" shouted Coffman. "I think I see water!"

"O.K. How close?"

"Can't tell."

Spalding's hand rested lightly on the throttle, ready to instantly advance. At 50 feet, Coffman shouted that he sees waves, as do they all. The ceiling was low, but it was clear; visibility was about half a mile. The Hudson skated along at about 150 miles per hour, a few dozen feet above the ocean, suspended between two horizons. They began a search pattern, flying an ever-widening grid over the ocean. Spalding divided his attention between the windshield and the engine and navigation instruments. It was nerve-wracking.

Looking up after an engine check, he was thoroughly rattled to find the Hudson rocketing along in a forest of ship masts, seeming to appear out of nowhere. The Hudson bounced around, weaving around the onrushing structures.

"Hell!" someone sputtered. "It's a convoy!" They were close enough to see American flags pass under their wingtips.

The fog lifted a bit, a situation deemed miraculous by Spalding, and he saw a destroyer riding herd on the convoy. He flew toward it, began circling. The destroyer began flashing Morse at the Hudson, far too quickly for Spalding to follow. He noticed also that every gun on

ADVANCE FORCE — PEARL HARBOR

the destroyer had been unlimbered and was tracking the bomber. He hoped the crews weren't trigger-happy. Spalding ordered Coffman to signal back something reassuring.

The Hudson passed over the convoy a couple more times, and then on the third pass, the ships disappeared. More low passes failed to flush them out. "This is crazy," decided Spalding. "Let's go home."

Their course set once again beneath the ceiling of fog, the bomber rolled over the ocean. Spalding had just settled down into the routine when rocks appeared directly ahead. He applied full throttle, horsed the plane upward; it squirted out of the fog bank a few feet away from the Pigeon Point lighthouse, maybe 15 feet, he estimated, from the edge of the cliff.

There had been no time to get frightened, and the Hudson had reacted smoothly. Leveling off at 4,000 feet, Spalding was feeling rather smug when he noticed that the port throttle linkage had slipped in the maneuver. He could no longer control both engines with one hand movement.

The only approach approved by the Navy tower at Alameda was over Oakland, with two enormous gas tanks in the glidepath. Spalding had to make several passes while experimenting with the unruly throttle control. Finally, the wheels touched halfway down the field. Close enough, figured Spalding, who began tapping the brakes. He could see the bay lapping at rocks ahead. As soon as the tailwheel touched, Spalding slammed down on the left brake and the Hudson spun around in the sand just at the end of the runway, facing the tower.

"Looks like we made it," said Spalding.

"Nice going, lieutenant," said Coffman, who looked pale.

The brakes took several minutes to cool. Spalding then taxied toward the tower, using the port brake to counteract the revving left engine, which tended to pull the plane too quickly. Spalding attempted to get the Hudson back in line with the other bombers, a maneuver which required two left turns. On the second, the left brake exploded and the bomber surged ahead. Spalding jabbed down on the right brake, and the bomber wheeled in that direction, the port propeller eating up several feet of the wing of the Hudson next to it. Aluminum splinters rained down as Spalding's Hudson lurched to a halt.

A sailor ran up and began spraying the plane's smoking brakes with a fire extinguisher. Spalding stuck his head out the cockpit window and bawled, "Hey cut that out! You'll ruin it!" Then, feeling like an idiot, he ducked back in.

Damn. Damn. Damn. Spalding stewed. It wasn't just another day of anti-submarine patrol. Instead of spotting 17 Jap subs, he had nailed two American airplanes.

STRIKING AT AMERICA

SUBMERGED SCARES

27

PHANTOM SUBMARINES AND SUSPICIOUS BEHAVIOR

Earl Kraft, an insurance investigator and member of the Hawaii Businessmen's Training Corps, was standing guard at Kula Sanitarium on Maui, on the evening of Dec. 8, 1941. He was alerted by a telephone call just short of 9 p.m. A light was reported flashing under a water tank near the hospital, a violation of the just-imposed blackout. As Kraft charged over to the water tank, the flashing stopped, then started again a few moments later inside the hospital.

Ward worker Marie Dupont was making her rounds in the hospital at the moment and noticed flashes under the closed door to room 401-B. Curious, she opened the door and found patient Shigeo Furukawa in the window, a pile of burnt matches at his feet. Knowing that he did not smoke, she asked what he was up to, and Furukawa said he was trying to see what time it was. Through the window, Dupont spotted the tank.

The district intelligence officer thought this was mighty suspicious, especially since Furukawa had been regularly visited by a couple of "enemy aliens" named Hamada and Matsuda, and Furukawa's name had been found the previous summer among the effects of Mainland spy Lieutenant Commander Sadatomo Okada. Also, although this was unknown on Maui, spy Otto Kuehn's signaling scenario with Japanese submarines had called for lights on Maui between 9 and 10 p.m. if the Lanikai site was unavailable. This particular signal meant that the battle force had left Pearl Harbor.

Upon being discovered at the hospital window — which looked down on Lahaina Roads, and coincidentally, an Imperial Navy rendezvous point — Furukawa tried to commit suicide "by drinking an excessive amount of Listerine." He was placed in isolation.

Because of this incident, the slopes of Haleakala volcano, including Kula, were placed under close nighttime scrutiny. Signals were spotted in Kula on Dec. 11, but when officers converged on the area, the signaler doused the light and was heard scrambling away.

Kula Sanitorium, at the beginning of World War II, was one of the largest buildings on Maui, affording one of the best views of the ocean.

On Dec. 14, at the same time of night Furukawa had tried signaling from the sanatorium, Fish and Game Warden H.E. Anderson and Maui police officers Albert Wong, Louis Fernandez and Charles Ledward observed lights at Maalaea Bay on Maui flash on and off. A moment later, lights in the sea answered. This went on for several minutes.

Anderson placed the seaward light on the uninhabited island of Kahoolawe, but the police officers, who saw the signal from a different vantage point, placed it in the channel between Kahoolawe and Lanai.

Kahoolawe was deserted except for some horses owned by the Baldwin family. The Baldwins before the war had visited the island once a week on a sampan they owned, *Maisie C.*, which was skippered by an alien Japanese, last name Yamauchi. Since the attack on Pearl, the sampan had been tied up on Maui. The signal triggered an armed search of Kahoolawe by Maui guardsmen, who were taken to the island on the only craft available — *Maisie C.*

These incidents, happening on top of each other on a Hawaiian island far from the action at Pearl Harbor, are typical of the kind of suspicion engendered by the Advance Force's underwater assault. The threat of submarine action is often as damaging as an actual attack, tying up men, resources and time and creating a mood of hysteria. In the waning days of December, no one knew where the next torpedo would appear.

After studying the captured midget at Pearl Harbor, it became obvious that she had not reached Hawaii under her own power. During interrogation, prisoner Sakamaki confirmed it. Japanese submarines seemed to be everywhere, and there were fears the Imperial Navy might try to slip another one under the net.

A month after the attack, the crew of a search plane 600 miles west of the harbor breathlessly reported "a mother ship towing three small submarines." This seemed like a solution that explained how midget submarines may have reached Hawaii from Japan, and antisubmarine forces began to scramble.

A check with the Combat Intelligence Unit, however, revealed this apparition was actually *Arthur Foss*,[1] a tugboat towing three empty barges. She had escaped from Wake Island only hours before the attack and had resolutely plugged across the war-torn Pacific at her maximum towing speed of two and a half knots. She narrowly escaped being tagged as an enemy on her last leg home.

This skill in divining ship identities was typical of the the newly sensitized Combat Intelligence Unit. Though CIU concentrated on keeping track of Japanese submarines, the position of all ships at sea became a guessing game as radio silence went into effect. Probable courses were plotted by informed imagination.

CIU knew, for example, that freighter *Steel Voyager* was nearing Honolulu from Panama a few days after the attack. A radio message from a Japanese submarine was intercepted and direction finders

[1] *Arthur Foss is still around, a National Historic Landmark in Seattle, Washington.*

SUBMERGED SCARES

placed her directly in *Steel Voyager's* course. Honolulu's port director sent out a blind warning to the freighter, who obligingly changed course and skirted the sub's position.

By the end of December, convoys were formed, the first setting out from San Francisco on Dec. 28. The 21 ships were initially escorted by light cruiser *Detroit* and destroyers *Clark* and *Cummings*, and met halfway by Pearl Harbor ships heavy cruiser *Portland*, and destroyers *Farragut* and *Phelps*. Their orders concluded, "Enemy submarines are known to be operating in the vicinity of the Hawaiian Islands and off the West Coast of the United States. Enemy raiders and submarines may be encountered en route …"

As the war ground on, intelligence officers were able to accurately and quickly determine an enemy submarine's position from translating the traffic patterns. They were stymied by a scarcity of anti-submarine vessels. Even quite close to the islands, Japanese submarines would pop to the surface, send out a quick message over the radio and submerge before strained anti-submarine patrols could reach the location. American intelligence units didn't discover until later that many of these Japanese submarines also carried light observation aircraft, which made the submarines dangerous to land targets as well as seagoing.

In late December, Japanese submarines were returning from the West Coast — with unexpended ammunition still weighing them down — and paused off Midway Atoll for a midnight bombardment. Based on radio traffic, CIU warned the Marines on Midway that something might be up, and they returned the submarine gunfire so quickly and accurately that the Japanese aborted the mission.

As the I-boats left, they ran into American submarine *Gudgeon*, which cautiously stole into the combat zone on Jan. 26, warned in advance by the intelligence unit. *Gudgeon* was returning to Pearl Harbor from patrolling off Japan. One of the surfaced Japanese submarines waddled across her bow, and *Gudgeon* sank *I-73* with a spread of three torpedoes.

The next day, *I-23* was caught by American destroyers north of Hawaii. She was the seventh Japanese submarine sunk since the war opened, and the last to be sunk for the next three months.

In the meantime, the black shapes were everywhere. A week after the war started, W.R. Spear, a retired Navy lieutenant,[2] spotted a light about 300 yards outside the reef fronting Niu Valley, to the east of Diamond Head. On Jan. 12, Spear saw it again, in the same location, as did Lieutenant (jg) Floyd C. Bryant, who saw it from the different direction of Maunalani Heights.

One night, an enemy submarine cruised just beyond the reef near Diamond Head, leisurely recharging her batteries. Lieutenant Holmes of the Combat Intelligence Unit lived nearby on Black Point, an artists' colony also attracting the families of submariners. Less than a block away from his home, up the slopes of Diamond Head, was an ancient coastal defense battery of two 8-inch guns, which covered the

[2] *Spear had distinguished himself fighting fires in Drydock No. 1 on Dec. 7, 1941.*

Kahala reef area — including the enemy submarine under their noses.

This was the first opportunity for American coastal defense guns to fire at a real target since the Civil War, recalled Holmes, and the crews excitedly swung the barrels around and pointed them at the submarine's reported position. The gun-pointers took aim, and discovered they were looking directly into the windows of "George Hunter's old house," a hundred feet or so away. And directly under the barrel blast were 20 or so homes filled with sleeping families and fragile glass windows.

The commanding officer at Fort Ruger decided to evacuate the area. By the time all the sleepy families had been safely tucked out of harm's way, the submarine was long gone. The next morning, so was George Hunter's house, courtesy an Army demolition crew.

The surprise shellings on Kauai, Maui and Hawaii during December 1941, brought the danger home. The spasmodic shelling contributed to an island-wide blackout that lasted nearly to war's end, which caused innumerable hardships for island families. The shellings were treated as a coup by Japanese propagandists, which backfired on them. The Japan Radio broadcast of Dec. 31, 1941 — heard in Hawaii by shortwave radio — announced, *Since the 17th of this month, the Japanese have damaged ships, planes, wireless stations and piers on the American islands of Maui, Johnston and Palmyra ...*

Here is the big news — a happy new year present to the subjects of Japan. Through the courtesy of the Imperial Navy, a newsreel picture of the history-making attack of Pearl Harbor is released. It shows the Japanese aircraft carrier heading to Hawaii and the instant sinking of American capital ships by bomb and torpedo. Navy photographers risked their lives to take these pictures ...

Claims of extravagant damage caused by the shore-directed shelling were easily disproven by anyone in the area, and did much to discredit Japanese propaganda from the beginning of the war.

Nanakuli and Waianae on the leeward coast of Oahu were favorite locations to imagine submarines offshore. On March 7, 1942, projectiles rained on Nanakuli, destroying a mango tree and sprinkling homes and stores with metal fragments. Navy ships rushed to the area and pulverized the blue water offshore with depth charges, killing thousands of fish called *akule*. The shells turned out to be American anti-aircraft rounds with faulty fuses. Dead *akule* drifted ashore, creating a huge stink.

Long suspected as rendezvous points for Japanese submarines, sampans continued to be dangerous places to work. Sampans off Barbers Point were later strafed by Army A-20s and shelled by a Coast Guard cutter when they were suspected of aiding a submarine. Several fishermen were wounded.

In 1942 the Navy seized sampans to use as coastal patrol vessels. By 1943, most had been returned, or sold to Hawaiian Tuna Packers, which patriotically changed the ship's Japanese names. *Kasuga Maru*, for example, became *Marlin*, and *Kiyo Maru* became *Skipjack*.

Submerged Scares

Rumors grew immediately that the midget submarine on display at Pearl Harbor had entered the port disguised as an American vessel. A few days after the attack, as heavy cruiser *Indianapolis* entered Pearl Harbor and the crew witnessed the devastation for the first time, Ensign William C. McCain noted the event in a diary:

"We passed the entrance buoy and noticed that the guard barge was very alert, and well armed. Two PT boats were tied up at the barge. Quite a shake up since last Sunday, when they let a Jap submarine disguised as an American into the channel ..." [3]

In February 1942, naval investigators made what they considered a shocking discovery among the personal effects of one Ernest Shigeru Matsusaka, an "espionage suspect." Matsusaka, a naval-history buff, had a collection of *Kaigun-Kenkyusha* magazines, including the 1938 issue of *Navy Graph* with the American midget sub article. This was the first time Naval Intelligence saw the article, and the similarities between it and the HA-boat attack were uncomfortable. Matsusaka was promptly interned.

Knowing too much about submarines could get you in trouble. Not knowing enough was bad for morale. A civilian named Leslie Eichelberger, testifying to the Roberts Commission, complained that "if there could be more frankness officially about submarine operations in the vicinity it would be reassuring. We get news that submarines have shelled nearby cities. We get great volumes that submarines have been sunk, but no official statements. If we could know that a submarine was sunk the day after Lahaina was shelled, or some such thing, it would be very reassuring to the civilian population!"

Another civilian, Bernard Butler from Maui, said the population wasn't afraid of Japanese invasion. They were instead "apprehensive." He complained that Japanese subs had shelled Maui on two occasions with no response from shore.

He gave an example. During the Dec. 15 attack, his factory in Kahului took five shell hits that knocked down the stack and put holes in the roof. Lining them up later, he realized the apparent target was a ship in the harbor, and the factory strikes were overshoots. The last round struck the pier right next to the ship.

During the shelling, Colonel William T. Lyman, military commander of the district, was on his way to make an address over the Maui police radio, because Army radios were constantly breaking down. As the shells rained down, the colonel ran into the police station and used the radio to try and reach Honolulu. Within seconds, nearly everyone on Maui knew an attack was under way, and those in Kahului rushed outside to get a glimpse of the submarine. There it was, beyond the reef, muzzle flashes twinkling in the darkness.

Lyman also tried to transmit to Puunene, where utility squadron VJ-3 was stationed. No one was there to take the message.

Before the end of the month, the survivors of freighter *Lahaina* came ashore without being challenged and the island was shelled again. Butler came to testify to the Roberts Commission about the

[3] *That Sakamaki had a handmade American flag on board his craft was widely known, and added fuel to the rumor.*

"amateur" defense preparations on Maui. The *Lahaina* crew rowing offshore and shooting up flares really startled Maui residents — here was a lot of commotion on the ocean and "no means absolutely of investigating them, no boats or anything else."

It is impossible to estimate how many of the hundreds of sightings were genuine. Most of the Japanese submarines stayed away from shore if possible. Though all the I-boats were briefed on Otto Kuehn's Lanikai signaling location, only *I-75* stayed in the area close enough to watch the Kailua shore.

By that time, Kuehn was long gone. One of the prominent names on the FBI's master list of suspects, Kuehn was picked up within a few hours of the attack and promptly spilled the beans. All residences on the beach in Lanikai were canvassed in the week following the attack. Kuehn's house was rented by Army Lieutenants Chapman and Stuppy and their wives, attached to Schofield hospital. None had any contact with Kuehn other than as a landlord, nor did they observe any mysterious signals.

On the other hand, Mrs. R.C. Waldron, a neighbor two houses down, distinctly remembered seeing a man of Japanese extraction on the beach the morning of Dec. 7. The man was carrying a fishing pole, she said suspiciously.

John A. Burns of the Honolulu Police Department Espionage Squad[4] went door to door in the area, checking on the "Japanese-ness" of the residents. In one house that had a splendid view of the ocean, he found 10 Japanese; two families and a couple of young women. Most were citizens, and a couple had been strafed while tending their farm at Makapuu on the morning of Dec. 7. He left them alone.

Japanese consulate secretary Kimie Doue was debriefed and said that she saw a white man visit the office in mid-November. FBI head Robert Shivers thought this interesting and placed Doue in a stenographer's room at FBI offices, advising her to watch the doorway. Kuehn was led to the doorway and engaged in conversation. Doue gasped and grabbed a piece of carbon paper to hold it over her face so she wouldn't be recognized. Afterward she claimed with conviction that the "haole" — white foreigner — at the consulate had been the same man who was in the doorway.[5]

With both German and Japanese spy networks down, the Imperial Navy resorted to direct means of gathering intelligence. The mid-December Glen flight from *I-7* showed Pearl Harbor being repaired. The next flight was Jan. 6, from *I-19*. In late February another flight from *I-9* confirmed blackout conditions were island-wide except for Pearl Harbor, where the repair lights were so bright they prevented the airmen from getting good looks at the ships.

Repairs were proceeding quickly and Imperial Navy planners thought another air strike would slow down the pace. The attack was dubbed Operation K and given to the 24th Air Flotilla to carry out, using the new long-range "Emily" flying boats, only the two prototypes of which were available. The plane had a 3,000-mile range, so it

[4] Burns later became governor of Hawaii largely on the strength of Japanese-American votes.

[5] Doue recognized Kuehn, she claimed, because he "looked Jewish."

A pre-war Imperial Navy maneuver with a "Mavis" flying boat and a submarine. These inter-service operations were predicted by author Wilfred "Jasper" Holmes in his novella "Rendezvous." See page 126.

could make a long bombing mission with a refueling stopover some-where quiet. French Frigate Shoals was chosen by *I-22*, which had reconnoitered possible routes northwest of Oahu in late February.

The plan called for departure from Wotje in the Marshalls, each plane burdened with four 550-pound bombs. They'd fly 1,600 miles to French Frigate Shoals to be refueled by submarines *I-15* and *I-19*. The two planes were then to proceed to Pearl, dump their bombs and race back to Wotje while the American shipyard — presumably — went into panic.

I-9 took up position between Jaluit and French Frigate Shoals to act as a radio homing beacon.

Emilys flown by Ensign Tomano and flight leader Lieutenant Toshio Hashizume took off from Wotje before dawn on March 3. Hashizume damaged his plane slightly on take-off. They met up with the submarines at the Shoals at sunset. Hoses, buoyed by floats, fed the thirsty seaplanes. Water was rough in the lagoon, and mooring lines broke. The Emily engines were fired up and the planes used the props to backpedal, reducing strain. Tomano and Hashizume lifted off at 9:38 p.m.

Unusually heavy radio traffic in that direction had alerted Pearl that something was up. Kauai radar stations picked up incoming planes shortly after midnight as they thundered in from the northwest. Hawaii air controllers, now mindful of the lesson of Dec. 7, quickly determined that the blips weren't friendly. It was assumed that the planes came from a carrier, so five PBYs armed with torpedoes were

The La Perouse Pinnacle at French Frigate Shoals.

scrambled at 1:15 a.m. to hunt down the ship. A few minutes later, four P-40s were scrambled to intercept the invaders. By the time the fighters were airborne, the Emilys were already passing over Kaena Point, the northwest tip of Oahu, using the lighthouse there to set up their bombing run on Pearl.

In the darkness and clouds, everybody missed. The P-40s poked around in the gloom and were disappointed. The ship the PBYs were searching for didn't exist. The two Emilys overshot the harbor, and when Hashizume realized the error he radioed Tomano to turn north. The wingman apparently did not hear the message, and when he noticed Hashizume missing, Tomano turned north anyway and guessed at Pearl Harbor's location, jettisoning his bomb load at 2:30 a.m.

The Kawanishi H8K flying boat was the largest in the Imperial Navy and considered superior to the British Short Sunderland and the American PBY. Maximum range was 4,445 miles!

Tomano's bombs disappeared into the darkness, unheard and unseen by any Americans, perhaps falling into the ocean. Hashizume, who had turned north earlier, was over Oahu when he dumped his bombs, at 2:10 a.m. The explosions racked up and down Tantalus, a forested hill above Honolulu, and some five miles east of the harbor.

"Surprise attack successful!" radioed Hashizume.

The flying boats, separated, flew back by slightly different routes, Tomano going back to Wotje, and Hashizume going directly to the repair facilities at Jaluit. [6]

[6] *Hashizume was killed on March 10, 1942, shot down by Marine Buffalos near Midway.*

Although the physical damage was slight — a few dozen kiawe trees — there was psychological fallout from the raid, which in some respects resembled the more famous Doolittle raid on Japan two months later. The Army and Navy on Oahu each blamed the other for the damage, convinced that the bombs were lost by an American pilot, who, naturally, must have been flying for the other service.

Another attack was immediately planned by the Japanese, then canceled when American forces bombed Wake Island. The refueler submarines were ordered away from the Shoals to intercept the returning American task force.

Intelligence officer Edwin Layton's radio whizzes eventually hammered out the details of Operation K, and American patrol boats were posted at French Frigate Shoals. Curiously, Lieutenant Holmes, using the pen name Alec Hudson, had predicted just such a maneuver in a fiction piece the previous August for the *Saturday Evening Post*.

Another K-operation had been planned prior to the Midway

SUBMERGED SCARES

American soldiers inspect bomb craters on Tantalus, a hillside neighborhood overlooking downtown Honolulu.

assault, but when Japanese submarines approached the islet on May 30, they were scared away. All planned reconnaissance of Oahu was canceled, and the Japanese missed Admiral Raymond Spruance's carriers steaming north of Midway, to lie in wait for the Japanese.

Japanese submarines continued to refuel reconnaissance aircraft during the war, notably south of the Guadalcanal area following Allied landings there in August 1942. Americans also used submarines to refuel PBY patrol bombers.

After the war, it was discovered that a fourth submarine had served as a navigational beacon for the flying boats, and a fifth, *I-23*, was supposed to lie off Oahu and report weather conditions, as well as pick up downed crews if necessary. *I-23* had been sunk by American destroyers, however, and the Emily bombers flew blindly into the unreported rainstorm.

Another event, in June of 1942, confirmed the worst fears of military intelligence — enemy submarines deposited eight saboteurs on American beaches. They quickly melted into the population, even getting past Coast Guardsman John Cullen, who hailed a group of four spies as they were busily burying high explosives in the sand.

The saboteurs were German; the landing sites Amagansett, Long Island, and Vero Beach, Florida. Their mission was to bomb aluminum and magnesium plants in Tennessee, and when that was completed, to take advantage of racial hysteria then taking place on the West Coast against Japanese-Americans. Planning for the mission began the week of the attack on Pearl Harbor, and Japanese news releases about the exploits of the midget submariners gave it additional impetus. Small, highly visible and bloody acts of sabotage in the East, the Nazi command figured, would result in a similar crackdown on Americans of German descent. The country would be split.

When Cullen challenged them on the Long Island beach, they claimed to be stranded fishermen, and offered the unarmed young guard $260 to keep quiet. Cullen doubted their tale — besides, he'd

heard chattering in a foreign language, and could see something floating offshore that looked like a submarine. He took the bribe, and hurried off to report the incident.

Cullen's superiors waited until dawn to investigate, and at the landing site found German uniforms, brandy, a raft and a variety of explosive devices, some in the form of pen-and-pencil sets.

All eight saboteurs were rounded up within days of landing by the Federal Bureau of Investigation. Bureau head J. Edgar Hoover took the lion's share of credit, citing his agency's brilliant detective work. It was considered quite a coup, and helped create an omnipotent image for the agency.

Six of the eight Germans were executed within two months of the landing. Surviving saboteurs George Dasch and Ernest Burger were quietly released from prison in 1948 and sent to Germany. Dasch, who had been the leader of the two groups, began telling an interesting story. Within moments of landing at Amagansett, he claimed, he had gotten cold feet over the affair, and had straightaway telephoned the FBI. The agent on the other end listened patiently, then observed, "Yesterday, Napoleon called," and hung up.

Dasch went to Washington, demanding to see J. Edgar Hoover. Even while meeting with FBI assistant director "Mickey" Ladd, the agent in charge of the manhunt for the Abwehr saboteurs, Dasch had trouble convincing them of his claims until he had tipped over a portmanteau containing the saboteurs' travel expenses. With $84,000 in their laps, the FBI agents agreed something must be afoot.

Hoover personally falsified the details of the Nazi agents' capture to reflect credit on the FBI. Details of the Dasch mission began to leak out in 1945, when Tom Clark, Truman's new attorney general, entered into a long-time feud with Hoover. Clark spilled the beans, and FBI efforts at damage control included demanding advance peeks at press coverage of the incident.

Dasch claimed that the $84,000 handed over to the FBI disappeared. He also claimed that the information he had volunteered about German submarine operations was largely responsible for turning the tide against the U-boats in the Atlantic.

Fears over submarine-launched foreign saboteurs were genuine. In February of 1942, passenger liner *Normandie* burned and capsized at her pier in New York harbor. The ship was in the midst of being converted into troop transport *Lafayette*. Sabotage was suspected, but not proved.

The Germans still tried to land agents via submarine, but the easy approaches of 1942 to American shores had vanished. The FBI got into the act again in August of 1944, when the Navy sank a U-boat and an Abwehr secret agent was among the survivors. Hoover demanded that the German be turned over to the FBI; the Navy refused because the man was a commissioned officer in the Kriegsmarine. Giving a military prisoner to the FBI would set a legal precedent, and the Gestapo would feel justified in interrogating American POWs. The

SUBMERGED SCARES

turf argument ranged all the way up to the White House. Roosevelt agreed with Hoover — in itself a historic moment — and the German officer was quietly given to the FBI.

In 1943, Richard Sakakida, a Japanese-American from Hawaii working for the Imperial Army in Manila, was ordered by Japanese officers to land on Oahu via submarine. Sakakida could then easily sabotage American ships in Pearl Harbor, or so the Army officers believed.

Sakakida talked his way out of the plan, and the Japanese dropped it, presuming Sakakida didn't have enough courage. What they didn't know was that Sakakida was a double agent, a prewar plant by the Military Intelligence Service, and far more valuable in Manila, where he routinely pilfered Japanese war plans.

Soon after the German saboteur incident, Japanese alien Giichiro Uyeno was killed at Waimanalo on Oahu in what appeared to be similar circumstances.[7] Shortly before midnight on July 25, 1942, he was spotted near a machine gun emplacement, and a sentry called out several times. Uyeno began to run, tossing away something into the bushes, and was shot by the sentry.

[7] Perhaps Sakakida was to have been a replacement for Uyeno.

The item thrown away by Uyeno turned out to be a flashlight. Traces of colored cellophane around the bulb showed that it had once been "blacked out," though the cellophane had been since removed. Subsequent investigation revealed that Uyeno was a yardman living on a private estate nearby, and was always promptly in his quarters by the 8 p.m. curfew.

"He was a recluse, but considered sane," the report on the incident concluded. "Uyeno knew he was risking death. The probability is that his mission at the time justified assuming that risk."

At the same moment Uyeno was shot, surface radar operators at Kaneohe, about 10 miles away across the water, reported "a strange surface vessel or submarine" appearing on their plots. Shore batteries fired at the presumed location, and the signal disappeared. The next night, the suspected submarine reappeared inside Kaneohe Bay, was observed from shore, and was peppered with gunfire. The craft dashed out of the shallow water and ducked behind Moku Manu, a steep islet north of the Kaneohe peninsula, where it was shielded from shore-based guns. Though aircraft were roused from the air station, the submarine had disappeared by the time they reached Moku Manu.

Across the bay, near Kahaluu, a swimmer was seen heading for shore. A company of soldiers was dispatched to the area to head off the fellow, whom, it was presumed, had been dropped off by the submarine. They found only swampy, heavy underbrush. Footprints were discovered coming out of the ocean, made by rubber-soled shoes.

The coincidence of Uyeno's clandestine foray near the beach and the possible submarine sightings in the same area placed Hawaii intelligence officers in a state of profound self-justification. Reports at the time pointed out that good swimmers could slip ashore almost

anywhere on Oahu and return to the ocean just as easily. Oahu had many small islands that would shield host submarines from shore. Intelligence speculators noted that such a method of landing spies or saboteurs was actually easier than a rendezvous with the suspected sampans, as the fishing boats were by then strictly regulated and regularly inspected.

Because of these incidents, beach patrols around Oahu were maintained to the end of the war.

This excitement led credence to another sighting in late September 1942, when a submerged object broke the surface off Kahuku, on the windswept northeast coast of Oahu. A series of small rocky islands along the shore led to speculation that swimmers or shielded shortwave transmitters could use them as cover, and the 298th Infantry was detailed to cover the beaches. No one could use the beach without a written pass from the commanding officer.

The Kahuku submarine was seen diving and surfacing four times during a week, each time working its way along the reef. Odd behavior for a submarine, though not unusual for a whale.

On April 6, 1943, a Kaneohe crash boat, searching for survivors from an airplane downed off the bay, were surprised to see a submarine conning tower broach briefly near them. In the late morning of April 10, a submarine was spotted by a PBY near Kahuku Point. As the Catalina approached, the craft dove. Later that night — between 9 and 10 p.m. — Kaneohe radar picked up an echo off the bay. The shore guns were readied, and star shells launched. In the sputtering glare, a conning tower was seen at 7,000 yards, and every gun within range opened up. Amid the shell splashes, the conning tower was seen to slide smoothly under the water and disappear. The next night, a submarine was reported off Maui, though PBYs from Kaneohe were unable to confirm it.

The isolation of the Territory of Hawaii made such reports more ominous than they were in the continental United States, where, if invaded, a population would always have an avenue of retreat. Hysteria reached such levels after the attack on Pearl Harbor that a dog barking on the beach was seriously reported to be sending treasonous messages to Japanese submarines, woofing in Morse code.

The presumed danger contributed to the territory being placed under martial law until nearly the end of the war. "Invasion by stealth, by submarine, commando raids, espionage parties, I consider it not only probable, but imminent. It is always impending," said Admiral Nimitz, in mid-1944.

Submarines, because of their ability to show up unexpectedly and then vanish, could press the clouds of uncertainty into deluge. Lieutenant Elmer Oettinger, newly attached to communications security at CINCPAC[8] in 1944, was sleeping soundly when "all hell broke loose. Guns — big guns — were booming within sight of the BOQ. Over the loudspeaker system, turned on at top-decibel level, a voice of doom ordered, "Lights out! We are under attack! Man battle stations!"

[8] The title was changed from CINCUS to Commander in Chief, Pacific Fleet, in the spring of 1942.

370

SUBMERGED SCARES

Oettinger whipped on his uniform and ran to the CINCPAC code room to ask where his battle station was. No one seemed to know, and he felt naked without a helmet, "something I had not been issued or indeed seen before. I soon discovered there was good reason, for falling flak from our own guns seemed to constitute the only danger from the sky."

The new lieutenant was assured there was an attack under way, and there was no need for him at CINCPAC. Crouched in the stairway of the Base Officers' Quarters, he fell asleep, and eventually the guns quieted. The next morning, Oettinger learned that Army patrol planes had witnessed a fleet of Japanese submarines massing 200 miles north of Oahu. Navy attack aircraft had found only a pod of whales in the same location.

"I never heard a word about the costly mistake later," recalled Oettinger. "It was as though the evening never happened."

The night scare wasn't Oettinger's first encounter with phantom submarines. On board commandeered troop ship *President Johnson*, Oettinger had been ordered to the South Pacific along with 2,000 Seabees and 4,500 other servicemen in early 1944, leaving from Long Beach. The liner was scheduled to make 14 knots and sprint across the ocean unescorted and under radio silence, the speed and stealth of which would be sufficient to outrun Japanese submarines.

A few days out of California, however, the liner began to wallow, slowing to 4 knots or drifting. A typhoon struck, and the ship was not able to make headway. The ship was a fat target. "Daily, as the ship slowed and smoke and sparks belched up into the sky from our laboring stacks … our dialogues began to include segments devoted to the condition of the ship and the manifest danger to us all. There was no fear or panic, but a sense of awareness was omnipresent," recalled Oettinger.

The passengers were well aware of blame-passing going on in the ship's unified command structure, which consisted of Army, Navy and Merchant Marine officers.

One day Oettinger was ordered to report to the troop commander, a Commander Hill. "This ship's in grave peril!" barked Hill. "We're gonna save it!"

"Yessir," said Oettinger. "You and I?"

"You and me and Navy Communication. Thank God for Navy Communications," said Hill. "Did you know that Jap subs have sunk two ships within 50 miles of us?"

Oettinger was alarmed, not knowing that Hill was probably referring to 1941, not 1944.

"Those sons of bitches don't want to break silence, but we have to. We're going to. Despite that milquetoast colonel and that bullhead Merchant Marine commodore, we're going to see that 6,500 fighting men on this ship are going to live to fight the war."

Oettinger was ordered to draft an emergency message for Pearl Harbor, in code. "You're going to ask for instructions — *most urgent!*

— or our ass will be dragging the bottom of this goddamn ocean," said Hill. "Draft it short and straight, one-syllable words, so those bastards at Pearl will understand and give it a priority!"

Oettinger did as he was told,[9] and *President Johnson* diverted to Honolulu for repairs. The ship muddled north, seeming to go slower by the day, and Hill gossiped daily about intercepting distress calls from ships torpedoed nearby by Japanese I-boats. "We clearly were sitting ducks … it did not make me any more comfortable about our chances," said Oettinger.

If escort ships were sent, they missed *President Johnson*. The liner was well into Hawaiian waters before being spotted by an aerial patrol, which prepared to dive-bomb the ship before being convinced, via signal lantern, that the troopship was American.

President Johnson moored in Honolulu, in the shadow of Aloha Tower, for several weeks while repairs were made. The sequestered troops were allowed ashore only to march in circles around the block, as the 14th Naval District declined leave.

Oettinger was shanghaied off the ship by a Communications acquaintance in CINCPAC, and was the only man left behind when *President Johnson* finally left port.

More typical of the submarine rumor mill was the case of Frederick Arthur Dunkley, an expatriate Englishman living in Waikiki. On Oct. 8, 1943, Dunkley telephoned the Radio and Radar Laboratory at Pearl Harbor. Lieutenant Ralph K. Rhyan answered the call, and Dunkley told him that Pearl Harbor would be reconnoitered by a submarine-launched airplane between the 13th and 16th of October. Rhyan passed on the message to Naval Intelligence.

Dunkley claimed to have been General Edmund Allenby's intelligence officer in the Near East during World War I, and later an office manager at Pearl Harbor. Lieutenant Commander Harold S. Burr, then the District Intelligence Officer, dutifully filed the prediction, noting that Dunkley had "a low reliability rating."

A month earlier, submarine *I-36* was "ordered to leave Yokosuka immediately upon taking on supplies and to proceed to the Hawaiian area to reconnoiter the enemy's condition, observe and attack his fleet, and destroy his commerce," rather a tall order for single submarine.

The orders — later captured on Kwajalein — were signed by a Commander Takero Kouda, and went on to push for an aerial "reconnaissance on a moonlit night about 21 September," as well as two more sorties on Oct. 8 and Oct. 20. Suggested take-off sites included southwest of Kawaihae Bay and south of Kealakekua Bay both on the Big Island — and south of Kahoolawe and west or south of Niihau.

And if Pearl Harbor was busy, Lahaina Roads off Maui was to be surveyed as well.

"Observation of the enemy fleet is to be carried out principally by aerial reconnaissance; but during periods when no aerial reconnaissance is in progress observation of the enemy fleet is to be carried out as thoroughly as possible on the sea-routes likely to be used to the Fiji

SUBMERGED SCARES

area; and at the same time destruction of his commerce will be undertaken," ordered Kouda.

"On the occasion of the second and third aerial reconnaissance flights a bombing attack is to be made simultaneously with the reconnaissance mission ... carriers will be considered the most desirable target for both submarine attack and bombing raids by the airplane."

I-36 rushed to the area and attempted several flights between Sept. 20 and 27, each of which were tagged by American radar and the Glen returned to its hangar submarine. Desperate, *I-36* finally launched a one-way flight on Oct. 17 from 300 miles out, which reported Pearl Harbor swarming with four battleships, four aircraft carriers, five cruisers and 17 destroyers. The U.S. Navy was preparing to invade the Gilbert Islands. The aircraft was picked up by searchlights at Barbers Point, and it immediately dived, reversed course and sped away just above the wavetops. Japanese records indicate the aircraft radioed its report and then disappeared.

The next day, *I-36* fell in with a large American convoy going southeast. As the submarine wheeled in pursuit, the Pearl Harbor report was radioed in. Submarines *I-35, I-19, I-169* and *I-175*[10] were ordered to speed toward Hawaii, but contact was lost. The convoy turned up in the Gilberts on Nov. 19, and the submarines then rerouted to this area.

After the flight on Oct. 17, District Intelligence officer Burr hustled Ensign H.S. Larsen over to debrief Dunkley. The Englishman claimed the prediction was based on "general situations ... each grain of sand being gathered to make a beach." One key grain, according to Dunkley, was a scheduled Shriners football game that week, just like one on Dec. 6, 1941, and that he'd heard Japanese maids were quitting their jobs.

He made another prediction for the ensign — the Japanese Navy would strike full force at Pearl Harbor on either Oct. 30 or 31. Another football game was scheduled.

Wilder guesses have come true — the set-up is OK, Burr wrote in the margin of Larsen's report.

Pearl Harbor went on full alert.

Nothing happened.

[10] *Despite the high numbers, these are Advance Force veterans —* I-69 *and* I-75 *were in a submarine class renumbered during 1942.*

28 HERO GODS

WISHFUL THINKING OF THE HIGHEST ORDER

News of the successful attack on Pearl Harbor rolled across Japan like a thunderclap.

The sense of stifling pressure building up in the island empire was burst by the news. It was as if a snap decision had crystallized instantly in the minds of millions; the feeling of uncertainty was gone; the national mood was euphoric. Their empire had finally taken the plunge, deeply dangerous and daunting, exhilarating in its scope.

While the American reaction was one of baffled outrage, the attack on Pearl Harbor, to the Japanese, was a metaphor, a heroic symbol of Yamato spirit, of Asian sacrificial triumph over Western arrogance and materialism.

Commander Sadamu Sanagi of the Naval General Staff's Operations Section wrote in his diary Dec. 8th; "Our air force, together with the submarine force, achieved a great success unprecedented in history by the Pearl Harbor attack … Nothing could hold back our Imperial Navy, which kept silent for a long time. But once it arose, it never hesitated to do the most difficult thing on this earth. Oh, how powerful is the Imperial Navy!"

One fleet-sized submarine and five midgets were lost, as well as 29 aircraft. The only survivor was Sakamaki, and he was an accident. Fifty-five airmen, nine midget submariners, an unknown number on the large submarine — acceptable losses, considering the result.

An apotheosis of the midget submarine crews began at once.

Without any way of knowing for certain, Vice Admiral Chuichi Nagumo added to his report; "It is certain that, in addition to this, the Special Attack Unit of the Advance Force inflicted much damage by its bravest attack …"

Wishful thinking of the highest order — it certainly affected both admirals Yamamoto and Matome Ugaki as well, champions of the brave, useless submariners.

Aviator Fuchida's assessment of the midgets was more succinct — "Not worth a damn," he said.

The year ended with an accidental minus for the Japanese. On New Year's Eve, *RO-60* arrived at Kwajalein in horrible weather and

slammed aground with such force that her hull split like a banana. All hands were saved, but the sub went down.[1]

So, by the end of 1941, three fleet-class submarines were lost, as well as the five midgets. *I-70* had been sunk by *Enterprise* planes, and *RO-62* was lost near Wake, an accident like *RO-60*. *I-24tou* and Sakamaki had been captured. The fates of *I-70* and the rest of the midgets were complete mysteries to the Imperial Fleet. The time was fast approaching when Imperial press attaches needed to start inventing history, before the questions started.

The first general announcement of the attack mentioned that submariners had carried the attack "to penetrate the very vitals of the American naval base." No other details were given.

The night message from midget pilot Masaji Yokoyama that called the surprise attack a success, coupled with the huge explosions seen from sea on the evening of Dec. 8, plus the devastating loss of battleship *Arizona*, melded into a propagandists' dream package. It was decided, fairly quickly, to credit the *Arizona* to the midget submarines of the Advance Force. It was a way of deflecting attention from the 100 percent loss among the HA-boat crews. The only ones who knew better were the airman of Fuchida's aerial force, who credited a carrier bombardier for the kill.

During the first months of 1942, the Imperial Navy Office of Public Relations coyly alluded to "the glorious, incomparable, strong attack on Pearl Harbor by the Special Naval Attack Flotilla ... at the time of the iconoclastic blow against outrageous America, which disregarded our great motive and mission of world peace."

But there were no details. The first press release concerning the attack on Pearl Harbor simply stated that, "Five vessels of the Japanese Special Attack Flotilla have not returned yet."

A communique describing the attack, issued March 6, was the first time the Japanese nation was alerted to the role the midget submarines played in the attack — or the role Imperial propagandists wished the "Special Attack Flotilla" had played. The five missing submarines were played for dramatic effect in the battle description. "These words were contained in the last paragraph of the historic Imperial Headquarters announcement of the Battle of Hawaii — the paragraph which threw, and is still throwing, the whole Japanese nation into a crucible of indescribable excitement," the press release began, referring to the December release. "The great task of annihilating the United States Pacific Fleet was thus accomplished ... the entire nation prostrates itself in paying deepest respect to their souls."

It is also entirely possible that, had Sakamaki's submarine not been captured and then been the subject of a highly public tour of the United States, the little submersibles would have remained a secret weapon. The opinion-makers in the Imperial Navy decided instead to inflate the submarines' role, turning the nine dead submariners into "hero-gods," a mortal ranking that has no equivalent in any society outside Japan, but consists of equal parts Emperor-worship, Shinto

[1] *Another source claims the submarine was lost on Dec. 9, 1941. The wreck is visible on a reef 14 miles from Roi-Namur Island.*

Here is the pantheon of Hero Gods, with Iwasa at the peak, surrounding a romantic view of the devastation at Pearl Harbor. This kind of devout iconography is generally reserved for saints and holy men, and gives a hint of the intense ritualiization surrounding Imperial Japanese warmaking.

belief, Bushido-inspired brainwashing, martial magic and a smug conviction that "Japanese-ness" was next to godliness. It was an indication how closely allied the military and religious drives of Imperial Japan were. To question the submariners' sacrifice would be an insult to higher beings, not just officers and politicians, but to the gods themselves.

The nine were jumped two places in rank, and Yokoyama given official credit for *Arizona's* sinking. Sakamaki, captured and in disgrace, vanished from Imperial Navy records as if he were an unpleasant shadow.

As the communique continued: "Theirs really was a training of gods, not human beings, and this was responsible for the great success they reaped in the Battle of Hawaii."

It also described how the midgets "proceeded with suppressed eagerness, deeper and deeper into the harbor," where they spotted the double row of battleships at Ford Island. The work of Captain Hideo Hiraide of the Imperial Navy Press Section, the release embellished the tale even further, saying that the midgets actually took up positions between battleships moored next to each other. The official line was that the midgets actively contributed to the initial shock of attack, and even saw Imperial Navy aircraft through their periscopes. So many torpedoes were whizzing around the harbor that the hero gods were obliged to settle on the harbor bottom. There, "impatiently awaiting the sunset, the men probably spent their time playing with wooden toys which they had brought on board with them. To be forced into inaction this way must have been very trying for them …"

And then the waited-for description that proved the submarines' success; " … just two minutes after the moon rose, a tremendous explosion occurred in Pearl Harbor, sending fiery columns high into the air, scattering red hot splinters. In a few minutes the fiery columns

HERO GODS

disappeared whereupon the enemy anti-aircraft batteries went into action, apparently mistaking the raid of the Special Attack Flotilla for that of the Japanese Aerial Force.

"There is not the slightest doubt that the Special Attack Flotilla attained supreme results amidst the confusion reigning in Pearl Harbor ... at present, however, it is difficult to distinguish the results attained by the Special Attack Flotilla from those of the air force.

"The instant sinking of the warship *Arizona* by them at night was so spectacular that it was clearly recognized by the Japanese forces located far off Hawaii then."

It was a prime example of wartime emotionalism, bent to steer the citizenry along the path to victory.

"This noble spirit of self-sacrifice is the essence of bushido; this is the embodiment of the Yamato spirit. Search though one may, he will never find a parallel case in the history of the world. The mere thought of the great deed performed by these nine men makes our hearts throb with emotion." Anyone who was not moved by these words, obviously, simply wasn't Japanese.

Hiraide also claimed that the midget submariners had designed and built their craft themselves, as if they were gods who fashioned their own lightning bolts. The nine hero-gods were compared to others in history, such as the famous 47 Ronin, who faced death calmly for supporting their feudal lord.

Hero-god-for-life Emperor Hirohito's only public pronouncement on the midget attack was a simple, "We appreciate this exploit." Upon this statement, Imperial Navy opinion-molders built a grand

Depictions of Yokoyama's fabled sinking of battleship Arizona *became a profitable sideline of Japan's propaganda industry. This version is from "Special Attack Flotilla." Also see the back cover.*

framework of platitude. "How grateful they must be in their watery graves to hear the gracious words!" went the official line. "This fulfilled their fondest hopes."

Released through neutral countries, the press release was widely distributed in America. In Hawaii, an Associated Press story printed on the front page of the *Honolulu Advertiser* was headlined, "Now Tokyo Tells How Attack on P.H. Was Made — Weird Story of Operations of a Special Flotilla Accompanies After-Death Citations." Curiously, the newspaper inserted an editorial aside at the head of the story, which asserted that, "The following account is obviously propaganda. It is, as well, studded with lies. No 'Special Attack Flotilla' entered Pearl Harbor during the Dec. 7 battle ..."

There were nine hero-gods, and five midget submarines. Something didn't add up, even for the propagandists. Edwin T. Layton later noted smugly that "the Japanese press subsequently was forced to announce that one of the members of these crews had been taken prisoner, because many Japanese knew these were 2-man submarines, and nine men could not be divided into two."

The American destroyer crews who had struggled with at least one midget submarine and dozens of suspects within Pearl Harbor must have felt the same way when the *Honolulu Advertiser* stated firmly no submarines entered the naval base. [2]

[2] Lorrin Thurston, publisher of the newspaper, was also the military governor's public-relations adviser during the war.

The Santa Barbara shelling also was hailed by the Japanese press, which announced that the entire West Coast was gripped by fear. The seacoast cities were deserted; President Roosevelt had ordered factories to relocate behind the safety of the Rockies. This national panic was somehow symptomatic of deep flaws in American character. Radio Tokyo announced on March 3 that "sensible Americans know that the submarine shelling of the Pacific coast was a warning to the nation that the Paradise created by George Washington is on the verge of destruction."

The relocation of Japanese-Americans from seacoast areas further armed Imperial propagandists. "Farms in California are facing total destruction since the Japanese have moved out," bemoaned Radio Tokyo, engaging in a bit of race-baiting on its own; were Japanese the only people capable of farming?

The Santa Barbara shelling was an icon of Imperial action, returned to again and again. "The expanse of water between Hawaii and the United States is under control of Japanese warships," Radio Tokyo flatly declared on April 9.

In a report on Imperial Japanese subversion in the islands, Army Intelligence Chief Lieutenant Colonel Kendall H. Fielder explained how such radio propaganda tended to backfire. "For example, the Japanese story of the great damage done by the submarine attack on Hilo, Hawaii, was clearly false and the Japanese residents of that city knew this to be a fact. In a comparatively short time these facts also became known to all the residents of other islands of the Hawaiian group. This also was true in the case of the single-plane night raid

HERO GODS

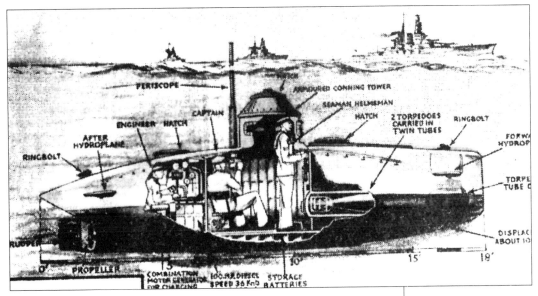

against the island of Oahu, March 4, 1942, when the Tokyo Broadcast falsely claimed extensive damage done at Pearl Harbor. Instances of this type have resulted in the local Japanese to greatly discredit propaganda emanating from that source ..."

Much credit was given to Japanese motherhood as a political concept, and every detail of the life of a hero-god's mother was analyzed as if she were the Virgin Mary. "Without such great mothers, there would never have been such loyal Japanese warriors," explained Hiraide. "At the root of this difference, be it noted, lies the selfish and hedonistic temperament of American and British mothers, which has naturally found reflection in the character of their children. In America, naval men are defined as a class of people who see the sights of the world, free of charge, who are paid very handsomely and who are, thus, in a position to lead very pleasant and happy lives."

The tough, self-sacrificing Japanese fighting man and the self-centered, buttery American, said Hiraide, were "as different as chalk and cheese."

The subtext was that Japanese mothers who lost children in battle were more highly thought of than mothers whose children still lived. This "spiritual power" was discussed in detail, and often offered up as a reason Japanese women should not be allowed to vote.

Those connected with the nine martyrs were swept up in the war of words. Sadamu Uyeda's old skipper on board *Chiyoda* wrote a widely publicized letter to the slain submariner's father, in which he claimed that "by the wonderful result of his heroic deeds we could recognize by our observations how the enemy fleet was disturbed in great confusions."

More interestingly, he claimed that Uyeda sank a battleship, but that his comrades blew themselves up in frustration when they were unable to do the same.

The reverses at Midway revived the legend of midget-submarine

This newspaper graphic is quite a fanciful cutaway of a midget submarine, considering that photographs of the real thing were distributed immediately by U.S. Navy public-relations wranglers.

exploits at Pearl Harbor, and Hiraide codified his persuasive skills in an English-language volume called "Special Attack Flotilla — Bushido in the War of Greater East Asia." A product of the staff of *Japan Times*, it was quickly printed and distributed in late 1942.

"Dashing courageously into Pearl Harbor they completed their task and then calmly awaited death," reads one passage. "It came, and they faced it with smiles on their faces. When our thoughts dwell on their gallant deed and we recall their great act of sacrifice, how can we help but become overcome with the deepest feeling of emotion?"

Public attention was directed to the uniquely Japanese character of the sacrifice.

"Something was needed to accomplish the impossible — something special was needed. But what?" said Hiraide, in an interview with Eiji Yoshikawa, a Japanese novelist. "That which is special is also fraught with danger. It also had to be something which the enemy could not duplicate. It had to be something only the Japanese could do. This was the Special Attack Flotilla."

Even the Nazis tumbled for the midget submariner mystique. Here is a German painting of two fierce Hero Gods penetrating Pearl Harbor.

"The nine heroes of the Pearl Harbor attack not only silently and patiently waited for death, but they took on the added burden of actually drilling and practicing to perfect their technique," chimed in Yoshikawa. "When I think of this, I really am at a loss for words."

This fatalistic conceit would have been a surprise to Yamamoto and the other Navy men who demanded the midget crewmen be given every chance to return alive. They did not, so their deaths were treated as a spiritual triumph instead of tragedy, on a plane so elevated only a true Japanese could understand.

These words presaged desperate *kamikaze* attacks later in the war. But there was a difference in temperament between the two that Yoshikawa and Hiraide recognized, and took pains to erase. *Kamikaze* attacks took place at thrilling speeds with blood boiling in one's veins, while midget attacks took place quietly, deliberately, precisely. It took a different sort of man from the *kamikaze*, a soul well-trained, indefatigable, able to stare down his own death.

"They reached the highest domain man is able to reach," said Hiraide. "These youths went one step further than that plane of spiritual perfection reached by the 70- or 80-year-old priest. How did they, then, in such a short period, attain such perfection of spiritual being? The answer lies in His Majesty the Emperor; it lies in the Imperial Virtues and Glory."

And then Hiraide gets to the nut of it: "The elimination of the Anglo-American way of thinking from East Asia is one of the prime

HERO GODS

A national day of mourning was held in Japan on April 8, 1942, when the nine Hero Gods were ceremoniously interred at Hibiya Park in Tokyo. These pavilions were constructed for the occasion, and a parade of Shinto priests, honor guards and naval officials filed onto the sacred grounds.

objectives of the War of Greater East Asia. Self-interest, love of material wealth, untrammeled pursuit of pleasures must be completely wiped out of the Japanese mind. The nine heroes out of their pure and self-sacrificing act set an example for us to follow. If there are men who would still cling to the Anglo-American ideals despite the initiative taken by these nine heroes, they should die of mortification and shame. The attack on Pearl Harbor was not only a great blow at the enemy, but was at the same time an assault on the Anglo-American-mindness of some Japanese people …"

In other words, in these post-Midway declarations — if you are a true Japanese, be prepared to sacrifice. Through failure and death, the nine midget submariners continued to serve the purposes of their government.

During the war years, the heroics of midget submariners became the subject of a best-seller called "Navy," by Toyoo Iwata. Other popular writers invoked the ghosts of the hero gods. Jihei Asai, who had lived in prewar Hawaii, wrote wishfully of an invasion of the islands. "Panicked at the surprise attack by Imperial forces, the American Navy won't have a chance to throw leis overboard as it departs. Even if the Navy did throw leis, they would sink and turn to seaweed on the ocean floor. But the spirits of our young eagles[3] who scattered cherry blossoms around the entrance of Pearl Harbor are awaiting the arrival of Imperial forces and shall help turn Hawaii into a forward base for our navy."

In fact, a plan for invading Hawaii was set into motion less than two days after the attack. It required a starve-out to succeed — Japanese plans for invading Hawaii foundered on the daunting prospect of keeping inhabitants fed. In 1941, nearly three million tons of food were shipped to Hawaii from the American mainland, 2,300 miles away. With a Japanese occupying force, the amount of food

[3] The deceased submariners — Japanese fighting men were popularly called "eagles."

necessary would rise, and would have to be shipped nearly 4,000 miles, in waters already teeming with American submarines.

In the 100-day shipping strike of 1936-1937, Hawaii had only a 14-day food supply left when the strike ended.

The Japanese plan called for seizure of Midway, with a later sweep on Hawaii. It was estimated that the minimum force required would include an extraordinary 14 carriers and 300 submarines, a number far beyond the capabilities of *Dai Nippon* shipyards. The submarines, long-range models capable of a 9,000-mile sortie, would create an undersea tripwire between Hawaii and West Coast.

In any case, the carrier debacle north of Midway in June 1942 scuttled the scheme. If the blockading submarines of the Advance

Navy Minister Admiral Shigetaro Shimada made a public pilgrimage to the holiest of holies, Naoji Iwasa's home. Here he burns incense at an altar devoted to Iwasa in the home.

Force had been kept in place, instead of sprinting around after carriers, the scheme might have succeeded. On Dec. 9, 1941, General Short estimated 37 days of food remained in the islands. Within a week of the attack, he busied himself by demanding shipments of foodstuffs. "It is essential that allocation for shipping space be made immediately," he pleaded with the adjutant general.

By late December, the general staff concluded that Hawaii was safe, beyond the occasional shelling attack or bomb run. The territory was assigned a shipping priority below that of Australia, and soon, below that of the "ferry islands," colonized by Pan Am in the '30s.

Shipping to Hawaii dropped off dramatically, and naval insistence on Atlantic-like convoys kept individual ships in port until they could all leave together. General Delos C. Emmons, commander of the Hawaii garrison, was quite bitter about this practice. He complained in January 1942 about supply ships loafing on the West Coast. In reply, General George C. Marshall denied that there was a problem.

Part of the fault lay with the practitioners of martial law in Hawaii, who had no experience in running a complex island economy. Soon after taking over from Short, for example, Emmons ordered a quantity of sulfanilamide greater than the total capacity of the American pharmaceutical industry, as well as 37,000 brand-new Garand rifles to hand out to the civilian populace.

By the end of March 1942, the Army's handling of supplies to Hawaii had "broken down completely," according to an investigation by the War Production Board. Fewer than 18 days' worth of gasoline remained, spare parts for the important search aircraft were non-existent. Cement was in such short supply that the Board estimated it would take "73 freighters, plying continuously for three months, to remedy it."

The Board declared that the problem had two roots — the low priority assigned to Hawaiian resupply, and the refusal of Army and Navy commanders to cooperate. Hawaii's priority was bumped up, and ships began to pour into Honolulu Harbor. The Army was put in

HERO GODS

charge of ports, the Navy given control of shipping, and they were forced to work together.

The Battle of Midway and a shift of focus to the European theater in the fall of 1942 slowed the flood to a trickle, and for the rest of the war Hawaii was passive. The opportunity gone, I-boats never again had the rich targets available in Hawaiian waters.

Even so, there was no relaxing of martial law. As University of Hawaii psychology professor Stanley Porteus pointed out in a 1947 book: "Invasion, the threat of blockade, were convenient bogeys with which to scare civilians."

Military and business leaders in Hawaii worked together to develop a "scorched earth" proviso that would devastate the islands' industrial infrastructure should Imperial troops pour ashore. Castle &

Sailors present arms in honor of the Hero Gods at the public funeral. The ceremony included a covered gun carriage, a traditional military honor inherited from the Royal Navy.

Cooke, Ltd., consulting engineer S.T. Hoyt was given the job of designing the plan in early 1942. Hoyt studied on it, and decided that a surprise attack by surface ships or aircraft would be discovered and defeated, given the now-alert state of Hawaii troops.

Submarines were another matter. "A surprise attack by troops landed by submarine is not an impossibility, with types now in use," he wrote on April 3, 1942. "The Japanese can crowd more men into a given space than we consider possible … Fifty submarines carrying 500 men each traveling on the surface at night, and submerging by day might succeed in reaching Oahu from points outside the areas most intensively patrolled."

Hoyt hoped that "the patrols on the shore would see and halt" the attacking Japanese, but that "the nights are dark at the time of the full moon. If the attack were successful, it would succeed quickly" in overrunning island defenses.

A similar scheme was given the go-ahead by the Imperial Navy,

Posing in front of a shrine to their son, Kiyoshi Inagaki's parents read his last letter home.

a Dieppe-like raid dreamed up by Lieutenant Commander Daiji Yamaoka. Several hundred volunteers of "Yamaoka's Parachute Brigade" would be smuggled across the Pacific in gigantic submarines; they would storm ashore in Santa Barbara; then blast their way into Los Angeles. They would wreck the big aircraft factories of Lockheed and Douglas, taking as many Americans with them as possible, but eventually they would be wiped out. Training began in earnest in December 1944, and shifted emphasis in May 1945 when the target was changed to the Marianas. In any case, there was no transport available by that late date.

The concept of blockade was a popular war-game option, and well understood. As it became easier to get from one side of the Pacific to the other in the 1800s, Hawaii was no longer isolated. As the chain of islands grew in strategic importance, and conversely unable to replenish a modern economy, the islands became dependent on outside forces. The nature of warfare became such that a battle of attrition would overwhelm Hawaii; the islands were essentially indefensible without the support of a world power. The question a century ago was when, not if, the kingdom of Hawaii would be grabbed by another country.

That the Pacific Ocean is an adjunct to the islands of Japan is a popular belief that persists to this day. "The Pacific Ocean is the *furosato* — native place-of the Japanese people," wrote reporter Soen Yamashita in a 1942 book on Hawaii. Tetsuji Kada, a sociologist at Keio University, taught that all the Pacific islands were homogeneous, "extensions" of the Japanese home archipelago.

Japanese officials, such as Diet member Yusuke Tsurumi, who toured the United States on lecture tours before the war, spread the government line that Polynesians were actually Asian. The Pacific War that followed was simply a noble attempt to keep the area all in the family. Books appeared postulating that Japanese mariners had

HERO GODS

landed in Hawaii hundreds of years before James Cook, and had intermarried with Polynesians, begetting Hawaiians.

These weren't radical concepts in Japan. The leading thinker of Japan's geopolitical university system was Saneshige Komaki of Kyoto Imperial University, who argued that the Japanese — as "the greatest maritime people in the world" — were uniquely qualified to rule over all the oceans.

The very word "Pacific," insisted Komaki, should be tossed out and replaced with "New Sea of Japan." And all the world's continents were extensions of Asia, with Japan at its center.

In this context, an Oct. 30, 1945, article in *Yomiuri Hochi* stating

that "long before" the attack, "Japan's submarine offensive on Pearl Harbor were (sic) going on and several eerie periscopes were feeling out movements of American fleets from the rough sea" was acceptable behavior for a country claiming to want peace.

These concepts were far removed from the reality of war, a conflict that the Imperial Navy had sought to avoid. With a Pacific war forced upon them, the truth of Advance Force operations was studied in detail and disseminated.

Claims by the returning I-boats of the Advance Force were somewhat exaggerated, not surprising given the hit-and-run circumstances of submarine warfare.

The grand total claimed by the Imperial Navy through Dec. 25, 1941, was 10 ships sunk, about 70,000 tons' worth, three vessels run aground (about 30,000 tons), and five probables. The actual number was eight sunk, seven damaged.

Japanese losses included the five HA-boats, the two RO-boats lost by accident, and *I-70*, which seemed to have vanished. The last known position was within a few miles of Pearl Harbor on Dec. 8, when it radioed "one ship which appears to be an enemy aircraft carrier is entering Pearl Harbor. Our position is a bearing of 230 degrees and a distance of four miles from Diamond Head." Flagship

As the war continued, so did interest in midget submarines. This example was captured by the U.S. Navy on Guadalcanal and closely examined before it was lost. For some reason, Navy censors have painted a pair of loose trousers on the sailor examing the torpedo tubes.

The business end of the midget submarine found on Guadalcanal. Shrouds have been extended over the torpedo tubes and the draft markings now appear to be spot-welded onto the hull.

Katori radioed back an acknowledgment, but nothing further was heard from *I-70*.

The carrier was *Enterprise*; on Dec. 10, an SBD bomber from that ship sank *I-70* north of Oahu.

Two I-boats were lightly damaged. *I-69* was caught in "anti-sub nets" on Dec. 8; it escaped but damaged "various electrical instruments" for measuring distance and speed, for flood control, and the periscope. Even so, *I-69* completed her sortie, and returned to Kwajalein on Dec. 26.

I-68 was depth-charged in the forward patrol sector of Pearl Harbor on Dec. 15, with "flooding in aft torpedo tubes and such places." Two depth charges went off "within 10 meters" of the hull, directly overhead. Light bulbs burst throughout the submarine, watertight hatches began to seep seawater, and sensitive electronic instruments became scrambled. Despite the horrific drumming, the submarine was found to be remarkably intact, and her patrol resumed.

A report on Advance Force experiences pointed out that U.S. depth charges were, "by previous investigations," ascertained to trigger at 35 meters, therefore Japanese submarines should dive to least 50 to 70 meters. *I-16* had three charges go off directly above her and suffered no damage. "The bursting charge of America's depth charges appeared to be feeble …

"It seems as if American destroyers are equipped with accurate and good sound detectors and they, for the most part, are executing stationary or slow patrol speed. Even when an American destroyer is stationary, be on guard."

Accordingly, on future patrols near enemy shores, I-boats skippers were urged to proceed at "slowest speed, ventilation stopped, in steering mechanical power only on dive planes, otherwise manpower, charge batteries same distance from attack area and return undercover of darkness."

The rough water around Hawaii appeared to be a surprise. *I-7* originally tried to launch her Glen floatplane on Dec. 8 near Niihau, and was prevented by rough weather. The submarine stole south to the protected lee of the Big Island and launched the aircraft a few days later. To cover such eventualities, it was determined that many aircraft-carrying submarines may be necessary for any extended operation.

Onshore current at Barbers Point was very strong. *I-68* raised her periscope one day to look around, and sighted breakers dead ahead. She turned quickly to avoid being dashed onto the reef. Waves in

386

HERO GODS

Hawaii were heavier than expected, and several I-boats had conning towers broach embarrassingly close to American patrol boats. It was hard to maintain underwater position. The I-boat skippers were unanimous — periscopes should be made as long as possible.

On the way back to Kwajalein after 30 days of operations, 20 of which were submerged, *I-16* test-fired her deck machine guns. One worked perfectly, the other balked after one round.

These lessons of battle were to later prove valuable to the fleet-sized submarines. But despite the outpouring of glorious propaganda, the Imperial Navy still had no solid data to direct midget submarine operations. Once a midget was launched, the crew never reported back.

This situation was hinted at when a midget submarine later salvaged in Visale Bay on Guadalcanal was studied by the Americans; documents from the submarine interior were rescued, but a storm rattled salvage ship *Ortolan* and the midget broke loose and sank again.

Included were instructions to the "Yatsumaki Butai" from Satoru Harada, then commander of *Chiyoda*. They were unusually cautious for what previously had been unstated suicide missions:

"As there is at present no information for the evaluation of the true worth of the midget submarine, it is expected that each man will, both in the attack and the withdrawal, exert his every effort, and in this way (do his part) in supplying this information.

"Be confident in the August Virtue of His Majesty, in Providential Assistance, and in your ability which you have constantly developed. Go forth undaunted. 'Heaven helps those who help themselves.'"

An American sailor tries the Guadalcanal midget on for size. The snug passage through the sail is evident.

29 | LAST OF THE CLASS

Lives Light As Feathers

The Advance Force actions around Pearl Harbor and the West Coast of America continued to have reverberations throughout the war. A pair of midget submarine assaults launched just before the Battle of Midway wiped out the first class of trained submariners, and the cavalier Merchant Marine sinkings of the early part of the war turned deadly, highlighting profound philosophical differences between the combatants.

The Japanese continued to build several brands of midget submarines, using them occasionally to harass American invasion fleets from the Aleutians to Australia. On May 31, 1942, midget submarines penetrated both Sydney Harbor in Australia, and Diego Suarez, Madagascar. None of these midgets survived their attacks either, and there are other interesting parallels to the Pearl Harbor assault.

At Sydney, a large, deep bay with a wide throat, midgets launched from mother subs *I-22*, *I-24* and *I-27* crept toward the harbor in the early evening of May 31. In charge was Captain Hanku Sasaki, commander of the Special Attack Unit at Pearl. A report from a Glen launched from *I-21* on May 29 confirmed the harbor was crowded with warships. Sasaki decided to assault Sydney within 48 hours.

One midget, containing Lieutenant Kenshi Chuma and Petty Officer Takeshi Ohmori from *I-27*, got hung up in an anti-torpedo net stretched between George's Head and Green Point. Australian ships began to investigate, but not too closely, because they thought it was a mine. At 10:35 p.m., as harbor craft closed in on the object, it suddenly blew up. The Japanese had set off the scuttling charge.

While attention was directed toward the net, the other two midgets slipped into the harbor. One, holding Lieutenant Katsuhisa Ban and Petty Officer Namori Ashibe from *I-24*, broke surface 500 yards from U.S. cruiser *Chicago*, which opened wildly inaccurate but spectacular fire with tracers. Ten minutes later, at 11:10 p.m., *HMAS Geelong* also began firing at Ban's midget, and also missed.

Ban didn't fire his torpedoes at *Chicago* until 11:30 p.m., plenty of time to get lined up. Both torpedoes, however, swerved to starboard. One slithered up on the shores of Garden Island without

exploding. The other struck a retaining wall beneath *HMAS Kuttabul*, a converted ferry. The explosion ripped off *Kuttabul's* stern and she sank quickly. Twenty sailors drowned. The Dutch submarine *K-9*, moored nearby, had several battery jars cracked by the shock bubble.

Nearly an hour and half later, at 1:58 a.m., the magnetic detector at the channel entrance recorded Ban's midget leaving the harbor. It was not seen again.

The third midget contained Petty Officer Masao Tsuzuku and, at the helm, Lieutenant Keiu Matsuo, the doctor-spy who had wanted so desperately to go along on the Pearl Harbor raid.

At 11:07 p.m. near the torpedo net, Matsuo's midget was bracketed by six depth charges from *HMAS Yandra,* who then lost contact. At 3:01 a.m., the midget's magnetic field set off the detector at the harbor entrance — she had presumably recovered from the earlier attack. Australian ships scrambled around the harbor with no luck.

At 5 a.m., *HMAS Sea Mist* spotted a mysterious shadow in Taylor Bay. She hit the spotlights and caught Matsuo's midget in the glare. *HMS Yarroma* and *HMS Steady Hour* then charged in, and the three ships boiled the bay with depth charges.

At 8:27 a.m., black oil and debris belched onto the surface. *Steady Hour* dragged her anchor across the bay until it caught on something beneath the surface.

The next day a diver went down and discovered the midget's screws still turning, slowly. Slings were quietly placed around the hull — the Australians remembered the other midget suddenly self-destructing on the harbor net — and the midget was raised on June 4.

Reporter William J. Dunn of CBS[1] was there and filed a radio report. It reflected a growing public fascination with the small craft, and an account of midget salvage missing from Pearl Harbor records:

"Today I saw the job completed and the battered steel cylinder that had once been a menacing weapon deposited on dry land. Although it was previously indicated that this particular midget was probably identical with those used at Pearl Harbor, when the craft was lifted out of the water it was found to be a slightly larger type.

"Only two-thirds of the submarine were raised, the tail section having been torn away by the force of the depth bombs or by the salvage operations that followed. The sub, intact, would probably be close to 65 feet long. It is almost needle-like in its proportions, being barely five and a half feet in diameter, capped by a conning tower two and half feet tall.[2]

"As it rose from the water in the arms of a huge crane, the marks of its terrific beating were apparent. Steel plates were battered badly, and water poured from several seams as well as the open section at the rear and a hatch cover on the bottom which had warped open. Below the conning tower it carried two numerals, but there were no Japanese characters of any kind in evidence.

"From the battered nose peered the shining tip of a live torpedo, as though it had jammed in the act of firing. Actually, naval observers

[1] *Dunn is the only bareheaded man in the famous picture of General Douglas MacArthur going ashore at Leyte.*

[2] *These midgets were essentially identical to Pearl midgets and had the same proportions.*

One of the midget submarines is pulled from Sydney harbor. Aboard are the bodies of Matsuo and Tsuzuku.

doubt that the tube had been fired, because closer inspection indicates its cover probably had been blown away by the blast which had obviously crushed the covering of the second torpedo directly below it. On both the nose and the conning tower were steel cutting edges designed to aid the craft in getting through anti-submarine nets.

"The entire craft gave the appearance of great flimsiness and could not be compared in careful construction with its larger brothers.

"The question of whether the probable two-man crew is still aboard is not yet answered. Naval officers who inspected the craft briefly through the open hatches reported the first object they were able to identify through the mud was a neatly folded umbrella!"

The "umbrella" turned out to be a samurai sword. "I still wonder which of the two items would be the biggest asset in an underwater sortie into enemy territory," Dunn later wrote.

The U.S. Navy made a thorough examination of the Sydney submarine — which was essentially identical to the Pearl Harbor model — noting that:

"Access hatch in the bottom of the midget evidently was made to make a watertight fit over the deck hatch of the mother …

"Battery charging leads and telephone wires passed through glands in the midget from the mother. When casting off they are cut, leaving about three-foot lengths trailing when the boat is launched.

"Vertical and horizontal rudders are drilled with holes to match holes in the fins which permit securing by a steel strap …

"A cutter on the torpedo head is in the form of a cross whose center portion is knife-edged. A pyramidal device of four cutters is removable from additional saw-like cutters extending back the full length of the torpedo. An inertia pistol is fitted to the side of the head.

"Water sealing caps provided in each tube are released by hydraulic pressure acting on holding down clamps with a push rod acting on the upper cap."

LAST OF THE CLASS

The Sydney midget submarine separated at the aft joint between the battery compartment and the engine housing.

Two demolition charges were discovered, one forward, the other aft. Apparently the Imperial Navy was not going to let another HA-boat get captured.

"It is believed probable that this modified type of midget submarine was built as a result of the unsuccessful performance of the smaller type at Pearl Harbor," concluded the Navy.

Also aboard were the bodies of Matsuo and Tsuzuku, dead of gunshot wounds to the head. A week later, *I-24* resurfaced and fired 10 rounds in the general direction of the city. As the first rounds impacted, the bright city lights winked out and searchlights began playing on the water from shore installations. They focused on *I-24* and the submarine quickly withdrew to the north. Down the coast, *I-21* repeated the attack scenario on the steel works and shipyards at Newcastle.

While this going on in Australia, on the other side of the Indian Ocean Rear Admiral Ishizaki in flagship *I-8* cruised the Mozambique Channel, off the east coast of Africa. His force consisted of four I-boats. On May 30, a plane from *I-10* reported there were British warships in Diego Suarez, a placid, clover-shaped bay on the north-ernmost tip of Madagascar. Only a few weeks earlier, British forces had landed there against Vichy French forces in a comic-opera invasion that produced no injuries beyond scraped knees. The British were busily arranging a convenient truce that would surrender the rest of Madagascar while leaving it still in French hands.

Ishizaki ordered an immediate midget assault the next night. The timing, occurring in exact conjunction with the Sydney attack, was apparently a coincidence.

I-16, *I-18* and *I-20* were all Pearl Harbor Special Attack veterans. *I-18* had been stalking the Madagascar channel for more than a month, but when the time came to let loose her midget, the craft balked with a frozen engine.

HMS Ramillies *is hit in Diego Garcia in another wishful Imperial Navy propaganda painting.*

[3] *Ironically, during the War of 1812, the 74-gun sailing warship* HMS Ramillies *was attacked in July 1813 by a "diving boat" that succeeded in poking a hole in the warship's copper plating.*

So, only two midgets were sent into the harbor, where they expected to find British battleships and cruisers. Commander Kaoryu Yamada of *I-16* launched Ensign Katsusuke Iwase and Petty Officer Kozo Takada, and from *I-20*, Commander Takashi Yamada launched Lieutenant Saburo Akieda and Petty Officer Masami Takemoto.

Akieda had been Naoji Iwasa's fellow test-pilot during the early days of midget submarine shakedowns, and considered the leading master of midget theory after Iwasa's disappearance at Pearl Harbor.

At Diego Suarez, the midgets' torpedoes succeeded in damaging British battleship *HMS Ramillies* and sinking tanker *British Loyalty*, and didn't return to their mother subs. Their movements are as much a mystery as the Pearl Harbor midgets. [3]

Ramillies retired rapidly to Durban, South Africa, and when the scout plane from *I-10* came nosing around again a few days later, empty mooring buoys gave the Japanese the impression that the British battleship had sunk. The Japanese left the area and sailed north, to blockade the Suez Canal.

The British, knowing nothing about mother submarines, assumed the midgets had sailed from Vichy ports to the south. Using bombers from South Africa, raids were launched against these ports and the carefully orchestrated truce fell apart. Madagascar suffered three more bogus invasions before the French threw in the towel. Embarrassed by the exaggerated claims of Pearl Harbor, Ishizaki's crews carefully monitored British radio traffic as they sailed away. They learned the actual disposition of the battleship, and something else as well; British gossip about two Japanese sailors who had waded ashore at Diego Suarez and attempted to attack the shore garrison.

The sailors had thrown themselves at the fort, despite calls for surrender, and were shot.[4] Imperial Navy submariners decided without evidence that these two were Akieda and Takamoto, the most highly trained of the midget submariners, and naturally — it follows — the most brave.

The simultaneous, nearly successful attacks at Sydney and Diego Suarez brought to a close the aggressive actions of the Advance Force. Everything to follow in the war would be a reaction to those opening months. The first group of midget submariners had been wiped out; the only survivor was Kazuo Sakamaki, cold, friendless and in a deep funk in an American POW camp.

At Camp McCoy, Wisconsin, snow covered the ground, and the Hawaii internees exclaimed over it. Each was given three blankets, two sheets and a pillow. The clothing was Army woolen trousers and Mackinaw coats, handed down from the Civilian Conservation Corps.

The commandant was Lieutenant Colonel Horace Ivan Rogers, a Detroit lawyer with connections in Army Intelligence. Keenly interested in his charges, Rogers allowed the Japanese to observe holidays and plan educational seminars. Ironically, the camp was cleared out in June 1942, to make way for the 100th Infantry, newly organized from the Hawaii National Guard and other volunteers.

The first night in the snowy camp, Sakamaki was escorted to the Hawaii group. There were no separate facilities for a prisoner of war. The guards left Sakamaki with the Japanese "enemy aliens" from Hawaii, requesting that they explain the situation to him.

"Of course," said Dr. Kazuo Miyamoto. This would give Miyamoto and other internees their first chance to talk to Sakamaki.

"Sakamaki-san, this is not Sand Island. At that camp you were forbidden to talk to us. But here at this camp, the commander is asking that you stay with us until a barracks can be prepared for you — you cannot sleep in an unheated barracks!" said Miyamoto.

Sakamaki bowed stiffly. The burns under his eyes were nearly healed.

With the guards gone, the internees pelted Sakamaki with questions. The POW was suspicious and begged off. The next day, Sakamaki was taken away to a solitary barracks. The Hawaii internees talked among themselves about the Imperial Navy officer, and agreed that he seemed to be in a trance. He talked as if drugged.

Sakamaki has no memories of this period of imprisonment.

By March, the Combined Imperial Fleet had discovered Sakamaki's capture. Admiral Yamamoto called submarine staff officer Captain Takayasu Arima into his cabin and then raged loudly and

[4] *The British version claimed the two submariners swam ashore after their craft hit a reef, and that they hid in the jungle for three days before being surrounded and killed.*

long. The admiral "literally stormed," recalled Arima. "He got red in the face and stamped his feet on the deck in anger. According to the code of a Japanese warrior it was a disgrace to be captured." Yamamoto also assumed the Americans had wrung valuable military information out of Sakamaki, when in fact all they had gotten was confused, miserable ramblings.

By then, Sakamaki was deep in the heartland of the enemy. Most of the other prisoners were civilians; internees and Axis nationals swept up in the outbreak of war.

Sakamaki wasn't a difficult prisoner for the Americans, but he was a hard one to understand. He insisted on cold-water bathing in the dead of winter. He kept to himself, and did not speak even to the other Japanese captives. When other prisoners and internees would gather at the camp canteen and sing nostalgic Japanese folk songs — including songs Sakamaki had sung in the Navy — Prisoner of War Number One stayed on the sidelines and sneered. "They were merely songs, just as all hills were hills to me. I had no aesthetic or sentimental feelings," he recalled.

Sakamaki refused to speak at all to the Americans except to say, "Good morning, Colonel" every day to Commandant Rogers. The

Americans decided Sakamaki might be insane. A psychiatrist was called in, and spoke to Sakamaki through an interpreter.

There was a cultural and psychological schism that each party was barely aware of. The psychiatrist was unable to treat a man who, from the day he'd entered the seclusion of the Naval Academy at Eta Jima, had devoted himself to strict conditioning of mind and body.

Sakamaki didn't mind the cold-water baths — he'd trained his body to ignore changes in temperature. He also had hammered his soul into a "complete separation from understanding of other human beings, except those of my own kind in the services."

An actor portraying Kazuo Sakamaki meditates in his cell in the Nippon-TV docudrama "P.W. 1: In the Footsteps of a Midget Submarine Captain." There are no official records or photographs of Sakamaki's imprisonment.

This is why he kept away from the Japanese civilian internees in the camp — they were as alien to him as the Americans.

After a few futile attempts to draw Sakamaki out, the psychiatrist left him alone, which was exactly what Sakamaki wanted.

When Rogers signed over the internees to a Captain Laemmle, they gave him a rousing *banzai*.

The prisoners were sent south, to Camp Forrest in Tullahoma, Tennessee, near the tri-state border with Georgia and Alabama. Sakamaki began to warm up when he was treated kindly by Red Cross workers on the trip, and even watched a Deanna Durbin movie at the USO. New clothing was issued, tailored green shirts and trousers, part of a uniform shipment for Filipino scouts that didn't get to the Philippines in time.

Sakamaki snapped out of his shell in Camp Forrest. After a visit

LAST OF THE CLASS

from the International Red Cross, the prisoner was allowed to talk to others, to attend movies and lectures, to roam the compound, as long as he was escorted.

Sakamaki discovered a mentor in the Reverend Ninryo Nago, a former cavalry soldier in the Russo-Japanese war, who had been wounded and captured in Manchuria decades before. "To be a captive is not a disgrace. Alive we can serve our country again," Nago told him one day.

"Dying for our country may be the supreme sacrifice, but it is not for the greatest good. We can serve our country in many ways."

Sakamaki was then moved to Camp Livingston, Louisiana, an internee camp filled with Spanish-speaking Japanese-Panamanians. Later, a few Japanese POWs trickled in from Pacific campaigns. Many proved hostile and ignorant, and a couple were so crazed they even frightened Sakamaki. He was given the task of keeping them in line, which he did with schooling and hard work.

At first, pocket-sized New Testaments were distributed to the Japanese prisoners, who accepted them eagerly; the pages were the right thickness and size for rolling cigarettes.

Sakamaki passed on Nago's advice to the thoroughly rattled men. Their leader, a Captain Nagamune, attempted suicide by slashing his own throat. He failed, which made him despair even more.

"I did not carry out my responsibilities well enough!" he shouted at Sakamaki. "That's why we lost!"

"Do you mean the fate of the battle at Midway depended on one ship, one man?" countered Sakamaki. "Was the responsibility for the outcome all yours? Would you have taken all the acclaim in case Japan had won?

"Of course not. Battles are cooperative efforts. You fought the best you could, and the Americans fought the best they could. That's all we in the military can do — to do our best with what we have."

The words spilled out of Sakamaki. They had been locked in his mind for months.

Sakamaki became friendly with Kumaji Furuya, who owned a furniture store in Honolulu. The two enjoyed dissecting the intersecting cultures. One day, while strolling in a pine grove, he called Furuya a "lucky American."

Furuya stopped short. He had lost his business, been separated from his family, all because he had made himself a leader in the Japanese community. "American?" he snapped. "We're not Americans. We often think we are, but during emergencies such as this, look at what happened to us. We're really Japanese."

"You have a Japanese face and name, and you use the Japanese language, but inside you're no longer Japanese," said Sakamaki. "You have a different philosophy.

"For example, we in Japan don't feel much responsibility for others, although we're taught to fight and die for our country. But then country — the term country — is an ideal, a nebulous idea. We're

trained from an early age to believe our country comes first. Before ourselves, before our families. We must be able to sacrifice ourselves and our families for our country."

Sakamaki gathered steam. Could he have chatted this way at Eta Jima, been able to express self-doubt?

"But we're not relating to individual people , to our friends, our neighbors … people who have names and faces and sorrows and joyful experiences and worries. Our country comes first. But within it are these people …" mused Sakamaki.

"That's another way of looking at it. These people are precious; these people are worth fighting for, and these people constitute our country. It's like looking from both ends of a kaleidoscope.

"I think that's what makes this country — America — great. You care for each other. I see you sharing your sad moments, your happy moments. You almost live each other's lives."

Furuya was fascinated. He sensed that Sakamaki was lonely, not fitting in with either the Americanized Japanese or the recent Pacific prisoners, still steely in their self-deprecation.

"Well, there's so few of us, and nothing else to do," rationalized Furuya. "We have to listen to others and to our own conscience. We're given the time and opportunity to evaluate our past and our values, our expectations, our goals in life, our relationships with others."

"You are Japanese, and yet you are American."

"It's probably the Hawaiian influence, more than the American influence. In Hawaii, we have what we call *ohana* — extended family. There's a large family relationship where members care and share with each other," said Furuya, and he described a cooperative work-and-family ethic that sounded wildly exotic to the Japanese POW.

"Ohana? In Japanese it means a flower," said Sakamaki. "That relationship, of caring and sharing, is as beautiful as a flower."

"And Hawaiians have what is called a 'calabash cousin.' I used to hear Hawaiians say, 'So and So is my calabash cousin,' and I would ask, 'On your father's side or your mother's side?' and they'd say 'Neither! He's a calabash cousin.'"

Sakamaki had never heard of calabashes. Furuya explained that it was a gourd, hollowed out and used by ancient Hawaiians as a vessel. During times of emergency, Hawaiians would pass the calabash and givers would make anonymous offerings into the gourd.

"There's no way the receiver can know how much the giver gave. That way the giver gives from his heart, according to what he can share," said Furuya. "That's a true friend — a calabash cousin!"

"There's no way of knowing who gave $1 or who gave $50?"

"It doesn't matter to the giver, because he's giving because he wants to share in that happy or sad occasion, not because he wants to be acknowledged," said Furuya. "In Japan — and in Hawaii — we put our money in envelopes with our name and address on the outside."

The two walked quietly awhile in the rustling woods. Sakamaki's mind was in overdrive. He found himself bursting with questions.

LAST OF THE CLASS

But he asked only one. "Furuya-san," he said. "May I be your calabash cousin?"

In contrast to Sakamaki's quiet months of reflection, Allied prisoners captured by Japanese submarines often did not survive — and those that did brought back ghastly tales of butchery on the high seas. The ruthless but disorganized Advance Force operation off the American West Coast was transformed into a bloody free-for-all — Vice Admiral Ichioka of Submarine Squadron 8 had given orders to kill all survivors of sinking ships.

The senseless machine gunning of the civilian crew of *Donerail*, three days after Pearl Harbor, was unusual, but it was quickly followed by the sinking of Dutch freighter *Langkoeas* on Jan. 1, 1942. Three survived of *Langkoeas'* 94 seamen, executed by the crew of *I-58*. *I-58* and four other boats of the 4th squadron were on patrol off Java — not part of the Advance Force — and were looking for targets of opportunity. *I-58* also sunk Dutch freighter *Boero* on Feb. 25, near the Sunda Strait, this time leaving no survivors.

Plainly marked Australian hospital ship *Centaur* was attacked May 14, 1943, by *I-177,* skippered by Lieutenant Commander H. Nakagawa. *Centaur* sailed with all lights on to broadcast her non-combatant status, including floodlit red crosses on her sides. Her route and description had also been reported in advance to the Japanese, so there would be no mistakes. The hospital ship was torpedoed and went down within three minutes. Of the ship's complement of 360, including crew, patients and medical personnel, 64 survived.

RO-110 added a new twist after sinking *Daisy Moller* on Dec. 14, 1943. The British ship went down quickly, within three miles of the Eastern Ghats, a coastal plain fronting the Bay of Bengal. The entire crew managed to escape the sinking ship. With lifeboats and rafts intact and the jungly shore within sight, they had an excellent chance of surviving.

RO-110 surfaced and began to ram the lifeboats with her prow. When all were splintered, the Japanese opened fire on the merchant seamen with machine guns, sinking the inflatable rafts and killing 55 of the 71 civilians.

Tanker *British Chivalry* was sunk on Feb. 22, 1944, by *I-37,* skippered by Nakagawa, who had sunk hospital ship *Centaur.* It was the beginning of an extraordinarily bloody week for Nakagawa.

Of the tanker's crew, 53 of 59 survived the sinking itself. *I-37* opened fire on the lifeboats with her deck gun and with machine guns. The Japanese spent nearly two hours patrolling the area, shooting the floating bodies again and again, and sledding the submarine's rudder back and forth so that the I-boat's twin screws chopped the bodies to pieces. *British Chivalry* skipper Walter Hill was forced to stand on the deck of the submarine and watch.

Nakagawa suddenly called off the massacre and steamed away. Most of the men had swum away from the scene, and they returned to find, surprisingly, that the Japanese had killed only 13 and injured 5,

despite the effort. A riddled boat was patched and the crew attempted to make for Madagascar; they were rescued after 37 days at sea. Hill remained a prisoner of the Japanese for the duration.

On Feb. 26, Nakagawa and *I-37* torpedoed motorship *Sutlej,* carrying a load of phosphates across the Indian Ocean. The ship went down in minutes, dragged by the heavy ore. The attack was at night; it's unknown how many got off the freighter before it went down. After Nakagawa's men finished firing on the heads bobbing in the water, 22 survived of the crew of 73.

On Feb. 29, Nakagawa struck again, this time sinking British cargo steamer *Ascot.* Nakagawa took *Ascot's* master Jack Travis on board and began to slash at the prisoner with a sword, which kicked off two hours of slaughter. Both of the ship's lifeboats were rammed and sunk. Eight civilian seamen of 56 aboard *Ascot* survived.

In seven days, Nakagawa and *I-37* had killed 118 civilian seamen after they had escaped their sinking ships.

On March 18, *I-165* sank steamship *Nancy Moller.* Survivors were taken aboard the submarine and tortured; others were gunned down as they flailed in the water. Of the British ship's complement of 65, only 32 survived.

The most notorious rampage involved Commander Tatsunosuke Ariizume and *I-8,* which had been with the Advance Force positioned north of Oahu on Dec. 7 and had led the final Advance Force assault on Madagascar. But this cruise, during the spring of 1944, was to be a low point for Advance Force veterans.

I-8 again was prowling the Indian Ocean, picking off solitary merchant ships. On March 26, Ariizume torpedoed Dutch freighter *Tjisalak.* On board the ship, making a run from Melbourne to Ceylon, were a mixed group of Allies; Dutch sailors, Australian soldiers, Indonesian and Hindu civilians, and a British gunner. Also aboard were American nurse Verna Gordon Britten, a Red Cross worker who had toured the Far East before the war as a dancer and who was trying to rejoin her British husband in India, and radio officer James Blears, a British merchant seaman whose Olympic swimming hopes had been scuttled by the war.

Blears stood the midnight-to-four radio watch and retired below. As he dozed off, *Tjisalak* was slammed amidships by a torpedo at 5:30 a.m. Blears ran to his primary emergency post in the radio shack and determined that the operator was still alive and was sending out a distress call. Neither radioman knew that the explosion had sprung the

SLAUGHTER AT SEA

The worst massacre presided over by the Imperial Navy occurred not aboard submarines, but on the heavy cruiser Tone, *also a veteran of Pearl Harbor. Passenger and cargo vessel* Behar, *owned by the Hain Steamship Company, was caught in a tactical net strewn by three cruisers.* Tone *opened fire on the cargo ship, killing three. The crew and passengers, 111 in all, escaped safely, but were pulled on board the cruiser. During six days of beatings, while the cruiser made for Batavia, three of the prisoners died. In port,* Behar's *officers and passengers were separated from the rest and transferred to cruiser* Aoba. *The 72 remaining civilian seamen were taken to sea aboard* Tone, *lined up and beheaded, one by one.*

ship's antennae, making it useless. Blears went to his combat post at the four-inch gun, and from there went to a lifeboat and wrestled a "portable" radio aboard. "In those days, they were like a gigantic suitcase, and weighed about 50 to 80 pounds," he recalled.

Tjisalak was rapidly settling on an even keel. As waves washed across the deck, the lifeboats were cut free, the four boats holding 103 survivors of the initial attack. Three men in the engine room were not

Dutch freighter Tjisalak.

accounted for, and Blears thought about them as *Tjisalak* sank into the ocean, bleeding debris and oil as she broke up below the surface.

It was now light out, the flat, white tropical scrim of dawn near the equator, and the sailors clearly saw a periscope knifing through the swells, circling, shark-like.

I-8 surfaced nearby, disgorging Japanese sailors on deck. Blears heard an officer on the conning tower bridge call out on a megaphone — in English — "Captain! Captain!"

The skipper of the *Tjisalak* stood up, and the Japanese motioned him over. The skipper's boat had a small motor, and Blears distinctly heard the engine wheeze softly on the silent ocean. The captain, the ships officers and nurse Britten were hauled out and taken below. The man with the megaphone ordered the other boats to row toward the submarine. As they pulled alongside, the seamen were stripped of jewelry and clothing, and marched naked onto the foredeck of *I-8*.

Blears marveled at how big the submarine was — there was room for all the survivors to kneel together, looking forward at the empty sea. He had never seen a Japanese man before, and thought they looked like the caricatures in the *Saturday Evening Post*, short and fierce, with swords dragging on the deck. They wore kepis with a havelock, and many had pistol-lanyards around their necks. They posed and shouted, slapping the prisoners with the flats of swords. To Blears, the Japanese appeared to be enjoying themselves immensely.

Below, Ariizume and Lieutenants Sadao Motonaka and Masanori Hatori tortured *Tjisalak* officers for information. This was witnessed by Jiro Nakahara, a Hawaii resident serving in the Imperial Navy. When they were finished, the bodies were dumped over the side. Nurse Britten was asked if she wanted a blindfold; she told her captors to go to hell. She was shot.

Blears heard laughter as her body fell into the sea.

I-8 began to move away from the area. As the submarine plowed forward, Motonaka and Hatori began to pick through the prisoners kneeling on the forward deck. Any who looked large and dangerous were prodded aft at sword point. One at a time, they were killed as they disappeared around the conning tower. The Japanese took turns — the skulls of some prisoners were crushed by sledgehammer; others were beheaded and the writhing torsos kicked into the spinning screws; a few were shot by officers lounging in deck chairs; some had the backs of their skulls chopped open and brains exposed. The sailors were amused by every dying contortion. *I-8* left a bloody trail.

None of this was visible to the prisoners still facing forward on the bow, though the screams and laughter from the stern made them weep in rage and frustration. Blears was slapped with the flat of a sword and told to stand. His hands were tied together behind his back, and he tensed his wrists, which made the knots go slack when released. He was tied to Peter Brunger, a Dutch friend who had escaped from Nazi-occupied Holland. The two were pushed toward the back of *I-8*.

As they rounded the tower, Blears saw the bloody deck and the grinning sailors. "Some bastard's back here waiting for us," Blears muttered to Brunger.

Brunger screamed — *or was it a samurai shout?* — as a sword slashed the Dutchman open. Blears instinctively dove over the side of *I-8*, dragging Brunger with him. He went deep, as the crusty hull of *I-8* hurtled by, and he saw the ripping probes of bullets lance through the water. The submarine's screws chopped water, and he went deeper — the propeller blades thrashed overhead. It was all extraordinarily slow-moving and vivid to Blears; the ocean seemed limitlessly transparent, an inverted horizon, as the twin screws spun away and the viper-strikes of bullets reached for him.

He burst to the surface, saw officers still shooting at him, not bothering to rise from their deck chairs. He went low, until the submarine was out of range. One hand was free, and Blears worked on the knots that bound him to Brunger. His friend was dead, completely split open and gushing blood into the sea. Blears didn't know if Brunger had been killed by the sword blow or by gunfire. Afraid of sharks, Blears freed himself and said goodbye to Brunger, letting the ocean claim the dead. Blears swam away quickly, in the opposite direction from *I-8*.

Blears swam all day, his youth and Olympic breaststroke training serving him well. In late afternoon, Blears came across wreckage from *Tjisalak*, but couldn't find the lifeboats. He began to panic, looking around wildly as swells picked him up. Blears saw black spots in the water, made for them, found the oak card table from the ship's canteen. "Jesus!" he shouted.

Floating atop the card table, he spotted an emergency raft. Aboard it was Frits de Jong, one of the Dutch officers. De Jong, a big man and one of the first to be shot, was alive despite a seeping hole in the back of his head. Blears dressed the wound with sulfa powder, and as he did

LAST OF THE CLASS

so he heard a shout. It was an engineer named Spuybroek, who had escaped while being struck with a sword.

The three decided to look for a lifeboat — preferably the one with the radio — and began to row. Night fell, and the ocean twinkled with dozens of lights around them, like a Christmas tree, recalled Blears. The emergency light beacons on abandoned life vests had been triggered by salt water. The scene was eerie and surreal and years later still made Blears' voice swell with wonder.

In the dark they found a nearly submerged lifeboat. Another cry revealed First Officer Jan Dekker, also with a pistol wound to the head, and a Hindu seaman Blears knew only as Dhange. Dekker had revived after rolling off the deck; the Hindu was one of the last 20 prisoners on the submarine. They had been tied together in a row, and the leader tied to the conning tower. *I-8* then dove, dragging them under. Dhange, last in line, pulled himself free as the submarine went deep. No one else came to the surface.

The lifeboat had plenty of food and a radio, which they were afraid to use lest it alert the submarine. After three days of sailing toward Ceylon, nearly 1,000 miles away, Dekker was paralyzed and delirious. Blears decided to risk using the radio. He put up the antennae, keyed a signal and reported good news to his shipmates; the radio worked. They decided to wait until darkness, when the signal could be thrown farther, and celebrated by sharing a can of peaches.

There was enough for one peach each.

Blears had just begun sending another distress signal when a shell exploded near them, throwing up a column of water into the night. Rounds began dropping all around them, bracketing the lifeboat. Blears' heart sunk; he was ready to give up. A dark shape moved toward them from the horizon. Suddenly it loomed out of the night and groaned as the screws reversed.

"C'mon, goddammit!" came an American voice. "Get up here! We're not supposed to stop!"

The ship was *James A. Wilder*, a Liberty ship also on the Calcutta run. Dekker was taken aboard the Liberty first and was promptly arrested, taken to the bridge at gunpoint. The skipper of the American ship was furious because the survivors had not made any distress signals. He thought the lifeboat had been a sub's conning tower.

The five survivors were taken to Columbo, and Blears was sent to Bombay. Just as his train was about to enter the city, it was stopped, and remained there all night. A munitions ship had exploded in Bombay Harbor, a horrific cataclysm that killed more than 8,000 sailors and threw freighters through the air like toys. Blears had just missed being assigned there.[5]

I-26, another Advance Force veteran, sank liberty ship *Richard Hovey* on March 29, 1944. The Japanese crew came on deck and opened fire on the survivors with rifles and machine guns. Lieutenant Harry Goudy, of *Richard Hovey's* small armed guard, was startled to see a Japanese on the bridge filming the incident, and to see a turbaned

[5] *The Great Bombay Explosion of 1944, as it was called, was hushed up by military authorities.*

[6] Most survivors stated a cameraman was generally present. To date, none of this film has turned up publicly in Japanese archives.

representative of the Indian National Army taking part.[6] Lifeboats were rammed or shot up. Extraordinarily, none of the 39 sailors to survive the sinking were hit, though one died of exposure a few days later. Goudy wondered if the Japanese crew were either terrible shots or paying lip service to the standing order to kill survivors.

In addition to *Tjisalak*, *I-8* had scored conventional but poor victories during the spring of 1944, including the tiny *City of Adelaide*, an unidentified civilian sailing ship and British liner *Nellore*. Liberty ship *Jean Nicolet* was hit by I-8 on July 2, repeating the slaughter aboard *Tjisalak*. All 100 men aboard the freighter escaped safely, only to be brought aboard *I-8*. Ariizume's first act was to execute 16-year-old deck boy William Musser with a pistol shot in the eyes.

Others were slowly tortured over the course of the evening, or forced to run a gauntlet of laughing Imperial Navy sailors raining down blows with clubs and blades. An alarm rang suddenly and *I-8*'s crew scuttled below. The submarine crash-dived, leaving at least 30 men still tied up on deck. A PBY Catalina swept overhead, alerted by *Jean Nicolet*'s distress call. Had the aircraft not shown up when it did, more civilians would likely have been killed.

As it was, 23 survived out of 100.[7]

After the war, Blears learned that the murder of 101 aboard *Tjisalak* was not an isolated incident. Japanese submarines had routinely butchered survivors of merchant ship sinkings, explaining during the war crimes trials in Tokyo that they had done it because "death was kinder than the shame of being sunk." Defense teams also pointed out that Japan had not ratified the "International Convention Relative to the Treatment of Prisoners of War," commonly known as the Geneva Convention after the city where it originated. Although 47 countries had agreed to sign it in 1929, including Japan, the issue had been repeatedly passed over until 1941. In any case, the Japanese were formally bound by the Fourth Hague Convention of 1907, which they had ratified while flush with the success of the Russo-Japanese War.

[7] Missing purser Francis J. O'Gara turned up in a Japanese POW camp at the end of the war, only to discover that a Liberty ship had been named in his honor four months earlier. The *Francis J. O'Gara* was the only Liberty ship to have been named — in error — for a living person. O'Gara was later presented with the ship's builder's plate.

The Hague Convention contained most of the provisions of the Geneva pact, including rules against torture, murder and starvation of enemy prisoners. All of these Japan did routinely during the war. Four percent of Allied prisoners were killed in the notoriously harsh Nazi camps; more than 27 percent did not live through the Japanese camps. The percentage is actually much worse, as it is skewed by civilian camps holding women and children. In some military camps run by the Japanese, no prisoners survived the war.

These cruelties existed on a face-to-face level, however. Despite the horrific details of bloodbaths like the "Rape of Nanking" and the siege of Manila — during which Imperial troops bayoneted women and raped the dying bodies, or killed infants by digging out their eyes — the Japanese seemed incapable of long-term killing strategies like those of the Nazi Holocaust. The acts were simply inflicted upon those which the Japanese considered sub-human; that is, anyone not Japanese. The very few Japanese histories that touch on this subject

LAST OF THE CLASS

today portray the Imperial troops as victims, forced into this kind of behavior by Western economic pressure.

The code of Bushido, the steel spine that pushed this island empire across half of Asia, was inculcated into soldiers from birth — and all Japanese considered themselves soldiers. Japanese warriors "looked upon it as shame to themselves not to die when their Lord was hard-pressed," explained Jukichi Inouye in "Introduction to Chushingura." "Their own shame was the shame of their parents, their family, their house and their whole clan, and with this idea deeply impressed upon their minds, the Samurai, no matter of what rank, held their lives light as feathers when compared with the weight they attached to the maintenance of a spotless name."

With this mind-set, it was impossible to treat Western prisoners in Western ways. They were handled the way Japanese believed any prisoner of war should be handled — with degradation and death. In some notorious cases, American fliers were executed and Japanese officers ate their flesh.

The *I-8* incident, in which bundled prisoners were drowned, was not unique. This was a favorite method of disposing of large numbers of POWs. Dutch prisoners were regularly herded aboard barges at Kota Radja in Indonesia and taken on a final voyage.

While inspecting Kure naval base the day before the Japanese surrender aboard battleship *Missouri*, American submarine commander Admiral Charles Lockwood picked up a number of steel-pointed arrows, and joked with his Marine guards that it must be a new Japanese secret weapon. He later learned that captured American sailors had been used for archery practice.

The London Naval Treaty of 1930 between the United States, Britain, France, Italy and Japan hammered out strict codes regarding submarine warfare, primarily where merchant passengers were involved. In early 1942, Hitler ordered his U-boats to surface after sinking a target and shoot up the lifeboats. This order — heartily disliked and widely ignored by the U-boat crews — was adopted by Ambassador Oshima and transmitted to Japan for approval. A year later, on March 20, 1943, the commander of the 1st Submarine Force at Truk ordered his I-boats to "carry out the complete destruction of the crews of the enemy's ships; if possible, seize part of the crew and endeavor to secure information about the enemy." This was the excuse under which Ariizume tortured prisoners.

Over the next year, nine ships were torpedoed — eight in the Indian Ocean and one in the Pacific — and the submarine commander took the downed ship's captain and a few crew on board for interrogation. This finished, life boats were destroyed and the prisoners turned

Merchant seaman James Blears was typical of the young men killed by Imperial Navy submariners for sport. By sheer luck and athletic stamina, Blears survived.

over to the Imperial sailors for slaughter. At the time, official protests through neutral channels were met with blanket denials by the Japanese. "It is clear that Japanese submarines had nothing to do with the facts alleged in these protests," protested Mamoru Shigemitsu, Minister for Foreign Affairs.

Japanese submarine atrocities against civilian seamen have been largely overshadowed by their general poor record at harboring military prisoners of war, because most of the killings took place in the faraway backwater of the Indian Ocean, and simply because most of the victims were not Americans.

The cruelties laid on the survivors of I-boat attacks, however, had a horrific impact far beyond the few sinkings they achieved. It tended to color their activities so thoroughly that the Imperial Navy's submarines came to be despised more than they were feared.

Even at the height of the Atlantic Campaign, Nazi submariners were rarely described in the baited terms their Japanese counterparts were. On occasion, the Japanese lived up to the propaganda. In no other theater, in no other service, were civilian seaman targeted, tortured and killed — often for the sport of the submariners — with the bloody ferocity exhibited by the Imperial Japanese Navy.

One of the original Advance Force commanders, Tatsunosuke Ariizume's legacy is that of a notorious Japanese war criminal.

Most of the Japanese skippers who had slaughtered civilian sailors were never brought to trial. Some disappeared without a trace. Only four officers were eventually charged in the War Crimes trials; Vice Admiral Naomasa Sakonju and Captain Haruo Mayazumi for beheading 72 of *Behar's* crew, and Lieutenants Sadao Motonaka and Masanori Hatori for aiding Ariizume in the *Tjisalak* massacre. Sakonju and Mayazumi were hanged. Motonaka and Hatori served six years in Sugamo Prison.

I-8 skipper Ariizume committed suicide at war's end, before he could be captured.

After VJ Day, Blears was contacted by the War Crimes Tribunal and gave a statement, as did Imperial Navy sailor Nakahara in a plea arrangement. *Why didn't they just leave us in the middle of the ocean?* wondered Blears. *It wasn't right, what they did — there was no point to it, except cruelty.*

It was war. American submarine skipper "Mush" Morton on board *Wahoo* occasionally fired on Japanese sailors adrift. American aircraft often gunned down Japanese seamen escaping from sinking

vessels; the logs of the 345th Bomb Group speak glowingly of turning the water red with blood.

As for Kazuo Sakamaki, Prisoner of War Number One, he was interviewed by Army Intelligence authorities as the war ended. They were anxious to find out if Japanese POWs would make complaints about their imprisonment.

He said, "In Japan there are many problems because of the cruel treatment of the POWs, but the POWs in the United States were treated very fairly, in compliance with the terms of the Geneva Convention. The commandants of the camps made these provisions known, not only to the camp staff but to all of us by means of posters, etc. Mess consisted of bread, milk, butter and meat in sufficient quantity. I had a rice meal once a day. The sanitation and health facilities, air raid shelters and all living facilities were good.

"If anything did not meet the provisions of the Geneva Convention, we were free to point it out. We were allowed to take our morning ceremonies, bows toward the palace, and *banzais* on the four big holidays until the end of the war. It was a free and lenient life."[8]

Buffered from the harshness of the war, Sakamaki only became aware of gradual changes within himself. The war was going badly for Japan. Upon hearing of the fall of Saipan, Sakamaki thought, *What can I do?* as he stared at some little white flowers growing among the weeds. The flowers winked back at him. He imagined himself as one of the many flowers, lost among the weeds, with no control over the war's path.

"What can I do?" he decided. "Nothing. I can control only my own destiny."

By the time he was shipped back again to Camp McCoy, the sullen, incommunicative prisoner had metamorphosed into a leader of dispirited men. One day, a new prisoner thanked him, saying, "This camp life is better run than the Army life in Japan … this is not a military life. This is more like a spiritual training camp."

Kazuo Sakamaki, the "peace boy," had quietly come full circle in his soul, an internal battle that may have been more difficult than assaulting Pearl Harbor. Both had dark hours.

The end of the war came with Sakamaki in Camp Kennedy, Texas. By the new year of 1946, he was on the Pacific Ocean again, a whole man sailing home to a shattered Japan. Someone had to help pick up the pieces of empire.

[8] *As it turned out, the only Japanese POWs to complain were held by the British in Malaya. The Japanese pointed out that they were given only 280 grams of food a day. The British pointed out that this was more food than they got as soldiers in the Japanese Army.*

30

THE SPLINTERED SWORD

Ignoring the Obvious

On Jan. 15, 1942, in from its war patrol of the American coast, *I-15* arrived at Kwajalein, its first combat base of the Pacific War. "Our contribution to the war effort had been exactly zero," wrote officer Zenji Orita. "Our crew was cheerful, though. In spite of a very rough first Pacific crossing that had wrecked some submarine-borne aircraft, the success of the 1st Air Fleet's smash at Pearl Harbor buoyed us up during weeks that passed without any major accomplishments by 6th Fleet submarines."

The crews rested. Orita noted that in eight weeks of wartime cruising, there had not been any major injuries, illnesses or maintenance problems. Fresh water had been successfully conserved, so much so that the men had been allowed showers every three days, and every five days they were allowed to wash their underwear. "Except for no drinking or recreation," announced one keyed-up crewman, "I much prefer wartime cruise to peacetime!" The long, hard days of schooling had ended, with the Pearl Harbor assault as the final exam. Everyone passed.

As soon as *I-15* arrived at Kwajalein, a conference was held on board flagship *Katori* and the submarine skippers compared notes. The 1st Squadron was credited with 11 ships sunk, 2 damaged. The 2nd Squadron was credited with 4 sunk, 1 damaged, this last being the limping *Saratoga*. The 3rd Squadron was credited with 2 ships sunk, balanced against the loss of *I-70*.

The grand total was 17 ships claimed sunk and 3 damaged — the actual total was naturally lower — and when Vice Admiral Shimizu compared this with German successes in the Atlantic, he was disappointed. The submarine skippers nodded and vowed to do better.

The conversation turned to American anti-submarine tactics and marksmanship, both of which were ridiculed. Then, curiously, under pressure from above, they decided that Imperial Navy submarines should concentrate on sinking enemy merchant ships while avoiding enemy warships. The request had come from Germany, then on the ropes in the Atlantic.

This dilemma, representing an about-face in Japanese submarine

strategy, was indicative of confused strategy carried out by the I-boats. The Japanese navy would regret losing not only the striking power of its submarines, but its long-range scouting ability as well. The broad Pacific was not the same as the narrow, U-boat-infested corridors of the Atlantic, and the theaters could not be compared.

Japanese skippers constantly complained that American merchant ships seemed unreasonably difficult to sink. In May 1942, *I-26* cornered a merchant ship off Dutch Harbor and fired 50 rounds into the bigger ship's hull. The deck gun grew too hot to continue, and the submarine was forced to sink the freighter with a valuable torpedo.

I-21, fresh from shelling Australia in June 1942, ran across a merchant ship off Noumea. While the crew took to lifeboats, the I-boat circled leisurely around the merchant, firing more than 60 rounds. The ship wouldn't sink. The submarine nudged up close enough to the bigger ship to count the shell holes, and finally sailed away in frustration.[1]

Tankers seemed toughest. Submarine skippers who roamed the West Coast of the United States early in the war reported that tankers seemed to shrug off torpedoes. One submarine fired one torpedo after another at a target until the six forward tubes were empty, and then surfaced and shot at the tanker with the deck gun. When the injured tanker replied with gunfire of its own, the submarine withdrew. After this engagement, the rule of thumb for attacking tankers was to use both gunfire and a full spread of torpedoes.

The Advance Force submarines around Hawaii were given strict rules of engagement, a precise number of torpedoes for given targets. One torpedo each for merchantmen and destroyers — the reason why some merchants after the Hawaii operation were sunk with deck guns — three torpedoes for cruisers and full spread of six reserved for battleships and carriers. Second shots were forbidden. Under these conditions, I-boats were expected to be cautious in their tactics.

The Japanese oxygen-powered torpedoes were very fast and wakeless, but when set for shallow-water running, they often enthusiastically leaped into the air, like porpoises. After Pearl Harbor, Imperial Navy torpedo officers drafted a memo suggesting the torpedoes be slowed down slightly, have shallow-water stability designed in, and the warheads switched to magnetic exploders so they could detonate near a ship instead of directly against it. No more near misses, and the shock effect of the explosion caused more damage. They also lobbied for more promiscuous use of the weapons — the single shot loosed at merchant ships usually missed and called down the attentions of escort ships.

Merchant ships were to be considered legitimate targets only if there were no warships around to shoot at. Only early in the war did the Imperial Navy have enough resources to attack these secondary targets. American submarines sank as many Japanese ships as possible, whatever their combat status.

In an interrogation of Rear Admiral Shigeyoshi Miwa after the

[1] *Survivors of Japanese sinkings often told of I-boats hanging around, long after their target's fate was sealed, in order to fire shells at the sinking hulk. Invariably, they also claimed Japanese marksmanship was terrible.*

war, he stated that Imperial Navy submarines were used primarily as auxiliaries with the fleet, and merchant attacks were secondary. The reasons for attacking merchants at all, he said, were that American warships simply weren't available, and that the Germans wished it so. Some in the Imperial Navy wanted to gather all the submarines together to hound American battleships, but the Nazis wanted to kill merchants in the Indian Ocean, which were resupplying British forces in North Africa. Over the course of the war, there were few attacks in the central and south Pacific zones because of aggressive behavior by American aircraft, as well as too few submarines to make a difference.

Following the brief period of merchant attacks, Japanese submarines were drafted to run supplies to island outposts, a decision influenced by Imperial Army leaders in Tokyo.

During one of these runs, Takeo Kuboaki, an engineer on *I-1* during the Pearl Harbor attack, was pulled from the water in February 1943, after the submarine was sunk near Guadalcanal. He had been drifting for 24 hours and his feet and forearms had been shredded by sharks. Kuboaki told interpreters that *I-1* shot several torpedoes at transports in the Hawaiian area, and all had missed.

Another failure during the Advance Force assault involved stationing *I-74* off Niihau to wait for downed airmen. The tactic predated similar American tactics by several years. President George Bush, then a very young Navy flier, was rescued by submarine *Finback* after losing his plane on a Pacific raid. The failure in *I-74's* case may have been a simple lack of nerve; there are several Japanese aircraft crash sites ringing Kauai and Niihau; one pilot set down on Niihau and terrorized the island for a week before being killed by citizens who did not know war had been declared, but knew when they'd had enough.

I-74 picked up no airmen, fired no torpedoes, made no reports.

The Americans also had been careful about minesweeping, and had minecraft in nearly continuous operation in Hawaii. Yet the Advance Force had deployed no minelayers. With less than a month of food left, a ring of mines could have really isolated the islands.

Mine-laying was normally carried out by the specially designed *I-121, I-122, I-123* and *I-124* boats, a class laid down in 1925 and thoroughly disliked for their tricky handling characteristics. These submarines squirted mines from the stern, another German innovation from World War I, and were rather delicately balanced.

If a mine were launched from the stern track, for example, an equal weight in water needed to be shipped aboard, otherwise the stern would break surface like a broaching fish. Mochitsura Hashimoto served aboard one of these craft in 1940, and primarily remembers being grateful that no one was injured during his watch — sailors were often crushed by runaway mines when the I-boat rollercoastered.

In 1940, these ungainly craft were saddled with aviation fuel tanks on the decks, giving them an additional capability. On Nov. 30, 1941, the mine-laying unit left its base at Hainan, the last Imperial Navy unit to deploy before the simultaneous attacks on Dec. 7. That

THE SPLINTERED SWORD

day, *I-123* and *I-124* laid 40 mines in Balabac Strait and off Manila. *I-124* stood by and rescued aircraft crews shot down during the raids on Manila — the task *I-74* never accomplished during the Pearl Harbor raid — while *I-121* and *I-122* laid mines off Singapore, which claimed a merchant ship on Dec. 11.

I-123 went on to lay some mines at the north end of Surabaya Strait, and *I-121* visited Manila Bay, to be scared off by the few remaining destroyers of the Asiatic Fleet. *I-124* was sunk off Darwin.

In the spring of 1942, *I-6* learned another trick from the Germans and laid mines off Brisbane, holding them three to a torpedo tube. They weren't immediately successful, and the Imperial Navy essentially gave up on mine-laying for the duration. Stealthy mine operations are something submarines excel at, and aggressively mining the coastlines of Allied strongholds like Pearl Harbor could have been a potentially devastating strategy.

But mine-laying didn't have the cachet of doing battle, honorably, with an enemy warship.

At the outbreak of hostilities with America, Germany, Italy and Japan divided up the world among them. The 70th meridian, which bisected the Indian Ocean, was the agreed-upon line of demarcation. German and Italian submarines were to prowl the area west of the line; the Japanese took the ocean east and into the Pacific, from the Arabian Sea to South Africa, and east to the coast of the Americas.

I-boats entered the Indian Ocean without waiting for Singapore to fall, attacking merchant shipping. Hunting was safe in the balmy waters of the Indian Ocean, Penang was a very modern base and skippers preferred duty there. "The Indian Ocean campaign was regarded almost as a paradise compared to the 'Hell War' in the Pacific," said Hashimoto.

They shared it with the Nazis. The Germans had been surprised by the Pearl Harbor raid; Joachim von Ribbentrop, awakened because of the news, angrily called the information an enemy propaganda trick and went back to sleep.[2]

Hitler took the event in better spirits, slapping his thighs in delight and chattering about the new world order. The shift in power had come at just the right time, he exclaimed. The thorough drubbing Japan had inflicted upon the United States would energize the Pact of Steel, then reeling under difficulties on the Russian front.

"The turning point!" said Hitler. "Now it is impossible for us to lose the war; we now have an ally who has never been vanquished in three thousand years, and another ally" — Italy — "who has constantly been vanquished but has always ended up on the right side."

Almost immediately, Hitler ordered the Kriegsmarine to open fire on any ships flying the American flag. On Dec. 11, Germany formally declared war. Hitler had acted on his own, without the opinion of his general staff, without consideration of consequences. His eagerness for a triumphant new ally had struck him strategically blind. His major weapon, the deadly U-boats, were dispatched for the

[2] *The first ship downed in World War II was British liner* Athenia, *sunk by U-boat* U-30. *Fleeing for the safety of America, 128 civilian refugees lost their lives; a pattern that would repeat throughout the war. At the time, the Germans claimed the British had destroyed the liner themselves in order to embarrass the Kriegsmarine.*

A U-boat heads for the Far East. The cartoonish quality of the paint scheme is exacerbated by the large swastika on the sail and white stripes on the deck, used as recognition signals for the Japanese.

American east coast without delay.

Caught without an operational plan for the area, the first four U-boats weren't sent to the Indian Ocean until the summer of 1942. The patrol was dubbed *Eisbaer* — Polar Bear — and lost *U-156* en route. The three remaining submarines sank 24 allied ships by October. They were followed quickly by another patrol of Nazi submarines, which sank 36 merchant ships without a loss. Both patrols then returned to the sub pens of France.

Compared to Japanese efforts, the Indian Ocean was a rich hunting ground for the Germans. Early 1943 saw a force of five U-boats and five Italian submarines cruising Far Eastern waters, sinking 24 ships. A second group sank 34 merchantmen within three months. Of the two U-boat packs, only *U-182* was lost.

A favorite Japanese trick was to eject rubber slippers and sake bottles through the torpedo tubes during depth chargings. German U-boats were known to carry yards of animal intestines, which would be jettisoned to float to the surface, fooling submarine hunters into thinking their depth charges had successfully cracked the egg. It was rumored on both sides that the Germans also carried severed arms and legs, to add detail to the horror, but this is unlikely; intestines float, arms and legs generally sink.

Allied ships began steaming in convoy and hunting became hairier. The Atlantic also had become a more dangerous stalking ground. The Japanese invited the Germans to port at Singapore, Batavia, and Penang, an island off the Malay coast. U-boat patrols already in the Indian Ocean returned to Europe, except for *U-178*, which headed east to Penang.

Fregattenkapitan Wolfgang Lueth's orders were to establish a U-boat base at the isolated island. Admiral Karl Donitz, Commander of Submarines and Hitler's chosen successor, decided the Far East would be fertile fields — the early successes seemed to confirm this — and would be an easier site from which to run raw materials. German surface ships were being easily picked off by the British. The new German blockade runners were to be submersible, the Type XB and Type XIV cargo-carrying submarines. The campaign was named Monsoon, and kicked off in July of 1943.

Eleven U-boats set out for the Indian Ocean; six were lost en route. The remaining five were joined by Lueth's *U-178*, out of Penang, and they cruised the Madagascar straits and the Gulf of Aden, eventually sinking 21 Allied ships.

A second fleet of four Monsoon U-boats were dispatched from France, and were decimated in the Atlantic — only *U-510* reached Penang, though it sank five Allied ships.

THE SPLINTERED SWORD

When Italy surrendered in September, 1943, two of her sub-marines in the Far East were taken over by the Germans and designated *UIT-23* and *UIT-24*. When Germany surrendered, the Imperial Navy inherited the craft. They were refurbished, manned by a mixed crew, and commanded by German officers. They were utilized as cargo carriers, running between Japan and Malaya.

By the spring of 1944, Donitz had 42 U-boats and the converted Italian submarines posted to the Far East. During this first year of Monsoon, 12 submarines were lost on sortie, 23 had eventually returned home, six were still on station, and *U-511* had been presented as a gift to the Emperor. Allied losses during this period were 33 ships. Bases and sortie routes were well-established. Penang was the hub, Kobe and Singapore were repair berths, Djakarta was where the cargo-carrying submarines were filled up, and Soerabaja was both a repair facility and cargo port.

Later groups of Monsoon boats also had trouble fighting their way into the Indian Ocean. The third fleet of seven boats lost four en route; the fourth fleet of 11 lost seven; the fifth fleet of seven lost five. Three U-boats were lost while operating in the Indian Ocean. As 1944 closed, 19 of the 24 U-boats posted to the region had been sunk, most before firing a shot. Allied shipping losses were 28. The "Happy Time" was over.

Essentially cut off from Europe by the invasion of Normandy, the Kriegsmarine boats languished at Malaya. Continual problems with maintenance, poor intelligence, and misdirected cooperation between the Axis partners increased the Germans' sense of being marooned. Only *U-861* and *U-862* were still operational at year's end; another eight were undergoing repairs or loading cargo during the winter.

The last German submarine victory in the Pacific theater was Feb. 6, 1945, when *U-862* sank American troopship *Peter Sylvester* 700 miles west of Perth. *U-183* was refurbished and left Penang in April to harass American forces off the Philippines. Within a few weeks, it was sunk by American submarine *Besugo* in the Java Sea, becoming the only German submarine to face the U.S. Navy in the Pacific.

U-861 and cargo boats *U-510* and *U-532* were ordered home in the spring of 1945, and were advancing through the Atlantic when the war ended in Europe. The eight U-boats left in the Far East were seized by the Imperial Navy, and the German crews interned, though that didn't prevent them from training the new Japanese crews.

In the final spreadsheet, U-boat operations in the Indian Ocean, which didn't begin until the third year of war, were moderately successful. Kill ratios were roughly equal to that of Atlantic hunting, but the long Allied gauntlet around the Cape of Good Hope proved to be spectacularly dangerous. U-boats could hunt in the Indian Ocean, but first they had to get there, and then return. With Rommel already rolled up in North Africa, their presence in the Far East made no strategic sense.

The same scenario applied to cargo-carrying U-boats, and the scheme became a fiasco. Fewer than 1,000 tons of cargo from the rich

mines of Indochina reached the German war machine. German U-boats were far more successful at hunting ships than the Japanese I-boats, even in waters under the Japanese sphere of influence. Of 323 Allied ships sunk in the Indian Ocean, 171 were credited to the Nazis, and another five to the Italians.

The big success of the Hawaii raid, at least according to Radio Tokyo broadcasts, was the midget submarine. Although stern launchings of midgets from *Chiyoda* were never actually used, mother submarines continued to carry them into combat. In the fall of 1942, Lunga anchorage was attacked by midgets carried by *I-16, I-20* and *I-24*, under-the command of Captain N. Ota. The midgets were attached at Truk or Shortland and then proceeded to the north entrance of Indispensable Strait, there to launch at targets of opportunity. Survivors were to head for Marovovo, on the north end of Guadalcanal, to land. *I-16* and *I-20* each launched midgets on Nov. 15, 1942, claiming a transport and a destroyer sunk. One midget returned.

Each submarine made two more launches during the next month, running up a combined claim of two more transports, one destroyer and two craft of unknown type. One midget submarine had a torpedo misfire, similar to Sakamaki's at Pearl, and had to call off its attack. Of the six midget submarines launched by mid-December off Guadalcanal, half vanished.

Some submarine cargo-towing containers were mistaken for midgets, and many Americans believed that the midgets were towed to location by the mother submarine, like the British X-craft.

Another weapon carried by mother submarines made its appearance when the weight of armament was irretrievably swinging to the Allies. It was the *kaiten*, a one-way piloted torpedo, an underwater *kamikaze* and a weapon forced by desperate circumstance. Like the nine hero-gods at Pearl Harbor, publicity surrounding the weapon far outweighed its actual deployment.

On Nov. 20, 1944, five *kaiten* launched by mother submarines *I-36* and *I-74* stole into the Ulithi Atoll anchorage at dawn. Four were picked off immediately by alert Americans, but a *kaiten* piloted by Ensign Mishida struck oiler *Mississinewa*, killing 150 of her crew.

The only other ship confirmed killed by a *kaiten* was destroyer escort *Underhill*, on July 24, 1945 in the Philippines. A *kaiten* was launched within 1,000 yards of the American ship, which spotted the midget craft immediately and, apparently thinking it to be a full-sized I-boat, tried to ram it. This mistake in judgment resulted in heavy loss of life as the DE's bow was blown off.

Confusion over deployment and an unimaginative strategy limited the midget submarine's usefulness. As the war ground on, the Imperial Navy abandoned true midget craft in favor of *kaiten* and *kairyu*, suicide submersibles designed to fall upon the Allied fleet like a flight of arrows. Superior anti-submarine tactics employed by the U.S. Navy negated their use, and the Japanese turned to the airborne *kamikaze* as the suicidal weapon of choice.

THE SPLINTERED SWORD

With mother submarines becoming *kamikaze* carriers, midget submarines were posted to local defense duties. This scheme became somewhat theoretical in isolated arenas like the Solomons and the Aleutians. In the Philippines, however, a country of hundreds of islands and thousands of underwater anchorages, midget submarines came into their own. Their highly successful deployment during the Allied invasion of the Philippines is lost in the smoke of the larger naval engagements.

Four midgets were stationed at Cebu, two at Zamboanga, two at Davao, all to defend the Surigao and San Bernardino straits north of Mindanao. The Allied invasion of the archipelago spurred these craft into action, and they were moved to Dumaguete. The idea was to pinch Allied shipping between the south tip of Negros and the north tip of Mindanao. A lookout station at Surigao reported likely targets.

In the time period between Dec. 8, 1944, and March 21, 1945, 14 Allied ships were reported sunk by this force, including two cruisers, one seaplane tender, five destroyers, five transports and one other. On March 20, Americans landed at Davao, and the midget crews scuttled their craft and joined the fight ashore.

Samuel Eliot Morison's account of this period[3] notes that American ships were hassled by Japanese submarines near Mindoro, primarily older, smaller RO-class submarines. According to Morison, *RO-115* and *RO-55* were attacked and considered sunk, but incredibly

An indication of how seriously the Imperial Navy considered midget submarines — dozens of advanced five-man Koryu line the shipways at Kure, 1945.

[3] *"The Liberation of the Philippines"*

survived to fight — and be sunk — another day. It's possible that some of these attack victims were actually midgets, whose actions under local commanders weren't charted by Tokyo. The only solid midget submarine encounters reported by the Americans appear to have been counterattacks.

On the afternoon of Jan. 5,1945, three midget submarines sortied from Cebu and attacked an American task force.[4] The Allied force was formidable, including headquarters ship *Wasatch* and light cruisers *Boise, Phoenix, Montpelier* and *Denver*, and nine destroyers. On board *Wasatch* were Admiral Thomas Kinkaid, commander of the 7th Fleet, and Lieutenant General Walter Krueger, commander of the 6th Army. On board *Boise* was General Douglas MacArthur, Allied

[4] *Their serials are thought to be* HA-69, HA-81 *and* HA-82.

Another view of the Koryu sheds at Kure.

Supreme Commander, who watched the afternoon's action while "calmly puffing on a corncob pipe."

At 3:08 p.m., destroyer *Nicholas* spotted torpedoes arrowing toward the cruisers. On board *Boise*, Lieutenant Commander Willard M. Downes pushed the cruiser to flank speed while pulling the ship to starboard — the torpedoes narrowly missed. Destroyers *Nicholas* and *Taylor* charged down on the intruder. She was *HA-82*, which had popped to the surface while succumbing to the fatal flaw in midget design, an inability to trim properly after firing torpedoes. Commander Nicholas J. Frank, skipper of *Taylor*, rammed the submarine with his destroyer. The midget submarine tore in half and sank. The other two midget submarines disappeared.

In the late afternoon of the Cebu landing on March 26, destroyer *Conyngham* spotted a periscope in the offshore channel. Rear Admiral Albert Sprague, task group commander, assumed the worst and ordered the invasion force into cruising formation, providing moving targets, and detailed two destroyers and two patrol craft to massage the contact, which by now provided a fat sonar return.

Conyngham and *Flusser* closed on the periscope, which rode enough out of the water to show part of a small conning tower,

414

THE SPLINTERED SWORD

confirming it to be a midget craft. Both destroyers straddled it with gunfire, from about 3,000 yards out. No hits were seen and the midget, now warned, disappeared. *PC-1133* dashed in for a sonar-directed kill and beached itself on a shoal in Cebu Harbor. The submarine return vanished from sonar screens.

At a half-hour past midnight that evening, destroyer *Newman* surprised a midget submarine on the surface, about seven miles south of the first sighting. It was probably the same craft. The American ship fixed the little submarine in the glare of its searchlights, closed in to 100 yards and shredded it with automatic weapons. The conning tower burst open, and the midget sub was swallowed by the sea.

When all the midget submarines in the Philippines had been expended, the remaining crews were given weapons and reassigned to infantry units.

During the Okinawa invasion in the early summer of 1945, a "midget submarine pen" was bombed on the north shore of the island, putting it out of action. These might have *kaiten*-type suicide craft or later, "Type C" midget submarines — Navy accounts of the period don't make any distinction between these *kamikaze* craft and small, sea-going submarines.

The wide press and apparent effectiveness of midget submarine operations put pressure on the Americans to develop their own craft. In July of 1944, Admiral Ernest King and his war plans chief, Rear Admiral Charles M. Cooke, visited Pearl Harbor and leaned on Admiral Charles Lockwood — head of American submarine operations in the Pacific — to create a midget submarine program. "This was an idea I had been battling all during the war," Lockwood complained. "The Japs had midgets, the Germans had midgets, the Italians had midgets and now the British had used XE craft, four-man submarines, to attack the *Tirpitz* at Alten Fjord in Norway — therefore we should have midgets."

Lockwood believed that a midget product would siphon away needed materials and construction time on full-sized fleet boats, which had already bottled up the Japanese merchant fleet. American aircraft could then pick off the harbored merchants, he argued. Sending Americans into foreign harbors in midget submarines was a needlessly risky enterprise.

Cooke told Lockwood that the midgets were coming whether he liked it or not. The British were going to reverse lend-lease a couple of XE craft, and Lockwood agreed to deal with them when the craft were received. But nothing more ever came of the scheme.

By the time the American war was a year old, a Navy intelligence essay for the invasion of the Philippines pointed out, midgets had been reported in nearly every theater of the war, had accounted for knocking out a battleship and a tanker, giving a cruiser a bad scare, and had caused an American cargo ship to beach itself on Guadalcanal. Though the midgets had largely disappeared, "the Philippines area offers the midget sub far more favorable operating conditions … the

The smallest of Japan's submarines attacked Pearl Harbor, and the largest were towed into the American base for study after the war. These are the monster I-400 boats, built as underwater aircraft carriers to attack the Panama Canal.

restricted waters will reduce the maneuverability and hamper the effectiveness of our ASW vessels. The indentions of the coast offer adequate concealment. At the same time, the distance from base is greatly reduced." This assessment also contained "Jap midget doctrine" salvaged from the midget submarine found on Guadalcanal. "The Time for Resolute Attack!" as it was called, contained guidelines for submariners, including immediate attacks on "powerful ships and transports" as soon as they were spotted, rather than waiting for an advantage.

Curiously, the document stresses escape and evasion as a tactic. "Do not uselessly throw away your lives but do your utmost to seek a means of escape and endeavor to return. Such as these are truly brave men and are faithful to the cause of their country."

Such advice ran counter to the spirit of sacrificial bushido that drove the *kaiten* pilots. But it is realistic. The loss of trained midget submariners in the first year of war nearly curtailed operations. As feared by the U.S. Navy, the Philippines proved to be an ideal theater for midget tactics, with enough trained crews on hand to throw a scare into Allied operations. The new success led to a crash program of midget-building in Japan, with hundreds of Type D midgets being constructed. These were excellent craft, with all the experience of four years of war poured into their design. With Japan's sudden surrender, none were utilized in combat.

THE SPLINTERED SWORD

UNDERWATER NINJA

31

Mysteriouser and Mysteriouser

It's the right size. It's the right shape. It's lying right where it should be. The midget submarine sunk by destroyer *Ward* may still be intact, lying in more than 800 feet of water. During the last day of a 1988 underwater survey of Pearl Harbor, sonar returns from deep water outside the harbor indicated something that appeared to be a midget submarine.

"It could be anything," said Arizona Memorial Superintendent Bill Dickinson at the time. "Even a bunch of oil drums in a line. But it looks promising. We're very happy."

The survey, called Operation Seamark, was a cooperative effort of the Navy and the National Park Service, with the Arizona Memorial Association bankrolling the Park's end. It fulfilled a federal requirement that historical artifacts in a National Historic Landmark be cataloged. Pearl Harbor has been such a landmark since 1964.

The Navy's contribution included providing electronic mine-detecting equipment and experts from Pearl Harbor's Explosive Ordnance Disposal (EOD) unit under the command of Commander Steve Epperson and divers from the Mobile Diving and Salvage Unit (MDSU) under the command of Captain David McCampbell. The Park Service's expert was Larry Murphy of the Submerged Cultural Resources Unit (SCRU) in Santa Fe, N.M.

Seamark to date has been the only major archeological assessment of a major naval battle, and was a remarkable cooperation that went against the built-in grain of federal bureaucracy. The five-year program, directed by Dan Lenihan of the Park Service and enlisting the talents of McCampbell and Otto Orzech of the Navy, revealed details of battleships *Utah* and *Arizona* long buried in the mud.

Electronic and hands-on searches inside the harbor didn't produce much, said Dickinson, except for metal "junk" and a lot of silt. "But that, in its own way, has been instructive. At least we know where things aren't." Park rangers are often asked if Japanese planes from the attack still lie at the bottom of Pearl Harbor.

Searches outside the harbor itself were plagued by equipment problems, which were resolved on the last day of the search. The

equipment was loaded on board *TR-6*, a 125-foot torpedo retriever ship from Pearl Harbor's Submarine Base.

Following charts designed by Pearl Harbor survivor Ray Emory and NPS historian Daniel Martinez, *TR-6* shadowed the probable course of the midget submarine. Emory reconstructed the ships' paths using sightings, action reports, probable speed and direction of the different ships involved in the action.

Side-scan sonar painted a shape on the bottom in a "high probability area" for the tiny submarine, said Dickinson. The shape matched what is known about submarines involved in the attack. However, a later search by a University of Hawaii deep-diving submarine failed to locate the target. This was probably because of the long tethering cables deployed on the sonar blimp, which tended to wander while being pulled behind the Navy boat. The signal came from a general area, not a specific location.

The submarine pilot believed the Park Service was mistaken about the sonar return, though he said there was a "lot of junk" on the bottom, including 1930s vintage aircraft and tanks. A Park Service historian said the University search was too brief and looked in the wrong place.

A short search in the summer of 1991 by a *National Geographic* television crew, co-directed by Lenihan and Chris Nicholson, was plagued by technical problems and halted before the midget submarine hulk was found. The completed television program made much of the submarine's unwillingness to cooperate.

The seabed approach to Pearl Harbor is littered with the wreckage of military aircraft, vehicles, boats and weapons, as it was the designated dumping spot for "surveyed," or written-off materiel. Aircraft during the 1930s were regularly stripped of engines and instruments, placed on barges and pushed over the side a few miles off the harbor entrance. Many have been covered by seafloor subsidence.

No archeological survey has yet been made of this area. Still under Navy control, it also holds the junction grids for SOSUS, the Navy's top-secret submarine listening apparatus, the computer-analysis headquarters of which are on Ford Island.

The search teams hoped the midget sank straight down after being depth-charged by *Ward*. If the hull remained intact, with its finned, dart-like shape, it might have arrowed through the water as it plunged to the bottom. The final resting place could be a considerable distance from the initial action. In the meantime, Seamark remains the only effort to answer 50 years of historical debate with solid evidence rather than speculation.

There is also no way of knowing whose midget submarine it was. Based on departure times, submariner Zenji Orita believes the midget sunk by *Ward* was Iwasa's, as does Pearl Harbor submarine historian Ray de Yarmin. David Aiken, a historian who has made a close study of attack movements, believes the craft is *I-20tou*, piloted by Hiro-o.

Sakamaki and Inagaki's *I-24tou* was bombed by American air-

UNDERWATER NINJA

I-24tou is prepared for shipping at Pearl Harbor. The craft is essentially complete and has been repaired with pieces of the midget submarine sunk inside Pearl Harbor. In the back is one consequence of the Advance Force assault — anti-torpedo nets.

craft as it rested on the reef, which accidentally succeeded in dislodging it. The scuttling charge was neutralized and the submarine pulled ashore at Bellows. Photos of it lolling in the shorebreak gave the impression it had drifted ashore easily, when in actuality the salvage operation was difficult and dangerous. The submarine looks weathered and scruffy, the black paint chipped off and revealing the red lead paint beneath. The submarine also became slightly fouled on the initial dash across the Pacific, giving the craft a greenish sheen.

Sakamaki's maps were captured. The penciled routes gave intelligence operatives the impression he had entered the harbor and circled Ford Island, perhaps days before the attack, something which the prisoner refused to discuss until after the war. Many histories of the Pearl Harbor attack still believe this to be the case, though they ignore the fact that similar routes were found on maps in Japanese aircraft. Most likely the "routes" are dredging plans faithfully copied from a stolen prewar map. Sakamaki's maps were themselves stolen.

After being examined from net-cutter to stern, *I-24tou* was propped up on a pedestal at Pearl Harbor's Submarine Base, where it was to become a memorial. Within two months, it became a traveling war-bond attraction, ironically giving aid to the American enemy. "I was possessed by a terrible, uncontrollable shame," Sakamaki wrote about discovering his midget being captured. "I trembled with the fear that through my fault the invaluable secret weapon had fallen into the enemy's hands …"

Parts of the midget submarine rammed by *Monaghan* were installed on Sakamaki's sub, including the torpedo tube guard, a figure-eight construction that on Sakamaki's sub had been reduced to scrap-metal spaghetti by running it into reefs.

Pictures of *I-24tou* during this period show that considerable

On its special wagon, I-24tou *arrives in Times Square, New York City, beneath a gigantic poster reminding war bond purchasers to "Remember Pearl Harbor."*

effort was made at Pearl Harbor to show off this craft. The care taken is inconsistent with the short time it was there, for the midget submarine was supposedly shipped to the American mainland in February, 1942. But a photograph showing it being prepared for shipping at Pearl Harbor is dated Aug. 29, 1942; this later date makes more sense.

As Secret Service agents stand guard, President Roosevelt inspects I-24tou *at Mare Island. In the car with FDR are admirals J.W. Greenslade and W.L. Friedell.*

Once it was on the coast, 22 small windows were torched in the side and fake motors and batteries installed, as well as two mannequins wearing fierce samurai expressions. By the end of the war, it had rolled through 41 states on a specially constructed wagon, selling war bonds.

Admission to the "Japanese suicide sub" was through buying a war bond or some war stamps. These bond drives were planned as thoroughly as amphibious landings, "in which just about every promotional stunt the combined brains of Madison Avenue, Hollywood and the Treasury Department's War Finance Division — plus hundreds of thousands of local drive chairmen — could dream up was employed ..." wrote Richard Lingeman in "Don't You Know There's a War On?" Possibly the first public outing of *I-24tou* was a mass enlistment of Chinese-American naval recruits, on the piers of San Francisco, on Navy Day, 1942.

The Japanese secret weapon was a huge public-relations success, crystallizing the "epitome of the Japanese obsession with smallness and precision — the mechanical counterpart of the bonsai tree," wrote historian Gordon Prange, who had the opportunity to examine the Ha-boats after the war.

This concept of "littleness" became a potent propaganda tool to hurl at the Japanese, a way of pointing out differences between the two

UNDERWATER NINJA

peoples in solidly racist terms. The American press fell right in line, using the concept of the "little Jap" as a convenient pigeonhole. Within a few weeks of Pearl Harbor, for example, *Time* editorialized that the Japanese were "big only in their fury," marching through Malaya "in miniature scale," using "tiny one-man tanks and two-gun carriers. The British even said that their doctors cut miniature Japanese bullets out of miniature British wounds …"

"Americans detested the Japanese the most," pointed out Paul Fussell in "Wartime," "for only they had the effrontery to attack the United States directly, sinking ships, killing sailors, and embarrassing American pretenses to alertness and combat adequacy. They must be animals to behave thus, and cruel ones at that …

"Americans in Japanese prison camps noticed the way their captors liked to get up on something, a box, podium, platform, or stand, when haranguing their prisoners,"

wrote Fussell. "Americans of standard height could understand the Japanese problems immediately as the 'Runt's Complex,' familiar from high school, the need of the short to 'get back at' people of normal height and their customary use of guile or fraud to do so. The 'sneak attack' on Pearl Harbor thus explains itself."

Sakamaki's midget submarine seemed to be proof of the concept. Americans could peer into the cramped, fetid interior and feel secure in their bigness.

In 1947, after the midget was discovered rusting and lonely at a Navy pier in Chicago, the commander of the U.S. submarine base at Key West arranged to have it barged there. In 1964, it was transferred to the Lighthouse Military Museum in Key West, across the street from Ernest Hemingway's house. At this point, *I-24tou's* periscope was removed.

In the early 1980s, as the Arizona visitor center was becoming established, some Park historians and veterans proposed that the submarine be moved from Key West to Pearl Harbor, a notion endorsed by U.S. Sen. Daniel Inouye of Hawaii. The idea was put on the back-burner when the Key West museum decided to keep the artifact. In 1988, Park Service Maritime Historian James Delgado visited the Arizona site in conjunction with Operation Seamark and superintendent Dickinson fired him up about moving the submarine. At the same time, the Key West museum decided to narrow its focus, and seemed willing to let *I-24tou* go. The Arizona Memorial Museum Association funded a stabilization survey, occurring at the same time Delgado applied for National Historic Landmark status for the craft.

The survey indicated that *I-24tou* was reasonably intact, and

Mare Island Navy Yard workers also inspect I-24tou. Problems with lighting and perspective hint that this is probably a retouched and composite photograph.

Sakamaki's midget submarine is disassembled at Key West, waiting for its future to be decided.

[1] *It should be noted that the Arizona Memorial exists in a kind of limbo, being the only National Park site in the country existing without the benefit of "enabling legislation," the operating statement that spells out specifically what message and context the site should convey. As a result, interpretations of the goals of the Arizona Memorial Visitor Center tend to change with administrations. The public, however, continues to perceive the site as a de facto museum of the Pacific War, a role clearly beyond the Center's original scope.*

because of its historical significance as a war prize, was awarded the Landmark designation. Delgado djinned up a permanent loan from the Navy to the Memorial, and met with a national committee of veterans' groups at an American Legion function. The plan was to display it as a prize of war during its days as a war-bond fund-raising vehicle. Though interested, the veterans neither endorsed or condemned the move.

In 1989, *I-24tou* was set to be moved for permanent display at the Visitor Center, but a variety of circumstance conspired against it. Two key players dropped out of the picture. Bill Dickinson left, and was replaced by Gary Warshefski as an "acting" superintendent at the Visitor Center, with all of the responsibility and none of the power the post required. The Park Service regional director was replaced by Park Service veteran Stan Albright. Albright reversed the decision to acquire the submarine, a move that spurred staff outrage.

Albright's rationale was that the memorial should remain a memorial, and not incorporate controversial artifacts.[1]

Albright's superiors in Washington were unwilling to step on his regional prerogatives. A press release explaining the decision was scuttled, and rumors began to fly. A Veterans of Foreign Wars chapter got the impression that *I-24tou* was to be refloated and berthed above the sunken *Arizona*, an image that horrified any veteran who heard it described. A letter-writing campaign snowballed; the avalanche rolling into Albright's office. The VFW complaint was that the war prize, being Japanese, is an inappropriate artifact to be placed near an American memorial.

A letter from the Ladies Auxiliary to the Veterans of Foreign Wars post in Tumwater, Washington, was typical. Rosemary Hartwell, secretary of the post auxiliary, was outraged: "It has come to the attention of our auxiliary that the National Park Service has proposed moving a Japanese two-man submarine into the U.S.S. Arizona Memorial at Pearl Harbor," she wrote the director of the Park Service in 1989.

"'Inappropriate' is too mild a word to describe the intentions of the National Park Service in this plan. 'Vulgar disregard of the feelings of the veterans of the U.S. Armed Services,' is more like it. Add to that the anger of the relatives and friends of those who lost their lives at Pearl Harbor and you may begin to understand what we are trying to say; that so blatant a disrespect for the feelings of the

UNDERWATER NINJA

surviving veterans and their families cannot be ignored nor disregarded in this display of cynical insensitivity."

Hartwell then demanded the Park Service be barred from further desecrations of the Arizona Memorial, and sent copies of this letter to President George Bush and every congressman in Washington.

Hundreds of similar letters descended on the National Park Service, which as bureaucracies go, is a creature unusually sensitive to public ill will.[2] Rather than stir the flames, the NPS backed down.

A new Park Service director, Jim Ridenour, listened to an impassioned plea by NPS Chief Historian Ed Bearss — a Marine wounded in the New Britain campaign — and ordered the submarine acquired.

Other museums, thinking the Park Service was out of the running, began to lobby for the artifact, including the Nimitz Center museum in Texas, the Air Force base at Bellows Field and the *U.S.S. Bowfin* museum, next door to the Arizona Memorial Visitor Center. The Nimitz Center lobbied hardest, with members being heard by another Texan in the White House. President Bush deferred to the Navy, which stuck to the original plan. Park historian Daniel Martinez arranged a compromise solution: While the Park Service prepared a home for the craft — safely after the politically sensitive 50th anniversary of the attack on Pearl Harbor — it was to be kept at the Nimitz Center's Pacific War Museum in Fredericksburg, Texas.

In 1988, a similar storm arose in Australia when veterans of the Japan Midget Submarine Association journeyed to the Australia War Memorial and presented brass plaques honoring the submariners who died in Sydney harbor. The Royal Australia Navy accepted the plaques despite loud protests from Australian veterans, who called the gesture "grotesque and outrageous."

The custody battle may not be over. Nimitz Center's long-range plans show the craft as a permanent fixture. "If they want our sub, they'll have to come get it," a Nimitz Center employee said during a Pearl Harbor commemoration.

I-24tou is currently suffering from years of corrosion, and requires a massive stabilization effort. An exhaustive rivet-by-rivet documentation of the vessel is planned.

Part of *I-24tou* may already be at the Visitor Center. In 1989, the Park Service was given what is supposed to be the midget submarine's periscope. This instrument, however, which was acquired through the carrier *Intrepid* floating naval museum in New York, does not match contemporary photographs of *I-24tou's* periscope. It's possible that it is from another midget submarine. According to Park Service curator Bob Chenoweth, "there is no proof either way." Each of the midget periscopes appears to be unique.

The *Bowfin* museum also has some artifacts in its collection that may have come from *I-24tou*, including most of the notorious gyrocompass and a model of a HA-boat fashioned from lead ballast from a midget submarine. These items were obtained from the Navy, which did not keep adequate documentation.

[2] *Part of the problem stemmed from park usage of "Arizona Memorial" to describe the entire complex, including the Memorial Visitor Center, which is across the harbor from the Memorial. This is actually the intended site.*

A display of midget submarine gadgets at Bowfin Museum Park that includes I-24tou's balky gyrocompass and a lead submarine model.

Sometime during the war, a bronze plaque was installed at the base of the flagpole at Bellows Field. "Japanese Midget Submarine Number 19, captured 8 December 1941 by Army and Navy personnel after grounding on reef off Bellows Field, T.H.

"The commanding officer was captured by Lt. P.G. Plybon and Corporal D.M. Akui of the 298th Infantry as he swam ashore. The other member of the crew was found dead." The plaque was moved near the base officers' club at a later date, and is the only midget submarine artifact in Hawaii that names *HA-19*.

Alex Campbell shows off some interesting scrap metal found by accident in Waikiki — Sakamaki's propeller.

Pieces keep turning up, sometimes in surprising places. A crew from the Fletcher Pacific construction company was clearing an overgrown lot on Lewers Street in Waikiki on Feb. 27, 1992, when a hundred-pound propeller was found in the tall grass. "They would have tossed it into the bin with all the other trash, but it was too heavy," said Alex Campbell, project manager.

On closer inspection, one of the mangled steel blades had neat black lettering that read, *Two-Man Sub Prop, Ran Aground at Pearl Harbor Hawaii, Dec. 7th 1941 on Coral Reef.* Campbell decided not to toss the prop until a historian looked at it. He then spent a fruitless weekend trying to contact the Arizona Memorial and getting only prerecorded tour schedules. A friend suggested Campbell call the *Bowfin* submarine museum, where Collections Manager Mary Jo Valdes accessioned the artifact sight unseen. The propeller is an exact match for the aft half of the contra-rotating propellers used on the Type #A midget submarine. Damage to the screw blades is consistent with that described on *I-24tou* — chances are excellent this is Sakamaki's propeller, dinged on the reef.

The mystery is how it wound up in Waikiki.

Campbell said that the propeller was found behind an Outrigger Hotels annex at 409 Lewers. When a tall building was constructed nearby, the water table was lowered and walls sagged in the area. He speculated that the propeller was found in the rubbish when the annex wall was rebuilt.

Valdes said that many buildings in the area were taken over by the Navy during World War II. The Royal Hawaiian hotel, only a few blocks away, was used by submariners on leave. It is possible that the propeller might have adorned the wall of a Navy office as a trophy, and was tossed out when the war ended.

"I think this prop is absolutely from the Sakamaki midget," said Delgado, who shows the excitement of Indiana Jones whenever World War II debris is discovered. "We know that the torpedo guards and propeller were replaced because they were too banged up, and that these various pieces disappeared as souvenirs or whatever.

"The circumstantial evidence certainly points that way — the various pieces of the puzzle are coming back into the picture. This is very excellent!"

The most-intact of the other Advance Force midget submarines is also the most mysterious. On June 13, 1960, Navy diving instructor GM/2 Jerry Galloway decided to take his students on a long-distance diving exercise on the Pearl Harbor side of Keehi Lagoon, just outside the channel's mouth. The water here was generally murky from Pearl silt, but on this day it was clear.

Navy diver SK/l C.F. Buhl surfaced and announced he had spotted a submerged submarine. Doubtful, Galloway followed him down and confirmed it — a tiny craft sitting upright, 76 feet down.

On July 13, 1960, she was raised by bridles from salvage ship *Current*. The torpedoes were still in the tubes and the hatches, curiously, were open. Captain H.A. Thompson of ComSubPac was the first to cautiously climb into the dripping, slippery interior, where he discovered bent piping, shattered instruments and the big electric engine twisted from its mount. This midget had suffered serious depth-charge damage.

There was no sign of the crew's remains or possessions. Not a

In the rush to display the coveted midget submarine at Nimitz Center in Fredericksberg, Texas, the center section was assembled backwards.

At left is the sail as it currently appears, in the war museum's Peace Garden.

Navy divers inspect the midget submarine found in Keehi Lagoon during the summer of 1960. Almost two decades after the Pearl Harbor attack, the craft was still in relatively good condition.

tooth or a belt buckle or a document, items forensic experts said would have had no trouble lasting underwater. Sulfur still present in the scuttling fuse indicated it had never been lit.

Bizarre speculation arose that the crew may have swum ashore and melted into the local Japanese populace — an unlikely event in light of the prewar FBI's close tabs on Hawaii's Japanese-Americans. They may have instead drowned while trying to reach the surface, and their bodies swept out into the trackless Pacific. It is possible that the two bodies picked up in the same area by destroyer *Ward* a week after the attack came from this midget submarine, although the uniforms, as described, matched those of Imperial Navy flight suits.

On Dec. 23, 1941, in the same general area, a tugboat struck a large, rounded object just under the water. The "operator was quite certain object struck was not a submerged log," noted the report. On Jan. 1, 1942, tug *Hercules* "reported striking a submerged object which felt as if it were round, and rolled off of it." The recorded position tallies closely with the midget craft found in 1960.

It also could have been the mysterious harbor-bottom object *Plunger* ran her grapnel over on Dec. 10, 1941.

This may have been Yokoyama's craft, which was still prowling late on Dec. 7; if so, why were the torpedoes unused? His radio message said the surprise attack was successful.

Or could it be the phantom submarine of Dec. 12, 1941, escaping the harbor only to settle just outside? It's remotely possible that a

UNDERWATER NINJA

midget could have idled away five days on minimum battery power, waiting for a clear shot inside the harbor.

On the other hand, the Dec. 12 "attack" could have simply been a case of military mass hysteria. Even though the midget apparently never broke surface, and never fired its torpedoes, most of the crews involved in the hunt believed they were after the genuine article.

Vice Admiral Kazuo Ueda, Secretary General of the *Tokusenkai* — Japan Midget Submarine Association — says the Keehi midget is that of either Furuno or Hiro-o; de Yarmin believes it is Hiro-

o's. Aiken thinks it is Iwasa's. Zenji Orita admits it is possible that Hiro-o or Furuno got into the harbor, only to get away again.

The area where it was found is now filled with an artificial island holding Honolulu International Airport's "Reef Runway." Prior to

The mysterious midget submarine is floated to the surface, drained ...

building the runway, very few — if any — surveys of the reef bottom were made. According to the Hawaii State Department of Transportation, the majority of the filled area was directly on the reef, in depths ranging from two to 25 feet. "Little chance something as large as a submarine could have been overlooked in water that shallow," said an engineer who worked on the project.

The depth-charge damage on the Keehi Lagoon midget could have come from the furious action in the harbor on Dec. 12. It's possible that the torpedo tubes, like Sakamaki's, were crimped from this pounding and unable to fire.

This last possibility was too dangerous to investigate. The section with the potentially dangerous torpedoes, each with 790 pounds of

... and then lifted out of the water with a sea-going crane. No one at this point had any idea what is inside the craft.

Worried-looking Navy EOD officer Lieutenant (j.g.) James Connor pries open the craft. No crew remains or artifacts were found, though the thoroughness of the search is open to question. Japanese consul Masayuki Harigai and Pacific Fleet chief of staff Captain Paul Stimson discuss the find at right.

high explosive, was unbolted and dumped at sea, along with 50 pounds of scuttling charge. Even after more than 7,000 days in salt water, the bolts turned easily. The rest of the vessel was shipped to Japan on LST *Shiretoko*, where — with a false nose and a coat of paint — it currently rests on a concrete pedestal at Eta Jima. It has become a shrine of sorts, and a curious twist on the veterans' furor that arose over *I-24tou* in 1990. "The submarine was given a place of final repose in its present position for reason that the Maritime Self-Defense Force Officer Candidate School is also in the same area which, incidentally, was the site of the former Japanese Naval Academy," wrote JMSDF head Admiral Sadayoshi Nakayama in a letter of thanks for the craft. "I firmly believe that it will serve as a silent source of remembrance of

UNDERWATER NINJA

the past for the young officers, midshipmen and men in these schools as well as a means of furthering the close bond between the navies of the United States and Japan."

The midget submarine rammed by *Monaghan* was raised from the harbor two weeks following the attack and dumped at the Submarine Base. It sat there for a couple of days with the crew still rotting inside, a horrific scene that drew many sightseers.

"It was a weird-looking thing, with the hull crushed and the conning tower damaged by gunfire," remembered E.E. Blyth, then serving in destroyer *Phelps*. "They didn't bother to remove the bodies

either. Only one body was visible from the roped-off area and it was badly mangled … the stench was terrible."

Marine Lieutenant Cornelius C. Smith wrote in his diary, "Today we went over to the sub base to take a look at one of the midget submarines the Japs

The Keehi Lagoon midget submarine's bow was inspected and found to hold live torpedoes. This section was unbolted and dumped at sea. The aft two-thirds, already waving a Japanese flag, was taken back to Japan, where it was restored and placed on display at the naval academy at Eta Jima. One unexpected find was a bottle placed in a hole in the submarine's skin — at the time, the bottle was rumored to hold sake.

Inspecting the Monaghan midget: *note the severe washboarding of the hull from the depth charge attack. Navy censors deleted the background in the bottom picture.*

used. She's out of the water, resting on chocks, and doesn't look like much because she's so small. Still, she was able to get off a couple of torpedoes successfully. The conning tower is tiny, with room enough for one man to steer the craft. He's still in there. One of our ships rammed him, broadside, and he's caught, dead, with his legs still hanging out; I guess they'll have to cut him free with a blowtorch. I suppose the torpedoman inside is dead, too …"

The monocoque hull was heavily washboarded from the shallow-water depth charge attack, the thin steel dished in between the ribs and stringers. There are two notable exceptions to this damage. One is the aft connection between the engine and battery compartments, where the submarine bolted together. The circular framework here was

430

UNDERWATER NINJA

virtually intact, indicating great rigidity. The other exception is the forward part of the hull, a great chunk of which was blown open, the jagged edges curling outward like a blossom. This damage is inconsistent with the external pressures obvious on the rest of the hull. It matches, however, the damage evident in other midget submarines when the scuttling charge was set off.

It is possible that the crew of this midget submarine deliberately self-destructed, hoping to take *Monaghan* with them as the destroyer rolled over their heads.

Japanese historians and Sakamaki believe the crew were midget expert Iwasa

and his helmsman, Naoji Sasaki. Sakamaki wrote after the war that Iwasa's shoulder insignia was placed on display somewhere at Pearl Harbor, although there is no record of this. Later, he said that had been a poor translation; it was meant as a metaphor.

De Yarmin says the craft is *I-18tou*, piloted by Furuno. Orita and Aiken think the midget submarine was piloted by Yokoyama, despite the late-night message supposedly sent by the midget operator.

This midget was raised west of Ford Island, and *Plunger's*

Muck and oil stream from the Monaghan *midget, which lay on the bottom of Pearl Harbor for two weeks. The shell hole in the sail that supposedly decapitated the pilot is visible. At left are the relatively undamaged screws.*

mystery object was hooked north of the Navy airfield. It is possible that they are the same.

Sakamaki's midget was repaired with parts from this wreck, particularly the torpedo guard and the lower fin. The sailors who did this work noticed no bodies within the rammed midget, even though they spent much time inside it. It's likely they were removed, and the violent stench from the corrupted battery acids contrib-

[3] *The bow of* HA-21, *the submarine recovered in Sydney Harbor, was mated to pieces of the one that self-detonated on the net, and sent on an Australia-wide war bond tour. They can be seen at the Australian War Memorial.*

uted to the legend of the crew being buried with the midget. Any technical report on this midget, including its HA-number, has not been located.[3]

The shattered midget submarine was used as landfill, lowered by crane into a new pier while a brief military funeral service was held. The service was broadcast by radio across the United States and the Territory of Hawaii. Among the audience was a deeply embarrassed Sakamaki. One source claims that the crew were buried separately and honorably, that spectators assumed the smell of fouled batteries and decomposing sea growth were that of the dead seamen.

In 1952, while excavating a dockside area, a civilian dragline

Workmen prepare to roll the Monaghan *midget submarine into a landfill area at Pearl Harbor's submarine yards. The screws and periscope are missing. In the background, I-24tou is being cleaned up and reassembled. Barely visible on the hull is "19," the Ha-boat's serial number. Rumors persist to this day that other midget submarine hulls are buried in the harbor.*

punched into something too big to move. The boggling stench of chlorine gas hissed out, and workmen tumbled out of the pit, gagging.

The dragline's teeth were stuck fast. Lieutenant Earl Dean Bronson, who had been on *Plunger* during the Pearl Harbor assault, recalled that a midget had been used as landfill in the area and told the foreman of the construction crew. A smaller excavator cleared away the muck, and Bronson's suspicions were confirmed.

The excavator had penetrated the battery compartment. Gas masks were provided to the work crew and a trench dug alongside the interred midget submarine. The midget was rolled over into the pit and covered up.

Today, this midget — and perhaps her crew — still lies beneath the asphalt near the Pearl Harbor Submarine Base Officers' Club.

The fifth midget submarine simply vanished in the moil of smoke and battle. It may be the one shot at by *St. Louis* after expending its torpedoes. It may also be the one that waited for so long outside the harbor, made a radio report on Dec. 8 and possibly sprinted into the harbor later that week.

De Yarmin says the night message not only came from Yokoyama aboard *I-16tou*, but that it was transmitted from *inside* the harbor! *I-68* and *I-69*, he adds, were ordered to loiter at the harbor entrance to rescue Yokoyama.

Aiken believes the fifth midget is *I-18tou*, and that crewmen Furuno and Yokoyama went away someplace to commit *jibaku*, ritual suicide.In all probability, this midget was wounded by a destroyer and sank quietly. There are also reports of an object resembling a midget

432

submarine deep in a murky bay at Maui, reasonably near the mother submarine rendezvous area. The underwater survey of Pearl Harbor during the summer of 1988 turned up nothing that could be a midget submarine, but the survey also only covered the heavily-trafficked portion of the harbor.

On May 2, 1991, a Japanese aerial torpedo came to the surface in the jaws of a bottom dredger, near the quays where battleships *Maryland* and *Oklahoma* were damaged in the attack, and an area surveyed in 1988. All ship operations in the harbor were halted when the torpedo was reported to port operations at 9 a.m. The ferry ride to Ford Island, the path of which passes directly by the spot, was shut down, trapping people on either side. After a momentary halt, boat tours to the Arizona Memorial were resumed without interruption.

By mid-afternoon, the torpedo had been moved to an isolated area in West Loch and "rendered safe," according to public-affairs officer Commander Joel Keefer. West Loch is the location of the harbor's naval magazine and the Explosive Ordnance Disposal team has a "small branch office out there," said Commander Keefer. That night, the torpedo was moved again, to an area considered safer by the Navy, though they didn't reveal the location.

The National Park Service expressed interest in acquiring the torpedo. "There are very few intact artifacts from the attack," said curator Chenoweth. "All that's usually left is bits and pieces."

The dredging project had picked up several smaller items related to the Pearl Harbor attack, including an ammunition ready locker and pieces of a "Kingfisher" scout plane from battleship *Oklahoma*, "but this one was a bit of a surprise," said Keefer.

Despite assurance from EOD experts that the torpedo could be rendered safe, the Navy took it out to sea on May 3, 1991, and blew it up. While it was being destroyed — without the knowledge of naval historians in Washington — Navy public-affairs crews at Pearl Harbor deliberately misled interested citizens about the weapon's fate. At one point, a Navy officer collected Park Service photographs of the torpedo before a television news crew could see them.

When the EOD team revisited the area, they were surprised to discover, among the bits and pieces, the shredded aft end of the torpedo. The Navy loaned this piece to the Arizona Memorial Visitor Center, where it was displayed for the 50th anniversary of the attack.

Apparently, the power of these unusual underwater weapons to tie up men and resources has not diminished, even after half a century.

On July 27, 1992, a team of aircraft wreck salvors, working with the University of Hawaii's Undersea Research Lab (HURL) on a hunt for the Douglas flying boat hulls, accidentally stumbled over a piece of midget submarine.

"We looked at it and asked ourselves, 'Is that what we think it is?'" said Gary Larkins of the Institute of Aeronautical Archaeology and Research, a Sacramento-based aircraft recovery firm. "I've spent 20 years looking for aircraft—and this pops up!"

I-24tou *on display at Nimitz Center, deep in the heart of Texas. Apparent are the rewelded viewing ports on the fuselage flank.*

What they found is the rear third of a midget submarine, neatly sheared off at a bolted joint, the same joint that is intact on the midget submarine run over by destroyer *Monaghan,* and the same seam along which the midget submarine depth-bombed in Sydney Harbor popped open. This may be a weak design feature — the rigidity of the structure exacerbates tension on the bolts holding it together.

Visible through the opening is the engine and reduction gear; the propellors and fins on the tail are damaged as if the piece impacted the bottom tail-first. The rest of the submarine fuselage seems undamaged except for plant growth.

The exact location of the find is being treated as proprietary

UNDERWATER NINJA

information by IAAR, which quickly instituted complete salvage claims to the wreck while simultaneously disclaiming ownership. The coordinates given in the salvage claim place it well outside the Prohibited Area, making it unlikely this craft is the one sunk by *Ward*.

Without the forward end, which contains the conning tower, torpedoes and serial number, it's impossible to tell for sure which midget submarine this is.

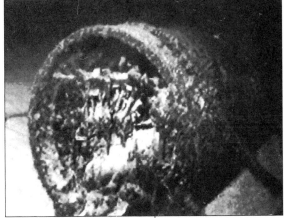

Larkins and associate George Carter were scouring the bottom in the University of Hawaii's *Pisces V* submarine, and the submarine was found as they reached the end of their battery power. They had time only to make a videotape before leaving.

"I feel sorry for the people who searched so hard for it before and didn't find it," said Larkins. "We weren't even looking for it!"

Delgado pointed out that the submarine is technically still "the property of the empire of Japan. It is not our property unless it surrendered or was boarded and seized."

The legal petition to claim dominion over the find caught Pearl Harbor historians by surprise, as IAAR salvors Larkins and Carter had previously professed willingness to work closely with the National Park Service.

The petition, filed in mid-August 1992 in the United States District Court in Hawaii, claimed the IAAR had "for some time" been searching for the lost submarine. Larkins and Carter told local media that they were on assignment for the Naval Air Museum in Pensacola, Florida, to look for the abandoned flying boat hulls. The National Park Service provided IAAR with data to aid the search for aircraft.

A video image of the midget submarine hull spotted in the summer of 1992. Barely visible through the muck and growth in the opening is a motor mount like the one below, this one inside I-24tou.

"Our only objective is to map the object and find out about its history," said Chenoweth. "We're not fretting about who owns it — although we've been looking for it longer than anybody."

The petition asked that IAAR be awarded "complete dominion and control" over possible salvage of the midget submarine hulk, as well as denying access to the wreck to other deep-sea researchers. The California salvors also demanded $5 million in recovery fees should the hulk be salved by another party.

Larkins said the legal petition was a standard step to "keep someone from circumventing us—so we can keep in on the deal. Lots of different factions are trying end runs, trying to grab the submarine from us."

Maritime historians say that the legal status of a midget submarine wreck, as a warship of a sovereign nation that was neither surrendered nor boarded and seized in wartime, is an interesting legal dilemma.

"It is the property of Japan under the principle of sovereign immunity; it is an extension of Japanese soil," said Delgado. "Any legal motions on this wreck simply do not apply unless the government of Japan decides not to press their claim."

As of this writing, the Japanese government had not announced its decision. A source with access to the Japanese ambassador to the United States said that — extremely unofficially — the Japanese government's position is that the wreck is ancient history.

"There is already legal precedent, regarding the Confederate raider *Alabama,* which was sunk in battle within the territorial waters of France in 1863," said Delgado. "The United States has signed an agreement with France declaring that the *Alabama* remains the property of the American government. The same thing has been done with U-boats off the East Coast of the U.S.—they remain the property of the German government.

"This is really troubling, and it's not just a question of finders-keepers. Who does history belong to? Pearl Harbor, of course, was an intensely personal event for the people who were involved, but it has transcended that, and become an important part of our cultural history. The artifacts of Pearl Harbor are temporal touchstones, one of the rare bits of history that you can actually touch, and should be beyond the taint of commercial exploitation," said Delgado.

"To turn this vessel in to a ... privately owned *thing* ... is a fundamental betrayal of why we preserve history."

The mystery of the midgets has grown since the attack on Pearl Harbor. Even those already found are ciphers. The ships carried no markings. Reflecting their expendable nature, the midgets had no discernable numbers or names. The crews carried no personal belongings. They were the stealth fighters of their day, the underwater ninja.

Unless positive ID is made of crew remains, there is no way of telling which midget did what. The midget submarine used as landfill in 1941 lies deep on a busy Navy base, and the midget submarine recovered and cursorily examined in 1960 contained no trace of the crew. If the midget submarine sunk by *Ward* is discovered, or the front two-thirds of the craft found by the HURL deep-diver is uncovered, careful forensic examination will be needed to sort things out.

To wreck salvors, the bits of torn steel on the bottom of the ocean represent dollar signs. To historians, the wrecks are interesting pieces of data, more loose ends in the knot of Pearl Harbor. To the families of the men who fought in these waters, however, the military wreckage of all nations is sacred ground.

To disturb their sleep may be defilement. Perhaps once the curious have learned what they need to learn from these rusting shrouds, they should draw away, and let the drifting, dark waters, the unimaginable pressures of the deep, reclaim the faraway dreams of empire and the fading glory of battle.

UNDERWATER NINJA

ECHOES

32

Listening For Ghosts

Mochitsura Hashimoto looked out the window of the Royal Hawaiian Hotel, a fading sun polishing his face. The last time Hashimoto saw Hawaii, he drank in the lights of Waikiki across the waves, listened to music drifting from the hotels by the beach. As torpedo officer of Imperial Japanese Navy submarine *I-24*, he then launched *I-24tou* toward Pearl Harbor, in the predawn murk of Dec. 7, 1941.

Forty-nine years later, music from Del Courtney's band drifted up from the hotel's Monarch Room, then called the Persian Room. The music is '41-vintage Glenn Miller.

Ironies on ironies.

Pearl Harbor was the beginning of the Pacific War. Near the end, as skipper of submarine *I-58*, Hashimoto fired a spread of torpedoes at a ship looming by in the night. It was heavy cruiser *Indianapolis*, which quickly went under. Most of the crew perished in the days following the sinking, as the U.S. Navy flush with expectations of war's end simply forgot to look for an overdue ship.

Sunk with *Indianapolis* was the reputation of Captain Charles B. McVay, who was blamed by the Navy for the ship's loss.

Hashimoto was the guest in Hawaii of Kimo McVay, son of the *Indianapolis*' skipper.

"I'm just tired of all the Japan-bashing that goes on nowadays," said McVay, a local show business promoter. "Captain Hashimoto was just doing his duty, as was my father. They were both good sailors, loyal to their country."

The *Indianapolis* sinking was the U.S. Navy's worst open-sea disaster, as the battleship *Arizona* remains the Navy's greatest peacetime disaster — the country was still technically at peace during the attack. Hashimoto was present at both.

Hashimoto was flown to Washington by the U.S. Navy to testify against Captain McVay. His testimony, that there was nothing McVay

Mochitsura Hashimoto with Hawaii's "Ambassador of Aloha," entertainer Danny Kaleikini, who is fluent in Japanese.

could have done to avoid the incoming torpedoes, turned out to be beneficial to the defense. Hashimoto was quietly returned to Japan, and the charges against McVay reduced. The damage to the American's career had been done, however, and years later he shot himself in the head while clutching the figure of a toy sailor.

Hashimoto became a Shinto priest. Nearly 90, he made his own videotape chronicle of his Hawaii visit. He claimed the memories of war do not haunt him.

The Pearl Harbor attack, that hinge of history that marks the beginning of the modern world, has affected him more than he knows. The actions that began in the dark waters of a Hawaiian night have bent the trajectory of lives, have shaped destinies, have colored the memories of those who prefer to see things in black and white.

Kazuo Sakamaki, whose war started and ended at Pearl Harbor, returned to Japan after the war and was snubbed by his colleagues. He received many letters from men, suggesting that he kill himself, and several letters from women, suggesting sex. He married a neighbor on Aug. 15, 1946 — the first anniversary of VJ Day — had children and went to work for Toyota. He became an executive, heading Toyota's Sao Paulo, Brazil, office. He recently returned to Japan. He has spent the last half-century trying to forget the war.

The very model of a corporate warrior — Kazuo Sakamaki in the 1950s with son and new Toyota.

He returned to Hawaii a number of times anonymously. The first time, in the 1950s, was to make sure Inagaki's remains were properly remembered.

In the spring of 1991, Sakamaki attended a symposium on the Pearl Harbor attack held in Austin, Texas. The event was something of an eye-opener. The Americans were genuinely interested in his exploits, honored his bravery, and did not consider his capture shameful. A dignified man who seems focused on some inner horizon, Sakamaki experienced complicated feelings in Texas.

He seemed worried and sad that the history of World War II is mentioned briefly, if at all, in Japanese schools. "Young people don't know the war," he said. "And many forget Pearl Harbor. (General Douglas) MacArthur pressed to change the constitution after the war — no more war, no more soldiers — so there is no war in the schools.

"So now young men don't know about war or Pearl Harbor. They just don't know what it is like."

A few minutes later, a radio reporter rushed up to Sakamaki and breathlessly asked if he was "one of the Japs that bombed Pearl Harbor."

"No," said Sakamaki. He seemed amused.

Kazuo Sakamaki at a veteran's symposium in Austin, Texas, in the spring of 1991, watching American pilots of the Confederate Air Force pretend to bomb Pearl Harbor.

Walter Burke returned to Baker Island in 1943, and located the flag he had buried there two years before. He took it home, where it remained until Burke passed away in 1990. The Amelia Earhart Lighthouse was restored to operating condition by the Coast Guard in 1963, part of a nationwide observance of Earhart's 65th birthday. In the 1950s, the bodies of Richard Whaley and Joe Keliihahanui were exhumed on Howland and reburied in the military cemetery at Schofield Barracks.

"When I reminisce about those times, I realize that we were young and naive," says Abraham Piianaia. "I realize now that we were there to strengthen our position in the Pacific, and I'm only beginning to appreciate how important that was.

"The opportunity to be left in nature is something youngsters don't have any more. Our companions were the birds. All we .had were the four of us and nothing else. Perhaps that's how Adam and Eve could have felt in the Garden of Eden. Everything was … so pristine."

Piianaia later became head of the Hawaiian Studies department at the University of Hawaii.

On occasion, the veterans of the brief colonization of the Equatorial Islands meet in the cemetery to remember their boyhood friends, and they unroll the flag and let it fly over the graves of Whaley and Keliihahanui.

Within 10 days of landing on Maui, most of the survivors of the *Lahaina* sinking were again at sea. An elegantly printed souvenir copy of Doug McMurtry's log was distributed to each. Rumors flew that the Navy had intercepted *Lahaina*'s distress signal and refused to believe the sinking ship was in its reported position.

After the war, Matson tried to collect $615,000 in damages from the government for the loss of *Lahaina*. A federal district court ruled that the War Damages Corporation was set up to reimburse companies for property lost in transit, and that the law applied only to cargo, not ships. Since *Lahaina* was virtually empty at the time of sinking, Matson was owed nothing. The court also remarked Matson should have applied for "war risk" insurance prior to hostilities.

Although *Lahaina's* Japanese-American crewman Richard Hirashima was repeatedly described by several sailors as "a fine boy and a real American," he was banned from going to sea. In frustration, the Honolulu shipping commissioner and Hirashima made a direct appeal to Rear Admiral Claude Bloch, commandant of the 14th Naval District, who sympathized, saying, "I know how you feel, but there's nothing I can do. We have orders from Washington — no Japanese at sea until the war is over."

Hirashima learned to be a plumber, sticking to it until 1946, when he again became a seaman. This embarrassment, as well as a legal scrape when he was a teenager, prodded the seaman into changing his name to Haru. Richard Hirashima-Haru didn't come home from the sea until 1983.

Despite a commission as a Naval Reserve lieutenant, Hans O. Matthiesen was promptly stripped of command. He had relatives in the German military, and some of the sailors had complained to interrogators of Matthiesen's anti-American attitudes. The proof lay in his joke about U.S. Navy aircraft while landing on Maui.

To make ends meet, Matthiesen washed bottles in a brewery. Within two years, on appeal to the Navy, he was appointed lieutenant commander, skippering *Deimos*, an ammunition carrier. It too was sunk by a Japanese submarine, off Guadalcanal in 1943.

Such was engineer Mike Locke's regard for Matthiesen that he requested duty with him, serving as an engineer on Matthiesen's next Navy command, Liberty ship *Ruticulus*, called the "S.S. Ridiculous" by her crew. The ship and the two men served out the war, supporting the invasion of Saipan and Tinian and weathering *kamikaze* attacks off Okinawa.

Matthiesen eventually became a well-liked Matson captain, commanding the liner *Lurline*. In this capacity, he was once visited by Locke and his family. "This is the captain, and when he says jump, you do it," Locke explained to his daughters.

The conversation went on for awhile, and suddenly Matthiesen turned to the girls and said , "Jump!" They looked puzzled.

"See, I'm not so powerful," Matthiesen laughed. He retired in 1970 as commodore of the Matson fleet.

McMurtry worked for Matson until February 1942, and then went into the Navy, becoming an intelligence officer and skippering a ship. He finally "swallowed the anchor" and wound up back in the San Francisco area, operating the family masonry business.

In 1979, when the business could take care of itself for a few days,

Douglas and Peggy McMurtry took a vacation in Kahului. They visited the beach where the lifeboat had grounded.

That night, in the hotel room, Peggy heard her husband exclaim, "Oh, no!" as he stepped out of the shower. She found him looking at an Army surplus towel, provided by the hotel. Stenciled across the edge was the soldier's name: *McMurtry.*

And, as it happened, the date was Dec. 11. The day *Lahaina* had been attacked, nearly four decades before. To McMurtry, just for a moment, the hotel floor seemed to pitch like a small boat on the ocean.

The men who captured Sakamaki on the Waimanalo beach had distinguished combat careers. David Akui became a ranger with Merrill's Marauders, passing away in the early 1980s. Paul C. Plybon was wounded on Kwajalein and in December, 1991, attended the 50th commemoration of the Pearl Harbor attack.

In 1961, Steve Weiner wrote to Sakamaki but received no response. In 1991, the two met again at the Texas symposium. Across a "peace garden" donated by the Japanese to a Pacific War museum, Weiner recognized his former prisoner. "Look!" he said. "That's Sakamaki! I'd know him anywhere — he looks like he's *still* out of it."

Weiner was introduced to Sakamaki, who listened intently while Weiner explained how they'd first met. Sakamaki had to take Weiner's word for it; the former midget submariner appears to have no memories of this period.

Claude Bloch was possibly the only command-level American naval officer involved in the attack on Pearl Harbor who subsequently escaped criticism. That is a tribute either to Bloch's superior naval skills, or to his talent for safely navigating the halls of Congress, and probably both.

On a Sunday in December 1941, Admiral James O. Richardson had breakfast with his wife in Washington D.C. Still bitter over his dismissal from the U.S. Fleet 11 months earlier, and feeling helpless in the rush of events, he said to her, "We are on the verge of a war which may break out any minute. About eight years ago, when I was a student at the war college, I wrote a thesis on Japanese policy. After breakfast, I'm going to find that thesis and read it, to see if my opinions have changed."

He found it, read it, and was going over the summary — "That should it appear to (Japan's) advantage to do so, she will strike viciously, effectively and unexpectedly prior to any declaration of war ..." — when the telephone rang. The caller advised Richardson to turn on his radio.

Like most of America, the one-time Commander-in-Chief of the

U.S. Fleet found out about the attack on Pearl Harbor from a radio news flash.

The next day he went down to the Navy Department, and listened to the other officers ponder the attack. Asked for his view, Richardson said, "Every day from now on, I am going to pray for two things. The first is for success of our arms; the second is that I shall keep my mouth shut."

Richardson served briefly as part of the Special Committee for Reorganization of National Defense. When the committee recommended that the military be headed by a single individual who reported to the President, Richardson disagreed. He spent the rest of the war as an adviser to the Navy General Board and as an executive in the Navy Relief Society.

At the congressional hearings following the war, Admiral Richardson was asked, "Can you account for the fact that the Navy was *not* alerted and the Army *was* alerted" during the false alarm of June 17, 1940?[1] He answered, "That passes my comprehension."

[1] See pages 31 and 32.

At the same hearings, General Marshall denied that the alert had been an exercise, and of telling Richardson so in 1940. They were just two of many commanders with selective memories of the months prior to the attack.

Richardson, in later years, laid the blame for the Pearl Harbor debacle on Washington, squarely in the lap of Admiral "Betty" Stark. The two met often after the war, though neither had any inclination to discuss Pearl Harbor.

Shigemi Furuno's parents at the shrine of their dead son.

When Shigemi Furuno was installed as a hero-god, "a guardian deity of the country," the reaction from his mother was, "I should like to visit Hawaii with my husband and honor the memory of those who laid down their lives for the cause of the State."

At Akira Hiro-o's death, his mother was stunned, and spent the rest of the war consoling families similarly bereaved.

The silver watch from Shigenori Yokoyama's torpedo school was sent to his eldest brother, Tsurumi. Money left behind by Shigenori was used by his mother to buy war bonds. At the news of his death, she left straight-away for the family altar and reported to her ancestors that one of her maternal duties was fulfilled.

In 1942, Japanese filmmakers made a solemn movie version of the Pearl Attack called "Hawaii Sakusan," or "Hawaii-Marei Oki Kaisen," a documentary-like retelling of Pacific victories which added to the luster of the nine hero-gods. After the war, Sakamaki's part in the attack was lampooned in a film comedy called "Human Bullet."

Dr. Tokue Takahashi, the Japanese alien who entertained Imperial naval officers in a home that commanded a view of both Pearl and Honolulu harbors, declared his allegiance to Japan well before war broke out. Promptly interned, he returned to Japan in 1943 and gleefully described the Dec. 7 attack for Japanese radio.

"The pilot of a plane with the insignia of the Rising Sun, finding his craft afire, immediately crashed his plane into an enemy ship and destroyed himself," reported Takahashi. "It seemed at this time the pilot lifted both arms to the sky and shouted, *'Banzai! Banzai!'* But due to the loud noise all about, and the great confusion, I was not able to hear his voice. This was really regrettable."

Perhaps Takahashi's keen eyesight had divined the plane crash onto *Curtiss'* crane area, but this is doubtful. The doctor's beautiful home, which still stands, is nearly nine miles from Ford Island.

After the war, Honolulu physicians debated whether to revoke Takahashi's medical license should he return to Hawaii. Takahashi died — in Japan — in 1951.

Akira Hiro-o's father draws the blade of his son's sword.

Among the curious crowd at the Kewalo pier on Dec. 8, 1941, when the sampans arrived were the Kidas' nephew, who recognized the burnt, ripped bodies on board *Kiho Maru*. He immediately called the family. Kida's wife was catatonic with grief, and positive identification of the bodies in the police morgue was made by daughter Kimie Shidaki.

A week later, as prayer services were being held in the Kida home, military policemen knocked on the door and demanded to talk to Sutematsu and Kiichi Kida. Informed that the two had recently been killed, the MPs saluted pictures of the dead men, bowed toward the family and left.

Seiki Arakaki was later called on to testify at an insurance hearing. He had

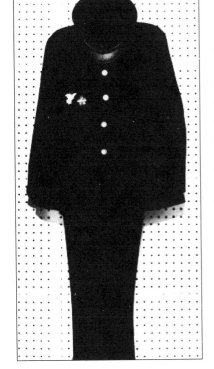

Like a ghost forever bowing toward the Emperor, Furuno's uniform remains on display in his home town.

heard Kiichi moaning after the first strafing run by the SBD, while Sutematsu had not made a sound. On this basis, Kiichi was determined to have survived his father, though by moments. In 1967, the insurance company paid out $8,000 to the Kida family.

Kenji Takumi received approximately $2,500 for the seizure of his sampan, plus proceeds from the fish catch already on board the boat on Dec. 8.

Sannosuke Onishi was not compensated for his injuries or the loss of his sampan.

Hawaii congressional delegate Joseph R. Farrington later introduced measures to compensate the Kida family for the deaths of the two men and the loss of the family sampan. More than 25 years after the incident, attorney Clarence Shimamura filed a similar request of the U.S. government. Neither were successful.

Sampan movements were sharply restricted after the attack. The 1942 fish catch plummeted to one percent of the 1941 catch, at a time when Hawaii could have used the food most. The sampan-based fishing industry never recovered. Despite efforts by Hawaii preservationists, many of the surviving sampans are being broken up.

On Feb. 21, 1942, Otto Kuehn was found guilty on eight counts of spying by a military court and sentenced to death by firing squad. The trial was top secret, so much so the White House was fed disinformation about it; U.S. Attorney General Francis Biddle told the President on March 4 it was actually consul Nagao Kita who was to be shot.

The news shocked Roosevelt. Sumner Welles argued that if Kita was executed, then the Japanese would certainly kill U.S. diplomats still in Japan. J. Edgar Hoover was eventually called upon to straighten things out with the president.

It was still thought executing Kuehn might rebound against American nationals in Germany and Japan. Later in 1942 Kuehn's sentence was commuted to 30 years in prison.

Honolulu residents discovered Kuehn's spying activities only when his son-in-law, a Navy officer, filed for divorce in 1943, on grounds that he didn't know his in-laws were spies. The divorce was swiftly granted, unusually so in martial-law Hawaii.

After the war, Kuehn returned to Germany and died there. His widow Friedel attempted unsuccessfully to recover Hawaii assets seized by the U.S. government — and originally paid for by the Japanese government.

During the last year of war, Wyman Spalding was still on the West Coast, flying brand-new B-25Hs in exercises and developing maneuvers. The planes were stripped of all armament, so he was mildly curious when the squadron was told to knock down Japanese balloons, should they come across one. The wind-driven weapons

were launched in Japan and rode the jet stream across the Pacific. Hundreds came down in North America, as far east as Michigan and Texas. The balloons carried thermite bombs, and a minister's wife and five children were killed by one during a Sunday outing.[2] It is possible forest fires breaking out in the Pacific Northwest today are caused by these weapons, long-forgotten, still hanging in trees.

Spalding still lives in the bay area, and is a volunteer guide at the Presidio. If his name sounds familiar, it may be because his father and grandfather were both involved in baseball.

Kumaji Furuya returned to Honolulu and the furniture business, eventually being honored by both Japanese and American governments for his civic works. He recalled later that waving goodbye to Sakamaki at Camp Livingston was like saying farewell to a brother. He never saw his "calabash cousin" again.

A well-known professional wrestler and surfing enthusiast, "Lord James Tallyho" Blears moved to Hawaii in 1947. While touring on the first international wrestling event in Japan in 1955, he appeared on television and challenged lieutenants Motonaka and Hatori to came down to the station. "I'll arm-wrestle ya and then I'll *strangle* ya, ya *bastards!*" he roared into the camera.

Every year on the anniversary of the sinking, Blears takes a long, long swim, and then wife Lee feeds him peaches.

Fireman Bill Ellis and other crewmen of supply ship *Antares* stayed on board Dec. 7 in Honolulu Harbor, and the next went to Pearl Harbor, where the magnitude of the devastation was emotionally overwhelming. By the time the ship left the base in March 1942 it had been outfitted with weapons.

"Doc" Nash of Coast Guard cutter *Tiger* saw the midget submarine rammed by *Monaghan* and was surprised by its size. *It's more of a big torpedo,* he thought. Later that month, *Tiger* helped rescue crews of *Manini* and *Prusa,* and Nash watched the survivors wolf down stew prepared by the cutter's cook as they returned to Honolulu.

The second time *Ward* gunner Richard Phill saw a midget submarine was in St. Paul after the war, as *I-24tou* promoted war bonds. He reflected on the irony of the craft stuck out of water in the Midwest, while he, a born Midwesterner, spent the war at sea, including a stint in cruiser *Augusta* as she ferried President Roosevelt to Yalta.

In the four-stacker's wardroom, the *Ward* crew mounted the shell

[2] *On Gearhart Mountain in south-central Oregon, May 5, 1945. Five years later, the Weyerhaeuser Timber company erected a small monument on the site containing the names of the dead — Elsye Winters Mitchell, 26; Edward Engen, 13; Jay Gifford 13; Sherman Shoemaker, 11; Joan Patzke, 13; and Dick Patzke, 14.*

casing from the shot that hit the midget, a memento of the first naval engagement of the war, and they intended to take it back to the reserve armory in St. Paul. "When I visited aboard the *Ward*, the officers proudly showed me their four-inch shell casing," remembered then-ensign Adrian Marks of *Sacramento*, another ship manned by an all-reserve crew. "It was certainly a brave staff officer who dared venture into the wardroom of that ship for a cup of coffee!"

Ward was hit by a *kamikaze* on Dec. 7, 1944, and had to be sunk by destroyer *O'Brien* — which was commanded by a somewhat surprised William Outerbridge, *Ward's* skipper in 1941.

Admiral Husband Kimmel was relieved of command in a manner that made him a target for blame in the Pearl Harbor debacle. General Walter Short got similar treatment, and quietly retired. But Kimmel's combative nature wouldn't allow him to go quietly. Much of the controversy that still taints Pearl Harbor comes from the routing of these two men, deserved or not.

Paul Stillwell, author of "Air Raid: Pearl Harbor" and editor of *Naval History,* believes the Roberts Commission, which initially fixed blame, "was a kangaroo court. Its members blamed Kimmel and Short wholly, when there was enough blame to go around. They were charged with dereliction of duty." If Kimmel and Short were replaced, it was suggested, the nation could get on with winning the war.

"There's an obvious term for this — scapegoating. Kimmel was vilified. To the day he died, he received mail suggesting he commit suicide to atone for the deaths at Pearl Harbor. Kimmel made mistakes, but the same mistakes were made by leaders in Washington — he prepared for an enemy's presumed intentions, rather than its capabilities. And even if the fleet had sortied to sea, it probably wouldn't have changed the results of the attack.

"And what of an Army general named MacArthur? The whole business of Kimmel and Short smacks of monumental unfairness. When it comes to the verdict of history, I feel considerable sympathy for Admiral Kimmel. He deserved a better fate than he received."

Army historian Charles Anderson, author of a biography of Short, said that "by 1949, Gen. Short had retreated to such obscurity that his neighbors did not know who he was. But during the war years, Short was unjustly vilified as the man who was asleep at the switch, who allowed (the attack on) Pearl Harbor to happen. No amount of new information has managed to shake this damning and unjustified impression.

"Marshall had appointed Short to Hawaii precisely because Short was a shaker of the complacent. Short spent the rest of the war testifying across polished conference tables, a waste of a bright career. President Truman stated, 'The blame for Pearl Harbor must be shared by all Americans.'"

A move by Pearl Harbor veterans to posthumously restore Kimmel

ECHOES

and Short to four-star rank — the rank they held as Hawaii commanders — has been stonewalled in Washington. Said one historian, bitterly, "this upholds the American tradition of accountability — which goes up to the top, as well as down."

In late 1991, 50 U.S. senators appealed to the White House to have command rank reinstated for Kimmel and Short. President Bush rejected the notion, explaining that he did not want history reversed.

As for the single reason Americans were caught unprepared at Pearl Harbor, historian John Costello neatly summed it up with a Texas saying: "Everyone was focusing, but in the wrong direction. In the phrase of a bumper sticker — Shit Happens."

Submarine *I-6* was sunk on July 14, 1945, by destroyer escort *William C. Miller,* named after the SBD radio operator who had died bravely over Ewa on the morning of Dec. 7.

The "mother" submarines that participated in the Pearl Harbor attack were all of the C-l type, small by Japanese standards but still quite a bit larger than American fleet submarines.

None of the mother submarines survived the war. *I-16* was sunk by destroyer escort *England* on May 19, 1944, 140 miles northeast of Cape Alexander. She had been modified to carry *daihatsu* landing craft abaft of the conning tower. *I-18* was sunk by destroyer *Fletcher* on Feb. 11, 1943, 200 miles south of San Cristobal. *I-20* was sunk Oct. 10, 1943, 150 miles north of Espiritu Santo. *I-22* was never heard from again after Oct. 5, 1942. *I-24* was rammed by *PC-487* on June 11, 1943, near Attu in the Aleutians.

Because unsuccessful submarine sorties tend to disappear without a trace, many details of Japanese naval operations of World War II may never be known.

The Japanese also built three enormous submarines capable of carrying light bombers, the *I-400* series, with New York City and the Panama Canal targeted. They were on their way to attack American warships at Ulithi Atoll when the war ended. Their commander was Tatsunosuke Ariizume, the murderous I-boat skipper of *I-8*.

The captured monsters were brought to Pearl Harbor, examined and scuttled eight miles south of Barbers Point, along with smaller I-boats *I-14, I-201* and *I-203*. The jingoistic *Honolulu Advertiser* carried a fascinating (for the wrong reasons) account of their sinking, writer Buck Buchwach subheading his story with the lines *Subs Inferior To Ours* and *Nip Subs Immense.*

"Experts found no unusual construction or equipment which might prove valuable to the U.S. in any of the subs," Buchwach wrote. "However, some of the parts were removed and sent to Washington for further research," which seems to be a contradiction of sorts.

The irony of the Imperial Navy's smallest and largest submarines beginning and ending the war at Pearl Harbor escaped him.

At the other end of the scale, in the last month of the war, a tiny

kaiten suicide submarine was found on the beach at Panama. Instead of a warhead, it contained hundreds of pounds of pure silk. There was no trace of crew, and it is unlikely that Japanese seamen would melt easily into the population of Panama.

Kaiten had very limited range, and there are no records of Japanese mother submarines in the area. Officially, there was no way for it to be there. When the U.S. Army museum in Panama shut down

Standing at what they assume is a safe distance, tourists at the Hilton Hawaiian Village in Waikiki inspect a torpedo washed ashore in 1964. It turned out to be a runaway Coast Guard "target simulator."

in the late '70s, the sub wound up warehoused by the Army Museum in Hawaii. A former *kaiten* mechanic inspected the craft, and declared it was a reconnaissance type rather than a suicide type. The mysterious kaiten went to Japan, where it is on display near the midget submarine raised from Keehi Lagoon.

In 1946, a torpedo was discovered sticking out of the sand at the south base of the Golden Gate bridge. Shipping was detoured from under the bridge and traffic halted overhead while a Navy demolition team strapped a charge onto the missile. When it exploded, six-inch scraps of metal showered the area.

The Navy speculated that a Japanese submarine had aimed a torpedo at the bridge base, and missed. Despite the heavy warheads of Japanese torpedoes, it's doubtful that a single shot could topple the Golden Gate, and San Francisco newspapers snootily pointed out that a torpedo is a "watertight vessel; it can drift anywhere between here and the coast of Asia …"

A cylindrical object found washed ashore on Lanai in 1959 was immediately assumed to be a Japanese midget from the attack. It was actually a Navy practice torpedo.

Pat's Used Cars, a lot on Nimitz Highway near Pearl Harbor, displayed a "midget submarine" during the mid-'60s as a come-on for customers. It was actually a Japanese torpedo from the *I-400* boats, liberated when the submarines were examined at the shipyard in 1946. Lot owner Pat Muller bought the surplus torpedo from a scrap yard, added a sail and periscope made from an oil drum and scrap metal and painted the creation up in fanciful markings, including a rising sun flag on the conning tower. After complaints from the Japanese consulate, the flag was removed.

ECHOES

In 1990, Seto town, whose isolation and similarity to Pearl Harbor made it the ideal site to train midget submariners, proposed to Pearl City, an Oahu community snuggled against Pearl Harbor, that the two towns became sister-cities. Shigehisa Abe, the town's headman, said that he would "do my best to realize this relationship for the sake of world peace and as a pledge not to repeat that sort of tragedy again." As of this writing, Pearl City — whose population is predominantly Japanese-American — has avoided taking Seto up on the offer.

The ersatz midget submarine parked at a used car lot near Pearl Harbor in the '60s. Many local residents remember it as the real thing.

Submarines continue to prowl Hawaiian waters. Pearl Harbor, which began as a submarine base prior to World War I, remains a vital link in America's underwater defense system. Just as important are anti-submarine forces arrayed at the Navy base of Barbers Point; Russian submarines passing near the islands are common.

A tour submarine called *Atlantis VII* began operating in Hawaii during the 1980s. Capable of carrying 28 sightseers, it can dive to shallow depths. Modern technology has made it roughly comparable in size to the small submarines of WWII. There are now four of these craft operating in Hawaiian waters, the most recent being named, ironically, *Lahaina*.

The University of Hawaii also operates a small submarine called *Pisces V*. It is primarily used for deep-water oceanographic research. At the request of the Park Service, it once made a search for the midget submarine sunk by *Ward*. Nothing was found, though the author was told that the sea bottom off Pearl Harbor is littered with "junk — old cars, tanks and aircraft."

On Aug. 22, 1945, a week after the surrender, *Taishun Maru,* a ship repatriating Japanese homesteaders from Sakhalin Island, mysteriously exploded and sank. More than 1,700 were lost. It was not until Oct. 1, 1992, that Soviet submariners owned up to the sinking, as well as those of two other Japanese cargo ships after the end of the war.

Japan surrendered unconditionally on Sept. 2, 1945, and General Douglas MacArthur became de facto ruler of the shattered country. "My directive read, 'Japan is not to have an Army, Navy, Air Force, Secret Police organization or civil aviation,'" said MacArthur, who proceeded to exorcise militarism from Japanese souls. Some 1,128

Japanese were tried for war crimes, and seven were executed. In Manila, generals Tomoyuki Yamashita and Masaharu Homma also were killed. Anyone suspected of promoting militarism in the Japanese government was purged, some 210,000 officials. The Japanese constitution codified this trend, stating "the Japanese people forever renounce war as a sovereign right of the nation ... land, sea and air forces, as well as other war potential, will never be maintained."

This suited the Allies until the Korean War, when MacArthur backtracked and said the earlier rules were "aimed entirely at eliminating Japanese aggression." He also suggested that Japan create a defense force. Soon, a National Police Reserve of 75,000 paramilitary men was created, complete with infantry weapons. In 1952, Japan's sovereignty was restored by treaty, and the soldiers renamed the National Safety Force. Rules against militarism quietly evaporated in the face of the North Korean threat, and Japan became the "Far East Arsenal of the Free World," with three-quarters of its industry tied up in defense work.

After the Korean War ended, separate land, sea and air forces were dubbed "Self Defense" forces, and today, number some 300,000 troops. The Maritime Self-Defense Force, successor to the Imperial Navy, now has nearly as many ships patrolling the Pacific as the United States.

The Reagan era influenced Japan to pay its own way, and today Japan's defense outlay is just behind France, Germany and Great Britain. If the domino effect of defense spending is counted, Japan's self-protection budget of $39 billion follows only that of the United States and the former Soviet Union. Nearly half of Japan's military budget goes for salaries; the actual number of troops is exceeded by 24 other countries, including Taiwan and Indonesia.

If the United States were to pull out of the Far East — a process started with the Philippines — and Japan were to face new security considerations, such as a hostile, unified Korea or a new hegemony in the China Seas, the Japanese constitution may well have to be reconsidered. As of this writing, China is dickering to buy an aircraft carrier from the Soviets.

The Persian Gulf War of 1991 brought pressure on Japan to participate in the conflict. Though Japan gets 70 percent of its oil from the region, and thus had a vested interest in the outcome, the country declined to send troops, instead sending money and some hospital corpsmen. In 1992, Japan sent soldiers abroad for the first time since World War II, as peacekeepers in Cambodia.

Since the war, many countries have continued midget development. The former Soviet Union returned to the concept with vigor, realizing that midget submarines represented a cost-effective way of throwing covert operations across the globe. They now have an estimated 200 midget craft. Soviet midgets figure largely in their

ECHOES

strategic plans as well. The Russians have a number of midgets fitted with tank-like tracks and quarters for Spetsnatz marine commandos, designed to crawl along the bottom of enemy harbors and cause havoc. The cutting of telephone lines near the end of World War II by midget submarines could easily be duplicated today, and cause just as much mischief.

This Soviet design owes much to the Nazi *Seeteufel* (sea-devil), of which one was built and tested before the end of World War II. Today, harbor-defense is a nearly forgotten art, and the threat of Soviet-designed Seeteufel are overlooked in the overall strategic picture.

Sweden's problems with bottom-crawling intruders are well-known; in the summer of 1987 no less than four alerts were issued in waters around sensitive Swedish defense installations. The Soviet response

A midget submarine used by a new enemy — smugglers used this craft to bring drugs into the United States.

had been to demand proof. "The Russians may want us to believe we've got giant prehistoric centipedes here," said an exasperated Swedish officer. "But they certainly make peculiar noises that tally with the noise-prints of Soviet submarines in our archives."

Less well-known are the discovery of mysterious underwater tracks off Brazil, inside San Francisco Bay, inside most Japanese harbors and encircling South Korea. The prehistoric centipedes are found world-wide. North Korea has the largest number of midget submarines in service, and virtually nothing is known about them.

The official U.S. venture into midget submarine development was the *X-1*, based on a British X-craft loaned to the Navy. *X-1* was an

unarmed research craft and was powered by hydrogen peroxide, a volatile chemical that also propelled the rocket-powered Nazi aircraft Me-163. *X-1* suffered an internal explosion in 1958 which tore the craft into three pieces. She was rebuilt, given a conventional diesel power plant and painted bright orange. She lasted until 1973.

Both the United States and the former Soviet Union have developed DSRVs — Deep Submergence Rescue Vehicles — to rescue submariners trapped on the bottom. In design, these aren't so different from midget submarines, and Soviet India-class submarines are de-

A DSRV carried on the back of a modern mother submarine.

signed to carry DSRVs in dorsal wells. American DSRVs can be carried strapped piggyback on SSNs, looking startlingly like *kaiten*.

The U.S. Navy has admitted to having 15 or so Swimmer/Seal Delivery Vehicles (SDV), for naval commando operations.

The American submarine fleet has continued its reliance on a global strategy for war. American submarines are sophisticated, nuclear-powered, independent, prepared for an atomic Armageddon or a wide-ocean conflict. The only American submarine to fire a weapon in combat since World War II was *Louisville*, which launched Tomahawk cruise missiles at Iraqi positions on Jan. 19, 1991 — a purely tactical use of a strategic weapon, repeated a half century after the attack on Pearl Harbor.

Submarines are now the capital ships of any navy, a role made possible only by recasting their mission. The surface-ship hunters of the World Wars became, during the Cold War, high-tech listening agents and nuclear spear carriers. The oceans belong to those who control the deep. Did the developing technology lead us to this point, or was the precipice reached by pushing developers to the edge?

To stay viable in the post-Glasnost world, the Silent Service is casting for a new mission for its approximately 34 missile submarines, 89 attack submarines and 61,000 submariners. The new undersea battlefields will move from the oceans back to the coasts, from strategic to tactical uses, in stealthy, shallow-water sorties. A new generation of midget submariners, delivered by mother submarine, can seize control of an enemy's sea approaches, disrupt their shipping, slaughter their navy and even assault their soil under cover of water. The development of cruise missiles has multiplied the killing stroke of even the smallest submarine by hundreds of miles.

In the summer of 1991, a combined exercise was held in the Caribbean that used three American submarines and Special Forces troops from each branch of the service. The successful maneuver drilled in night landings, rescue attempts and the shootdown of a drone aircraft, from a shoulder-launched Stinger missile on the deck of a submarine. At least three American submarines have been refitted as troop carriers.

The simplicity and low cost of midget submarines make them ideal for smaller countries as well. In the midst of a decade-long war with Iraq, Iran ordered X-craft plans from the Royal Naval Subma-

All the rage in Germany during the 1960s, the tiny, James Bond-like volksunterseeboote *carried one scuba diver.*

rine Museum and embarked on a building program. Their first two products reportedly looked much like the Japanese *ko-hyoteki* of World War II, an ideal design if Iran planned on slashing, deep-water attacks on shipping in the Persian Gulf. The outline reportedly resembles an A-type with the X-boats facility for carrying side loads of limpet mines, and a wet-dry compartment for divers. The prototype was completed in 1987 and assembled at the port in Bandar Abbas, though diving tests were unsuccessful.

In June 1988, a midget constructed by DPRK of North Korea was delivered to Iran, one of 20 such built since 1974. A midget-sized explorer-type submarine from West Germany was purchased in 1988, ironically, only a few months after the Pentagon prevented the sale of the same submarine to North Korea.

Teething troubles, however, supposedly caused Iran to cancel the program and order *R-1* (one-man) and *R-2* (two-man) midget submarines directly from Yugoslavia. Iran's small midget fleet is supposedly stationed at Bushehr.

Yugoslavia also has supplied R-midgets to Sweden — presumably to go mano-a-mano with Soviet bottom-crawlers — to Libya, and test vehicles to the Soviet Union. Yugoslavia's M-100-D midgets owe much to WWII designs. The *R-1* "wet chariots" can be launched out of a conventional torpedo tube with a single pilot. The plexiglass and light aluminum *R-2* carries two in relative comfort. The instrument array includes aircraft-type gyro compass, a magnetic compass, its own sonar system and echo finder, and searchlights, all of which aid it in nighttime stealth operations. Yugoslavia itself has six *Una*-class MD-100 type midgets in service.

Italy has successfully built at least three midget-sized Maritalia-designed submarines, ostensibly small-scale test vehicles for the radical toroidal propulsion system, in which oxygen stored in the pressure hull fuels an anaerobic diesel engine. The design is nearly silent and leaves no exhaust, and allows the submarine to roam far afield without surfacing, the usual problem for a diesel design.

Colombia has two small submarines named *Intrepido* and *Indomable*, about 75 feet long. They're designed to carry out midget-type raids, holding up to eight attack swimmers, or, more interestingly, two small "swimmer-delivery vehicles."

In the early 1980s, Taiwan acquired a West German-built midget, the Tows 64 DGK/300, a commercial craft which is just 22 feet long. There is speculation that Taiwan may have used this craft as a blue print for building a line of military midgets.

Saudi Arabia has huddled with Egypt about acquiring midgets and then pooling the training program.

Pakistan has at least five SX 404-class midgets, purchased in 1972 from Cosmos, an Italian manufacturer. Capable of carrying 12 "passengers," the craft are 52 feet long. Another four midgets, of the updated SX 756 class, are also on the Pakistani Navy roster. Cosmos is heavily staked by the notorious Chilean arms company Cardoen,

[3]*When the author asked U.S. Navy information services in Washington if Allied forces had uncovered any evidence of Iraqi midget submarines, he was told, "No! Of course not. But if you've got any reporters in the area, and they see anything — could you let us know?"*

which announced after the Iran-Iraq cease-fire that diversifying into midget submarine design was the wave of the future.[3]

Virtually any seagoing vessel can carry a midget or two in her belly without being noticed. Soviet freighters, for example, often seem to draw deeper drafts than necessary for their tonnage, and Howard Hughes' *Glomar Explorer* had an entire deep-sea salvage apparatus built into her without looking different in any way.

Defense industry analysts have long predicted that small submarines, operated by Third World countries, may become a headache for the U.S. Navy. As early as 1950, former Pacific Fleet submarine commander Charles Lockwood warned of atomic bombs hidden aboard midget submarines. Newly designed propulsion systems and relatively small sonar cross-sections make them difficult to detect for the American hunter-killer fleet, which are accustomed to tracking large Soviet submarines. A current design by Maritalia of Italy is 80 feet in length, displaces 150 tons, has an operating range of 1,600 miles at 8 knots and can sprint at 25 knots. It carries two torpedoes, and is capable of carrying Harpoon- or Exocet-like anti-ship cruise missiles. If the basic Ko-Hyoteki design had remained in development, it would be very much like the Maritalia product.

Advances in off-the-shelf robotic design eliminate the need for one-way suicide missions. The idea still may be attractive to religiously motivated terrorist groups, however; in the hands of an Abu Nidal the chariot designs of World War I could still cause significant damage and be almost impossible to sense on the inbound track. The only roadblock is psychological. The pilot would be alone in the cold sea, without the buoying power of fellow terrorists.

In other words, wartime weapons aren't of interest to terrorists — they're fighting for intangibles, not specific objectives. But in the hands of someone striking a zealous blow, a midget submarine is as formidable a weapon as it was in World War II. You prepare for what the enemy is capable of, not what you believe he will do. You go against your instincts. That is the lesson of Pearl Harbor.

It's almost dark at the Royal Hawaiian, and Mochitsura Hashimoto is very tired. The war is a memory. The submariner closes his eyes, listening, perhaps, to faraway thunder. There is only the sound of music and of people laughing on the beach.

"In the Pacific, the Indian Ocean, and the Atlantic we remember the multitude of resentful sleeping warriors; in our ears we hear the whisper of the voice from the bottom of the sea," wrote Hashimoto in "Sunk!," his account of the I-boat war. *What does he hear?* The interpreter is unable to translate.

This night at the Royal Hawaiian Hotel, Kimo McVay, the son of the man Hashimoto ruined by an act of war, takes the Shinto priest down to the Monarch Room to hear the music first-hand, and the old warrior gathers his strength and goes smilingly.

ECHOES

THE SCRIM
OF MEMORY

33

OVERTAKEN BY SHADOWS

The last ship to be sunk between Hawaii and the West Coast was *John A. Johnson,* a Liberty steaming out of San Francisco. Carrying a full load of provision and ammunition, and a deck crammed with trucks, *John A. Johnson* encountered heavy swells on Oct. 28, 1944, and radioed that one of her liferafts had been carried away. The signal was picked up by *I-12,* under the command of Lieutenant Commander Kaneo Kubo. The submarine intercepted the freighter that evening, and snapped her keel with a torpedo.

The Liberty ship began to break up and all 70 of the crew abandoned her safely. *I-12* then began to ram the lifeboats and turned a machine gun on the merchant seamen, silhouetted by the flames of the burning ship. The half of the ship containing the ammunition suddenly exploded, sending flames hundreds of feet in the air.

The explosion was spotted by a Pan American Boeing 314 "clipper," and the pilot began to buzz *I-12.* The submarine dove quickly and vanished, and the airplane radioed a distress message, which was picked up by aircraft transport *Argus,* 90 miles away.

Scouts from *Argus* found 60 survivors the next morning. Ten had been killed, and many of those still alive had bullet wounds.

I-12 was one of the Imperial Navy's largest and best-equipped submarines. It carried the Glen reconaissance aircraft and German-built radar. Despite this, and the massive number of Allied ships in the Pacific at the time, *I-12* had been three months on station without scoring. *John A. Johnson* was her only proven kill; the submarine vanished in the Central Pacific during January, 1945.

The short, inglorious career of *I-12* was a paradigm of Japanese submarine strategy during the war. A capable ship was frittered away on timid attacks, the actual accomplishment of battle overshadowed by what the Allies considered barbarous behavior.

The opposite was true of American submarine tactics. "No battleship would accomplish anything of significance during the Pacific naval war," wrote Zenji Orita. "Submarines and aircraft would write the story."

Even so, Japan's limited amount of available steel went to build

the giant battleships and carriers — the smaller submarines had a crippled building program, which wasn't helped by the wide variety of underwater designs desired by the Imperial Navy. The Americans had a successful boilerplate design — the *Gato/Balao* class — and a simple strategy as well, summed up in the Pacific submariner's slogan "Sink 'em All!"

"American submarine crews were very well trained, skillful and brave. It was unexpected, we did not expect such skillfulness. This is not a compliment but the truth," testified Admiral Miwa. "I expected your submarine forces would be all on the same level with Japanese crews and likewise the devices of submarines; but they were superior to the Japanese."

At the outset of war, Japanese submarines seemed to be everywhere. They terrorized the West Coast of America far out of proportion to their numbers. Although Yamamoto resisted using submarines at first, by the time his favored carriers in Kido Butai were underway, 42 percent of Japan's submarine force was already in or near Hawaiian waters. Considering the extraordinary demands on the Imperial Navy during this time period, that's an inequitable spread of projected power. Clearly, Yamamoto and his staff placed the I-boats where they expected to do the most damage.

Except for token shellings of isolated islands and scattered sinkings of merchant ships, the Advance Force's role in the assault on America seems sputtering and ineffective. The U.S. Navy's own estimate of I-boat effectiveness was succinct: The Japanese lost one full-sized submarine and five midget submarines were lost, while Americans "suffered no known damage from submarines. Balanced against this is the fact that the submarines served an important scouting function and tied up American naval units."

The actual damage inflicted by the submarines was wildly disproportionate from what commanders of both sides expected they would achieve. On the morning of Dec. 7, the American fleet was trapped in Pearl Harbor and its scouting forces solely arrayed against the underwater threat expected on its doorstep. A devastating aerial attack had proved to be a possibility in war games for years, but it was still only a possibility. When the balloon went up, Kimmel and his staff knew — *absolutely* — that Japanese I-boats would be waiting outside the safe harbor. And they were.

The psychological dimension of underwater warfare has an impact far beyond that of actual deployment. A killer that cannot be seen, that can strike at any moment and slip away — this is the stuff of nightmare. If the Japanese wanted to exploit this effect, they need only to have placed a few submarines in Hawaii, and carried out scattered raids similar to those off the coast of the United States.

Use of the Advance Force submarines should be seen in the context of the Imperial Navy's overall undersea strategy.

"In Japanese tactics, we are told when we have two enemies, one in front and one in the back, first we must cut the one in front by

456

THE SCRIM OF MEMORY

sword," explained a Japanese navy commander after the war. "Only cut and not kill, but make it hard. Then we attack the back enemy and kill him. Then we came back to the front enemy and kill him. This time we took that tactic, having no aim to capture Pearl Harbor but just to cripple it …"

It should be remembered that Kido Butai simply sought to knock the U.S. Fleet out of the Pacific ring long enough to seize Indochina. The Pearl Harbor attack was a immediate tactical victory, without regard to long-range strategy. They expected the U.S. would soon cede the Pacific, at least the west end of it, and the war would be over within months. If there was a showdown, it would be in the mid-Pacific, with battleships slugging it out. Destroying the enemy's supply routes would presage a war that pitted civilians as well as military professionals. Besides, these were the same merchant ships that supplied Japan prior to the war.

The Imperial Navy was modeled after that of another empire, Great Britain, so much so that the Naval Academy at Eta Jima is a replica of Dartmouth, with bricks imported from England and a lock of Nelson's hair on display in the memorial hall.

The British traditionally looked upon war against commerce as a ungentlemanly use of naval force. Also influential was the American strategic wizard Mahan, whose studies of naval warfare were highly regarded by the British, and so also by the Japanese. Mahan pointed out that wars were never won unless a navy could control the seas, which British and Japanese strategists took to mean point-to-point engagements between combatants, while merchant ships sailed blithely around the fray.

This narrow view was not strictly Mahan's, and also didn't take into account the German experience in World War I, when U-boats terrorized Britain's commerce lines.

As a result, as Japan plunged into war with the west, Imperial Navy policy called only for tactical use of submarines, as an auxiliary to a battle fleet, meaning they were usually used only in direct combat with Allied forces. It led to the development of many different kinds of Japanese submarines, including underwater supply ships, troop transports and aircraft-carrying ships that bombed the U.S. mainland.

Using submarines as supply ships was a political decision, created to keep peace between the navy and army factions at Imperial Headquarters. "It was very important for them to supply even isolated and ineffective bases because the Army, which was a partner in the (war) planning, would have refused to send additional strength to the South Pacific if the Navy had left the men to starve … Another point was that this use of submarines as supply weapons fitted in with our overall strategic planning for fighting delaying actions on all islands," explained Commander Chikataka Nakajima, a staff officer.

The view of many in Japan was that the submarine service was a sacrificial arm of the Imperial Navy. The submariner sailed forth in joyful self-destruction, and Japanese newspapers printed transpar-

ently provocative novels such as "Kaigun (The Navy)," which in 1942 immortalized the nine "hero gods" of Pearl Harbor.

Thus Japanese essentially ignored the strategic value of submarines, something Germans and Americans were quick to seize upon. Using only one type of submarine, the U.S. Navy was able to economically isolate Japan from her own sea lanes. Japanese anti-submarine measures also lagged far behind those of America and Great Britain.

Of 2,828 merchant ships sunk during World War II, only 175 were sunk by Japanese submarines, 907,351 tons out of a global tally of 14,687,231 tons. Allied subs sunk 1,153 Japanese merchants, almost 5 million tons.

With the declaration of war on the United States, the Kriegsmarine moved U-boats closer to America. Between Dec. 21, 1941, and Feb. 9, 1942, five Nazi submarines managed to dominate waters off the East Coast. So great was their devastation that official Allied estimates pegged U-boat numbers as four times greater than their actual count, and so great was their potential for terror that the U.S. claimed to have sunk 28 U-boats and damaged many more. In fact, all of the U-boats returned home safely from the first patrol of Operation Drumbeat, as Admiral Donitz called the assault.

It was the nightmare war plan Rainbow 5 was created to defend against. The U-boats seemed unstoppable, each sinking two or three freighters a night while the few American destroyers available wandered aimlessly or spent the period in harbor. Soon, U-boat crews were fighting among themselves for the chance to spend a week in the East Coast shooting gallery. They called it the "Happy Time."

During the six-month period of Drumbeat, 397 Allied merchant ships were lost. Only *U-85* was eventually caught, surprised on the surface by destroyer *Roper* and dispatched with quick gunfire.

The almost unbelievable success of the initial U-boat offensive caused a flurry of cover-up in Washington. The famous "Sighted Sub, Sank Same" message during this period was the invention of a Navy PR officer from VP-82, stationed at Argentia. Even today, Navy histories tend to gloss over the failure of American warships to halt — or slow — the freighter sinkings.

The same easily could have happened on the West Coast. Though the reluctance of Imperial Navy I-boats to engage anything less than a capital warship was certainly different from the Kriegsmarine's goal of starving England, the I-boats and U-boats had much in common. Their submarines had long legs. Their crews were motivated and efficient. Their torpedoes exploded when they were supposed to.[1] Their opponent navies were off doing something else; the Atlantic fleet was escorting convoys, and the Pacific fleet was in Hawaii. The coasts were wide open. During December 1941, while nine I-boats prowled off the West Coast, there were six destroyers stationed at Mare Island and three in San Diego, not nearly enough for patrol. The load fell on conscripted vessels.

[1] American submariners, stuck with balky warheads, did not become efficient until the torpedo problem was rectified.

458

And yet, despite the highly publicized sinkings in the Pacific during the first two months of war, the I-boats were only marginally successful compared to the U-boats. The Japanese commanders even complained that freighters, particularly tankers, were too hard to sink.

Worse, during the week following the Pearl Harbor attack, when Hawaiian waters were infested with Imperial Navy submarines, not one torpedo strike was recorded against a U.S. warship, the stated objective of the Advance Force. It's tempting to attribute this to the finely honed anti-submarine skills and daring of the Pacific Fleet, particularly the destroyer crews who had practiced with the problem for more than a year, but the Atlantic fleet had had much of the same training. Some of the destroyer crews had been transferred from the Pacific to the Atlantic, already trained, and over Kimmel's objections.

The difference may have been in the style of command. Kimmel's forces were bent on the offensive; the plan against "Orange" dictated taking the war to the enemy. The Navy's destroyers were deployed defensively, riding shotgun with convoys in the stormy mid-Atlantic — where the U-boats were not — or waiting in harbor for assignment.

Kimmel's positive genius for gunnery seems to have percolated down as well. During the two instances when his ships had a chance to shoot at the tiny, darting sails of the midget submarines, destroyer *Ward* and tender *Curtiss* each put a shell round through the conning tower in short order. By any standard, this was superb shooting.

Attacks on merchant ships between Hawaii and the U.S. Mainland immediately after the Pearl Harbor assault were considered flanking actions of that particular battle, not actions in their own right. Japanese submarine doctrine called for an all-out assault on Allied merchant shipping only between the months of April and November 1942, after which they were primarily used as underwater supply ships to remote garrisons. The murderous rampage carried out in the Indian Ocean in 1944 tied up relatively few I-boats.

The tactical offensive was stressed at the expense of strategic defense. Also misunderstood was the role played by shipping, despite the valuable lesson being played out by the U-boat fleet strangling England. Though the Imperial Navy was modeled on the Royal Navy, the similarity didn't end there. Both were island economies, weak in natural resources. A determined submarine blockade would sever the arteries of supply.

While being debriefed after the war, German Vice Admiral Paul H. Wenneker, the Nazi naval attache in Japan, was bitter about German efforts to make Japanese war planners change their tune.

"It was the expressed desire of the German Naval Ministry that every possible effort be made to induce the Japanese to exert their maximum effort in attacks against U.S. merchant shipping in the Pacific," he said. "The Japanese had one invariable answer, namely, that they must conserve their submarines for attack against the U.S. Fleet ... if they were to hazard their subs, it must be against the U.S. Navy."

The midget submarines ranged all over the Pacific, limited only by their battery capacity. Here, three midgets are examined by American soldiers shortly after Kiska Island was recaptured in September 1943. All three midgets have been gutted by scuttling charges.

Wenneker complained also that the "Japanese had poor types of submarines in the war ... they were too big for easy handling under water when under attack, and consequently were too easily destroyed."

As the war progressed, Japanese submarines became increasingly ineffectual. They were hampered by confused strategy, bumbling communications, poor allocation of resources and an overly zealous adherence to a passive patrol regime — which dictated that the submarines were to lie quietly and wait for targets to cross their sights. The prideful officers of Eta Jima, who smilingly went to die for their empire, had no idea how to think for themselves.

Despite the poor results, there was no trouble with submariner morale throughout the war, Admiral Miwa explained later to curious Allied intelligence officers. The Imperial Navy's silent service never lacked for volunteers. In another debriefing, staff officer Captain Y. Watanabe confirmed — "It was a morale factor. Young naval officers very much admired the bravery of Italian officers in torpedo boats and small submarines. Because of their admiration of Italian officers, they also wanted to show bravery in submarines ..."

"Compared with the Europeans the Japanese ... preferred colorful and offensive fighting to monotonous and defensive warfare," wrote Miwa. "It was only natural that convoy-escorting and anti-submarine warfare were not jobs welcomed by Japanese naval men."

Admiral Fukudome, bitterly summing up after the war, wrote, "the Japanese Navy expected much from its submarines, and for this reason alone both officers and men were carefully selected and put through the most rigorous training. They considered themselves superior in technique in the field of submarine warfare to any in other navies. But when it came to the test of actual warfare, the results were deplorable."

"The Japanese high command had the wrong idea — they didn't use submarines to disrupt supply and communication lines, as the

THE SCRIM OF MEMORY

Americans and Germans did. We learned too late, to our disgrace," lamented Masataka Chihaya, an aide to Yamamoto.

The very nature of submarine warfare dictates that it charge into enemy waters. Japanese aircraft purposefully ignored American submarines at Pearl Harbor, showing that they didn't understand the potential threat themselves. Although the Hawaiian Sea Frontier was filled with Japanese I-boats, the Imperial Navy was surprised when the tables were turned. This, American submarines did a very few weeks after Pearl Harbor, fueled by the oil Fuchida's bombers had failed to burn. Though every drop of oil in Hawaii had to be shipped from the Mainland, the oil tank farms were not touched on Dec. 7, and neither were the tankers.

Also passed over were the U.S. Fleet destroyers, the deadliest threat to the Advance Force. Only three of the 29 destroyers at Pearl Harbor were put out of action, and they all eventually returned to duty.

It is not known, in spite of numerous and contrary intelligence claims, if Japanese submarines actually visited Hawaii prior to the Advance Force sortie. Chihaya claims they didn't, as does Professor Teruaki Kawano of the military history department within the Japanese government. The ocean-level drawings of Oahu's south shore found aboard Sakamaki's *I-24tou* could have been made aboard an NYK liner, or by a consulate employee pretending to fish from a sampan. There is no proof one way or another.

It's hard to believe, however, that the Imperial Navy's long-range fleet boats never at least passed through the Sea Frontier. One of the most valuable missions of a submarine is its ability to scout silently and invisibly. Nagumo skipped his own submarine screen during the battle at Midway, six months after Pearl Harbor, and missed spotting the American carriers flanking his forces. It was a dreadful error, one that contributed to the loss of the world's best-trained, hardest-hitting assault force — the carriers *Akagi, Kaga, Hiryu* and *Soryu*.

How much damage midget submarines could have inflicted at Pearl Harbor is one of those impossible what-if questions of history. The Japanese Imperial Navy had high hopes for them, and indeed had counted on them and the fleet-class submarines to make a killing stroke. As it turned out, the midgets were massacred and the fleet subs that ringed Oahu proved to be remarkably timid.

The midget submarines failed at Pearl Harbor due to a triple-punch. Their own inexperience and too-brief training period, Pearl Harbor's difficult waterways and the alert, dogged response of American destroyers mitigated against success. They also were fixated on grand targets, an attitude that began at the top.

"Yamamoto was absolutely obsessed with battleships," said Chihaya. "They were the force we expected to do battle with. It's only my assumption, and my belief, that he attacked the U.S. fleet to lessen

The midget submarine in the foreground on the opposite page still lies where it was scuttled on Kiska, wild grass pulling it gradually into the earth. Jagged parts of the hull from the scuttling explosion are peeled back alongside the sail.

the morale of Americans. Yamamoto was supposedly the one who understood Americans, who knew about (your) country, but even he underestimated the fighting spirit of Americans."

Ironically, because the American carriers were off delivering aircraft to Wake and Midway, and couldn't provide anti-submarine patrols, all of the American battleships were in port at Pearl Harbor the morning of the attack — to keep them safe against submarine attack. Usually, only a third of the battleships were there at one time. One of the reasons Japan considered the attack successful was that so many of the feared battleships were caught together, an unexpected bonus.

The chokeway of Pearl Harbor proved to be nearly impossible to negotiate. Against another target the midgets had trained for — like the wide-open waterways of San Francisco or Singapore — things might have turned out differently. If the ships had been in Lahaina anchorage, the midget submarines could have been devastating.

But they would have had to be very stealthy in those other harbors. Due to their shallow-running characteristics, the midget submarines were easily spotted from the air, and Japanese Zeros cleared the skies over Oahu that morning. On the other hand, American air-sea tactics needed some practice. Navy planes dropped at least ten bombs on Sakamaki's midget while it was a fat target, immobile on the reef off Bellows. All missed.

Submarines continue to seize the Japanese popular imagination. Here, a modern submarine struggles against a Hokusai sea in this illustration from the popular manga *comic book series "Chinmoku no Kantai," or "The Silent Fleet."*

The narrow, twisting throat into Pearl Harbor, flat landscape and numerous lochs of the Naval Base made sea-level navigation difficult at best. Their inability to make headway into Pearl also may have been a design malfunction in the craft itself. The only midget submarine's progress which we know exactly is Sakamaki's, and it went wildly out of control due to faulty trim. Other midget skippers could have had the same trouble.

The midget submarines were least successful at what they were supposed to do best — delivering a quick, killing stroke with a torpedo. Each boat packed two oxygen-powered "long-lance" torpedoes, at the time the world's deadliest underwater weapon. Aerial torpedoes, which ironically did the greatest damage at Pearl, can't be precisely aimed from an aircraft jitterbugging through the sky. The midgets were there at Pearl to administer a tightly fired *coup de grace*, in conjunction with the scattershot aerial attack.

The midget submarine that had the cruiser *Chicago* in its sights in Sydney Harbor had nearly half an hour to aim carefully, and the torpedoes still missed by a wide margin, both fore and aft of the target. Perhaps the recoil from the jetting torpedo produced enough yaw to

THE SCRIM OF MEMORY

throw the submarine off by a degree or two before the weapon was completely out of the tube.

Another possibility of failure is that the delicate, single-hull construction of the midget did not adequately protect her torpedo tubes. As the battle accounts suggest, midget submarines involved in depth charging or rough water subsequently had trouble firing their torpedoes. Perhaps concussion effects crimped the tube throats just enough to make the torpedoes stick.

Assuming that the midget sunk by *Ward* still holds her torpedoes, at least six of the ten torpedoes carried by the midgets were never fired. Two were fired inside Pearl Harbor, and missed targets completely in the heat of attack. Another two were claimed fired at *St. Louis* (if you accept the cruiser crew's account of the incident). If this is the case, then the torpedo attack against *Breese* the evening of Dec. 7 could not have come from a midget. *Breese* actually may have been targeted by playful porpoises, turned menacing by the visors of panic.

Since the mother submarines quietly stole over to Lanai for the rendezvous, any additional torpedoes fired on Dec. 7 would have to have come from other Imperial fleet-class submarines, and records are sketchy on that point. Destroyers claimed additional submarine sightings throughout the day of Dec. 7, and fired depth charges without much provocation. While some of these could have been enemy ships, it is unsettling to think of how many innocent whales may have been targeted during the war.

On the basis of available evidence, it is likely only one midget penetrated the harbor. The others may have hovered outside, unable to get in, and unwilling to fire their precious torpedoes at piddling targets like the patrolling destroyers. Cruiser *St. Louis* must have seemed awfully tempting indeed, to try a bank shot against a coral reef.

Virtually every book written about the Pearl Harbor campaign points out that the valuable American carriers were missed by the Japanese, a circumstance that would eventually haunt them. This is a semantic distinction at best — the Advance Force hit on carrier *Saratoga* is ignored. The ship did not sink, but she was laid up for four months during the most critical period of the Pacific War. Although the attack happened a month after the assault on Pearl Harbor, *Saratoga* was hit by one of the original vanguards of Kido Butai, which had remained on station in enemy waters until the moment was right. This wait-and-shoot strategy was part and parcel of Yamamoto's original Pearl Harbor strike plan, and so this crippling of *Saratoga* should be reconsidered. Battles do not begin and end as promptly as a football game. *Saratoga* was as much a victim of Pearl Harbor as any of the battleships.

Despite its failures, which were primarily due to dogged and ruthless American anti-submarine tactics, the Advance Force expedition was the only cohesively planned Japanese submarine operation of the war, the only undersea assault that worked in concert with a

On the other side of the Pacific, the lure of hurtling alone through the deep is just as potent. Here's a 1990 design for the home submariner.

tactical operation. That it even came close to succeeding is as much due to the vagaries of pure luck as to American training.

There are also victories that cannot be measured by sunken steel. Japanese propaganda like "Special Attack Flotilla" drove home the point, again and again, that the midget submarine attack on Pearl was a success, and that it could only have succeeded because of the Japanese-ness of the Imperial Navy sailors who pressed it to victory. Credit is duly given to "the blue blood of their race."

The propaganda war had racial undertones, used in different ways. The thrust of the Allied campaign stressed that victory was inevitable because the inferiority of the Japanese; Japanese propaganda stressed that victory was inevitable because of the superiority of the Japanese.

Naval propagandist Hideo Hiraide, in conversation with novelist Eiji Yoshikawa, postulated grandly that, "something special was needed. But what? That which is special is also fraught with danger. It also had to be something which the enemy could not duplicate. It had to be something only the Japanese could do. This was the Special Attack Flotilla."

The strike at Pearl Harbor was presented as a kind of philosophical parry against the West. As a point of pride it could be focused, like the pure, hot shaft of a laser beam, against the perceived influence of decadent thought. On this level, despite the reality of history, the emotional power of the Advance Force submariners — ten small men in tiny boats assaulting a mighty American naval base — charged the souls of the Japanese public. Against such spirit, only the atomic bomb had power.

The Japanese dashed into war without long-range strategy, their ultimate goals obscured by the instant gratification of immediate victory. The plan was nurtured on a slim hope, that the Americans would roll over and quit when things didn't go their way. They didn't believe that *Yogeki sakusen*, the preamble of nibbling attrition before the big shoot-out, would be turned against them by American submarines, and become the touchstone of the Pacific War.

The Imperial Army's goal was to construct a massive, self-supplying "sphere" that would allow Japan to wait out American willpower. The Imperial Navy wanted a decisive battle that would quickly end the war. The divergence was fundamental.

In "Global Positioning for the Twenty-First Century: Rethinking Strategic Planning," Leonard Caum Moffitt wrote:

"Like Germany, Japan was caught between the oceanic might and resilience of America and Britain and the unconquerable vastness of China and Russia. Japan's initial mistake lay in trying, as an oceanic country, to defeat a continental foe, China …

"Dominated by military officers, Japan's government never grasped Yamamoto's warning and never prepared a strategic plan tailored for a prolonged war, only one for seizing area. Steeped in the samurai tradition of individual valor in battle, Japanese generals

THE SCRIM OF MEMORY

sorely neglected the unheroic matter of logistics ... Japan not only failed to protect its own logistical net with appropriate naval units, it failed to appreciate the vulnerability of long U.S. supply lines. Never did its admirals use their superior subs and torpedoes to cut U.S. shipping when they had the chance. Instead, they continued like samurai of old to think in terms of gambling all on one grandiose confrontation, in the end using battleships even though their own Admiral Yamamoto had proven them obsolete."

Moffitt also credits "Japanese myopic arrogance and insensitivity to people of other cultures" for their eventual defeat. The Japanese refused to believe other countries might not play the war game by their rules, and a game it was, until the Japanese themselves began to suffer. The horror of war, that omnivorous eater of lives and resources and national pride, was fine as long as it was applied to others.

"We should at least pose the question of whether there is also a psychological factor, deeply embedded in Japan's samurai heritage, that made taking a 'suicide leap' into the Pearl Harbor attack so exciting and dramatic a war game that once it was proposed as a possibility it had to be tried," wrote Hilary Conroy in "Pearl Harbor Reexamined."

"This was certainly an element in the psychology of General Tojo. Brought up by samurai values, his entire schooling and adult life spent on military 'duty,' he had once admonished an ambivalent Konoye that there might come a time in a man's life when he must take a huge risk and, with his eyes closed, jump 'from Kiyomizu temple' (a tall building in Kyoto) into the ravine below."

This short-sighted view of global strategy was Japan's undoing. The island empire traded relatively peaceful coexistence with America, Britain and rest of the Allies for an unproductive relationship with Germany and Italy, primarily to seize control of raw materials in countries too far from the home islands to safely ship. This failure to think things through provided America with its greatest strategic weapon, the long-range submarine.

The Japanese are credited today with their superb, long-range business strategies. They have learned from their mistakes, and have profited by them. They have done this by turning their back on the past, by channeling their hustle into the business arena. After all, to dominate another country in a global economy, you do not have to invade it anymore, you just have to control its markets. The Japanese now have a heightened appreciation of the power of merchant ships — by the 1950s, Japan was the world's leading merchant shipbuilder.

On the 40th anniversary of the attack on Pearl Harbor in 1981, a poll by a Japanese newspaper revealed that 80 percent of Japanese men and women in their 20s were unable to associate "Pearl Harbor" with the date of the attack. Asked what images "Pearl Harbor" conjured, the common response was honeymoon trips to Hawaii.

A recent phenomenon in Japan has been the runaway success of backward-looking techno-thrillers, Tom Clancy in reverse, in which

Imperial Forces win World War II by concentrating on technology instead of spirit. All that was needed, these novels suggest, were better killing machines. [2]

The "Deep Blue Fleet" series, for example, which has sold more than 200,000 copies, has Japan developing workable radars, computers and giant submarines, which turn the tide. Japanese forces are treated as liberators when they invade other Asian countries; Americans and Europeans are painted as evil colonialists. Rape and murder are unknown, actually held in check by Japan's "moral police."

This is wishful nonsense, but it is nonsense that exists in a vacuum of knowledge. It's as if a curtain of selective amnesia has fallen across Japanese memories of the Greater East Asia War. In Japanese school textbooks, the 1937 to 1945 period of history has simply vanished. A 1991 exhibition in Osaka of Japanese wartime excesses was on view only five days; the cities of Nagasaki and Hiroshima have full-time employees devoted to public display of atomic-bomb horrors, finessing American guilt over ending the war too easily.

With the atomic holocausts in 1945, the circle that began in the dark waters off Pearl Harbor began to close. Balanced against the world-ending power of nuclear war, the weapons of the Advance Force and of Kido Butai seem insignificant. But they were the shots that began the process, fired by men in love with their killing machines. It was seduction by technology.

Who's controlling who?

What's controlling what?

Humankind cannot allow samurai mentalities to control the triggers of total war. It will require good sense, and a sense of history.

As for the nine hero-gods — and Kazuo Sakamaki, a confused, thoroughly human being — their actions are as unknowable today as they were on Dec. 7, 1941. What really happened has been obscured by time, politics, the clouds of battle and the fading scrim of memory.

That they never returned, not one, to the mother submarines is either blindingly heroic or damning, and probably both. They wasted themselves on an impossible target, unable to return with torpedoes unfired because of a moral code that equated the life of a sailor with that of his weapon. They could not succeed, and it was unthinkable to fail — and so they vanished into darkness.

[2] "If the Japanese ever apply their efficiency to the military in the same way they have applied it to their economy, we've had it!" said Bilveer Singh, director of the Institute of International Affairs in Singapore.

THE SCRIM OF MEMORY

PERSONNEL OF THE ADVANCE FORCE

First Submarine Division (Special Attack Unit)

In Command: Capt. **Hanku Sasaki**
Mission: Midget mother ships

I-16	Cmdr. **Kaoryu Yamada,** skipper	
I-16tou	Lt. Cmdr. **Masaji Yokoyama,** skipper	
	W.O. **Sadamu Uyeda,** crew	
I-18	Cmdr. **Kiyonori Otani,** skipper	
I-18tou	Lt. Cmdr. **Shigemi Furuno,** skipper	
	Sub.Lieut. **Shigenori Yokoyama,** crew	
I-20	Cmdr. **Takashi Yamada,** skipper	
I-20tou	Lieut. **Akira Hiro-o,** skipper	
	W.O. **Yoshio Katayama,** crew	
I-22	Cmdr. **Kiyotake Ageta,** skipper	
I-22tou	Cmdr. **Naoji Iwasa,** skipper	
	Sub.Lieut. **Naokichi Sasaki,** crew	
I-24	Lieut. Cmdr. **Hiroshi Hanabusa,** skipper	
I-24tou	Ens. **Kazuo Sakamaki,** skipper	
	W.O. **Kiyoshi Inagaki,** crew	

Second Submarine Division

In Command: Capt. **Kijiro Imaizumi**
Mission: Screen for attack fleet.

I-19	Cmdr. **Takaichi Kinashi,** skipper
I-21	Cmdr. **Kanji Matsumura,** skipper
I-23	Cmdr. **Genichi Shibata,** skipper

Sixth Fleet (Submarine)

In Command: VAdm. **Mitsumi Shimizu**
Mission: Flagship on cruiser *Katori*

First Submarine Squadron

In Command: RAdm. **Tsutomu Sato**
Mission: Oahu blockade, raiding operations

I-9	Cmdr. **Akiyoshi Fujii,** skipper
I-15	Cmdr. **Nobuo Ishikawa,** skipper
I-17	Cmdr. **Kozo Nishino,** skipper
I-25	Cmdr. **Meiji Tagami,** skipper

Second Submarine Squadron

In Command: RAdm. **Shigeki Yamasaki**
Mission: Oahu blockade, raiding operations

I-1	Cmdr. **E. Ankyu,** skipper
I-2	Cmdr. **Hiroshi Inada,** skipper
I-3	Cmdr. **K. Tonozuka,** skipper
I-4	Cmdr. **K. Nakagawa,** skipper
I-5	Cmdr. **T. Utsuki,** skipper
I-6	Cmdr. **Tsuso Inaba,** skipper
I-7	Cmdr. **K. Koizumi,** skipper

Third Submarine Squadron

In Command: RAdm. **Shigeoshi Miwa**
Mission: Oahu blockade, raiding operations.

I-8	Cmdr. **T. Ariizume,** skipper
I-68	Cmdr. **Y. Tanabe,** skipper
I-69	Cmdr. **Katsuji Watanabe,** skipper
I-70	Cmdr. **Takashi Sano,** skipper
I-71	Cmdr. **T. Kawasaki,** skipper
I-72	Cmdr. **I. Togami,** skipper
I-73	Cmdr. **Akira Isobe,** skipper
I-74	Cmdr. **N. Nanbu,** skipper
I-75	Cmdr. **Sunao Tabata,** skipper

Independent Reconnaissance

In Command: Cmdr. **Yasuchika Kayahara**
Mission: Pacific and Aleutian intelligence.

I-10	Cmdr. **Yasuchika Kayahara,** skipper
I-26	Cmdr. **Minoro Yokota,** skipper

BIBLIOGRAPHY

BOOKS AND ARTICLES

Ah! Special Small Submarines! Japan Midget Submarine Association, 1971.

Aldinger, Charles. "U.S. Preparing Attack Submarines for Third World Role." Reuters, 1991.

Bagnasco, Ermino. *Submarines of World War Two.* Naval Institute Press, 1973.

Beechert, Edward D. *Honolulu: Crossroads of the Pacific.* University of South Carolina Press, 1991.

Borghese, J. Valerio. *Suicide Squad Sea Devils.* Henry Regnery, 1954.

Byas, Hugh. *The Japanese Enemy.* Knopf, 1942.

Carpenter, Dorr, and Norman Polmar. *Submarines of the Imperial Japanese Navy.* Conway, 1986.

Carus, Clayton D., and Charles L. McNichols. *Japan: Its Resources and Industries.* Harper and Brothers, 1944.

Chenoweth, Robert P. "Hawaii's Aku Sampans: Historic Treasures Still at Work." Unpublished paper. University of Hawaii at Manoa.

———. "Kaiten Raids." Unpublished notes.

Cohen, Stan. *East Wind Rain.* Pictorial Histories, 1981.

Coleman, Mark. "Businessmen and Military Plotted to Destroy Hawaii." *Pacific Business News,* April 7, 1980.

Collins, Edward. "Survival By Lifeboat: The Sinking of the S.S. *Manini.*" *Amp&rsand,* Winter 1991.

Compton-Hall, Robert. *Sub vs. Sub.* Orion, 1988.

Congress of the United States. *Pearl Harbor Hearings.* 40 vols. U.S. Government Printing Office.

Curran, Bob. "Pearl Harbor Display Irks Veterans." *Buffalo News,* May 1989.

Dasch, George J. *Eight Spies against America.* Robert M. McBride, 1959.

Dawson, Don. "Enemy Sub? . . . Or Moby Dick?" Seven parts. *The Ketchikan Record,* April–June 1990.

Delgado, James P. "The Japanese Midget Submarine HA-19: A Unique Artifact That Helps Us 'Remember Pearl Harbor.'" Unpublished article, 1991.

de Yarmin, Ray. "Japanese Midget Subs Joined December 7th Attack." *Navy News,* 1966.

Dickinson, Clarence L. *The Flying Guns.* Zenger, 1942.

Drake, Hal. "POW No.1." *Pacific Stars and Stripes,* 1966.

Dull, Paul S. *A Battle History of the Imperial Japanese Navy.* Naval Institute Press, 1978.

Dunn, William J. *Pacific Microphone.* Texas A&M University Press, 1988.

Dybdal, Victor. "Anti-Submarine Warfare, Pre–WWII, Pacific." Unpublished paper.

———. "Encounters With a Midget Submarine." Unpublished paper.

Edwards, Bernard. *Blood and Bushido.* Self Publishing Association, Great Britain, 1991.

Evans, David C., ed. *The Japanese Navy in World War II.* Naval Institute Press, 1969.

Farago, Ladislas. *The Broken Seal.* Random House, 1967.

Fields, Rick. *Code of the Warrior.* HarperPerennial, 1991.

Francillon, Rene J. *Japanese Aircraft of the Pacific War.* Naval Institute Press, 1970.

Gentry, Curt. *J. Edgar Hoover—The Man and the Secrets.* Norton, 1991.

Gleason, James, and Tom Waldron. *Midget Submarine.* Ballantine, 1975.

Goette, John. *Japan Fights for Asia.* MacDonald, 1942.

Goldstein, Donald M., Katherine V. Dillon, and J. Michael Wenger. *The Way It Was: Pearl Harbor.* Brassey's, 1991.

Graham, Donald. *Keepers of the Light.* Harbor Publishing, 1985.

Grieves, Billy. "Peril at Fifty Fathoms." *Naval History,* Fall 1988.

Hashimoto, Mochitsura. *Sunk!* Henry Holt and Co., 1954.

Hiraide, Hideo. "Special Attack Flotilla." *Japan Times,* 1942.

Holmes, W. J. *Double-Edged Secrets.* Naval Institute Press, 1979.

Honan, William H. *Visions of Infamy.* St. Martin's Press, 1991.

Ienaga, Saburo. *The Pacific War.* Pantheon, 1978.

I-Go, RO-Go, HA-Go. Kojinsha/Maru Ship, 1990.

Ito, Masanori, and Roger Pineau. *The End of the Imperial Japanese Navy.* Norton, 1962.

Jackson, Charles L. *On to Pearl Harbor—And Beyond.* Pacific Ship and Shore, 1982.

Jahn, George. "Rendezvous With Destiny: The S.S. *Lurline*'s Pearl Harbor Voyage." *Amp&rsand,* Winter 1991.

Jentschura, Hansgeorg, Dieter Jung, and Peter Mickel. *Warships of the Imperial Japanese Navy.* Naval Institute Press, 1977.

Karig, Walter, and Welbourne Kelly. *Battle Report—Pearl Harbor to Coral Sea.* Farrar and Rinehart, 1944.

Kemp, Paul J. *Midget Submarines.* Arms and Armour Press, 1990.

Kimmel, Husband E. *Admiral Kimmel's Story.* Henry Regnery, 1955.

Kiralfy, Alexander. *Victory in the Pacific—How We Must Defeat Japan.* John Day, 1942.

Knaster, Mirka. "The Panala'au." *Honolulu,* November 1988.

Kobayashi, Hidejiro, ed. *Naval Strategies Photographic Record, Great Asian War.* Imperial Navy Press Office, 1942.

LaForte, Robert S., and Ronald Marcello, eds. *Remembering Pearl Harbor.* Scholarly Resources, 1991.

Layton, Edwin T., Roger Pineau, and John Costello. *And I Was There: Pearl Harbor and Midway—Breaking the Secrets.* William Morrow and Company, 1985.

Lockwood, Vice Admiral Charles A. *Sink 'Em All.* E. P. Dutton, 1951.

Lory, Hillis. *Japan's Military Masters.* Viking, 1943.

Marks, R. Adrian. *Selected Speeches of R. Adrian Marks.* Privately printed memoir, 1990.

Martin, James J. *The Saga of Hog Island and Other Essays in Inconvenient History.* Ralph Myles, 1977.

McKinney, John. "A Beach Shelled by the Japanese in 1942." *Los Angeles Times,* February 20, 1988.

Moffitt, Leonard Caum. *Global Positioning for the 21st Century—Rethinking Strategic Planning.* Michigan State University Press, 1990.

Moosa, Eugene. "Authors Make Killing on 'Japan Wins World War II' Novels." Reuters, 1991.

Murphy, William S. "Memories of Fort MacArthur's War Years Linger." *Los Angeles Times,* May 22, 1988.

National Park Service. "Pearl Harbor Survivor Questionnaires." Filled out by survivors visiting the *Arizona* Memorial.

National Security Agency. Miscellaneous declassified documents.

Nicholson, Brian. "Captured at Pearl Harbor." United Press International, December 3, 1981.

Oettinger, Elmer. *Hush Most Secret.* Unpublished manuscript.

Olson, Donald W. "Pearl Harbor and the Waning Moon." *Sky and Telescope,* December 1991.

O'Neill, Richard. *Suicide Squads of World War II.* Military Heritage, 1981.

Orita, Zenji. *I-Boat Captain.* Major, 1976.

Prange, Gordon W., Donald M. Goldstein, and Katherine V. Dillon. *At Dawn We Slept.* McGraw-Hill, 1981.

———. *Dec. 7 1941: The Day the Japanese Attacked Pearl Harbor.* McGraw-Hill, 1988.

———. *Pearl Harbor, The Verdict of History.* McGraw-Hill, 1986.

"PW No.1—Footsteps of a Midget Submarine Captain." Nippon Golden Network. Television documentary.

Richardson, James O., and George C. Dyer. *On The Treadmill To Pearl Harbor.* Naval Historical Division, Department of the Navy, 1973.

Rohwer, Jürgen. *Axis Submarine Successes, 1939–1945.* Naval Institute Press, 1983.

Roscoe, Theodore. *United States Destroyer Operations in World War II.* Naval Institute Press, 1953.

Rusbridger, James, and Eric Nave. *Betrayal at Pearl Harbor.* Summit, 1991.

Russell, Lord, of Liverpool. *The Knights of Bushido.* Berkley, 1958.

Saiki, Patsy Sumie. *Ganbare! An Example of Japanese Spirit.* Kisaku, 1982.

Sakamaki, Kazuo. *I Attacked Pearl Harbor.* Association Press, 1949.

Sakurai, Tadayoshi. *Human Bullets.* Teibi, 1907.

Seth, Ronald. *Secret Servants.* Farrar, Straus and Cudahy, 1957.

Slackman, Michael. *Target Pearl Harbor.* University of Hawaii Press, 1990.

Spalding, Wyman. "Anti-Submarine Patrol, California 1942." Unpublished article, 1991.

Stephan, John J. *Hawaii under the Rising Sun—Japan's Plans for Conquest after Pearl Harbor.* University of Hawaii Press, 1984.

Stewart, A. J. "Those Mysterious Midgets." *Proceedings,* December 1974.

Stillwell, Paul, ed. *Air Raid: Pearl Harbor!* Naval Institute Press, 1981.

Submarine Operations Dec. 1941–April 1942. Japanese Monograph 102. Japanese Research Division, 1952.

Toland, John. *Infamy.* Berkley, 1982.

Tompkins, Tom. *Yokosuka—Base of an Empire.* Presidio, 1981.

U.S. Army Air Force. "History of Bellows Field from Time of Inception to 31 March 1944."

U.S. Department of the Interior. "HA-19." National Register of Historic Places Registration Form.

U.S. Navy. Action reports, December 1941. Reports from all ships and shore installations in the Territory of Hawaii.

———. "Description and Photographs of Japanese Midget Submarine No. 19." Navy Intelligence, December 26, 1941.

———. 14th Naval District. Naval Intelligence Files. World War II National Archives, San Bruno, Calif.

———. 14th Naval District Watch Log, December 1941.

———. Ship's Histories. Division of Naval History (OP09B9).

U.S. Strategic Bombing Survey. "Interrogations with Japanese Officials." U.S. Government Printing Office, 1946.

Warner, Denis, and Peggy Warner. *Sacred Warriors.* Avon, 1982.

Webber, Bert. *Silent Siege II.* Webb Research Group, 1988.

Weintraub, Stanley. *Long Day's Journey Into War.* Dutton, 1991.

Wenger, Michael, and Robert J. Cressman. *Steady Nerves and Stout Hearts.* Pictorial Histories, 1991.

Williams, John A. "The Night That Shook Sydney." *After the Battle,* 1985.

Willmott, H. P. *Empires in the Balance.* Naval Institute Press, 1982.

Willoughby, Malcolm F. *Rum War at Sea.* Treasury Department, 1964.

Windrem, Robert. "Iraq's Most Lethal Weapons." *Popular Science,* 1991.

Young, Donald. *December 1941.* Pictorial Histories, 1992.

INTERVIEWS AND CORRESPONDENCE

David Aiken, Forrest R. Biard, James Blears, James P Delgado, Dave Dingeman, Victor Dybdal, Richard Geiger, Mochitsura Hashimoto, Richard Hirashima, Teruaki Kawano (Center for Defense Studies), Ernest Kurosawa (Department of Transportation), Jean K. Lambert, Mike Locke, Douglas McMurtry, Sadayoshi Nakayama (Japan Defense Agency), Ralph "Doc" Nash, Elmer Oettinger, Richard Phill, Abraham Piinaia, Kazuo Sakamaki, Wy Spalding, Steve Weiner.

INDEX

E

Earhart, Amelia *aviatrix* 312—314, 439
Earle, John B. *Captain* 143, 179—183, 186, 201, 218, 264, 270
Eastern Ghats *India* 397
Eastman, Richard *Ensign* 218
Ebesu Maru No. 2 sampan 174
Eckstrom, Olaf *First Mate* 338—339
Eddy, Daniel T. *Lieutenant Commander* 270
Edgers, Dorothy *cryptographer* 120
Eichelberger, Leslie 363
Eifler, Carl *Captain* 304
Eiji Goto *sampan crewman* 247
Electric Boat Company 76
Ellis, Bill *fireman* 167—171, 201, 208, 445
Ellis, Earl "Pete" *spy* 12
Ellison, John *Captain* 330
Elwood Oil Field *California* 349
Emidio merchant ship 331—332
Emily H8K *Kawanishi* 364—366
Emmons, Delos C. *General* 382
Emory, Ray *historian* 418
Enderbury Island 313
England 188, 447
English Channel 85
Enterprise aircraft carrier CV-6 148, 163, 177, 180, 203, 209—210, 227—229, 240—241, 245, 256—261, 266—268, 342, 375, 386
Epperson, Steve *Commander* 417
Equatorial Line Islands 310, 314
Espiritu Santo 324, 447
Estero Bay *California* 338
Estevan Point *lighthouse* 351
Eta Jima *Naval Academy* 54—59, 66—68, 251, 394, 396, 428, 457, 460
Etter, Charles *Machinist's Mate* 219
Eureka *California* 109, 331, 338
Ewa *Oahu* 40, 209, 210
Explosive Ordnance Disposal *EOD* 417, 433

F

F2A Buffalo *Brewster* 266
F4F Wildcat *Grumman* 148, 180, 241
Fanning destroyer DD-385 260
Farallon Islands *California* 326, 332
Farragut destroyer DD-348 150, 185, 219, 240, 361
Farrill, Ray *operator* 176
Farrington, Joseph R. *Territorial congressman* 444
Farrow, Clark A. *Captain* 331
Federal Bureau of Investigation *FBI* 17, 109, 114—117, 121, 277—281, 309, 364, 368, 426
Ferguson, Homer *Michigan senator* 269
Fernandez, Louis *policeman* 360
Ferrier, A. *Leading Signalman* 80—81
Fielder, Kendall H. *Lieutenant* 113, 252—253, 304—306, 309, 378
Fiji Islands 131, 353, 372
Finback submarine 408
Fink, Carl K. *Commander* 201, 226
Finlay, Gordon T. *Commander* 145, 218
Fiona Shell merchant ship 78
Fisher, George E. *guard* 309
Fitzpatrick, Ernest Hugh *author* 19
Fleck, Francis E. Jr. *Lieutenant* 210
Fleet Problem 21 27—30
Fleming, Ian *Commander* 117—118
Fletcher Pacific *construction company* 424

Flusser destroyer DD-368 87, 414
Foote, W.S. "Sparks" *Radioman* 331
Ford Island *Oahu* 40, 155, 173, 195—199, 203, 205, 210, 212, 214, 218, 224—225, 235—236, 257, 278, 281, 376, 419, 431—433, 443
Fort Armstrong *Oahu* 145
Fort Camosun merchant ship 347
Fort Kamehameha *Oahu* 185, 202, 238, 281, 292
Fort McDowell *California* 309
Fort Ord *California* 357
Fort Ruger *Oahu* 362
Fort Shafter *Oahu* 252—253
Fort Stevens *Oregon* 294
Foxworth, Percy *FBI agent* 117
Franciosa, Anthony *gunner* 357
Frank, Nicholas J. *Commander* 414
Fraser, I.E. *Lieutenant* 83
Fredericksburg *Texas* 423
Freedman, Herman *seaman* 303, 333—335
Freel, J. *Leading Seaman* 80
French Frigate Shoals 365—366
French, Howard C. *Boatswain's Mate* 225
French Indochina 14, 46, 412
Fuchida, Mitsuo *Commander* 8, 54, 223—224, 263, 374—375, 461
Fuetsch, Bernhart A. *Lieutenant* 230
Fujii, Akiyoshi *Commander* 295
Fujita, Nobuo *Flying Officer* 135, 342, 353—354
Fukudome, Shigeru *Vice Admiral* 50, 460
Fukunaga, Kyosuke *Lieutenant Commander* 21
Fulton submarine 76
Furukawa, Shigeo *sanitarium inmate* 359
Furuno, Shigemi *Lieutenant Commander* 60, 65—66, 159, 427, 431—432, 442
Furuya, Kumaji *internee* 395—396, 445
Fushimi, Prince Hiroyasu 71
Fuso battleship 66
Fussell, Paul *historian* 421, 471

G

Galapagos Islands 110
Galloway, Jerry *diver* 425
Gamble destroyer/minesweeper DM-15 147, 236
Garrett and Nordenfelt *manufacturers* 76
Gearin, H.F. *Quartermaster* 168
Geelong warship 388
Geiger, Richard *seaman* 216
Genda, Minoru *Commander* 8, 153
General Albert Lyman airfield *Hawaii* 345
General Royal T. Frank troop ship 345—346
Geneva Convention 305, 402, 405
Gerner, Louis *Gunner's Mate* 169—170
Gerow, Leonard *Brigadier General* 147
de Geus, Leonard *Radioman* 296, 298, 302
Gianella, Lawrence H. *Radioman* 329
Gibraltar 78—79
Gilbert Islands 330, 373
Gill, P.W. *Ensign* 213—215
Gilpin, J.W. *Communications officer* 214, 217
Glen E14Y1 *Yokosuka* 135, 294, 342, 353—354, 364, 373, 386, 388, 455

Glomar Explorer salvage ship 454
Gneisenau cruiser 11
Goebbels, Josef *Nazi propgandist* 119
Goepner, Oscar *Lieutenant* 149, 160, 168—171
Gojo *Japanese village* 68
Gold Beach *Oregon* 347
Goleta oil field *California* 351
Gonclaves, Frederick *Captain* 332
Goudy, Harry *Lieutenant* 401
Graciosa Bay *Solomons* 323
Graham, Donald *historian* 352
Grand Congress of Overseas Compatriots 19
Grannis, Lawrence C. *Commander* 167—168, 185, 194, 202, 206—208
Great Britain 104, 313, 458
Greater East Asia Co-Prosperity Sphere 12, 14
Green Point *Sydney* 388
Greenland 354
Greenland, R.T.G. *Lieutenant* 80—81
Greenwald, Harry *seaman* 340
Gridley destroyer DD-380 261
Grogan, Leslie *Radioman* 176, 178
Grover, William Dell *seaman* 148, 181, 229, 235
Guadalcanal 323, 367, 387, 408, 412, 415, 440
Guadalupe Island 343
Guam 20, 41, 142, 190
Guano Act of 1856 310
Gudgeon submarine 361
Guilio warship 81

H

H.M. Storey merchant ship 337
HA-1 submarine 71
HA-2 submarine 71
HA-3 submarine 71
HA-13 submarine 282
HA-19 submarine 62, 282
  See I-24tou
HA-44 submarine 71
HA-46 submarine 72
HA-61 submarine 72
HA-82 submarine 414
Hagen, Bernard *Captain* 351
Hague Convention 402
Halsey, William *Vice Admiral* 149, 195, 222, 235, 258—260, 346
Hamaguchi, Yuko *politician* 13
Hanabusa, Hiroshi *Captain* 135, 154, 165, 229, 322
Handler, Frank *Quartermaster* 197, 202, 206
Hara, Genji *seaman* 348—350
Hara, Takashi *politician* 13
Harada, Kaku *Captain* 49, 55, 60—61, 70
Harada, Satoru *Commander* 387
Harashijima *Japanese port* 55, 223, 257, 265
Hardon, Gilbert S. "Al" *Chief Torpedoman's Mate* 198, 212—216
Hart, "Tommie" *Admiral* 101
Hartwell, Rosemary *letter writer* 422—423
Hashimoto, Mochitsura *Lieutenant* 10, 132, 137—139, 166, 316, 322, 351, 408—409, 437—438, 454
Hashizume, Toshio *Lieutenant* 365—366
Hatori, Masanori *Lieutenant* 399—400, 404, 445
Havana *Cuba* 76
Hawaii Businessmen's Training Corps 359
Hawaii Suisan Kaisha Fishing Co. 174
Hawaiian Air Force 95, 97, 195
Hawaiian Sea Frontier 95, 313, 461

ABOUT THE AUTHOR

William G. "Burl" Burlingame was born in Alaska bush territory and raised on a former Imperial Japanese Navy air base in Taiwan. While still a student in Hawaii schools, he worked with environmental and preservation associations, both as an activist and a journalist, and went on to major in journalism and anthropology at the University of Missouri. Burlingame has also worked as chief photographer for the Sun Press Newspapers, media adviser for Hawaii Pacific College, and editor of *Hawaii Coastal Zone News*. He joined the *Honolulu Star Bulletin* in 1979, and his reporting on cultural, historic, and preservation issues has won several awards.

In 1989 Burlingame founded Pacific Monograph, a company specializing in historic interpretation. His company published *Advance Force Pearl Harbor* in 1992, and a year later the book was voted one of the top five nonfiction books of the last decade from Hawaii by the Hawaii Book Publisher's Association. Burlingame has also cowritten *Coverama: The Collector's Guide to Antique Hawaiian Milk Covers*, which discusses the Hawaiian origins of the "Pog" phenomenon. Written with cap collector DeSoto Brown and published by Pacific Monograph, it was named one of "Hawaii's Best Books" in 1995. *Da Kine Sound: Conversations With People Who Create Hawaiian Music*, a book Burlingame wrote just after college and among the first on ethnic Hawaiian music, is still in print more than twenty years later.

Along with his writing, Burlingame serves as Director of Collections and Interpretation for the Pacific Aerospace Museum, and has designed or built exhibits for the Pacific Aerospace Museum, the U.S. Army Museum of Hawaii, the Bowfin Museum, the Arizona Memorial, the Maritime Center, and the upcoming Hawaii Museum Center. He also serves as chairman of the Barbers Point Museum Task Force. In addition, Burlingame restores antique military vehicles, has won national awards for scale-model building, and plays in the blues band Honolulu Blue Devils. He lives in Kailua with his wife, Mary, who is an editor, daughters Amelia and Katie, two rabbits, and a dog that is half-Kelpie, half something else.

The Naval Institute Press is the book-publishing arm of the U.S. Naval Institute, a private, nonprofit, membership society for sea service professionals and others who share an interest in naval and maritime affairs. Established in 1873 at the U.S. Naval Academy in Annapolis, Maryland, where its offices remain today, the Naval Institute has members worldwide.

Members of the Naval Institute support the education programs of the society and receive the influential monthly magazine *Proceedings* and discounts on fine nautical prints and on ship and aircraft photos. They also have access to the transcripts of the Institute's Oral History Program and get discounted admission to any of the Institute-sponsored seminars offered around the country.

The Naval Institute also publishes *Naval History* magazine. This colorful bimonthly is filled with entertaining and thought-provoking articles, first-person reminiscences, and dramatic art and photography. Members receive a discount on *Naval History* subscriptions.

The Naval Institute's book-publishing program, begun in 1898 with basic guides to naval practices, has broadened its scope to include books of more general interest. Now the Naval Institute Press publishes about one hundred titles each year, ranging from how-to books on boating and navigation to battle histories, biographies, ship and aircraft guides, and novels. Institute members receive significant discounts on the Press's more than eight hundred books in print.

Full-time students are eligible for special half-price membership rates. Life memberships are also available.

For a free catalog describing Naval Institute Press books currently available, and for further information about subscribing to *Naval History* magazine or about joining the U.S. Naval Institute, please write to:

Membership Department
U.S. Naval Institute
291 Wood Road
Annapolis, MD 21402-5034
Telephone: (800) 233-8764
Fax: (410) 269-7940
Web address: www.navalinstitute.org

WITHDRAWN